The revised
edition of
C'est à toi! is
a three-level
textbook

m with unique communicative

es. Its truly functional approach to

ge learning makes French personal

levant to your students. Featuring

stic mix of activities covering all

sic skills, *C'est à toi!* helps your

ts to develop proficiency as

erform meaningful tasks in the

ge. With *C'est à toi!*, learning

becomes an exciting adventure

ur students will find irresistible!

C'EST À TOI!

Written by current and experienced high school French teachers, **C'est à toi!** is a function-based textbook series that uses a communicative approach to teach students French within the context of the francophone world. While developing cultural sensitivity to the everyday activities of French-speaking people throughout the world, students acquire proficiency in listening to, speaking, reading, and writing French. From day one, students practice communicating easily and confidently with their peers in paired activities or in cooperative learning groups.

FLEXIBLE

The goal of **C'est à toi!** is to meet the needs of the wide range of ability levels in your classroom. Because most classes are diverse, you need to provide students with opportunities to interact in small groups and work together toward communicative competency. **C'est à toi!** offers a variety of options and approaches for teaching students at multiple ability levels and with diverse learning styles.

Revised Edition
C'EST À TOI!

The Most Comprehensive, Up-to-Date French Textbook Program Available

REVISED
C'EST À TOI!
Level Two

REVISED
C'EST À TOI!
Level Three

REVISED
C'EST À TOI!
Level One

2002 Copyright

PROFICIENCY BASED

The *C'est à toi!* program provides a series of proficiency activities in which students can experience situations in a range of contexts that they would most likely encounter in the francophone culture. Proficiency activities presented in this program act as a catalyst for the authentic use of French, as students begin to internalize and master the language. This ability to interact with others using listening, speaking, reading, and writing skills, all integrated with culture, give students the confidence to use the language "on their feet." Students will find that *C'est à toi!*, like no other program before, encourages and enhances their ability to communicate and understand the communicated message.

BROAD CULTURAL COVERAGE

In-depth coverage of various francophone cultures in *C'est à toi!* gives students a solid understanding of and appreciation for the language within its multicultural, diverse contexts. This new series provides the broadest and most complete reflection of the lifestyles and cultural subtleties found every place in the world where French is spoken. Authentic cultural situations, used as the vehicle for proficiency-based role-playing and creative expression, appear throughout the program to encourage students to widen their cultural horizons as they develop their proficiency in French. You'll find that the cultural topics grab your students' interest, while preparing them to use French functionally.

UNIQUELY BALANCED

Listening, speaking, reading, and writing are all important skills in learning a language, and *C'est à toi!* offers the most balanced approach to developing these skills. Each lesson carefully blends creative oral and written exercises to build expressive skills, while culture-based reading and listening exercises provide practice to develop receptive skills. *C'est à toi!* has a carefully controlled vocabulary and bridging of structures that allow for constant recycling of basic information to form the foundation for developing proficiency.

APPROACH TO READING

C'est à toi! incorporates a unique and refreshing approach to teaching reading, writing, and organizational skills. In the beginning units, students read simplified texts focusing on the functions, vocabulary, and structures covered in those units. Readings found in later units are followed by achievable tasks, such as responding to content questions or using reference materials successfully. This interactive approach to the reading process encourages in-depth thought. The *C'est à toi!* program suggests assessing students' answers or responses to reading questions on a holistic basis, with superior scores given to students who produce more creative or thought-provoking answers. As students become more proficient in French, they can diagnose both their own learning process and their achievement in the language in order to become independent learners.

TEXTBOOK

C'est à toi! uses an eclectic mix of activities to integrate the four basic skills with culture. Through all three levels of the program, thematic units are subdivided into brief, function-driven lessons that are easy to teach. With *C'est à toi!*, your students will begin to use French immediately in authentic contexts while having fun building their communicative proficiency from the first day of class.

Communicative functions are listed at the beginning of each unit and each lesson. They preview the tasks students will be able to accomplish when they complete each section.

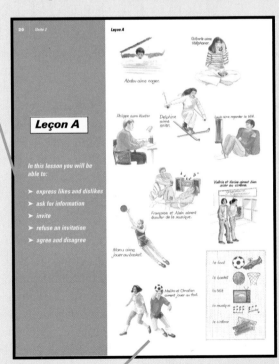

Colorful illustrations introduce all new vocabulary groupings and expressions in each lesson. Vocabulary is presented in a meaningful context.

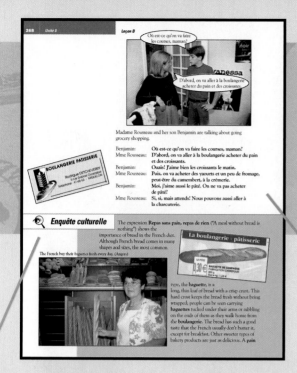

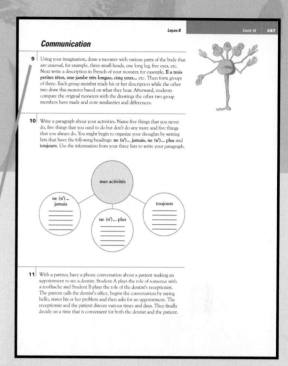

Dialogues at the beginning of each lesson illustrate how the communicative functions, new vocabulary, and structures are expressed in brief, real-life situations.

Enquête culturelle (Cultural inquiry) highlights certain cultural subtleties in the francophone world that are introduced in the *Dialogues*. Accompanying photos and authentic materials help to expand the students' cultural horizons.

Communication sections, following each lesson's *Pratique* activities, provide opportunities for students to develop oral and written proficiency. Paired and cooperative learning activities as well as activities that encourage the development of multiple intelligences foster the creative use of French to practice the unit's communicative functions.

Structure presents the lesson's main grammatical topics concisely and precisely. Colorful charts provide eye-catching reinforcement as do photo captions that illustrate how the specific structures are used. Examples in French are presented along with their English equivalents for reference.

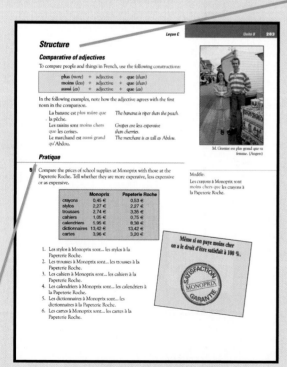

Pratique sections follow the presentation of each grammar topic. Contextualized activities allow students to practice both oral and written skills. The *Modèle*, in the side margin, demonstrates a correct response to help students succeed immediately.

TEXTBOOK

Sur la bonne piste
(On the right track) presents various reading strategies in French. Each unit focuses on a different technique to help students experience success as they read in French. Students are carefully guided before and as they read authentic French texts (realia, ads, poetry, narratives).

Mise au point sur...
(Spotlight) features in-depth cultural material related to the unit's theme. Current, topical information in English broadens students' understanding of and appreciation for francophone culture.

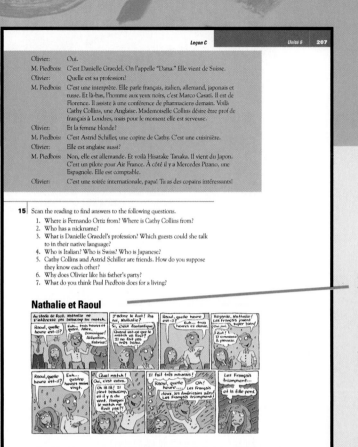

Nathalie et Raoul, an original cartoon series at the end of each unit, features a continuous story line and additional, current vocabulary that will appeal to your students.

C'est à moi! (It's my turn!) is the unit's seven-section review. First comes a checklist to see if students know how to perform the unit's functional objectives. Next, a quiz checks cultural comprehension. Then, the *Communication orale* and *écrite* sections evaluate oral and written proficiency as students express the unit's functions using appropriate vocabulary and structures. The *Communication électronique* section allows students to practice their language skills as they explore authentic realia and read up-to-the-minute information about francophone culture on the Internet. Finally, a cumulative writing section called *À moi de jouer!* gives students the opportunity to show what they can do by putting together everything they have learned so far. Capping off the review section is a list of the unit's vocabulary.

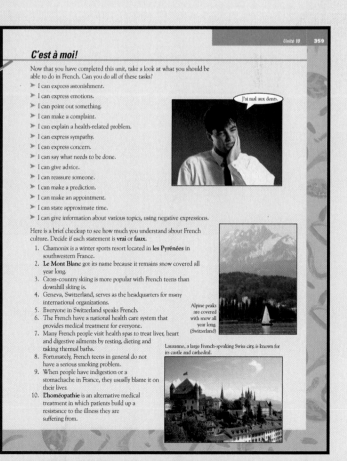

TEXTBOOK

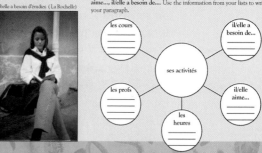

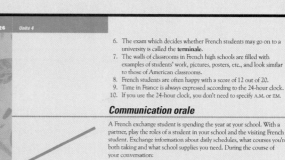

7. French teenagers drink as much milk as American teens do.
8. French people now do all of their grocery shopping in large supermarkets instead of going to small shops and markets.

Since French people generally drink more mineral water than Americans, they often buy enough for one or two weeks.

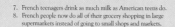

9. French supermarkets sell more bottled water and usually have a smaller variety of cold cereal than American supermarkets.
10. Because of its climate, Guadeloupe must buy most of its fresh fruits and vegetables from France.

Communication orale

With a partner, play the roles of a student who is planning to have a party to celebrate his or her friend's birthday and a grocer at the corner store. The student is going to order by phone several trays of party food and some beverages. During the course of your phone conversation, turn away from each other and talk as though you are on the phone.

1. The student dials the number of the grocery store, saying the numbers out loud in pairs.
2. The grocer answers the phone by saying hello and giving the name of the store.
3. The student identifies himself or herself and explains that he or she needs to buy some meat and cheese, fruits and vegetables, desserts and beverages for a party.
4. The grocer asks what day the party is.
5. The student gives the date of the party and then asks for the prices of specific items.
6. The grocer gives the prices.
7. The student orders the amount of the kinds of meat and cheese, fruits and vegetables, desserts and beverages that he or she wants.
8. The grocer gives the price of each item and then gives the total.
9. The student thanks the grocer and both say good-bye.

Communication écrite

Imagine that you are going to give a party to celebrate a special event. The first step in getting ready for your party is to design and write an invitation to send to your guests. On the invitation say that you're having a party and what special event you're celebrating. Be sure to mention what day and where the party is and at what time. Also include the foods and beverages you'll be serving. Remember to add RSVP and your name and phone number at the end of the invitation.

Communication orale is the unit's cumulative oral proficiency activity. Usually in the form of a role-play, the activity combines all the unit's elements into one contextualized situation.

6. The exam which decides whether French students may go on to a university is called the **terminale**.
7. The walls of classrooms in French high schools are filled with examples of students' work, pictures, posters, etc., and look similar to those of American classrooms.
8. French students are often happy with a score of 12 out of 20.
9. Time in France is always expressed according to the 24-hour clock.
10. If you use the 24-hour clock, you don't need to specify A.M. or P.M.

Communication orale

A French exchange student is spending the year at your school. With a partner, play the roles of a student in your school and the visiting French student. Exchange information about daily schedules, what courses you're both taking and what school supplies you need. During the course of your conversation:

1. Greet each other in French and introduce yourselves.
2. Ask each other how things are going and respond.
3. Ask and tell each other which courses you are taking now.
4. Ask and tell each other the teacher's name for each of these courses.
5. Ask and tell each other when each of these classes begins.
6. Ask and tell each other which courses you like.
7. Ask and tell each other what supplies you need.
8. Tell each other good-bye and say that you'll see each other soon.

Communication écrite

As a follow-up to your conversation, write a paragraph telling what you have discovered about your partner's daily schedule, courses and needed school supplies. You might begin to organize your thoughts by writing lists that have the following headings: **les cours, les profs, les heures, il/elle aime..., il/elle a besoin de....** Use the information from your lists to write your paragraph.

Isabelle a besoin d'étudier. (La Rochelle)

Communication écrite is the written equivalent of the *Communication orale*. Graphic organizers guide students as they prepare their memos, notes, invitations, reports, letters, and compositions.

les cours

il/elle a besoin de...

ses activités

les profs

il/elle aime...

les heures

Communication active

To express need, use:
J'ai besoin de dormir.	*I need to sleep.*
J'ai besoin d'étudier.	*I need to study.*

To ask what something is, use:
Qu'est-ce que c'est?	*What is it/this?*

To identify something, use:
C'est le cahier de maths.	*This is the math notebook.*

To tell location, use:
Il/Elle est **devant** le café.	*It's in front of the café.*
Il/Elle est **derrière** la chaise.	*It's behind the chair.*
Il/Elle est **sur** le bureau.	*It's on the desk.*
Il/Elle est **sous** le sac à dos.	*It's under the backpack.*
Il/Elle est **dans** la trousse.	*It's in the pencil case.*
Il/Elle est **avec** le stylo.	*It's with the pen.*
Il/Elle est **là.**	*It's there/here.*

To ask for information, use:
Où est la trousse?	*Where is the pencil case?*
Quoi?	*What?*
Tu as juste un cours le mercredi?	*Do you have just one class on Wednesday?*

To give information, use:
Je finis à 10h00.	*I finish at 10:00.*

To disagree with someone, use:
Si, j'aime la biologie.	*Yes (on the contrary), I like biology.*

To express emotions, use:
Tant mieux.	*That's great.*
J'en ai marre!	*I'm sick of it! I've had it!*
Zut!	*Darn!*

To describe daily routines, use:
J'ai une heure de chimie.	*I have one hour of chemistry.*
J'ai trois cours.	*I have three classes.*
Je commence à 8h00.	*I begin at 8:00.*
Je finis à 17h30.	*I finish at 5:30.*

To invite someone to do something, use:
On mange ensemble?	*Shall we eat together?*

To state exact time, use:
Il est deux heures **et quart.**	*It's 2:15.*
Il est deux heures **quinze.**	*It's 2:15.*
Il est quatre heures **et demie.**	*It's 4:30.*
Il est quatre heures **trente.**	*It's 4:30.*
Il est six heures **moins le quart.**	*It's 5:45.*
Il est cinq heures **quarante-cinq.**	*It's 5:45.*
Il est sept heures **dix.**	*It's 7:10.*
Il est neuf heures **moins vingt.**	*It's 8:40.*
Il est huit heures **quarante.**	*It's 8:40.*

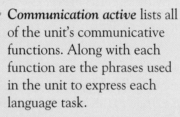

Tant mieux!

Zut! La géographie commence à 8h45.

Communication active lists all of the unit's communicative functions. Along with each function are the phrases used in the unit to express each language task.

Communication électronique, a new technology section of the unit review, features an exploratory Internet activity correlated specifically to the cultural content of the unit. Students are directed to a specific Web site, given careful directions on how to proceed, and then asked questions about what they have discovered. These questions range from those that check content comprehension to more open-ended, discovery questions.

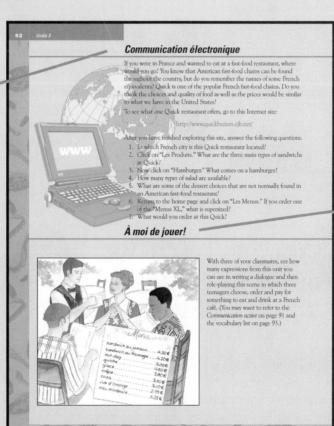

Communication électronique

If you were in France and wanted to eat at a fast-food restaurant, where would you go? You know that American fast-food chains can be found throughout the country, but do you remember the names of some French equivalents? Quick is one of the popular French fast-food chains. Do you think the choices and quality of food as well as the prices would be similar to what we have in the United States?

To see what one Quick restaurant offers, go to this Internet site:

http://www.quickbeziers.cjb.net/

After you have finished exploring this site, answer the following questions.

1. In which French city is this Quick restaurant located?
2. Click on "Les Produits." What are the three main types of sandwichs at Quick?
3. Now click on "Hamburger." What comes on a hamburger?
4. How many types of salad are available?
5. What are some of the dessert choices that are not normally found in an American fast-food restaurant?
6. Return to the home page and click on "Les Menus." If you order one of the "Menus XL," what is supersized?
7. What would you order at this Quick?

À moi de jouer!

With three of your classmates, see how many expressions from this unit you can use in writing a dialogue and then role-playing this scene in which three teenagers choose, order and pay for something to eat and drink at a French café. (You may want to refer to the *Communication active* on page 91 and the vocabulary list on page 93.)

À moi de jouer! is a cumulative writing section in which students draft dialogues or descriptive narratives based on a visual cue and using the functions and vocabulary in the unit. Students' writing for this section will be more open-ended and creative than in the *Communication écrite* section.

SUPPLEMENTARY MATERIALS

ANNOTATED TEACHER'S EDITION

The **Annotated Teacher's Edition** includes the full-sized student pages with an abundance of useful and practical teaching suggestions in the margins. An introduction to the Annotated Teacher's Edition provides a Scope and Sequence Chart, lesson plans for a model unit that cover both regular class periods and block scheduling, and the *C'est à toi!* program's philosophy and learning strategies. Easy-to-use marginal notes suggest when to use ancillary materials and offer a wealth of additional cultural information, grammar explanations, and suggestions for expanding the lesson's content. Each page of the Annotated Teacher's Edition contains a correlation of the activities and information on that page to the National Standards.

The *C'est à toi!* Annotated Teacher's Edition contains numerous activities on various topics corresponding to and supporting the material students are studying in each unit, including the following:

- Comparisons (critical thinking skills)
- Paired activities
- Cooperative group practice
- Connections (cross-curricular activities)
- TPR
- Games
- Activities to develop students' multiple intelligences
- Ideas for modifying and expanding activities

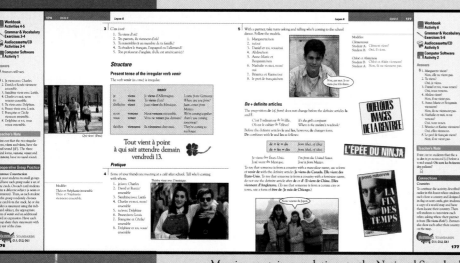

Margins contain correlations to the National Standards and colorful icons cross-referencing *C'est à toi!* components.

ANNOTATED TEACHER'S EDITION ON CD-ROM

A TRULY GREAT PLANNING TOOL FOR THE NEW MILLENNIUM

The Annotated Teacher's Edition is available on CD-ROM for easy access to the textbook and its components. Pages can be printed out or viewed on screen by means of clicking on icons that also cross-reference supplementary materials.

WORKBOOK AND WORKBOOK TEACHER'S EDITION

Innovative activities correlated to each section in the textbook help students become proficient in written French as they further practice the functions, vocabulary, and structures in each unit. The **Workbook** recombines previously learned language concepts and broadens students' understanding. Realia-based activities prepare students to use the language in authentic situations.

The **Workbook Teacher's Edition** contains the answers for all of the exercises in the student workbook. The Annotated Teacher's Edition contains icons that note where each workbook activity best fits in.

TEACHER'S RESOURCE KIT

The **Teacher's Resource Kit** contains a variety of useful and practical tools to help you make your daily lesson plans. This easy-to-use kit includes a program manager with daily lesson plans, additional listening comprehension activities on reproducible blackline masters (with answer key/teacher's edition), audiocassettes or CDs with listening activities, a teacher's edition of the workbook, and an audiocassette/CD program manual.

Innovative exercises correlated to the lessons in the textbook offer an exciting way to hone language skills.

Realia prepares students for language use in authentic situations.

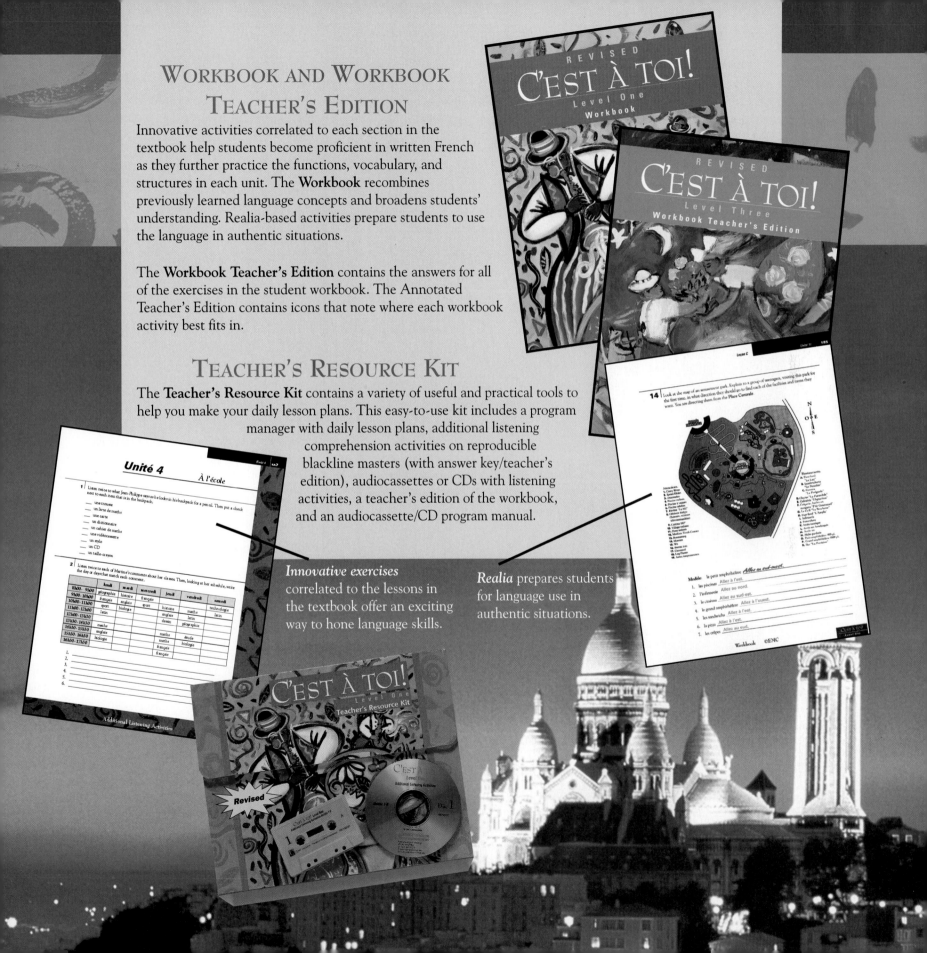

SUPPLEMENTARY MATERIALS

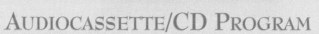

AUDIOCASSETTE/CD PROGRAM

The **Audiocassette/CD Program** is an integral part of *C'est à toi!* Appropriate icons in the Annotated Teacher's Edition designate which material in the textbook has been recorded on audiocassettes or compact discs by native speakers of all ages from a variety of francophone countries. This program will help your students develop an ear for the many nuances of the French language. Recorded material in each unit includes:

- Introduction of new words and expressions
- *Dialogue*
- *Pratique*
- *Prononciation*
- *Sur la bonne piste*

The Audiocassette/CD Program Manual includes the complete script of the recorded material for each unit in the textbook.

ASSESSMENT PROGRAM

The unique format of the **Assessment Program** allows you to design tests that evaluate what you have taught in the way you have taught it. Choose to use whatever sections you feel are relevant: vocabulary, structure, proficiency writing, culture, listening, speaking, and reading. You can even choose which parts of these seven sections fit your needs. For example, to evaluate listening, you might choose an activity on video or an activity on audiocassette or CD. Or to evaluate speaking, you might choose a paired activity or a teacher/student interview. The Assessment Program includes: Lesson Quizzes (with answer key/teacher's edition), Unit Tests, Unit Tests Teacher's Edition, Listening Comprehension Tests Video, Listening Comprehension Tests Audiocassette or CD, and Portfolio Assessment with Proficiency Tests.

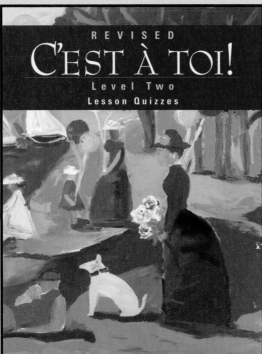

LESSON QUIZZES

Included within the Assessment Program, the **Lesson Quizzes** contain quizzes correlated to each lesson of the textbook. The quizzes include sections that evaluate speaking, vocabulary, structure, and culture. These quizzes provide students with excellent practice before they take the unit test. Appropriate icons in the Annotated Teacher's Edition designate at what point in the lesson the quiz may be given.

PORTFOLIO ASSESSMENT WITH PROFICIENCY TESTS

Included within the Assessment Program, the **Portfolio Assessment with Proficiency Tests** contains a variety of forms for both students and teachers to complete, featuring rubrics for oral and written work as well as semester and year-end tests that measure proficiency in all five skill areas in order to monitor students' progress.

SUPPLEMENTARY MATERIALS

TPR STORYTELLING MANUAL

Total Physical Response (TPR) Storytelling is a teaching strategy that ensures greater fluency in and comprehension of the target language as well as better long-term vocabulary retention. The **C'est à toi!** **TPR Storytelling Manual** provides everything French teachers need to incorporate TPR Storytelling into their classrooms.

- Philosophy and teaching techniques are thoroughly described for teachers who have little or no background in teaching TPRS.
- Preparation time is kept to a minimum because step-by-step instructions walk teachers through the teaching of each story.
- Basic and advanced stories provide teachers and students with flexibility.
- Recommended gestures for new words help teachers convey meaning.
- Numerous illustrations are included.
- Authors are classroom teachers who have used these materials with their students.

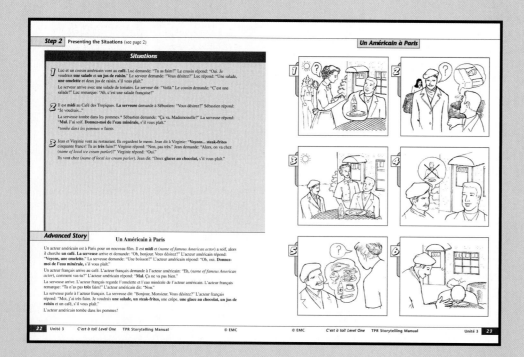

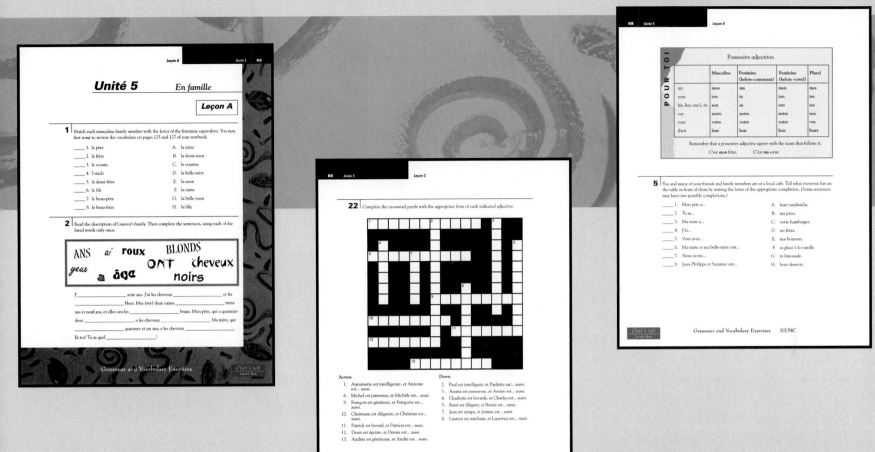

GRAMMAR AND VOCABULARY EXERCISES

Grammar and Vocabulary Exercises, available for levels one and two of *C'est à toi!*, provide an ideal format for additional practice of the basic structures and topics presented in first- and second-year French. Each unit is correlated to the textbooks, and both the grammar and vocabulary sections give students excellent practice in preparing for the quizzes and tests in the *C'est à toi!* program.

The Grammar and Vocabulary Exercises:

- supplement the *C'est à toi!* textbook with 250 pages of additional thematic practice in vocabulary and grammar
- review basic structures in the *Pour toi* sections before students practice them
- expand on the structures presented in the textbook (for example, additional *–ir* and *–re* verbs)
- offer a variety of fun activities, such as word searches and crossword puzzles
- provide flexibility for students at all ability levels
- build a solid foundation for continuing in French

SUPPLEMENTARY MATERIALS

VIDEO PROGRAM

Filmed entirely on location in La Rochelle and Paris, this exciting **Video Program** with a continuous story line is closely coordinated with the functions, vocabulary, and structures of each unit. Your students will easily become involved with their francophone contemporaries in interesting, realistic situations and be eager to discover what happens to them in the next episode. The accompanying Video Manual contains both innovative viewing and post-viewing activities as well as transcripts of the video units.

Students become involved with their francophone contemporaries and can't wait to discover what happens in the next episode.

OVERHEAD TRANSPARENCIES

Full-color **Overhead Transparencies,** correlated to
the content of each lesson, offer illustrations of scenes,
objects, and maps to provide an outstanding method
of visually reinforcing the lesson's content. These
transparencies can be used to teach or review the
lesson's content in a creative, communicative manner.
The Annotated Teacher's Edition contains icons that
designate where each transparency best fits in.

COMPUTER SOFTWARE

The **Computer Software Program** (Macintosh and
IBM), closely coordinated with the textbook, is
ideal drill and practice for reviewing and reinforcing
each lesson's structural information. At the end of
each lesson, a comprehensive quiz checks students'
understanding of each concept. The Computer
Software Program Manual provides additional
details on how to use the program effectively.

SUPPLEMENTARY MATERIALS

CD-ROM PROGRAM

EMC/Paradigm's **C'est à toi!** series features a highly interactive multimedia **CD-ROM Program** designed to enhance students' skills in speaking, listening, writing, and reading within a functional and cultural context. As journalistic interns for a publication about the French-speaking world, students face the many communicative challenges of news reporters. The program expands on the context of the textbook and also offers real-life tasks that assess students' proficiency in the language.

Interactive Dialogues

- Native French speakers engage students in conversations on a variety of topics.
- An innovative recording feature allows students to record conversations for playback.
- Students can check their speaking ability and fluency by listening to models of native speakers.

Innovative Assignments

- Observation and listening skills are honed as students watch videos and gather information to solve problems encountered by journalists.
- Vocabulary and fluency improve as students become immersed in authentic, animated conversations.

Publication Pages

- Engaging assignments motivate students to do research and write about the geography, history, and culture of French-speaking countries.

- Reading and writing skills improve as students read faxes and encyclopedia articles to prepare the pages for publication.

- Futuristic online reference materials allow immediate access to a dictionary, a colorful atlas, and an encyclopedia for all cultural and publication activities.

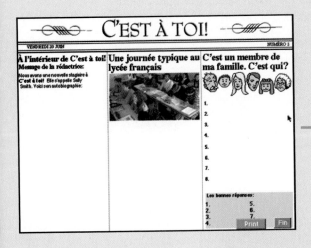

SUPPLEMENTARY MATERIALS

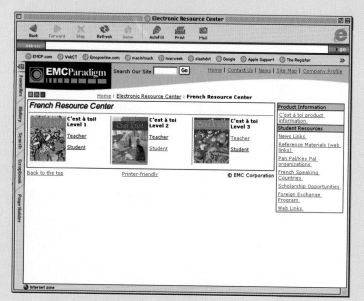

INTERNET RESOURCE CENTER

Internet activities and answers, self-quizzes, review exercises, and Web links, all correlated to the units of the *C'est à toi!* textbooks, can be found on the Internet Resource Center, accessible from **www.emcp.com**. In addition, general student resources include links to scholarship sources, travel Web sites, pen pal and key pal organizations, and reference materials. In the general teacher resources are links to professional organizations, grant opportunities, state adoption information, and teaching resources.

Each Internet activity is linked to a French Web site that students can access and review to complete the activity worksheet.

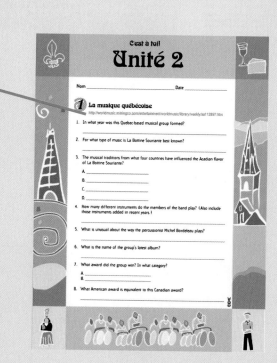

INTERNET ACTIVITIES

Internet activities in French and English enhance students' language skills and cultural knowledge as well as develop their Internet research skills.

To review the *C'est à toi!* Internet activities online:

1. Go to **www.emcp.com/cestatoi/**.
2. Click on level one, two, or three.
3. Click on Student Internet Activities.
4. Choose an activity from one of the units.
5. Print out the worksheet.
6. Instruct students to open the link to the Web site address within the Internet activity and use the Web site to answer the questions on the worksheet.

The *C'est à toi!* Program

Choose the Best French Program for You and Your Students

C'est à toi! **will make your students' experiences with French an exciting adventure and your job easier and more rewarding!**

- Teacher-friendly to minimize your preparation time

- Flexible to meet the needs of students at all ability levels

- Proficiency based to enhance students' real-world skills

- Up-to-date, broad cultural coverage

- Balanced approach to skill development

- Comprehensive and numerous supplementary materials

- Great service and support

C'EST À TOI!

Level One

About the Cover

Woman with Jazz Musicians, the cover for the first level of *C'est à toi!*, is an original acrylic by Kelly Stribling Sutherland. Reminiscent of *Woman with Hat* by Henri Matisse, the figure in the foreground comes alive with brilliant clashes of pure color in the style of the French expressionists. Created expressly for *C'est à toi!*, this painting captures the **joie de vivre** for which the French are famous. World music, one of the textbook's themes, is reflected in this scene that brings to mind the festive Mardi Gras celebration in New Orleans, complete with swirling confetti.

C'EST À TOI!
Level One

Annotated Teacher's Edition

Authors

Karla Winther Fawbush

Toni Theisen

Dianne B. Hopen

Sarah Vaillancourt

Contributing Writer

Linda Klohs

EMC/Paradigm Publishing, Saint Paul, Minnesota

ISBN 0-8219-2256-4

Published by EMC/Paradigm Publishing
875 Montreal Way
St. Paul, Minnesota 55102
800-328-1452
www.emcp.com
E-mail: educate@emcp.com

Printed in the United States of America
2 3 4 5 6 7 8 9 10 XXX 07 06 05 04 03 02

Contents

SCOPE AND SEQUENCE CHART

Unité	Leçon	Fonctions	Vocabulaire	Enquête culturelle
1 *Salut! Ça va?*	**A**	greeting someone introducing yourself introducing someone else asking someone's name telling someone's name	greetings introductions names	greetings register levels school courtyard
	B	introducing yourself greeting someone leaving someone thanking someone giving telephone numbers restating information	greetings leave takings numbers from 0 to 20 alphabet	phone numbers leave takings
2 *Qu'est-ce que tu aimes faire?*	**A**	expressing likes and dislikes asking for information inviting refusing an invitation agreeing and disagreeing	activities sports	cognates school schedules movies
	B	expressing likes and dislikes agreeing and disagreeing asking for information	adverbs of degree activities sports	free-time activities music driving *le Tour de France*
	C	asking for information expressing likes and dislikes giving opinions inviting	activities sports	sports
3 *Au café*	**A**	asking how someone is telling how you are asking what time it is telling time on the hour inviting accepting and refusing an invitation	physical well-being time	fast-food restaurants healthy eating
	B	ordering food and beverages	food beverages	*le boulevard Saint-Michel* French fries mineral water coffee crêpes
	C	asking for a price stating prices	numbers from 20 to 100	*service compris* money

Structure	Prononciation	Mise au point sur...	Sur la bonne piste
subject pronouns *tu* vs. *vous* infinitives present tense of regular verbs ending in *-er*	unpronounced consonants		
position of adverbs		la musique	
negation with *ne (n')... pas*			beginning reading strategies: context, cognates, guessing
present tense of the irregular verb *aller* telling time on the hour	[a], [i]		
gender of nouns and indefinite articles		la cuisine française	
definite articles plurals			cognates

Unité	Leçon	Fonctions	Vocabulaire	Enquête culturelle
4 *À l'école*	A	expressing emotions expressing need asking for information telling location asking what something is identifying objects	classroom objects classroom expressions prepositions	school supplies short French words names of schools terms for "student"
	B	expressing emotions describing daily routines agreeing and disagreeing asking for information giving information	days of the week numbers from 100 to 1,000 school subjects	slang expressions French calendar school subjects schools in Canada
	C	inviting describing daily routines stating exact time	time	24-hour clock difference between A.M. and P.M.
5 *En famille*	A	asking for information giving information pointing out family members asking and telling how old someone is describing physical traits	family relationships colors (hair and eyes) age	proverbs prefix *beau-*
	B	asking and telling what the date is telling location pointing out family members	pets numbers over 1,000 dates months	Nantes Guadeloupe and Martinique metric system vacations pets
	C	explaining something telling when someone's birthday is expressing emotions describing character	adjectives	birthday celebrations saint's day
6 *Tu viens d'où?*	A	asking for information asking and telling where someone is from identifying nationalities	birthdays countries nationalities	Tours travel within Europe
	B	identifying professions asking for information giving information explaining something	professions	working in France
	C	giving information inviting expressing emotions	seasons weather	Celsius scale bicycles and mopeds

Structure	Prononciation	Mise au point sur...	Sur la bonne piste
present tense of the irregular verb *avoir* expressions with *avoir*	[y], [u]		

present tense of regular verbs ending
  in *-ir*
		l'enseignement
		  secondaire en France	

telling exact time			context
possessive adjectives expressions with *avoir*	liaison		
present tense of the irregular verb *être* dates		les familles françaises	
agreement of adjectives			cultural viewpoint
present tense of the irregular verb *venir* *de* + definite articles forming questions	intonation		
indefinite articles in negative sentences the interrogative adjective *quel* *c'est* vs. *il/elle est*		la France et ses voisins	
present tense of the irregular verb *faire* forming questions with inversion			skimming and predicting

Unité	Leçon	Fonctions	Vocabulaire	Enquête culturelle
7 *On fait les magasins.*	A	expressing intentions expressing need inviting expressing likes and dislikes	clothing types of stores	specialized stores teenagers and fashion *le Quartier latin* open-air markets
	B	expressing likes and dislikes inquiring about and comparing prices agreeing and disagreeing	colors adjectives	Montreal *soldes*
	C	choosing and purchasing items asking someone to repeat asking for information giving information	shopping	how to ask someone to repeat sizes French words used in English
8 *On fait les courses.*	A	asking for information giving information agreeing and disagreeing identifying objects asking for permission	vegetables seafood	Marseille regional dishes healthy ingredients
	B	agreeing and disagreeing expressing likes and dislikes insisting giving information	food specialty food stores expressions of quantity	bread cheese yogurt
	C	asking for a price stating prices making a complaint inquiring about and comparing prices negotiating choosing and purchasing items	fruits comparative of adjectives	Guadeloupe shopping for fruits and vegetables
9 *À la maison*	A	inviting identifying objects	types of housing rooms in a house furniture	apartments *une armoire* teens' bedrooms bathrooms public restrooms
	B	inviting accepting and refusing an invitation greeting someone greeting guests introducing someone else offering and accepting a gift excusing oneself offering food and beverages	parts of a house introductions	styles of houses floors of a house vacation homes gifts for the hosts before-dinner snacks
	C	expressing intentions describing daily routines telling location agreeing and disagreeing	meals table setting	*le Maghreb* Morocco Ramadan

Structure	Prononciation	Mise au point sur...	Sur la bonne piste
aller + infinitive *à* + definite articles	[ɔ], [ɔ̃]		
irregular adjectives position of adjectives present tense of the verbs *acheter* and *préférer*		les vêtements	
present tense of regular verbs ending in -*re*			critical reading
present tense of the irregular verb *vouloir* present tense of the irregular verb *pouvoir* demonstrative adjectives	[ø], [œ]		
the partitive article the partitive article in negative sentences expressions of quantity		les courses	
comparative of adjectives			thinking in French
de + plural adjectives	[ə], silent "e"		
present tense of the irregular verb *prendre* the imperative		les repas	
present tense of the irregular verb *mettre*			inference

Unité	Leçon	Fonctions	Vocabulaire	Enquête culturelle
10 *La santé*	**A**	expressing astonishment and disbelief expressing emotions expressing reassurance pointing out something expressing need and necessity giving advice	parts of the body physical well-being	Chamonix *le Mont Blanc* skiing proverb
	B	making an appointment stating exact and approximate time explaining a problem congratulating and commiserating giving information	negative expressions parts of the head ailments	Lake Geneva Switzerland
	C	expressing concern making a complaint explaining a problem expressing need and necessity making a prediction giving advice	ailments parts of the body	*une crise de foie* health expressions pharmacy herbal remedies homeopathy
11 *En vacances*	**A**	describing past events telling location	European countries nationalities travel by train	*la Toussaint, le jour des Morts* travel by train Belgium Brussels
	B	writing postcards expressing emotions telling location describing past events sequencing events expressing likes and dislikes stating a preference	African countries nationalities travel by plane ordinal numbers	Paris airports Ivory Coast Senegal
	C	inquiring about details identifying objects telling location giving addresses asking for information giving directions	places in the city compass directions	Luxembourg the Camargue region les Saintes-Maries-de-la-Mer Mistral changing money post office *le tabac*
12 *À Paris*	**A**	writing journal entries describing past events sequencing events	places in the city travel by subway	Tahiti *le Drugstore* *Mona Lisa* *le métro* *Père-Lachaise* Statue of Liberty
	B	describing past events sequencing events expressing need and necessity	Bastille Day expressions	*la Défense* Bastille Day celebration
	C	asking for information giving opinions comparing things sequencing events	superlative of adjectives	public parks in Paris districts of Paris *le Forum des Halles* *la Villette*

Structure	Prononciation	Mise au point sur...	Sur la bonne piste
present tense of the irregular verb *falloir*	[s], [z]		
verbs + infinitives negative expressions		la santé	
present tense of the irregular verb *devoir*			pictures and illustrations
passé composé with *être*	[ɛ̃], [jɛ̃]		
ordinal numbers prepositions before cities, countries and continents		le monde francophone	
present tense of the irregular verb *voir*			review of reading strategies
passé composé with *avoir*	[k]		
irregular past participles		Paris	
superlative of adjectives			dictionary skills

Introduction

C'est à toi! is a revised three-level French program that has been developed in response to needs expressed by teachers throughout the country who are looking for the latest in a communication-based, functional approach to teaching French language and culture. Based on detailed surveys involving hundreds of experienced educators and information gleaned from focus groups conducted in various parts of the country, *C'est à toi!* offers an innovative, creative approach to meeting the needs of students in the twenty-first century.

When the *Goals 2000: Educate America Act* provided funding for improving education in 1994, a K-12 Student Standards Task Force was formed to establish content standards in foreign language education. The National Standards in Foreign Language Education Project brought together a wide array of educators, organizations and interested individuals to discuss and establish a new national framework of standards for foreign language education in the United States. The resulting document, titled *Standards for Foreign Language Learning: Preparing for the 21ˢᵗ Century*, provides a bold vision and a powerful framework for understanding language learning. These standards will help shape instruction and assessment for years to come.

The National Standards identify and describe 11 content standards that correspond to the organizing principle of five interconnected Cs: Communication, Cultures, Connections, Comparisons and Communities. The *C'est à toi!* program was specifically designed to address these standards, and they are cross-referenced in the lower left- and lower right-hand corners of the pages of *C'est à toi!*, using the numbering system as it appears in the standards:

Communication

Communicate in Languages Other Than English
Standard 1.1: Students engage in conversations, provide and obtain information, express feelings and emotions and exchange opinions.

Standard 1.2: Students understand and interpret written and spoken language on a variety of topics.

Standard 1.3: Students present information, concepts and ideas to an audience of listeners or readers on a variety of topics.

Cultures

Gain Knowledge and Understanding of Other Cultures
Standard 2.1: Students demonstrate an understanding of the relationship between the practices and perspectives of the culture studied.

Standard 2.2: Students demonstrate an understanding of the relationship between the products and perspectives of the culture studied.

Connections

Connect with Other Disciplines and Acquire Information
Standard 3.1: Students reinforce and further their knowledge of other disciplines through the foreign language.

Standard 3.2: Students acquire information and recognize the distinctive viewpoints that are available only through the foreign language and its cultures.

Comparisons

Develop Insight into the Nature of Language and Culture

Standard 4.1: Students demonstrate understanding of the nature of language through comparisons of the language studied and their own.

Standard 4.2: Students demonstrate understanding of the concept of culture through comparisons of the cultures studied and their own.

Communities

Participate in Multilingual Communities at Home and Around the World

Standard 5.1: Students use the language both within and beyond the school setting.

Standard 5.2: Students show evidence of becoming life-long learners by using the language for personal enjoyment and enrichment.

C'est à toi! features a fresh approach to function-based communication in all three modes: interpersonal, interpretive and presentational. Written by active and experienced high school French teachers who deal daily with students just like yours, the *C'est à toi!* program provides a realistic balance among all five skill areas that will develop proficiency in each one. Paired, small group and cooperative group activities are at the heart of today's student-centered classroom. In the *C'est à toi!* program, students assume a more active role in their learning, working with each other to accomplish linguistic tasks, with teachers serving primarily as facilitators.

The comprehensive *C'est à toi!* program, composed of the textbook and its fully integrated set of additional components, offers instructors and students the most complete materials possible to teach and learn French. The accompanying ancillaries may be used as enrichment, additional practice or reinforcement. These tailor-made materials, which fit individual students' needs and learning styles, include the annotated teacher's edition, annotated teacher's edition on CD-ROM, workbook, grammar and vocabulary exercises, assessment program (with quizzes, tests, portfolio assessment with proficiency tests, and test generator on CD-ROM), audiocassette/CD program, teacher's resource kit, program manager (with daily lesson plans), video program, overhead transparencies, computer software program, total physical response storytelling manual, Internet activities, Internet resource center and interactive CD-ROM program. One of the greatest challenges that teachers face today is reaching students with varying abilities, backgrounds, interests and learning styles. The extensive instructional program of *C'est à toi!* recognizes, anticipates and provides for these differences.

About This Annotated Teacher's Edition

The front section of this Annotated Teacher's Edition contains:

- a description of each section of the textbook along with a list of the other *C'est à toi!* components
- a Scope and Sequence Chart that gives a complete overview of each unit in *C'est à toi!*
- relevant information about the program's authors
- authors' philosophy of proficiency, culture, structure and reading
- the *C'est à toi!* program's philosophy and learning strategies that are incorporated in the textbook
- model lesson plans for both regular class periods and block scheduling
- a list of practical classroom expressions (**Expressions de communication**)
- a phonetic representation of the French alphabet (**L'alphabet phonétique**) and a list of the French expressions for basic punctuation marks (**La ponctuation**)
- a list of all the communicative functions covered in *C'est à toi!* and the units in which they are first practiced
- suggestions and ideas for using the Internet
- a list of additional sources for information

The annotated version of the expanded student textbook contains:

- correlations of ancillary materials to the textbook

    a. **Workbook Activity**

    b. **Grammar & Vocabulary Exercise**

    c. **Audiocassette/CD Activity**

    d. **Transparency**

    e. **Listening Activity**

    f. **Quiz**

    g. **Computer Software Activity**

    h. **Video**

- correlations of the textbook to the National Standards

- answers to both oral and written activities (except where answers are personalized)
- cultural notes (information that may be useful to teachers and interesting to students)
- additional background information
- linguistic and pronunciation notes
- teaching suggestions
  a. paired activities
  b. cooperative group practice
  c. TPR
  d. comparisons (critical thinking skills)
  e. connections (cross-curricular activities)
  f. games
  g. activities to engage students' multiple intelligences
  h. ideas for modifying and expanding activities

Components

C'est à toi! is a comprehensive three-level French language program written to meet the needs of French students as they enter the twenty-first century. The first-level program includes the following components:

- Textbook
- Annotated Teacher's Edition
    - Annotated Teacher's Edition on CD-ROM
- Workbook
- Workbook Teacher's Edition
- Grammar and Vocabulary Exercises
- Teacher's Resource Kit
    - Additional Listening Activities
    - Additional Listening Activities Teacher's Edition
    - Audiocassettes/CDs with Additional Listening Activities
    - Workbook Teacher's Edition
    - Audiocassette/CD Program Manual
    - Program Manager with Daily Lesson Plans
- Audiocassette/CD Program
    - Audiocassettes/CDs
    - Audiocassette/CD Program Manual
- Assessment Program
    - Lesson Quizzes
    - Lesson Quizzes Teacher's Edition
    - Unit Tests Booklet
    - Unit Tests Booklet Teacher's Edition
    - Unit Tests Video
    - Unit Tests Audiocassettes/CDs
    - Portfolio Assessment with Proficiency Tests
    - Test Generator on CD-ROM
- Video Program
    - Videos
    - Video Manual
- Overhead Transparencies
- Computer Software Program (IBM or Mac)
    - Disks
    - Manual
- TPR Storytelling Manual
- Internet Activities
- Internet Resource Center
- CD-ROM Program (IBM or Mac)

Textbook

This revised textbook contains 12 **unités**. Each **unité**, except the first one, is composed of three **leçons**, labeled **A**, **B** and **C**. At the end of the textbook you will find a grammar summary, an end vocabulary section (French/English and English/French) and a grammar index. All the **unités**, except the first one which contains only two **leçons**, have been designed in a similar manner so that students will be familiar with the format and know exactly what to expect. Each lesson gives students the communicative functions, vocabulary, structures and cultural information necessary to communicate in authentic French about a variety of everyday situations that interest teenagers. The entire textbook's active vocabulary is less than 1,000 words, and grammatical structures are recycled systematically to help students bridge from the known to the unknown.

Unit Opener — The unit begins with a list of communicative functions. This provides a preview of the tasks that students will be able to accomplish when they complete the unit. Functions are continually recycled from one unit to the next, with functions repeated only when a different way of expressing that specific function is introduced. A two-page photo visually prepares students for one of the main cultural components of the unit.

Lesson Opener — Each lesson begins with a list of the communicative functions that pertain to that lesson. Next come colorful illustrations or photos with speech bubbles that introduce all the new vocabulary groups and expressions in the lesson in a meaningful context. Students should be told that illustrations and photos in the lesson opener are part of the basic textbook material, visually explaining words and expressions that students are expected to know.

Dialogue — Next comes a short dialogue, telephone conversation, postcard or journal entry that follows a natural format and dramatizes a situation typical of everyday life in francophone regions. Speakers represent a cross section of age groups, although the emphasis is on activities of teenagers. The dialogue is introduced with a colorful illustration or photo that reinforces the cultural content and makes each situation more meaningful. The dialogue contains an example of how each one of the lesson's communicative functions is expressed. (This is summarized for students in the **Communication active** section in the **C'est à moi!** review section at the end of every unit.) Each dialogue has been carefully designed not only to present authentic speech but also to contain at least one instance in which each of the new structures in the lesson is used. All words in the dialogue are active vocabulary; that is, students are expected to produce the words in **Pratique** and **Communication** activities and use them again in following units. To understand the lesson's new vocabulary words, students can refer back to the introductory illustrations or photos as well as infer meaning from the dialogue's context. Previously learned words and structures are regularly recycled.

Enquête culturelle — Directly after the dialogue, a group of notes highlights certain cultural subtleties or presents more detailed information about the French-speaking world. These notes are not related to each other; they refer to various sentences in the dialogue and expand on the information presented there. These comments are intended to heighten students' interest in, appreciation for, and understanding of certain aspects of francophone culture and to provide insight into the daily activities of French speakers. Accompanying photos and realia help to expand students' cultural horizons.

Activités — Following the **Enquête culturelle** is a series of activities that checks comprehension of the dialogue's content and new vocabulary that has been presented either visually or in the dialogue. Some of the activities in early lessons also evaluate students' understanding of information presented in the **Enquête culturelle**. Following the comprehension activities, students are challenged to answer personalized questions dealing with the dialogue's theme in the **C'est à toi!** activity. All of these activities may be done orally, in writing or both.

Structure — This section presents the lesson's main grammatical topics in a concise, clear manner. Examples in French are presented along with their English equivalents to help students' comprehension. Colorful charts provide reinforcement as do photo captions that illustrate how the specific structures are used in context.

Pratique — Following the presentation of each grammar topic is the **Pratique** section, composed of contextualized activities that allow students to practice both oral and written skills. Realistic situations as a basis for the activities make students' communication more relevant. You may choose whether students respond orally, in writing or both. The more mechanical activities precede those that allow students more creativity or are open-ended. The type of activities in the **Pratique** section varies— those based on visual cues and realia, dehydrated sentences, paired activities and sentence completion. The **Modèle**, in the side margin, demonstrates a correct response to help students succeed immediately.

Communication — A series of proficiency-based activities appears at the end of each lesson following the last **Structure** and **Pratique** section. These activities provide opportunities for students to develop oral and written proficiency using the functions that are presented in each lesson. Task-based paired and cooperative learning activities as well as activities that encourage the development of multiple intelligences foster the creative use of French to practice using the lesson's vocabulary and structures to express specific functions. For example, students may be asked to write shopping lists, design menus, order at a restaurant, conduct a survey or an interview, label photos, do role-plays, design postcards, make posters or give directions.

Prononciation — This section is presented at the end of **Leçon A** in each unit. It gives students the opportunity to practice and perfect their pronunciation of certain French sounds and intonation patterns. Sounds that may be especially difficult for English speakers to master have been highlighted and may be contrasted with related sounds. Only words previously introduced are used as models.

Mise au point sur... — Written in English, this section at the end of **Leçon B** in each unit features in-depth cultural material related to the unit's theme. Current, topical information broadens students' understanding of and appreciation for francophone culture. Different from the **Enquête culturelle**, the topics are more general (for example, world music, sports, shopping and Paris) and are presented in greater depth. On-location photography reinforces the cultural content. Two activities follow each **Mise au point sur...**. The first checks students' comprehension of the content of the reading. The second features a piece of realia relating to the section's theme that students use to answer questions.

Sur la bonne piste — Various reading strategies in French are highlighted; for example, skills in skimming and scanning, identifying cognates, determining meaning from context and using a dictionary. Each unit focuses on a different technique to help students experience success as they read in French. Students are carefully guided before and as they read authentic French texts, such as realia, ads, poetry and narratives, so that they can apply the strategies presented in each unit. A series of questions follows, some calling for specific answers and others calling for some interpretation. The Annotated Teacher's Edition gives suggestions on how to holistically grade these answers and also optional activities where students can further practice each reading strategy.

Nathalie et Raoul — This original cartoon series featuring a continuous story line offers a light-hearted approach to using each unit's functions, vocabulary and structures. Additional, current vocabulary that appeals to students but is not a part of the unit vocabulary is introduced. English equivalents of the cartoons are found in the Annotated Teacher's Edition.

C'est à moi! — The first of the seven-part review section at the end of each unit, **C'est à moi!** consists of a personalized checklist of all the functions that have been introduced in the unit. If students are unsure of how to express a certain function, they should look for an example of it in the following **Communication active** section. **C'est à moi!** also has a true-false quiz on the cultural information presented in the unit's **Enquêtes culturelles** and **Mise au point sur...**.

Communication orale — This cumulative oral proficiency activity usually takes the form of a paired role-play. Students are carefully guided as to what each partner should include in the conversation. The activity combines all the elements in the unit — functions, topics, vocabulary and structures — into one final, contextualized situation.

Communication écrite — This cumulative proficiency-based writing activity is the written equivalent of the **Communication orale**. Again, students are carefully guided as to what they should include in their memos, notes, invitations, reports, letters and compositions.

Communication active — The fifth part of the review section summarizes all of the unit's communicative functions. Along with each function are the phrases used in the unit to express each language task. English equivalents are also given for easy reference. The words in boldface type are the invariable elements; those not in bold may change depending on the specific information that students want to express.

Communication électronique — This new technology section features an exploratory Internet activity correlated specifically to the cultural content of the unit. Students are directed to a Web site, given careful directions on how to proceed and then asked questions about what they have discovered. These questions range from those that check content to more open-ended, discovery questions. Students practice their language skills in French as they explore authentic realia and read up-to-the-minute information about francophone culture. (Note that the Internet is a fast-paced technology, and Web pages and Web addresses are constantly changing or disappearing. You may need to substitute different addresses from the ones given in the **Communication électronique** throughout the textbook.)

À moi de jouer! — In this new cumulative writing section, students have the chance to show what they can do by putting together everything they have learned so far. Illustrations give students a visual clue as to what they should include in writing their dialogues or descriptive narratives based on the functions and vocabulary in the unit. Students' writing will tend to be more open-ended and creative than in the **Communication écrite** section.

Vocabulaire — The final part of the review section is a list of all the new active words and expressions (with English equivalents) that are introduced in the unit.

Grammar Summary (end of the textbook) — This useful reference section summarizes for students' convenience the structures introduced in *C'est à toi!* Present tense forms of all irregular verbs are also included.

Vocabulary (end of the textbook) — All words and expressions introduced as active vocabulary in *C'est à toi!* appear in this end vocabulary. The number following the meaning of each word or expression indicates the unit in which it appears for the first time. For convenient and flexible use, both French-English and English-French vocabularies are included. Passive vocabulary found in the direction lines to activities and in authentic readings is not included.

Grammar Index (end of the textbook) — A complete index of all the grammar points covered in *C'est à toi!* is provided for easy reference and location.

Annotated Teacher's Edition

This Annotated Teacher's Edition contains a front section and an annotated version of the student textbook.

Front Section:
- description of all the program's components
- Scope and Sequence Chart
- information about the authors
- authors' philosophy of proficiency, culture, structure and reading
- program philosophy and learning strategies
- model lesson plans (regular and block scheduling)
- classroom expressions
- phonetic alphabet and punctuation marks
- communicative functions
- Internet suggestions
- additional sources for information

Annotated Version of the Student Textbook:
- correlations of ancillary materials to the textbook
- correlations of the textbook to the National Standards
- answers to both oral and written activities
- cultural notes
- additional background information
- linguistic and pronunciation notes
- teaching suggestions (paired activities, cooperative group practice, TPR, comparisons (critical thinking skills), connections (cross-curricular activities), activities to engage students' multiple intelligences, games)

Annotated Teacher's Edition on CD-ROM

The annotated version of the student textbook is available on CD-ROM for convenient access to the book. Each page can be viewed on screen and printed out so that teachers don't have to carry the textbook home to plan their classes. Teachers can also click on each of the icons to view and print out pages of the supplementary materials that support each page of the textbook.

Workbook

The workbook reviews and expands on the material covered in the textbook with additional written exercises that reinforce students' language skills and cultural awareness. These innovative activities help students become proficient in written French as they further practice the functions, vocabulary and structures in each unit. The workbook also recombines previously learned language concepts to broaden students' understanding. Again, many of these activities are written situationally to make them more realistic and relevant to students. Realia-based activities prepare students to use French in authentic situations. Exercises in the workbook are carefully coordinated with the textbook. The Annotated Teacher's Edition contains icons that tell where each workbook activity best fits in.

Workbook Teacher's Edition

An answer key for all exercises contained in the workbook is available.

Grammar and Vocabulary Exercises

This workbook provides additional practice with basic structures and topics presented in first-year French. Each unit is correlated to the same unit in the textbook to give students more opportunities to use what they have learned. Conceptualized to make them more meaningful and relevant, these activities are preceded by a telescopic restatement of the grammar point being explained or the verb being presented along with several examples. Vocabulary that has been introduced in the textbook is also reviewed. Word games and puzzles give students the chance to identify and write the new vocabulary groupings. Both grammar and vocabulary sections offer excellent practice in preparing for quizzes and tests and provide a solid foundation for continuing in French. An answer key is at the end of the workbook.

Teacher's Resource Kit

The Teacher's Resource Kit contains a variety of useful and practical tools to help teachers make their daily lesson plans. The following components are included in the Teacher's Resource Kit:

- **Additional Listening Activities (on blackline duplicating masters)**

  There are four additional listening comprehension activities in each unit, one for each lesson and a cumulative dialogue. They check students' ability to understand authentic French speech in the form of narratives or conversations. Students have an answer sheet on which they respond in writing either by completing a checklist or by answering true-false, multiple-choice or matching questions. These activities help to prepare students for the listening comprehension sections of the Unit Tests in the Assessment Program. The Annotated Teacher's Edition contains icons that tell where each listening activity best fits in.

- **Additional Listening Activities Teacher's Edition**

  The complete text for the recorded additional listening activities as well as an answer key is available.

- **Audiocassettes/CDs with Additional Listening Activities**

  These audiocassettes/CDs contain the additional listening activities for each unit.

- **Workbook Teacher's Edition**

  An answer key for all exercises contained in the workbook is available.

- **Audiocassette/CD Program Manual**

  This manual contains the complete script of the recorded material (introduction of new words and expressions, **Dialogue**, **Pratique**, **Prononciation** and **Sur la bonne piste** sections) for each lesson in the textbook.

- **Program Manager with Daily Lesson Plans**

  The Program Manager pulls together the textbook and all the ancillary materials with daily lesson plans for organizing, preparing and teaching the *C'est à toi!* program. Each day's lesson plan presents the core material from the textbook in the left-hand column. In the right-hand column, across from each core element, are the specific ancillary materials that are appropriate for expansion. There are separate lesson plans for both traditional 45- to 55-minute class periods as well as for classes on the block scheduling system.

Audiocassette/CD Program

The various components included in the Audiocassette/CD Program are:

- **Audiocassettes/CDs**

  The Audiocassette/CD Program is an integral part of *C'est à toi!* Appropriate icons in the Annotated Teacher's Edition designate which material in the textbook has been recorded on cassettes or CDs by native speakers of all ages from a variety of francophone countries. Recorded material in each unit includes:

  Introduction of new words and expressions (for student repetition)
  Dialogue (recorded first as a listening experience and then broken into manageable phrases for student repetition)
  Pratique (selected activities for student response)
  Prononciation (for student repetition)
  Sur la bonne piste (recorded as a listening experience)

- **Audiocassette/CD Program Manual**

  This manual contains the complete script of the recorded material (introduction of new words and expressions, **Dialogue**, **Pratique**, **Prononciation** and **Sur la bonne piste** sections) for each lesson in the textbook.

Assessment Program

The *C'est à toi!* Assessment Program contains the following components:

- **Lesson Quizzes**

  There are three quizzes for each unit, one at the end of every lesson. Each quiz consists of four sections: speaking (role-playing activities or personalized questions), vocabulary, grammar (both mastery and proficiency activities) and culture. These quizzes provide students with excellent practice before they take the unit test. Appropriate icons in the Annotated Teacher's Edition designate at what point in the lesson the quiz may be given.

- **Lesson Quizzes Teacher's Edition**

  A complete answer key for the Lesson Quizzes is available.

- **Unit Tests Booklet**

  The Unit Tests in the *C'est à toi!* program evaluate to what degree students are attaining the program's goals and objectives. A unique format in assessment allows teachers to design tests that evaluate what they have taught in the way they have taught it. Teachers may choose to use whatever sections reflect their students' learning styles and their teaching style: vocabulary, structure, proficiency writing, culture, listening, speaking and reading. For example, to evaluate students' listening ability, teachers can choose an activity on video or an activity on audiocassette. Or to evaluate their students' speaking ability, teachers can choose a paired activity or a teacher/student interview.

- **Unit Tests Booklet Teacher's Edition**

  The Teacher's Edition of the Unit Tests Booklet contains the text of the material recorded for the listening comprehension section (audiocassette/CD and video) and answer keys to the listening comprehension section and written sections (vocabulary, structure, proficiency writing, culture, speaking and reading) of each Unit Test.

- **Unit Tests Video**

  Teachers may choose to use the Unit Tests Video to evaluate students' listening and cultural comprehension. A short segment of the *C'est à toi!* Video Program has been recorded as part of the Assessment Program. After students watch this segment, they answer questions that evaluate their cultural understanding and their ability to comprehend what they have heard.

- **Unit Tests Audiocassettes/CDs**

  Teachers may choose to use the Unit Tests Audiocassettes/CDs to evaluate students' listening comprehension. Students hear authentic French in conversations or narratives and respond by choosing the best answer or continuation to the conversation. They may also see a visual and respond by choosing the best answer to a related question.

- **Portfolio Assessment with Proficiency Tests**

  The first section of the *C'est à toi!* Portfolio Assessment is a rationale for using portfolios in the French class and tips on how to implement this form of evaluation. Next comes a variety of forms for both students and teachers to complete, such as a learner profile, peer evaluation sheet, communicative functions checklist and suggested rubrics for evaluating oral and written production. The final section contains a proficiency-based exam evaluating all five skills for use at the end of the first semester, and another for use at the end of the year.

- **Test Generator on CD-ROM**

  The IBM- and Macintosh-compatible test generator allows teachers to test exactly as they have taught, allowing for differences in instructional emphases, teaching approaches and students' learning styles. Teachers can select and modify sections from the existing Assessment Program, including Units Tests, Lesson Quizzes and Proficiency Tests, in order to create and print their own customized tests. The CD also allows teachers to add their own test questions as well as edit existing questions.

Video Program

The various components included in the Video Program are:

- **Videos**

  Filmed entirely on location in La Rochelle and Paris using professional actors, these exciting, live-action videos with a unique, continuous story line are closely coordinated with the functions, vocabulary and structures of each unit of the textbook. Students see and hear situations related to themes in *C'est à toi!* that review, reinforce and expand on the material they have just learned.

Becoming involved with their francophone contemporaries in interesting, realistic situations, students can't wait to discover what happens to Aurélie, Julien and Leïla in the next episode. There is one video episode for each unit in the textbook. The Annotated Teacher's Edition contains icons that tell where each video best fits in.

- **Video Manual**

  The Video Manual is included in the Video Program. It contains transcripts of the video units as well as a variety of innovative pre-viewing and post-viewing activities, some based on additional authentic materials.

Overhead Transparencies

A set of 64 full-color transparencies offers illustrations of scenes (as a stimulus for conversation), objects (with identifying overlays) and maps. These transparencies provide an outstanding method of teaching, visually reinforcing or reviewing the lesson's content in a creative, communicative manner. Students can apply their knowledge of vocabulary and culture using different visual stimuli. The Annotated Teacher's Edition contains icons that tell where each transparency best fits in.

Computer Software Program (IBM or Mac)

Included in the Computer Software Program are:

- **Disks**

  The Computer Software Program, closely coordinated with the textbook, is ideal for drill and practice to review and reinforce each lesson's structural information. At the end of each unit is a comprehensive quiz that checks students' understanding of each concept. The Annotated Teacher's Edition contains icons that tell where each activity best fits in.

- **Manual**

  The Computer Software Program Manual provides additional details on how to use the program effectively.

TPR Storytelling Manual

In EMC/Paradigm's TPR Storytelling Manual, teachers present new vocabulary through gestures, then students practice this vocabulary in short situations before finally using it to tell and act out a story. This "hands-on" manual has everything teachers need to incorporate TPR Storytelling into their classrooms. In the beginning of the manual, TPRS philosophy and teaching techniques are thoroughly explained for instructors who have little or no experience with this strategy. Then step-by-step instructions guide teachers through the presentation of the basic and advanced stories, one of each correlated to every unit in the textbook. Gestures are given for new words and phrases to help teachers convey meaning as they present the situations and the stories. Numerous illustrations guide students as they recreate the stories. Additional teaching suggestions, strategies and assessment options are also provided for each story.

Internet Activities

The *C'est à toi!* Internet Activity Web site features contemporary, interesting Internet activities. There are three activities correlated to each unit in the textbook. These Internet activities enhance students' language skills and cultural knowledge as well as develop their Internet research skills. Students are carefully guided through the various links in each activity. Teachers receive a password to allow them to access all the activities' answers. Since the Internet is a changing medium, activities are constantly being added, deleted and modified. To view these activities, visit **www.emcp.com/cestatoi**/.

Internet Resource Center

Internet activities and answers, self quizzes, review exercises and Web links, all coordinated with the units of the *C'est à toi!* textbooks, can be found on the Internet Resource Center, accessible from **www.emcp.com**. The site also features general resources for teachers and students, including useful Web links, teaching tips and study aids. The content of the Internet Resource Center is continually being updated.

CD-ROM Program (IBM or Mac)

The innovative, interactive CD-ROM Program with video reinforces and enriches students' skills in all five areas within a functional context. Students actively play the roles of interns at a newspaper and are asked to complete various hands-on assignments for the editor-in-chief. As interns, they face an array of challenges that any news reporter would encounter. This business setting allows students to solve meaningful, real-world problems as they improve their proficiency in French. Authentic French video clips stimulate students' responses on a variety of topics. An innovative recording feature allows students to record all their conversations for playback. Students' vocabulary and fluency improve as they become immersed in authentic, animated conversations. An abundance of additional geographical, historical and cultural information expands students' understanding of the francophone world.

About the Authors

Karla Winther Fawbush has taught French, English and Journalism at Brooklyn Center High School in Brooklyn Center, Minnesota, since 1975. She has served on the Executive Boards of the Minnesota Council on the Teaching of Languages and Culture and the Minnesota Chapter of the American Association of Teachers of French (AATF). Fawbush received her M.Ed. degree in Second Languages and Cultures from the University of Minnesota. She has worked with the Minnesota Humanities Commission, organizing teacher workshops and speaking to the state legislature urging implementation of the Minnesota Institute for the Advancement of Teaching. She has been awarded a Rockefeller Fellowship, a National Endowment for the Humanities Summer Seminar Fellowship and a Council for Basic Education Interdisciplinary Fellowship. Recently, she has been selected to be included in *Who's Who Among America's Teachers*. Fawbush has led many student groups on her extensive travels to francophone areas, including France, Belgium, Switzerland, Quebec, New Orleans and Martinique.

Toni Theisen teaches French and World Cultures at Loveland High School and Turner Middle School in the Thompson R2J School District in Loveland, Colorado, where she is also the district's foreign language subject area leader. Active in the foreign language profession throughout her career, Theisen has given many presentations and workshops at national, regional and state foreign language conferences. She has served as president of the Colorado Congress of Foreign Language Teachers (CCFLT) and the Colorado AATF, member of the Central States Conference (CSC) Board of Directors, program chair for the CSC and local arrangements chair for the CSC, SWCOLT and CCFLT Joint Conference. Theisen has traveled extensively throughout the francophone world and spends many summers in France organizing and leading student travel/homestay programs. She has received numerous honors and awards, including the ACTFL Nelson Brooks Award for the Teaching of Culture, the Governor's Award for Excellence in Teaching, SWCOLT's Outstanding Teacher Award and the Excellence in Teaching Award from the CCFLT.

Dianne Hopen has been a French teacher for 31 years at Humboldt Senior High School in St. Paul, Minnesota, where she has also served as her school's specialty planner for the International Studies and Communications Program. She earned her M.A. degree in French from the University of Minnesota, where her continuing Ph.D. studies have focused on the psychology of learning and teaching. Named an Honor Roll Teacher in the search for Teacher of the Year in Minnesota, Hopen has received the Rotary Educator of the Year Award and the Gordon M. A. Mork Award as an Outstanding Educator. She has devoted more than 25 years to the Concordia College Language Villages Program as a designer, director and teacher in the residential French programs and a leader of their biking in France program. Hopen most recently created a summer high school credit program for American students in Avignon, France. Many times a guest speaker at teacher education seminars, she has also given presentations at national and local foreign language conferences on informal educational immersion experiences, based on her more than 40 trips to France.

Sarah Vaillancourt is French Editor at EMC/Paradigm Publishing. She is a graduate of Macalester College and the recipient of two NDEA Foreign Language Institute grants, studying in Paris, Tours and Grenoble. She taught French I-V at East High School in Madison, Wisconsin, for 22 years where she received the Bassett Award for Excellence in Teaching. As a program administrator for various student travel organizations, she has taken high school students on more than 20 study-travel tours to Europe, Africa and Canada. Vaillancourt authored the textbooks in the series *Perspectives françaises*, and has been the editor of the textbooks and ancillary materials in the series *Le français vivant* and *C'est à toi!* She has spoken at many state, regional and national foreign language conventions and workshops on topics such as using paired activities for proficiency, engaging students' multiple intelligences and weaving culture through the French curriculum.

Foreign Language Proficiency

by Toni Theisen

Proficiency as an organizing concept and as a thoughtful philosophy for second language acquisition has given our content area new life and meaning since its realization in the 1980s with the advent of the ACTFL Proficiency Guidelines. We as language instructors and facilitators are becoming more and more aware of the power, meaning and relevancy of knowing a second language. It is an exciting time to be a part of the profession as we begin to see enrollments increase steadily. We are also encouraged by the growing number of people who value communication skills in our global society. Therefore, the *C'est à toi!* program provides a series of proficiency activities in which students can experience situations in a range of contexts that they would most likely encounter in the francophone culture. Language learners actually use French to solve language tasks.

The ACTFL Proficiency Guidelines

The ACTFL Proficiency Guidelines have given us a clearer definition of the manner and degree in which language is acquired at different levels. We now know the appropriate language tasks and the level of accuracy we can expect from our students in all language skills, ranging from novice-low to superior levels. Proficiency activities involve all language modalities—from listening and reading to speaking and writing, with culture naturally integrated into each language task. We expect novice-mid language learners to function only with limited accuracy in simple survival situations using vocabulary that deals with high-frequency phrases. For example, novice-mid students can successfully order in a café or listen to a set of directions to arrive at a given place. Language learners at the advanced level are able to function at a higher degree of accuracy in situations with a problem or twist, often using circumlocution to negotiate meaning. For example, advanced students are able to write a narrative describing a situation that occurred in the past, such as retelling the events of an accident that they might have witnessed and then relating their reaction to the situation. These guidelines help us design realistic and attainable goals for our language learners.

The Rationale for Proficiency Activities

In order for students to truly own a language, they need to be able to interact with it on successful terms. Proficiency activities act as a catalyst for authentic language use, and students begin to identify with the real purpose of language learning. This ability to interact with others using any of the skills of listening, speaking, reading and writing, all integrated with culture, gives language learners a true sense of accomplishment in French.

Research shows that the optimum scenario for learning is actually doing or experiencing. Through lecture and passive reception, students retain only about 10 percent of the material, whereas with experiential, active learning, students can achieve a 90 percent retention rate. Learning through experience involves students in such a way that vocabulary, structures and functions are put into long-term memory.

Responsibilities of the Learner and Teacher

When incorporating proficiency activities into a lesson, the instructor or facilitator turns over the responsibility of the cognitive learning process to the language learners. It is this opportunity to create with the language that motivates students not only to successfully complete the task, but also to do it with a certain amount of risk involved. As teachers, it is then a part of our job to encourage and effectively praise our students for taking that risk with their acquired language skills and cultural knowledge. In this process, students will discover more ways to negotiate meaning in French. They will arrive at a clear understanding of the linguistic task and all its variables.

Using Many New Strategies

Proficiency is a philosophy and not a strategy. Using proficiency as an organizing principle opens the doors to many new learning strategies. This is a great forum for the use of cooperative learning activities that encourage language learners to work together to complete a given task and to depend on and trust each other in order for the group to be successful. The use of pairs and cooperative groups has proved to be tremendously effective in foreign language classrooms. Proficiency also encourages student-centered activities in which the teacher becomes the facilitator of the language. Many instructors integrate authentic materials into their lesson plans as ways to more easily negotiate meaning. Using authentic materials, teachers have learned to change the task rather than change the text.

Proficiency links the learner with language. This real-world use of language framed in real-life situations makes learning French even more relevant. As students strive for higher and higher levels of proficiency, our country will feel more a part of the whole world. In the words of the French Canadian singer Michel Rivard, "C'est la langue de mon cœur et le cœur de ma vie." Hopefully, our students will also feel this way about French.

The Teaching of Culture

by Karla Winther Fawbush

It is impossible to understand another culture thoroughly without speaking its language. Language and culture are directly linked to each other. Words themselves have cultural connotations. For example, the word **marché** evokes an image of a bustling marketplace, the scent of flowers and spices in the air, people bumping into one another as they shop for the freshest produce and the shouts of vendors advertising their wares. What does this say about the value of fresh food in French-speaking households? How do the colors, smells and animation of the marketplace compare to the efficient, sterile atmosphere of the contemporary supermarkets that are springing up in many francophone countries? In what ways does the visual image of the word **marché** help students to understand the deeper aspects of both traditional and contemporary francophone culture?

Ask most students what picture comes to mind when they think of Paris, and they will usually respond "the Eiffel Tower." Built for the World's Fair in 1889, this famous landmark certainly represents the traditional view of French culture: Paris as the center for the best in art, literature, music and architecture. Although historically valid to a point, this definition of culture must be expanded. Culture is more than the great masterpieces of one city; it is how a variety of francophone people speak and behave in everyday situations.

Communicative competency includes both linguistic and cultural proficiency. Therefore, the teaching of culture must extend to every aspect of instruction in a proficiency-based classroom. Certainly there remains a place for the formal, "big C" study of the fine arts in French civilization. Students of all levels of French can appreciate the paintings of Monet, the poems of Prévert, the music of Debussy and the stained glass windows and flying buttresses of Chartres Cathedral. However, the definition of culture needs to extend to a more anthropological view of daily life and language in the francophone world. Why is it inappropriate to bring chrysanthemums as a gift to a dinner party in France? Why should the expression **je suis pleine** be avoided when you have had enough to eat? Why might a young person in Cameroon refer to an adult as Mama Renée or Papa Jean?

Cultural instruction should: (1) expand the study of isolated facts to include a deeper understanding of the various values, beliefs and behavior of French speakers; (2) recognize similarities, as well as differences, among cultures; (3) help students to develop critical thinking skills so that they learn to notice details and work toward independence in novel social situations; and (4) be entwined with the language as a means of communication.

French teachers cannot be expected to be the authority on every aspect of francophone culture. Native guest speakers or teaching assistants, radio and television programs, magazines, newspapers, computer networks, videos and other forms of realia are helpful sources of cultural information.

Moving from the identification of the various components of a cultural program to its implementation in the classroom can be done in several ways. In order to integrate culture into the study of the French language, students should be encouraged to: (1) keep a cultural notebook and make culture a component of their language portfolio; (2) reflect on their own cultural background; and (3) practice questioning and hypothesizing in order to recognize patterns that will help them interact successfully in the francophone culture. Culture engages the heart, and students are most motivated to learn French when it is taught through relevant, meaningful content.

From their first day of French, students should learn to integrate cultural information with the study of the language. By maintaining a cultural notebook, students can explore their own cultural self-awareness as they expand their appreciation of other cultures, learn to express what they have observed, examine their attitudes and enhance their ability to make choices.

As they become exposed to various aspects of francophone culture, students need to examine their own background. For example, students can form groups to select ten items for a time capsule that would represent American culture. Or, students can compare French and American TV commercials to identify the methods used to sell various products in the two cultures. What do these methods say about the subjective values, beliefs and behavior of these two groups? To what extent are the goals (i.e., the need for food, shelter, clothing and education) the same in both cultures?

Students also need to utilize critical thinking skills in order to identify patterns and act appropriately in novel situations. For example, after listening to a foreign exchange student from France, American students may observe that French teenagers seem to rely on automobiles less than they do. Why? At what age do young people in various countries get their driver's license? Is gas more expensive in French-speaking countries than in the United States? Do French-speaking high school students have part-time jobs that would help them pay for the expenses of driving a car? What is public transportation like in francophone countries? Do people often walk or bike to their destination? Finding out the answers to these questions will help students learn to understand francophone culture, while realizing how much of their personal behavior stems from their own geographical and socioeconomic background.

In *C'est à toi!* culture is integrated into the study of French. Dialogues are placed in a variety of francophone settings, as a backdrop for the language itself. Cultural information corresponds to the topics and vocabulary introduced in each unit. Realia engages students to use both inductive and deductive reasoning. Teacher's notes offer supplementary cultural information and suggestions on how to make culture an integral part of each day's activities. For example, in the comparisons activities (critical thinking), questions are provided that students might think about and answer in their cultural journals. Organized on the premise that awakening student interest in the diverse aspects of the francophone world can only enhance linguistic growth, *C'est à toi!* encourages students to widen their cultural horizons as they develop their proficiency in French.

Structural Practice

by Dianne Hopen

> ## Achievement = Personal Experience and Ability + Practice

Each student is the sum of his or her previous learning through a variety of educationally and noneducationally oriented situations, plus his or her ability to process new learning. Student achievement depends on the *amount of practice* available to the student in order to compensate for differing amounts of previous learning and the student's natural ability to learn.

Each of our students enters the language learning setting with a unique set of personal experiences and a differing ability to participate successfully in each new learning situation. As teachers we cannot change our students' previous experience, nor can we alter their ability to learn. What we can do is provide adequate practice.

Research on cognitive learning style preferences has validated foreign language educators' long-held belief that a variety of learning activities is necessary for students to realize their objectives in language learning. Activities that provide contextually meaningful practice are appropriate for all students. Those students with a structured approach to learning benefit the most from structured practice, but all students increase their level of confidence with such practice.

Controlled structural practice or the practice of the mechanics of a language in a contextually meaningful activity allows students to master communicative patterns that lead to the development of free-flowing speech. Students are not logically capable of responding appropriately or accurately in all language settings until they have had the opportunity to practice the functions and vocabulary relating to each particular setting.

Each time a student miscommunicates, it reinforces the importance of accuracy and serves to motivate the student to practice the structure of the language. In a learning setting where both the teacher and the student seek quality control of French for accurate communication, mechanical practice serves as one of the building blocks to success.

Identifying appropriate language components and providing varied and sufficient practice with each one is the goal of the **Structure** sections in the *C'est à toi!* program. Once students have had the opportunity to experience authentic French in realistic situations, structured practice becomes meaningful by providing increasingly more thoughtful practice with manageable portions of communication. This is how students work toward achieving their goal of communicating in French.

Reading
by Linda Klohs

Reasons for Reading

We read for two basic reasons: (1) for pleasure, and (2) for information. In order to read for pleasure, we must first understand what we are reading, that is, read for information. There are various strategies that our students can use to efficiently glean appropriate information from what they read. Unfortunately, these strategies do not come easily to many of them. It is part of our job as educators to find and teach these methods, techniques or strategies.

Learning to Infer: Part of the Reading Act

Many students believe that they must understand each word of every sentence in order to proceed to the next one. In many real-life reading acts, this need to understand each word is not necessary. Furthermore, such dependence is self-defeating, culminating in students' reluctance or refusal to continue when they encounter new or forgotten information or structures. Students need to be encouraged to read for the main idea and to infer meaning from previous sentences or paragraphs or ones that follow.

The Role of the Student and Teacher in the Reading Process

At one time, reading was called a "passive" skill. Many still refer to it as a "receptive" skill. But it is important for students to know that reading is, in fact, an "active" skill. Students must take an active part in the reading process, constantly inferring, deducing, anticipating, guessing, predicting, checking and asking themselves questions about the text. How we, as teachers, encourage them in this process requires us to ask a broader range of questions and accept a wider range of responses than those required by traditional multiple-choice or fill-in-the-blank tests.

Reading Progression in *C'est à toi!*

In the first level of *C'est à toi!* the beginning units ask students to read simplified texts written by native speakers. These texts focus on the functions, vocabulary and structures on which these early units are based. Readings found in later units come from original texts that are followed by achievable tasks, such as responding to content questions about a poem or using a French-English dictionary successfully. Having students read authentic French in the first year does not imply a much more difficult task on their part. The difficulty of a reading passage depends greatly on what is required of the student after reading the text.

Assessment of the Reading Process

Students bring various personal experiences from life and past reading, both in English and in French, to the reading task. The temptation to lead students toward a single interpretation may curtail thought and enjoyment of a reading passage. If they believe that there is only one answer or way to perceive the reading, many will be discouraged from developing idiosyncratic thought or offering well-thought-out answers. Depending on their level of reading proficiency, students may arrive at various acceptable answers to the activities that follow some of the readings in *C'est à toi!* If students believe that delving deeper into a reading will result in a superior score, many will take the risk to do so. Assessment of students' answers or responses should be judged on a holistic basis, with superior scores given to students who produce more creative or thought-provoking answers. While holistic grading is new to some teachers, suggestions on how to implement this means of assessment are made in the Annotated Teacher's Edition.

Some students depend entirely on teachers for assessment and approval of their work. It becomes increasingly important that as students become more proficient in French, they must be able to diagnose both their own learning process and achievement in the language in order to become independent learners. Teachers can decide when students are ready to self-assess, and will find techniques in the Annotated Teacher's Edition of *C'est à toi!* that will help them in the process.

Philosophy and Learning Strategies

C'est à toi! is a function-based textbook series that uses a communicative approach to teach students the French language within the context of the francophone world. Students acquire proficiency in listening to, speaking, reading and writing French while developing cultural sensitivity to the everyday activities of French-speaking people throughout the world. Since the focus of the classroom is student interaction, from day one students practice communicating easily and confidently with their peers in paired or cooperative learning groups. A balance of activities, both in the textbook and in the comprehensive ancillary program, allows students with a variety of learning styles to be successful in French as they progress from carefully structured practice to more creative expression. The five "Cs" addressed in *Standards for Foreign Language Learning: Preparing for the 21ˢᵗ Century* are artfully interwoven throughout each section of the textbook, integrating the principles of COMMUNICATION, CULTURES, CONNECTIONS, COMPARISONS and COMMUNITIES to help prepare students for an active, informed role as world citizens in the new millennium.

Many activities in the student textbook, as well as additional activities suggested in the color-coded sections of the Annotated Teacher's Edition, incorporate the following learning strategies and techniques to make learning more actively student centered and relevant to those with diverse learning styles.

- **Paired Activities**

  As the teacher-centered classroom moves toward the student-centered classroom where students are directly involved in and responsible for their own learning, teachers find that paired activities (in which one student is paired with a partner):

  1. give students markedly increased practice time in using French
  2. promote cooperation with others to achieve clearly stated goals
  3. instill in students greater self-confidence in their language abilities by placing them with their peers in less-threatening situations
  4. place students in more realistic, communicative settings
  5. lead to increased student involvement and motivation
  6. provide for a variation in classroom routine
  7. allow the teacher to assume a facilitating role, circulating throughout the room to answer questions and assist those who can benefit from individual help

  In order to assure students' success in a paired activity, teachers should make certain that the activity's goal is clearly communicated to students, tell them how to proceed in order to achieve their goal (provide a model), announce how much time they have to finish their task and inform them how their learning will be evaluated at the end of the activity. Paired activities appear in the **Pratique**, **Communication** and **C'est à moi!** sections of the textbook as well as in the color-coded Paired Practice section of the Annotated Teacher's Edition.

- **Cooperative Group Activities**

  Cooperative learning involves students working together to access, share and process knowledge, increase academic competencies and develop interpersonal and small group social skills. Putting students in cooperative learning groups makes them individually accountable for the outcome of their learning. Each member of a cooperative group must assume some responsibility for completing his or her task in order for the group to attain the stated goal. Students practice positive interdependence as they interact face-to-face with each other. Usually cooperative learning groups consist of four students who are grouped heterogeneously. As with paired activities, the teacher's role is to clearly communicate the activity's goal, tell how to proceed, set time limits and clarify evaluation procedures. When assigning group roles, the teacher should divide up responsibilities to ensure students' interdependence and cooperation. Each group should have a leader or facilitator, recorder and reporter. The final step in a cooperative group activity is to share the group's product with the rest of the class, who, along with the teacher, should assess the quality of the group's production. Cooperative learning activities are provided in the **Communication** and **C'est à moi!** sections of the textbook as well as in the color-coded Cooperative Group Practice section of the Annotated Teacher's Edition.

- **TPR Activities**

In the TPR (Total Physical Response) approach to second language acquisition, students are actively engaged in listening comprehension activities while limiting their responses to physical rather than to verbal demonstrations of comprehension. The teacher initially gives commands or verbal cues that elicit specific student behavior. Students may respond, for example, by pointing, gesturing, moving around the classroom or manipulating objects. This is an effective method of introducing new vocabulary words and expressions as well as new structures. This physical response to verbal stimuli aids students' comprehension of new elements and helps students to internalize and remember them longer. A list of practical classroom commands (**Expressions de communication**) that are useful in doing TPR activities is located on page TE45 of the Annotated Teacher's Edition. There are TPR activities in the color-coded TPR and Games sections of the Annotated Teacher's Edition.

- **Connections Activities (Cross-curricular)**

The French language and francophone culture are artfully interwoven into other areas of the secondary school curriculum so that students form connections to additional bodies of knowledge that may be unavailable to the monolingual English speaker. For example, students use their knowledge of French language and francophone culture as a stepping stone to a deeper understanding of geography, history, mathematics, art, music and science. Cross-curricular activities help to expand students' global thinking and understanding as enlightened world citizens. Connections activities are found in the **Pratique** and **Communication** sections of the textbook as well as in the color-coded Connections section of the Annotated Teacher's Edition.

- **Comparisons Activities (Critical Thinking)**

It is essential to emphasize the development of critical thinking skills, or higher order thinking skills, if our students are to succeed in school and later in life. There are many activities in *C'est à toi!* in which students practice comparing French with English and critical thinking. The cognitive abilities and their associated critical thinking skills included in the program are: knowledge acquisition (locate, describe, identify, list, match, name); comprehension (summarize, rewrite, rearrange, paraphrase); analysis (compare and contrast, order, categorize, distinguish); evaluation (conclude, justify); synthesis (associate, combine, compile, plan, generalize); and application (compose, create, design, produce). Comparisons activities appear in both the **Pratique** and **Communication** sections of the textbook and in the color-coded Comparisons section of the Annotated Teachers' Edition.

- **Activities to Engage Students' Multiple Intelligences**

Many factors affect learning. For years teachers have recognized that students' intelligence, social environment and motivation all need to be considered. In addition, not all students learn the same way. Students' diverse learning styles need to be addressed in different ways in order to maximize individual potential.

Recent explorations in how the brain works and human intelligence have provided a wealth of valuable information that is changing the perspectives of learning and teaching. Howard Gardner's Multiple Intelligences Theory proposes a pluralized way of understanding the intellect. It states that people have varying abilities in many different areas of thought and learning, and these abilities affect people's interests and how quickly they assimilate new information and skills. Gardner says that our brain processes and uses information either separately or together in concert through eight different intelligences: verbal-linguistic, logical-mathematical, visual-spatial, bodily kinesthetic, musical-rhythmic, interpersonal, intrapersonal and naturalist. The general characteristics associated with each of these intelligences are described below along with suggested instructional strategies.

Verbal-Linguistic: These students demonstrate a strong appreciation for and fascination with words and language. People who display verbal-linguistic intelligence enjoy writing, reading, word searches, crossword puzzles and storytelling.

Teaching Strategies:
Tell a story.
Summarize a magazine or newspaper article.
Write a poem.
Discuss the meaning of a song.
Write to a keypal on the Internet.

Logical-Mathematical: These students like establishing patterns and categorizing words and symbols. Students with logical-mathematical intelligence enjoy mathematics, experiments and games that involve strategy or rational thought.

Teaching Strategies:
Calculate the temperature in degrees Celsius.
Double or triple a recipe.
Write an analysis of an event.
List the reasons why something happened.
Tabulate the total cost of a shopping trip.

Visual-Spatial: These students think in pictures and can conceptualize well. They often like complicated puzzles and may be seen drawing a picture, doodling, constructing something from the objects that surround them or daydreaming. They are able to imagine how something would look from a verbal description.

Teaching Strategies:
Write a summary comparing the artistic styles of two paintings.
Draw the ideal house.
Design a theme park.
Identify a shape based on a classmate's description.
Do a creative presentation using video and slides.

Bodily-Kinesthetic: Students who are athletic may demonstrate bodily-kinesthetic intelligence. They learn best by doing what they enjoy and want to learn through movement and touch. They express their thoughts with body movement. They are good with hands-on activities, such as sewing, woodworking, dancing, athletics and crafts.

Teaching Strategies:
Perform a dance from a francophone country.
Act out a part from a play.
Build a housing structure that is reminiscent of one that appears in the textbook.
Perform an activity as directed by a classmate or the teacher (TPR).
Create artwork that represents some aspect of the francophone world.

Musical-Rhythmic: These students can be observed singing or tapping out a tune on a desk or other nearby object. They are discriminating listeners who can hear a song once and then are able to play or sing the tune. Students who demonstrate musical intelligence catch what is said the first time, whereas others around them may need to hear the same thing repeated a number of times.

Teaching Strategies:
Write a song.
Listen to and describe a musical piece.
Perform a song.
Identify musical styles of several musicians from the francophone world.
Prepare a comparison of the music of two or more musicians.

Interpersonal: Students with interpersonal intelligence are natural leaders. They communicate well, empathize with others and often know what someone is thinking or feeling without having to hear the person speak.

Teaching Strategies:
Role-play a vendor making a sale.
Lead a discussion.
Debate an issue.
Organize and direct a poll.
Negotiate a settlement.

Intrapersonal: People with intrapersonal intelligence may appear to be shy. They are self-motivated and are very aware of their own thoughts and feelings about a given subject.

Teaching Strategies:
Write answers to questions about personal life.
Prepare a written plan for a career path.
Determine the pros and cons of an issue.
Create a list of favorite activities.
Write a poem expressing feelings.

Naturalist: Students with naturalist intelligence might have a special ability to observe, understand and apply learning to the natural environment. For example, students with naturalist intelligence may collect data about the environmental conditions for a particular place and instinctively know what crop would grow best there.

Teaching Strategies:
Draw or photograph and then present to the class an object found in nature.
Collect and categorize objects from the natural world.
Do research and present findings about a wildlife protection project.
Keep a notebook of observations of nature.
Go on a nature hike or field trip.

It is important to understand that these intelligences exist in everyone in different degrees and in different combinations. These intelligences do not relate specifically to content areas, but rather to the ability to process information. The Multiple Intelligences Theory reflects a way of thinking about people that not only allows for similarities, but also for differences. It fosters inclusion, increases opportunities for enrichment, builds self-esteem and develops respect for individuals and the gifts they bring to the classroom. In a setting that fosters the multiple intelligences, all students are allowed to learn through their strengths and to share their expertise with others.

Weaving the magic of the diversity of learning with the intent of "intelligence fair" strategies challenges all teachers to explore new possibilities to honor human potential. There are activities to engage students' multiple intelligences in the **Communication** and **C'est à moi!** sections of the textbook as well as in the color-coded Teacher's Notes and Connections sections of the Annotated Teacher's Edition.

- **Games**

Games in French are excellent motivational tools that give students the opportunity to learn in a context that varies from the daily routine. During this "learning pause," students review and reinforce previously introduced material as they expand on their language skills. French songs are also presented in the color-coded Games section of the Annotated Teacher's Edition.

Model Lesson Plans

Because instructional approaches and the length of class periods vary greatly among teachers and schools, it is difficult to provide a detailed plan for each individual lesson that would apply to all students using *C'est à toi!* Many school districts offer traditional 45- to 55-minute daily class periods. Other districts have implemented a block scheduling system in which class periods range from 75 to 110 minutes. These block schedules may involve consecutive days for a whole semester, alternate days for a year or other variations.

We offer some suggested guidelines to effectively use the materials in **Unité 2**, the first unit to include all the different sections of a typical unit. The first schedule suggests how the textbook might be used in a traditional 50-minute class period. In this case, 15 days are allotted for each **unité**: four to five days for each lesson plus one day for assessment. Assuming 180 days of 50-minute class periods, *C'est à toi!* can be covered entirely in one year at the high school level.

The second schedule demonstrates how you might use the textbook in a 4/4 semester block scheduling plan. In this case, eight days are allotted for each **unité**: approximately two and one-half days for each lesson plus one day for assessment. Assuming 90 days of 90-minute class periods, *C'est à toi!* can be covered entirely in one year at the high school level.

To see lesson plans for each **unité** in the *C'est à toi!* program, consult the Program Manager with Daily Lesson Plans.

Model Unit *(Unité 2)*
Traditional Class Period (50 minutes)

Day 1 — *Leçon A*

Textbook	Ancillary materials/activities
1. Warm-up: Review numbers 0-20 and introductions from *Unité 1*	
2. Introduce the functions for *Leçon A* and vocabulary, p. 20	Audiocassette/CD: *Qu'est-ce qu'ils aiment faire?* (A) (Side A, Track 1) Transparencies 4-7 ATE: TPR, p. 20
3. *Dialogue*, p. 21	Audiocassette/CD: *Dialogue* (Side A, Track 2)
4. *Activités* 2-3, pp. 22-23	Audiocassette/CD: Activity 3 (Side A, Track 3)
5. *Enquête culturelle*, pp. 21-22	ATE: Comparisons, p. 52
6. *Activité 1*, p. 22	

Day 2 — *Leçon A*

Textbook	Ancillary materials/activities
1. Warm-up: Review *Dialogue*, p. 21	
2. Review vocabulary, p. 20	Workbook Activities 1-2, pp. 13-14
3. Subject pronouns, p. 23	Computer Software Activity 1 Grammar and Vocabulary Activity 1, p. 9
4. *Pratique* 4-5, p. 24	

5. *tu* vs. *vous*, p. 25

Workbook Activity 3, p. 15
Computer Software Activity 2
ATE: Comparisons, p. 25
Grammar and Vocabulary Activity 3, p. 11

6. *Pratique* 6, p. 25

Day 3 — *Leçon A*
Textbook

Ancillary materials/activities

1. Warm-up: Review subject pronouns and *tu* vs. *vous*

Grammar and Vocabulary Activities 2 and 4, pp. 10-11

2. Infinitives, p. 26

Grammar and Vocabulary Activities 5-7, pp. 12-14

3. *Pratique* 7-8, pp. 26-27

Audiocassette/CD: Activity 8 (Side A, Track 4)

4. Present tense of regular verbs ending in -*er*, pp. 27-28

Computer Software Activities 3-4
ATE: Comparisons, p. 27
Workbook Activities 4-6, pp. 16-17
Grammar and Vocabulary Activities 10-11, pp. 15-16

Day 4 — *Leçon A*
Textbook

Ancillary materials/activities

1. Warm-up: Review infinitives and present tense of regular verbs ending in -*er*

ATE: Game, p. 29
Grammar and Vocabulary Activities 8-9 and 12-13, pp. 14-17

2. *Pratique* 9-12, pp. 28-29

Audiocassette/CD: Activities 9 and 12 (Side A, Tracks 5-6)

3. *Communication* 13-16, pp. 30-31

ATE: Paired Practice, p. 31

4. *Prononciation*, p. 31

Audiocassette/CD: *Prononciation* (Side A, Track 7)

Day 5 — *Leçon A/Leçon B*
Textbook

Ancillary materials/activities

1. Warm-up: Review all of *Leçon A* for quiz

Listening Activity 1, p. SA3

2. Quiz *Leçon A*, pp. 4-6

Quiz *Leçon A*, pp. 4-6

3. Introduce the functions for *Leçon B* and vocabulary, p. 32

Audiocassette/CD: *Qu'est-ce qu'ils aiment faire?* (B) (Side A, Track 8)
Grammar and Vocabulary Activities 14-15, p. 18

4. *Dialogue*, p. 33

Audiocassette/CD: *Dialogue* (Side A, Track 9)

Day 6 — *Leçon B*
Textbook

Ancillary materials/activities

1. Warm-up: Review vocabulary, p. 32 and *Dialogue*, p. 33

Workbook Activity 7, p. 18
Grammar and Vocabulary Activities 16-17, pp. 19-20

2. *Activités* 2-3, p. 35

Audiocassette/CD: Activities 2-3 (Side A, Tracks 10-11)

3. *Enquête culturelle*, pp. 33-34

ATE: Comparisons, p. 34
Workbook Activity 8, pp. 18-19

4. *Activité* 1, p. 35

5. Position of adverbs, p. 36

Workbook Activity 9, pp. 19-20
Computer Software Activity 5
Grammar and Vocabulary Activity 18, p. 21

Day 7 — *Leçon B*
Textbook

Ancillary materials/activities

1. Warm-up: Review position of adverbs

ATE: Cooperative Group Practice, p. 37
Grammar and Vocabulary Activity 19, p. 21

2. *Pratique* 4-6, pp. 36-37

Audiocassette/CD: Activity 4 (Side A, Track 12)

3. *Communication* 7-8, pp. 37-38

4. Introduce French music to prepare for *Mise au point sur... la musique*

Day 8 — *Leçon B*
Textbook

Ancillary materials/activities

1. Warm-up: Review position of adverbs

2. *Mise au point sur... la musique*, pp. 39-40

Workbook Activity 10, p. 21
ATE: Connections, p. 40

3. *Activités* 9-10, p. 41

Day 9 — *Leçon B/Leçon C*
Textbook

Ancillary materials/activities

1. Warm-up: Review all of *Leçon B* for quiz

Listening Activity 2, p. SA3

2. Quiz *Leçon B*, pp. 7-8

Quiz *Leçon B*, pp. 7-8

3. Introduce the functions for *Leçon C* and vocabulary, pp. 42-43

Workbook Activity 11, p. 22
Audiocassette/CD: *Qu'est-ce qu'ils aiment faire?* (C) (Side B, Track 13)
Grammar and Vocabulary Activity 20, p. 22

Day 10 — *Leçon C*
Textbook

Ancillary materials/activities

1. Warm-up: Review vocabulary, pp. 42-43

Workbook Activity 12, p. 23
Grammar and Vocabulary Activity 21, p. 23

2. *Dialogue*, p. 44	Video
	Audiocassette/CD: *Dialogue* (Side B, Track 14)
3. *Activités* 1-3, p. 45	Audiocassette/CD: Activities 1 and 3 (Side B, Tracks 15-16)
4. *Enquête culturelle*, p. 44	Workbook Activity 13, p. 24

Day 11 — *Leçon C*
Textbook

Ancillary materials/activities

1. Warm-up: Review *Dialogue*, p. 44

Video

2. Negation with *ne (n')... pas*, p. 46

Workbook Activity 14, p. 25
Computer Software Activity 6
ATE: TPR, p. 46
ATE: Paired Practice, pp. 47-48
Grammar and Vocabulary Activity 22, p. 24

3. *Pratique* 4-7, pp. 46-47

Audiocassette/CD: Activities 4-7 (Side B, Tracks 17-20)

4. *C'est à moi!*, p. 52

ATE: Comparisons, p. 22

Day 12 — *Leçon C*
Textbook

Ancillary materials/activities

1. Warm-up: Review negation with *ne (n')... pas*

Video
Grammar and Vocabulary Activity 23, p. 25

2. *Communication* 8-10, pp. 48-49

3. *Communication orale*, pp. 52-53

4. *À moi de jouer!*, p. 54

Day 13 — *Leçon C*
Textbook

Ancillary materials/activities

1. Warm-up: Review negation with *ne (n')... pas*

Grammar and Vocabulary Activity 24, p. 26

2. Cartoon, p. 51

3. Review all of *Leçon C* for quiz

Listening Activity 3A, p. SA3
Computer Software Activity 7

4. Quiz *Leçon C*, pp. 9-11

Quiz *Leçon C*, pp. 9-11

Day 14 — *Leçon C*
Textbook

Ancillary materials/activities

1. Warm-up: *Communication écrite*, p. 53

ATE: Paired Practice, p. 53

2. *Communication électronique*, p. 54

3. *Sur la bonne piste*, pp. 49-51   Audiocassette/CD: *Sur la bonne piste* (Side B, Track 21)
Workbook Activity 15, p. 25

4. *Activité* 11, p. 51

Day 15 — Assessment
Textbook

Ancillary materials/activities

1. Warm-up: *Communication active*, p. 53

     Listening Activity 3B, p. SA4

2. Review highlights of unit

     ATE: Game, p. 53

3. *Unité 2* test, pp. 11-25

     Unit Tests Booklet, pp. 11-25, Unit Tests Video, Unit Tests Audiocassette/CD

Model Unit *(Unité 2)*
Block Scheduling (90 minutes)

Day 1 — *Leçon A*
Textbook

Ancillary materials/activities

1. Warm-up: Review numbers 0-20 and introductions from *Unité 1*

2. Introduce the functions for *Leçon A* and vocabulary, p. 20

     Audiocassette/CD: *Qu'est-ce qu'ils aiment faire?* (A) (Side A, Track 1)
Workbook Activities 1-2, pp. 13-14
Transparencies 4-7
ATE: TPR, p. 20

3. *Dialogue*, p. 21

     Audiocassette/CD: *Dialogue* (Side A, Track 2)

4. *Activités* 2-3, pp. 22-23

     Audiocassette/CD: Activity 3 (Side A, Track 3)

5. *Enquête culturelle*, pp. 21-22

     ATE: Comparisons, p. 52

6. *Activité* 1, p. 22

7. Subject pronouns, p. 23

     Computer Software Activity 1
Grammar and Vocabulary Activity 1, p. 9

8. *Pratique* 4-5, p. 24

9. *tu* vs. *vous*, p. 25

     Workbook Activity 3, p. 15
Computer Software Activity 2
ATE: Comparisons, p. 25
Grammar and Vocabulary Activities 3-4, p. 11

10. *Pratique* 6, p. 25

Day 2 — *Leçon A*
Textbook

1. Warm-up: Review subject pronouns

2. Infinitives, p. 26

3. *Pratique* 7-8, pp. 26-27

4. Present tense of regular verbs ending in *-er*, pp. 27-28

5. *Pratique* 9-12, pp. 28-29

6. *Communication* 13-16, pp. 30-31

7. *Prononciation*, p. 31

Ancillary materials/activities

Grammar and Vocabulary Activity 2, p. 10

Grammar and Vocabulary Activities 5-7, pp. 12-14

Audiocassette/CD: Activity 8 (Side A, Track 4)

Computer Software Activities 3-4
ATE: Comparisons, p. 27
Workbook Activities 4-6, pp. 16-17
ATE: Game, p. 29
Grammar and Vocabulary Activities 10-11, pp. 15-16

Audiocassette/CD: Activities 9 and 12 (Side A, Tracks 5-6)

ATE: Paired Practice, p. 31

Audiocassette/CD: *Prononciation* (Side A, Track 7)

Day 3 — *Leçon A/Leçon B*
Textbook

1. Warm-up: Review infinitives and regular verbs ending in *-er*

2. Review all of *Leçon A* for quiz

3. Quiz *Leçon A*, pp. 4-6

4. Introduce the functions for *Leçon B* and vocabulary, p. 32

5. *Dialogue*, p. 33

6. *Activités* 2-3, p. 35

7. *Enquête culturelle*, pp. 33-34

8. *Activité* 1, p. 35

Ancillary materials/activities

Grammar and Vocabulary Activities 8-9 and 12-13, pp. 14-17

Listening Activity 1, p. SA3

Quiz *Leçon A*, pp. 4-6

Audiocassette/CD: *Qu'est-ce qu'ils aiment faire?* (B) (Side A, Track 8)
Grammar and Vocabulary Activities 14-15, p. 18

Workbook Activity 7, p. 18
Audiocassette/CD: *Dialogue* (Side A, Track 9)

Audiocassette/CD: Activities 2-3 (Side A, Tracks 10-11)

ATE: Comparisons, p. 34
Workbook Activity 8, pp. 18-19

Day 4 — *Leçon B*
Textbook

1. Warm-up: Review vocabulary, p. 32

Ancillary materials/activities

Grammar and Vocabulary Activities 16-17, pp. 19-20

2. Position of adverbs, p. 36	Workbook Activity 9, pp. 19-20 Computer Software Activity 5 ATE: Cooperative Group Practice, p. 37 Grammar and Vocabulary Activity 18, p. 21
3. *Pratique* 4-6, pp. 36-37	Audiocassette/CD: Activity 4 (Side A, Track 12)
4. *Communication* 7-8, pp. 37-38	
5. *Mise au point sur... la musique*, pp. 39-40	Workbook Activity 10, p. 21 ATE: Connections, p. 40
6. *Activités* 9-10, p. 41	

Day 5 — *Leçon B/Leçon C*
Textbook

Ancillary materials/activities

1. Warm-up: Review position of adverbs	Grammar and Vocabulary Activity 19, p. 21
2. Review all of *Leçon B* for quiz	Listening Activity 2, p. SA3
3. Quiz *Leçon B*, pp. 7-8	Quiz *Leçon B*, pp. 7-8
4. Introduce the functions for *Leçon C* and vocabulary, pp. 42-43	Workbook Activities 11-12, pp. 22-23 Audiocassette/CD: *Qu'est-ce qu'ils aiment faire?* (C) (Side B, Track 13) Grammar and Vocabulary Activity 20, p. 22
5. *Dialogue*, p. 44	Video Audiocassette/CD: *Dialogue* (Side B, Track 14)
6. *Activités* 1-3, p. 45	Audiocassette/CD: Activities 1 and 3 (Side B, Tracks 15-16)
7. *Enquête culturelle*, p. 44	Workbook Activity 13, p. 24

Day 6 — *Leçon C*
Textbook

Ancillary materials/activities

1. Warm-up: Review vocabulary, pp. 42-43	Video Grammar and Vocabulary Activity 21, p. 23
2. Negation with *ne (n')... pas*, p. 46	Workbook Activity 14, p. 25 Computer Software Activity 6 ATE: TPR, p. 46 ATE: Paired Practice, pp. 47-48 Grammar and Vocabulary Activities 22-23, pp. 24-25
3. *Pratique* 4-7, pp. 46-47	Audiocassette/CD: Activities 4-7 (Side B, Tracks 17-20)
4. *Communication* 8-10, pp. 48-49	
5. Cartoon, p. 51	

6. *C'est à moi!*, p. 52

7. *Communication orale*, pp. 52-53

8. *À moi de jouer!*, p. 54

Day 7 — *Leçon C*
Textbook

ATE: Comparisons, p. 22

Ancillary materials/activities

1. Warm-up: Review negation with *ne (n')... pas*, p. 46

Video
Grammar and Vocabulary Activity 24, p. 26

2. Review all of *Leçon C* for quiz

Listening Activity 3A, p. SA3
Computer Software Activity 7

3. Quiz *Leçon C*, pp. 9-11

Quiz *Leçon C*, pp. 9-11

4. *Sur la bonne piste*, pp. 49-51

Audiocassette/CD: *Sur la bonne piste* (Side B, Track 21)
Workbook Activity 15, p. 25

5. *Activité* 11, p. 51

6. *Communication écrite*, p. 53

ATE: Paired Practice, p. 53

7. *Communication électronique*, p. 54

Day 8 — Assessment
Textbook

Ancillary materials/activities

1. Warm-up: *Communication active*, p. 53

Listening Activity 3B, p. SA4

2. Review highlights of unit

ATE: Game, p. 53

3. *Unité 2* test, pp. 11-25

Unit Tests Booklet, pp. 11-25, Unit Tests Video, Unit Tests Audiocassette/CD

EXPRESSIONS DE COMMUNICATION

À demain.	*See you tomorrow.*
Allez au laboratoire.	*Go to the laboratory.*
Allez au tableau.	*Go to the board.*
Attention.	*Be careful.*
Bon appétit.	*Have a good meal.*
Bonne journée.	*Have a good day.*
Bon weekend.	*Have a good weekend.*
C'est bien.	*That's good.*
Comment dit-on...?	*How do you say . . . ?*
Comment s'appelle-t-il?	*What's his name?*
Comment s'appelle-t-elle?	*What's her name?*
Continuons.	*Let's continue.*
Écoutez.	*Listen.*
Écrivez.	*Write.*
Encore.	*Again.*
Épelez.	*Spell.*
Fermez la porte.	*Close the door.*
Fermez le livre.	*Close your books.*
Je ne comprends pas.	*I don't understand.*
Lisez.	*Read.*
Maintenant, une dictée.	*And now a dictation.*
Montrez-moi....	*Show me . . . .*
Ouvrez la porte.	*Open the door.*
Ouvrez le livre à la page....	*Open your book to page . . . .*
Prenez votre (vos) livre(s).	*Take out your book(s).*
Présentez-moi....	*Introduce me . . . .*
Présentez-nous....	*Introduce us . . . .*
Répétez.	*Repeat.*
Répondez.	*Answer.*
Tous ensemble.	*All together.*

L'ALPHABET PHONÉTIQUE

A   [a]
B   [be]
C   [se]
D   [de]
E   [ə]
F   [ɛf]
G   [ʒe]
H   [aʃ]
I   [i]
J   [ʒi]
K   [ka]
L   [ɛl]
M   [ɛm]
N   [ɛn]
O   [o]
P   [pe]
Q   [ky]
R   [ɛr]
S   [ɛs]
T   [te]
U   [y]
V   [ve]
W   [dubləve]
X   [iks]
Y   [igrɛk]
Z   [zɛd]

LA PONCTUATION

,   = une virgule
.   = un point
?   = un point d'interrogation
;   = un point virgule
:   = deux points
( )   = les parenthèses
" "   = les guillemets
'   = une apostrophe
—   = un tiret
-    = un trait d'union

Functions

in *C'est à toi!*

The number following the communicative function indicates in what unit a specific way to express that function is presented for the first time.

accept and refuse an invitation 3, 9
agree and disagree 2, 4, 7, 8, 9
ask and tell someone's age 5
ask and tell the date 5
ask and tell where someone is from 6
ask for a price 3, 8
ask for information 2, 4, 5, 6, 7, 8, 11, 12
ask for permission 8
ask how someone is 3
ask someone to repeat 7
ask someone's name 1
ask what something is 4
ask what time it is 3

choose and purchase items 7, 8
compare things 12
congratulate and commiserate 10

describe character 5
describe daily routines 4, 9
describe past events 11, 12
describe physical traits 5

excuse oneself 9
explain a problem 10
explain something 5, 6
express astonishment and disbelief 10
express concern 10
express emotions 4, 5, 6, 10, 11
express intentions 7, 9
express likes and dislikes 2, 7, 8, 11
express need 4, 7, 10, 12
express reassurance 10

give addresses 11
give advice 10
give directions 11
give information 4, 5, 6, 7, 8, 10
give opinions 2, 12
give telephone numbers 1

Suggestions and Ideas for Using the Internet

Because of its widespread and instantaneous nature, the Internet offers endless potential as a tool for teaching and learning. In French classrooms, the Internet can help teachers meet the challenge of providing students with materials that are up-to-date and culturally authentic. With virtually no lag time, information from the culture of francophone countries can be accessed and utilized in a variety of ways. In a lesson about Paris, for example, you and your students can:

- access city and subway maps
- view photographs of major landmarks of the city
- obtain news from French newspapers
- visit museums and view works of art
- obtain tourist information
- participate in discussion groups on French culture and civilization
- access current weather information and forecasts
- exchange e-mail correspondence

By using the Internet as a supplement to *C'est à toi!*, you also will create exciting learning opportunities for students that simply did not previously exist. The activities your students will be able to do are limitless. Here are some sample activities and various supplementary materials that illustrate the vast possibilities of the Internet.

E-mail Projects

Consider arranging e-mail exchanges to complement the use of *C'est à toi!* Have students participate in a number of exchanges that allow them to apply the concepts, vocabulary and cultural information studied in a given lesson. Here are some sample exchanges.

1. After studying expressions about the weather, students write a weather report for their city or state and send it to a collaborating keypal. They also inquire about the weather and climate in the region where the keypal lives. Subsequent exchanges could deal with:
   - sports and activities related to different seasons of the year
   - outdoor activities that students enjoy
   - the school calendar and how the local climate may affect it
   - weather conditions in different francophone countries

2. As part of a food unit, students develop an e-mail exchange sharing the following information about their culture or family:
   - a typical meal schedule at home
   - a typical meal schedule in their country
   - a menu for a typical day and one for a special celebration

3. After learning about leisure-time activities, students share with their keypals what they do during a typical weekend or vacation.

4. Students write a description of a well-known individual in sports, music, politics or the movies. Then they send the description to their keypal who tries to guess the mystery person's identity.

5. Students conduct surveys in order to explore cultural comparisons. Topics may include:
   - the level of independence given to teenagers
   - access and admittance to clubs or discotheques
   - the legal age for driving
   - the number of students who work
   - the minimum wage paid to teenagers who work

6. Examples of other possible exchange topics for beginning students include school, daily life, family, friends, travel, sports, clothing and popular music. Topics for more advanced students may include current events, politics, household rules, curfew and educational aspirations.

Suggested Sites for E-mail Projects:

International Tandem Network
http://marvin.uni-trier.de/Tandem/email/engfra/engfraen.html

E-pals
http://www.epals.com/

Linguistic Funland
http://www.linguistic-funland.com/penpalpostings.html

International Pen Friends for Schools
http://www.europa-pages.co.uk/school_form.html

Model Unit for an E-mail Exchange: Ma Famille
This unit allows students to share information about their families and learn about the families of their keypals. While the unit is appropriate for learners at various levels of proficiency, teacher expectations and student performance will vary accordingly.

Academic Goals
Students will be able to:
1. Use vocabulary related to the family.
2. Use possessive and descriptive adjectives and appropriate verbs.

Social Goals
Students will be able to:
1. Share information about their families.
2. Find out about the families of their keypals.
3. Recognize similarities and differences between families in the United States and families in cultures where French is spoken.

Procedures for a Beginning French Class
1. Teach and practice specific vocabulary pertaining to family members. Show pictures and begin by describing your real family or a fictitious family in terms of members, roles, names, ages, likes, dislikes and professions. After your description, see what students are able to remember. This questioning gives students a chance to use basic expressions.

2. Then have students describe their own families. As preparation for class, have students prepare notes about their families (real or imaginary) according to the specifications given in advance.

3. After further practice in class, have students write descriptions of their families. Possible information includes:
   - family name
   - number of people in the family
   - description of each member of the family (name, age, occupation, personality)
   - family activities and traditions

4. Once the documents are completed and revised (by peers and by the teacher), send the descriptions to keypals abroad. When the replies are received, have students compare families in both cultures and find similarities and/or differences.

Locating Keypals

Possible keypals can be found in the same school building or district, in another city or around the world. Here are some strategies for locating keypals.
- Place ads in professional organization newsletters and journals.
- Attend professional conferences and technology workshops in order to network with colleagues.
- Search the Web for Collaborating Classrooms, Cultural Classroom Connection or Exchanges.
- Post messages in French newsgroups.
- Subscribe to listservs pertinent to francophone areas.
- Check related www home pages or Internet Guides.
- Write to American Schools Abroad. (A listing may be obtained from the Department of State in Washington, D.C.).

Netiquette Tips

- To see whether or not you and your students practice good "netiquette," take this quiz:
  http://www.albion.com/netiquette/netiquiz.html

- To find out whether or not you are safe at work when on the Web, take this quiz:
  http://sladen.hfhs.org/library/education/netiquette.html

- If you missed any questions on these two quizzes, review the rules at:
  http://www.albion.com/netiquette/corerules.html

Overcoming E-mail Limitations

Hardware Limitations: When a limited number of computers are available, students can work in pairs or individual students can access computers at other times (for example, while others in class are working on an assignment, after completing a test, during lunch periods, study hall, time in the media center or before and after school). Assignments made well in advance of their due date will allow students to choose their work time and produce final products of high quality.

Time Limitations: When computer lab time is limited, schedule individuals or groups in such a way that at least one exchange can be completed per quarter, trimester or semester.

Access Limitations: If you have one computer with access to the Internet using a modem and a single phone line, get the project ready and transmit it when the line is available. A designated student can be the mailer. If there is no access in school, a teacher or student who has access to the Internet or other commercial service can be the mailer for the group. This will ensure that the outgoing and incoming mail will involve only one supervised e-mail account.

Surfing the Web

To search or "surf" the Web, use the latest version available of the Web browser of your choice. Web browsers provide a harmonious interface for text and graphics. You have different options for general search engines. Some search titles or headers of documents, others search the documents themselves, and still others search indexes or directories. To locate a desired resource, do a Net Search. Here is a list of some popular and powerful search engines.

(**Note**: The following addresses may change at any time. Visit sites to verify they are active before using them in class.)

AltaVista	**http://www.altavista.fr/**
Excite	**http://fr.excite.com/**
InfoSeek	**http://infoseek.go.com/**
Lokace	**http://www.lokace.com/**
Lycos	**http://www.lycos.fr/**
Mamma	**http://www.mamma.com/**
Méga francité	**http://mega.francite.com/fr/**
Moteurs de recherche	**http://www.chez.com/ordicom/Moteurs.htm**
Nomade	**http://www.nomade.fr/**
Webcrawler	**http://www.webcrawler.com/**
Yahoo	**http://www.yahoo.com/**
Yahoo France	**http://fr.yahoo.com/**

Sample Web Site and Activities

City Net is a World Wide Web home page that archives or stores information about cities around the world. This resource can be particularly helpful in creating cultural units because the information found at this site might include historical events, transportation, maps, pictures and sites of interest (including schedules, addresses and telephone numbers). Once the user has clicked on the city of choice, graphics and text that support these categories are accessible by clicking on highlighted areas on the screen.

Virtual City Tour

It's easy to take your students on a virtual city tour using the City Net home page. First, determine your objectives for this activity: What will your students learn from this work? What cultural awareness and knowledge will they develop? What language skills will they practice? How will students practice critical thinking and problem solving? How will they further process their conclusions and share what they have learned with others?

Procedures for Initiating a Virtual City Tour
1. Open the Web browser and go to City Net by entering **http://www.excite.com/travel/**
2. Select the desired continent, then country, then city.
3. Locate a map of the city and identify specific sites of interest that your students might "visit" during a virtual tour of the city.
4. If the city has a subway system, find a subway map or a subway planner. (The latter allows you to enter specific points of origin and destination. Then you receive the routing path and trip duration.)

Here are some other suggestions for a virtual city tour using small groups.

1. Have students visit a certain city that you have chosen. Each group selects a different section of the city. Their task is to determine what sites to visit during a 48-hour period while staying within a specific budget. One group may choose to visit museums while another group may travel to a park to see sculptures and attend a particular event.

2. Have each group visit a different city in the same country. When each group has processed the information, have them present their city's attractions to the entire class. To extend the activity, you might ask students to share their information with the class in written or visual form. Finally, have each group design a quiz pertaining to their city.

3. Have small groups design a travel brochure for their city that includes information on some of the following topics:
   - entertainment opportunities
   - shopping and dining
   - brief historical facts about the city
   - airlines serving the city
   - special events
   - weather
   - typical cuisine

When doing Web-based activities, keep in mind that vocabulary and structures will vary according to level. You may ask beginning students to identify numbers, times, days of the week, cognates and vocabulary related to daily activities. More advanced students may be asked to imagine and narrate a special experience from their virtual city tour.

Cultural/Historical Studies and Presentations

Students work in small groups to become "experts" on a country where French is spoken. The objectives of the activity are to help students get acquainted with the history, geography, economics, climate, attractions and current events of the target country and culture. Working in groups, students search for information pertaining to a francophone country that is assigned or chosen. Once the search is completed, groups summarize the information and present it to the class. The information can be found by doing searches at the sites listed previously or by visiting these URLs:

Les Pages de Paris	**http://www.paris.org/**
France on the Web	**http://www.u.arizona.edu/~kurzer/french242.html**
Découvrons Canada	**http://www.geocities.com/Paris/Bistro/7445/dbesite.htm**
Tennessee Bob's famous French links	**http://www.utm.edu/departments/french/french.html**
Parlez-vous?	**http://members.yourlink.net/kappa/espanole/french.html**
Newcastle University Links	**http://www.ncl.ac.uk/~nsml/links/french.htm**

Suggest that students include specific information in their presentation:
- maps
- geography
- history
- climate/weather
- major cities and tourist attractions

- popular events
- airlines serving the country
- economic activity and exchange rate
- major newspapers (include a copy of recent headlines)

In addition to sharing their findings with the class, students should submit:
1. a printed copy of the material found and used for the presentation
2. a copy of the final presentation
3. a listening comprehension or reading quiz prepared by the group and based on the presentation. Students can do the listening comprehension exercise while the presentation is being given. They can do the reading comprehension exercise at the end of the presentation after the group has distributed printed copies of their presentation to the entire class. The quiz should also include a key with the correct answers.

Virtual Museums and Works of Art

When teaching colors, emotions, description and even history, works of art may be viewed and/or copied to teach, illustrate and reinforce a variety of concepts. Students may be assigned to search for works of certain artists to illustrate the concepts and/or vocabulary studied in class. When considering the works of a given artist, students may also be assigned to give a presentation on that artist that includes:
- country of origin
- biographical information about the artist
- period in history when the artist lived
- style of work
- colors and shapes used by the artist
- feelings and aspects of life represented by the artist's work
- examples of the artist's work

Suggested sites:

    http://www.intermusees.com/
    http://www.louvre.fr/
    http://www.toile.qc.ca/quebec/qcart_mu.htm

Weather Reports

Weather reports, including satellite and infrared maps, are available through the Net. When teaching about weather and weather conditions, have students access weather reports from francophone countries and regions of the United States. Students then use this information to give weather reports or forecasts to the class. If used throughout the year, such information can be included in different units of the curriculum to link weather conditions with seasons, clothing, sports and outdoor activities.

As with other projects, students' ability level will be a factor in assigning specific tasks and content. Beginning students may give simple weather reports, including temperatures and precipitation, while advanced students may explore the relationship between weather conditions and lifestyle, tourism and the economy.

Suggested sites:

    http://www.weather.com/
    http://www.letemps.com/
    http://www.meteo.fr/temps/
    http://cnn.com/weather/
    http://www.intellicast.com/search/

Newspapers and Magazines

The many newspapers and magazines on the World Wide Web are another outstanding resource for students and teachers in the French classroom. Here is one possible activity using newspapers and magazines.

1. Locate appropriate newspapers and magazines from countries where French is spoken.
2. Familiarize yourself with their format and content.
3. Divide the class into small groups.
4. Assign a content area to each member of the group or allow the students to choose an area of interest. Possible areas include international news, national news, politics, entertainment, weather and sports.
5. According to the number of groups in class, the level and the time allotted, develop a schedule that allows each group to present news from its newspaper or magazine on a regular basis. You may ask a different group to do this at the beginning of class every day or you may prefer to identify a day of the week for several group presentations. The activity should not take more than 5-10 minutes per group. It is helpful to give specific instructions about what you expect to hear in the presentations and to post a calendar of presentation dates in the classroom.

To vary this activity, divide students in small groups and have them summarize the school newspaper in French. Then send the summary via e-mail to a collaborating class with whom you have contact. Such an exchange of news can become an activity to be done throughout the year.

Suggested sites:
> **http://globegate.utm.edu/french/topics/newspapers.html**
> **http://globegate.utm.edu/french/topics/magazines.html**
> **http://libraries.mit.edu/humanities/flnews/french.html**
> **http://prensa.hypermart.net/europe/france.html**

Assessing Internet Projects

Here are some helpful guidelines when developing and assessing e-mail and Web projects.

1. Give specific instructions in writing about the project.
2. Post a calendar or time line for the project.
3. Remember that some flexibility may be necessary if students encounter difficulties (for example, with access or printing).
4. Develop clear criteria for grading and evaluation. Depending on the project, some factors to consider may include:
   - appropriate content, length, etc.
   - completion of the project on time
   - quality of the presentation and/or written assignment(s)
   - printed copies of materials from the Web, with graphics where possible
   - participation

Being specific about how student work will be evaluated will make it easier to assign a grade that will require very little explanation at the end of the project. Again, it is a good idea to post the project's requirements, deadlines and evaluation procedures.

Teacher Resources on the World Wide Web

City/Country Information:

City Guide	**http://cityguide.lycos.com/**
Travel Guides	**http://www.excite.com/travel/**
	http://www.lonelyplanet.com/
	http://travel.discovery.com/dest/dest.html
	http://www.virtualtourist.com/
Tourism Offices	**http://www.towd.com/**
Embassies	**http://www.embassyworld.com/**

Culture/Education:

Classroom Connections for E-mail Partners	**http://www.stolaf.edu/network/iecc/**
French Studies Virtual Library	**http://www.library.usyd.edu.au/Guides/Arts/French/**
La Bibliothèque Universelle	**http://cedric.cnam.fr/ABU/**
Food (French recipes)	**http://listes.cru.fr/arc/cuisine-fr@cru.fr/index.cgi**
	http://www.teutates.com/cuisine/

Foreign Language Professionals:

FLTEACH is designed to facilitate networking and dialogue among foreign language professionals. To subscribe to the list, send the following message: SUBSCRIBE FLTEACH first name last name to: **LISTSERV@UBVM.CC.BUFFALO.EDU.**

American Association of Teachers of French	**http://aatf.utsa.edu/**
L'Alliance Française	**http://fmc.utm.edu/~rpeckham/ALLIANCE.HTM**
Association canadienne d'éducation de langue française	**http://www.acelf.ca/**
Agora language marketplace	**http://agoralang.com/agora/prof.html**

Other Sites of Interest:

Web 66: International School Registry	**http://web66.coled.umn.edu/schools.html**
Daily guide to Paris	**http://www.pariscope.fr/**
France Pratique	**http://www.pratique.fr/**
Versailles	**http://www.chateauversailles.fr/fr/114.asp**
Québec	**http://globegate.utm.edu/french/globegate_mirror/quebhist.html**
Montréal	**http://globegate.utm.edu/french/globegate_mirror.montreal.html**
Switzerland	**http://www.myswitzerland.com/**
French language	**http://french.about.com/homework/french/**
Language games	**http://www.transparent.com/games/index.htm**
	http://www.quia.com/french.html

Additional Sources for Information

Teachers interested in obtaining realia such as brochures and posters as well as other pedagogical aids may contact the agencies listed below.

Tourist offices

French Government Tourist Office
444 Madison Avenue
16th Floor
New York, NY 10022
Tel: (212) 838-7800
Fax: (212) 838-7855
Web site: **http://www.francetourism.com**

French Government Tourist Office
676 North Michigan Avenue, Suite 3360
Chicago, IL 60611
Tel: (312) 751-7800 or (410) 286-8310
Fax: (312) 337-6339
Web site: **http://www.francetourism.com**
E-mail: fgto@mcs.net

French Government Tourist Office
9454 Wilshire Boulevard, Suite 715
Beverly Hills, CA 90212
Tel: (310) 271-6665
Fax: (310) 276-2835
Web site: **http://www.francetourism.com**
E-mail: fgto@gte.net

Tourisme Québec
900 Boulevard René Lévesque Est
Office 400
Québec, Québec G1R 285
Tel: (418) 643-5959
Fax: (418) 646-8723
Web site: **http://www.bonjourquebec.com**
E-mail: communications@tourisme.gouv.qc.cq

Office du Tourisme et des Congrès de la Communauté Urbaine de Québec
399, rue Saint-Joseph Est
Québec, Québec G1K 8E2
Tel: (418) 522-3511
Fax: (418) 529-3121
Web site: **http://www.quebecregion.com**
E-mail: info@quebecregion.com

Belgian Tourist Office
780 Third Avenue
New York, NY 10017
Tel: (212) 758-8130
Fax: (212) 355-7675
Web site: **http://www.visitbelgium.com**
E-mail: info@visitbelgium.com

Luxembourg National Tourist Office
17 Beekman Place
New York, NY 10022
Tel: (212) 935-8888
Fax: (212) 935-5896
Web site: **http://www.visitluxembourg.com**
E-mail: lux.nto@aol.com

Switzerland Tourism Office
608 Fifth Avenue
New York, NY 10020
Tel: (212) 757-5944
Fax: (212) 262-6116
Web site: **http://www.myswitzerland.com**
E-mail: info.usa@switzerlandtourism.com

Monaco Government Tourist Office
565 Fifth Avenue
New York, NY 10017
Tel: 800-753-9696
Fax: (212) 286-9890
Web site: **http://www.monaco-tourism.com**
E-mail: mgto@monaco1.org

Caribbean Tourism Association
80 Broad Street, 32nd Floor
New York, NY 10004
Tel: (212) 635-9530
Fax: (212) 635-9511
Web site: **http://www.caribtourism.com**
E-mail: get2cto@dorsai.org

Embassies

French Embassy
4101 Reservoir Road NW
Washington, D.C. 20007-2181
Tel: (202) 944-6000
Fax: (202) 944-6072 (press and information)
Web site: **http://info-france-usa.org**
E-mail: info@amb-wash.fr

Canadian Embassy
501 Pennsylvania Avenue NW
Washington, D.C. 20001
Tel: (202) 682-1740
Web site: **http://www.canadianembassy.org**

Consulates

(Each consulate gives information only for its district.)

French Consulate General
737 North Michigan Avenue, Suite 2020
Chicago, IL 60611
Tel: (312) 787-5359
Fax: (312) 664-4196
Web site: **http://www.france-consulat.org/chicago**
E-mail: chicago@france-consulat.org

French Consulate General
540 Bush Street
San Francisco, CA 94108
Tel: (415) 397-4330
Fax: (415) 433-8357
Web site: **http://www.accueil-sfo.org**

French Consulate General
10990 Wilshire Boulevard, Suite 300
Los Angeles, CA 90024
Tel: (310) 235-3200
Fax: (310) 477-0416 (cultural service)
Web site: **http://www.info-france-usa.org**
E-mail: consulat-la@etats-unis.com

Canadian Consulate General
1251 Avenue of the Americas
New York, NY 10020-1175
Tel: (212) 596-1600
Fax: (212) 596-1790
Web site: **http://www.canada-ny.org**
E-mail: cngnylib@pipeline.com

Cultural services

French Cultural Services
972 Fifth Avenue
New York, NY 10021
Tel: (212) 439-1400
Fax: (212) 439-1455
Web site: **http://www.frenchculture.org**
E-mail: mail@frenchculture.org

Audio-visual materials, such as documentary and language teaching films as well as feature-length films, radio and television programs on cassettes, are available through FACSEA (Society for French-American Cultural Services and Educational Aid) at the French Cultural Services in New York. Call the French Cultural Services for catalogues of traveling exhibits your school may borrow.

Also contact French Cultural Services for information on *au pair* positions in France. These are arrangements where young women (and occasionally young men) perform various household duties and care for children in France in exchange for a monthly allowance and the experience of living with a French family.

Cultural Services of the French Consulate
737 North Michigan Avenue, Suite 1170
Chicago, IL 60611
Tel: (312) 664-3525
Fax: (312) 664-9528
Web site: **http://www.france-consulat.org/chicago**
E-mail: chicago@france-consulat.org

French Cultural Services
Park Square Building
31 St. James Avenue, Suite 750
Boston, MA 02116
Tel: (617) 292-0064
Fax: (617) 292-0793
Web site: **http://www.franceboston.org**
E-mail: bclebos@ix.netcom.com

French Cultural Services
1 Biscayne Tower, Suite 1710
2 South Biscayne Boulevard
Miami, FL 33131
Tel: (305) 372-1615
Fax: (305) 577-1069
Web site: **http://www.info-france-usa.org/miami**

French Cultural Services
777 Post Oak Boulevard, Suite 600
Houston, TX 77056
Tel: (713) 985-3263
Fax: (713) 572-2914
Web site: **http://www.consulatfrancehouston.org**
E-mail: martine.sperry@diplomacy.fr

Airlines

Air France
125 West 55th Street
New York, NY 10019-5384
Tel: 800-237-2747
Fax: (212) 830-4390
Web site: **http://www.airfrance.com**

Air Canada
P.O. Box 14000
Station Airport
Dorval, Québec H4Y 1H4
Tel: 800-813-9237 or 800-247-2262 (reservations)
Fax: 800-463-5251
Web site: **http://www.aircanada.ca**

Air Afrique
1350 Avenue of the Americas
New York, NY 10019
Tel: (212) 541-7474
Fax: (212) 541-7539
Web site: **http://www.airafrique.com**

Swissair
41 Pine Lawn Road
Melville, NY 11747-8910
Tel: (516) 844-4500
Fax: (516) 844-4874
Web site: **http://www.swissair.com**

Commercial sources

Food and Wines from France, Inc.
215 Park Avenue South, Suite 1600
New York, NY 10003
Tel: (212) 477-9800 (items for purchase) or (914) 928-7529 (promotional materials)
Fax: (212) 473-4315
Web site: **http://www.frenchwinesfood.com**

French language newspaper

France Press, Inc.
Journal Français d'Amérique
1051 Divisadero Street
San Francisco, CA 94115
Tel: 800-232-1549
Fax: (415) 921-0213
Web site: **http://www.journalfrancais.com**
E-mail: info@francentral.com

French language radio broadcasts

Radio Canada
CP 6000, Succursale (station) A
Montréal, Québec H3C 3A8
Tel: (514) 597-7825
Fax: (514) 597-7862
Web site: **http://www.radio-canada.ca**
E-mail: teleform@montreal.radio.canada.ca

News, weather and sports broadcasts in French are aired on shortwave frequencies 5960, 9755 and 11955 (kHz).

Pen pals

American Association of Teachers of French
Bureau de Correspondance Scolaire—AATF
Mail Code 4510
Southern Illinois University
Carbondale, IL 62901
Tel: (618) 453-5732
Fax: (618) 453-5733
Web site: **http://aatf.utsa.edu/**
E-mail: abrate@siu.edu

Slides for purchase

Documentation Photographique
29-31 quai Voltaire
75344 Paris Cédex 07
Tel: 01.40.15.72.30
Web site: **d-bataille@ladocfrancaise.gouv.fr**

REVISED

C'EST À TOI!

Level One

Authors

Karla Winther Fawbush

Toni Theisen

Dianne B. Hopen

Sarah Vaillancourt

Contributing Writer

Linda Klohs

EMC/Paradigm Publishing, Saint Paul, Minnesota

Credits

Editor
Sarah Vaillancourt

Associate Editor
Diana Moen

Language Specialist
Sandrine Noyelle

Desktop and Composition
The Nancekivell Group
Bradley J. Olsen
Desktop Solutions

Illustrator
Hetty Mitchell

Cartoon Illustrator
Steve Mark

Consultants

Augusta DeSimone Clark
St. Mary's Hall
San Antonio, Texas

Michael Nettleton
Smoky Hill High School
Aurora, Colorado

Mirta Pagnucci
Oak Park River Forest High School
Oak Park, Illinois

Ann J. Sorrell
South Burlington High School
South Burlington, Vermont

Nathalie Gaillot
Language Specialist
Lyon, France

EMC/Paradigm World Language Consultants
Dana Cunningham
Robert Headrick

ISBN 0-8219-2255-6

Published by EMC/Paradigm Publishing
875 Montreal Way
St. Paul, Minnesota 55102
800-328-1452
www.emcp.com
E-mail: educate@emcp.com

Printed in the United States of America
2 3 4 5 6 7 8 9 10 XXX 07 06 05 04 03 02

To the Student

C'EST À TOI! (*It's Your Turn!*), as your book's title suggests, invites *you* to express yourself in French by interacting with your classmates. Either in pairs or in small groups, you'll be talking right away about subjects that interest both you and French-speaking teens: music, sports, leisure activities, food, etc. Don't hesitate to practice your French every chance you get both during and outside of class. You will make mistakes, but your ability to speak French and your confidence will improve with continued practice.

Bienvenue au monde francophone! (*Welcome to the French-speaking world!*) You are beginning an exciting journey of discovery. You will not only visit many of the countries where people speak French every day, but you will also learn how to communicate and interact with them. In addition, as you are exposed to new ways of thinking and living in other cultures, your horizons will widen to include different ways of seeing and evaluating the world around you. Learning how to speak French will not only open the door to the French-speaking world, it will give you a knowledge, insight and appreciation of French culture. Language and culture go hand in hand, and together they reflect the spirit of the francophone world. An appreciation of French culture helps you understand what we have in common with French speakers and how we differ. And learning about an important world culture and its language will help you appreciate your own culture and language even more.

People speak French well beyond the borders of France itself. Nearly 200 million people worldwide use French in their daily lives. On our continent, French speakers live in places like Louisiana, New England and Quebec. Besides in Europe, people also speak French in Africa and Asia, as well as in the Caribbean. Obviously, these diverse French speakers come from a wide variety of cultural backgrounds. Communicating with them will help you understand their way of life and give you a more global perspective. During your lifetime, you will hopefully be able to use your French as you visit at least one of these lands. But even if your travels abroad are limited to "living the language" in your classroom, you will be exposed to a new way of viewing the world.

Internationally, French is one of the primary languages, and people who speak and understand it are an asset in the world of work. Knowing French can expand your career options in areas such as international trade or law, investment, government service, technology and manufacturing. Multinational companies hire hundreds of thousands of Americans who have proficiency in at least one world language. Just knowing French will not assure you of the job you want, but, combined with another specialization, it will increase your employment opportunities. French may be the key that gives you the competitive edge in the global marketplace. Whatever your reasons for learning French, **bon voyage** as you begin to discover the culture and language of the French-speaking world, and **bonne chance** (*good luck*)!

Table of Contents

Unité 1 Salut! Ça va? 1

Unité 2 Qu'est-ce que tu aimes faire? 19

Unité 3 Au café 57

Unité 4 À l'école 95

Unité 6 Tu viens d'où? 171

Unité 7 On fait les magasins. 215

Unité 8 On fait les courses. 255

Unité 9 À la maison 295

Unité 10 La santé 333

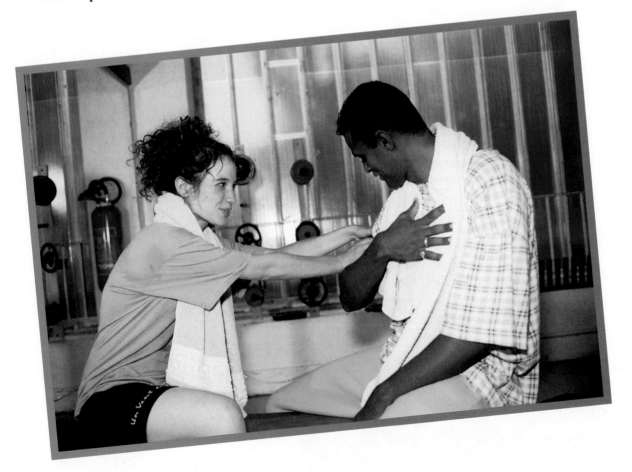

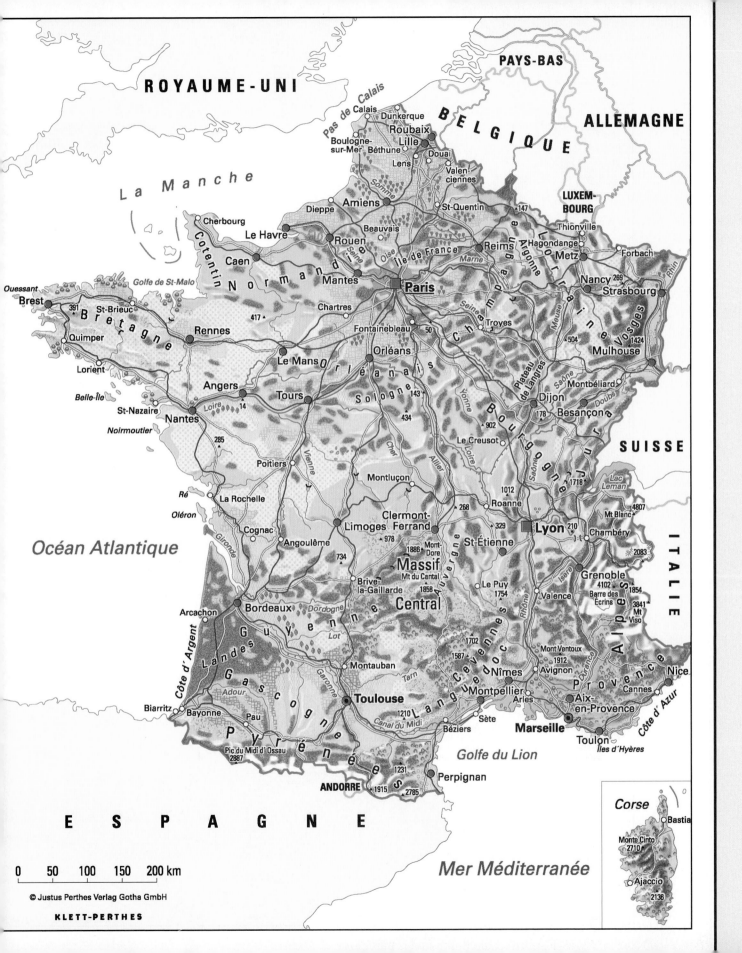

ROYAUME-UNI

PAYS-BAS

ALLEMAGNE

BELGIQUE

LUXEM-BOURG

La Manche

Pas de Calais

Dunkerque
Roubaix
Lille
Boulogne-sur-Mer
Béthune
Douai
Lens
Valen-ciennes

Dieppe
Amiens
St-Quentin
▲147
Thionville
Forbach

Cherbourg
Beauvais
Hagondange
Metz

Le Havre
Rouen
Île de France
Reims
Nancy 269
Strasbourg

Caen
Seine
Marne
Rhin

Golfe de St-Malo
Mantes
Paris

Ouessant
Brest
391
St-Brieuc
Chartres
Troyes
▲504
1424
Mulhouse

Bretagne
417 ▲
Fontainebleau
50

Rennes
Orléans
Plateau de Langres
Montbéliard

Quimper
Le Mans
Sologne
143
Dijon
Doubs
Besançon

Lorient
Orléanais
434
178

Angers
Tours
Loire
14
Vienne
902

Belle-Île
285
Le Creusot
Bourgogne

St-Nazaire
Nantes
Poitiers
Cher
Allier
Loire
1718
Lac Léman

Noirmoutier
Montluçon
1012
4807

Ré
La Rochelle
Roanne
Mt Blanc
Chambéry

Oléron
Cognac
268 ▲
329 ▲
Lyon 210
2083

Océan Atlantique
Angoulême
Clermont-Ferrand
Limoges
St-Étienne
Grenoble
4102

734 ▲
978 ▲
1886 ▲ Mont-Dore
Barre des Écrins 1854

Brive-la-Gaillarde
Massif
Mt du Cantal
1858
Le Puy
1754
Valence
3841 Mt Viso

Arcachon
Bordeaux
Dordogne
Central
Auvergne
Grenoble

Côte d'Argent
Lot
1702
Mont Ventoux
1912

Gascogne
Montauban
Garonne
1587
Cévennes
Avignon
Nice

Landes
Tarn
Nîmes
Provence
Cannes

Biarritz
Bayonne
Pau
1210
Montpellier
Arles
Aix-en-Provence
Côte d'Azur

Pyrénées
Canal du Midi
Sète
Marseille
Toulon

Pic du Midi d'Ossau
2887
Toulouse
Béziers
Îles d'Hyères

ANDORRE
1231
1915
2785
Perpignan
Golfe du Lion

SUISSE

ITALIE

E S P A G N E

Mer Méditerranée

| 0 | 50 | 100 | 150 | 200 km |

Corse
Bastia
Monte Cinto 2710
Ajaccio
2136

© Justus Perthes Verlag Gotha GmbH

KLETT-PERTHES

XV

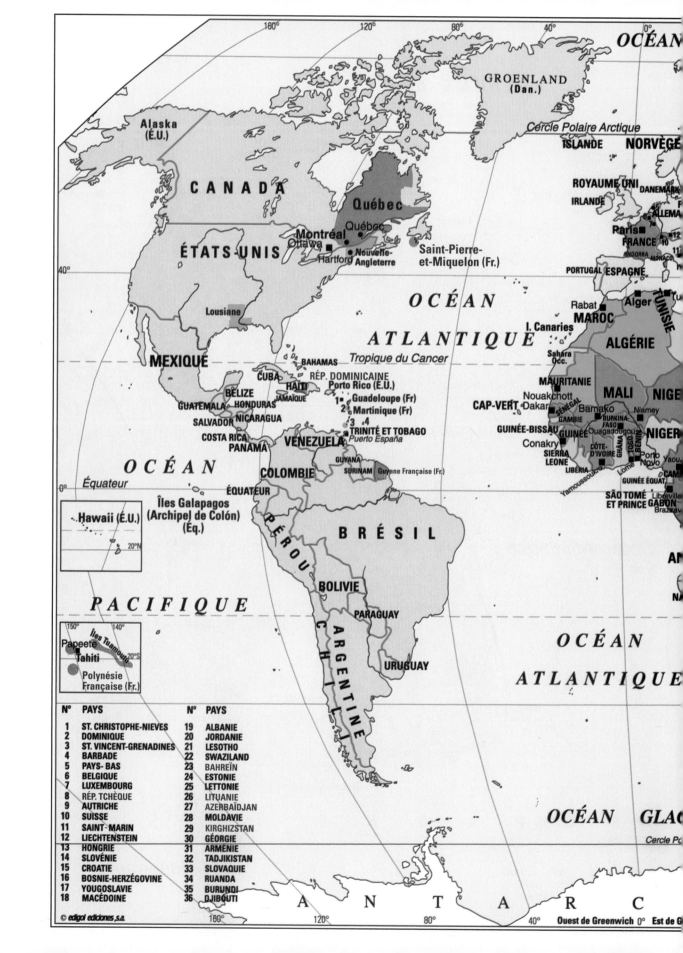

OCÉAN

GROENLAND
(Dan.)

Cercle Polaire Arctique

ISLANDE   NORVÈGE

Alaska
(É.U.)

ROYAUME UNI   DANEMARK
IRLANDE

CANADA

Québec

Québec

Montréal   Paris
Ottawa   FRANCE
Hartford   Nouvelle-   PORTUGAL   ESPAGNE
Angleterre

Saint-Pierre-
et-Miquelon (Fr.)

ÉTATS-UNIS

40°

OCÉAN   Rabat   Alger
MAROC   TUNISIE
I. Canaries

Lousiane   ATLANTIQUE   ALGÉRIE
Sahara
Occ.

MEXIQUE   Tropique du Cancer   MAURITANIE   MALI   NIGE
BAHAMAS
CUBA   RÉP. DOMINICAINE   Nouakchott
HAÏTI   Porto Rico (É.U.)   CAP-VERT Dakar
BÉLIZE   JAMAÏQUE   1   Guadeloupe (Fr)   SÉNÉGAL   Bamako   Niamey
GUATEMALA   HONDURAS   2   Martinique (Fr)   GAMBIE   BURKINA-   NIGER
SALVADOR   NICARAGUA   3 4   GUINÉE-BISSAU   FASO
COSTA RICA   TRINITÉ ET TOBAGO   Conakry   GUINÉE Ouagadougou
PANAMÁ   Puerto España   SIERRA   CÔTE-   GHANA
VENEZUELA   LEONE   D'IVOIRE   Porto Yaou
GUYANA   LIBÉRIA   Novo   CAMP
COLOMBIE   SURINAM Guyane Française (Fr.)   Yamoussoukro Lomé   GUINÉE ÉQUAT.

0°   Équateur   ÉQUATEUR   SÃO TOMÉ   Libreville
ET PRINCE GABON
Brazzav

Îles Galapagos
(Archipel de Colón)
(Éq.)

Hawaii (É.U.)

BRÉSIL   AN

20°N   NA

OCÉAN   PÉROU

BOLIVIE   OCÉAN

PACIFIQUE   PARAGUAY

150° 140°   ATLANTIQUE
Îles Tuamoutu
Papeete
Tahiti   20°S

Polynésie   URUGUAY
Française (Fr.)

OCÉAN   GLAC

Cercle Po

Nº	PAYS	Nº	PAYS
1	ST. CHRISTOPHE-NIEVES	19	ALBANIE
2	DOMINIQUE	20	JORDANIE
3	ST. VINCENT-GRENADINES	21	LESOTHO
4	BARBADE	22	SWAZILAND
5	PAYS- BAS	23	BAHREÏN
6	BELGIQUE	24	ESTONIE
7	LUXEMBOURG	25	LETTONIE
8	RÉP. TCHÈQUE	26	LITUANIE
9	AUTRICHE	27	AZERBAÏDJAN
10	SUISSE	28	MOLDAVIE
11	SAINT- MARIN	29	KIRGHIZSTAN
12	LIECHTENSTEIN	30	GÉORGIE
13	HONGRIE	31	ARMÉNIE
14	SLOVÉNIE	32	TADJIKISTAN
15	CROATIE	33	SLOVAQUIE
16	BOSNIE-HERZÉGOVINE	34	RUANDA
17	YOUGOSLAVIE	35	BURUNDI
18	MACÉDOINE	36	DJIBOUTI

A   N   T   A   R   C

© edigol ediciones, s.a.   180°   120°   80°   40°   Ouest de Greenwich 0° Est de G

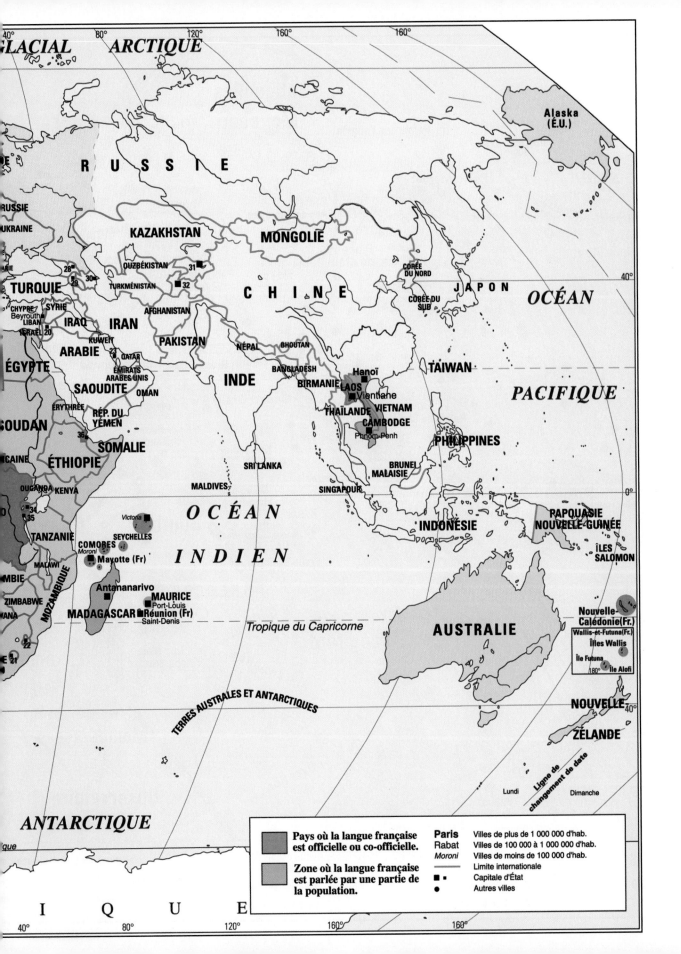

OCÉAN GLACIAL ARCTIQUE

Alaska (É.U.)

R U S S I E

RUSSIE
UKRAINE

KAZAKHSTAN

MONGOLIE

OUZBÉKISTAN 31

28
30
29

TURKMÉNISTAN 32

C H I N E

CORÉE DU NORD

J A P O N

OCÉAN

TURQUIE

40°

CORÉE DU SUD

CHYPRE
SYRIE
Beyrouth
LIBAN
ISRAEL 20

AFGHANISTAN

IRAQ

IRAN

PAKISTAN

TAIWAN

PACIFIQUE

ARABIE

KUWEIT
QATAR
23

NÉPAL

BHOUTAN

EMIRATS
ARABES UNIS

ÉGYPTE

SAOUDITE

OMAN

INDE

BANGLADESH

BIRMANIE

LAOS

Hanoï

ÉRYTHRÉE

RÉP. DU
YÉMEN

THAÏLANDE

Vientiane
VIETNAM

SOUDAN

36

SOMALIE

CAMBODGE

PHILIPPINES

CAINE

ÉTHIOPIE

Phnom Penh

OUGANDA KENYA

SRI LANKA

BRUNEI
MALAISIE

MALDIVES

SINGAPOUR

0°

34
35

Victoria

OCÉAN

INDONÉSIE

PAPOUASIE
NOUVELLE-GUINÉE

TANZANIE

COMORES
Moroni

SEYCHELLES

ÎLES
SALOMON

MALAWI

Mayotte (Fr)

I N D I E N

MBIE

MOZAMBIQUE

Antananarivo

ZIMBABWE

MAURICE

WANA

MADAGASCAR

Port-Louis
Réunion (Fr)
Saint-Denis

Nouvelle-
Calédonie(Fr.)

Tropique du Capricorne

AUSTRALIE

Wallis-et-Futuna(Fr.)
Îles Wallis

22

Île Futuna

180°
Île Alofi

21

NOUVELLE

40°

ZÉLANDE

TERRES AUSTRALES ET ANTARCTIQUES

Ligne de changement de date

Lundi

Dimanche

ANTARCTIQUE

que

	Pays où la langue française est officielle ou co-officielle.	**Paris**	Villes de plus de 1 000 000 d'hab.
		Rabat	Villes de 100 000 à 1 000 000 d'hab.
		Moroni	Villes de moins de 100 000 d'hab.
	Zone où la langue française est parlée par une partie de la population.		Limite internationale
		■ ·	Capitale d'État
		●	Autres villes

I Q U E

40° 80° 120° 160° 160°

xvii

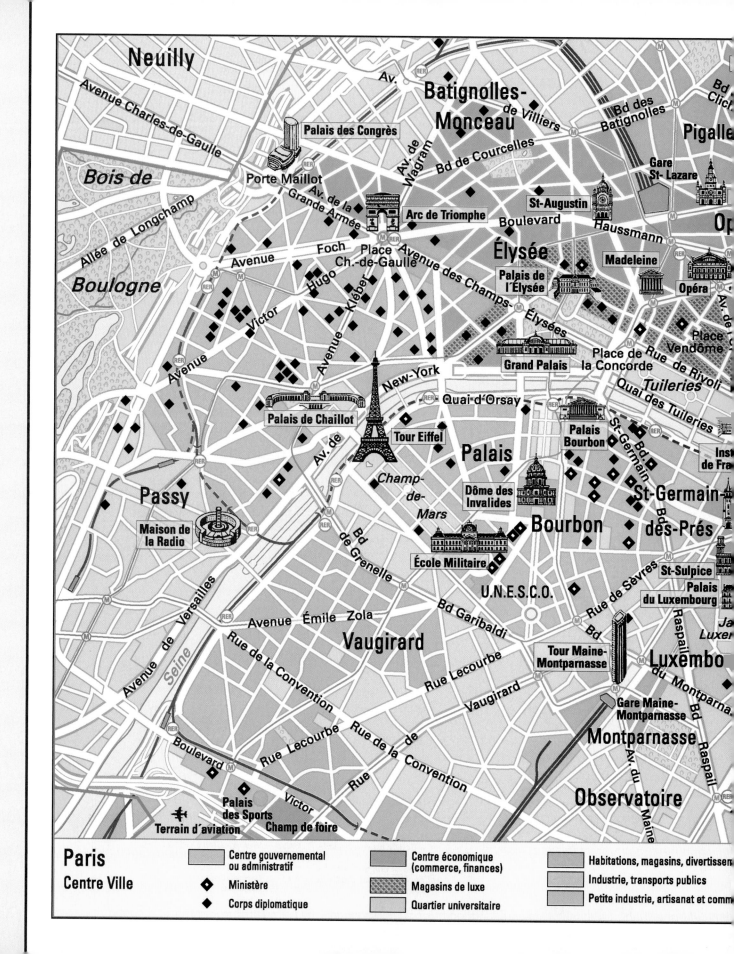

Paris

Centre Ville

◆ Ministère

◆ Corps diplomatique

Centre gouvernemental ou administratif

Centre économique (commerce, finances)

Magasins de luxe

Quartier universitaire

Habitations, magasins, divertissem

Industrie, transports publics

Petite industrie, artisanat et comm

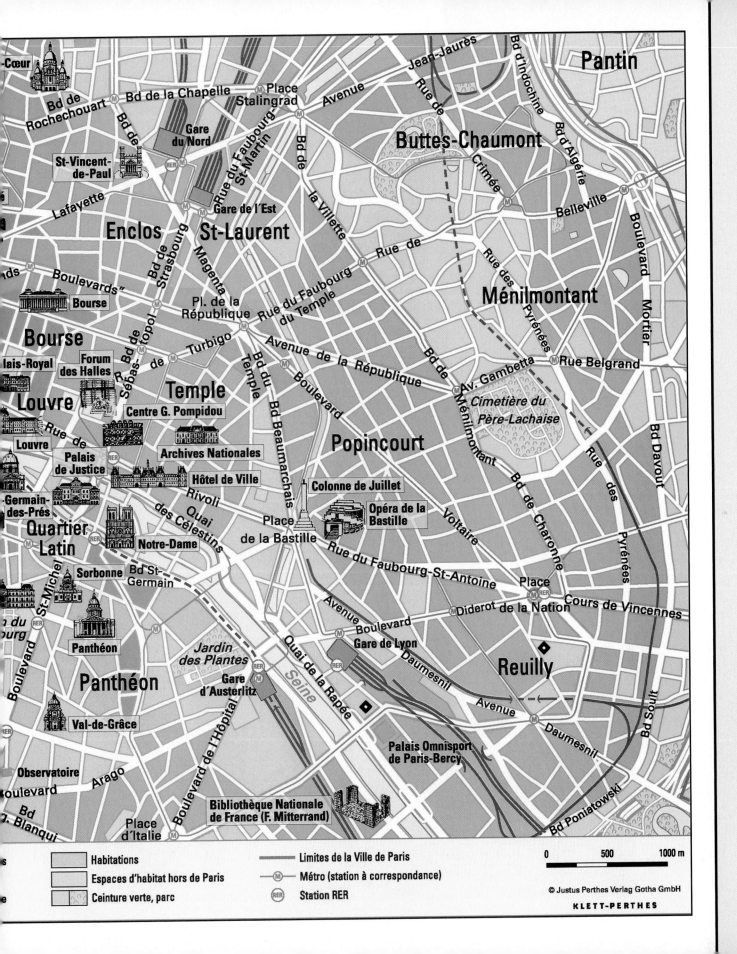

Sacré-Cœur

Bd de Rochechouart Bd de la Chapelle Place Stalingrad Jean-Jaurès Bd d'Indochine **Pantin**

Gare du Nord Avenue Rue de Bd d'Algérie

St-Vincent-de-Paul **Buttes-Chaumont**

Lafayette Gare de l'Est Rue de la Villette Crimée Belleville Boulevard Mortier

Enclos St-Laurent Rue du Faubourg St-Martin Bd de Strasbourg Magenta Rue de Rue des Pyrénées

Boulevards" **Bourse** Pl. de la République Rue du Faubourg du Temple **Ménilmontant**

Bourse Bd de Sébastopol de Turbigo Avenue de la République Bd de Ménilmontant Av. Gambetta Rue Belgrand Bd Davout

lais-Royal **Forum des Halles** **Temple** Bd du Temple Boulevard Bd de **Cimetière du Père-Lachaise** Rue des Pyrénées

Louvre Centre G. Pompidou Bd Beaumarchais **Popincourt**

Louvre Rue de Archives Nationales

Palais de Justice Hôtel de Ville Colonne de Juillet Voltaire Bd de Charonne

-Germain-des-Prés Rivoli Quai des Célestins Place de la Bastille Opéra de la Bastille

Quartier Latin Notre-Dame Rue du Faubourg-St-Antoine Place Cours de Vincennes

St-Michel Sorbonne Bd St-Germain Diderot de la Nation Rue des Pyrénées

n du ourg **Panthéon** Avenue Boulevard

Boulevard Jardin des Plantes Quai de la Rapée Gare de Lyon **Reuilly**

Panthéon Gare d'Austerlitz Seine Daumesnil

Val-de-Grâce Avenue Daumesnil

Observatoire Arago Boulevard de l'Hôpital Palais Omnisport de Paris-Bercy Bd Poniatowski

oulevard Bd J. Blanqui Place d'Italie Bibliothèque Nationale de France (F. Mitterrand)

Habitations	Limites de la Ville de Paris
Espaces d'habitat hors de Paris	Ⓜ Métro (station à correspondance)
Ceinture verte, parc	Ⓡ Station RER

0 500 1000 m

© Justus Perthes Verlag Gotha GmbH

KLETT-PERTHES

The Francophone World

near the Arch of
Triumph (Paris)

windsurfing in the Mediterranean
(Saint-Tropez)

a ski resort in the French Alps (Chamonix)

a picturesque Swiss alpine setting (Lake Brienz)

horseback riding on the beach (Corsica)

a soccer team (Belgium)

the Casino in Monte Carlo (Monaco)

a tropical paradise (Haiti)

dressed for the Carnival
(Martinique)

an open-air market in Tahiti (Papeete)

traveling by camel in Morocco (Agadir)

the village market day
(Senegal)

shopping in the old quarter of a Tunisian city (Mahdia)

the Ice Palace at the Winter Carnival (Quebec City)

Mardi Gras (New Orleans)

Unité 1

Salut! Ça va?

In this unit you will be able to:

➤ greet someone

➤ leave someone

➤ thank someone

➤ introduce yourself

➤ introduce someone else

➤ ask someone's name

➤ tell someone's name

➤ give telephone numbers

➤ restate information

NATIONAL STANDARDS
C2.1

Grammar & Vocabulary
Exercise 4

 Audiocassette/CD
Greetings

Transparencies 1-2

Teacher's Notes

1. To help you communicate in French as much as possible from the first day, we have provided a list of useful classroom expressions **(Expressions de communication)** on page TE45. You may want to develop a gesture for students to associate with each one of these commands. Another suggestion is to introduce one of these expressions each day by writing it on the board and having students repeat it. You may want to make a flash card of each expression in English and then, as each expression is learned, put it in a paper bag. At the beginning of each class period, have a student reach into the bag and pull out an expression, which he or she must then say in French. You might also want these expressions to become "passwords" that students must say as they enter or leave the classroom. 2. Make sure that your students realize that many of the new expressions and vocabulary words in each lesson are presented visually at the beginning of the lesson before the opening dialogue. These new expressions and vocabulary words are introduced by means of illustrations or photos. Therefore, students should carefully study the visuals that begin each lesson. All other new expressions and vocabulary words are presented contextually within the dialogue itself. 3. **Allô** is a greeting used only when answering the telephone. 4. Note that **Unité 1**, the introductory unit, has only two lessons and does not include all the sections that future **unités** will have.

 **NATIONAL STANDARDS**
C1.2

2

Leçon A

In this lesson you will be able to:

➤ **greet someone**

➤ **introduce yourself**

➤ **introduce someone else**

➤ **ask someone's name**

➤ **tell someone's name**

■ **Workbook**
Activities 1-2

✎ **Grammar & Vocabulary**
Exercises 5-7, 15

📼 **Audiocassette/CD**
Dialogue, Enquête culturelle

André is talking with Nadine in the school courtyard between classes.
André's friend Abdou joins them.

Abdou: **Eh, salut, André!**
André: **Tiens, bonjour, Abdou! Je te présente Nadine.**
Abdou: **Pardon, tu t'appelles comment?**
Nadine: **Je m'appelle Nadine.**
Abdou: **Bonjour, Nadine.**

Teacher's Note

Comment t'appelles-tu? is another way of phrasing the question **Tu t'appelles comment?**

Cooperative Group Practice

Wagon Wheel Introductions

Have students form two circles with the same number of students in each circle, one inside the other. Students face their partner. Partners greet each other by saying **Bonjour** or **Salut** and then say **Je m'appelle....** (giving their new French name, if students have already selected them). After both students have given their greetings, say **Changez**. Then the outside student moves one person to the right, setting up a new pair. Continue until students return to their original partners.

Cultural Differences

Divide students into small groups with one student in each group acting as the recorder. Have them discuss how people greet each other, noting similarities and differences between French and American cultures. For example, students may include comments on how they greet their family in the morning, their friends and teachers at school, and a salesperson at a local store. Then compare this information with the explanations given in the **Enquête culturelle.** Groups may share their responses.

 *Enquête culturelle*

French people often shake hands when they greet and say good-bye to each other. Their handshake consists of just one up-and-down motion, unlike the American handshake which involves several movements. Friends and family members say hello and good-bye to each other with two to four kisses (**bises**) on alternating cheeks. Girls and women kiss each other and male friends as well. The number of kisses varies according to the region of the country. Boys and men usually shake hands with each other instead of kissing.

NATIONAL STANDARDS
C1.1, C1.2, C2.1, C4.2

bonjour

French speakers change the way they talk depending on the situation. They will often use slang and casual speech when talking to friends and family. Teenagers will use more formal words with adults as a sign of respect. For example, a student would say hi to a friend with either **Salut** or **Bonjour**, but would generally say **Bonjour, Monsieur** (*Mr.*), **Bonjour, Madame** (*Mrs.*) or **Bonjour, Mademoiselle** (*Miss*) to a teacher. In writing, these titles are abbreviated as follows:

Monsieur = M.   Madame = Mme   Mademoiselle = Mlle

The school courtyard, **la cour**, is a very popular meeting place for French students between classes and before and after school. Teenagers talk with their friends and play games there.

1 Answer the following questions.

1. What are three words for saying hello in French? Which one can you say only when talking on the phone?

2. What do boys do when they say hello to each other?

3. What do girls do when they say hello to friends?

4. Where can students meet between classes? Does your school have one?

French teens get together in *la cour* during lunch hour. (Verneuil-sur-Seine)

2 | *Choisissez la bonne réponse.* (Choose the correct answer.)

1. How does Abdou say hello
   to André?
   a. Pardon.
   b. Tiens.
   c. Salut.

2. How does André introduce
   Nadine to his friend?
   a. Je te présente Nadine.
   b. Je m'appelle Nadine.
   c. Bonjour, Nadine.

3. What does Abdou say
   when he doesn't hear
   Nadine's name?
   a. Eh....
   b. Tiens....
   c. Pardon....

4. What does Abdou say to
   Nadine to find out her name?
   a. Tu t'appelles comment?
   b. Je te présente Nadine.
   c. Je m'appelle Nadine.

5. How does Nadine give
   her name?
   a. Tu t'appelles comment?
   b. Je m'appelle Nadine.
   c. Je te présente Nadine.

6. What does Abdou say after
   meeting Nadine?
   a. Tiens, Nadine.
   b. Bonjour, Nadine.
   c. Eh, Nadine.

3 | What do you say in French when . . .

1. you greet a friend in the hall at school?
2. you introduce your friend to another classmate?
3. you ask a new student his or her name?
4. you tell your teacher the new student's name?
5. you tell someone your name?
6. someone tells you his or her name?

Bonjour! Je m'appelle Antoine.

6

Tu t'appelles comment?

prénoms de filles

Je m'appelle Anne.

Adja	Laïla
Aïcha	Lamine
Amina	Latifa
Anne	Magali
Anne-Marie	Malika
Antonine	Margarette
Arabéa	Marie
Ariane	Marie-Alix
Assia	Martine
Béatrice	Michèle
Caroline	Myriam
Catherine	Nadia
Cécile	Nadine
Chloé	Nathalie
Christine	Nicole
Claudette	Nora
Clémence	Patricia
Delphine	Renée
Denise	Sabrina
Diane	Saleh
Élisabeth	Sandrine
Fatima	Sonia
Florence	Sophie
Françoise	Stéphanie
Gilberte	Sylvie
Isabelle	Valérie
Jamila	Véronique (Véro)
Jeanne	Yasmine
Karima	Zakia
Karine	Zohra

Je m'appelle Malick.

Je m'appelle Zakia.

prénoms de garçons

Abdel-Cader	
Abdou	Jean-François
Abdoul	Jean-Philippe
Ahmed	Jérémy
Alain	Karim
Alexandre	Khaled
Amine	Khadim
André	Laurent
Assane	Louis
Benjamin	Luc
Bruno	Mahmoud
Charles	Malick
Christophe	Mamadou
Clément	Marc
Damien	Max
Daniel	Michel
David	Mohamed
Dikembe	Nicolas
Djamel	Normand
Édouard	Olivier
Emmanuel (Manu)	Ousmane
Éric	Patrick
Étienne	Paul
Fabrice	Pierre
Fayçal	Raphaël
Frédéric (Fred)	Robert
Guillaume	Salim
Hervé	Théo
Jean	Thibault
Jean-Christophe	Thierry
	Vincent

Je m'appelle Karine.

Je m'appelle Frédéric.

Je m'appelle Salim.

What's in a name?

First names can reflect a person's religious or cultural background. For example, children called Paul and Anne may have been named after saints, while the names Charles and Catherine may refer to former French royalty.

Last names, or surnames, often explain where a family was from originally or the family's occupation. The name Dubois ("from the woods") means that the family lived near a forest; the name Meunier ("miller") indicates that the family milled flour.

M. Dumont

Mme Charpentier

Today, names reflect the multicultural makeup of French society. When looking up a last name in the phone book or on the Minitel (a telecommunication system), you will find family names from a variety of French-speaking countries and other areas of the world.

PACHOUTINSKY Alexandre · 01 49 59 63 71
PAFUNDI Danièle · · · · · · 01 45 31 35 90
PAGANELLI Paul · · · · · · 01 40 44 55 08
PAGET Christèle · · · · · 01 42 50 87 29
PAI Thérèse · · · · · · · · 01 43 58 26 61

French-Canadian families pass along first names, such as Serge, Robert, Muguette and Céline, from generation to generation. Paquette, Charbonneau, Levesque and Poitras are examples of surnames from Quebec.

In French-speaking Africa, first names may indicate on what day a child was born, his or her birth order or the name of a nearby lake or town. For example, a boy called Fez or Fes would be named after a city in Morocco. African surnames vary from country to country: Kourouma (the Ivory Coast), Moutawakel (Morocco), Senghor (Senegal).

Il s'appelle Serge Desrosiers.

Workbook Activity 4

Grammar & Vocabulary Exercise 2

Connections

Family Research

You might have your students spend some time talking to their parents and/or extended family about their personal history. Then they may respond in writing to the following questions, in preparation for a class discussion. A. Names. What is the origin of your family name, both geographically and in meaning? (For example, "Donaldson" is an English or Scandinavian name that originally meant "the son of Donald.") Were there any changes in your family surname if your ancestors came from another country? How did you receive your first name? Do you have a nickname, and if so, is there a meaning behind it? Is there a French equivalent for your first name? B. History. What do you know about the background of your parents and grandparents? (For example, their childhood, education, marriage(s), politics, religion, hobbies.) From what part(s) of the world did your ancestors come? When did your ancestors arrive in this country? Why did they come here? C. Traditions. What customs does your family have for holidays, birthdays, weddings and other special celebrations? D. Events. How have historical events such as World War I and II, the Vietnam War and/or the Persian Gulf War affected your family? Has your family experienced any natural disasters, such as hurricanes or earthquakes? Have the Civil Rights Movement and the Women's Liberation Movement affected your family?

NATIONAL STANDARDS
C1.2, C2.1, C3.2

Listening Activity 1

Communication

Comparisons

Coat of Arms

Have students create their personal coat of arms by making a shield which they divide into six sections and number consecutively. Then have students answer the first five questions that follow by drawing simple pictures that symbolize their responses. Have them write out the response for the last question in the last section. (You may want to demonstrate by making your own coat of arms first.) When students finish, they may share their responses with the rest of the class and then display their projects in the classroom. 1. What is your greatest personal achievement? 2. What are your three most prized possessions? 3. What are two things that you are good at and that you enjoy doing? 4. Who is your hero or heroine? 5. What is something that other people can do to make you happy? 6. If you died today, what three things would you most like to be said about you?

Modèle:

Nicolas (shaking hands with Sandrine):   Bonjour.
Sandrine (shaking hands with Nicolas):   Salut.
Nicolas: Tu t'appelles comment?
Sandrine: Je m'appelle Sandrine.
            Tu t'appelles comment?
Nicolas: Je m'appelle Nicolas.

4   It's the first day of school and you're in French class. You have already chosen a French name and now you want to practice asking and giving names with a classmate before you meet the new French exchange student. With your partner:

1. Shake hands (the way French people do).
2. Greet each other.
3. Ask each other's new French name.
4. Answer.

Modèle:

Janine: Tiens, salut!
Zakia: Bonjour, Janine.
Janine: Je te présente Pierre.
Zakia: Bonjour, Pierre.
Pierre: Salut. Tu t'appelles comment?
Zakia: Je m'appelle Zakia.
Pierre: Bonjour, Zakia.

5   With two of your classmates, play the roles of a student, the student's friend and the new French exchange student who's attending your school this year. The student must introduce this new exchange student to his or her friend in French class.

1. The student and exchange student greet each other.
2. The student introduces the exchange student to the friend.
3. The exchange student greets the friend by name.
4. The friend greets the exchange student. Then the friend asks for the exchange student's name again.
5. The exchange student gives his or her name.
6. The friend greets the exchange student by name.

NATIONAL STANDARDS
C1.1, C1.2

= zéro

 = un

 = onze

 =deux

 = douze

 = trois

 = treize

 = quatre

 = quatorze

 =cinq

 =quinze

 = six

 = seize

 = sept

 = dix-sept

 = huit

 =dix-huit

 = neuf

 = dix-neuf

 = dix

 = vingt

Leçon B

In this lesson you will be able to:

➤ introduce yourself

➤ greet someone

➤ leave someone

➤ thank someone

➤ give telephone numbers

➤ restate information

Grammar & Vocabulary
Exercises 8-14

Audiocassette/CD
Numbers 0-20

Teacher's Note

Number Song

Students learn easily by using music and rhythm as a mnemonic device. Have them sing the numbers 1-10 to the tune of "Frère Jacques" as follows: Un, deux, trois; un, deux, trois; quatre, cinq, six; quatre, cinq, six; sept, huit; sept, huit; neuf, dix; neuf, dix.

TPR

Tic, Tic, Tic, Boom

In this game students practice the numbers from one to ten using the TPR (Total Physical Response) approach. In TPR activities, students actively engage in listening comprehension while responding only physically, not verbally. (This physical response helps to establish and ensure comprehension of new vocabulary or structure.) In this game each student takes a sheet of paper, tears it into ten pieces, labels each piece with a number from one to ten and then places the ten small pieces of paper on his or her desk. You call out a number from one to ten (in French or in English). Then begin timing aloud by saying *Tic, Tic, Tic,* (etc.), *Boom.* Students who hold up the appropriate piece of paper within the time allotted earn one point. Students who hold up an incorrect piece of paper or no paper within the time allotted receive no points.

NATIONAL STANDARDS
C1.1, C1.2

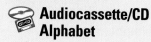

Workbook Activities 5-6

Audiocassette/CD Alphabet

Teacher's Notes

1. You may want to tell your students that in France, students often refer to the **accent circonflexe** as **un chapeau**. 2. You may want to point out to your students that when French speakers count on their fingers, they indicate "1" with their thumb.

Game

Machine à écrire

You might play this game once you have presented the French alphabet and your class has practiced it, using the vocabulary of **Unité 1**. Divide the class into two teams. Then assign a letter of the alphabet to individual members of each team. Assign accent marks, too. In doing this, be sure each team has members that represent the whole alphabet and all accent marks. (If the class is small, then assign several letters or accent marks to single players.) Start the game by giving one team a word from the lesson to spell orally. They must do this so fast that they sound like a typewriter; hence, the name of the game. (You may set a time limit for calling out letters, say one or two seconds.) For example, if the word is **Bonjour**, the student with the letter **b** calls out that letter in French, and teammates with the appropriate letters complete in turn the spelling of **Bonjour**. By doing this, the team earns one point. Then the other team gets their turn at a word. Whenever a team fails, its rival gets a chance to spell the same word and win another point.

NATIONAL STANDARDS
C1.1, C1.2, C4.1

a = a   b = bé   c = cé

d = dé   e = e   f = effe

g = gé   h = hache   i = i

j = ji   k = ka   l = elle

m = emme   n = enne   o = o

p = pé   q = ku   r = erre

s = esse   t = té   u = u

v = vé   w = double vé   x = iks

y = i grec   z = zède

é = e accent aigu

à = a accent grave

ï = i tréma

ô = o accent circonflexe

ç = c cédille

Jessica Miller, an American high school student, is planning to visit her French pen pal, Stéphanie Dufresne. Jessica calls Stéphanie to tell her when she will be arriving.

Jessica:	... seize, zéro trois.
Stéphanie:	**Allô, oui?**
Jessica:	**Stéphanie? Bonjour! C'est Jessica Miller.**
Stéphanie:	**Ah, salut, Jessica! Ça va?**
Jessica:	**Ça va bien, merci. Écoute, j'arrive le dix.**
Stéphanie:	**Pardon, le six?**
Jessica:	**Non, pas le six, le dix, d... i... x.**
Stéphanie:	**Ah, d'accord.**
Jessica:	**À bientôt, Stéphanie.**
Stéphanie:	**Au revoir.**

Enquête culturelle

Note that Stéphanie Dufresne's phone number is 01.42.60.16.03. Phone numbers in France have ten digits and are divided into five groups of two numbers, which are often separated by periods. In 1996 France was divided into five regions from "01" to "05." The first two digits of a phone number for Paris and the surrounding region (Île-de-France) are "01." When calling Paris from the United States, Jessica begins by dialing "011" (international long distance), "33" (the country code for France) and then "1" (not "01") before the remaining eight digits.

Answers

1 1. a
2. c
3. e
4. b
5. d
6. f

2 1. c
2. a
3. b
4. a
5. b

3 Possible answers:

1. Allô, oui?
2. Ça va bien, merci.
3. J'arrive le (*number*).
4. Pardon?
5. Answers will vary.
6. À bientôt.

AlloCiné
01 40 30 20 10
Les salles, les horaires, les films

Although **Au revoir** may be used at any time to say good-bye in French, teenagers often say **Salut**. Two other words you may hear are **Ciao**, borrowed from Italian, and even "Bye." **Allô** is used only when answering the phone. **À bientôt** (*See you soon*) may also be said to end a conversation in French.

1 | *Choisissez la bonne réponse.*

1. What word for hello is used when you answer the phone?
2. What do French speakers say when they want someone to repeat something?
3. How many digits are there in a French phone number?
4. What are the first two digits in a Parisian phone number?
5. What word means both hello and good-bye in French?
6. What is the Italian word for good-bye that French people use?

a. Allô.
b. "01"
c. Pardon?
d. Salut.
e. ten
f. Ciao.

Salut! Ça va?

2 | *Choisissez la bonne réponse.*

1. Allô, oui?
   a. J'arrive le dix.
   b. À bientôt.
   c. Bonjour! C'est Philippe.

2. C'est Myriam.
   a. Salut.
   b. Écoute.
   c. Ciao.

3. Ça va?
   a. Ah, d'accord.
   b. Ça va bien.
   c. Merci.

4. J'arrive le sept.
   a. Pardon, le dix-sept?
   b. Tu t'appelles comment?
   c. Pas le sept?

5. À bientôt.
   a. Tiens, bonjour.
   b. Au revoir.
   c. N... e... u... f.

3 | What would you say in French in the following situations?

1. You answer the phone.
2. Someone asks you how it's going.
3. Someone asks you when you're arriving.
4. You're not sure you've heard someone correctly.
5. Someone asks you to spell your first and last names.
6. Someone tells you good-bye.

NATIONAL STANDARDS
C1.1, C1.2, C2.1, C4.1

Communication

4 You are going to make a name tag for the new French exchange student, but you aren't sure how to spell his or her name. With a partner, play the roles of the student and the exchange student. In the course of your conversation:

1. The student greets the exchange student.
2. The exchange student greets the student and asks how things are going.
3. The student says things are going well and then asks if the exchange student's name is spelled a certain way (incorrectly).
4. The exchange student says no and spells his or her name correctly.
5. The student repeats the correct spelling.
6. The exchange student agrees.
7. The student says OK, thank you, and says he or she will see the exchange student soon.
8. The exchange student says he or she will see the student again soon.

Bonjour! Je m'appelle Stéphanie

Modèle:

Laura:	Bonjour, Stéphanie.
Stéphanie:	Salut, Laura. Ça va?
Laura:	Ça va bien, merci. Ah... Stéphanie, c'est S... t... e... f... a... n... e... e?
Stéphanie:	Non, c'est S... t... e accent aigu... p... h... a... n... i... e.
Laura:	S... t... e accent aigu... p... h... a... n... i... e.
Stéphanie:	Oui!
Laura:	D'accord, merci. À bientôt.
Stéphanie:	À bientôt.

5 You need to call certain people but you don't have their telephone numbers. Fortunately, your partner does. As your partner reads you each person's telephone number in French, use the accompanying telephone to dial these ten-digit numbers, touching each set of numbers in order. For example, you say **Stéphanie?** Your partner replies **Ah... Stéphanie... zéro un, vingt, zéro neuf, quinze, zéro cinq**. Then you dial 01.20.09.15.05 on the phone. Your partner will watch to see that you dial correctly.

1. M. Paquette:
   zéro quatre, dix-neuf, zéro huit, zéro sept, douze
2. Marie-Alix:
   zéro un, vingt, quinze, seize, zéro un
3. Théo:
   zéro trois, treize, dix, quatorze, dix-sept
4. Mme Bérenger:
   zéro deux, zéro six, zéro quatre, onze, dix-huit

Nathalie et Raoul

Listening Activity 2B

Workbook Activity 9

Answers

1. false
2. true
3. true
4. false
5. true
6. false
7. false
8. true

Teacher's Note

The checklist in the **C'est à moi!** section relates to the communicative functions that are presented in each unit. If students are unsure of how to express any of them, tell students to look for help in the **Communication active** section that follows.

Comparisons

Cultural Journal
You may want to encourage your students to keep a cultural journal during the course of the year in which they record observations they have made about francophone cultures, similarities and differences between francophone and American cultures, and personal reflections. Collect and comment on your students' observations regularly. A suggestion for an entry in the cultural journal for this **unité** is to have students list some French words or expressions that are commonly used in English. (For example, hors d'œuvre, à la carte, bon voyage, faux pas, fiancé, gourmet, R.S.V.P., etc.) Then have them note in what situations people use these expressions. Also have students try to figure out why so many English words have been borrowed from French.

NATIONAL STANDARDS
C1.1, C1.2, C2.1, C4.2, C5.1, C5.2

14

Friends greet each other with kisses (*bises*) on the cheek. (French West Indies)

D'accord. Au revoir.

C'est à moi!

Now that you have completed this unit, take a look at what you should be able to do in French. Can you do all of these tasks?

➤ I can say hello, hi, thanks and good-bye, and can greet my friends and adults appropriately.

➤ I can introduce myself.

➤ I can introduce my friends to each other and tell their names.

➤ I can count from 0 to 20.

➤ I can spell names and other important information.

Here is a brief checkup to see how much you understand about French culture. Decide if each statement is true or false.

1. When French teenagers talk to each other, they say **Monsieur**, **Madame** or **Mademoiselle**.
2. In French-speaking Africa, a child's first name may be the name of the weekday on which he or she was born.
3. You say **Allô** when answering the phone in French.
4. The French shake hands the same way Americans do.
5. French last names, such as Meunier and Dubois, indicate what work the family did or where they came from.
6. As soon as you meet someone in France, you should greet that person with two to four kisses on his or her cheeks.
7. French teenagers talk to their friends only in class or on the telephone.
8. French-Canadian first names are passed along from grandparents to parents to children.

Communication orale

Imagine that a family in your town or city has a French teenager staying with them. The teenager speaks very little English. With a classmate, play the role of an American student who is a friend of this family and the role of the visiting teenager. The family has asked the American student to phone this French teenager so that he or she will have someone to talk to who can speak French. The American student agrees to do this because he or she is eager to practice speaking French.

Before beginning, the French person writes his or her American phone number on a small sheet of paper and gives it to the American student without saying anything. As the student pretends to dial the phone number, he or she says the numbers out loud in French one at a time. During the course of the phone call, turn away from each other to talk as though you are on the phone.

1. The French student answers the phone.
2. The American student greets the French student and introduces himself or herself.

3. The French student greets the American student.
4. Tell each other your name and spell it so that the other person is sure to understand.
5. Ask each other how things are going.
6. Tell each other that things are going well.
7. Tell each other good-bye and that you will see each other soon.

Communication écrite

After you and your partner finish talking on the phone in the preceding activity, your teacher wants to know exactly what each of you said. Begin by writing out the French words for the phone number of the French student, digit by digit. Then write out in dialogue form the entire conversation you had with your partner to give to your teacher. As you write out the conversation, remember to write the name of the person speaking before each line of dialogue.

Communication active

To greet someone, use:

Salut!   *Hi!*
Bonjour!   *Hello!*
Allô?   *Hello? (on telephone)*
Ça va?   *How are things going?*

To say good-bye to someone, use:

Au revoir.   *Good-bye.*
Ciao.   *Bye.*
Salut.   *Good-bye.*
À bientôt.   *See you soon.*

To introduce yourself, use:

Je m'appelle Valérie.   *My name is Valérie.*
C'est Patrick.   *This is Patrick.*

To introduce someone else, use:

Je te présente Malika.   *Let me introduce you to Malika.*
C'est Luc.   *This is Luc.*

To ask someone's name, use:

Tu t'appelles comment?   *What's your name?*

To tell someone's name, use:

Il s'appelle Mahmoud.   *His name is Mahmoud.*
Elle s'appelle Yasmine.   *Her name is Yasmine.*

To thank someone, use:

Merci.   *Thanks.*

To give a telephone number, use:

Zéro un, dix-neuf, zéro cinq, dix, douze.   *Zero one, nineteen, zero five, ten, twelve.*

To restate information, use:

Raoul, R... a... o... u... l.   *Raoul, R . . . a . . . o . . . u . . . l.*

Bonjour! Je m'appelle Jérémy.

NATIONAL STANDARDS
C1.1, C1.2, C4.1

Communication électronique (answers)

Communication électronique

1. Possible answer: Telecommunications, the airlines, import-export companies, the foreign service and international investments are five areas in which knowing French will give you a competitive edge in the job market.
2. About 125 million people around the world speak French.
3. Possible answer: The Le Mans automobile race, the French Open tennis tournament and the Tour de France bicycle race attract spectators from all over the world.
4. Possible answer: Learning French will help you to improve your memory, self-discipline and self-esteem as well as increase your problem-solving skills.
5. By knowing French you can become an educated tourist, for example, you can ask for directions, get a hotel room and order at a restaurant.
6. Answers will vary.

À moi de jouer!

Possible conversations:

— Salut, Olivier! Je te présente Amélie.
— Bonjour, Amélie.
— Bonjour, Olivier. Ça va?

. . . .

— Au revoir, Bruno.
— À bientôt, Éric.

Communication électronique

What were your reasons for choosing to study French? Are you aware that learning French may help you now and in the future by...

▸ increasing your employment opportunities?

helping you understand how people think and live in other cultures?

offering you a new perspective on your own language and culture?

enhancing your skills in English?

To learn ten reasons why knowing French is an asset in the new millennium, go to this Internet site:

http://www.info-france.org/kids/apprend2.htm

After you have finished exploring this site, answer the following questions.

1. What are five occupations in which knowing French will give you a competitive edge?
2. How many people around the world speak French?
3. What are three sports competitions in France that attract spectators from all over the world?
4. What important life skills will you acquire by learning French?
5. How can a knowledge of French help you in your travels?
6. In your opinion, what are the three most important reasons for you to study French?

À moi de jouer!

Now it's your turn! Put together everything that you have learned so far by completing the two short dialogues below with appropriate expressions from this unit. (You may want to refer to the *Communication active* on page 15 and the vocabulary list on page 17.)

Vocabulaire

À bientôt. See you soon.
ah oh
allô hello (on telephone)
arriver to arrive
au revoir good-bye

bien well
bonjour hello

c'est this is, it's
ça
    Ça va? How are things going?
    Ça va bien. Things are going well.
ciao bye
cinq five
comment what

d'accord OK
deux two
dix ten
dix-huit eighteen
dix-neuf nineteen
dix-sept seventeen
douze twelve

écoute listen
Eh! Hey!

huit eight

j' I
je I

le (+ *number*) on the (+ ordinal number)

m'appelle: je m'appelle my name is
Madame (Mme) Mrs., Ma'am
Mademoiselle (Mlle) Miss
merci thanks
Monsieur (M.) Mr., Sir

neuf nine
non no

onze eleven
oui yes

pardon excuse me
pas not
présenter to introduce

quatorze fourteen
quatre four
quinze fifteen

s'appelle: elle s'appelle her name is
    il s'appelle his name is
salut hi; good-bye
seize sixteen
sept seven
six six

t'appelles: tu t'appelles your name is
te to you
Tiens! Hey!
treize thirteen
trois three

un one

vingt twenty

zéro zero

NATIONAL STANDARDS
C2.1, C2.2

Unité 2

Qu'est-ce que tu aimes faire?

In this unit you will be able to:

➤ **express likes and dislikes**

➤ **agree and disagree**

➤ **give opinions**

➤ **ask for information**

➤ **invite**

➤ **refuse an invitation**

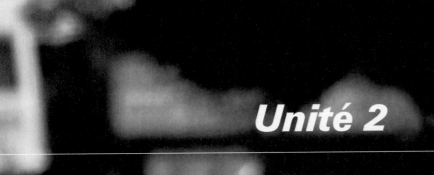

NATIONAL STANDARDS
C2.1, C2.2

Workbook Activities 1-2

Audiocassette/CD
Qu'est-ce qu'ils aiment faire? (A)

Transparencies 4-7

Teacher's Notes

1. You might develop a gesture for each verb, do the gesture and have students repeat the verb after you, then do the gesture again and have students say the verb without you. 2. Some words in French are shortened, for example, **le foot (football)** (point out **le football américain**), **le basket (basketball)** and **la télé (télévision)**. 3. The technical word for a television set is **un téléviseur**, but in current French, people commonly use **la télévision** to refer both to the set and to television (TV) in general. 4. A communicative function that is recycled in this lesson is "giving information." Those functions that are recycled from unit to unit will not be specifically listed in the **Communication active** section unless students learn a new way to express that function.

TPR

Tu aimes...?

You might have each student draw a heart on a piece of paper and cut it out. Then ask students individually the question **Tu aimes...?** Students respond that they like a particular activity by holding up their hearts.

NATIONAL STANDARDS
C1.2

20

Leçon A

In this lesson you will be able to:

➤ **express likes and dislikes**

➤ **ask for information**

➤ **invite**

➤ **refuse an invitation**

➤ **agree and disagree**

Abdou aime nager.

Gilberte aime téléphoner.

Philippe aime étudier.

Delphine aime skier.

Louis aime regarder la télé.

Valérie et Karine aiment bien aller au cinéma.

Françoise et Alain aiment écouter de la musique.

Manu aime jouer au basket.

Malika et Christian aiment jouer au foot.

le foot

le basket

la télé

la musique

le cinéma

Qu'est-ce que tu aimes faire?

J'aime aller au cinéma.

Audiocassette/CD
Dialogue

Teacher's Notes

1. In the context of this dialogue **passer** means "to show." Its more common meanings are "to pass by" and "to spend (time)." 2. **Bon** and **bonne** are introduced as active vocabulary in this **unité**. Their structure will be explained in **Unité 6**. 3. **Une interro** is the abbreviated form of **une interrogation**. 4. Other ways to refuse an invitation are to say **Impossible** or **Désolé(e)**. 5. You can disagree by saying **Pas d'accord**. 6. The reading strategy for learning to recognize cognates will be discussed again in the **Sur la bonne piste** section of this **unité** and will be more fully developed in the **Sur la bonne piste** section of **Unité 3**.

It's Wednesday afternoon. Since Valérie and Karine don't have classes, they talk about what they're going to do this afternoon.

Valérie: **Dis, qu'est-ce que tu aimes faire?**
Karine: **J'aime aller au cinéma. Pourquoi?**
Valérie: **On passe un bon film au Gaumont. On y va?**
Karine: **Pas possible. J'étudie pour l'interro, demain.**
Valérie: **D'accord. Alors, à demain.**

Enquête culturelle

It's not hard to figure out what the French word **musique** means. **Musique** is a cognate, a word that has a similar spelling and meaning in both French and English. Originally, many of these words may have been borrowed from one language to another. Words like **basketball, télévision, skier** and **téléphoner** are examples of cognates. Learning to recognize cognates is an easy way to increase your French vocabulary.

"Pizza" is a cognate. Can you find another? (Angers)

French teenagers usually don't have school on Wednesday afternoon, but they may attend classes on Saturday morning. Students use Wednesday afternoon to see their friends, practice sports, shop and study. Few French teens have part-time jobs. They need to study quite a bit each evening because teachers often assign a lot of homework.

NATIONAL STANDARDS
C1.2, C2.1, C4.1

Answers

1 1. Valérie and Karine don't have classes on Wednesday afternoon but do have classes on Saturday morning.
2. You can say **Pas possible** to refuse an invitation.
3. A French speaker says **À demain** when he or she will see the person the next day.
4. Most students in France don't have part-time jobs because they have a lot of homework to do each evening.
5. No, movies from many countries are shown in France.

2 1. a
2. b
3. a
4. b
5. c
6. a
7. c

Comparisons

Cultural Journal

If your students are keeping a cultural journal, you might have them write answers to these questions: What are some of the activities that you do during your leisure time? How do you get to most of your activities away from home (on foot, by bike, by car, etc.)? If you had the choice between buying a car or going on a trip anywhere in the world, which one would you choose? Why?

NATIONAL STANDARDS
C1.2, C2.1, C2.2, C3.2, C4.2

22

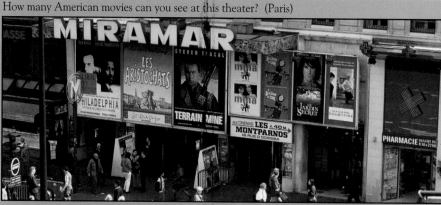

How many American movies can you see at this theater? (Paris)

Going to movies is a popular leisure activity for French speakers of all ages. Paris has the largest number of movie theaters of any city in the world. Many films from countries other than France are shown as well. On certain days of the week movie theaters offer reduced prices for students.

French teenagers have many hours of homework each night.

1 Answer the following questions.

1. How is the daily school schedule of Valérie and Karine different from yours?
2. What can you say in French to refuse an invitation?
3. How does a French speaker say good-bye when he or she will see the person the next day?
4. Why is it difficult for students in France to have part-time jobs?
5. Are only French movies shown in France?

2 *Choisissez la bonne réponse.*

1. What word does Valérie use to get Karine's attention?
   a. Dis.
   b. D'accord.
   c. Alors.

2. How does Valérie ask Karine what she likes to do?
   a. Pourquoi?
   b. Qu'est-ce que tu aimes faire?
   c. On y va?

3. How does Valérie say that there's a good movie?
   a. On passe un bon film.
   b. J'étudie pour l'interro.
   c. J'aime aller au cinéma.

4. What does Karine say to refuse Valérie's invitation?
   a. D'accord.
   b. Pas possible.
   c. Alors.

5. When does Karine have a test?
   a. À demain.
   b. Le six.
   c. Demain.

6. How does Valérie respond when Karine says she has to study?
   a. D'accord.
   b. Ciao.
   c. Pas possible.

7. How does Valérie tell Karine when they'll see each other again?
   a. Au revoir.
   b. Salut.
   c. À demain.

✎ **Grammar & Vocabulary Exercises 1-2**

📷 **Audiocassette/CD Activity 3**

💾 **Computer Software Activity 1**

3 | *C'est à toi!* (It's your turn!) *Questions personnelles.*

1. Qu'est-ce que tu aimes faire?
2. Tu aimes aller au cinéma?
3. Tu aimes jouer au foot?
4. Tu aimes jouer au basket?
5. Tu aimes écouter de la musique?
6. Tu aimes regarder la télé?

CINÉMA LE VAUBAN à SAINT-MALO
02 36 68 69 21*
Le nouveau numéro de répondeur vocal interactif.

Structure

Subject pronouns

To talk to or about people, use subject pronouns to replace their names. Subject pronouns are either singular (referring to one person) or plural (referring to more than one person). In French the singular subject pronouns are **je**, **tu**, **vous**, **il**, **elle** and **on**. The plural ones are **nous, vous, ils** and **elles**.

Singular		Plural	
je	*I*	**nous**	*we*
tu		**vous**	*you*
vous	*you*		
il	*he*	**ils**	
elle	*she*	**elles**	*they*
on	*one/they/we*		

Tu aimes aller au cinéma?   *Do you like to go to the movies?*

Oui, j'aime aller au cinéma.   *Yes, I like to go to the movies.*

Note that **je** becomes **j'** when the next word begins with a vowel sound.

The pronoun **on** is singular even though it often refers to more than one person.

On passe un bon film au Rex.   *They're showing a good movie at the Rex.*

Il replaces a masculine name; **elle** replaces a feminine name.

Valérie? Elle va au cinéma.   *Valérie? She is going to the movies.*

Elles refers to two or more women. **Ils** refers to two or more men or to a combination of men and women.

Nicolas et Renée? Ils aiment skier.   *Nicolas and Renée? They like to ski.*

RESERVE AUX ABONNES

SKETBA!

TU AIMES LE BASKET?
TU AS ENTRE 13 ET 18 ANS?
PARTICIPE AU FRANCE BASKET TOUR!

Du 3 avril au 3 septembre, dans plus de 30 villes de France, CANAL+ et la Fédération française de Basket-Ball te proposent une grande compétition de basket 3 X 3.

Pour t'aider à participer, **CANAL+** te réserve ta place en priorité et t'offre la "carte basket", assurance obligatoire qui te permet de t'inscrire à **tous les tournois de basket en liberté** jusqu'à la fin de l'année. En plus de cette "carte d'identité de basketteur", une casquette te sera offerte! Que tu sois un garçon ou une fille, si tu es un as des playgrounds dans ta ville le jour de la compétition, tu seras invité(e) pour **la grande finale à Paris**, le week-end des **5 et 6 novembre**, et tu assisteras à un grand rendez-vous de basket avec les plus grandes stars.
Tu es intéressé(e)?
Alors renvoie-nous ce coupon avec une photocopie de ta carte d'identité et une photo d'identité pour ta carte basket à
CANAL+ BASKET, BP 129, 59009 Lille cedex
1 mois avant la date de rencontre te concernant (voir liste des villes).

LISTE DES VILLES ET DATES DES RENCONTRES

Renseignements 📺 36 15 CPLUS rubrique PLUS ☎ 01 49 87 20 40

Nous recyclons. Et vous? (Canada)

Answers

3 Answers will vary.

Teacher's Notes

1. In order to contextualize the examples in the **Structure** sections, vocabulary relates to the lesson's theme and functions whenever possible. 2. You may want to indicate subject pronouns with gestures rather than with verbal cues. For example, **je** can be expressed by pointing the thumb of the right hand toward the speaker. To express **tu**, point the index finger of the right hand toward the listener. To express **il**, point the index finger of the right hand to the right side. To express **elle**, point the index finger of the left hand to the left side. To express **nous**, point both thumbs toward the speaker. To express **vous**, point both index fingers toward the listener(s). To express **ils**, point both index fingers to the right. To express **elles**, point both index fingers to the left.

NATIONAL STANDARDS
C1.1, C1.2, C3.2, C4.1

Pratique

4 While paging through a French magazine, you come across the following headlines and advertisements. Tell what subject pronoun is found in each one.

Il jouait du piano assis...
1.

5. **Nouvelle Peugeot 405 MI 16. Elle met tout son talent à vos pieds.**

—Vous avez gagné 20 €
2.

On aime... on déteste *fleurs CD tomates*
6.

JE DESIRE M'ABONNER A **PARIS MATCH**
3.

Ils ont dit « oui », comme au cinéma !
7.

TU AS JOUÉ ?
4.

Nous allons à la plage!
8.

5 You are describing various people at your new school to a family member. Unfortunately, you can't remember any of their names. Select the appropriate subject pronoun you could use to describe each person or group of people from the following list:

> il   elle   ils   elles

1.

3.

5.

2.

4.

6.

tu vs. *vous*

In French **tu** and **vous** both mean "you," but they are used in different ways. When you talk to one person,

use **tu** with:
1. a friend
2. a close relative
3. a person your own age
4. a child
5. a pet

use **vous** with:
1. an adult you don't know
2. a distant relative
3. a person older than you
4. an acquaintance
5. a person of authority, such as a teacher

Bonjour, Mlle Dufresne! Vous skiez?

Dis, Toutounne, qu'est-ce que tu aimes faire?

When you talk to more than one person, always use **vous**.

Qu'est-ce que **tu** aimes faire, Nadine?   *What do you like to do, Nadine?*

Vous skiez, Mlle Dufresne?   *Do you ski, Miss Dufresne?*

Karine et Luc, **vous** étudiez?   *Karine and Luc, are you studying?*

Pratique

6 Since Karine can't go to the movies, Valérie has asked you to go with her. On the way to the theater, you meet and speak French with many different people. Indicate whether you should use **tu** or **vous** with each person or group of people.

1. Karine's mother
2. a lost five-year-old
3. your math teacher
4. your friend Bruno
5. Bruno's dog, Milou
6. two secretaries from the office at school
7. your 15-year-old cousin Thierry
8. your grandfather's brother
9. your classmates Sophie and Béatrice
10. a police officer

Sophie et Béatrice, vous aimez aller au cinéma?

Workbook Activity 3

Grammar & Vocabulary Exercises 3-4

Computer Software Activity 2

Answers

6 1. vous
  2. tu
  3. vous
  4. tu
  5. tu
  6. vous
  7. tu
  8. vous
  9. vous
 10. vous

Comparisons

Formal vs. Informal Address
Ask students to think of ways in which English speakers differentiate between the concept of **tu** and **vous**. (Possible answers: register levels, tone of voice, forms of address, body language, etc.) Then discuss with students the benefits of being able to distinguish this in French because of the two different words for "you."

NATIONAL STANDARDS
C1.2, C2.1, C4.1

25

Grammar & Vocabulary Exercises 5-9

Answers

7 parler, passer, payer, préférer, préparer, présenter, regarder, rencontrer, rentrer, répéter, rester, retourner

Teacher's Notes

1. Ask your students to draw a picture for each **-er** verb that they have learned. Then, take the best picture for each one, laminate it and use it as your visual cue for that verb. 2. You may want to indicate infinitives ending in **-er** with gestures rather than with verbal or visual cues. Here are some suggestions.

étudier	Act as if you are opening a book, then place your right hand on your cheek as if you are concentrating.
nager	Make an overhand crawl stroke with both arms.
jouer	Pretend that you are boucing a ball.
skier	Make a cross-country ski motion.
regarder	Point your right index finger to your right eye.
écouter	Cup your right hand behind your right ear.
téléphoner	Hold an imaginary phone up to your left ear and dial with your right hand.
aimer	Place your right hand over your heart.
passer	For the meaning "to show a movie," act as if you were filming, holding the camera with the left hand and winding the film with the right hand.

NATIONAL STANDARDS
C1.2, C4.1

26

Infinitives

A verb expresses action or a state of being. The basic form of a verb is the infinitive, the verb form found in the end vocabulary of this textbook and in French dictionaries. Many French infinitives end in **-er**. Some of the verbs you have already seen that end in **-er** are **présenter**, **arriver**, **étudier**, **nager**, **jouer**, **skier**, **regarder**, **écouter**, **téléphoner**, **aimer** and **passer**.

Pratique

7 List the infinitives ending in **-er** that are found on the following page taken from a beginning French dictionary.

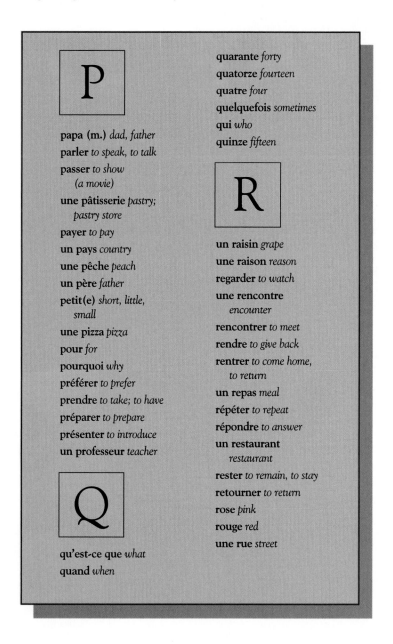

P

papa (m.) *dad, father*
parler *to speak, to talk*
passer *to show (a movie)*
une pâtisserie *pastry; pastry store*
payer *to pay*
un pays *country*
une pêche *peach*
un père *father*
petit(e) *short, little, small*
une pizza *pizza*
pour *for*
pourquoi *why*
préférer *to prefer*
prendre *to take; to have*
préparer *to prepare*
présenter *to introduce*
un professeur *teacher*

Q

qu'est-ce que *what*
quand *when*

quarante *forty*
quatorze *fourteen*
quatre *four*
quelquefois *sometimes*
qui *who*
quinze *fifteen*

R

un raisin *grape*
une raison *reason*
regarder *to watch*
une rencontre *encounter*
rencontrer *to meet*
rendre *to give back*
rentrer *to come home, to return*
un repas *meal*
répéter *to repeat*
répondre *to answer*
un restaurant *restaurant*
rester *to remain, to stay*
retourner *to return*
rose *pink*
rouge *red*
une rue *street*

8 Tell what some of your friends like to do, according to the illustrations.

1. Marc aime....

4. Vincent aime....

2. Fatima aime....

5. Caroline aime....

3. Louis aime....

6. Anne aime....

Modèle:

Karima aime aller au cinéma.

Present tense of regular verbs ending in -*er*

Many verbs whose infinitives end in -**er** are called regular verbs because their forms follow a predictable pattern. Regular -**er** verbs, such as **jouer**, have six forms in the present tense. To form the present tense of a regular -**er** verb, first find the stem of the verb by removing the -**er** ending from its infinitive.

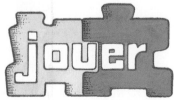

Now add the endings (-**e**, -**es**, -**e**, -**ons**, -**ez**, -**ent**) to the stem of the verb depending on the corresponding subject pronouns.

Grammar & Vocabulary Exercises 10-13

Audiocassette/CD Activity 8

Computer Software Activities 3-4

Answers

8 1. jouer au foot
2. nager
3. téléphoner
4. regarder la télé
5. skier
6. écouter de la musique

Teacher's Note

Some conjugated verb forms are also found in the end vocabulary of this textbook. These forms appear in the end vocabulary because their infinitives have not yet been introduced as active vocabulary.

Comparisons

Inductive Thinking
You may prefer to teach -**er** verbs by using the inductive method. Give each student a sheet of paper containing about 25 sentences that use different subject pronouns and an assortment of -**er** verbs that students have already seen. Put students in pairs, telling them to work together to try to sort out the sentences so they can recognize various patterns. Have pairs work together until several of them have discovered the relationship between subject pronouns and verb endings and can explain it to the entire class.

NATIONAL STANDARDS
C1.1, C1.2, C4.1

Workbook Activities 4-6

Audiocassette/CD Activity 9

Answers

9 1. Karim joue au basket.
2. Vous jouez au foot.
3. Je joue au foot.
4. Florence et Alexandre jouent au basket.
5. Tu joues au foot.
6. Mlle Larue joue au basket.
7. David et Jean-François jouent au foot.
8. Nous jouons au basket.

Teacher's Notes

1. The irregular verb **aller** will be presented in **Unité 3**. 2. Tell students that of the six verb endings, only **-ons** and **-ez** are pronounced; the others are silent. There are only three different oral forms of **jouer**. 3. You might have students orally practice the regular **-er** verbs already introduced. Ask them questions in the **tu** form to establish the **tu — je** pattern as an automatic response. 4. If students ask about the verb **s'appeler**, you might tell them that it is irregular and will be explained later. 5. If students ask why the **nous** form ends in **-eons** for infinitives ending in **-ger**, tell them that an **e** is added before the ending to keep the same [ʒ] sound as there is in the infinitive. 6. You might have students bring pictures from back issues of magazines (or they can make drawings) in which people are participating in the activities taught in this **leçon**. Then students, one at a time, show their picture and read its caption, for example, **Elle joue au basket.**

NATIONAL STANDARDS
C1.1, C1.2, C4.1

28

Ils jouent au basket.
(Paris)

Modèles:

nous
Nous jouons au foot.

Sandrine
Sandrine joue au basket.

jouer

Subject Pronoun +	Stem +	Ending		
je	jou	e	Je **joue** au foot.	*I play soccer.*
tu	jou	es	Tu **joues** bien.	*You play well.*
il/elle/on	jou	e	Elle **joue** le six.	*She plays on the sixth.*
nous	jou	ons	Nous **jouons** au basket.	*We play basketball.*
vous	jou	ez	Vous **jouez** demain?	*Are you playing tomorrow?*
ils/elles	jou	ent	Ils **jouent** au tennis.	*They are playing tennis.*

Remember that **je** becomes **j'** when the next word begins with a vowel sound: **J'étudie pour l'interro.**

Each present tense verb form in French consists of only one word but has more than one meaning.

André **nage** bien.
{ *André swims well.*
{ *André is swimming well.*

André **nage** bien? *Does André swim well?*

If an infinitive ends in **-ger**, its **nous** form ends in **-eons**.

Nous **nageons**. *We are swimming.*

Pratique

9 Tell whether the following people play soccer or basketball.

 1. Karim

 2. vous

 3. je

 4. Florence et Alexandre

 5. tu

 6. Mlle Larue

 7. David et Jean-François

 8. nous

0 Complete each short dialogue with the correct form of the appropriate verbs from the following list. Try to use each verb at least once.

regarder	étudier	aimer	passer	écouter	jouer	arriver

1. Qu'est-ce que vous... faire?
   Nous... nager.
2. Tu... la télé?
   Non, j'... de la musique.
3. Tu... au basket?
   Non, je... au foot.
4. Vous... le sept?
   Non, nous... le neuf.
5. On... un bon film au Gaumont. On y va?
   Pas possible. J'... pour l'interro.

11 The Bouchards have invited the Robidoux family to spend the day at their cabin. Describe what everyone is doing.

12 With a partner, talk about what various people are doing right now. Student A asks questions and Student B answers them. Follow the model.
1. Mme Gagner (regarder la télé/téléphoner)
2. Karine et Manu (étudier/jouer au basket)
3. tu (jouer au foot/écouter de la musique)
4. Diane et Nadia (arriver le dix/arriver le neuf)
5. tu (aimer aller au cinéma/aimer regarder la télé)

Madame Doubtfire
Jamais un père n'avait été aussi proche de ses enfants !
ROBIN WILLIAMS
SALLY FIELD
_ MADAME _
DOUBTFIRE
UGC Gaumont les 5 lumières

Modèle:
Édouard joue au basket.

Modèle:
Éric (nager/skier)
Student A: Éric nage?
Student B: Non, il skie.

Audiocassette/CD Activity 12

Answers

10 Possible answers:
1. aimez, aimons
2. regardes, écoute
3. joues, joue
4. arrivez, arrivons
5. passe, étudie

11 Claudette et Marie jouent au foot.
Mme Bouchard téléphone.
Normand et Robert nagent.
Mme Robidoux écoute de la musique.
M. Robidoux et Minou regardent la télé.

12 1. Mme Gagner regarde la télé?
   Non, elle téléphone.
2. Karine et Manu étudient?
   Non, ils jouent au basket.
3. Tu joues au foot?
   Non, j'écoute de la musique.
4. Diane et Nadia arrivent le dix?
   Non, elles arrivent le neuf.
5. Tu aimes aller au cinéma?
   Non, j'aime regarder la télé.

Game

Verb *Tic Tac Toe*
To practice regularly formed **-er** verbs, have students work in pairs. Each of the two students plays with a different-colored pen. Pass out a copy of the *Tic Tac Toe* worksheet to each pair. The heading of the worksheet is the infinitive of the verb to be conjugated. In the grid each of the nine boxes contains one subject pronoun (**je, tu, il, elle, on, nous, vous, ils, elles**). Students write the correct verb form in the box to match the given pronoun. If a student makes a mistake, his or her opponent can correct the mistake, steal the square and proceed with his or her regular turn.

NATIONAL STANDARDS
C1.1, C1.2

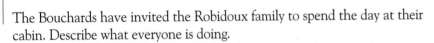

Communication

13 You would like to know what some of your classmates' favorite activities are. Draw a grid like the one that follows. In the grid write the question you will ask and add any three activities you can express in French. Then poll ten of your classmates to determine which of these three activities is the most popular. In your survey:

1. Ask each classmate what he or she likes to do, giving him or her your three choices.
2. As each classmate answers your question, make a check by the appropriate activity to indicate that he or she likes to do it. (You may check as many activities as your classmate names.)
3. After you have finished asking questions, count how many people like each activity and be ready to share your findings with the rest of the class.

Modèle:

Cécile: Qu'est-ce que tu aimes faire? Nager? Jouer au basket? Regarder la télé?

Daniel: J'aime nager.

Qu'est-ce que tu aimes faire?

	1	2	3	4	5	6	7	8	9	10
nager	✔									
jouer au basket										
regarder la télé										

14 Working in pairs, take turns asking each other what you like to do. Make a grid like the one that follows and mark your partner's responses with a check in the appropriate column.

Modèle:

Frédéric: Tu aimes aller au cinéma?

Laurent: Oui.

Tu aimes étudier?

Tu aimes...	oui	non
aller au cinéma?	✔	
étudier?		
nager?		
jouer au foot?		
jouer au basket?		
skier?		
regarder la télé?		
écouter de la musique?		
téléphoner?		

Audiocassette/CD
Prononciation

 Listening Activity 1

Quiz
Leçon A

15 Which of the nine activities whose names you have learned in this lesson are your favorites? Classify these activities by making a list of them beginning with the one you like the most and ending with the one you like the least. (You may need to refer back to Activity 14 to remember all nine of these activities.) When you have finished, read your list to a partner and compare your preferences.

16 It's the last class of the day. You and a friend pass notes back and forth to find out about your plans for after school. In these notes:

1. Student A tells Student B what two other friends are doing and asks Student B if he or she would like to do it also.
2. Student B either accepts Student A's invitation or refuses it and gives a reason for his or her refusal.
3. Student A says OK and that he or she will see Student B either soon or tomorrow.

For example:

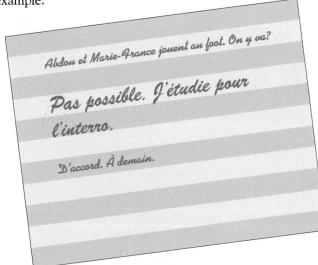

Abdou et Marie-France jouent au foot. On y va?

Pas possible. J'étudie pour l'interro.

D'accord. À demain.

Paired Practice

You might have students do Activity 16 again, this time orally with a partner.

Prononciation

Unpronounced consonants

A consonant in French generally is not pronounced when it is the last letter of a word. Say each of these words:

salut   alors   comment   pas   pardon   d'accord

The consonant **h** is never pronounced in French. Say each of these words:

Catherine   Hervé   Nathalie   Thierry

Grammar & Vocabulary
Exercises 14-17

 Audiocassette/CD
Qu'est-ce qu'ils aiment faire? (B)

Teacher's Notes

1. Another way to say "to go in-line skating" is **faire du roller-blade**. In-line skates are **les patins en ligne (m.)** or **les roller-blades (m.)**. 2. A popular winter activity in France is **le snowboarding** (*snowboarding*). The verb is **faire du snowboarding** (*to go snowboarding*). 3. You may want to indicate new verbs with gestures rather than with verbal or visual cues. Here are some suggestions.

faire du roller	Bend over and clasp hands behind the back as professional skaters do.
faire du footing	Run in place.
faire du vélo	Lean forward and put your hands out as if you are holding the handlebars of a bike.

4. Another way for students to visualize the difference in meaning of the adverbs of degree is to use appropriate body language or gestures to illustrate each one. 5. A communicative function that is recycled in this lesson is "giving information."

NATIONAL STANDARDS
C1.2

Leçon B

In this lesson you will be able to:

➤ **express likes and dislikes**

➤ **agree and disagree**

➤ **ask for information**

Ils aiment faire du sport.

Malick et Nicole aiment faire du roller.

Marc et Renée aiment faire du footing.

Fabrice et Karine aiment faire du vélo.

le roller

le footing

le vélo

M. Vinay aime un peu le camping.

Yasmine et Anne-Marie aiment bien les sports.

Patrick aime beaucoup les films.

Workbook Activities 7-8

Audiocassette/CD Dialogue

Jérémy wants to ask Sophie out. To find out what Sophie likes to do, he asks her friend Martine some questions.

Jérémy: **J'aime bien Sophie. Elle aime faire du sport?**

Martine: **Oui. Elle aime bien faire du roller, du footing, du vélo.**

Jérémy: **Elle écoute de la musique?**

Martine: **Oui. Elle aime beaucoup le rock et le reggae. Elle aime un peu le jazz.**

Jérémy: **Super! Moi aussi, j'aime beaucoup le rock. Bon, je téléphone à Sophie.**

After school many French teenagers play sports, listen to music or watch TV. When they have free time in the evening, they often get together with their friends at sidewalk cafés or at home. Many high school students like to dance at weekend parties, called **soirées.** Younger teens usually call their parties **boums.** Older teens and adults often go out to dance and listen to music at **les boîtes** and **les clubs** (*dance clubs*).

Enquête culturelle

Many French speakers listen to music from other countries, including England and the United States. Teens may like **le rock, le rap, le reggae, la techno, le jazz, le hard, le funk, la dance** or **la musique classique,** for example.

Teacher's Notes

1. Another word for **le footing** is **le jogging.** Other related terms include **la marche** (*walking*)**, la randonnée** (*hiking*) and **la course** (*running, racing*). 2. When French speakers use the expression **aimer les sports,** they mean that they like many different kinds of sports. To say that they like sports in general, they use **aimer le sport.** 3. Note that the verb **téléphoner** must be followed by **à** before someone's name. 4. There are seven main television channels in France: **TF1** (the largest and first privately owned television station), **France 2** and **France 3** (state owned), **La Cinquième** and **M6** (privately owned), **Canal+** (featuring movies and sports for a monthly fee) and **Arte** (owned with Germany). Cable television is becoming more and more popular in France, with many of the approximately 30 channels coming from other countries in Europe. French television is no longer completely funded by the viewing public, but also by commercials, which are generally quite creative. International television will be brought to Europe by telecommunication satellites. The first European television channel, **La Sept,** began in 1989.

Comparisons

Cultural Journal

If your students are keeping a cultural journal, you might have them write answers to these questions: Do you and your friends organize casual parties at home? What do you serve to eat? Many French teens dance at their parties. What do you and your friends do when you get together? What kind(s) of music do you listen to?

In France teenagers can't get a driver's license until they are 18 years old. They often walk, bike, ride mopeds, use inexpensive public transportation or even hitchhike to get to school or to recreational activities.

Racers in the *Tour de France* fall into one of two categories: *grimpeurs*, who excel in scaling mountains, and *sprinters*, who do best in speeding over short distances.

Le **Tour de France**, the most prestigious sporting event in France, is an annual endurance test of bicycling skill that was first organized in 1903. For 24 days in July, racers cover over 2,000 miles. The distance covered each day depends on the difficulty of the terrain. The most challenging laps wind through the mountain passes of the Alps and the Pyrenees. The **Tour de France féminin** also takes place in July.

TOUR DE FRANCE : DUEL AUX SOMMETS !

1 | *Choisissez la bonne réponse.*

1. What is the French word for "running"?
2. Where do French teenagers often get together after school or in the evening?
3. What is the word 11- to 13-year-old students use for a "party"?
4. What do older students call a "party"?
5. Where would you go to dance in a French-speaking country?
6. Name a kind of music that is popular in France.
7. At what age can the French get a driver's license?
8. What is the name of the most famous sporting event in France?

a. boîte
b. 18
c. techno
d. Le Tour de France
e. café
f. boum
g. soirée
h. footing

Where do the French often meet with their friends? (Paris)

2 | *Répondez en français.* (Answer in French.)

1. Jérémy aime bien Sophie?
2. Qu'est-ce que Sophie aime faire?
3. Sophie écoute de la musique?
4. Sophie aime un peu le rock?
5. Jérémy aime aussi la musique?
6. Jérémy téléphone à Martine?

3 | *C'est à toi!*

1. Tu aimes faire du sport?
2. Tu aimes le roller?
3. Tu aimes le footing?
4. Tu écoutes de la musique?
5. Tu aimes le reggae?
6. Tu aimes regarder la télé?
7. Tu aimes le camping?
8. Tu nages bien?

J'aime beaucoup nager!

Sophie aime bien faire du vélo.

Audiocassette/CD Activities 2-3

Answers

1 1. h
2. e
3. f
4. g
5. a
6. c
7. b
8. d

2 1. Oui, Jérémy aime bien Sophie.
2. Sophie aime bien faire du roller, du footing, du vélo.
3. Oui, Sophie écoute de la musique.
4. Non, Sophie aime beaucoup le rock./Non, Sophie aime un peu le jazz.
5. Oui, Jérémy aime aussi la musique.
6. Non, Jérémy téléphone à Sophie.

3 Answers will vary.

Teacher's Note

Family Interviews

You might have your students interview their family members about what activities they like to do and what kinds of music they like to listen to. Students should make a list of ten activities and kinds of music, limiting themselves to the new vocabulary from this **unité**. (For example, one question might be **Tu aimes les films?**) After students have completed their interviews, they can write a summary in French describing what their family members like. (Since possessive adjectives and names of family members have not yet been introduced, you might tell students to use first names in all their sentences.)

NATIONAL STANDARDS
C1.1, C1.2, C2.1

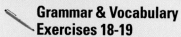

Workbook
Activity 9

Grammar & Vocabulary
Exercises 18-19

Audiocassette/CD
Activity 4

Computer Software
Activity 5

Answers

4 Answers will vary.

5 Sylvie aime un peu le footing, le roller, le foot et le basket. Elle aime un peu les sports.
Nadia aime beaucoup le footing, le foot et le basket. Elle aime un peu le roller. Elle aime beaucoup les sports.
Salim aime beaucoup le footing, le roller, le foot et le basket. Il aime beaucoup les sports.
Pierre aime beaucoup le foot. Il aime un peu le footing, le roller et le basket. Il aime un peu les sports.
Chloé aime beaucoup le roller. Elle aime un peu le footing, le foot et le basket. Elle aime un peu les sports.

NATIONAL STANDARDS
C1.1, C1.2, C4.1

36

Modèle:

le rock
J'aime beaucoup le rock.

Modèle:

Max aime beaucoup le footing. Il aime un peu le roller, le foot et le basket. Il aime un peu les sports.

Structure

Position of adverbs

Adverbs describe verbs, adjectives and other adverbs. Adverbs tell how, how much, where, why or when. Note that French adverbs usually come right after the verbs they describe.

beaucoup	J'aime **beaucoup** le rock.	*I like rock a lot.*
bien	J'aime **bien** la musique.	*I (really) like music.*
un peu	J'aime **un peu** le jazz.	*I like jazz a little.*
	J'aime **un peu** écouter le reggae.	*I like to listen to reggae a little.*

Pratique

4 Tell how much you like what is indicated by using **beaucoup, bien** or **un peu**.

1. faire du roller
2. regarder la télé
3. le jazz
4. faire du vélo
5. le camping
6. faire du footing
7. le reggae
8. téléphoner

On aime bien le camping. (Collonges-la-Rouge)

5 You just finished conducting a survey on how much your friends like running, in-line skating, soccer and basketball. Tell how much they like each individual sport and how much they like sports in general.

	le footing	*le roller*	*le foot*	*le basket*
Max	beaucoup	un peu	un peu	un peu
Sylvie	un peu	un peu	un peu	un peu
Nadia	beaucoup	un peu	beaucoup	beaucoup
Salim	beaucoup	beaucoup	beaucoup	beaucoup
Pierre	un peu	un peu	beaucoup	un peu
Chloé	un peu	beaucoup	un peu	un peu

6 People like to do the things that they do well. Tell what you and your friends like to do and then say that you do it well.

1. Bruno/jouer au foot
2. je/skier
3. Marc et Benjamin/ jouer au basket
4. Latifa/nager
5. Anne-Marie et Alain/skier
6. nous/étudier

Modèle:

Martine/jouer au basket
Martine aime jouer au basket. Elle joue bien.

Anne-Marie et Alain skient bien.

Communication

7 Try to guess how much your partner likes certain activities. On a sheet of paper number from 1 to 8 and predict whether your partner will say he or she likes each activity in the following list a lot or a little. Beside the number on your paper that refers to each activity, write **beaucoup** or **un peu.** When you have finished, get together with your partner to check the accuracy of your guesses. Ask each other questions based on your predictions. If your partner's answer matches your prediction, circle it. See who has the most correct guesses.

Modèle:

Emmanuel: Tu aimes beaucoup le camping?

Diane: Oui, j'aime beaucoup le camping.

Emmanuel: (Circles beaucoup on his sheet of paper.)

1. faire du vélo
2. le rock
3. le camping
4. faire du roller
5. le reggae
6. faire du footing
7. le jazz
8. les films

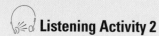
8   You have just put some photos of your friends in your album. Now you need to write captions for these photos. On a piece of paper, write a sentence for each one, giving the name of the person and telling what he or she likes to do. You may want to tell how much the person likes doing the activity by using **beaucoup, bien** or **un peu** in your caption. The first one has been written for you.

Marie-Alix aime bien écouter de la musique.

Mise au point sur... la musique

Music is an international language. **Le rock, le jazz** and **le reggae** sound familiar to teenagers all over the globe because of an increasing trend toward world music.

What kinds of music do you listen to? Chances are that French speakers listen to the same sounds that you do. Music is an important part of a teenager's life in French-speaking countries, just as it is for English-speaking teens. Of course, tastes in music vary from person to person.

Shopping for CDs or cassettes is a favorite activity of many adolescents in France. In fact, music lovers of all ages shop at a large music store in Paris that occupies four stories!

Performers from all over the world appear at the Zénith and at Bercy, two popular concert halls in Paris. When students' favorite artists perform at these halls, concerts sell out in no time.

Traditional French songs are usually poetic and melodious. The lyrics often have a message or a feeling to convey to the listener. The messages change, but the songs typically deal with love, peace, family, daily life and politics.

The Virgin Megastore on the Champ-Élysées sells music recordings of all kinds. (Paris)

Workbook Activity 10

Teacher's Note

If you are able to find a variety of francophone music, play it for your students and have them listen to the rhythms. Then have them compare the music they have just heard with types of music they hear in the United States.

NATIONAL STANDARDS
C1.2, C2.1, C2.2, C3.2, C4.2

Connections

Popular French Music

Your students will probably enjoy listening to French songs. Try to find a traditional French song, such as a ballad, as well as a more contemporary selection. The music should have words that are fairly clear and easy to understand. Before playing the songs in class, give a little background information on the singers and their songs. Next, you might pass out to each student a sheet of the lyrics. Leave blank spaces on the sheets for words that the students already know. Ask the students to write in the missing words as you play the selection several times. (If students have difficulty filling in the blanks, you could substitute a cloze activity where a list of possible words is provided at the top of the sheet.) Afterward, you may choose to give students the English version of the songs. Finally, you might have students give their opinions of the songs and what they liked or disliked about each one.

RAP, HOUSE, FUNK, TECHNO LA DANCE, C'EST

3 6 1 5 DE LA DANCE

LES RAVES, LES BONS PLANS, DES CD'S ET DES VOYAGES A GAGNER, ETC.

CHAQUE SEMAINE, LES CHARTS DE REFERENCE :

TOP DANCE
MAXI DANCE
FREQUENCE DANCE

POSEZ VOS QUESTIONS A
SPEEDY J

The words of contemporary songs are more daring than those of the past. Topics include women's issues, antiracism, the environment and the difficulty of city life. The music and the lyrics are fairly aggressive, especially those of **le rock** and **l'alternative**. Their strong rhythm encourages dancing. **Le rap**, still popular in France, was influenced by the same movement in the United States. In fact, many French-speaking teenagers listen to songs in English and know the words, even though they may not know what these words mean.

At dance clubs and on the radio, teenagers listen to a variety of music formats, such as **le disco**, **le funk**, **la new wave**, **le rock**, **le hard** and **l'alternative**. **La cold** is a type of music that originated in England and now has a certain following in France. **La techno**, another popular type of music, is based on an industrial, synthetic sound. **La dance** also has a synthetic sound and a rhythm that makes it popular for dancing. Even though **le jazz** originated in the United States, many teens in France listen to it as well. Clubs, such as Le Petit Journal Montparnasse, New Morning and the Jazz Club Lionel Hampton, have helped establish Paris as one of the jazz capitals of the world.

Le Petit Journal
MONTPARNASSE
13, rue du Commandant-Mouchotte
75014 PARIS ☎ 01.43.21.56.70

Le Petit Journal SAINT-MICHEL
71, Boulevard Saint-Michel
75005 PARIS ☎ 01.43.26.28.59

JAZZ CLUB LIONEL HAMPTON

Teenagers all over the world listen to a wide variety of sounds. A wave of multiculturalism has swept across the music scene, influencing and expanding tastes. For example, singers from Quebec, such as Céline Dion, have become international stars. Other examples of the trend toward international music are **la musique créole**, exported from Martinique, and **l'african beat** or **le world beat**, from French West Africa. A style of reggae, sometimes called **le raggamuffin**, has also attracted many listeners. But no matter where a song originates, its music and lyrics reflect the lifestyles of its writers and performers.

CWD PRESENTE
JEAN MICHEL JARRE
EUROPE EN CONCERT

AVEC
NRJ

2 France

28 JUILLET : MONT ST MICHEL
5 SEPTEMBRE : VITROLLES
(aéroport Marseille Provence)
25 SEPTEMBRE : CHATEAU DE VERSAILLES

LOCATIONS : FNAC, DANS TOUTE LA FRANCE,
OFFICES DE TOURISME, POINTS DE VENTE HABITUELS ET SUR MINITEL 3615 NRJ CLUB.
PARIS **MATCH** POUR CONNAITRE LA FREQUENCE NRJ DE VOTRE VILLE, TAPEZ 3615 CODE NRJ, RUBRIQUE STA.

MUSIC YOUR TOUR

9 Answer the following questions.

1. What is the major music trend in France?
2. What are the names of two concert halls in Paris?
3. What are two words that describe traditional French songs?
4. What are three topics that may be included in contemporary songs?
5. What are two styles of music that are based on a synthetic sound?
6. What kind of music is played at Le Petit Journal Montparnasse?
7. What is a type of music that has been exported from Martinique?
8. What is another name for **l'african beat**?

Eddy Mitchell *en concert*

juin
22 Clermont-Ferrand
23 Toulouse
24 Pau
25 Istres

juillet
1ER Sully / Loire
2 Maubeuge
3 Braine-L'Alleud (B)
5 Epinal
6 Grenoble
14 Le Touquet
15 Le Mans
16 La Rochelle
18 Carcassonne

juillet
19 Vienne
20 Cannes
21 Cahors
22 Nyon (S)
23 Abbeville
29 Bollène

août
2 Sauve
3 Ramatuelle
4 Antibes
5 La Seyne/Mer
6 Béziers
7 Arles
9 Pradelles
10 Annecy

NOSTALGIE C'est pour toujours

23 novembre Paris-Bercy COMPLET
concert supplémentaire le 22 novembre Paris-Bercy
location fnac, virgin megastore, agences, 36 15 nostalgie

10 Choose the best answer to each question based on the advertisement you see.

1. What is being advertised here?
   a. A restaurant.
   b. A café.
   c. A dinner theater.
2. What is the name of this place?
   a. Arlequin.
   b. Trio Dany Revel.
   c. Déjeuners Musicaux.
3. What is the name of the group that is playing here from April 24 to June 26?
   a. Carte Menu.
   b. Café Arlequin.
   c. Trio Dany Revel.
4. What time is this group performing? (Times are often given using the 24-hour clock.)
   a. 12:30 — 5:00.
   b. 12:30 — 3:00.
   c. 12:30 — 2:00.
5. How much does the suggested meal cost for each person?
   a. 25 euros.
   b. 150 francs.
   c. 15 euros.
6. What telephone number do you call to make reservations?
   a. 01.40.68.30.85.
   b. 25.
   c. 12.30.15.

DÉJEUNERS MUSICAUX

**Tous les dimanches
du 24 avril au 26 juin
découvrez les déjeuners musicaux
au**

Café **ARLEQUIN**

**ambiance musicale avec le
TRIO DANY REVEL**
de 12h30 à 15h

—

**Notre suggestion
CARTE MENU
25 €**
(par personne)
comprenant (1 entrée, 1 plat, 1 dessert et Café)

Information - Réservation 01.40.68.30.85

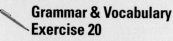

**Workbook
Activities 11-12**

**Grammar & Vocabulary
Exercise 20**

Audiocassette/CD
*Qu'est-ce qu'ils
aime faire?* (C)

Teacher's Notes

1. **Volley** is the abbreviated form of **volleyball**. 2. Another expression for **jouer aux jeux vidéo** is **faire des jeux vidéo**. 3. You may want to indicate new verbs with gestures rather than with verbal or visual cues. Here are some suggestions.

jouer au volley	Act as if you are bumping a volleyball with your hands and arms together in front of you.
jouer au tennis	Act as if you are hitting a tennis ball with a forehand swing while stepping forward.
danser	Do the twist.
manger de la pizza	Pretend that you are eating a slice of pizza.
dormir	Put both hands together under your cheek, tilt your head and close your eyes.
sortir	Pretend to open a door and step outside.
faire les devoirs	Pretend to open a book and write.
faire du shopping	Pretend to hold a shopping bag on your arm and put items in it.
jouer aux jeux vidéo	Pretend to hold a control device in your hands and press down your thumbs as if you were operating the buttons.
lire	Pretend to open a book and read, moving your head slowly from side to side.

NATIONAL STANDARDS
C1.2, C4.1

42

Leçon C

In this lesson you will be able to:

➤ **ask for information**

➤ **express likes and dislikes**

➤ **give opinions**

➤ **invite**

Fifi aime dormir.

Thierry et Christine aiment sortir.

M. Delon aime faire du shopping.

Adja aime faire les devoirs.

David et Mahmoud
aiment jouer aux jeux vidéo.

Mme Lafont et Delphine aiment lire.

le volley

le tennis

la pizza

les devoirs (m.)

le shopping

les jeux
vidéo (m.)

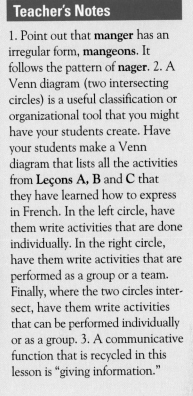

Teacher's Notes

1. Point out that **manger** has an irregular form, **mangeons**. It follows the pattern of **nager**. 2. A Venn diagram (two intersecting circles) is a useful classification or organizational tool that you might have your students create. Have your students make a Venn diagram that lists all the activities from **Leçons A, B** and **C** that they have learned how to express in French. In the left circle, have them write activities that are done individually. In the right circle, have them write activities that are performed as a group or a team. Finally, where the two circles intersect, have them write activities that can be performed individually or as a group. 3. A communicative function that is recycled in this lesson is "giving information."

NATIONAL STANDARDS
C1.2, C2.1

**Workbook
Activity 13**

**Grammar & Vocabulary
Exercise 21**

**Audiocassette/CD
Dialogue**

Video

J'invite tout le monde chez moi.

Paul, Éric, Émilie, Laurent and Chantal are making plans to get together over the weekend.

Paul: Qui aime danser?
Éric: Émilie et moi, nous aimons aller en boîte. Mais Laurent et Chantal, ils n'aiment pas danser.
Paul: Alors, qui aime jouer au tennis?
Chantal: Je joue au tennis. Mais je préfère jouer au volley.
Paul: Bon ben, j'invite tout le monde chez moi. Tout le monde aime manger de la pizza!

Enquête culturelle

The French love windsurfing.

Since sports are not usually associated with schools in France, students often go to **le club** to exercise. Many also take private lessons there. Local communities offer opportunities for students to participate in sports and arrange competitions as well. In Canada many teenagers ski or play hockey or ringette. On the Caribbean island of Martinique they play soccer or participate in many kinds of water sports, for example, **la planche à voile** (*windsurfing*).

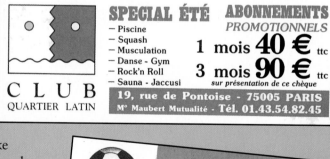

NATIONAL STANDARDS
C1.2, C2.1, C3.2

1 *Répondez en français.*

1. Émilie et Éric aiment danser?
2. Qui aime aller en boîte?
3. Qui n'aime pas danser?
4. Qui joue au tennis?
5. Qu'est-ce que Chantal préfère?
6. Qui invite tout le monde à manger de la pizza?
7. Tout le monde aime manger de la pizza?

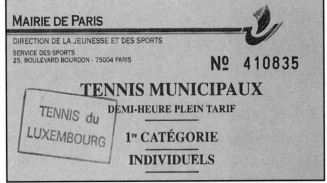

MAIRIE DE PARIS

DIRECTION DE LA JEUNESSE ET DES SPORTS

SERVICE DES SPORTS
25, BOULEVARD BOURDON - 75004 PARIS

N° 410835

TENNIS MUNICIPAUX

TENNIS du LUXEMBOURG

DEMI-HEURE PLEIN TARIF

1re CATÉGORIE

INDIVIDUELS

2 *Complétez le dialogue suivant.* (Complete the following dialogue.)

Aimée:	Bonjour. Ça va?
Danielle:	Ça va.... Tu aimes faire...?
Aimée:	..... Je préfère....
Danielle:	Qui aime...?
Aimée:	Moi, je n'aime pas....
Danielle:	..., à bientôt.
Aimée:	....

3 Say in French whether you like or don't like to do the following activities.

Thierry aime jouer aux jeux vidéo.

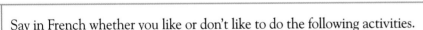

1.

4.

7.

Modèle:

J'aime aller au cinéma.
Je n'aime pas aller au cinéma.

2.

5.

8.

3.

6.

9.

10.

Audiocassette/CD Activities 1, 3

Answers

1 1. Oui, Émilie et Éric aiment danser.
2. Émilie et Éric aiment aller en boîte.
3. Laurent et Chantal n'aiment pas danser.
4. Chantal joue au tennis.
5. Chantal préfère jouer au volley.
6. Paul invite tout le monde à manger de la pizza.
7. Oui, tout le monde aime manger de la pizza./Non.

2 Possible answers:
Bonjour. Ça va?
Ça va bien. Tu aimes faire du sport?
Non. Je préfère faire du shopping.
Qui aime jouer aux jeux vidéo?
Moi, je n'aime pas jouer aux jeux vidéo.
Alors, à bientôt.
Ciao.

3 1. J'aime manger de la pizza./ Je n'aime pas manger de la pizza.
2. J'aime étudier./J'aime faire les devoirs./Je n'aime pas étudier./ Je n'aime pas faire les devoirs.
3. J'aime faire du shopping./Je n'aime pas faire du shopping.
4. J'aime jouer aux jeux vidéo./ Je n'aime pas jouer aux jeux vidéo.
5. J'aime dormir./Je n'aime pas dormir.
6. J'aime regarder la télé./Je n'aime pas regarder la télé.
7. J'aime skier./Je n'aime pas skier.
8. J'aime jouer au tennis./Je n'aime pas jouer au tennis.
9. J'aime écouter de la musique./Je n'aime pas écouter de la musique.
10. J'aime faire du roller./Je n'aime pas faire du roller.

NATIONAL STANDARDS
C1.1, C1.2, C3.2

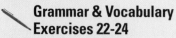
Answers

4 1. André n'aime pas jouer aux jeux vidéo.
2. Anne n'aime pas jouer au tennis.
3. André n'aime pas lire.
4. Anne n'aime pas faire du roller.
5. André n'aime pas sortir.
6. André n'aime pas dormir.
7. André n'aime pas faire les devoirs.
8. Anne n'aime pas skier.
9. André n'aime pas aller en boîte.

5 1. Tu n'aimes pas manger de la pizza.
2. Vous aimez lire.
3. Clément n'aime pas téléphoner.
4. Sandrine et moi, nous aimons danser.
5. J'aime dormir.
6. M. et Mme Meunier n'aiment pas faire du shopping.
7. Malika n'aime pas jouer au tennis.

TPR

Tu aimes...?

You might have each student draw two hearts on a piece of paper and cut them out. On the first heart students write **J'aime**; on the second heart they write **Je n'aime pas**. Then ask students the question **Tu aimes...?** Students respond that they like or don't like an activity by holding up the appropriate heart.

NATIONAL STANDARDS
C1.1, C1.2, C4.1

46

Modèle:

faire du shopping
André n'aime pas faire du shopping.

Modèles:

Béatrice/jouer au volley
Béatrice aime jouer au volley.

nous/faire du footing
Nous n'aimons pas faire du footing.

Structure

Negation with *ne (n')... pas*

It takes two words to make a verb negative in French: **ne** and **pas**. Put **ne** before the verb and **pas** after it.

ne	+	verb	+	pas

Jérémy **ne** danse **pas**.   *Jérémy does not (doesn't) dance.*

Tu **ne** joues **pas** au tennis.   *You do not (don't) play tennis.*

Ne becomes **n'** before a vowel sound.

Je **n'**aime **pas** le footing.   *I do not (don't) like running.*

Vous **n'**aimez **pas** faire du shopping?   *You don't like to go shopping?*

Pratique

4 Although they are twins, Anne and André are very different. André likes only sports. Anne likes all activities except sports. Tell which twin doesn't like each activity.

1. jouer aux jeux vidéo
2. jouer au tennis
3. lire
4. faire du roller
5. sortir
6. dormir
7. faire les devoirs
8. skier
9. aller en boîte

5 Tell whether or not the following people like the indicated activities.

1. tu/manger de la pizza   5. je/dormir

2. vous/lire   6. M. et Mme Meunier/ faire du shopping

3. Clément/téléphoner   7. Malika/jouer au tennis

4. Sandrine et moi, nous/danser

6 Your mother has called you at camp to see how you are and to find out what you and the other campers do. Answer her questions.

1. Vous regardez la télé?
2. Vous mangez beaucoup?
3. Vous jouez au tennis?
4. Vous écoutez de la musique?
5. Vous dansez?
6. Vous jouez au volley?
7. Vous téléphonez?

Modèles:

Vous nagez?
Non, nous ne nageons pas.

Vous jouez au foot?
Oui, nous jouons au foot.

7 Find out what you have in common with your partner. Ask each other if you participate in the indicated activities.

1. skier
2. jouer au volley
3. danser
4. étudier
5. écouter le rock
6. nager
7. jouer au basket

Modèle:

Stéphanie: Tu écoutes le jazz?
Daniel: Non, je n'écoute pas le jazz. Tu écoutes le jazz?
Stéphanie: Oui, j'écoute le jazz.

Tu écoutes le rock? (Montréal)

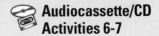

Modèle:

Jérémy: Tu joues au volley?
Laurence: Oui, je joue au volley.
            (Writes his name beside
            number 1.)

Communication

8 *Trouvez une personne qui....* (Find someone who . . . .) Interview your classmates to find out who participates or likes to participate in various activities. On a separate sheet of paper, number from 1 to 20. Circulate around the classroom asking your classmates one at a time the questions that follow. When someone says that he or she participates or likes to participate in a certain activity, have that person write his or her name next to the number of the appropriate question. Continue asking questions, trying to find a different person who participates or likes to participate in each activity.

Tu...

1. joues au volley?
2. préfères jouer au tennis?
3. manges de la pizza?
4. aimes beaucoup dormir?
5. aimes jouer aux jeux vidéo?
6. nages beaucoup?
7. préfères lire?
8. aimes faire du shopping?
9. écoutes le jazz?
10. danses beaucoup?
11. aimes bien le camping?
12. aimes faire du vélo?
13. skies?
14. aimes sortir?
15. aimes jouer au basket?
16. étudies?
17. joues au foot?
18. regardes la télé?
19. aimes faire les devoirs?
20. aimes beaucoup la musique?

Modèle:

Laurence joue au volley. Jean-Claude et moi, nous ne skions pas. Nathalie et Bernard aiment sortir.

9 You are going to write an article in French for your school newspaper in which you give the results of the survey you conducted in Activity 8. Tell what activities the students in your French class like, dislike and prefer and also which ones they do or don't participate in. To tell about one person, use that person's name and the **il** or **elle** form of the verb. To tell that you feel the same way about a certain activity that someone else does, use the **nous** form of the verb. To say that several people feel the same way, use the **ils** or **elles** form of the verb.

10 To make plans for the weekend, get together with four of your classmates and find out what they want to do. Everyone in the group must suggest one activity that he or she would like to do. At the end of the conversation, the group should agree on one activity that they will do together.

Tout le monde aime manger de la pizza!

Modèle:	
Karine:	Qui aime faire du vélo?
Véro:	J'aime beaucoup faire du vélo.
Renée:	Moi, je préfère jouer au tennis.
Michel:	J'aime jouer au volley. On y va?
Stéphanie:	D'accord. Nous jouons au volley et j'invite tout le monde chez moi. On mange de la pizza?

  Workbook Activity 15

 Audiocassette/CD *Sur la bonne piste*

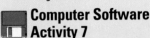 **Listening Activity 3A**

Quiz *Leçon C*

Computer Software Activity 7

Teacher's Note

There will be new passive vocabulary words presented contextually in each reading that will not be listed in the end vocabulary. As your students read the first passage on page 50, you may want to go through the guessing approach with them in class, step by step. Here are some suggestions.

1. Figure out the context (setting or purpose) of the reading. The essay on page 50 is written by a young person, perhaps someone 14 years old.
2. Digest the title, don't just look at it. "A typical week in my life." Whose life? A 14-year-old's life.
3. Before reading the passage in detail, begin by thinking about what the author might logically write.
4. First order guessing: In scanning the reading as a whole, you discover that each paragraph begins with a word you don't know (**lundi, mardi, mercredi, jeudi, vendredi**). Since you know little French at this point, it would seem logical that a person would organize his or her writing and would start at the beginning of a week. A week contains days, like Monday, etc. Perhaps these are names for the days of the week.

Sur la bonne piste

Wouldn't it be wonderful to pick up something written in French and be able to read it as though it were in English? Have you ever asked yourself what it is that makes reading in English relatively simple? Obviously, the words themselves must be the reason for your understanding. But is it only the words? What you probably don't notice is that you take many factors into consideration that set you up for success. Look at the following paragraph:

Why? Hello, my name is Inigo. See you later. Let's go. Homidas swims very well. I'm studying for a quiz. That's not possible.

Even though this paragraph is written in English, it makes very little sense. You may not have recognized the names that are used, but you probably knew they are names because of where they are found in the sentences. Still, there are three factors that may have made you say "Huh?" First, there is no context for the reading. Context refers to the setting or purpose of the reading. Is this part of a letter? Is this a conversation? Are the two people friends? Is the author a teenager communicating with another teenager? Second, the sentences are not in a logical order. And third, it appears that there are some sentences that are missing.

When you begin to read in another language, you are often so caught up in trying to understand the words that you skip around, trying to find anything you understand. By skipping around, you read things out of order, you miss whole sentences and you probably ignore the context. You understand very little and soon may become discouraged. Ignoring the context and skipping around lead only to frustration. Before you attempt to read something in French, look at the suggestions on page 50.

 **NATIONAL STANDARDS**
C1.1, C1.2, C3.1

Other guessing skills:

Read the paragraph beginning with **Le lundi** again. With the week in mind, some things are more likely to happen to 14-year-olds on Monday, such as going to school where they greet their friends (**Je salue mon amie Christine**) and waiting until after school to do some favorite activities (**Nous décidons d'écouter de la musique**). Listening to music with a friend is more likely to happen after school. Could this have something to do with **après les cours**?

Read the paragraph beginning with **Le mardi** again. You have just studied most of these words, but **parce qu'il fait beau** is new. Here is a hint: What kind of weather is desirable in order to play volleyball?

Read the paragraph beginning with **Le mercredi** again. This paragraph requires a little more guessing. **Trois heures de classe.** The French school system is run a little differently than ours. In France, students spend only half the day at school on Wednesday. **Je dis "Bonjour" à Jean-Marc.** Since quotation marks come right after **dis**, it's likely that this word means "say."

This detailed approach should go on until you have finished the entire reading more than once. Some students will feel comfortable after reading it only two times. Others will have to read the passage many times.

How to approach (or sneak up on) a reading:

1. Figure out the context (setting or purpose) of the reading.
2. Look at the reading as a whole. (It's all right to skip around at this point because you are going to look at things in order in the next step.)
3. Read the sentences in order. Try to read everything in one sentence before moving on to the next one. Look for cognates, words that look the same and have the same meaning in both French and English.
4. Pick out the sentences that you don't understand and try to fit them into the rest of the reading.
5. Read the passage three times.

Here is a short essay. Using the preceding suggestions, read this account of a typical week in a student's life.

Ma Vie Hebdomadaire (A Typical Week in My Life)

Le lundi. Je salue mon amie Christine. Nous décidons d'écouter de la musique après les cours. Je préfère l'alternative, mais pas Christine. Alors, nous écoutons du reggae.

Le mardi. J'invite tout le monde chez moi. Qu'est-ce que nous aimons faire? Alors, nous jouons au volley parce qu'il fait beau.

Le mercredi. Trois heures de classe. À l'école, je dis "Bonjour" à Jean-Marc. Il demande "Tu joues au foot aujourd'hui?" Mais je refuse parce que j'ai une interro vendredi. "Non. Désolé. J'étudie pour l'interro de maths."

Le jeudi. J'adore regarder la télé lundi, mardi, mercredi, jeudi... mais c'est pas possible. J'aime aussi nager en été, skier en hiver et jouer aux jeux vidéo. Qui aime étudier? Pas moi. Mais j'ai une interro.

Le vendredi. L'interro? Pas trop difficile! Après les cours, je téléphone à Serge. Je lui demande "Qu'est-ce que tu aimes faire?" Serge aime faire du roller. Alors, nous invitons Thibaud, Karim et Nathalie aussi et nous allons faire du roller. Et comme d'habitude, j'invite tout le monde chez moi. Tout le monde arrive chez moi. "On y va?" dis-je. "D'accord. Faisons du roller!" Super!

Ça, c'est ma vie hebdomadaire.

Beginning to use approach skills:

How did you do? You probably didn't understand everything. You must learn to guess when all else fails, since you don't want to look up each word you don't know in the dictionary. Use approach skills to help you. For instance, would it have been likely to find sentences about elephants in the reading? It would have been more likely if the title were "My Day at the Zoo." The title is meant to help you understand. If a title is given, read it first! Then stop. Ask yourself "What would be some usual things that someone would write on the topic?" Also, consider the fact that "A Typical Day in My Life" would be written differently by someone else, for example, a presidential candidate. A 14-year-old may have in-line skating on his or her agenda, but it would be less likely for a 65-year-old. Continue this guessing approach, step by step, as you look at the reading again. Read the passage until your guesses seem to make sense based on the title and the context of the reading. If you spend more time when you first start reading, you will develop some reading habits that will allow you to enjoy reading. If you try to pass over the reading as quickly as possible, you will get very little out of it and feel very uncomfortable when asked about its contents.

11 Can you answer some general questions about this reading?
1. Are all the days of this person's typical week mentioned?
2. Does this person have any friends?
3. Does this person like a variety of activities? What is his or her least favorite activity?
4. Is this person a good student? How do you know?

Nathalie et Raoul

Answers

11 Possible answers:
1. The first five days of this person's typical week are mentioned.
2. This person has many friends.
3. This person likes a variety of activities. His or her least favorite activity is studying for a quiz.
4. This person is a good student because he or she spent two days studying for a quiz, and, consequently, did very well on it.

Teacher's Note

Here is the English version of this cartoon: Excuse me, uh . . . Marcel . . . who is that girl? What's her name? It's Nathalie! Do you think she has a boyfriend? Well, Raoul, she likes Thomas. Thomas who? What's his name? Dupont . . . Thomas Dupont. He plays soccer. Well or badly? He plays very well. But Thomas likes Cécile, and they are going out together. I'm an idiot. She's not interested in me. She likes Thomas better! She doesn't like me, but . . . . A note for you, Nathalie. Raoul! Yes, Ma'am. (A poem for you. You are as beautiful as a rose. Shall we go to the movies? Shall we go to the café? Shall we go to the Pink Floyd concert? Answer me!)

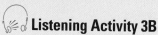

Answers

1. faux
2. vrai
3. vrai
4. faux
5. faux
6. vrai
7. vrai
8. vrai
9. faux

Comparisons

Stereotypes

As your students find out about how French-speaking teens spend their free time, they will realize that some French leisure-time activities are the same as theirs and some are different. Your students may already have some ideas about the French culture. Some of these ideas may indeed be true, while others may be stereotypes based on first impressions. First, you may want your students to answer these two questions: What characteristics would I use to describe myself? What characteristics would I use to describe Americans in general? Next, have your students look at some typical stereotypes of Americans: 1. Americans are informal. 2. Americans are materialistic and greedy. 3. Americans don't believe in fate. Rather, they think they can personally control the future. 4. Americans believe in equality. 5. Americans like sports. 6. Americans eat too much. Ask your students these questions: Which of these stereotypes seem positive? Which of these stereotypes seem negative? Are all of these assumptions true for you and/or your friends? Do you like being labeled in this manner? What are some of the dangers of labeling a whole society based on the same stereotypes?

NATIONAL STANDARDS
C1.1, C1.2, C2.1, C2.2,
C4.2

52

C'est à moi!

Now that you have completed this unit, take a look at what you should be able to do in French. Can you do all of these tasks?

➤ I can tell what I like and what I dislike.

➤ I can give my opinion by saying what I prefer.

➤ I can agree or disagree with someone.

➤ I can ask for information about "who," "what" and "why."

➤ I can invite someone to do something.

➤ I can refuse an invitation.

Here is a brief checkup to see how much you understand about French culture. Decide if each statement is true (**vrai**) or false (**faux**).

1. Most French teenagers don't go to school on Wednesday afternoons and spend this time at their part-time jobs.
2. Movies are a popular leisure activity for French teens.
3. High school students often dance at parties called **soirées**.
4. French teenagers limit their interest in music to **le rock** and **le funk**.
5. In France you have to be 21 years old to get a driver's license.
6. **Le Tour de France** is a 2,000-mile French bike race that takes place every summer.
7. Music in France has a multicultural influence that makes it very international.
8. Many French teens know the words to songs in English even if they don't know what the words mean.
9. Just as they do in the United States, organized sports play an important role in a French teenager's life at school.

Do French teens go to the movies very often? (Paris)

Communication orale

Imagine that you have applied to be a junior counselor at a camp in France where French teenagers practice speaking English. The camp needs native speakers of English who can also communicate in French. You want to practice your French before your interview with a camp official. Have a classmate play the role of the camp official. During the course of your brief practice interview:

1. Greet each other in French and introduce yourselves.
2. Ask each other how things are going.
3. The camp official asks the student what he or she likes to do.
4. The student tells the camp official at least three activities that he or she likes to do (which are appropriate for camp) and how much he or she likes to do each one.
5. The camp official asks the student what he or she does not like to do.
6. The student tells the camp official at least one activity that he or she does not like to do.
7. The camp official asks the student if he or she likes to listen to music.

8. The student tells the camp official that he or she likes to listen to music and specifies what kinds.

9. Thank each other and tell each other good-bye.

Communication écrite

As a follow-up to your interview with the camp official for the job of junior counselor, write a letter to the director of the camp, Mr. Desrosiers, highlighting the information you supplied in your interview. Begin your letter with **Monsieur**. After you introduce yourself, tell what things you like to do and how much you like to do each one. Then name the things you don't like to do. Finally, tell what kinds of music you like and don't like to listen to. Thank the director and sign your letter.

Communication active

To say what you like, use:

J'aime le rock.	*I like rock (music).*
J'aime danser.	*I like to dance.*
J'aime aller au cinéma.	*I like to go to the movies.*
J'aime faire du sport.	*I like to play sports.*

To say what you dislike, use:

Je n'aime pas le camping.	*I don't like camping.*
Je n'aime pas étudier.	*I don't like to study.*
Je n'aime pas aller en boîte.	*I don't like to go to the dance club.*
Je n'aime pas faire du footing.	*I don't like to go running.*

To agree or disagree with someone, use:

D'accord.	*OK.*
Oui.	*Yes.*
Moi aussi.	*Me, too.*
Non.	*No.*

To give your opinion, use:

Je préfère le jazz.	*I prefer jazz.*
Je préfère jouer au volley.	*I prefer to play volleyball.*

To ask for information, use:

Qu'est-ce que tu aimes faire?	*What do you like to do?*
Qui aime skier?	*Who likes to ski?*
Pourquoi?	*Why?*

To invite someone to do something, use:

On y va?	*Shall we go (there)?*
J'invite tout le monde chez moi.	*I'm inviting everybody to my house.*

To refuse an invitation, use:

Pas possible.	*Not possible.*

On aime faire du footing. (Bayonne)

7es INTERNATIONAUX DE VOLLEY-BALL

OPEN PATRICE BEGAY

17-18 SEPTEMBRE
HALLE CARPENTIER
81, boulevard Masséna 75013 Paris

LE TOP MONDIAL DES CLUBS

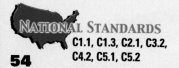
Communication électronique

Are you curious to find out how teenagers live and what they like to do in countries where French is spoken? Have you thought of how interesting it would be to have a French-speaking keypal? Can you think of ways in which this friendship could be mutually beneficial?

To see lists of possible keypals from a variety of francophone countries, go to this Internet site:

http://www.franceworld.com/fw2/en/recherche.asp

Now click on option 1 ("Look for a pen pal"). Then select any French-speaking country. You may want to modify your search by specifying an area of the country, the person's age and sex. Finally, select "See the fiches" to read the biographies. After browsing and then choosing your keypal, answer the following questions.

1. Were any students your age listed? Which of your leisure activities and sports do they share?
2. From what city or region is the person with whom you are going to correspond?
3. Does your future keypal want an American correspondant?
4. What did this person say about himself or herself in the "Notes"?

Using the French you have already learned, prepare a short message to your keypal in which you introduce yourself and tell what you like to do. See how quickly you receive an answer. Print out the reply you receive and share it with your class.

À moi de jouer!

It's your turn to show what you have learned in this unit!

Begin by writing what Delphine likes to do.

In terms of sports, tell what Christophe and Malick do and don't do.

Complete the short dialogue below in which Luc asks out Karine. Use appropriate expressions that you have learned so far. (You may want to refer to the *Communication active* on page 53 and the vocabulary list on page 55.)

Vocabulaire

à to
   À demain. See you tomorrow.
aimer to like, to love
aller to go
alors (well) then
au to (the), at (the)
aussi also, too

le **basket (basketball)** basketball
beaucoup a lot, (very) much
ben: bon ben well then
bien really
une **boîte** dance club
bon, bonne good
   bon ben well then

le **camping** camping
chez to the house/home of
   chez moi to my house
le **cinéma** movies

danser to dance
demain tomorrow
les **devoirs (m.)** homework
dis say
dormir to sleep

écouter to listen (to)
   écouter de la musique to listen to
     music
elle she, it
elles they (f.)
en to (the)
et and
étudier to study

faire to do, to make
   faire du footing to go running
   faire du roller to go in-line skating
   faire du shopping to go shopping
   faire du sport to play sports
   faire du vélo to go biking
   faire les devoirs to do homework
un **film** movie
le **foot (football)** soccer
le **footing** running

il he, it
ils they (m.)
une **interro (interrogation)** quiz, test
inviter to invite

le **jazz** jazz
des **jeux vidéo (m.)** video games
jouer to play
   jouer au basket to play basketball
   jouer au foot to play soccer
   jouer au tennis to play tennis

jouer au volley to play volleyball
jouer aux jeux vidéo to play video
   games

l' the
la the
le the
les the
lire to read

mais but
manger to eat
   manger de la pizza to eat pizza
moi me, I
la **musique** music

nager to swim
ne (n')... pas not
nous we

on they, we, one
   On y va? Shall we go (there)?

passer to show (a movie)
(un) **peu** (a) little
une **pizza** pizza
possible possible
pour for
pourquoi why
préférer to prefer

qu'est-ce que what
qui who, whom

regarder to watch
le **reggae** reggae
le **rock** rock (music)
le **roller** in-line skating

le **shopping** shopping
skier to ski
sortir to go out
un **sport** sport
super super, terrific, great

téléphoner to phone (someone), to
   make a call
la **télé (télévision)** TV, television
le **tennis** tennis
tout le monde everybody
tu you

un a, an

un **vélo** bicycle, bike
le **volley (volleyball)** volleyball
vous you

Unité 3

Au café

In this unit you will be able to:

➤ invite

➤ accept and refuse
   an invitation

➤ order food and beverages

➤ ask for a price

➤ state prices

➤ ask what time it is

➤ tell time on the hour

➤ ask how someone is

➤ tell how you are

NATIONAL STANDARDS
C2.1, C2.2

Workbook Activity 1

 Grammar & Vocabulary Exercise 1

 Audiocassette/CD *Comment vas-tu?, Quelle heure est-il?*

Transparencies 8-11

58

Leçon A

In this lesson you will be able to:

➤ ask how someone is

➤ tell how you are

➤ ask what time it is

➤ tell time on the hour

➤ invite

➤ accept and refuse an invitation

Il est une heure.   *Il est neuf heures.*   *Il est minuit.*

Il est quatre heures.   *Il est midi.*

Workbook Activities 2-4

 Audiocassette/CD *Dialogue*

Caroline runs into her classmate Malika downtown.

Caroline:	**Bonjour, Malika. Comment vas-tu?**
Malika:	**Très bien, merci. Et toi?**
Caroline:	**Pas mal, mais j'ai faim.**
Malika:	**Moi aussi. Quelle heure est-il?**
Caroline:	**Il est déjà une heure. On va au café ou au fast-food?**
Malika:	**Moi, je préfère aller au fast-food.**
Caroline:	**D'accord, allons-y!**

After school or when they are out with their friends, French teenagers sometimes stop at a fast-food restaurant for something to eat. Restaurants like Quick, Free Time and Pizza del Arte serve food and beverages that many teenagers like: hamburgers, French fries, pizza, hot dogs and soft drinks. American fast-food restaurants can also be found in the French-speaking world; teenagers often eat at McDonald's and Domino's.

Enquête culturelle

NE VOUS ENDORMEZ PAS SANS PASSER CHEZ PIZZA DEL ARTE!

Le Big bacon :

Un pain rond et moelleux au froment, un steak haché juteux recouvert de chester fondant et de bacon grillé, une sauce bacon aromatisée aux tomates et à la sauce Worcester.

Quick

Teacher's Notes

1. Remind students that they have already learned one way to ask people how they are: **Ça va**? In more formal situations people say **Comment allez-vous**? and answer with **Je vais bien (mal)**, etc. 2. **Quel** and **quelle** are introduced as active vocabulary in this **unité**. Their structure will be explained in **Unité 6**. 3. In the plural **un fast-food** becomes **des fast-foods**. The French government would prefer that people use the expression **restauration rapide** instead of **fast-food**. 4. To accept an invitation you can also say **Chouette; C'est une bonne idée; Oui, je veux bien; Volontiers** (more formal) and **Okay**. To refuse an invitation you can also say **Je suis désolé(e), mais...; Je regrette, mais...; Désolé(e); Non, merci** and **Non, je vais voir**. 5. To make the conversation more realistic, Caroline could have specified a certain fast-food restaurant to go to. But in the *C'est à toi!* series, unnecessary commercialism has been avoided in the dialogues. However, certain American and French fast-food restaurants are discussed in the **Enquête culturelle** section that follows. You may alter the dialogue by using the name of one of them, if you wish. 6. The command form **allons-y** (*let's go there*) is presented here as a lexical item. The command structure will be explained in **Unité 9**.

NATIONAL STANDARDS
C1.2, C2.1, C2.2, C3.2, C4.2

Comparisons

Cultural Journal

If your students are keeping a cultural journal, you might have them write answers to these questions: At what times do you eat breakfast, lunch and dinner? If you eat a snack after school, what do you have? What is your idea of a perfect meal? How many times each week do you eat at fast-food restaurants? The trend of eating at fast-food restaurants has spread from the United States to many other countries in the world. What do you think of this trend? (If you prefer to use these questions as the basis for a class discussion, you might use the "think-pair-share" format: 1. You ask the question. 2. Students have a moment to think of an answer. 3. Students form pairs and discuss their responses. 4. Students share responses with the entire class.)

It's easy to find an American-style burger in France. (Lyon)

Love Burger is one of the French versions of an American fast-food restaurant. (Paris)

McDonald's, familiarly called Macdo, was the first American fast-food restaurant to cross the Atlantic. Approximately 300 McDonald's restaurants have opened in France since 1974.

French families often end their meals with fruit and cheese.

When French families sit down for meals together at home, there is an emphasis on healthy eating and good-tasting food. Fresh bread and vegetables are frequently purchased each day. Dessert often consists of fruit, cheese or yogurt. More and more products are appearing with the expression **light** in the name. You can find **Coca-Cola light**, **ketchup light** and even **chocolat light** at supermarkets in France.

Fresh bread is no more than a few blocks from home for most people in the city. (Bayonne)

1   How do you feel when the following things happen? Answer using **Très bien, Pas très bien** or **Comme ci, comme ça**.

1. You get an "A" on a math test.
2. It rains on the day of your trip to the amusement park.
3. You win your tennis match.
4. You have to clean your room.
5. It's the first day of school.
6. You win concert tickets from a local radio station.
7. Your date cancels at the last minute.
8. You receive an unexpected gift.

2   Based on the dialogue, match the expression on the left with whom it describes on the right.

1. Pas mal.
2. Très bien.
3. J'ai faim.
4. Elle préfère aller au fast-food.
5. On va au fast-food.

    a. Malika
    b. Caroline
    c. Malika et Caroline

3   How do you ask your friend in French...

1. what time it is?
2. how he or she is feeling?
3. if he or she wants to go to the café?
4. what he or she likes to do?
5. if he or she likes to go to the fast-food restaurant?
6. who likes to eat pizza?

Quelle heure est-il? (Lyon)

4   *C'est à toi!*

On va au fast-food?

1. Comment vas-tu?
2. Tu aimes aller au fast-food?
3. Qu'est-ce que tu préfères, Le Macdo ou Domino's?
4. Tu préfères aller au fast-food ou au café?
5. Tu aimes le Coca-Cola light?

NATIONAL STANDARDS
C1.1, C1.2

Teacher's Notes

1. A mnemonic device to help students remember the meaning of **aller** (and to later differentiate between **aller** and **avoir**) is to write **aller** with two little legs that represent the **ll**. 2. Have students repeat after you the forms of **aller**, stressing liaison with **nous** and **vous**. Remind students that **ne** becomes **n'** in the negative forms **nous n'allons pas** and **vous n'allez pas**. 3. Point out to students that each present tense form of **aller** has three meanings, just as other present tense **-er** verb forms do. For example, **je vais** can mean *I go, I am going* or *I do go*. 4. Explain that liaison is optional between the **je, tu, nous, vous** and **ils/elles** present tense forms of **aller** and a word beginning with a vowel sound, for example, **Je vais au café, Tu vas au café, Nous allons au café**, and so on. 5. Point out the command form **allons-y** (*let's go there*) used in the dialogue of this lesson.

TPR

On va...?

You might put pictures or drawings around the classroom to represent the places where your students can say they can go: **au cinéma, au café, au fast-food, en boîte** and **chez moi**. As you say a complete sentence using a form of **aller** and the name of one of these places, have small groups of students, pairs or individuals go to that picture.

Structure

Present tense of the irregular verb *aller*

The verb **aller** (*to go*) is called an irregular verb because its forms follow an unpredictable pattern. It's the only **-er** verb that is irregular.

Une montre... pour aller à l'école.

aller			
je	**vais**	Je **vais** bien.	*I'm fine.*
tu	**vas**	Comment **vas**-tu?	*How are you?*
il/elle/on	**va**	On y **va**?	*Shall we go?*
nous	**allons**	Nous **allons** au café.	*We're going to the café.*
vous	**allez**	Comment **allez**-vous?	*How are you?*
ils/elles	**vont**	Elles ne **vont** pas au cinéma.	*They're not going to the movies.*

Nous allons au café?

CINDY ET RICHARD VONT A LA PLAGE

As you can see, the verb **aller** has more than one meaning. It can be used:

1) to talk about going somewhere.
   On **va** au café.   *We're going to the café.*

2) to talk about how things are going in general.
   Ça **va**?   *How are things going?*

3) to talk about someone's health.
   Comment **vas**-tu?   *How are you?*
   Je **vais** bien, merci.   *I'm fine, thanks.*

Pratique

5 Tell whether or not the following people are feeling fine.

1. Sylvie

5. Marie-Christine et Laïla

2. nous

6. vous

3. Vincent et Nicolas

7. Mohamed

4. je

Modèles:

Guillaume
Guillaume va bien.

tu
Tu ne vas pas bien.

6 It's Saturday night. Tell where the following people are going, according to the illustrations.

1. Tu....

4. Vous....

2. Tout le monde....

5. Je....

3. Théo et Martine....

les 300 films de la semaine
cinéscope
BILL MURRAY — ANDIE MacDOWELL
UN JOUR SANS FIN
Groundhog Day

7 With a partner, play the roles of each of the following pairs of people. Student A and Student B ask and tell how they are feeling and then talk about where Student B is going.

Modèle:

Student A: Comment vas-tu?
Student B: Très bien. Et toi?
Student A: Pas mal. Tu vas au fast-food?
Student B: Non, je vais en boîte.

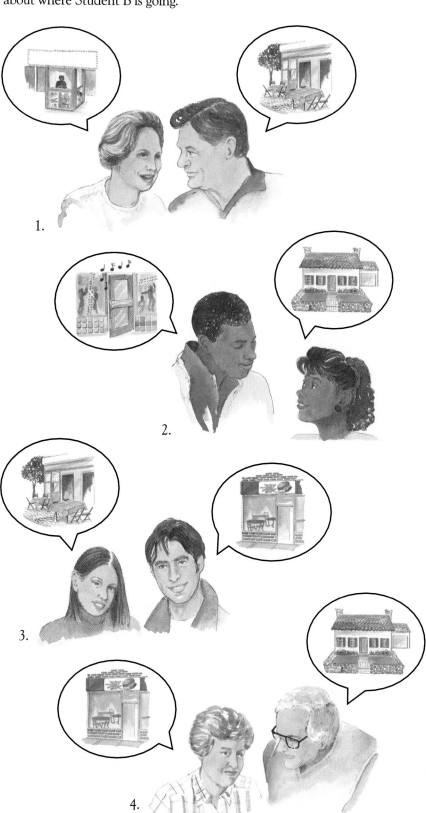

Telling time on the hour

To ask what time it is in French, say **Quelle heure est-il?** To tell what time it is, say **Il est... heure(s).** You must always use the word **heure(s)**, even though the expression "o'clock" may be omitted in English. To say that it's noon or midnight, use **Il est midi** or **Il est minuit.**

Quelle heure est-il?	*What time is it?*
Il est une heure.	*It's one (o'clock).*
Il est neuf heures.	*It's nine (o'clock).*

The abbreviation for **heure(s)** is **h**: **1h00 = 1:00.**

Quelle heure est-il?

Pratique

8 Looking at each clock or watch, answer the question **Quelle heure est-il?**

Modèle:

Il est cinq heures.

1.

2.

3.

4.

5.

6.

7.

8.

Workbook
Activities 6-7

Grammar & Vocabulary Exercises 6-8

Audiocassette/CD Activity 8

Computer Software Activity 2

Answers

8 1. Il est trois heures.
2. Il est midi.
3. Il est cinq heures.
4. Il est dix heures.
5. Il est sept heures.
6. Il est une heure.
7. Il est minuit.
8. Il est six heures.

Teacher's Notes

1. In conversational French you may often hear the question **Il est quelle heure?**, **Quelle heure il est?** or **Est-ce que tu as l'heure?**
2. Point out to students that after the number **une**, use **heure**. After all other numbers, use **heures**.
3. Point out that there is liaison between the final consonant sound of a number and the word **heure(s)**. Point out the sound [v] of the **f** in **neuf heures**. Use a clock with movable hands while asking the question **Quelle heure est-il?** 4. Although the 24-hour time system isn't presented at this point, you may mention that: A) it is the official system of schedules (school classes, planes, trains, TV programs, etc.) and appointments; B) digital clocks are making the 24-hour time system more popular; and C) the 24-hour time system uses only numbers for all hours, for example, **douze heures** for **midi** and **vingt-quatre heures** for **minuit**.

NATIONAL STANDARDS
C1.1, C1.2, C4.1

Teacher's Note

As a follow-up to or substitute for Activity 9, students might enjoy creating their own personal agenda for a summer day. Have them include at least eight activities, listing them according to time on the hour.

TPR

Clock

Have each student make his or her own clock, using a paper plate for the face and construction paper for the hands. The hands can be attached to the face with a round-head fastener. As you say a certain time, students show you the time on their clocks by holding them up. (This activity can also be done in pairs with one partner saying the time and the other partner showing the time.)

Paired Practice

Quelle heure est-il?

You might put students in pairs to practice telling time on the hour. One student randomly holds up one to ten fingers, and his or her partner gives the appropriate time. Switch roles for the next round.

NATIONAL STANDARDS
C1.1, C1.2

---

9 Suzanne has made many plans for the first day of summer vacation. Looking at each illustration, tell what time it is, based on the information she has written in her daily planner.

MERCREDI 25	
(6) Juin	
9h00	*faire du footing*
10h00	*téléphoner à Caroline*
11h00	*faire du vélo*
12h00	*faire du shopping*
1h00	*manger au fast-food*
2h00	*jouer au tennis*
3h00	
4h00	*nager*
5h00	
6h00	
7h00	
8h00	*sortir*

1.

2.

3.

4.

5.

6.

7.

8.

Communication

10 You meet one of your friends on the street after school. In the course of your conversation you decide to go to a café to get something to drink because you both are thirsty. With your partner:

1. Greet each other.
2. Find out how each other is feeling.
3. Student A says he or she is thirsty.
4. Student B agrees and suggests going to a fast-food restaurant.
5. Student A prefers to go to a café.
6. Student B agrees and suggests they go.

Modèle:

Student A:	Bonjour, Marie-Claire.
Student B:	Salut, Claudine. Comment vas-tu?
Student A:	Pas mal. Et toi?
Student B:	Très bien, merci.
Student A:	Dis, j'ai soif.
Student B:	Moi aussi. On va au fast-food?
Student A:	Moi, je préfère aller au café.
Student B:	D'accord, allons-y!

11 Cédric lives on the island of Martinique. His project for French class is to illustrate how he spends a typical vacation day. Help Cédric write captions to accompany his pictures, telling when he does each activity. The first caption has been done for you.

The sound [a]

The sound of the French vowel **a** is similar to the sound of the letter "a" in the English words "calm" and "father." However, the French sound [a] is shorter than the English "a" sound. In fact, all French vowels are shorter than English vowels. Say each of these words:

　　　mal　　　Malika　　　déjà　　　d'accord　　　allons-y　　　basket

The sound [i]

The sound of the French vowel **i** is similar to the sound of the letters "ee" in the English word "see." Say each of these words:

　　　midi　　　merci　　　Christine　　　idée　　　cinéma　　　musique

Prononciation

Workbook Activities 8-9

Grammar & Vocabulary Exercises 9-11

Audiocassette/CD *Au café*

Transparencies 12-13

Teacher's Notes

1. **Hamburger** is pronounced [ˈɑ̃buʀɡœʀ] and **hot-dog** is pronounced [ˈɔtdɔɡ]. Both words begin with an aspirate **h**. When an article precedes an aspirate **h**, there is neither liaison nor contraction. 2. Point out to your students that **un sandwich au fromage** and **un sandwich au jambon** are usually served cold. 3. **Un jus de fruit** is commonly used for "fruit juice." 4. **Limonade** is a false cognate. 5. You may want to point out to students that **eau** forms its plural by adding an **x**. 6. A communicative function that is recycled in this lesson is "greeting someone."

Cooperative Group Practice

Au fast-food

After reading about French fast-food restaurants in the **Enquête culturelle** of **Leçon A**, your students might like to create their own commercials for a French fast-food restaurant. Put students in groups of three or four. Each group will create and perform a commercial in simple French about either one product at that restaurant or about that restaurant in general. In each cooperative group one person serves as the recorder, another person plays the role of a customer and the third person takes the part of an employee.

NATIONAL STANDARDS
C1.2, C1.3

Leçon B

In this lesson you will be able to:

➤ **order food and beverages**

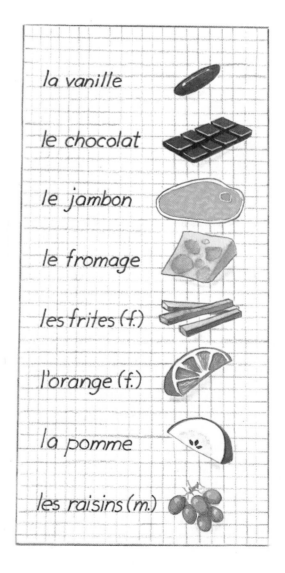

la vanille

le chocolat

le jambon

le fromage

les frites (f.)

l'orange (f.)

la pomme

les raisins (m.)

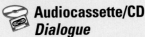

**Workbook
Activities 10-12**

**Audiocassette/CD
*Dialogue***

Monsieur and Madame Paganini are having lunch at a small café on **le boulevard Saint-Michel** in Paris. The server arrives to take their order.

Serveur:	**Bonjour, Messieurs-Dames. Vous désirez?**
Madame Paganini:	**Je voudrais une salade et un jus de pomme, s'il vous plaît.**
Serveur:	**Et pour vous, Monsieur?**
Monsieur Paganini:	**Je voudrais un steak-frites et une eau minérale, s'il vous plaît.**
Serveur:	**Et comme dessert?**
Monsieur Paganini:	**Je voudrais une glace au chocolat. Donnez-moi aussi un café, s'il vous plaît.**

Teacher's Notes

1. Some French cafés serve both food and beverages; others serve only beverages. 2. Meat can be ordered **saignant** (*rare*), **à point** (*medium*) or **bien cuit** (*well done*). 3. The terms **garçon** and **serveur** may be used to refer to a male server, but to address him, you say **Monsieur**. To address a female server, you say **Mademoiselle** or **Madame**. Often the **serveur** in a café is a male. However, at a fancier restaurant, the server may be male or female. 4. Storekeepers or servers often greet their customers by saying **Messieurs-Dames**, an abbreviation of **Messieurs** and **Mesdames**. This greeting is standard no matter how many customers there are, whether they are male or female, or whether or not the storekeeper or server knows them. This greeting creates a friendly atmosphere, but customers may not respond to the greeting. 5. To make the conversation more realistic, Madame Paganini could have named the brand of mineral water she wanted. Again, to avoid unnecessary commercialism, *C'est à toi!* has avoided brand names in dialogues. (Various brands are named, however, in the following **Enquête culturelle** section, and you may alter the dialogue, if you wish.) 6. Another way of saying **Donnez-moi un café** is **Apportez-moi un café**.

Enquête culturelle

Le boulevard Saint-Michel runs through the heart of the Latin Quarter in Paris. Located near France's most famous university, **la Sorbonne**, this street is one of the centers of student life.

Steak-frites refers to a steak that is served with French fries. *Frites* are also popular in Belgium, where they originated. French fry snack bars in Belgium are called **friteries**.

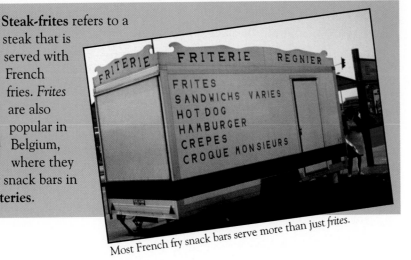

Most French fry snack bars serve more than just *frites*.

NATIONAL STANDARDS
C1.2, C2.1, C2.2, C3.1, C3.2, C4.2

Game

Pictionnaire

In this French version of the American game, students will orally identify in French, through sketched clues, as many French names for foods and beverages as possible in a designated time period. Divide the class into three or four equal teams. Roll the die to determine the order of play. The highest roller starts. Each team selects an order for picturists (the ones who will draw clues on the board). Each student must participate in drawing. The picturist position must rotate every time a team sketches. When the timer is turned on, the picturist begins sketching clues for the team. The picturist may not use verbal or physical communication to teammates during the round. He or she may not use letters or numbers in the drawings. Sketching and guessing continue until the word is identified in French or until time is up. If the team guesses the word correctly, a point is awarded. Rotate to the next team whether the word is identified or not. At the end of the designated time period the team with the most points wins.

People of all ages drink mineral water. Some popular brands are Vittel, Perrier, Vichy, Contrex, Évian and Badoit. Fruit juices are not just for breakfast but are served throughout the day. Usually, only young children drink milk. **Un diabolo menthe** is a sweet drink made by mixing lemon-lime soda with mint-flavored syrup. Other drinks can be made with different flavored syrups. French speakers also buy soft drinks, such as Coke and Pepsi.

The French, even teenagers, have coffee at the end of a meal, rather than during it. They may order **un express** (*espresso coffee*) or **un café crème** (*coffee with cream*) during the day when at a café with their friends. Coffee is made and served one cup at a time rather than by the pot.

Students often stop with their friends at **crêperies** (*crêpe shops*), where they snack on a dessert crêpe. Resembling thin pancakes, crêpes can be

filled with jam or with butter and sugar or even with chocolate. They originated in the province of Brittany in northwestern France but are now a popular dessert throughout the country. As a meal, these pancakes can be made with buckwheat flour. Then called **galettes**, they may be filled with ham, eggs or cheese.

What would you like your crêpe filled with—chocolate, jam, whipped cream? (Paris)

1 Say in French whether you're hungry or thirsty, depending on whether you see a food or a beverage.

1.   4.   7.

2.   5.   8.

3.   6.

Modèle:

J'ai soif.

2 Complete each sentence by identifying the numbered item you see in the illustration.

Modèle:
C'est une....
C'est une omelette.

1. C'est une....
2. C'est un....
3. C'est un....
4. C'est un....

5. C'est une....
6. C'est une....
7. C'est un....
8. C'est un....

Audiocassette/CD Activities 1-2

Answers

1 1. J'ai soif.
2. J'ai faim.
3. J'ai faim.
4. J'ai soif.
5. J'ai faim.
6. J'ai faim.
7. J'ai soif.
8. J'ai faim.

2 1. crêpe
2. jus d'orange
3. sandwich au jambon
4. café
5. glace au chocolat
6. salade
7. steak
8. hamburger

TPR

J'ai faim ou j'ai soif?
To reinforce the expressions **avoir faim** and **avoir soif**, you may want to try an activity with flash cards or pictures of the foods and beverages that were introduced in this lesson. As you hold up a set of two pictures, one of a food item and one of a beverage, say either **J'ai faim** or **J'ai soif**. Depending on what you say, students respond by raising their left hand if the food item should be selected and their right hand if the beverage should be selected.

NATIONAL STANDARDS
C1.1, C1.2

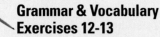

Teacher's Note

Make sure that students do not pronounce the **n** in **un** except in liaison with a following vowel sound.

TPR

Gender of Nouns

To practice listening skills, say a series of nouns and their indefinite articles. Have students raise their left hand if they hear a masculine noun; have them raise their right hand if they hear a feminine noun. As a follow-up activity, you might repeat the same list of nouns without their articles. Students again raise their left hand if the noun is masculine and their right hand if the noun is feminine.

Comparisons

Gender in Foreign Languages

Ask if there are any students in your class who know another foreign language. If there are, ask them which language they know and if this language designates nouns by gender. With your class make a list of languages in which nouns have a gender. Make another list of languages that do not designate nouns by gender. Ask your students if they have any ideas why certain languages show gender and others do not.

NATIONAL STANDARDS
C1.1, C1.2, C4.1

72

Modèle:

Vous désirez un café ou un jus d'orange?

Donnez-moi un jus d'orange, s'il vous plaît.

C'est une omelette.

3 If you had a choice between two items, say which one you would order.

1. Vous désirez une glace à la vanille ou une glace au chocolat?
2. Vous désirez un sandwich au fromage ou un steak-frites?
3. Vous désirez un jus de pomme ou un jus de raisin?
4. Vous désirez un coca ou une limonade?
5. Vous désirez une quiche ou une salade?
6. Vous désirez un hamburger ou un hot-dog?
7. Vous désirez une pomme ou une orange?

Structure

Gender of nouns and indefinite articles

A noun is the name of a person, place or thing. Can you pick out the nouns in the following sentences?

1. Je voudrais une salade et un jus de pomme.
2. Donnez-moi aussi un café, s'il vous plaît.

In the first sentence the nouns are **salade** and **jus de pomme**, and in the second sentence the noun is **café**.

Unlike nouns in English, every French noun has a gender, either masculine or feminine. You will need to remember the gender of each French noun that you learn. You can usually tell if a noun is masculine or feminine by what precedes it. For example, a noun preceded by **un** is masculine, and a noun preceded by **une** is feminine. **Un** and **une**, meaning "a" or "an," are called indefinite articles. In the two sentences above, you can tell that the noun **salade** is feminine because it is preceded by **une**; the nouns **jus de pomme** and **café** are masculine because they are preceded by **un**. If you don't know whether a noun is masculine or feminine, you can find out by looking it up in the end vocabulary of this textbook.

Pratique

4 Here are some café receipts. Count the number of masculine items and the number of feminine items on each one.

Café de l'Univers

un jus de pomme	2,29
un thé	2,74
une eau minérale	3,20
une salade verte	4,12
un steak-frites	10,67
une crêpe	3,51
Total	26,53

Café Olé

un coca	3,05
une limonade	2,90
un sandwich au jambon	4,27
un croque-monsieur	4,57
Total	14,79

Café Brocéliande

un diabolo menthe	3,35
un jus de raisin	2,29
une glace à la vanille	4,88
une glace au chocolat	4,88
Total	15,40

Café de la place de l'Horloge

un express	2,29
un café-crème	2,74
un chocolat	3,05
une tarte aux fraises	4,12
un croissant	1,37
Total	13,57

5 Using the café receipts from Activity 4, name one item you could order for each of the following prices.

1. 2,90
2. 3,20
3. 10,67
4. 3,51
5. 4,88
6. 3,05

Modèle:
2,74
un café-crème

Answers

4 Café de l'Univers: 3 masculine items, 3 feminine items
Café Olé: 3 masculine items, 1 feminine item
Café Brocéliande: 2 masculine items, 2 feminine items
Café de la place de l'Horloge: 4 masculine items, 1 feminine item

5 Possible answers:
1. une limonade
2. une eau minérale
3. un steak-frites
4. une crêpe
5. une glace à la vanille
6. un coca

Teacher's Notes

1. You might tell students that the prices listed on the café receipts are in euros. The French monetary system will be explained in **Leçon C**. 2. If you have flash cards, transparencies or pictures of the foods and beverages that were introduced in this lesson, you might show these pictures one at a time to the class. Have students take turns identifying each picture by giving the appropriate indefinite article and the item's name in French.

NATIONAL STANDARDS
C1.1, C1.2, C2.1

Audiocassette/CD
Activity 6

Answers

6 Possible answers:

1. Je voudrais un hot-dog et un coca, s'il vous plaît.
   Alors, un hot-dog et un coca?
   Oui, Monsieur.

2. Je voudrais un steak-frites, une salade et un café, s'il vous plaît.
   Alors, un steak-frites, une salade et un café?
   Oui, Monsieur.

3. Je voudrais un hamburger et une limonade, s'il vous plaît.
   Alors, un hamburger et une limonade?
   Oui, Monsieur.

4. Je voudrais une omelette et un jus de raisin, s'il vous plaît.
   Alors, une omelette et un jus de raisin?
   Oui, Monsieur.

5. Je voudrais une quiche et un jus d'orange, s'il vous plaît.
   Alors, une quiche et un jus d'orange?
   Oui, Monsieur.

Paired Practice

To simplify Activity 7, have one student play the role of a server at a café and the other student play the role of a customer who is going to order a snack or something to drink there. 1) The server and the customer greet each other. 2) The server asks what the customer would like. 3) The customer politely orders something to eat or drink.

NATIONAL STANDARDS
C1.1, C1.2, C2.1

74

---

6 With a partner, play the roles of various customers at a sidewalk café and a server. Student A orders certain things to eat and drink; Student B repeats each order to make sure everything is correct. Follow the model.

Modèle:

Student A: Je voudrais un sandwich au fromage et une eau minérale, s'il vous plaît.

Student B: Alors, un sandwich au fromage et une eau minérale?

Student A: Oui, Monsieur/ Madame/Mademoiselle.

1.

4.

3.

2.

5.

Alors, un sandwich au fromage et une limonade?

Communication

7 With two of your classmates, play the roles of two customers at a sidewalk café and the server who waits on them. The two customers are each going to order a snack and something to drink. In the course of the conversation:

1. The server and the two customers greet each other.
2. The server asks what the customers would like.
3. Each customer politely orders a snack and something to drink.
4. As the server repeats the two orders, he or she gets them mixed up, switching the beverages.
5. Each customer again says his or her order.
6. The server repeats both orders correctly.

8 | You and your family are traveling together in France. You decide to stop at a fast-food restaurant for something to eat and drink. Since you are the only one who knows any French, you have to order for the whole family. Before you place your order, make a list in French of what everyone wants. (You should order something for yourself that no one else has ordered.) You should organize your list by categories so that you can order efficiently at the counter.

> Your mother wants a salad and mineral water.
>
> Your father wants something hot to eat and a hot drink.
>
> Your sister wants ice cream and a cold drink.
>
> Your brother wants a sandwich and fruit juice.
>
> You want....

Tu aimes aller au fast-food? (Paris)

9 | Four of your friends are coming over to your house after school today to work on a group project. You know they will all be hungry, so you decide to pick up something to eat and drink at a fast-food restaurant on your way home. Decide what you are going to order and then write it down so that you will remember everything you want when you pull up to the microphone to place your order.

GRATUIT
1 GIANT
POUR 1 MENU GIANT ACHETÉ

Offre non cumulable, valable contre remise de ce bon à la caisse du restaurant jusqu'au 27 février 2002.

Quick

Entre vous et nous,
c'est une histoire de goût.

🎧 **Listening Activity 2**

Game

Memory Chain

After students are familiar with the vocabulary for foods and beverages that was presented in this lesson, you might play a memory game intended to practice higher order thinking skills. For example, start by saying **Je voudrais une salade**. The first student repeats what you have said and adds another item: **Je voudrais une salade et une omelette**. Every time a student is unable to repeat what has gone before, he or she is eliminated. If this game is played with teams, the team with the most players at the end of the allotted time is the winner. (Beginning classes composed of more visual learners may write down the items as they are said and read them off, adding their own contribution at the end. After students have become familiar with the material, they can also work from memory.)

NATIONAL STANDARDS
C1.1, C1.3, C2.1, C2.2,
C3.2, C5.1

75

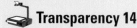

**Workbook
Activity 14**

Transparency 14

Teacher's Note

Inside the Café des Deux Magots are **magots**, statues of Chinese commercial agents. These statues are left over from a hosiery store that once stood there. The café was a favorite rendezvous of post-war existentialists, such as Albert Camus, Jean-Paul Sartre and Simone de Beauvoir. Ernest Hemingway and James Joyce also spent time there.

Connections

French Foods

In this lesson students learn about some French foods that are fairly easy to prepare. You may want to contact your Family and Consumer Sciences Department to ask the foods teacher if he or she would be interested in joining classes with you to hold an integrated lesson on French foods. You can be responsible for providing information on what foods the French typically eat, and the foods teacher can explain the preparation procedures for each dish. Finally your combined classes might prepare and sample one or more French foods or even prepare an entire French meal.

Mise au point sur... la cuisine française

When they are not enjoying meals at home with their families, French people like to eat out. French restaurants have earned the reputation of serving some of the best cuisine in the world. You can grab a sandwich from a sidewalk stand, spend some time at a café or eat a meal consisting of many courses at an elegant restaurant.

While walking downtown, people often grab a simple snack, such as a sandwich, hot dog, crêpe or slice of pizza, from a sidewalk stand. People with more time usually stop at a café where they can talk with friends, read the newspaper or watch people strolling by as they eat their food. Cafés are everywhere; you often see two or three of them in a row. Since menus are displayed outside cafés, you know in advance what is available and how much it will cost. In nice weather people usually sit on **la terrasse** (*terrace*) outside in front

Café **LE GLOBE**
BAR - BRASSERIE - GLACIER - COCKTAIL
DANS SON NOUVEAU DÉCOR 1900
34, rue Lenepveu - 49100 ANGERS
☎ 02.41.88.49.95
de 7 h à 2 h

DEPUIS 1885
LES DEUX MAGOTS
6, place Saint-Germain-des-Prés
75006 Paris - Tél. 01 45 48 55 25

Café terraces are crowded when the weather is warm and sunny. (Nice)

of a café. In winter most people eat inside. French cafés serve customers from early in the morning until late in the evening. In small towns, friends often gather at the local café, while tourists in Paris visit some of the world-famous cafés, such as the Deux Magots, the Café de Flore and Fouquet's.

NATIONAL STANDARDS
C1.2, C2.1, C2.2, C3.1, C3.2, C4.2

Since each region of France and each French-speaking country has its own specialty, there is something available for every taste and budget. You can order **choucroute garnie** (*sauerkraut with meat*) from the Alsace region near Germany, a **crêpe** from Brittany or a **salade niçoise** (*salad made with lettuce, cold vegetables, hard-cooked eggs, olives, anchovies, tuna and a vinaigrette dressing*) from the city of Nice on the Riviera. Of course, each region produces

Can you recognize what's in a salade niçoise? It gets its name from the city of Nice.

01.42.61.38.83 **LE MAROC** 01.42.61.48.83
UN DES MEILLEURS COUSCOUS DE PARIS
TAGINE, PASTILLA, EL KEFTA, MECHOUI
Fourchette d'Or de la Gastronomie Marocaine 90
9, rue Danielle-Casanova (av. de l'Opéra)
Son cadre unique ses très beaux salons climatisés

Couscous, a spicy meat stew on a bed of semolina, is a popular main course.

its own cheese, wine and even candy to share with the rest of the country. North African restaurants serve **couscous**, a dish of steamed semolina usually accompanied by a meat stew and a variety of sauces. Creole cuisine, from Martinique and Guadeloupe, is fairly spicy and uses many different fruits and seafoods. **La tourtière**, a meat potpie, originated in Quebec. Spicy Cajun cuisine from New Orleans is popular throughout the world.

Tourtière

- 1 livre de porc haché, maigre
- 1 oignon moyen, haché
- Sel et poivre
- ¼ c. à thé de sarriette
- ¼ c. à thé de clou de girofle moulu
- 1 feuille de laurier
- ¼ tasse d'eau bouillante
- Pâte brisée pour 2 abaisses

NATIONAL STANDARDS
C1.2, C2.1, C2.2, C3.1, C3.2, C4.2

Teacher's Note

If you would like Activity 11 on page 79 to have set answers, you could give your students certain prices for each menu item, for example, **salade** = 4,12 euros, **steak-frites** = 5,03 euros, **omelette** = 3,81 euros, **quiche** = 4,27 euros, **café** = 2,29 euros, **Badoit** = 4,27 euros and **coca** = 3,35 euros. The total would then be 27,14 euros.

Comparisons

Eating Out in the U.S.

You might have your students write an essay titled "Eating Out in the U.S." Tell students to model their essays after the cultural reading **Mise au point sur... la cuisine française.** They should treat the same subjects that are presented in the reading, for example, types of eating places, various regional specialties, different courses, etc. Tell students to write their essays from the point of view of someone who is describing American eating habits to a foreigner who is not

NATIONAL STANDARDS
C1.2, C2.1, C2.2, C3.1, C4.2

For a meal with several courses, people may go to a restaurant. The most popular kinds of restaurants feature typical, country-style dishes which are prepared with fresh ingredients. Good restaurants are often quite small and the chef may be one of the owners. In eating formally at a

A full-course meal at a restaurant may last several hours. (Château d'Isenbour

restaurant, people can choose either certain courses from the menu or a full-course meal at a fixed price. They may eat various courses, starting with an **hors-d'œuvre**, such as **crudités** (*raw vegetables, often shredded*), then a meat and vegetable course, a salad, cheese and finally dessert. Some fixed-price meals may have only three courses. Diners eat fresh bread throughout the entire meal. A small cup of espresso is served at the end. You can expect to wait a while between courses at a French restaurant. French people do not like to eat quickly and often spend hours at the table. They take great pleasure in eating well. It is often said that a good meal is composed of three parts: good food, plenty of time and good conversation.

~ **MENU à 11 €** ~

ENTRÉE AU CHOIX
Tartine du Baptiste
Salade aux noix
Salade au bleu
Crudités du marché
Champignons à la grecque (maison)
Oeufs durs mayonnaise
Cervelas en salade
Terrine de foies de volailles
Filets de harengs
Entrée du jour..... au tableau !

PLAT AU CHOIX
(Accompagné de frites ou garniture du jour)
Brochette de boeuf grillée, sauce maison
Tranche de gigot d'agneau grillée
Steak savoyard (boeuf haché, grillé gratiné)
L'idée poisson ou L'idée du jour
(Suivant l'humeur du Chef !!!)

DESSERT AU CHOIX
Crème caramel
Mousse au chocolat
Flan à la noix de coco
Terrine de fruits, au chocolat chaud ou au coulis de framboises
Glaces ou sorbets, deux parfums au choix
(vanille, chocolat, café, coco, citron vert, cassis, poire, passion)
Coupe damnation
(crème de marrons, chocolat chaud, crème fraîche)
Tarte au citron
Dessert du jour
(Autre dessert de la carte, plus 1,80 €)

~ **FORMULE à 9 €** ~
Une Entrée ou un Dessert du Menu à 11 €
avec un Plat de ce même menu

Prix nets - Service compris

Carafe d'eau gratuite

0 Answer the following questions.

1. What are three types of French eating establishments?
2. What can you order to eat at a sidewalk stand?
3. Besides eating, what do people do at cafés?
4. How can you decide where you want to eat before sitting down?
5. What are two regional specialties from France?
6. What is a specialty from North Africa?
7. Where do French people go for a larger meal?
8. What are five courses a typical French restaurant serves?
9. Why may the service seem slow to an American who dines at a French restaurant?
10. For a French person, what three ingredients compose a good meal?

1 Imagine that you are a server at the restaurant called Le Rétro. You must prepare the check for your table of three customers, using the receipt from the Chez Paul restaurant as a model. Your customers at Le Rétro ordered a salad, a steak with fries, an omelette, a quiche, a cup of coffee, a bottle of Badoit mineral water and a Coke. The check you make should show the name, address and phone number of the restaurant, the number of the table you have been serving, the number of people at the table (**couverts**) and a list of the food and prices as well as the total amount to be paid.

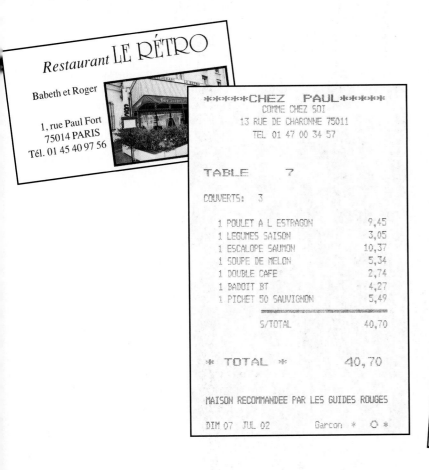

Workbook
Activity 15

Grammar & Vocabulary
Exercises 16-22

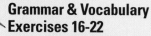
Audiocassette/CD
Numbers 20–100

Teacher's Note

Instead of teaching the numbers from 20 to 100 all at once, you might try the approach of teaching only 10, 20, 30, 40, 50, 60, 70, 80, 90 and 100 on the first day to help students realize that mastering all the numbers from 20 to 100 is not so impossible. Each day as you continue in **Leçon C**, you can fill in more of the sequence.

Game

Number Race

Make two sets of ten 12" x 12" pieces of construction paper with one numeral from zero to nine on each piece of paper. Divide students into two teams of ten each. Give each student a piece of paper with a numeral on it. The teams line up behind a marker. Call out a number in French from 0 to 98. (Double numbers, such as 77 or 88, will not work.) The students who are holding the numerals which make up that number run forward to another marker. The team to display the correct number first wins a point.

Leçon C

In this lesson you will be able to:

➤ **ask for a price**

➤ **state prices**

20 VINGT
21 vingt et un
22 vingt-deux
23 vingt-trois

30 TRENTE
31 trente et un
32 trente-deux
33 trente-trois

40 QUARANTE
41 quarante et un
42 quarante-deux
43 quarante-trois

50 CINQUANTE
51 cinquante et un
52 cinquante-deux
53 cinquante-trois

60 SOIXANTE
61 soixante et un
62 soixante-deux
63 soixante-trois

70 SOIXANTE-DIX
71 soixante et onze
72 soixante-douze
73 soixante-treize
74 soixante-quatorze
75 soixante-quinze
76 soixante-seize
77 soixante-dix-sept
78 soixante-dix-huit
79 soixante-dix-neuf

80 QUATRE-VINGTS
81 quatre-vingt-un
82 quatre-vingt-deux
83 quatre-vingt-trois

90 QUATRE-VINGT-DIX
91 quatre-vingt-onze
92 quatre-vingt-douze
93 quatre-vingt-treize
94 quatre-vingt-quatorze
95 quatre-vingt-quinze
96 quatre-vingt-seize
97 quatre-vingt-dix-sept
98 quatre-vingt-dix-huit
99 quatre-vingt-dix-neuf

100 CENT

Merci, Madame.

Je vous en prie.

**Workbook
Activity 16**

**Grammar & Vocabulary
Exercises 14-15**

**Audiocassette/CD
Dialogue**

Jean-François and Myriam have just finished eating and are ready to pay the bill.

Jean-François: Ça fait combien, Madame?

Serveuse: Voyons, le sandwich au jambon coûte quatre euros vingt-sept, la quiche… cinq euros trente-quatre, et les deux boissons… cinq euros dix-huit. Ça fait quatorze euros soixante-dix-neuf.

Myriam: Voilà quinze euros. Merci, Madame.

Serveuse: Je vous en prie.

On a menu the words **service compris** mean that the tip (a 15% service charge) is included in the bill, but most people leave some small change as an extra tip for good service.

Enquête culturelle

In January, 1999, the **euro** (**l'euro**) officially became the basic unit of money in France and in ten other European countries. In each of these 11 European countries **l'euro** has the same value. Previously, **le franc** was the national currency of France. During the transition period from 1999 to 2002, **francs** were still used for daily cash purchases, but the French could pay their bills either in **francs** or in **euros** when using checks or credit cards.

Teacher's Notes

1. To thank someone, you can also say **Merci bien** or **Merci beaucoup, Monsieur/Madame/ Mademoiselle; Je vous remercie** or **Merci mille fois**. To respond to someone's thanks, you can also say **De rien** or **Il n'y a pas de quoi**. 2. The 11 countries of the European Union that have chosen to use the **euro** are Austria, Belgium, Finland, France, Germany, Ireland, Italy, Luxembourg, the Netherlands, Portugal and Spain. These 11 countries have more than 300,000,000 inhabitants. The four EU countries that do not use the **euro** are Denmark, Greece, Sweden and the United Kingdom. 3. The price in **euros** of any item is found by dividing the price in **francs** by the official conversion rate: 6,55957. 4. The abbreviation of **euro** is EUR. The symbol € looks like the Greek letter epsilon that is intersected by two horizontal lines. The seven **euro** bills are of different colors: gray (5 **euros**), red (10 **euros**), blue (20 **euros**), orange (50 **euros**), green (100 **euros**), yellow (200 **euros**) and purple (500 **euros**). The images of doors, windows and archways on the front of the bills symbolize an opening to new ideas and economic opportunity. The bridges on the back of the bills symbolize the ties between the member countries of the European Union.

NATIONAL STANDARDS
C1.2, C2.1, C2.2, C3.1, C4.2

Audiocassette/CD Activity 2

Video

Answers

1 1. To ask how much something costs, you say **Ça fait combien?**

2. You say **Je vous en prie**.

3. **Service compris** means that the tip is included in the bill.

4. **L'euro** is the basic unit of money in France.

5. Ten other countries also use **l'euro**.

6. **Dix-huit euros cinquante** is written **18,50 €** or **18 € 50**.

2 1. Trente-cinq.
2. Cinquante-six.
3. Soixante-cinq.
4. Soixante-treize.
5. Quatre-vingts.
6. Quatre-vingt-un.
7. Quatre-vingt-dix.
8. Quarante-sept.

Teacher's Notes

1. All the **euro** coins have the same image on the "head" of the coin, but on the "tail" there are symbols representative of the specific country where the coin was minted. The French 1- and 2-**euro** coins portray a tree of life, the letters "RF" and the motto "Liberté, Égalité, Fraternité." On the 1-, 2- and 5-**cent** coins is the face of Marianne, symbol of the French Republic. The 10-, 20- and 50-**cent** coins show "RF" and a woman sowing seeds. 2. For more information on the **euro** and for calculators to convert **francs** to **euros**, visit **http://www.finances.gouv.fr/euro** or **http://europa.eu.int/euro**.

NATIONAL STANDARDS
C1.1, C1.2, C2.2, C3.1, C3.2, C4.2

82

It was decided to issue the new **euro** bills (**les billets**) and coins (**les pièces de monnaie**) in January, 2002.

Each **euro** is divided into 100 **cents** (or **centimes**). Bills are issued in denominations of 5, 10, 20, 50, 100, 200 and 500 **euros**. The greater the value, the larger the bill. There are also eight **euro** coins in denominations of one and two **euros** and 1, 2, 5, 10, 20 and 50 **cents**. Prices in **euros** are written with an **€** and sometimes a comma (**36,50 €** or **36 € 50** = **trente-six euros cinquante**). The value of the **euro** depends on the daily exchange rate, but roughly speaking, it is worth about the same as the American dollar. Some other currencies used in French-speaking countries are **le dinar** (Algeria and Tunisia), **le dirham** (Morocco) and **le dollar canadien** (Quebec).

1 Answer the following questions.

1. How do you ask in French how much something costs?
2. How do you say "You're welcome" in French?
3. What words appear on a menu to let you know that the tip is included in the bill?
4. What is the basic unit of money in France?
5. How many other countries use money with this name?
6. How do you write **dix-huit euros cinquante**?

2 *Ça fait combien? Répondez en français.*

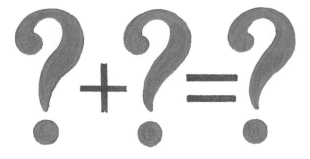

1. Douze et vingt-trois?
2. Quatorze et quarante-deux?
3. Trente-sept et vingt-huit?
4. Quarante et trente-trois?
5. Cinquante et trente?
6. Soixante et vingt et un?
7. Soixante-dix et vingt?
8. Treize et trente-quatre?

3 By looking at the menu and totaling prices, say how much the food and beverage combinations that follow cost.

sandwich au fromage	3,51 €
steak-frites	11,43 €
crêpe	3,20 €
quiche	3,66 €
omelette	4,27 €
salade	3,20 €
glace à la vanille	4,57 €
eau minérale	2,59 €
café	2,44 €
jus d'orange	2,74 €
jus de pomme	2,74 €
limonade	2,90 €
coca	3,05 €

1. une crêpe et un jus d'orange
2. un sandwich au fromage et un jus de pomme
3. une quiche et une limonade
4. un steak-frites et un coca
5. une glace à la vanille et un café
6. une salade et une eau minérale

4 *C'est à toi!*

1. Tu aimes aller au café?
2. Qu'est-ce que tu manges au café?
3. Tu aimes beaucoup aller au fast-food?
4. Qu'est-ce que tu manges au fast-food?
5. Qu'est-ce que tu aimes comme dessert?
6. Qu'est-ce que tu aimes comme boisson?

Qu'est-ce que tu voudrais comme dessert? (Angers)

Audiocassette/CD Activity 4

Answers

3 1. Cinq euros quatre-vingt-quatorze.
2. Six euros vingt-cinq.
3. Six euros cinquante-six.
4. Quatorze euros quarante-huit.
5. Sept euros un.
6. Cinq euros soixante-dix-neuf.

4 Answers will vary.

Game

Dring

Similar to the English game called "Buzz," *Dring* drills knowledge of numbers in French. The purpose of the game is to substitute the word *Dring* for predetermined numbers as students count aloud. The game starts with the students standing up and ends when only one of them remains on his or her feet. Students count off in French. (The first student says **zéro**, the second **un**, the third **deux**, etc.) They must watch out when an arbitrarily chosen number or its multiple comes up. Traditionally, the number is seven (although the game plays just as well with numbers like five, six or eight). When it's a student's turn to give either a number containing seven (for example, 17) or a multiple of seven (for example, 14, 21, 28), he or she must say *Dring* instead. The teacher spots those responding incorrectly and asks each in turn to sit down. Of course, a student can slip up and be seated even when the number to be given has nothing to do with seven. The count begins again after the next student in line corrects the error by saying *Dring* or the right number, depending on the type of mistake made.

NATIONAL STANDARDS
C1.1, C1.2, C2.1

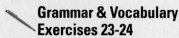

Workbook
Activity 17

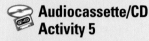

Grammar & Vocabulary
Exercises 23-24

Audiocassette/CD
Activity 5

Computer Software
Activity 4

Answers

5 Answers will vary.

Teacher's Notes

1. Explain the use of (*m.*) and (*f.*) in vocabulary lists of some books to indicate the gender of nouns that begin with a vowel sound. Point out that **un** and **une** indicate the gender of nouns in this book with a few exceptions, such as **l'anglais** (*m.*) *English*. 2. If you have flash cards, transparencies or pictures of the foods and beverages that were introduced in this unit, you might show these pictures one at a time to the class. Have students take turns identifying each picture by saying **Voilà** followed by the appropriate definite article and the name of the item.

TPR

Gender of Nouns

To practice listening skills, say a series of nouns and their definite articles from this or a previous lesson. Have students raise their left hand if they hear a masculine noun; have them raise their right hand if they hear a feminine noun. To vary this TPR activity, you might have students raise a green card if the noun is masculine or a red card if the noun is feminine.

NATIONAL STANDARDS
C1.1, C1.2, C4.1

84

J'aime bien la quiche.

La glace est délicieuse. (Biarritz)

Modèles:

J'aime la glace à la vanille.

Je n'aime pas le jus d'orange.

Structure

Definite articles

To refer to a specific person, place or thing, you use a definite article. In French the singular definite articles are **le, la** and **l'**, all meaning "the."
Le precedes a masculine word beginning with a consonant sound.

> Le sandwich au jambon coûte cinq euros. — *The ham sandwich costs five euros.*

La precedes a feminine word beginning with a consonant sound.

> La quiche est délicieuse. — *The quiche is delicious.*

L' is used instead of **le** or **la** before a masculine or feminine word beginning with a vowel sound.

> Je préfère l'eau minérale. — *I prefer mineral water.*
> L'omelette est pour Marie-Hélène. — *The omelette is for Marie-Hélène.*

A definite article may also designate a noun in a general sense.

> J'aime la glace. — *I like ice cream (in general).*

The subject pronoun **il** (*it*) may replace a masculine singular noun.

> Le dessert est superbe. — *The dessert is superb.*
> Il est superbe. — *It is superb.*

The subject pronoun **elle** (*it*) may replace a feminine singular noun.

> La salade est fraîche. — *The salad is fresh.*
> Elle est fraîche. — *It is fresh.*

Pratique

5 Tell whether or not you like the following foods and beverages.

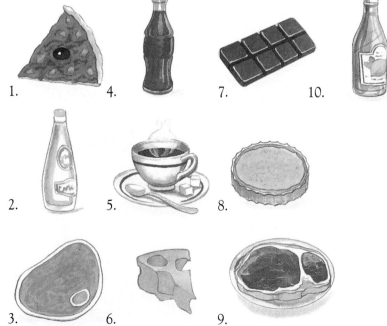

1.   4.   7.   10.

2.   5.   8.

3.   6.   9.

6 You and your partner are at a café. Student A, who has never been to this café before, asks how much certain things cost. Student B, who comes to this café almost every day, answers Student A's questions.

1. jus de pomme/2,74 €
2. omelette/4,27 €
3. steak-frites/6,10 €
4. salade/3,51 €
5. eau minérale/3,20 €
6. café/2,90 €
7. crêpe/4,57 €
8. glace à la vanille/4,88 €

Plurals

The plural form of the definite articles **le, la** and **l'** is **les** (*the*).

Les deux boissons coûtent six euros.	*The two drinks cost six euros.*

To form the plural of most singular nouns, add an **s**. This **s** is never pronounced. Nouns that already end in **-s** in the singular do not change in the plural.

la quiche	les quiches
le dessert	les desserts
le fast-food	les fast-foods
le jus d'orange	les jus d'orange

In spoken French the sound of **les** is often the only indication that the noun is plural. Always be careful to distinguish the sound of **les** from the sounds of **le** and **la**.

Voilà **le** sandwich.	Voilà **les** sandwichs.

The subject pronoun **ils** may replace one or more masculine plural nouns or a mixed group of nouns.

Les deux **cafés** coûtent cinq euros.	**Ils** coûtent cinq euros.
Le chocolat et **la limonade** coûtent sept euros.	**Ils** coûtent sept euros.

The subject pronoun **elles** may replace one or more feminine plural nouns.

Les boissons coûtent six euros.	**Elles** coûtent six euros.

The plural form of the indefinite articles **un** and **une** is **des** (*some*).

Vous désirez **des** frites?	*Do you want some French fries?*

Modèle:

sandwich au fromage/3,96 €

Student A: Combien coûte le sandwich au fromage?

Student B: Il coûte trois euros quatre-vingt-seize.

Voilà les desserts. (Angers)

Non, les deux cafés coûtent cinq euros.

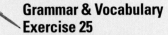

Answers

6 1. Combien coûte le jus de pomme?
   Il coûte deux euros soixante-quatorze.
2. Combien coûte l'omelette?
   Elle coûte quatre euros vingt-sept.
3. Combien coûte le steak-frites?
   Il coûte six euros dix.
4. Combien coûte la salade?
   Elle coûte trois euros cinquante et un.
5. Combien coûte l'eau minérale?
   Elle coûte trois euros vingt.
6. Combien coûte le café?
   Il coûte deux euros quatre-vingt-dix.
7. Combien coûte la crêpe?
   Elle coûte quatre euros cinquante-sept.
8. Combien coûte la glace à la vanille?
   Elle coûte quatre euros quatre-vingt-huit.

Teacher's Notes

1. Point out that the **s** of **les** and **des** is silent before a consonant sound and pronounced [z] before a vowel sound. 2. If you have pictures of the foods and beverages from this unit, you might show them to the class. If you show one food or beverage item, students say **Voilà** followed by the appropriate singular definite article and the name of the item. If you show two foods or two beverages, students say **Voilà** followed by the plural definite article and the names of the items.

NATIONAL STANDARDS
C1.1, C1.2, C2.1, C2.2, C4.1

Audiocassette/CD Activities 7-8

Answers

7 1. Il aime les sandwichs.
2. Elle aime les desserts.
3. Il aime les boissons.
4. Il aime les sports.
5. Il aime les films.
6. Elle aime les fast-foods.

8 Answers will vary.

9 1. Combien coûtent les deux jus de pomme? Ils coûtent cinq euros quarante-huit.
2. Combien coûtent les trois cafés? Ils coûtent sept euros trente-deux.
3. Combien coûtent les deux salades? Elles coûtent six euros soixante-dix.
4. Combien coûtent les deux quiches? Elles coûtent six euros quarante.
5. Combien coûtent les trois sandwichs? Ils coûtent dix euros cinquante-trois.
6. Combien coûtent les deux crêpes? Elles coûtent six euros dix.
7. Combien coûtent les trois glaces? Elles coûtent six euros quatre-vingt-sept.

Teacher's Note

In Activity 7 students apply their knowledge by using higher order thinking skills.

TPR

Singular or Plural?

Say a series of sentences containing singular or plural articles, such as **Voilà les salades** or **Voilà des salades,** and have students raise their left hand if they hear a singular article or their right hand if they hear a plural article.

NATIONAL STANDARDS
C1.1, C1.2, C2.2

86

Pratique

Modèle:

Sandrine désire une eau minérale et un café.
Elle aime les boissons.

7 Make a generalization about what each person likes.

1. André mange un sandwich au fromage et un sandwich au jambon.
2. Janine désire une glace et deux crêpes.
3. Khaled aime le jus de raisin et le coca.
4. Luc joue au foot et au tennis.
5. David aime *Aladdin* et *Dracula*.
6. Delphine n'aime pas les cafés. Elle préfère aller au Quick ou au Macdo.

Moi? J'aime beaucoup les sports!

Modèle:

hamburgers/steak
Student A: **Tu aimes les hamburgers?**
Student B: **Oui, j'aime les hamburgers. Tu aimes le steak?**
Student A: **Non, je n'aime pas le steak.**

8 Find out what your partner likes to eat. Ask each other if you like the indicated foods.

1. quiche/omelettes
2. sandwichs/salade
3. hot-dogs/jambon
4. pizza/frites
5. crêpes/glace
6. chocolat/raisins
7. pommes/oranges

Tu aimes le jambon?

Modèle:

3 cocas
Student A: **Combien coûtent les trois cocas?**
Student B: **Ils coûtent huit euros soixante-dix.**

9 With a partner, play the roles of a customer and a server at the Café Alexandre. Student A gets the receipt for the entire table. Because the receipt shows only the total price of the food and beverages ordered, Student A asks how much certain things cost. Student B answers these questions according to his or her handwritten list.

3 cocas @ 2,90 €	8,70 €
2 jus de pomme @ 2,74 €	5,48 €
3 cafés @ 2,44 €	7,32 €
2 salades @ 3,35 €	6,70 €
2 quiches @ 3,20 €	6,40 €
3 sandwichs @ 3,51 €	10,53 €
2 crêpes @ 3,05 €	6,10 €
3 glaces @ 2,29 €	6,87 €

1. 2 jus de pomme
2. 3 cafés
3. 2 salades
4. 2 quiches
5. 3 sandwichs
6. 2 crêpes
7. 3 glaces

10 Based on their orders, tell what each pair of café customers wants to eat or drink.

1. Mme Montand: Je voudrais une glace au chocolat, s'il vous plaît.
   Mme Arnaud: Et moi, je voudrais une glace à la vanille.

2. Anne: Donnez-moi une crêpe, s'il vous plaît.
   Sara: Et pour moi, une glace.

3. Dikembe: Donnez-moi un sandwich au jambon, s'il vous plaît.
   Lamine: Et moi, je voudrais un sandwich au fromage.

4. Marie: Donnez-moi un café, s'il vous plaît.
   Daniel: Et moi, je voudrais une eau minérale.

Communication

11 Picture what the menu of a small neighborhood café would look like. Create this menu in French, including at least seven beverages and ten food items, each with a price indicated in euros. Give your café a French name. One idea would be to use the word **chez** (meaning "the place of") plus your French name.

12 It's a law in France that all cafés and restaurants must post their menus outside for customers to see. You and your classmates should take the menus you made in Activity 11 and attach them to the walls in your classroom. Imagine that each menu is posted outside a different café in France. You and your partner have decided to go to a café for something to eat and drink. Walk around your classroom, noting menu prices and picking a café to eat at.

> Ça fait deux euros quarante-quatre.

> Et le jus d'orange, Monsieur?

1. Look at the menu of one of the cafés. You and your partner each name one beverage and one food item from the menu and say the prices. Do this for a total of five café menus.

2. After noting the prices at the five cafés, you and your partner each suggest one café to go to.

3. Agree on one café and go there.

Modèle:

Sophie: Je voudrais un coca, s'il vous plaît.
Jérémy: Donnez-moi une limonade, s'il vous plaît.

Sophie et Jérémy désirent des boissons.

> Donnez-moi une crêpe au chocolat, s'il vous plaît.

Modèle:

Bruno: Voyons... la limonade - deux euros cinquante-neuf, le sandwich au fromage - trois euros soixante-six.

Théo: Le jus d'orange - deux euros quarante-quatre, la glace au chocolat - un euro quatre-vingt-onze.

Bruno et Théo: (Name beverages, food items and their prices at four other cafés.)

Bruno: Alors, allons au café Chez Patricia!

Théo: Moi, je préfère aller au café Chez Christophe.

Bruno: D'accord. Allons-y!

 Audiocassette/CD Activity 10

Answers

10 1. Mme Montand et Mme Arnaud désirent des glaces.
2. Anne et Sara désirent des desserts.
3. Dikembe et Lamine désirent des sandwichs.
4. Marie et Daniel désirent des boissons.

Comparisons

Plurals

You might hold a class discussion in which you ask students to compare how we hear plurals in French (by listening for **les** instead of **le, la** or **l'**) and how we hear them in English (by listening for the sound [s] at the end of a noun).

Cooperative Group Practice

Scrambled Sentences

Write a series of scrambled sentences on an overhead transparency. Each sentence should contain at least one plural noun. (For example, **coûtent/les/euros/glaces/10/deux**.) Put students in small groups and have them unscramble each sentence as you uncover it on the transparency. Students can either say the reordered sentence or write it out. (To vary this exercise, you can write out these scrambled sentences on one slip of paper each and then cut each sentence up into single words. Distribute a set of cutout sentences to each group. The first group to put each sentence together correctly gets one point.)

NATIONAL STANDARDS
C1.1, C1.2, C2.2, C4.1, C5.1

**Workbook
Activity 19**

 Audiocassette/CD
Sur la bonne piste

Listening Activity 3A

Quiz
Leçon C

**Computer Software
Activity 6**

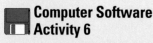
Teacher's Notes

1. You may have students read the text either silently in class or as homework. 2. You might mention to students that the word **thé** in the reading looks like the English word "the," but because it is listed with **café** and **coca**, you might assume that it is some sort of beverage. Considering this, the word "tea" would make more sense. 3. Ask students if they think that **addition** is a cognate or a false cognate. Taken out of context, it looks like a math term. But here it makes sense that the **serveur** may "add" up the "bill" (**addition** meaning "bill"). It becomes clear that paying attention to the context or big picture of a reading will help make smaller units like sentences and words make more sense. 4. There is a problem with making general statements about cognates and false cognates. What is a cognate for one person may not be a cognate for another. Some people may recognize a word because they have read more or different things in English than other people have. Even though people may disagree on whether some words are cognates, it is important to recognize the fact that cognates are still a powerful tool in understanding a new language.

NATIONAL STANDARDS
**C1.1, C1.2, C2.1, C2.2,
C3.1, C4.1, C4.2**

Modèle:

Serveur:	Bonjour, Messieurs-Dames. Vous désirez?
Bruno:	Je voudrais une limonade et un sandwich au fromage.
Théo:	Donnez-moi un jus d'orange et une glace au chocolat, s'il vous plaît.

Bruno:	La limonade, ça fait combien, Monsieur?
Serveur:	Ça fait deux euros cinquante-neuf.
Théo:	Et le jus d'orange?
Serveur:	Ça fait deux euros quarante-quatre.
Bruno:	Voilà. Merci.
Théo:	Et voilà. Merci.
Serveur:	Je vous en prie.

13 With two of your classmates, play the roles of two customers at a sidewalk café and the server who waits on them. The server asks what the customers would like, and each one tells the server the food item and the beverage that he or she wants. After the customers finish eating, they are ready to pay, but they have some questions about the bill. In the course of the conversation:

1. The server greets the two customers and asks what they would like.
2. Each customer orders something to eat and drink.
3. After they finish eating, the customers are ready to pay their bill, but they notice that the two beverages have been omitted. Since both customers have forgotten the beverage prices, they ask the server to repeat them.
4. The server gives the price of each beverage.
5. Each customer pays his or her share of the bill and thanks the server.
6. The server says you're welcome.

Sur la bonne piste

When reading, you naturally encounter new words. As you read in French, try not to look up the words you don't know in a dictionary. Instead, try to make sense of the reading as a whole by identifying cognates. "Cognate" is related to the word "recognize." If you recognize a word in French because there is a similar word in English, it may be a cognate. For instance, the words **invitation, table** and **café** are direct cognates; they mean the same thing in French as they do in English. For many people, the French word **préfère** looks enough like the English word "prefer" that they can quickly understand the sentence **Je préfère le chocolat**. The words **histoire** and **cours** are more or less direct cognates, although some people might not immediately recognize **histoire** as "history" or **cours** as "course." Unfortunately, there are words in French that are false cognates. A false cognate is a French word that looks like an English word but means something quite different. For example, the word **but** in French means "goal." **Chose** in French is not a verb ("to choose") but a "thing."

Here are two hints to help you make more educated guesses about possible cognates. 1) For words that contain a letter with a circumflex (^), imagine that there is an "s" that replaces or follows that letter. For example, if you add an "s" to the French word **coûter**, it starts to look like the English word "cost." 2) For French words that begin with an é, replace the é with an "s" to discover what the word means in English. For example, **école** means "school." Read the conversation that follows, remembering to pay attention to the title, the context, the order of sentences and possible cognates.

Au café

Isabelle rencontre son copain Michel à l'école.

— Salut, Michel. Ça va?

— Bien.

— Tu vas au café maintenant?

— Non, j'ai un cours.

Michel n'accepte pas l'invitation. Il va à son cours d'histoire. Isabelle a faim et elle va au café Printemps pour déjeuner.

À la terrasse du café Printemps, le serveur arrive à sa table.

— Qu'est-ce que vous désirez, Mademoiselle?

— Je ne sais pas. Qu'est-ce qu'il y a aujourd'hui?

— Des steaks-frites, des crêpes au jambon et au fromage, une belle salade niçoise, de la soupe du jour, des sandwichs....

— Combien coûtent les sandwichs?

— Trois euros quatre-vingt-un.

— Je voudrais un sandwich au thon, aux œufs et au maïs, avec de la mayonnaise, s'il vous plaît. Et puis, comme j'ai soif aussi, je prendrais....

— Du thé? Du café? Du coca? Une eau minérale? Un jus d'orange?

— Je voudrais un coca, s'il vous plaît, et une glace au chocolat. Merci!

Après le déjeuner, le serveur lui apporte l'addition.

— Ça fait combien?

— Ça fait six euros quatre-vingt-six.

— Voilà sept euros. Merci, Monsieur.

— À votre service, Mademoiselle.

Après son cours, Michel rencontre son amie Isabelle devant le café. Quelle bonne surprise!

---

14 Make a list of all the words that you encountered in the reading that are cognates. If the French word is not spelled the same as its English counterpart, write the English word next to it.

Nathalie et Raoul

Answers

14 Possible answers: (Remember that what is a cognate for one student may not be a cognate for another.)

café, **rencontre** reencounters, **copain** companion, **école** school, **salut** salutations, **non** no, **cours** course, **accepte** accept, **invitation**, **histoire** history, **faim** famished, **printemps** springtime, **terrasse** terrace, **serveur** server, **arrive** arrives, **table**, **désirez** desire, **steaks-frites** steak and fries, **crêpes**, **salade** salad, **soupe** soup, **sandwichs** sandwiches, **coûtent** cost, **euros**, **thon** tuna, **mayonnaise**, **plaît** please, **thé** tea, **café** coffee, **coca** Coke, **minérale** mineral, **jus d'orange** orange juice, **chocolat** chocolate, **addition** bill, **service**, **surprise**

Teacher's Notes

1. You may want students to work on Activity 14 in groups of four.
2. Optional activity. You might have students answer the following questions after finishing the reading: A. What are some foods and beverages that Isabelle could order at the café? B. How much does Isabelle's meal cost? C. Whom does she run into after eating? D. Are Michel and Isabelle friends? E. Why does Isabelle go to the café alone? F. How is the weather? You may want students to work on this activity in pairs. The first three questions have specific answers. However, there is still some room for subjectivity. For example, students may choose foods other than those in the reading. For the last three questions, students should be encouraged to come up with a variety of answers.

NATIONAL STANDARDS
C1.2, C3.1, C4.1, C4.2, C5.2

Listening Activity 3B

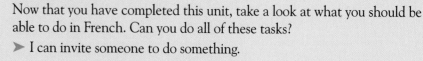

Answers

1. faux
2. vrai
3. faux
4. vrai
5. vrai
6. vrai
7. faux
8. vrai
9. vrai

Teacher's Note

Here is the English version of the cartoon on page 89: (Raoul poses as a reporter in order to talk to Nathalie.) My name is Raoul Robert. I'm a reporter for the school newspaper. Would you like to answer five questions? OK! Good! Question number one: Do you like to play sports? Yes, I really like to swim and to go in-line skating. Me, too! Question number two: Do you like going to fast-food restaurants? Yes, I like hamburgers and French fries a lot. Me, too! Question number three: Do you like rock? A little, but I prefer jazz. Not me. Question number four: Do you prefer boys . . . like Thomas? I prefer boys . . . like you. Wow! Well then, what are you going to do this weekend? I'd like to go to the movies. With whom? That's question number six. But the answer? With you, Raoul!

C'est à moi!

Now that you have completed this unit, take a look at what you should be able to do in French. Can you do all of these tasks?

➤ I can invite someone to do something.
➤ I can accept or refuse an invitation.
➤ I can order something to eat and drink.
➤ I can ask for and state the price of something.
➤ I can ask what time it is and tell time on the hour.
➤ I can ask people how they are and tell them how I am.
➤ I can say whether I'm hungry or thirsty.

Here is a brief checkup to see how much you understand about French culture. Decide if each statement is true (**vrai**) or false (**faux**).

1. Because France has strict rules about eating balanced meals, fast-food restaurants are not allowed in the country.
2. French families usually buy fresh bread and vegetables daily.
3. French fries originated in France.
4. Vichy, Perrier and Évian are popular brands of mineral water.
5. Crêpes resemble thin pancakes and can be filled with jam or with butter and sugar.
6. French cafés post their menus outside.
7. The French usually eat a salad before they begin their meat and vegetable course.
8. **Service compris** means that a service charge or tip is included in the price of the food and beverages.
9. **L'euro** is the basic unit of French money.

Communication orale

Imagine that the French classes in your school are planning to set up and run various French cafés for the upcoming International Day. Besides your classmates and other students, parents and community members (some of whom speak French) will also be coming to the event. You want to prepare and practice typical café conversations before the big day. With a partner, play the roles of a server and a customer. During the course of your brief practice conversation:

1. Greet each other in French.
2. Ask how each other is and respond.
3. The server asks the customer what he or she would like.
4. The customer orders something to eat and drink as well as something for dessert.
5. After the server brings the order and the customer finishes the meal, the customer asks the server how much it costs.
6. The server gives the price of each item and the total.
7. The customer says how much he or she is giving to cover the bill and tip.
8. The server thanks the customer.
9. Tell each other good-bye.

Communication écrite

To prepare for International Day and the cafés that you and other students are going to set up, divide into small groups. Each group will operate a café from one of the various regions of France. The menu of each café will reflect the types of food that are representative of that region. Begin by choosing a region of France and then, with members of your group, do research on what specific dishes come from that region. Next, determine a name for your café. Then design and write a menu that lists the food and beverages your café will serve, making the choices as authentic as you can for your region of France. Also give prices of the items in euros. To be as realistic as possible, find the current rate of exchange for the euro. (You can check the *Wall Street Journal* or other newspapers in your school library, or you may call a bank to learn the latest exchange rate.) Put that rate at the bottom of your menu so that your customers will be able to understand what their bill will be in dollars.

Communication active

To invite someone to do something, use:
On va au café? — *Shall we go to the café?*
Allons-y! — *Let's go (there)!*

To accept an invitation, use:
D'accord. — *OK.*

To refuse an invitation, use:
Moi, je préfère aller au fast-food. — *I prefer going to the fast-food restaurant.*

To order food and beverages, use:
Je voudrais une salade, **s'il vous plaît.** — *I would like a salad, please.*
Donnez-moi un café, **s'il vous plaît.** — *Give me (a cup of) coffee, please.*

To ask for a price, use:
Ça fait combien? — *How much is it/that?*

To state a price, use:
Ça fait trois **euros.** — *That's/It's 3 euros.*
Ça coûte neuf **euros** quinze. — *That costs 9,15 euros.*

To ask what time it is, use:
Quelle heure est-il? — *What time is it?*

To tell time on the hour, use:
Il est trois **heures.** — *It's three o'clock.*
Il est midi. — *It's noon.*
Il est minuit. — *It's midnight.*

To ask how someone is, use:
Comment vas-tu? — *How are you?*
Comment allez-vous? — *How are you?*

To tell how you are, use:
Très bien. — *Very well.*
Bien. — *Well.*
Pas mal. — *Not bad.*
Mal. — *Bad.*
Comme ci, comme ça. — *So-so.*
J'ai faim. — *I'm hungry.*
J'ai soif. — *I'm thirsty.*

Communication électronique

1. This restaurant is located in Béziers.
2. The three main types of sandwichs are hamburgers, chicken and fish.
3. Mustard, ketchup, pickles and onions are on a hamburger.
4. There are five types of salad.
5. Some dessert choices that are not normally found in an American fast-food restaurant include fruit salad, gosette and mousse au chocolat.
6. The fries and the beverage are supersized.
7. Answers will vary.

À moi de jouer!

Possible conversation:
— Bonjour, Messieurs-Dames. Vous désirez?
— Je voudrais un sandwich au fromage et un coca, s'il vous plaît.
— Et pour vous, Monsieur?
— Je voudrais un sandwich au jambon, une glace et un jus d'orange, s'il vous plaît.
— Et pour vous, Monsieur?
— Je voudrais un hot-dog et une eau minérale, s'il vous plaît.
— Ça fait combien, Monsieur?
— Voyons, pour Mademoiselle, le sandwich au fromage... quatre euros vingt et le coca... trois euros dix. Ça fait sept euros trente. Pour Monsieur, le sandwich au jambon... quatre euros trente, la glace... trois euros quatre-vingts et le jus d'orange... deux euros quatre-vingt-quinze. Ça fait onze euros cinq. Et pour Monsieur, le hot-dog... trois euros et l'eau minérale... trois euros vingt-cinq. Ça fait six euros vingt-cinq.
— Voilà vingt-cinq euros. Merci, Monsieur.
— Je vous en prie.

Communication électronique

If you were in France and wanted to eat at a fast-food restaurant, where would you go? You know that American fast-food chains can be found throughout the country, but do you remember the names of some French equivalents? Quick is one of the popular French fast-food chains. Do you think the choices and quality of food as well as the prices would be similar to what we have in the United States?

To see what one Quick restaurant offers, go to this Internet site:

http://www.quickbeziers.cjb.net/

After you have finished exploring this site, answer the following questions.

1. In which French city is this Quick restaurant located?
2. Click on "Les Produits." What are the three main types of sandwichs at Quick?
3. Now click on "Hamburger." What comes on a hamburger?
4. How many types of salad are available?
5. What are some of the dessert choices that are not normally found in an American fast-food restaurant?
6. Return to the home page and click on "Les Menus." If you order one of the "Menus XL," what is supersized?
7. What would you order at this Quick?

À moi de jouer!

With three of your classmates, see how many expressions from this unit you can use in writing a dialogue and then role-playing this scene in which three teenagers choose, order and pay for something to eat and drink at a French café. (You may want to refer to the *Communication active* on page 91 and the vocabulary list on page 93.)

Vocabulaire

allons-y let's go (there)

une **boisson** drink, beverage

ça that, it
    Ça fait.... That's/It's . . . .
    Ça fait combien? How much is it/
    that?
un **café** café; coffee
cent (one) hundred
le **chocolat** chocolate
cinquante fifty
un **coca** Coke
combien how much
comme like, for
    comme ci, comme ça so-so
comment how
    Comment vas-tu? How are you?
coûter to cost
une **crêpe** crêpe

déjà already
des some
désirer to want
    Vous désirez? What would you like?
un **dessert** dessert
donner to give
    Donnez-moi.... Give me . . . .

l' **eau (f.)** water
    l'eau minérale (f.) mineral water
est is

la **faim: J'ai faim.** I'm hungry.
fait
    Ça fait.... That's/It's . . . .
un **fast-food** fast-food restaurant
un **franc** franc
des **frites (f.)** French fries
le **fromage** cheese

une **glace** ice cream
    une glace à la vanille vanilla ice
    cream
    une glace au chocolat chocolate ice
    cream

un **hamburger** hamburger
l' **heure (f.)** hour, time, o'clock
    Quelle heure est-il? What time is it?
un **hot-dog** hot dog

le **jambon** ham
le **jus d'orange** orange juice
le **jus de pomme** apple juice
le **jus de raisin** grape juice

une **limonade** lemon-lime soda

mal bad, badly
Messieurs-Dames ladies and gentlemen
midi noon
minuit midnight

une **omelette** omelette
une **orange** orange
ou or

une **pomme** apple
prie: Je vous en prie. You're welcome.

quarante forty
quatre-vingt-dix ninety
quatre-vingts eighty
quel, quelle what, which
une **quiche** quiche

un **raisin** grape

s'il vous plaît please
une **salade** salad
un **sandwich** sandwich
    un sandwich au fromage cheese
    sandwich
    un sandwich au jambon ham
    sandwich
un **serveur, une serveuse** server
la **soif: J'ai soif.** I'm thirsty.
soixante sixty
soixante-dix seventy
un **steak** steak
    un steak-frites steak with French fries

toi you
trente thirty
très very

une a, an, one

voilà here is/are, there is/are
voudrais would like
voyons let's see

Unité 4

À l'école

In this unit you will be able to:

> express need

> ask what something is

> identify objects

> tell location

> ask for information

> give information

> agree and disagree

> express emotions

> describe daily routines

> invite

> state exact time

NATIONAL STANDARDS
C2.1, C2.2

Grammar & Vocabulary
Exercises 1-3

Audiocassette/CD
À l'école

Transparencies 15-16

Teacher's Notes

1. Other kinds of pens are **un stylo à bille** (*ballpoint*), **un stylo à plume** (*cartridge pen*) and **un stylo à encre** (*fountain pen*). Many French students use fountain pens. 2. The paper in French notebooks looks like graph paper, not like the lined paper used in American notebooks. 3. Instead of using the word **une stéréo**, many French speakers say **une chaîne**, which refers to **une chaîne stéréo**. 4. You may want to point out to students that **tableau** and **bureau** form their plurals by adding an **x**. 5. Review the words **les devoirs** and **la télé** that students learned in **Unité 2**. 6. Teenagers often refer to **un sac à dos** as simply **un sac**. 7. You may prefer to teach the word **une horloge** instead of **une pendule**. 8. Another word for **une affiche** is **un poster**. 9. Another computer-related word is **un clavier** (*keyboard*). A French keyboard is different from an American one. In France the letters AZERTY are the top letters on the left-hand side of the keyboard. 10. The command form **Montrez-moi** (*Show me*) is presented here as a lexical item. The command structure will be explained in **Unité 9**. 11. The words **un prof** and **une prof** are used in informal situations to refer to a male and a female teacher, respectively. The more formal word **un professeur** is always masculine even though it may refer to a female teacher. **Un proviseur** or **une directrice** is a principal, and **un professeur principal** is a homeroom teacher. 12. A communicative function that is recycled in this lesson is "agreeing and disagreeing."

NATIONAL STANDARDS
C1.2, C4.1

96

Leçon A

In this lesson you will be able to:

➤ **express emotions**

➤ **express need**

➤ **ask for information**

➤ **tell location**

➤ **ask what something is**

➤ **identify objects**

C'est une école.

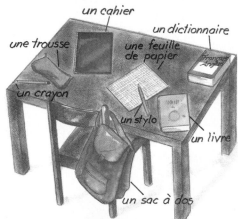

un cahier
un dictionnaire
une trousse
une feuille de papier
un crayon
un stylo
un livre
un sac à dos

C'est un professeur.
C'est un prof.

C'est une élève. C'est un élève

C'est un professeur.
C'est une prof.

C'est un étudiant. C'est une étudiante.

Montrez-moi une fenêtre.

Voilà une fenêtre.

une carte

une pendule

une affiche

une télé

un magnétoscope

une fille   un garçon

un tableau

une porte

un bureau

une stéréo

une corbeille

une vidéocassette

une disquette

une chaise

Qu'est-ce que c'est?

C'est un ordinateur.

un ordinateur

une fenêtre

un taille-crayon

une cassette

un CD

une salle de classe

Où est le livre de maths?

Dans le sac à dos.

Sur le sac à dos.   Sous le sac à dos.

Devant le sac à dos.   Derrière le sac à dos.   Avec le sac à dos.

Workbook Activity 1

Audiocassette/CD
Une salle de classe

Teacher's Notes

1. Other classroom items your students might like to learn the French names for are **un classeur** (*ring binder with pockets*), **un cahier d'exercices** (*workbook*), **une calculatrice** (*calculator*), **un lecteur de compact disc** (*CD player*), **un écouteur** (*headphone*), **un magnétophone** (*tape recorder*), **un morceau de craie** (*a piece of chalk*), **une table** (*table*), **une gomme** (*eraser*), **un trombone** (*paper clip*), **une agrafeuse** (*stapler*), **le scotch** (*adhesive tape*), **une machine à écrire** (*typewriter*) and **un carnet** (*small notebook*).
2. Other school-related expressions are **un terrain de sport** (*playing field*), **une bibliothèque** (*library*) and **un casier** (*locker*).

TPR

Montrez-moi....

Give students commands, such as **Montrez-moi un dictionnaire.** Students respond by pointing to a dictionary. (You may expand the activity by having students say **Voilà un dictionnaire** as they point to it. Or to avoid student verbalization, you might say **Voilà un dictionnaire**. If you have indicated a dictionary, students respond by giving the thumbs-up gesture. If you have not indicated a dictionary, they give the thumbs-down gesture.) As an alternate TPR activity, you might introduce the command **Mets** as a lexical item. You could give individual students commands, such as **Mets le crayon sur la chaise**. Students could then show comprehension by manipulating the objects as directed.

NATIONAL STANDARDS
C1.2, C4.1

Workbook Activity 2

Audiocassette/CD Dialogue

Teacher's Notes

1. Another word for **une interro** is **un quiz**. 2. The command form **étudions** (*let's study*) is presented here as a lexical item. 3. Younger students often carry **un cartable** (*book bag*), which is like a briefcase with a large flap that closes over the front.

Paired Practice

Qu'est-ce que c'est?

You might ask your students to make small drawings of items that are in their lockers, for example, **un crayon, un livre, un dictionnaire, une feuille de papier, un stylo, un cahier, une cassette, un CD, une disquette, une vidéocassette, un sac à dos, un taille-crayon, une affiche** and **une trousse.** Then have students cut out these items. Put students in pairs and have them take turns asking and answering the question **Qu'est-ce que c'est?** as they show one another each item they have cut out.

NATIONAL STANDARDS
C1.1, C1.2, C2.1, C3.1, C3.2

98

Où est le cahier?

Alexandre and Louis are doing homework together.

Alexandre:	**Zut! J'ai besoin d'étudier pour l'interro de maths, mais je n'ai pas le cahier. Où est le cahier de maths?**
Louis:	**Dans le sac à dos?**
Alexandre:	**Non, j'ai juste le livre de maths et la trousse dans le sac à dos.**
Louis:	**Tiens! Qu'est-ce que c'est?**
Alexandre:	**Quoi?**
Louis:	**Là, devant toi, sur le bureau.**
Alexandre:	**Oh, c'est le cahier de maths. Tant mieux. Bon ben, étudions!**

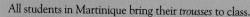

Enquête culturelle

French students often use **une trousse** to carry pens, pencils, rulers and other small school supplies. Students carry larger items in **un sac à dos.** In most French schools students do not have lockers; only teachers have a place to store their belongings.

All students in Martinique bring their *trousses* to class.

B
le sac à dos
19,67 €

Guide d'achat de LA RENTRÉE

Librairie Garneau

Just as you do, French speakers use short words to express strong emotion. For example, **zut!** shows disgust. You have already seen **eh!** and **tiens!** used to mean "hey!" when someone is surprised. Short French words are also used to fill pauses in conversations. For instance, **ben**, the shortened form of **bien**, means "well."

Many French schools are named after famous people, such as the rulers Henri IV, Saint Louis and Charlemagne. Although some buildings may be old, most of their facilities are very up-to-date.

Un élève refers to a male student; **une élève** refers to a female student. The words **un étudiant** and **une étudiante** traditionally refer to university students, but high school students like to use these terms to refer to themselves.

Would these girls refer to themselves as *élèves* or *étudiantes*?

1 | *Répondez en français.*

1. Qui étudie avec Alexandre?
2. Alexandre étudie pour l'interro de maths?
3. Le cahier de maths est dans le sac à dos?
4. Le livre de maths est dans le sac à dos?
5. Où est la trousse?
6. Où est le cahier de maths?

Answers

1 1. Louis étudie avec Alexandre.
2. Oui, Alexandre étudie pour l'interro de maths.
3. Non, le cahier de maths n'est pas dans le sac à dos.
4. Oui, le livre de maths est dans le sac à dos.
5. La trousse est dans le sac à dos.
6. Le cahier de maths est sur le bureau, devant Alexandre.

Comparisons

Cultural Journal

If your students are keeping a cultural journal, you might have them write answers to these questions: What is the name of your school? How did it get its name? Are any schools in your area named after famous people? If so, tell or find out three interesting facts about that person.

NATIONAL STANDARDS
C2.1, C3.1, C4.1, C4.2

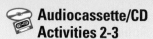

Audiocassette/CD Activities 2-3

Answers

2 1. C'est un tableau.
2. C'est un stylo.
3. C'est une carte.
4. C'est une prof./C'est un professeur.
5. C'est une chaise.
6. C'est un taille-crayon.
7. C'est un ordinateur.
8. C'est une feuille de papier.
9. C'est un élève./C'est un garçon.
10. C'est une porte.
11. C'est une fenêtre.
12. C'est un cahier.

3A. 1. Luc est sous le bureau.
2. Luc est devant le bureau.
3. Luc est derrière le bureau.
B. 1. La vidéocassette est dans le magnétoscope.
2. La vidéocassette est sur le magnétoscope.
3. La vidéocassette est avec le magnétoscope.

2 Identify each numbered person or object you see in the illustration.

Modèle:

C'est une pendule.

3 A. *Où est Luc?* Say where Luc is in relation to the teacher's desk.

Modèle:

Luc est sur le bureau.

1.   2.   3.

B. *Où est la vidéocassette?* Say where the videocassette is in relation to the VCR.

Modèle:

La vidéocassette est devant le magnétoscope.

1.   2.   3.

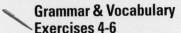

Workbook
Activities 3-4

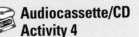

Grammar & Vocabulary
Exercises 4-6

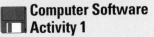

Audiocassette/CD
Activity 4

Computer Software
Activity 1

4 C'est à toi!

1. Tu étudies avec qui?
2. Tu aimes faire les devoirs?
3. Dans la salle de classe, qui est devant toi?
4. Dans la salle de classe, qui est derrière toi?
5. Qu'est-ce que tu préfères, un crayon ou un stylo?

le sac à dos
27,29 €

Structure

Present tense of the irregular verb *avoir*

The verb **avoir** (*to have*) is irregular.

avoir			
j'	ai	J'**ai** le cahier.	*I have the notebook.*
tu	as	Tu n'**as** pas la trousse?	*Don't you have the pencil case?*
il/elle/on	a	Luc **a** une heure de maths.	*Luc has one hour of math.*
nous	avons	Nous **avons** une interro.	*We have a quiz.*
vous	avez	Vous **avez** une feuille de papier?	*Do you have a sheet of paper?*
ils/elles	ont	Les Javert **ont** un ordinateur.	*The Javerts have a computer.*

Note the sound [z] in the plural forms of **avoir: nous‿avons, vous‿avez, ils‿ont, elles‿ont.**

J'ai une question, Madame.

J'ai
rendez-vous
avec vous.

Answers

5 1. Nous avons des stylos.
2. Daniel et Chloé ont des crayons.
3. Tu as des crayons.
4. Khaled a des crayons.
5. J'ai des stylos.
6. Les filles ont des stylos.
7. Vous avez des crayons.
8. Véro a des stylos.

6 1. Tu as deux livres et une trousse.
2. Ariane a deux disquettes, trois crayons et un taille-crayon.
3. Guillaume a deux cartes et quatre stylos.
4. J'ai un CD et deux cahiers.
5. Renée a deux stylos, trois cassettes et un dictionnaire.
6. Nicolas a deux vidéocassettes et une feuille de papier.

Cooperative Group Practice

Wagon Wheel

Have your students make small drawings of some items that are in their lockers and cut them out. Then have them form two circles with the same number of students in each circle, one inside the other. Students face their partner. Student A (in the inner circle) begins by asking Student B (in the outer circle) **Tu as un sac à dos?** If Student B has the requested item, he or she says **Oui, j'ai un sac à dos** and gives the drawing of it to Student A. If Student B does not have the requested item, he or she says **Non.** Then it's Student B's turn to ask Student A if he or she has a certain item. After both students have asked and answered questions, say **Changez.** Then the outside student moves one person to the right, setting up a new pair.

NATIONAL STANDARDS
C1.1, C1.2

102

Pratique

Modèles:

Jérémy

Jérémy a des crayons.

Diane et Anne-Marie

Diane et Anne-Marie ont des stylos.

5 | Tell whether the following students have pencils or pens in their pencil cases.

1. nous

2. Daniel et Chloé

3. tu

4. Khaled

5. je

6. les filles

7. vous

8. Véro

---

6 | Tell what the following students have in their backpacks.

Modèle:

Abdoul

Abdoul a deux cassettes et un cahier.

1. tu

2. Ariane

3. Guillaume

4. je

5. Renée

6. Nicolas

7 Your French class is going on a picnic today. Everyone who was supposed to bring food remembered. Unfortunately, everyone who was supposed to bring beverages forgot. Tell which people have what they were supposed to bring and which people don't.

1. Nicole et Olivier/la salade
2. vous/la limonade
3. nous/les hot-dogs
4. tu/le fromage
5. les garçons/le coca
6. je/les pommes
7. Michèle/la glace
8. le prof/l'eau minérale

Modèles:

Delphine et Saleh/les sandwichs
Delphine et Saleh ont les sandwichs.

Théo/le jus de pomme
Théo n'a pas le jus de pomme.

Expressions with *avoir*

You have already seen that forms of **avoir** are used in some French expressions where the verb "to be" is used in English. Two of these expressions are **avoir faim** (*to be hungry*) and **avoir soif** (*to be thirsty*).

J'ai faim. — *I'm hungry.*
Vous avez soif? — *Are you thirsty?*

To say that you need to do something or that you need something, use the expression **avoir besoin de** (*to need*). Remember that **de** becomes **d'** before a word beginning with a vowel sound.

Tu as besoin de téléphoner? — *Do you need to call?*
Oui, et j'ai besoin d'un euro. — *Yes, and I need a euro.*

Véro a besoin d'étudier.

Pratique

8 Tell whether the students and teachers in the school cafeteria are hungry or thirsty, based on what they have on their trays.

1. Théo et Nadia....

2. Nous....

3. Monsieur Bobot....

4. Yasmine....

5. Vous....

6. J'....

7. Les professeurs de maths....

8. Tu....

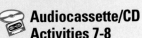
Workbook Activity 5

Grammar & Vocabulary Exercises 7-8

Audiocassette/CD Activities 7-8

Computer Software Activity 2

Answers

7 1. Nicole et Olivier ont la salade.
2. Vous n'avez pas la limonade.
3. Nous avons les hot-dogs.
4. Tu as le fromage.
5. Les garçons n'ont pas le coca.
6. J'ai les pommes.
7. Michèle a la glace.
8. Le prof n'a pas l'eau minérale.

8 1. ont faim
2. avons soif
3. a faim
4. a soif
5. avez faim
6. ai soif
7. ont soif
8. as faim

Teacher's Notes

1. To reinforce the expressions **avoir faim** and **avoir soif**, you may want to try an activity with flash cards, transparencies or pictures of the foods and beverages that were introduced in **Unité 3**. As you hold up a visual, students respond with either **J'ai faim** or **J'ai soif**, as appropriate.
2. Using the names of the school-related objects students have learned how to express in French, you might ask students whether or not they need certain items. For example, **Tu as besoin d'un dictionnaire? Oui, j'ai besoin d'un dictionnaire.**

NATIONAL STANDARDS
C1.1, C1.2, C4.1

Answers

9 1. Salim a besoin d'étudier?
Non, il n'a pas besoin d'étudier.
2. Paul et Charles ont besoin d'étudier?
Oui, ils ont besoin d'étudier.
3. Nora a besoin d'étudier?
Oui, elle a besoin d'étudier.
4. Christine et Sonia ont besoin d'étudier?
Non, elles n'ont pas besoin d'étudier.
5. Fatima a besoin d'étudier?
Non, elle n'a pas besoin d'étudier.
6. Éric a besoin d'étudier?
Oui, il a besoin d'étudier.
7. Jean-Philippe et Anne ont besoin d'étudier?
Non, ils n'ont pas besoin d'étudier.
8. Arabéa et Cécile ont besoin d'étudier?
Oui, elles ont besoin d'étudier.

Modèles:

Alexandre
Student A: Alexandre a besoin d'étudier?
Student B: Oui, il a besoin d'étudier.

Sophie et Karine
Student A: Sophie et Karine ont besoin d'étudier?
Student B: Non, elles n'ont pas besoin d'étudier.

9 Mme Vaillancourt's students have a test tomorrow. M. Messier's students are going on a field trip. With a partner, talk about who needs to study tonight. Student A asks questions and Student B answers them.

Les élèves de Mme Vaillancourt	Les élèves de M. Messier
Arabéa	Jean-Philippe
Charles	Fatima
Nora	Sophie
Alain	Christine
Éric	Salim
Paul	Sonia
Alexandre	Karine
Cécile	Anne

1. Salim
2. Paul et Charles
3. Nora
4. Christine et Sonia
5. Fatima
6. Éric
7. Jean-Philippe et Anne
8. Arabéa et Cécile

Communication

10 School supply stores are having their back-to-school sales. You decide to go shopping before classes begin to buy supplies that you know you will need this year. Make a list in French of what items you plan to buy.

Tu as besoin de quoi?

LIBRAIRIE - PAPETERIE
CARLIER
Beaux livres - Nouveautés - Articles cadeaux - "cuirs" - "stylos" - Menus - Faire-part...
61, rue Charles de Gaulle (grandes arcades) - 88200 REMIREMONT - Tél. 03.29.62.50.97

1 It is early in the school year, and your French teacher has passed out a list of supplies you need to bring to class tomorrow. You have checked off what you already have. After class you get together to compare lists with a classmate who has a different French teacher. Since you plan to go shopping with your classmate, compare what each of you has and what each of you needs to buy.

Modèle:

Student A: J'ai un dictionnaire. Et toi?

Student B: Moi, j'ai besoin d'un dictionnaire.

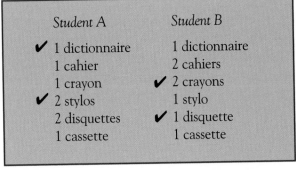

Student A	Student B
✔ 1 dictionnaire	1 dictionnaire
1 cahier	2 cahiers
1 crayon	✔ 2 crayons
✔ 2 stylos	1 stylo
2 disquettes	✔ 1 disquette
1 cassette	1 cassette

12 Write a paragraph in French in which you describe the people and items in your classroom and where they are located. For example, you might write **Le professeur, Madame Paquette, est devant le bureau.** Then, to check the accuracy of your description, find a partner and read your paragraphs to each other. As one of you reads, the other draws a picture illustrating the various people and items and their position in the classroom. After both of you have read your paragraphs and made sketches, compare them to see what similarities and differences you can find.

Prononciation

The sound [y]

The sound [y] of the French vowel **u** is similar, but not identical, to the sound of the first "u" in the English word "bureau." To make the sound [y], round your lips tightly and say the English sound "ew." Keep your mouth locked in one position and do not move your lips once the sound is made. Say each of these words:

     étudiant   musique   salut   juste   sur   pendule

The sound [u]

The sound [u] of the letters **ou** in French is similar to the sound "oo" in the English word "moo." To make the sound [u], keep your mouth locked in the "oo" position and do not move your lips once the sound is made. Say each of these words:

     jour   sous   cours   trousse   écoutons   vous

Audiocassette/CD
Prononciation

Listening Activity 1

Quiz
Leçon A

Teacher's Notes

1. After your students have completed Activity 12, you may want each set of partners to make a Venn diagram that shows the similarities and differences in their sketches. 2. To practice the sound [y] highlighted in this lesson, you might have students work on this tongue twister. They should say **As-tu vu le tutu de tulle de Lili d'Honolulu**? as fast as correct pronunciation will allow.

Cooperative Group Practice

Qui a...?

Put students in groups of four or five. Ask them to put on their desks at least three of the objects they learned how to express in French in this lesson. To begin, each student tells the others in the group what he or she has. For example, **J'ai deux crayons, un stylo, trois livres et trois cahiers**. Then, using as many different verb forms as possible, each person in the group says several sentences that tell what other group members have on their desks. For example, **Marie-Claire a un crayon. Jean et moi, nous avons trois livres. Daniel et Sylvie ont deux stylos.** This activity can be made more challenging by telling students that they may take notes as each one tells the others what he or she has. Next tell students to clear their desks or cover the objects they have listed orally. Then, using notes, each person in the group says as many sentences as possible that tell what other group members have. The people being talked about can verify the accuracy of each statement.

NATIONAL STANDARDS
C1.1, C1.2, C1.3, C4.1

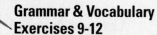

Workbook
Activities 6-9

Grammar & Vocabulary Exercises 9-12

Audiocassette/CD
Le Calendrier, Les cours, **Numbers 100-1,000**

Transparencies 17-18

NATIONAL STANDARDS
C1.1, C1.2

106

Leçon B

In this lesson you will be able to:

➤ **express emotions**

➤ **describe daily routines**

➤ **agree and disagree**

➤ **ask for information**

➤ **give information**

un calendrier

C'est quel jour?

lundi mardi mercredi jeudi vendredi samedi dimanche

une semaine

C'est vendredi.

Bonjour! | Hello! | Guten Tag! | ¡Hola!

le français | *l'anglais (m.)* | *l'allemand (m.)* | *l'espagnol (m.)*

Salve!

le latin | *la philosophie* | *l'histoire (f.)* | *la géographie*

1944 1789 1066 1918

la musique | *le dessin* | *le sport* | *les maths (f.)*

$(x+1)^2 = x^2 + 2x + 1$
$1/4 + 9/16 = 13/16$
$906 \div 6 = 151$

la biologie | *la physique* | *la chimie* | *l'informatique (f.)*

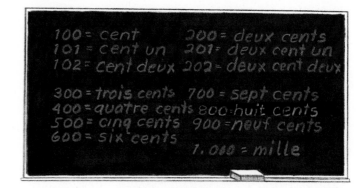

100 = cent	200 = deux cents
101 = cent un	201 = deux cent un
102 = cent deux	202 = deux cent deux
300 = trois cents	700 = sept cents
400 = quatre cents	800 = huit cents
500 = cinq cents	900 = neuf cents
600 = six cents	
	1.000 = mille

**Workbook
Activity 10**

**Audiocassette/CD
Dialogue**

Tu n'aimes pas les sciences?

Si, j'aime la biologie.

David is talking to Béatrice about his school schedule before their class begins.

David: **J'en ai marre! J'ai une heure de chimie le lundi, deux heures de physique le mardi et deux heures de biologie le samedi. Ça fait deux cent quarante minutes de sciences par semaine!**

Béatrice: **Tu n'aimes pas les sciences?**

David: **Si, j'aime la biologie, mais je n'aime pas la chimie.**

Béatrice: **Tiens, tu as juste un cours le mercredi?**

David: **Oui, géographie, de 9h00 à 10h00.**

Béatrice: **Tu finis à 10h00 le mercredi? Moi aussi.**

J'en ai marre! is a slang expression for "I'm sick of it!" or "I've had it!" Young French speakers frequently use slang when talking to friends and classmates.

Enquête culturelle

SEPTEMBRE

1	V	Gilles	16	S	Edith
2	S	Ingrid	17	D	Renaud
3	D	Grégoire	18	L	Nadège 38
4	L	Rosalie 36	19	M	Emilie
5	M	Raïssa	20	M	Davy Q.T.
6	M	Bertrand	21	J	Matthieu
7	J	Reine	22	V	Maurice
8	V	Nativité N.D.	23	S	AUTOMNE
9	S	Alain	24	D	Thècle
10	D	Inès	25	L	Hermann 39
11	L	Adelphe 37	26	M	Côme, Dam.
12	M	Apollinaire	27	M	Vinc. de Paul
13	M	Aimé	28	J	Venceslas
14	J	La Ste Croix	29	V	Michel
15	V	Roland	30	S	Jérôme

On French calendars the week traditionally begins with Monday. However, in Canada, Sunday is the first day of the week, just as it is in the United States. In French the names of days of the week usually are not capitalized.

J'en ai marre!

Teacher's Notes

1. Slang expressions, such as **J'en ai marre!** (*I'm sick of it! I've had it!*), are used idiomatically and usually aren't conjugated with different subject pronouns. 2. Tell your students that the word **le** before the name of a day of the week means "on" or "every." For example, **le lundi** means "on Monday" or "every Monday." 3. Point out to students that **si**, not **oui**, is the affirmative response to a negative question.

TPR

Les jours de la semaine

As a quick warm-up activity to practice the names of days of the week in French, you might say each day in French and have students stand if they like that day. You can vary this activity by calling out the days of the week again and having students stand if that day is their favorite (or least favorite) day.

Tic, Tic, Tic, Boom

Have each student take a sheet of paper, tear it into seven pieces, label each piece with a different day of the week in French and then place the seven small pieces of paper on his or her desk. You call out a day of the week (in French or in English). Then begin timing aloud by saying *Tic, Tic, Tic,* (etc.), *Boom*. Students who hold up the appropriate piece of paper within the time allotted earn one point. Students who hold up an incorrect piece of paper or no paper within the time allotted receive no points.

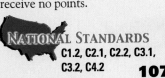

NATIONAL STANDARDS
C1.2, C2.1, C2.2, C3.1, C3.2, C4.2

107

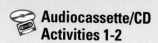
Answers

1 1. Le garçon est à l'école.
2. David est avec Béatrice.
3. David a 60 minutes de chimie par semaine.
4. Il a deux heures de biologie le samedi.
5. David aime la biologie, mais il n'aime pas la chimie.
6. Non, David a juste un cours le mercredi.

2 1. C'est lundi.
2. C'est samedi.
3. C'est jeudi.
4. C'est mardi.
5. C'est vendredi.
6. C'est dimanche.

Teacher's Note

Have your students say what day of the week precedes the one they see in Activity 2.

French high school students take certain required courses and some electives which relate to their specific area of study. Unlike most students in the United States, French students may take three courses in one subject area at the same time, for example, **la biologie, la chimie** and **la physique.** French students also study **la philosophie** and **la géographie,** subjects which are seldom offered in American high schools.

Jiro's favorite class is chemistry, but he also takes biology and physics.

In Canada, where people communicate in both French and English, the number of immersion schools grows steadily. Teachers conduct most or all classes in these schools in the language the student is learning. Immersion schools, in part, account for why many Canadians are bilingual.

1 | *Répondez en français.*

1. Où est le garçon?
2. David est avec qui?
3. David a combien de minutes de chimie par semaine?
4. Il a combien d'heures de biologie le samedi?
5. David aime les sciences?
6. David a trois cours le mercredi?

Serge et Daniel n'ont pas cours le mercredi.

2 | Say what day of the week follows the one you see.

1. dimanche
2. vendredi
3. mercredi
4. lundi
5. jeudi
6. samedi

Modèle:

mardi
C'est mercredi.

3 Marie-Ève is a 15-year-old girl who lives in France. Look at her **emploi du temps** (*schedule*) and then write the appropriate day (or days) of the week that matches each description.

Modèle:

Elle a musique.
le vendredi

EMPLOI DU TEMPS

heures	LUNDI	MARDI	MERCREDI	JEUDI	VENDREDI	SAMEDI
8h. - 9h.	Allemand	Géographie				
9h. - 10h.	Frs / E.E.	Mathématiques		Français	Sciences Naturelles	Latin (option)
10h. - 11h.	Mathématiques	Technologie		Français	Étude	Mathématiques
11h. - 12h.	Français			Latin (option)	Mathématiques	Sciences Physiques
12h. - 13h30	Repas	Étude		Étude	Anglais	Anglais
		Repas		Repas		
13h30 - 14h30	Étude	Allemand		Repas	Repas	
14h30 - 15h30	Sport	Anglais		Sciences Physiques	Allemand	
15h30 - 16h30	Histoire	Français		Latin (option)	Musique	
16h30 - 17h30	Dessin			Histoire	Sport	

1. Elle a juste quatre cours.
2. Elle a sport.
3. Elle n'a pas cours.
4. Elle a allemand.
5. Elle a histoire.
6. Elle n'a pas maths.
7. Elle a géographie.
8. Elle a anglais.
9. Elle a deux heures de français et deux heures de latin.

4 *C'est à toi!*

1. Tu préfères quel jour de la semaine?
2. Tu as combien d'heures de sciences par semaine?
3. Tu aimes un peu ou beaucoup les sciences?
4. Tu as combien de minutes de français par jour?
5. Tu as combien de cours le mercredi?

Audiocassette/CD Activity 4

Answers

3 1. le samedi
2. le lundi et le vendredi
3. le mercredi (et le dimanche)
4. le lundi, le mardi et le vendredi
5. le lundi et le jeudi
6. le jeudi (et le mercredi et le dimanche)
7. le mardi
8. le mardi, le vendredi et le samedi
9. le jeudi

4 Answers will vary.

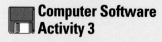

**Workbook
Activity 11**

**Grammar & Vocabulary
Exercises 13-18**

**Computer Software
Activity 3**

Answers

5 1. Tu finis la glace?
   Non, je ne finis pas la glace.
   Tu finis les frites?
   Non, je ne finis pas
   les frites.

2. Tu finis la quiche?
   Oui, je finis la quiche. Tu
   finis les raisins?
   Oui, je finis les raisins.

3. Tu finis le chocolat?
   Non, je ne finis pas le
   chocolat. Tu finis
   les pommes?
   Oui, je finis les pommes.

4. Tu finis le jambon?
   Oui, je finis le jambon. Tu
   finis le fromage?
   Non, je ne finis pas
   le fromage.

Teacher's Notes

1. Remind students that like present tense **-er** verb forms, each present tense **-ir** verb form consists of only one word in French but has more than one meaning in English. 2. You may want to point out that there are only four different oral forms of **finir**. 3. You might have students repeat after you the sentences in the chart. Be sure they pronounce **ss** as [s]. You might also do some exercises from affirmative to negative or from singular to plural. 4. Tell students that they will learn other regular **-ir** verbs (**choisir, obéir, réussir,** etc.) later on.

NATIONAL STANDARDS
C1.1, C1.2, C4.1

110

François finit les devoirs. (Martinique)

Modèle:

le steak/la salade
Student A: Tu finis le steak?
Student B: Oui, je finis le steak.
             Tu finis la salade?
Student A: Non, je ne finis pas
             la salade.

Structure

Present tense of regular verbs ending in -*ir*

The infinitives of many French verbs end in **-ir**. Most of these verbs, such as **finir** (*to finish*), are regular because their forms follow a predictable pattern. To form the present tense of a regular **-ir** verb, first find the stem of the verb by removing the **-ir** ending from its infinitive.

Now add the endings (**-is, -is, -it, -issons, -issez, -issent**) to the stem of the verb depending on the corresponding subject pronouns.

finir			
je	**finis**	Je **finis** le livre.	*I'm finishing the book.*
tu	**finis**	Tu **finis** à 10h00?	*Do you finish at 10:00?*
il/elle/on	**finit**	Le cours **finit** à midi.	*The class ends at noon.*
nous	**finissons**	Nous **finissons** les devoirs.	*We're finishing the homework.*
vous	**finissez**	Vous **finissez** à quelle heure?	*At what time do you finish?*
ils/elles	**finissent**	Les élèves ne **finissent** pas l'interro.	*The students don't finish the quiz.*

The final consonant of each form of **finir** is silent.

Pratique

5 Because you and your partner are the last two people to arrive for dinner, there is only a little bit of each type of food left. Student A likes only fruits and desserts. Student B likes everything but fruits and desserts. Determine who will finish what.

1. la glace/les frites
2. la quiche/les raisins
3. le chocolat/les pommes
4. le jambon/le fromage

Diane finit le sandwich au fromage?

6 A group of friends from school is meeting at a café at 3h30. David asks you who is going. Knowing that only those people who finish their last class of the day before 3h30 can go, answer his questions.

1. Et Catherine va au café? (5h00)
2. Et Laïla et toi, vous allez au café? (3h00)
3. Et Florence et Sabrina vont au café? (4h00)
4. Et Daniel va au café? (2h00)
5. Et André et Nicole vont au café? (3h00)
6. Et Max et moi, nous allons au café? (6h00)

Modèles:

Assane va au café? (2h00)
Oui, il finit à deux heures.

Et Élisabeth et Louis vont au café? (4h00)
Non, ils finissent à quatre heures.

Nous allons au café. Nous finissons à 2h30.

Communication

7 You want to know how much your classmates like various school subjects. Draw a grid like the one that follows. In the grid write the names in French of five common subjects. Then poll ten of your classmates to determine how much they like each subject. In your survey:

1. Ask each classmate if he or she likes each subject a lot, a little or not at all.
2. As each classmate answers your question, make a check by the appropriate response.
3. After you have finished asking questions, count how many people like each subject a lot, a little or not at all and be ready to share your findings with the rest of the class.

Modèle:

Henri: Tu aimes l'histoire?
Marie-Claire: J'aime beaucoup l'histoire.

. . . .

Henri: Six élèves aiment beaucoup l'histoire, trois élèves aiment un peu l'histoire et un élève n'aime pas l'histoire.

	beaucoup	un peu	ne...pas
Tu aimes l'histoire?	✔✔✔✔✔✔	✔✔✔	✔
Tu aimes...?			
Tu aimes...?			
Tu aimes...?			
Tu aimes...?			

Teacher's Note

You may want to have your students write a paragraph similar to the one Pierre-Jean has written in Activity 8 that describes their own weekly class schedules. Students can also record how many minutes they spend in each class and write the total number of minutes they spend in class each week.

Game

Verb Relay Race

As a review of **-er** verbs, **aller**, **avoir** and **finir**, you might play this game with your students. Put your students' desks in rows. Each row becomes a different team. As the first person from each row goes to the board, call out an infinitive and a pronoun subject, for example, **finir — nous**. The first person at the board to correctly write **nous finissons** earns one point for his or her team. Continue by calling out different infinitives and subjects for succeeding players. The team with the most points at the end of the game wins.

J'ai une heure de géographie à 15h00.

Modèle:

la chimie - trois cents minutes par semaine

8 You just received a letter from your French pen pal, Pierre-Jean, in which he describes his weekly class schedule. After reading his description, create on a separate sheet of paper his **emploi du temps** to show to your classmates and teacher. Here is the part of his letter in which he talks about his schedule.

J'ai dix cours différents par semaine. J'ai une heure de chimie le lundi à 10h00, de 10h00 à 12h00 le mardi et le jeudi, et de 9h00 à 10h00 le vendredi. Le lundi, le mardi, le mercredi, le jeudi et le samedi, j'ai une heure de maths à 9h00. Le français est de 14h00 à 15h00 le lundi et de 15h00 à 17h00 le jeudi. Le lundi, le mardi et le vendredi, j'ai une heure de géographie à 15h00. J'ai sport le mercredi de 14h00 à 17h00. J'aime beaucoup le sport! J'ai anglais de 10h00 à 11h00 le mercredi, le vendredi et le samedi, et j'ai une heure d'allemand le lundi et le mercredi à 11h00 et de 14h00 à 15h00 le vendredi. Le samedi à 11h00 j'ai une heure de musique. J'ai une heure de philosophie à 14h00 le mardi et le jeudi, et j'ai une heure d'histoire à 13h00 le lundi et à 11h00 le vendredi. Je finis à 12h00 le samedi.

9 Referring to the schedule you created in Activity 8, list in French the ten classes that Pierre-Jean has each week. Then figure out how many minutes he spends in each class and write this number in French words beside the appropriate class. Finally, write the total number of minutes he spends in class each week.

 ## Mise au point sur... l'enseignement secondaire en France

Métro, boulot, dodo!

"Métro, boulot, dodo!" This expression sums up how people who live in Paris describe their daily routine of taking the subway, going to work and then going to bed. This rhyme also describes the busy schedule of students, since education is a full-time job for French teenagers.

Secondary education begins when 11-year-olds enter **le collège**, or **C.E.S. (Collège d'Enseignement Secondaire)**. They stay here for four years: **sixième (6ème), cinquième (5ème), quatrième (4ème)** and **troisième (3ème)**. These years correspond to junior high school or middle school in the United States. (Note that the way of labeling school years is the opposite of the American system.)

COLLÈGE DE LA CATHÉDRALE ST MAURICE

collège de la Cathédrale St-Maurice

COLLEGE PRIVE - 6EME A 3EME
4E ET 3E TECHNOLOGIQUE
CLASSES AMENAGEES
MUSIQUE - CHANT - CHORALE
CLASSES DE PEDAGOGIE ADAPTEE

→ consultez l'Annuaire Electronique

2 r Jacobins
49000 Angers _ _ _ _ _ _ _ 02 41 87 48 42

Le collège begins with sixième and ends with troisième. Then students may go on to le lycée. (Créteil)

Since the public educational system is the same all over the country, all French students use similar textbooks, follow similar course schedules and take the same major tests. Students spend up to ten hours a day at school, since classes begin as early as 8:00 A.M. and sometimes continue as late as 6:00 P.M. However, all classes do not meet every day. For example, one day a student may have six classes, and another day just two; he or she may have history twice a week, French three times a week, and drawing once a week. Students have Wednesday afternoons off to study, play sports or meet friends. Some classes are held on Saturday mornings. Students must take a second language. They begin learning their first foreign language, usually English or German, in **sixième** and then add a second language a few years later. Teenagers usually have hours of homework to do every night.

At the end of **troisième**, students take their first big exam, **le brevet des collèges**. The results of this test do not affect entrance into high school (**le lycée**), but a high grade is naturally a morale boost. After four years at **le collège**, some students choose to go to a vocational school, while others who are academically inclined attend **le lycée**.

Laurent and André even do their homework on the bus.

COURS ALBERT CAMUS

Enseignement Secondaire Privé Mixte
de la 4ème aux baccalauréats

A B C D

ANNEE SCOLAIRE
COURS DE VACANCES

→ consultez l'Annuaire Electronique
Nom: COURS ALBERT CAMUS
Loc: NICE
Dpt: 06

70, avenue de la Californie
06200 NICE

04 93 37 16 76

Students go to **le lycée** in **seconde (2ème), première (1ère)** and **terminale**. Here they choose a major area of study in preparation for **le baccalauréat (bac)**, the national exam which usually determines whether or not students may continue their studies at a university. In **première**, students take the first part of **le bac**, which concentrates on the French language. The second half of **le bac**, given in **terminale**, focuses on each student's area of concentration.

NATIONAL STANDARDS
C1.2, C2.1, C2.2, C3.1, C3.2, C4.2

Cooperative Group Practice

Cultural Differences

Put your students in groups of four or five and have them discuss similarities and differences between French and American school systems. One person serves as each group's recorder and lists all the similarities and differences. After adequate discussion time, each group can appoint a spokesperson to share the group's list with the entire class.

Comparisons

Cultural Journal

If your students are keeping a cultural journal, you might have them write answers to these questions: French students often study philosophy, geography and several foreign languages, courses that are not always offered in American high schools. What are some courses that you would like to see offered at your school? Why would these courses be a good addition to your school's curriculum?

Different classes are often taught in the same classroom, so many rooms have bare walls.

A typical French **lycée** classroom is sparsely decorated. Students sit at tables instead of desks. Classroom instruction focuses on the teacher and textbook, with few of the visual aids seen on the walls of many American classrooms. Likewise, the relationship between teacher and students, which is often personal in the United States, is more formal in France.

As for grades, the French use a point system, with 20 points being the top score. Instead of an "A," a student might receive 18 out of 20. Teachers grade strictly and students are often happy when they get a score of 12 out of 20. Students need to have an overall average of 10 out of 20 to pass to the next grade, otherwise they must repeat it. Repeating a grade is fairly common in France: over half of the students in **le lycée** repeat at least one year of school. They may take **le bac** over if they don't pass it the first time, but if they fail a second time, they must repeat the whole school year.

SYNTHESE		
NOMS	*Moyenne Gén. Gént*	*classent*
GRANDJEAN Geoffroy	11,3	12ᵉ
HUSSON Gabrielle	13,4	1ᵉ
JOJOVIC Milan	11,8	7ᵉ
LEUVREY Christelle	11,8	7ᵉ
MANGEL Karine	12	4ᵉ

During the school day, students meet in the school courtyard or at lunch to talk with friends. A long lunch period in **la cantine** or **la caféteria** usually breaks up the school day. However, many students choose to leave the school grounds to have lunch in a café or at home. After school, teenagers may stop for **un goûter** (*afternoon snack*) at a sidewalk stand or for a beverage at a local café. Cocurricular activities generally take place away from school in France, and organized sports are less important in French **lycées** than they are in American high schools. Secondary schools are viewed as places to study and learn, and education is as important to teenagers as a job is to their parents.

Théo eats lunch every day in *la cantine*.

10 Answer the following questions.

1. What is junior high school called in France?
2. What is one similarity between French and American secondary schools?
3. What is one difference between French and American secondary schools?
4. What is the name of the test that students take at the end of **le collège**?
5. What is senior high school called in France?
6. What may French students do instead of attending a **lycée**?
7. Why is **le baccalauréat** so important?
8. What is one difference between French and American classrooms?
9. What overall score do students need to pass to the next grade?
10. Where might students go to eat lunch during the school day?

---

11 Michel goes to the **Collège Mongazon** in Angers. Look at his **bulletin de notes** (*report card*) for a three-week period and answer the questions that follow.

1. How many different courses did Michel take?
2. In what class did Michel receive the highest grade?
3. What were Michel's three scores in French composition?
4. What four languages did he take?
5. How many periods of science did Michel have?
6. What grade did Michel receive for his **leçons** (*lessons*) in art?
7. How many teachers signed the report card?
8. Was Michel an honor student?
9. The **appréciations** (*comments*), such as **très bien, bien, assez bien** (*fairly well*) and **vous pouvez mieux faire** (*you can do better*), show the teachers' opinions of Michel's efforts. What would your French teacher write about your efforts in class?
10. In what class did Michel do **assez bien**?

Institution mongazon
Collège et lycée
Classes préparatoires H.E.C.
Lycée technique privé
Externat et demi-pension
Internat : filles et garçons
1, rue du Colombier
49000 ANGERS   02 41 66 41 33

PÉRIODE DU _____ **AU** _____

Composition française	Leçons	Devoirs de contrôle	Autres devoirs	APPRÉCIATIONS
Composition française	14	16	15	
Orthographe Grammaire	17	17,5	18	C'est bien, Continuez.
Récitations	18	16	17	
Mathématiques	17,5	15,5	16	Bien, vous pouvez mieux faire.
Langue vivante I Anglais Allemand	17	19	18,5	Très bien.
Langue vivante II Anglais Allemand Espagnol	15,5	16	17,5	Bien, vous avez fourni des efforts.
Latin ou Grec ou langue renforcée	15	14,5	16	Bien, Continuez
Histoire Géographie	16	16	17	C'est bien. Apprenez plus la Géographie.
Biologie Géologie	17,5	15,5	16	C'est bien. Travaillez encore la Géologie
Sciences Physiques	18	15	17,5	Très bien.
Technologie	18	18	18	Très bien.
Dessin	17,5	17	17	
Musique	17	15,5	16	Assez bien
Education Physique	17	15	16	Continuez

Le Professeur Principal
Pr. De la Pastelle

TABLEAU D'HONNEUR   ENCOURAGEMENT

Les Parents

Grammar & Vocabulary Exercise 19

Audiocassette/CD
Quelle heure est-il?

Teacher's Note

Communicative functions that are recycled in this lesson are "giving information" and "agreeing and disagreeing."

TPR

Quelle heure est-il?

If your students have already made their own clocks, they can use them again in this lesson. (If not, have them make paper clocks as described in **Leçon A** of **Unité 3**.) As you say a certain time, students show you the time on their clocks by holding them up. (This activity can also be done in pairs with one partner saying the time and the other partner showing the time.)

NATIONAL STANDARDS
C1.2, C4.1

116

Leçon C

In this lesson you will be able to:

➤ **invite**

➤ **describe daily routines**

➤ **state exact time**

Il est une heure et quart.   *Il est deux heures et demie.*

Il est quatre heures moins le quart.

On finit à 12h40.

Nora and Patricia meet in the courtyard before school.

Nora: **On mange ensemble?**

Patricia: **Voyons, c'est vendredi. J'ai trois cours - musique, dessin et philosophie. Je finis à 12h30. On va à la cantine à 12h45?**

Nora: **D'accord. Tu as un bon emploi du temps.**

Patricia: **Mais c'est vendredi. Le lundi je commence à 8h00 et je finis à 17h30.**

Enquête culturelle

Many French-speaking countries use the 24-hour clock to give the times for TV programs, films, plays, sporting events, class schedules, plane and train schedules, etc. This 24-hour system eliminates the need for specifying A.M. or P.M. To convert the P.M. system to the 24-hour system, add 12 hours. For example, 3:00 P.M. is the same as 15h00. Conversely, to convert the 24-hour system to the P.M. system, subtract 12 hours.

France 3 13 mars **DIMANCHE**	
7.15 Bonjour les petits loups Les petits malins - 7.40 Les histoires du Père Castor - 7.55 Les aventures de Tintin: L'oreille cassée (4).	**13.00 Musicales** Elle s'appelle Anne Gastinel. La violoncelliste interprète *Concerto pour violoncelle et orchestre en la mineur opus 129* de Schumann.
8.00 Les Minikeums Le cristal magique - 8.25 Lucky Luke - 8.55 Les mondes fantastiques - 9.25 Les inventures des Minikeums - 9.35 Microkids.	**14.05 La croisière s'amuse** Série américaine. Rediffusion. L'amour de ses rêves.
10.05 C'est pas sorcier Drôles de savants et drôles de machines, avec Dominique Girard.	**14.55 Sport 3 dimanche** 15.05 Tiercé en direct d'Auteuil. 15.25 Cyclisme: Paris-Saint-Etienne-Nice, 8e et dernière étape - 16.35 Escrime: Challenge BNP, finale - 16.55 Athlétisme: Championnats d'Europe à Paris-Bercy.
10.30 D'un soleil à l'autre L'agriculture en Allemagne.	**17.50 Un commissaire à Rome** Série italienne inédite (2/9). Avec Nino Manfredi, Françoise Fabian, Dario Cantarelli, Sophie Carle. Secrets de bureau.
11.00 Mascarines Présenté par Gladys Says. 12.00 Flash 3 - Météo.	**19.00 19-20** 19.10 Le journal de la région.
12.05 Programme régional	**20.05 Yacapa** Avec Carlos, Annie Cordy, Brigitte Lahaie, Cendrine Dominguez, Georges Beller.
12.45 Le journal	XVII

To clarify the difference between A.M. and P.M., the French say **du matin** (*in the morning*), **de l'après-midi** (*in the afternoon*) and **du soir** (*in the evening*).

Workbook Activity 13

Audiocassette/CD *Dialogue*

Transparencies 19-21

Video

Teacher's Notes

1. You may want to point out that **une classe** means "classroom," **une matière** means "subject" and **un cours** means "course of study." 2. You might want to tell students that the **nous** form of the verb **commencer** is **commençons**. 3. If you have the opportunity to go to various train stations in France, try to collect sets of train schedules. Then, as a small group activity on the 24-hour system, give each group of students the same train schedule and have a contest to see which group can come up with the quickest route to get from one city to another.

Comparisons

Cultural Journal

If your students are keeping a cultural journal, you might have them write answers to these questions: Is being on time important to you? Why or why not? Do you like to follow a routine or do you prefer a varied schedule? When you invite someone to your house or apartment, how many minutes early is the earliest time that they should arrive? How many minutes late is the latest time that they should arrive? Do you think being late for an appointment or a date is rude or unimportant?

NATIONAL STANDARDS C1.2, C2.1, C2.2, C3.1, C3.2, C4.2   **117**

Answers

1 1. C'est vendredi.
   2. Patricia a trois cours.
   3. Patricia finit à 12h30.
   4. Nora et Patricia vont
      manger à la cantine.
   5. Patricia commence à 8h00
      le lundi.
   6. Patricia finit à 17h30
      le lundi.

3 Answers will vary.

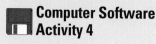
1. You may want to review with
your students the information
presented in the **Enquête
culturelle** of this lesson about the
use of the 24-hour clock. Remind
students that the 24-hour clock
uses only numbers for all times,
for example, **Il est douze heures
quarante-cinq** instead of **Il est
une heure moins le quart.** You
may also want to review briefly
the numbers in French up to 60.
2. Note that the adjective **demi**
is masculine following **midi** or
minuit but is feminine (**demie**)
after expressions using **heure(s)**.

1 | *Répondez en français.*

   1. C'est quel jour?
   2. Patricia a combien de cours?
   3. Patricia finit à quelle heure?
   4. Nora et Patricia vont manger où?
   5. Patricia commence à quelle heure le lundi?
   6. Patricia finit à quelle heure le lundi?

2 | Write your weekly **emploi du temps** in French. You may want to follow the
format of the schedule that appears on page 109. If you have courses for
which you don't know the French terms, ask your teacher or consult a
French dictionary.

3 | *C'est à toi!*

   1. Qu'est-ce que tu étudies à 9h00?
   2. Tu manges avec qui à midi?
   3. Tu manges à l'école?
   4. Tu as combien de cours le vendredi?
   5. Tu finis à 12h30 le vendredi?
   6. Qu'est-ce que tu aimes faire à 17h00?

Sandrine étudie le français
à 9h00.

Structure

Telling exact time

You have already learned how to ask what time it is and to tell time on the
hour in French.

Quelle heure est-il?	*What time is it?*
Il est dix heures.	*It's 10:00.*

To tell that it's quarter after the hour, add **et quart** or **quinze.**

Il est trois heures
et quart.

Il est huit heures **et quart.**	
Il est huit heures **quinze.**	*It's 8:15.*

To tell that it's half past the hour, add **et demi(e)** or **trente.**

Il est six heures
et demie.

Il est midi **et demi.**	*It's 12:30.*
Il est trois heures **et demie.**	
Il est trois heures **trente.**	*It's 3:30.*

To tell that it's quarter to the hour, add **moins le quart** before the next
hour or **quarante-cinq** after the hour.

Il est neuf heures
moins le quart.

Il est **six heures moins le quart.**	
Il est **cinq heures quarante-cinq.**	*It's 5:45.*

To tell that it's minutes after the hour but before the half hour, say the
number of minutes after the hour.

Il est **quinze heures vingt.**	*It's 3:20 P.M.*

To tell that it's minutes before the hour, say either **moins** and the number of minutes subtracted from the next hour or say the number of minutes after the hour. (With the increased use of digital clocks, it is becoming more and more common to express the time with minutes after the hour.)

> Il est quatre heures moins cinq.
> Il est trois heures cinquante-cinq. ⎱ *It's 3:55.*

To ask at what time something happens, use **à quelle heure**.

> On mange à quelle heure?   *At what time are we eating?*

Pratique

4   For each clock or watch, answer the question **Quelle heure est-il?**

1.

2.

3.

4.

5.

6.

7.

5   Because there is an assembly this afternoon, your school is on a special schedule. You and your partner have all the same classes. Student A, who doesn't know the special schedule, asks Student B if each class starts at a certain time. Student B, who *does* know today's schedule, answers.

1. le cours de biologie (8h30/8h40)
2. le cours de géographie (9h15/9h30)
3. le cours d'histoire (9h50/10h20)
4. le cours d'informatique (10h45/11h10)
5. le cours de maths (13h00/12h45)
6. le cours de français (13h25/13h35)

Modèle:

le cours d'anglais (8h00/7h50)

Student A: Le cours d'anglais commence à huit heures?

Student B: Non, il commence à huit heures moins dix.

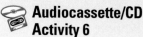

**Audiocassette/CD
Activity 6**

Answers

6 Answers will vary.

Paired Practice

Quelle heure est-il?

You might put your students in pairs to have them practice telling time. Have each partner draw five small rectangles on a sheet of paper and fill in five digital times that are not on the hour. Then students take turns pointing to their clocks, asking **Quelle heure est-il?** and answering accordingly. To vary this activity, you might have students use these same digital clocks as they take turns pointing to them, asking **Tu finis à quelle heure?** and answering accordingly.

Modèles:

Student A: Anne a deux cours de maths le lundi. Et toi?

Student B: Moi, j'ai juste un cours de maths le lundi.

Student B: Anne a latin le mardi de 8h00 à 9h00. Et toi?

Student A: Moi, je n'ai pas latin.

120

---

6   *C'est à toi!*

1. Tu arrives à l'école à quelle heure?
2. Tu as anglais à quelle heure?
3. Le cours d'anglais finit à quelle heure?
4. Tu vas à la cantine à quelle heure?
5. Tu finis à quelle heure le vendredi?
6. Tu préfères faire les devoirs à quelle heure?

> Je vais à la cantine à midi moins dix.

Communication

7   Anne Khoury, a classmate's French pen pal, has just faxed your class her school schedule. With a partner, look at this schedule and talk about what courses she takes, when they are, etc. Then compare Anne's weekly **emploi du temps** with your own. Take turns making a comment about one of Anne's courses and asking your partner if his or her schedule is the same.

EMPLOI DU TEMPS						
heures	**LUNDI**	**MARDI**	**MERCREDI**	**JEUDI**	**VENDREDI**	**SAMEDI**
8 à 9 h.	Histoire-Géo	Latin	Mathématiques	Mathématiques	Latin	Physique
9 à 10 h.	Histoire-Géo	Mathématiques	Mathématiques	Mathématiques	Anglais	
10 à 11 h.	Mathématiques	Mathématiques	Sport	Anglais	Physique	Sciences Naturelles
11 à 12 h.	Latin	Sciences Naturelles	Sport	Physique	Philosophie	
12 à 13 h.						
13 à 14 h.	Mathématiques			Espagnol	Mathématiques	
14 à 15 h.	Philosophie	Physique			Espagnol	
15 à 16 h.	Philosophie	Physique		Histoire-Géo	Mathématiques	
16 à 17 h.	Espagnol					

Anne a physique le mardi de 14h00 à 16h00, le vendredi de 10h00 à 11h00 et le samedi de 8h00 à 9h00.

You observe various signs in French-speaking countries that tell when places open and close, when trains or planes arrive and leave, etc. These times are usually given using the 24-hour system. Match each sign you see with the letter of its 12-hour system description.

1.

2.

3.

4.

5.

6.

7.

8.

a. quatre heures et quart
b. dix heures à six heures moins le quart
c. huit heures moins vingt
d. deux heures et demie

e. six heures cinq
f. sept heures
g. quatre heures moins cinq
h. onze heures moins douze

NATIONAL STANDARDS
C1.2

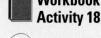
Workbook
Activity 18

Listening Activity 3A

Quiz
Leçon C

Computer Software
Activity 5

Answers

9 Possible answers:

1. douze heures trente
2. vingt heures
3. quatorze heures vingt
4. dix-huit heures
5. dix-sept heures
6. treize heures vingt-cinq
7. douze heures

10 Possible answers:

1. midi et demi
2. huit heures
3. deux heures vingt
4. six heures
5. cinq heures
6. une heure vingt-cinq
7. midi

Teacher's Note

Optional activity. To find out how your students feel about school, courses and leisure activities, have them complete the same questionnaire that the Tours students did, or have your students interview each other to gather this information. They could ask their classmates questions based on the items covered in the survey in the book, changing the subjects to **tu** and using appropriate verb forms with a rising intonation pattern. For example, **Tu as besoin d'étudier pour l'école? Oui, j'ai besoin d'étudier pour l'école./Non, je n'ai pas besoin d'étudier pour l'école.** At the end of the activity students might create a bar graph that gives the results of the survey visually.

NATIONAL STANDARDS
C1.1, C1.2, C2.1, C2.2,
C3.1, C3.2

122

Modèle:

"RAVEN"
dix-neuf heures

Modèle:

"RAVEN"
sept heures

 Sur la bonne piste

---

9 Here is a program listing for a French TV channel. You want to set your VCR to record specific programs. Using the 24-hour system, write the time in words to show when you will begin recording each program.

22 septembre VENDREDI M6		
	13.25	**Les rues de San Francisco** Une collection d'aigles. Un trafiquant de pièces de monnaies de collection se fait piéger par la police à cause d'un simple oubli.
	14.20	**Wolff, police criminelle** Coup monté.
	15.15	**Boulevard des clips**
REDIFFUSIONS R	17.00	**Hit machine** Animé par **Yves Noël** et **Ophélie Winter**.
5.45 **Boulevard des clips** 7.00 M6 Express.	17.30	**Classe mannequin** Un K de force majeure.
7.05 **Matin Express** Présenté par **Emmanuelle Gaume**. Avec à 8.00 et 9.00 M6 Express.	18.00	**Highlander** Jeux dangereux. Richie, le jeune protégé de Duncan, est à la recherche de sa famille qu'il n'a jamais connue. Enquêtant sur son passé, il apprend qu'il était un immortel et que son père naturel a stoppé son évolution.
9.05 **M6 Boutique** 9.35 **Boulevard des clips** Avec à 10.00 et 11.00 M6 Express - 10.55 Info-conso - 11.10 Passé simple.	19.00	**Raven** Apprenti cambrioleur. Engagé par la séduisante Erin Stuckey pour vérifier les systèmes de sécurité d'un musée, Ski finit par convaincre Raven de voler une ancienne s atue en or. 19.54 6 minutes - Météo.
11.20 **Les années coup de cœur** Chocolat et sympathie. 11.50 M6 Express - Météo.		
12.00 **Ma sorcière bien-aimée** Sur deux notes.	20.00	**Le grand zap** Divertissement présenté par **Olivier Carreras**. 20.35 Décrochages info ou Ciné 6.
12.30 **La petite maison dans la prairie** Promesses (2).		

1. "LA PETITE MAISON DANS LA PRAIRIE"
2. "LE GRAND ZAP"
3. "WOLFF, POLICE CRIMINELLE"
4. "HIGHLANDER"
5. "HIT MACHINE"
6. "LES RUES DE SAN FRANCISCO"
7. "MA SORCIÈRE BIEN-AIMÉE"

---

10 Do Activity 9 again, this time giving answers using the 12-hour system.

To help you understand what a reading in French is all about, it's important to determine its context (setting or purpose). Some readings just seem to fall into place when viewed from this larger perspective. For example, look at the results of the survey of French students that follows. If this questionnaire were written in English, you would expect to see items about school, courses and leisure activities. You would get the main idea without reading very carefully. Reading in French is no different. You can read for the big picture without reading thoroughly. Clues can be found throughout the reading if you pay attention to the subject or context before you begin to read. Section or paragraph titles can also help you anticipate what each one might be about.

Once you have figured out the meaning of individual words, how can you remember them? One way is to return to the context in which you originally encountered a word. For instance, if you read about attitudes toward school, let the reading set a scene in your mind and give you a feeling of what school or student life is like. It is better to think back on the context of what you read rather than simply repeating vocabulary words in English over and over again. Another way to remember vocabulary is to create mental images. Try to recall what you read by forming a picture in your mind of the what, who, where, when and why of the reading. Then try to label your mental pictures of things, people or activities in French while you review what you read. You will be surprised at what you can remember! More importantly, the words will start to come back to you in French rather than in English.

Voici un questionnaire distribué à quelques élèves âgés de 15 ans dans un collège à Tours en France.

Les réponses: 1 = Oui, tout à fait d'accord.
                   2 = Plutôt d'accord.
                   3 = Plutôt pas d'accord.
                   4 = Non, pas du tout d'accord.

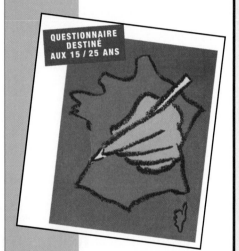

QUESTIONNAIRE DESTINÉ AUX 15 / 25 ANS

Mon opinion sur l'école et les études:	La moyenne des résultats:
J'ai besoin d'étudier pour l'école.	1,7
J'utilise un agenda.	1,2
J'ai beaucoup de devoirs.	1,0
J'en ai marre de l'école.	1,6
Je préfère:	
les maths.	3,2
les langues.	2,0
la littérature.	3,0
la biologie.	2,7
le dessin.	1,6
Mon opinion sur les sports et les loisirs:	
J'aime manger au resto.	2,5
J'aime aller au café.	1,2
J'aime sortir avec mes ami(e)s.	1,1
J'aime:	
le tennis.	2,0
le foot.	1,6
le basket.	2,0
le volley.	1,4
Je vais souvent au cinéma.	2,0
J'écoute de la musique.	1,2
Je skie souvent.	3,3
Je téléphone souvent.	2,4

Teacher's Notes

1. The average score for each item is given. If the number is 2,0 or lower, the students tended to agree with the statement. If the average is greater than two, students tended to disagree. 2. Optional activity. Have your students work in pairs, asking and answering questions based on the items covered in the survey in the book. Student A asks questions about school and courses; Student B asks questions about leisure activities. For example, **Tu aimes manger au resto**? 3. Optional activity. Have your students work in pairs and invent a "typical" French student (for example, Bernard) who took part in the original survey. Student A asks Student B what Bernard's opinion is on a specific topic. Student B answers, using the average score for that topic as a cue. For example, **Bernard écoute de la musique**? **Oui, il écoute de la musique.** (The response of 1,2 indicates that Bernard would answer affirmatively.) 4. Optional activity. Divide the class in five groups. Assign each group one department in a French school: science, language, math, art, social studies. Members of each group are responsible for drawing or bringing pictures of the kinds of objects that are found in that department. For instance, in the history department, there may be history books, notebooks, movies or videos, maps, etc. Each group's task is to label as many objects as they can that are found in that specific department. Groups should include as many items as possible from this **unité**; other items can come from the dictionary. Then group members quiz each other, asking **Qu'est-ce que c'est**? and answering **C'est un(e)....** or **Ce sont des....** Remind students to try to picture the objects and their context in their minds as they repeat the words.

NATIONAL STANDARDS
C1.2, C2.1, C3.1, C3.2, C4.2

Answers

Teacher's Note

Optional activity. Give each student a copy of the sheet with the labeled objects produced by his or her group in the optional activity on page 123. Then have students do this jigsaw or branching activity in cooperative groups. Form new groups, each with one member from former group 1, one member from former group 2, etc. Each member of the new group will present his or her objects to the other new group members. Each member is also responsible for quizzing new members, asking **Qu'est-ce que c'est?** and choosing someone to respond. After sufficient practice time, you may call on individual groups to present what they have learned to the entire class. To assess this activity, you can give a holistic grade of a check (✓), a plus (+) or a minus (-) to each individual in the group. You may prefer to give a holistic grade to the entire group or to both individuals and the group.

124

11 Everyone knows that opinions are subjective: the answers to a questionnaire are valid only for those students who are interviewed. The opinions expressed in the preceding questionnaire are not necessarily the same for students from all French-speaking areas. However, the statements that follow are generally correct or incorrect, according to the opinions expressed by the teenagers (**les adolescents**) surveyed in Tours. If a sentence is correct, write **vrai**. If not, write **faux**.

1. Les ados aiment sortir avec leurs ami(e)s.
2. Les ados aiment les sports.
3. Les ados vont souvent au ciné.
4. Les ados écoutent de la musique.
5. Les ados téléphonent souvent.
6. Les ados n'ont pas besoin d'un calendrier.
7. Les ados ont beaucoup de devoirs.
8. Les ados en ont marre de l'école.
9. Les ados préfèrent les maths et la biologie.
10. Les ados préfèrent les langues et le dessin.

Sylvie et Myriam écoutent souvent de la musique.

Nathalie et Raoul

C'est à moi!

Now that you have completed this unit, take a look at what you should be able to do in French. Can you do all of these tasks?

➤ I can say what I need.

➤ I can ask what something is.

➤ I can identify school objects.

➤ I can tell where people or things are.

➤ I can ask for information about "where" and "what."

➤ I can describe my school schedule.

➤ I can disagree with someone.

➤ I can express emotions.

➤ I can invite someone to do something.

➤ I can tell exact time.

Here is a brief checkup to see how much you understand about French culture. Decide if each statement is **vrai** or **faux**.

1. Students in French schools store their belongings in lockers, just as American students do.
2. French students often use slang expressions, such as **J'en ai marre!**, when they greet their teachers as they enter class each day.
3. French students study **la philosophie** and **la géographie**, subjects which are not always offered in high schools in the United States.
4. An 11-year-old French student enters **le collège** to begin a six-year university program.
5. French students usually don't have classes on Wednesday and Saturday afternoons.

French students often play sports on days when they don't have school. (Verneuil-sur-Seine)

Cooperative Group Practice

Team Dictation

As one of the final written activities in this **unité**, you might divide your class in groups of four or five. Dictate a passage in French that is composed of a series of sentences that includes a mixture of new vocabulary and structures from this **unité**. Put the passage together in such a way that students will not have seen those exact sentences before. Tell each student to write down as much of the passage as he or she can understand. Read the dictation one or more times, if necessary. Then have members of each group pool what they have written and produce a final copy of the passage to be handed in. (You may want to make overhead transparencies of some passages to be used in class as a group correction activity.)

6. The exam which decides whether French students may go on to a university is called the **terminale**.
7. The walls of classrooms in French high schools are filled with examples of students' work, pictures, posters, etc., and look similar to those of American classrooms.
8. French students are often happy with a score of 12 out of 20.
9. Time in France is always expressed according to the 24-hour clock.
10. If you use the 24-hour clock, you don't need to specify A.M. or P.M.

Communication orale

A French exchange student is spending the year at your school. With a partner, play the roles of a student in your school and the visiting French student. Exchange information about daily schedules, what courses you're both taking and what school supplies you need. During the course of your conversation:

1. Greet each other in French and introduce yourselves.
2. Ask each other how things are going and respond.
3. Ask and tell each other which courses you are taking now.
4. Ask and tell each other the teacher's name for each of these courses.
5. Ask and tell each other when each of these classes begins.
6. Ask and tell each other which courses you like.
7. Ask and tell each other what supplies you need.
8. Tell each other good-bye and say that you'll see each other soon.

Communication écrite

As a follow-up to your conversation, write a paragraph telling what you have discovered about your partner's daily schedule, courses and needed school supplies. You might begin to organize your thoughts by writing lists that have the following headings: **les cours, les profs, les heures, il/elle aime..., il/elle a besoin de....** Use the information from your lists to write your paragraph.

Isabelle a besoin d'étudier. (La Rochelle)

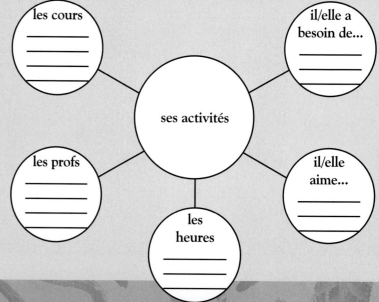

les cours

il/elle a besoin de...

les profs

ses activités

il/elle aime...

les heures

Communication active

To express need, use:

J'ai besoin de dormir.   *I need to sleep.*
J'ai besoin d'étudier.   *I need to study.*

To ask what something is, use:

Qu'est-ce que c'est?   *What is it/this?*

To identify something, use:

C'est le cahier de maths.   *This is the math notebook.*

To tell location, use:

Il/Elle est devant le café.   *It's in front of the café.*
Il/Elle est derrière la chaise.   *It's behind the chair.*
Il/Elle est sur le bureau.   *It's on the desk.*
Il/Elle est sous le sac à dos.   *It's under the backpack.*
Il/Elle est dans la trousse.   *It's in the pencil case.*
Il/Elle est avec le stylo.   *It's with the pen.*
Il/Elle est là.   *It's there/here.*

Tant mieux!

To ask for information, use:

Où est la trousse?   *Where is the pencil case?*
Quoi?   *What?*
Tu as juste un cours   *Do you have just one class*
le mercredi?   *on Wednesday?*

To give information, use:

Je finis à 10h00.   *I finish at 10:00.*

To disagree with someone, use:

Si, j'aime la biologie.   *Yes (on the contrary), I like biology.*

To express emotions, use:

Tant mieux.   *That's great.*
J'en ai marre!   *I'm sick of it! I've had it!*
Zut!   *Darn!*

Zut! La géographie commence à 8h45.

To describe daily routines, use:

J'ai une heure de chimie.   *I have one hour of chemistry.*
J'ai trois **cours.**   *I have three classes.*
Je commence à 8h00.   *I begin at 8:00.*
Je finis à 17h30.   *I finish at 5:30.*

To invite someone to do something, use:

On mange **ensemble?**   *Shall we eat together?*

To state exact time, use:

Il est deux heures **et quart.**   *It's 2:15.*
Il est deux heures **quinze.**   *It's 2:15.*
Il est quatre heures **et demie.**   *It's 4:30.*
Il est quatre heures **trente.**   *It's 4:30.*
Il est six heures **moins le quart.**   *It's 5:45.*
Il est cinq heures **quarante-cinq.**   *It's 5:45.*
Il est sept heures **dix.**   *It's 7:10.*
Il est neuf heures **moins vingt.**   *It's 8:40.*
Il est huit heures **quarante.**   *It's 8:40.*

NATIONAL STANDARDS
C1.2, C4.1

Communication électronique

1. There are both public and private schools in France.
2. The French term for "nursery school" is **maternelle**.
3. There are two kinds of **lycées**, general and vocational education **lycées** and also professional **lycées**. The first kind is the most popular.
4. No, a French **baccalauréat** is the equivalent of finishing the first year in an American university.
5. Some **Grandes Écoles** are the **Institut d'Études Politiques**, the **École Normale Supérieure**, the **Polytechnique** and the **HEC**.

À moi de jouer!

Possible paragraph:

C'est une salle de classe avec un professeur et des élèves. Il est huit heures et demie. Le professeur est devant le bureau. Le tableau est derrière le bureau. Un livre est sur le bureau. La corbeille est sous le bureau. Une fille est devant la porte. Le magnétoscope est sous la télé. Un sac à dos est sur une chaise. Un cahier est dans le sac à dos. Un ordinateur est avec une disquette.

Communication électronique

To find out more about the French educational system and to compare it to the American system, go to this Internet site:

http://www.info-france-usa.org/fprofile.htm

Under "Profile of France," click on "Education" and "Go." After reading the profile, answer the following questions.

1. Are there both public and private schools in France?
2. What is the French term for "nursery school"?
3. How many kinds of **lycées** are there? Which one is the most popular?
4. Is a French **baccalauréat** equivalent to the diploma from an American high school?
5. What are the names of several French **Grandes Écoles**?

Now click on "France." Under the heading "Nos écoles sur le Web," find a school that has an interesting Web site, explore it and then tell your classmates what you have learned about it (its name, location, special programs/activities). Would you like to attend this school?

À moi de jouer!

Now it's time for you to show how much French you have learned in this unit about school by writing a paragraph that describes what you see in this classroom. Use the names of as many classroom objects as possible and use prepositions to tell where these objects are. (You may want to refer to the *Communication active* on page 127 and the vocabulary list on page 129.)

Vocabulaire

à at
une **affiche** poster
l' **allemand (m.)** German (language)
l' **anglais (m.)** English (language)
avec with
avoir to have
 avoir besoin de to need
 avoir faim to be hungry
 avoir soif to be thirsty

le **besoin: avoir besoin de** to need
la **biologie** biology
un **bureau** desk

un **cahier** notebook
un **calendrier** calendar
une **cantine** cafeteria
une **carte** map
une **cassette** cassette
un **CD** CD
une **chaise** chair
la **chimie** chemistry
commencer to begin
une **corbeille** wastebasket
un **cours** course, class
un **crayon** pencil

dans in
de (d') of, from
demi(e) half
 et demi(e) thirty (minutes), half past
derrière behind
le **dessin** drawing
devant in front of
un **dictionnaire** dictionary
dimanche (m.) Sunday
une **disquette** diskette

une **école** school
un(e) **élève** student
un **emploi du temps** schedule
ensemble together
l' **espagnol (m.)** Spanish (language)
un(e) **étudiant(e)** student
Étudions.... Let's study . . . .

une **fenêtre** window
une **feuille de papier** sheet of paper
une **fille** girl
finir to finish
le **français** French (language)

un **garçon** boy
la **géographie** geography

l' **histoire (f.)** history

l' **informatique (f.)** computer science

jeudi (m.) Thursday
un **jour** day

juste just, only

là there, here
le **latin** Latin (language)
le (+ *day of the week*) on (+ day of
 the week)
un **livre** book
lundi (m.) Monday

un **magnétoscope** VCR
mardi (m.) Tuesday
marre: J'en ai marre! I'm sick of it!
 I've had it!
les **maths (f.)** math
mercredi (m.) Wednesday
mille (one) thousand
une **minute** minute
moins minus
 moins le quart quarter to
montrer to show
 Montrez-moi.... Show me . . . .

oh oh
un **ordinateur** computer
où where

par per
une **pendule** clock
la **philosophie** philosophy
la **physique** physics
une **porte** door
un(e) **prof** teacher
un **professeur** teacher

Qu'est-ce que c'est? What is it/this?
un **quart** quarter
 et quart fifteen (minutes after),
  quarter after
 moins le quart quarter to
quoi what

un **sac à dos** backpack
une **salle de classe** classroom
samedi (m.) Saturday
les **sciences (f.)** science
une **semaine** week
si yes (on the contrary)
sous under
une **stéréo** stereo
un **stylo** pen
sur on

un **tableau** (chalk)board
un **taille-crayon** pencil sharpener
Tant mieux. That's great.
une **trousse** pencil case

vendredi (m.) Friday
une **vidéocassette** videocassette

Zut! Darn!

Unité 5

En famille

In this unit you will be able to:

➤ **ask for information**

➤ **give information**

➤ **explain something**

➤ **point out family members**

➤ **describe physical traits**

➤ **describe character**

➤ **express emotions**

➤ **ask and tell how old someone is**

➤ **ask and tell what the date is**

➤ **tell when someone's birthday is**

➤ **tell location**

NATIONAL STANDARDS
C2.1, C2.2

Audiocassette/CD
Les cheveux et les yeux, L'âge

Teacher's Notes

1. The masculine singular forms **roux** and **gris** do not change in the plural. 2. Chestnut brown hair is **les cheveux châtain**. The adjective **châtain** is invariable. 3. Hazel eyes are **les yeux noisette**. The adjective **noisette** also is invariable. Dark brown eyes are considered to be **les yeux noirs** in French. Brown eyes are simply **les yeux marron**. The adjective is invariable. 4. A communicative function that is recycled in this lesson is "agreeing and disagreeing."

TPR

Family Members

You or your students might want to make flash cards of all the family members introduced on page 133. Then you might give students commands, such as **Montrez-moi le neveu**, while holding up the nephew card and another card. Students respond by pointing to the card representing the appropriate family member. Displaying all the cards for students to see, you might continue the activity by giving commands to individual students, such as **Mets le frère avec la sœur**. Students could then demonstrate comprehension by manipulating the flash cards as directed.

Leçon A

In this lesson you will be able to:

➤ **ask for information**

➤ **give information**

➤ **point out family members**

➤ **ask and tell how old someone is**

➤ **describe physical traits**

les cheveux (m.) blonds

les cheveux (m.) bruns

les yeux (m.) bleus

les yeux (m.) gris

Diane

M. Rihane

les cheveux (m.) roux

les cheveux (m.) noirs

les yeux (m.) verts

les yeux (m.) noirs

Mme Rihane

Mme Toussaint

Tu as quel âge?

J'ai trois ans.

Il a quel âge?

Il a neuf ans.

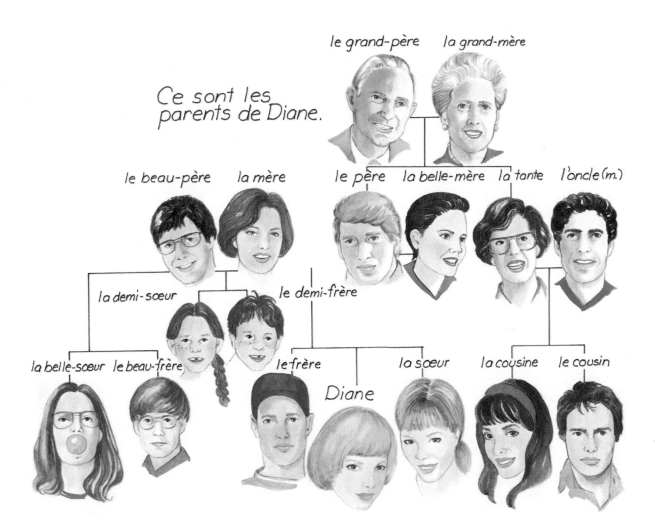

Ce sont les parents de Diane.

le grand-père   la grand-mère

le beau-père   la mère   le père   la belle-mère   la tante   l'oncle (m.)

la demi-sœur   le demi-frère

la belle-sœur   le beau-frère   le frère   la sœur   la cousine   le cousin

Diane

Ce sont les parents de M. Rihane.

M. Rihane   la femme
le fils
les enfants (m., f.)   la fille

Ce sont les parents de Mme Toussaint.

les parents (m.)   Mme Toussaint   le mari

**Workbook
Activity 1**

**Grammar & Vocabulary
Exercise 3**

 Audiocassette/CD
La famille

 Transparencies 22-23

Teacher's Notes

1. **Les parents** can mean both "relatives" and "parents." 2. Currently, the French often use **demi-frère** for either "half-brother" or "stepbrother" and **demi-sœur** for either "half-sister" or "stepsister." **Beau-frère** and **belle-sœur** are reserved for "brother-in-law" and "sister-in-law," respectively. 3. Tell students the following plural forms: **grands-pères, grands-mères, beaux-pères, beaux-frères, belles-mères, belles-sœurs, demi-frères, demi-sœurs.** 4. Remind students that they learned **une fille** (*girl*) in **Unité 4**. 5. Names of other **membres de la famille (m.)** (*family members*) in French include **le bébé** (*baby*), **le neveu** (*nephew*), **la nièce** (*niece*), **le petit-fils** (*grandson*), **la petite-fille** (*granddaughter*), **l'époux (m.)**, **l'épouse (f.)** (*spouse*), **l'ex-mari (m.)** (*ex-husband*), **l'ex-femme (f.)** (*ex-wife*), **les beaux-parents (m.)** (*stepparents, in-laws*), **les grands-parents (m.)** (*grandparents*), **les petits-enfants (m.)** (*grandchildren*), **les cousins germains (m.)** (*first cousins*), **les cousins éloignés (m.)** (*distant cousins*), **le fils unique** (*only son*), **la fille unique** (*only daughter*), **l'enfant unique (m., f.)** (*only child*) and **les kids, les gosses** (*children*). Other related terms are **la famille éloignée** (*distant relatives*), **la famille étendue** (*extended family*), **la famille nucléaire** (*nuclear family*), **la famille monoparentale** (*single-parent family*), **l'arbre généalogique (m.)** (*family tree*) and **divorcé(e)** (*divorced*).

NATIONAL STANDARDS
C1.2, C4.1

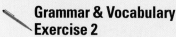

**Workbook
Activity 2**

**Grammar & Vocabulary
Exercise 2**

**Audiocassette/CD
Dialogue**

Teacher's Notes

1. **N'est-ce pas** is used as a lexical item in this unit. Formation of questions will be presented in **Unité 6**. 2. Point out that the verb **ressembler** is followed by the preposition **à**.

Comparisons

Family Relationships

You may want to show five minutes of a current TV program that deals with family relationships, such as "The Simpsons" or "Malcolm in the Middle." Then discuss with your students or have them write in their cultural journals the answers to these questions: What do these programs say about American families? What would someone from another culture think after watching these programs? Do these programs really reflect mainstream American family life?

NATIONAL STANDARDS
C1.2, C2.1, C4.1, C4.2

134

Max is looking at a photo of a young boy in Thierry's room.

Max: **C'est toi?**
Thierry: **Non, c'est Justin, mon demi-frère. Il a deux ans. C'est le fils de mon père et de ma belle-mère.**
Max: **Il a tes yeux bleus et tes cheveux bruns.**
Thierry: **Il est beau comme moi, n'est-ce pas? Nous ressemblons tous les deux à notre père.**

 Enquête culturelle

Proverbs demonstrate certain values or point out people's attitudes. The French proverb **Tel père, tel fils** means "Like father, like son." This proverb emphasizes the traditional belief that sons look and act like their fathers, follow in their father's footsteps by entering the same profession or carrying on the family business, and tend to marry women similar to the ones their fathers married.

Grammar & Vocabulary Exercises 1, 4

Audiocassette/CD Activity 1

The French use the same prefix, **beau-** or **belle-**, for members of stepfamilies and in-laws. For example, the word **beau-frère** means both "stepbrother" and "brother-in-law."

C'est la belle-famille de Delphine.

le beau-père

la belle-mère

Delphine

Francis

le beau-frère

la belle-sœur

Answers

1 1. Max est avec Thierry.
    2. Non, c'est une photo de Justin.
    3. Justin est le demi-frère de Thierry.
    4. Justin a deux ans.
    5. Justin/Thierry a les yeux bleus et les cheveux bruns./Justin et Thierry ont les yeux bleus et les cheveux bruns.
    6. Oui, il a aussi les yeux bleus.

2 1. verts
    2. oncle
    3. ressemble
    4. âge
    5. blonds
    6. grand-père
    7. sœur
    8. belle-sœur

1   *Répondez en français.*

    1. Qui est avec Thierry?
    2. C'est une photo de Thierry?
    3. Qui est Justin?
    4. Justin a quel âge?
    5. Qui a les yeux bleus et les cheveux bruns?
    6. Le père de Thierry a aussi les yeux bleus?

Teacher's Notes

1. Another word for "son-in-law" in French is **un gendre**. 2. If you would like to introduce some information on family relationships from other francophone countries, you might tell your students that the family structure is very important to French-speaking Africans. For example, people from Senegal see themselves as part of an unbroken chain; their ancestors are important, even after they die.

2   *Trouvez dans la liste suivante le mot qui complète correctement chaque phrase.* (In the following list find the word that correctly completes each sentence.)

grand-père	verts	sœur	âge	ressemble
belle-sœur	blonds	oncle		

    1. Pierre a les yeux....
    2. Le frère de ma mère est mon....
    3. J'ai les yeux gris et les cheveux blonds. Mon père a aussi les yeux gris et les cheveux blonds. Je... à mon père.
    4. Tu as quel...?
    5. Nicole a les cheveux....
    6. Le père de ma mère est mon....
    7. La fille de mon père est ma....
    8. La femme de mon frère est ma....

Bernard a les cheveux blonds.

NATIONAL STANDARDS
C1.1, C1.2, C4.1

135

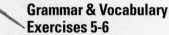

Workbook Activity 3

Grammar & Vocabulary Exercises 5-6

Audiocassette/CD Activity 3

Computer Software Activities 1-2

Answers

3 Answers will vary.

J'ai les yeux bleus.

DANY CARREL　JACQUES BALUTIN

LAISSE PARLER TA MÈRE !

Comédie d'YVES JAMIAQUE
Mise en scène d'ANNICK BLANCHETEAU
Décor de CHARLIE MANGEL

« On rit de bon cœur et sans arrière pensée » (PARISCOPE) - « Rire, émotion et tendresse » (FRANCE-SOIR) - « Ne pas manquer cette jolie pièce » (LE PARISIEN).

LOCATION : 01 48 78 63 47

SAUMUR SA RÉGION

3 | *C'est à toi!*

1. Tu as quel âge?
2. Tu ressembles à qui?
3. Tu as les cheveux blonds, bruns, noirs ou roux?
4. Tu as les yeux noirs, gris, verts ou bleus?
5. Tu as combien de cousins?

Structure

Possessive adjectives

Possessive adjectives show ownership or relationship, for example, "my" computer or "his" sister. In French, possessive adjectives have different forms depending on the nouns they describe. Note how possessive adjectives agree in gender (masculine or feminine) and in number (singular or plural) with the nouns that follow them.

	Singular		Plural
	Masculine	Feminine before a Consonant Sound	
my	mon	ma	mes
your	ton	ta	tes
his, her, one's, its	son (frère)	sa (sœur)	ses (parents)
our	notre	notre	nos
your	votre	votre	vos
their	leur	leur	leurs

The possessive adjective agrees with the noun that follows it, not with the owner.

C'est une photo de **mes** cousins et de **ma** tante. — *This is a picture of my cousins and my aunt.*

Leur père est très beau. — *Their father is very handsome.*

Son, sa and **ses** may mean "his," "her," "its" or "one's," depending on the gender of the owner.

Luc aime bien **sa** belle-mère. — *Luc really likes his stepmother.*
Claire et **son** frère étudient ensemble. — *Claire and her brother are studying together.*

Before a feminine singular word beginning with a vowel sound, **ma, ta** and **sa** become **mon, ton** and **son,** respectively.

Ton interro est demain? — *Is your test tomorrow?*
Ma sœur, Renée, a **mon** affiche. — *My sister, Renée, has my poster.*

NATIONAL STANDARDS
C1.1, C1.2, C4.1

Pratique

4 | Answer the questions about Sabrina's relatives, according to the family tree.

Modèles:

Nadine est la tante de Sabrina?
Oui, Nadine est sa tante.

Pierre est le père de Sabrina?
Non, Pierre est son grand-père.

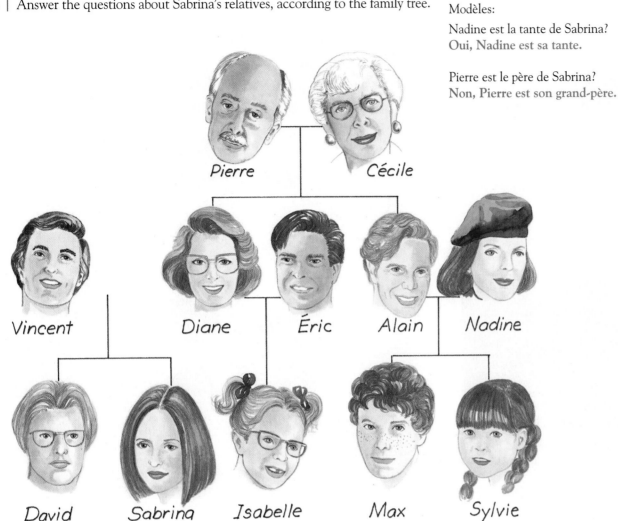

1. Max est le frère de Sabrina?
2. Éric est le beau-père de Sabrina?
3. Cécile est la grand-mère de Sabrina?
4. Isabelle est la cousine de Sabrina?
5. Vincent est l'oncle de Sabrina?
6. David est le cousin de Sabrina?
7. Diane est la mère de Sabrina?
8. Alain est le père de Sabrina?
9. Sylvie est la sœur de Sabrina?

Audiocassette/CD Activity 6

Answers

5 1. Abdoul a sa photo, son cahier et ses stylos.
2. J'ai ma photo et mon cahier. Je n'ai pas mes stylos.
3. Chloé a sa photo et ses stylos. Elle n'a pas son cahier.
4. Tu as ta photo, ton cahier et tes stylos.
5. Frédéric a sa photo et son cahier. Il n'a pas ses stylos.
6. Anne a son cahier et ses stylos. Elle n'a pas sa photo.

6 1. Je vais au café avec mes parents et mon grand-père.
2. Monsieur Eberhardt va au café avec sa femme et ses enfants.
3. Vous allez au café avec votre père et vos belles-sœurs.
4. Sophie et Ariane vont au café avec leur beau-père et leurs frères.
5. Manu et Christophe vont au café avec leur belle-mère et leurs sœurs.
6. Madame Magouet va au café avec son mari et sa fille.
7. Nous allons au café avec notre mère et nos cousins.

Modèle:

Benjamin

Benjamin a son cahier et ses stylos. Il n'a pas sa photo.

Philippe a ses livres et sa trousse. Il n'a pas son cahier. (Chelles)

Modèle:

Luc (mère/frère)
Luc va au café avec sa mère et son frère.

5 Your teacher told you and your classmates to bring a picture of your family, a notebook and two pens to class today. Tell which people have what they were supposed to bring and which people don't.

1. Abdoul

2. je

3. Chloé

4. tu

5. Frédéric

6. Anne

6 Tell which family members are going to the café with the following people.

1. je (parents/grand-père)
2. Monsieur Eberhardt (femme/enfants)
3. vous (père/belles-sœurs)
4. Sophie et Ariane (beau-père/frères)
5. Manu et Christophe (belle-mère/sœurs)
6. Madame Magouet (mari/fille)
7. nous (mère/cousins)

Danielle Steel
Leur promesse
Roman

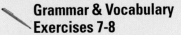 **Workbook Activity 4**

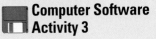 **Grammar & Vocabulary Exercises 7-8**

Computer Software Activity 3

Tell how much the following people look like their relatives. Complete each sentence with the appropriate form of the possessive adjective.

1. Je ressemble beaucoup à... cousins. Je ressemble un peu à... mère. Je ne ressemble pas à... oncle.
2. Michel et Karine ressemblent beaucoup à... demi-sœur. Ils ressemblent un peu à... père. Ils ne ressemblent pas à... cousins.

Michel ressemble beaucoup à sa sœur.

3. Vous ressemblez beaucoup à... grand-père. Vous ressemblez un peu à... parents. Vous ne ressemblez pas à... sœur.
4. Ahmed ressemble beaucoup à... mère. Il ressemble un peu à... sœurs. Il ne ressemble pas à... demi-frère.
5. Tu ressembles beaucoup à... frère. Tu ressembles un peu à... cousins. Tu ne ressembles pas à... tante.
6. Nous ressemblons beaucoup à... père. Nous ressemblons un peu à... grand-mère. Nous ne ressemblons pas à... cousins.

Expressions with *avoir*

You have already learned several expressions where the verb "to be" is used in English but forms of **avoir** are used in French. Two more of these expressions are **avoir quel âge** to ask someone's age and **avoir... an(s)** to tell someone's age.

Tu **as** quel âge?   *How old are you?*
J'ai quatorze **ans.**   *I'm fourteen (years old).*

LUNETTES NOIRES A VOTRE VUE !

Du 17 Avril au 31 Août.
56,41 €

J'ai quinze ans.

Teacher's Note

You may want to review the expressions **avoir faim** and **avoir soif** before beginning the section of expressions with **avoir.**

TPR

Tu as quel âge?

Conduct a brief survey on your students' ages. Post the expression **J'ai... ans** in various places in your classroom to reflect the ages of most of your students. As you ask students **Tu as quel âge?**, they go to the posted expression that represents their age. As a follow-up written activity, quickly count up how many students are in each category, write the number by the age expression and have students write sentences that tell how many are in each category. For example, **Dix élèves ont quatorze ans.**

NATIONAL STANDARDS
C1.1, C1.2, C4.1

Answers

8 1. Vincent a quel âge?
Il a quinze ans. Denise a quel âge?
Elle a vingt et un ans.
2. Christine et Christophe ont quel âge?
Ils ont huit ans. Madame Lafleur a quel âge?
Elle a quarante ans.
3. Magali a quel âge?
Elle a dix-sept ans. Raphaël a quel âge?
Il a trois ans.
4. Monsieur Charpentier a quel âge?
Il a trente-neuf ans. Marie-Alix a quel âge?
Elle a douze ans.
5. Madame Arnaud a quel âge?
Elle a cinquante-quatre ans.
Théo et Thierry ont quel âge?
Ils ont cinq ans.
6. Tu as quel âge?
J'ai... ans. Tu as quel âge?
J'ai... ans.

9 1. f
2. b
3. e
4. d
5. a
6. c

Cooperative Group Practice

Tu as quel âge?

Have your students conduct a survey on ages. Begin by having students choose an imaginary age for themselves between 1-21. Next have students write the names of ten classmates on a piece of paper. Then have students interview the ten people on their list, saying **Tu as quel âge?** Students write the answers next to the names. When everyone has finished, put students in pairs and have them tell each other what information they have found out, for example, **Stéphanie a 20 ans.** As a written check, students can hand in a summary of their surveys, for example, **Marc, Ariane et Guillaume ont 16 ans, Stéphanie a 20 ans,** etc.

NATIONAL STANDARDS
C1.1, C1.2, C1.3

Pratique

8 With a partner, take turns asking and telling how old certain people are.

Modèle:

M. Darrigues   Arabéa et Assia

Student A: Monsieur Darrigues a quel âge?
Student B: Il a soixante-cinq ans. Arabéa et Assia ont quel âge?
Student A: Elles ont six ans.

Vincent   Denise

1.

Christine et Christophe   Mme Lafleur

2.

Magali   Raphaël

3.

M. Charpentier   Marie-Alix

4.

Mme Arnaud   Théo et Thierry

5.

tu   tu

6.

Communication

9 You gave your friend a new photo album for her birthday. Help her organize some of her family pictures and their labels. Match each photo with the appropriate label. The first one has been done for you.

Modèle:

C'est ma sœur Claire. Elle a 6 ans.
g

a.

b.

c.

d.

e.

f.

g.

1. C'est mon grand-père.
2. C'est mon beau-père.
3. C'est mon frère, Alexandre.
4. C'est ma mère.
5. C'est ma grand-mère.
6. C'est ma sœur Anne. Elle a 19 ans.

10 The pictures that follow show some of the members of your imaginary family. Choose any two of these pictures, and write three sentences for each one on a separate sheet of paper. In each set of sentences, the first one should tell how this person is related to you; the second one should tell this person's approximate age; the third one should tell what color eyes and hair this person has. After you finish writing your descriptions, leave them on your desk, choose a partner and switch seats. Read the two sets of sentences on your partner's desk, and then write the letter of the appropriate picture next to each description. When you return to your seat, see if your partner correctly identified the two people you described.

Modèle:

C'est mon cousin.
Il a douze ans.
Il a les cheveux roux et les yeux verts.

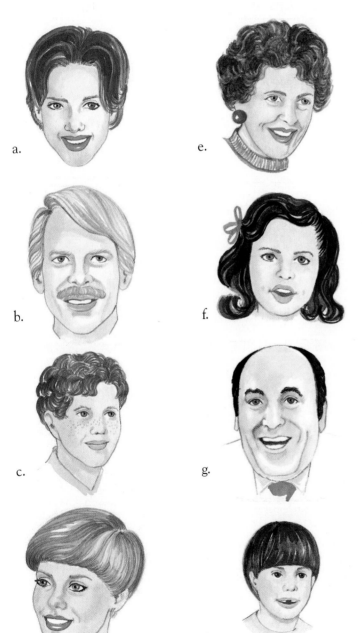

a.

b.

c.

d.

e.

f.

g.

h.

Audiocassette/CD
Prononciation

Listening Activity 1

Quiz
Leçon A

Paired Practice

Family Tree

If you believe it to be appropriate, you may want your students to make their own family tree, including names, family relationships and ages. Students could add a small photo or drawing beside the name of each person. Have partners exchange their family trees and take turns asking and telling who the people are. For example, **Qui est Sylvie?** **Sylvie est ma cousine.** You may also ask students to be prepared to describe their family tree to the entire class.

Teacher's Note

In general, the final consonants **c**, **r**, **f** and **l** (those in the word CaReFuL) are pronounced in French.

NATIONAL STANDARDS
C1.1, C1.2, C1.3, C3.1, C4.1

Modèle:

Moi, je m'appelle Derrick. J'ai 15 ans. Ma mère s'appelle Cynthia. Elle a 43 ans. Mon père s'appelle Glen. Il a 41 ans. Ma sœur s'appelle Ashley. Elle a 17 ans.

11 Write a brief description of each member of your real or imaginary family in which you tell each person's name, relationship to you and age. Then, with a partner, take turns reading your description aloud. While you listen to your partner's description, draw his or her family tree and label each person by name, family relationship and age, beginning with your partner.

sa mère, Cynthia, 43 ans — son père, Glen, 41 ans

Derrick, 15 ans — sa sœur, Ashley, 17 ans

 ## Prononciation

Liaison

You have already seen examples of liaison (linking of sounds) after some possessive adjectives when the next word begins with a vowel sound.

Leurs‿enfants ont faim.   Ton‿oncle s'appelle Michel.
[z]   [n]

In general, final consonants in French are silent. However, there is liaison between two words when the second one begins with a vowel sound: **a**, **e**, **i**, **o**, **u** and sometimes **h** and **y**. The final consonant of the first word is pronounced as though it were the first sound of the second word. Say each of these expressions:

les‿ordinateurs   On‿y va?
[z]   [n]

deux‿élèves   neuf‿ans
[z]   [v]

cinq‿heures   Il est‿au café.
[k]   [t]

les mois (m.)

janvier

février

mars

avril

mai

juin

juillet

août

septembre

octobre

novembre

décembre

Leçon B

In this lesson you will be able to:

➤ **ask and tell what the date is**

➤ **tell location**

➤ **point out family members**

■ **Workbook Activity 5**

✎ **Grammar & Vocabulary Exercises 9-10**

 Audiocassette/CD *Les mois*

Teacher's Note

Communicative functions that are recycled in this lesson are "asking for information" and "disagreeing with someone."

Cooperative Group Practice

Notre calendrier

Put students in groups and ask each group to design a calendar for the current school year in French. Individuals in each group could work on specific months, adding holidays, special school activities and community events for that period. When all calendars are completed, they can be posted for everyone to see.

NATIONAL STANDARDS
C1.2, C4.1

143

Workbook Activities 6-7

 Grammar & Vocabulary Exercises 11-13

Audiocassette/CD Numbers 1,000-1,000,000, Animals

Teacher's Notes

1. You may want to point out to students that **oiseau** forms its plural by adding an **x** and that the plural form of **un cheval** is **des chevaux**. 2. Other expressions dealing with pets include **les animaux domestiques (m.)** (*pets*) and **la perruche** (*parrot*). 3. You may want to point out to students that **mille** is invariable in the plural but **million** adds an **s**. 4. You might have your students practice numbers above 1,000 by giving them a numbers dictation. Compile a random sequence of 20-30 numbers over 1,000. Tell students to write each number using numerals as you say it in words. Read the list to your students at an even pace. After you have said the numbers once, repeat them a second time at the same speed so that students can fill in any numbers they missed. So that students can check their work, you might use a transparency that contains the correct numbers.

 **NATIONAL STANDARDS C1.2, C3.1**

144

1.000 = mille
1.001 = mille un
1.002 = mille deux
2.000 = deux mille
3.000 = trois mille
1.000.000 = un million
2.000.000 = deux millions
3.000.000 = trois millions

Miaou!

un chat

Glou glou!

un poisson rouge

Cui cui!

un oiseau

Ouaf ouaf!

un chien

Hî-hî-hî!

un cheval

Speech bubbles: Le chien ne va pas en vacances avec nous. — Mais si!

Monsieur and Madame Lévesque from Nantes are deciding where to go for their summer vacation.

Monsieur Lévesque:	**C'est quelle date?**
Madame Lévesque:	**C'est le 25 avril. Nous sommes jeudi. Pourquoi?**
Monsieur Lévesque:	**Nous allons en vacances dans trois mois, le 1ᵉʳ août.**
Madame Lévesque:	**Nous allons où? À Fort-de-France? À Pointe-à-Pitre?**
Monsieur Lévesque:	**Mais, la Martinique et la Guadeloupe sont à 7.000 kilomètres de Nantes. Le chien ne va pas en vacances avec nous?**
Madame Lévesque:	**Mais si! Milou est un membre de la famille.**

Restaurant La Martinique

75, rue du Mail
49000 ANGERS

📞 02.41.87.22.25

Spécialités Créoles Fruits de Mer
Cocktails exotiques Coupes glacées

Ouvert du lundi soir au dimanche midi.

Enquête culturelle 🔍

Nantes

Musique

La Folle Journée

4 et 5 février

The Lévesque family is from Nantes, a port city on the western coast of France near the mouth of the Loire River. Nantes was the site of the signing in 1598 of the Edict of Nantes, which gave French Protestants, called Huguenots, some religious freedoms. However, it was revoked by Louis XIV in 1685; consequently, about 200,000 Huguenots left France.

Workbook Activity 8

Audiocassette/CD Dialogue

Teacher's Notes

1. You may want to point out to students that **les vacances (f.)** is always plural. 2. The French abbreviation of **premier** (*first*) is **1ᵉʳ**. 3. The distance from Nantes to Martinique and Guadeloupe is only approximate. 4. Nantes is the birthplace of Jules Verne, the author of *Twenty Thousand Leagues under the Sea* and *Around the World in Eighty Days*. Nantes is also the city where the famous Lu cookies (**biscuits**) are made.

TPR

Birthdays

Post the names of the months in various places in your classroom. Have students go to the appropriate spot in the room to express what month their birthday is in. As a follow-up oral activity, each student could quickly say the date of his or her birthday. For example, **C'est le six mai.**

Martinique and Guadeloupe, two tropical islands in the Caribbean Sea, belong to France. The capitals of these two French overseas departments (**Départements d'Outre-Mer**) are Fort-de-France and Basse-Terre, respectively. Joséphine, the wife of Napoléon I (1769-1821), was born in Martinique.

Les Salines, the most beautiful beach on Martinique, is adjacent to a petrified forest.

The French use the metric system of measurement, developed by a commission of French scientists in the 1790s. In the metric system distance is measured in **kilomètres** instead of in miles. One kilometer equals .62 miles.

Most French workers get six weeks of paid vacation each year. Many families spend the entire month of July or August on vacation.

One out of every three households in France has a dog.

There are 35 million pets in France, more than double the number of French children! France has more dogs per person than any other country in western Europe. Paris has 40 animal clinics open day and night, animal ambulances, a therapy center for dogs and dog-sitter agencies. By law, the French must clean up after their pets. **Caninettes**, bright green motorbikes with rotating brushes and suction hoses, keep the city's sidewalks spotless.

Usually trained to behave very well, French dogs are welcome in hotels, stores and even the fanciest restaurants, where they may be served food prepared by the chef. They are often treated as part of the family and given affectionate nicknames. Some common names for dogs include Médor, Rex, Reine, Fidèle and Fifi. Pedigreed dogs born in a particular year must all have a name starting with a certain letter of the alphabet. In one recent year, the names of all pedigreed dogs began with the letter "H"; names such as Hercule and Hortensia were very popular.

Répondez en français.

1. C'est le 20 avril?
2. Les vacances de M. et Mme Lévesque, elles commencent le 25 avril?
3. Les Lévesque vont où en vacances?
4. Où sont la Martinique et la Guadeloupe?
5. Qui est Milou?
6. Qui va en vacances avec M. et Mme Lévesque? Pourquoi?

Milou est le chien de la famille Lévesque.

2 Using the information in the illustrations, answer the questions about these people and their pets.

Ariane et Bruno — *Prince*

Khaled — *Joséphine et Napoléon*

Laurent et Olivier — *Coco*

la famille Durocher — *Minou*

Denise — *Tornade*

Modèle:
Le chat de la famille Durocher s'appelle comment?
Leur chat s'appelle Minou.

CHANTILLY
MUSÉE VIVANT DU CHEVAL

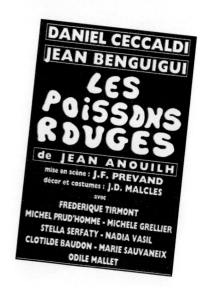

DANIEL CECCALDI
JEAN BENGUIGUI
LES POISSONS ROUGES
de JEAN ANOUILH
mise en scène : J.F. PREVAND
décor et costumes : J.D. MALCLES
avec
FREDERIQUE TIRMONT
MICHEL PRUD'HOMME · MICHELE GRELLIER
STELLA SERFATY · NADIA VASIL
CLOTILDE BAUDON · MARIE SAUVANEIX
ODILE MALLET

1. Qui a un cheval?
2. Combien de poissons rouges a Khaled?
3. La famille Durocher a un chien?
4. L'oiseau de Laurent et Olivier s'appelle comment?
5. Ariane et Bruno ont un chat?
6. Combien de chats a la famille Durocher?
7. Le cheval de Denise s'appelle Napoléon?
8. Qui a un chien?

Workbook
Activities 9-10

Grammar & Vocabulary
Exercises 14-17

Audiocassette/CD
Activity 3

Computer Software
Activity 4

Answers

3 Answers will vary.

Teacher's Notes

1. Have students repeat after you the forms of **être**. Remind students that **ne** becomes **n'** in the **tu, il/elle/on** and **vous** forms. 2. Point out that liaison is optional, but usually made, after the third person singular form of **être** before a word beginning with a vowel sound. Liaison is also optional after the other forms of **être**. 3. Once your students learn the forms of **être**, you may want to introduce the **passé composé** orally so that students can use it in classroom activities. Its presentation and uses could be limited to the verb **aller**. The **passé composé** will be explained in **Unités 11** and **12**.

Comparisons

Regular or Irregular?

Ask students if the verb "to be" is regular or irregular in English. Help them to begin thinking about this by saying or writing "I am, you are..." and having students continue. See if students can determine what makes a verb regular or irregular in English and in French.

148

3 | *C'est à toi!*

1. Tu préfères quel mois?
2. Tu vas où en vacances?
3. Tu vas en vacances avec qui?
4. Qu'est-ce que tu aimes faire en vacances?
5. Tu préfères les chats ou les chiens?
6. Qui sont les membres de ta famille?

Tu préfères les chats...

...ou les chiens?

Structure

Present tense of the irregular verb *être*

The verb **être** (*to be*) is irregular.

être			
je	**suis**	Je **suis** intelligent.	*I am intelligent.*
tu	**es**	Tu n'**es** pas timide.	*You aren't timid.*
il/elle/on	**est**	Il **est** beau.	*He's handsome.*
nous	**sommes**	Nous **sommes** au café.	*We're at the café.*
vous	**êtes**	Vous **êtes** ensemble?	*Are you together?*
ils/elles	**sont**	Elles **sont** à l'école.	*They are at school.*

Note that the **s** in **vous** is pronounced [z] before **êtes**:
Vous êtes professeur?
    [z]

Les filles sont ensemble. (Angers)

Elle est belle...

Pratique

Audiocassette/CD
Activity 4

4 Tell whether or not you think the following people are on vacation.

1. M. Simon

4. tu

2. Delphine et sa sœur

5. vous

3. la prof de français

6. M. et Mme Dupont

Modèles:

Karine

Karine est en vacances.

Luc et Ousmane

Luc et Ousmane ne sont pas
en vacances.

5 Complete each short dialogue with the appropriate forms of the verb **être**.

1. C'... quelle date?
C'... le 20 décembre. Nous... mercredi.
2. Tes chiens... en vacances avec toi?
Oui, Rex et Reine... des membres de la famille.
3. Tu... avec Étienne?
Oui, nous... ensemble.
4. C'... ton frère?
Oui, il... beau comme moi.
5. Tu... à l'école?
Non, je... au café.
6. Vous... les sœurs de Catherine?
Non, nous... ses cousines.
7. Vous... de Nantes?
Non, je... de Paris.

National Standards
C1.1, C1.2

Ils sont au fast-food.

6 Use appropriate forms of the verb **être** and the listed locations to tell where everyone is.

à l'école	au café	au cinéma	au fast-food

1. Les Maurel mangent des hamburgers et des frites.
   Ils....
2. J'écoute le professeur de biologie.
   Je....
3. Christine mange une quiche et une crêpe.
   Elle....
4. Nous étudions.
   Nous....
5. Tu es serveur.
   Tu....
6. Jeanne et toi, vous avez une interro.
   Vous....
7. Alain regarde un film.
   Il....

Dates

To express the date in French, follow this pattern:

le + number + month

C'est **le 12 décembre**.
Nous sommes **le 12 décembre**. } *It's December 12.*

An exception to this rule is "the first" of any month. Use **le premier** before the name of a month.

C'est **le premier mai**.
C'est **le 1er mai**. } *It's May first.*

When a date is abbreviated, note that the day precedes the month: 12/7 is July 12.

Pratique

The French teacher at the Lycée Carnot is very organized. She has already posted the dates of all the tests she will give throughout the school year. Give each date on the list in French.

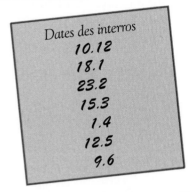

Dates des interros
10.12
18.1
23.2
15.3
1.4
12.5
9.6

Modèle:
3.11
le trois novembre

8 Give the date of each of the following holidays and events in French.

1. your birthday
2. Valentine's Day
3. New Year's Day
4. April Fools' Day
5. New Year's Eve
6. Saint Patrick's Day
7. Independence Day (U.S.)
8. Halloween
9. the last day of the school year

Modèle:
Christmas
C'est le 25 décembre.

9 With a partner, take turns asking and telling who is performing at the Zénith in Paris on certain dates. Follow the model.

Au Zénith...

18.1	DANY BRILLANT
13.2	VANESSA PARADIS
28.4	NEIL YOUNG
3.5	ALAIN SOUCHON
4.6	ALAIN CHAMFORT
30.7	JORDY
22.8	PATRICIA KAAS
26.9	TINA TURNER
1.10	KHALED
7.12	LITTLE BOB

Modèle:
4.6/1.10
Student A: Qui est au Zénith le 4 juin?
Student B: Alain Chamfort. Qui est au Zénith le premier octobre?
Student A: Khaled.

1. 7.12/30.7
2. 28.4/18.1
3. 3.5/26.9
4. 22.8/13.2

152

Answers

10 1. Two couples had daughters.
2. The baby boy's name is Étienne.
3. Malika's mother's name is Sabine Gié.
4. Étienne's last name is Vannier.
5. Étienne is the oldest.
6. Malika is the youngest.
7. Malika was not born in France.
8. Étienne's birthday is celebrated first each year.
9. Malika's birthday is in the summer.

Connections

Important Dates

Say in French a series of important dates in world history. Have students tell in English what event took place in each year. For example, 1066 (Norman Conquest), 1492 (Columbus discovered America), 1789 (beginning of the French Revolution), 1865 (end of the Civil War/assassination of President Lincoln), 1929 (stock market crash), 1941 (attack on Pearl Harbor) and 1963 (assassination of President Kennedy).

Cooperative Group Practice

C'est quelle date?

Tear the months off an old wall calendar and give one month to each cooperative group of three students. Have the first student point to two different days, one for each of the other group members to identify. For example, as the first student points to August 28, the second student says **C'est le vingt-huit août.** Each group member gets a turn to choose and point to two dates and have the others identify them.

NATIONAL STANDARDS
C1.1, C1.2, C2.1, C2.2, C3.1

Communication

10 When you were at your grandparents' house, you looked through an old scrapbook and found some birth annoucements. Based on these announcements, answer the questions that follow.

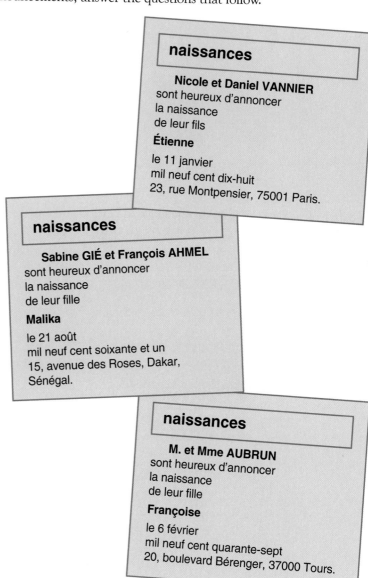

naissances

Nicole et Daniel VANNIER
sont heureux d'annoncer
la naissance
de leur fils
Étienne

le 11 janvier
mil neuf cent dix-huit
23, rue Montpensier, 75001 Paris.

naissances

Sabine GIÉ et François AHMEL
sont heureux d'annoncer
la naissance
de leur fille
Malika

le 21 août
mil neuf cent soixante et un
15, avenue des Roses, Dakar,
Sénégal.

naissances

M. et Mme AUBRUN
sont heureux d'annoncer
la naissance
de leur fille
Françoise

le 6 février
mil neuf cent quarante-sept
20, boulevard Bérenger, 37000 Tours.

1. How many couples had daughters?
2. What is the baby boy's name?
3. What is Malika's mother's name?
4. What is Étienne's last name?
5. Which of the three children is the oldest?
6. Which of the three children is the youngest?
7. Which child was not born in France?
8. Which person's birthday is celebrated first each year?
9. Which person's birthday is in the summer?

11 Your mother was sent to Aix-en-Provence in southern France on business for the month of July. Since you had vacation at the same time, you went along with her. Your mother traveled to many cities while she was based in Aix-en-Provence. Help her complete her mileage report for the month by telling the number of kilometers she traveled between Aix-en-Provence and each of the cities listed. (Note that the chart gives only one-way distances from Aix-en-Provence to each city.) Then give the total number of kilometers she traveled during the month. Follow the model.

Distances kilométriques d'Aix-en-Provence à:	
Antibes 165	Marseille 30
Arles 75	Montpellier 145
Avignon 75	Nice 190
Bordeaux 645	Orange 100
Cannes 155	Paris 765
Genève 430	Saint-Tropez . . .150
Grenoble 290	Toulon 80
Lyon 300	

Orange   Genève   Arles   Marseille   Montpellier
           Nice   Paris   Cannes

Modèle:

Lyon
six cents kilomètres

Paris est à 765 kilomètres d'Aix-en-Provence.

12 While reading the French newspaper *Le Parisien*, you find the lost and found section (**Perdu - Trouvé**) in the classified ads. Read the three ads about lost pets so that, if you spot one of them, you can call its owner. Answer the questions that follow.

> Perdu le 3/4, chien noir et brun, yeux gris. S'appelle Hugo. Contacter le 01.44.56.70.91. Forte récompense.

> Perdu le 31/3, grand chat gris, yeux verts. S'appelle César. Tél: 01.42.09.23.18.

> Perdu le 1/4, chien noir et brun, yeux noirs. S'appelle Rex. Porte un large collier noir. Contacter le 01.43.98.45.23.

1. What two kinds of pets are lost?
2. Which pet has been lost the longest?
3. What are the names of the other two animals?
4. In what way are the two dogs similar?
5. What is one difference in the appearance of the two dogs?
6. For which animal is there a reward?
7. Which animal is wearing a black collar?

Workbook Activity 12

Comparisons

Cultural Journal

If your students are keeping a cultural journal, you might have them react to the given situation by writing answers to the questions that follow: Think of three families that you know well. (They may live in an apartment, a house or a rural area.) If each of these families decided to host a foreign exchange student, what standards of behavior would each family expect? How do the attitudes of these families differ regarding issues such as religion, politics, dating and family responsibilities? What adjustments would *you* have to make to live with each of these families? How do you communicate with others? How do you deal with unexpected events and changes? How do you feel when you are expected to do what someone else wants? How willing are you to try out new things?

154

Mise au point sur... les familles françaises

Extended families still get together for important holidays.

When Americans talk about their families, they usually mean their immediate families: parents, children, brothers and sisters. In France, the term **la famille** is used to refer to the extended family, including grandparents, uncles, aunts, nephews, nieces and cousins. In the past, whole families often lived in the same town. They gathered together for Sunday dinners, important holidays and special events. The mother usually stayed at home to raise the children and take care of the household. But with today's ever-changing family structure, it has become more and more difficult to define the word **famille**.

The changing family structure is reflected by the decrease in the birth rate in France. In order to maintain the population at its current level, the French government gives money to families upon the birth of each child after the first two. French children often make adult decisions at a younger age than their parents did. Much advertising is aimed at teenagers, because they often help their families decide what cars, clothes, food, computers, etc., to buy.

In most cases today, family members don't all live in the same town, but they still enjoy getting together to celebrate special occasions, especially weddings. In France, couples often have two wedding ceremonies. First, there is a required official ceremony at **la mairie** (*town hall*). Instead of choosing a maid or matron of honor and a best man, the bride and groom select two or more witnesses to listen to their vows. Other family members and friends also attend this civil ceremony. A second, optional ceremony takes place at the couple's place of worship. The entire wedding celebration may last for several days and include dancing, singing and lots of good food. Couples with more modest tastes simply invite their friends and family to a restaurant for a special dinner afterward.

To celebrate a wedding in France, there are usually two ceremonies. The one at the church is optional.

> *Madame Joseph Rich*
> *Monsieur et Madame Jean-Pierre Jourda*
> *sont heureux de vous faire part du*
> *mariage de leur*
> *petite-fille et fille Frédérique, avec Monsieur*
> *Sébastien Martel.*
>
> *En vous priant d'assister ou de vous unir*
> *d'intention à la Cérémonie Religieuse qui sera*
> *célébrée le*
> *Samedi 21 Décembre 2002, à 15 h. 30, en*
> *l'Église de*
> *Saint-Suliac (Ille-et-Vilaine).*
>
> *Un Cocktail sera servi à l'issue de la*
> *Cérémonie.*
>
> *9, rue du Moulin aux Pauvres*
> *35300 Fougères*

In France, young women must be 15 years old (with parental permission) to marry; young men must be 18 years old. After her marriage, a woman may choose to keep her maiden name or to take the surname of her husband. She may also hyphenate her name, i.e., Martin-Dubois. But the legal name of a woman remains the name that she was given at birth.

French families don't need special occasions in order to get together. Some families have **une maison de campagne** (*country home*) to go to when they want to get away from the stress of city life. They often personalize this home with a name, such as **Mon Repos** (*My Place to Relax*).

Families usually spend a month-long summer vacation together. During July or August they head for their country home, go camping, travel, rent a home by the sea or visit relatives.

Reflecting both a gradually changing structure and a desire to preserve time-honored traditions, the family remains an important social institution in France.

Many French families go to their country homes in July or August. (Espelette)

13 Answer the following questions.

1. When Americans talk about their family, whom do they include?
2. When the French talk about their family, whom do they include?
3. Why does the French government give money to families upon the birth of each child after the first two?
4. Why is much advertising aimed at teenagers?
5. How are wedding ceremonies in France and in the United States similar?
6. How are they different?
7. How old must French people be in order to marry?
8. Where do French families go when they want to escape the stress of city life?

Francis and Isabelle Cazette were married in Beauregard.

Answers

13 Possible answers:
1. Americans include parents, children, brothers and sisters in the term "family."
2. The French include parents, children, brothers and sisters, as well as grandparents, aunts, uncles, nieces, nephews and cousins.
3. The French government gives money to families upon the birth of each child after the first two to maintain the population at its current level.
4. Teenagers often help their parents make decisions about what cars, clothes, food, computers, etc., to buy.
5. Friends and family in both France and the United States attend wedding celebrations where there may be dancing, singing and lots of good food.
6. The French often have two wedding ceremonies. Instead of a best man and a maid or matron of honor, French couples have witnesses at their civil wedding ceremony.
7. In France, young women must be 15 years old to marry; young men must be 18 years old.
8. When they want to escape the stress of city life, French families go to their **maison de campagne**.

Teacher's Note

Another expression for **une maison de campagne** is **une maison secondaire**.

NATIONAL STANDARDS
C2.1, C2.2, C4.2

155

Answers

14 1. Frédéric's last name is Meyer.
2. Anne's last name is Biancheri.
3. Colette is Anne's mother; Michel is Anne's father.
4. One of Frédéric's grandparents, his grandmother, will be at the wedding.
5. They will be married at **l'Église Notre-Dame du Monastère de Cimiez**.
6. The wedding is June 15, 2002.
7. The wedding begins at 4:00 P.M.
8. One of the bride's parents lives on the street where the church is located.
9. They live in Nice.
10. The zip code precedes the name of the city in a French address.

14 Here is a French wedding invitation. The bride's family is listed on the left side of the invitation; the groom's family is listed on the right side. The names of the grandparents come before the names of the parents. The parents' addresses are given at the bottom of the invitation. Answer the questions that follow about Anne and Frédéric's wedding.

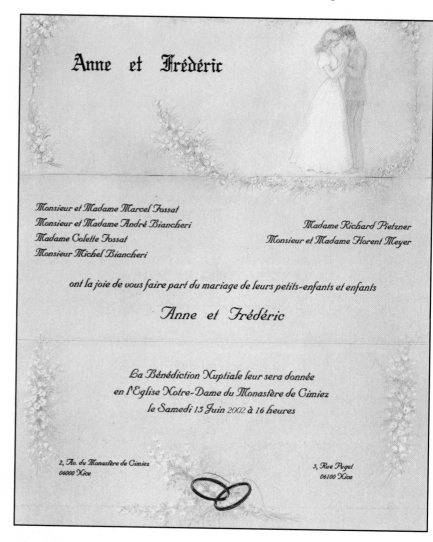

1. What is Frédéric's last name?
2. What is Anne's last name?
3. Who are Colette and Michel?
4. How many of Frédéric's grandparents will be at the wedding?
5. What is the name of the church where Anne and Frédéric will be married?
6. What is the date of the wedding?
7. At what time does the wedding begin?
8. Who lives on the street where the church is located?
9. In what city do Anne and Frédéric's parents live?
10. Where is the zip code placed in relation to the name of the city in a French address?

■ **Workbook Activities 13-14**

✎ **Grammar & Vocabulary Exercises 20-22**

💿 **Audiocassette/CD Adjectives**

Teacher's Notes

1. **Sympa**, the abbreviated form of **sympathique**, is invariable. 2. Communicative functions that are recycled in this lesson are "asking for information" and "asking and telling what the date is."

Cécile est sympa.

Françoise est méchante.

Paul est sympa.

Vincent est méchant.

Françoise est égoïste.

Cécile est généreuse.

Paul est généreux.

Vincent est égoïste.

Paul est intelligent.

Cécile est intelligente.

Françoise est bête.

Vincent est bête.

Cécile est diligente.

Françoise est paresseuse.

Paul est diligent.

Vincent est paresseux.

Cécile est timide.

Bla bla bla....

Bla bla bla....

Vincent est bavard.

Paul est timide.

Françoise est bavarde.

Leçon C

In this lesson you will be able to:

➤ **explain something**

➤ **tell when someone's birthday is**

➤ **express emotions**

➤ **describe character**

NATIONAL STANDARDS
C1.2, C4.1

Audiocassette/CD
Dialogue

Video

Sandrine brings her friend Jamila a gift.

Sandrine: J'ai un cadeau pour toi.
Jamila: Pourquoi?
Sandrine: Parce que c'est le 26 octobre. C'est ton anniversaire.
Jamila: Mais mon anniversaire est le 26 novembre.
Sandrine: Que je suis bête!
Jamila: Non, tu es généreuse.

 Enquête culturelle

The French often celebrate birthdays with a cake topped with candles, just as Americans do. To wish someone a happy birthday, they say **Joyeux anniversaire** or **Bon anniversaire**.

Joyeux anniversaire, Julien!

On French calendars the name of a saint is usually listed for each day, that particular saint's feast day (**fête**). Some French parents still follow the tradition of naming their child after the saint on whose feast day he or she was born. However, if the child is named after a saint whose feast day doesn't fall on the child's date of birth, he or she can celebrate twice each year. For example, a girl named Véronique born on May 14 may celebrate on that day and again on February 4, her saint's day. Children may receive a small gift from their family on their saint's day, while adults wish each other **Bonne fête** and may exchange cards.

FÉVRIER
☼ 7 h 23 à 16 h 46

1	M	Sᵉ Ella
2	M	Présentation
3	J	S. Blaise
4	V	Sᵉ Véronique
5	S	Sᵉ Agathe
6	D	S. Gaston
7	L	Sᵉ Eugénie
8	M	Sᵉ Jacqueline
9	M	Sᵉ Apolline
10	J	S. Arnaud
11	V	N.-D. Lourdes
12	S	S. Félix
13	D	Sᵉ Béatrice
14	L	S. Valentin
15	M	Mardi-Gras
16	M	Cendres
17	J	S. Alexis
18	V	Sᵉ Bernadette
19	S	S. Gabin
20	D	Carême
21	L	S. P. Damien
22	M	Sᵉ Isabelle
23	M	S. Lazare
24	J	S. Modeste
25	V	S. Roméo
26	S	S. Nestor
27	D	Sᵉ Honorine
28	L	S. Romain

1   Answer the following questions.

1. What is one similarity between French and American birthday celebrations?
2. How do the French wish each other a happy birthday?
3. Where are **fête** days listed?
4. Why may people named after saints celebrate twice each year?
5. When does a girl named Isabelle celebrate her **fête** day?
6. What do children receive on their **fête** day?
7. How do people wish each other a happy **fête** day?

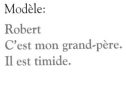

Answers

1 1. Both French and American birthday celebrations often include a cake topped with candles.
   2. The French say **Joyeux anniversaire** or **Bon anniversaire**.
   3. **Fête** days are listed on a calendar.
   4. They may celebrate once on the date of their birth and again on their **fête** day.
   5. A girl named Isabelle celebrates her **fête** day on February 22.
   6. Children often receive a small gift from their family.
   7. They say **Bonne fête.**

2   *Répondez en français.*

1. Qui a un cadeau?
2. Pour qui est le cadeau?
3. C'est l'anniversaire de Sandrine ou de Jamila?
4. Quelle est la date?
5. Quelle est la date de l'anniversaire de Jamila?
6. Sandrine, elle est bête ou généreuse?

Béatrice a un cadeau pour qui?

2 1. Sandrine a un cadeau.
   2. Le cadeau est pour Jamila.
   3. C'est l'anniversaire de Jamila.
   4. C'est le 26 octobre.
   5. L'anniversaire de Jamila est le 26 novembre.
   6. Sandrine est généreuse.

3 Answers will vary.

3   On a sheet of paper write the names of five of your family members. They may be members of your immediate family as well as distant relatives. Then write a sentence that tells how each person is related to you. Finally, describe each relative using an adjective from the list. Pick an adjective from the left-hand column for a male; pick one from the right-hand column for a female.

beau	belle
généreux	généreuse
intelligent	intelligente
timide	timide
bavard	bavarde
super	super
sympa	sympa
égoïste	égoïste
bête	bête
paresseux	paresseuse
diligent	diligente
méchant	méchante

Modèle:

Robert
C'est mon grand-père.
Il est timide.

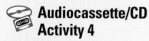

4 | *C'est à toi!*

1. Quelle est la date de ton anniversaire?
2. Qu'est-ce que tu aimes faire pour ton anniversaire?
3. Tu es timide?
4. Ta grand-mère, elle est généreuse ou égoïste?
5. Ton professeur de français est sympa?

Structure

Agreement of adjectives

Adjectives, words that describe nouns and pronouns, are either masculine or feminine, singular or plural. Masculine adjectives are used with masculine nouns and pronouns; feminine adjectives are used with feminine nouns and pronouns. In French, adjectives usually follow the nouns they describe.

M. Blot est un prof intelligent.   Mme Thibault est une prof intelligente.

Most feminine adjectives are formed by adding an **e** to masculine adjectives.

> masculine adjective + **e** = feminine adjective

Thierry est un élève diligent.   Latifa est une élève diligente.

If a masculine adjective ends in **-e**, the feminine adjective is identical.

Mon frère est timide.   Ma sœur est timide aussi.

If a masculine adjective ends in **-eux,** the feminine adjective ends in **-euse.**

Sébastien est généreux.   Sandrine est généreuse aussi.

Some common adjectives, like **beau**, precede the nouns they describe. The masculine adjective **beau** has an irregular feminine form, **belle.** Before a masculine noun beginning with a vowel sound, use **bel.**

Voilà un beau garçon.
Voilà un bel étudiant.
Voilà une belle fille.

Stéphanie est une élève diligente.

UNE BELLE PAGE D'HISTOIRE BRETONNE.
CHÂTEAU
LA BOURBANSAIS

If an adjective describes a plural noun, the adjective must be plural also. To form the plural of most adjectives, add an **s** to singular adjectives.

> singular adjective + **s** = plural adjective

Ton cousin est bavard.	Mes cousins sont bavards aussi.
Ma sœur est paresseuse.	Ses sœurs sont paresseuses aussi.

If a masculine singular adjective ends in **-s**, the masculine plural adjective is identical.

Le chat est gris.   Les chiens sont gris aussi.

The masculine singular adjective **beau** has an irregular plural form, **beaux.**

Jérémy a deux beaux chiens.

Pratique

5 Describe some of the people in your classroom. Use a different adjective to describe each one.

6 Brothers and sisters sometimes are very different. Say that these brothers and sisters are the opposites of their siblings.

1. Paul et Pierre sont bavards. Et Patricia et Pauline?
2. Judith et Claudette sont généreuses. Et Jean?
3. Myriam est intelligente. Et Max et Michel?
4. Fayçal est méchant. Et Fatima?
5. Anne-Marie et Ariane sont bêtes. Et Alexandre?
6. Christophe est égoïste. Et Christine et Chloé?
7. Florence est timide. Et Fred et Fabrice?
8. Delphine et Denise sont diligentes. Et David et Daniel?

Voilà deux beaux enfants. (Saint-Jean-de-Luz)

Modèle:
Jamila est bavarde.

Modèle:
Charles est paresseux. Et Caroline et Catherine?
Caroline et Catherine ne sont pas paresseuses. Elles sont diligentes.

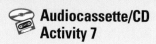

Answers

7 1. Monsieur Diouf, vous avez une belle femme!
2. Monsieur Diouf, vous avez un beau cheval!
3. Monsieur Diouf, vous avez trois beaux chiens!
4. Monsieur Diouf, vous avez un bel oiseau!
5. Monsieur Diouf, vous avez deux belles filles!
6. Monsieur Diouf, vous avez un beau fils!
7. Monsieur Diouf, vous avez quatre beaux poissons rouges!

Teacher's Notes

1. To make sure students give the date of their birthday correctly in Activity 8, have them fill out a sheet in class the preceding day on which they write their name and date of birth in French. You can compare what each student says with what date he or she has written. 2. You may want students to work in pairs as they answer the questions to **Sur la bonne piste** on page 164. Note that the first four questions have specific answers. However, there is still some room for subjectivity. The last two questions are interpretation questions, and students should be encouraged to come up with a variety of answers. To holistically grade this activity, either you or the students can give a check (✔) to an answer that comes directly from the reading passage, a plus (+) to an answer that requires thinking that goes beyond the text's answer and a minus (−) to an answer that is not at all related to the text. You or the students can give a zero (0) for no answer at all.

NATIONAL STANDARDS
C1.1, C1.2

162

Modèle:

deux chats
Monsieur Diouf, vous avez deux beaux chats!

Modèle:

Quelle est la date de ton anniversaire?
La date de mon anniversaire est le 25 septembre.

Modèle:

Tu t'appelles comment?
Je m'appelle Anne.

Tu as quel âge?
J'ai 15 ans.

Quelle est la date de ton anniversaire?
Mon anniversaire est le 10 juin.

Tu es timide ou bavarde?
Je suis timide.

Tu es diligente ou paresseuse?
Je suis paresseuse.

---

7 Flatter M. Diouf by telling him that his family members and pets are beautiful or handsome.

1. une femme
2. un cheval
3. trois chiens
4. un oiseau
5. deux filles
6. un fils
7. quatre poissons rouges

Monsieur Diouf, vous avez deux belles filles!

Communication

8 Your French teacher wants to know the birthdays of all the students in class in order to send birthday cards to everyone on the appropriate date. To make your teacher's job easier, ask your classmates their dates of birth in French and then arrange yourselves in a line in chronological order from left to right according to the information you obtain. Ask as many classmates as possible their dates of birth in order to know if you should stand to the right or left of them. When everyone is in the correct birth order, go down the line, one by one, saying your date of birth.

9 To get to know some of your classmates better, interview five of them, asking them their name, age, birthday and what they're like. To help you organize the information you gather, make a "sun" for each student you interview.

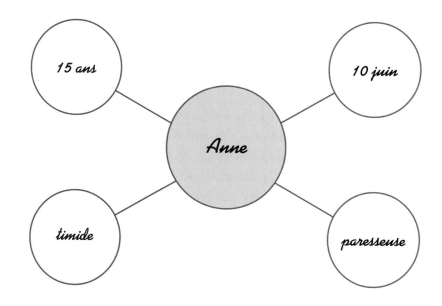

O Your French pen pal, Jérémy, sent you a picture of his family. Describe each person in the picture as completely as you can, mentioning a physical trait and a character trait.

Modèle:

Le grand-père de Jérémy a les cheveux noirs. Il est méchant.

When reading something, you naturally form mental pictures based on your own cultural viewpoint. If you are an American, this means that you "see" the reading through the eyes of an American: what's true or common in the United States seems like it should be true elsewhere in the world. Furthermore, your mind has a limited capacity and doesn't consider all the different possible definitions of a word. Instead, your mind tries to save thinking space by forming a very brief picture of what that word means and skipping by many other possible interpretations. The information that "slips by" may be important to other people, especially those from a different culture.

Here are two examples. When you see **une maison**, the French word for "house," you might picture a little white house with a garden, perhaps out in the country. You probably save the picture of an inner-city dwelling for the word "apartment." But many French people live in apartments and call them **une maison**. When you look at the number sequence 11-3-02 in English, it represents November 3, 2002. However, you already know that the French write 3.11.02 to represent this date. If you weren't aware of this, it's possible you could order tickets to the theater for the wrong night or wait for a train on the wrong day. You might ask "Why don't the French write the date the 'right' way?" The French believe they do, sequencing the date from the shortest period of time (the day) to the longest (the year).

In Marie-Claire's letter to her pen pal that follows, she tells about where she lives and gives the date. As you read her letter, remember that some words and ideas can be interpreted in more than one way. Writers give you many clues that can tell you whether or not you're on the right track. Keeping the context of the reading in mind will help guide you as you encounter events that are different in another culture.

Sur la bonne piste

 **Workbook
Activity 17**

 **Audiocassette/CD
*Sur la bonne piste***

 Listening Activity 3A

 **Quiz
*Leçon C***

**Computer Software
Activity 8**

Answers

10 Possible answers:
1. La grand-mère de Jérémy a les cheveux bruns. Elle est généreuse.
2. La mère de Jérémy a les cheveux roux. Elle est intelligente.
3. Le beau-père de Jérémy a les cheveux noirs. Il est bavard.
4. La sœur de Jérémy a les cheveux roux. Elle est égoïste.
5. La belle-sœur de Jérémy a les cheveux bruns. Elle est timide.
6. Jérémy a les cheveux blonds. Il est sympa.

Teacher's Note

Optional activity. Have students compare five things about Marie-Claire's family with either their own or a family on a popular TV series. Each student selects and copies five sentences from Marie-Claire's letter. Then, next to each of these five sentences, the student writes a related sentence or two in French that describes the family he or she has chosen. For example, next to **Mon père est brun, grand et intelligent**, a student might write **Mon père a les cheveux noirs et les yeux gris. Il est diligent, mais il n'est pas généreux.** Then collect these papers or have students exchange them. Students should be careful not to assess each other's opinions but rather to concentrate on language and culture.

NATIONAL STANDARDS
C1.2, C1.3, C2.2, C3.1, C4.2

Answers

11 Possible answers:
1. Marie-Claire wrote this letter July 12, 2002.
2. Gilberte's visit will take place in December, 2002.
3. Marie-Claire has one cat.
4. Marie-Claire's sister, Danielle, is 21 years old and is a student at the University of Nantes.
5. Marie-Claire is writing to Gilberte to tell her about her family. Gilberte, a Canadian exchange student, will be staying at Marie-Claire's house.
6. Marie-Claire has gifts for her mother because tomorrow is her birthday and for her father because tomorrow is his saint's day.

En famille

Marie-Claire va recevoir une jeune fille canadienne, Gilberte, pendant trois semaines en décembre. Gilberte fait partie d'un programme d'échanges. Voici la lettre de Marie-Claire à Gilberte.

12.7.02

Chère Gilberte,

Je suis très contente que tu viennes chez moi en décembre. J'ai 15 ans et je vais à l'école à Tours. Mes parents sont divorcés. J'habite dans une maison avec ma mère et mon beau-père. Ma mère est blonde aux yeux bleus. Demain c'est son anniversaire. Elle va avoir 42 ans. C'est aussi la fête de mon père. Quelle coïncidence, n'est-ce pas? Mon père est brun, grand et intelligent.

J'ai une sœur, Danielle. Elle a 21 ans. En ce moment, elle est à l'Université de Nantes. J'ai aussi un demi-frère. Il s'appelle Patrick et il a 9 ans.

J'adore les animaux. J'ai un chat, un chien et un canari chez ma belle-mère et mon père.

J'ai hâte de faire ta connaissance. Tu vas être comme un membre de la famille.

À bientôt,
Marie-Claire

11 Answer the following questions.
1. When did Marie-Claire write this letter?
2. When will Gilberte's visit take place?
3. How many cats does Marie-Claire have?
4. What is Marie-Claire's sister like?
5. Why is Marie-Claire writing to Gilberte?
6. Marie-Claire bought gifts for certain members of her family. For whom does she have gifts and why?

Nathalie et Raoul

C'est à moi!

Now that you have completed this unit, take a look at what you should be able to do in French. Can you do all of these tasks?

➤ I can ask for and give information about who someone is.

➤ I can identify family members, including pets.

➤ I can ask and tell how old someone is.

➤ I can describe someone's physical and character traits.

➤ I can express emotions.

➤ I can ask and tell what the date is.

➤ I can say when someone's birthday is.

➤ I can explain why.

➤ I can tell where places are located.

Here is a brief checkup to see how much you understand about French culture. Decide if each statement is **vrai** or **faux**.

1. The French word **beau-père** is used for both "father-in-law" and "stepfather."
2. Martinique and Guadeloupe are both located in French-speaking Canada.
3. Huguenots are the only French workers who get one month's paid vacation each year.
4. There are more pets than children in France.
5. French people usually have well-mannered dogs that are accepted even in hotels and restaurants.
6. Extended families in France live in the same towns or cities and get together every Sunday.

Why do extended families get together so often in France? ((Dinard)

7. French parents receive money from the government upon the birth of each child.
8. Couples in France must get married at **la mairie**.
9. The French often celebrate birthdays with cakes topped with candles.
10. Besides celebrating the day on which they were born, the French also celebrate their saint's feast day.

Listening Activity 3B

Teacher's Note

Here is the English version of the cartoon on page 164: Raoul, let me introduce you to my cousin Hélène. She's from Nantes. Hello, Hélène. Say, do you know a guy for Hélène? Hmmm . . . uhm . . . . Jacques? No, he's selfish. Bruno? No, he looks like my grandfather. Thierry? No, he's handsome, but dumb. Malick? No, he's too talkative. Fabrice! Intelligent . . . not stupid. Handsome . . . like me. Rich . . . but not a snob. Yes! (At Raoul's house) You have beautiful blue eyes, Raoul. He's fantastic! You're very beautiful, Nathalie. She's incredible! I have a gift for you, Hélène. What beautiful blond hair! Thanks, Fabrice. He's nice!

NATIONAL STANDARDS
C1.1, C2.1

Communication orale

Modèle:

Student A: Qu'est-ce que le prof d'anglais donne à l'école?

Student B: Le prof d'anglais donne un dictionnaire et des stylos. Il est généreux.

Imagine that a school in Martinique was recently destroyed by a hurricane. Your school's student government is collecting school supplies to send to the students and teachers there. They need everything from pens and pencils to VCRs and TVs. With a partner, ask and tell what various students and teachers, as well as your family members, are donating to this cause. As you take turns with your partner naming people who are contributing, give one more piece of information about each person, for example, a character trait. Follow the model.

Communication écrite

As a follow-up to your conversation with your partner about contributing to the relief fund for the school in Martinique, write a memo to your French teacher. Begin your memo with today's date. Then, based on your conversation, mention who is giving what to the students and teachers whose school was destroyed and tell something about each donor. Finally, ask your teacher what he or she is giving.

Communication active

To ask for information, use:

C'est toi? — *Is this you?*

Il est beau comme moi, **n'est-ce pas?** — *He's handsome like I am, isn't that so?*

To give information, use:

C'est Justin. — *It's Justin.*

To point out family members, use:

C'est mon père. — *This is my father.*
C'est ma mère. — *This is my mother.*
Ce sont mes parents. — *These are my parents.*
Milou **est un membre de la famille.** — *Milou is a member of the family.*

LES FRERES TALOCHE
Mise en scène Anne ROUMANOFF
BLANCS MANTEAUX 01 48 87 15 84

Mistigris est aussi un membre de la famille. (Paris)

To ask how old someone is, use:
Tu as quel âge? *How old are you?*

To tell how old someone is, use:
Il/Elle a quinze **an(s).** *He/She is fifteen years old.*

To describe physical traits, use:
J'ai les cheveux blonds. *I have blond hair.*
J'ai les yeux bleus. *I have blue eyes.*

To describe character, use:
Je suis généreux/généreuse. *I'm generous.*

To express emotions, use:
Que je suis bête! *How stupid I am!*

To ask what the date is, use:
C'est quelle date? *What's the date?*

To tell what the date is, use:
Nous sommes le 25 avril. *It's April 25.*
C'est le 1er août. *It's August 1.*

To tell when someone's birthday is, use:
Son anniversaire est le *His/Her birthday is October 26.*
vingt-six octobre.

To explain something, use:
Parce que c'est ton anniversaire. *Because it's your birthday.*

To tell location, use:
C'est à 7.000 **kilomètres** *It's 7,000 kilometers from Nantes.*
de Nantes.

J'ai les cheveux bruns
et les yeux noirs.

UN SOUHAIT D'ANNIVERSAIRE
Pour Toi,
Mon Frère

À moi de jouer!

Possible paragraph:

La famille de Sophie

Sophie a 15 ans. C'est la fille de M. et Mme Lanmeur et la sœur de Christophe. L'anniversaire de Sophie est le 23 juillet. Sophie a les cheveux blonds et les yeux bleus. Elle est bavarde et généreuse.

Mme Lanmeur est la mère de Sophie et Christophe, la femme de M. Lanmeur, et la fille de Mme St. Onge. Elle a 40 ans. Son anniversaire est le 4 décembre. Elle a les cheveux roux et les yeux verts. Elle est belle et sympa.

M. Lanmeur est le père de Christophe et Sophie et le mari de Mme Lanmeur. Il a 45 ans. Son anniversaire est le 30 octobre. Il a les cheveux bruns et les yeux noirs. Il est intelligent et diligent.

Christophe a 17 ans. C'est le fils de M. et Mme Lanmeur et le frère de Sophie. Son anniversaire est le premier avril. Il a les cheveux bruns et les yeux verts. Il est méchant et paresseux.

Mme St. Onge est la mère de Mme Lanmeur et la grand-mère de Christophe et Sylvie. Elle a 70 ans. Son anniversaire est le 25 août. Elle a les cheveux gris et les yeux bleus. Elle est sympa et généreuse.

Max est le chien de la famille Lanmeur. Il a 5 ans. Son anniversaire est le 8 mai. Il est timide et intelligent.

Communication électronique

To practice the French words for the days and months in preparation for your unit test, play this word search game by going to the following Internet site:

http://www.quia.com/custom/1237main.html

Now click on "Word Search" to begin the game.

À moi de jouer!

Show how much you have learned about describing family members in French by writing a paragraph about the family in the illustration. You can imagine either that you are one of the members of this family (the title of your paragraph would be **Ma famille**) or you can describe the family from the point of view of someone not in the illustration (your title would be **La famille de...**). In your paragraph identify everyone, tell how they are related, give their ages and birthdays, describe the color of their hair and eyes, and tell what kind of person they are. (You may want to refer to the *Communication active* on pages 166-67 and the vocabulary list on page 169.)

Vocabulaire

l'   **âge (m.)** age
     Tu as quel âge? How old are you?
un   **an** year
     J'ai... ans. I'm . . . years old.
un   **anniversaire** birthday
     août August
     avoir... ans to be . . . (years old)
     avoir quel âge to be how old
     avril April

     bavard(e) talkative
     beau, bel, belle beautiful, handsome
un   **beau-frère** stepbrother, brother-in-law
un   **beau-père** stepfather, father-in-law
une **belle-mère** stepmother, mother-in-law
une **belle-sœur** stepsister, sister-in-law
     bête stupid, dumb
     bleu(e) blue
     blond(e) blond
     brun(e) dark (hair), brown

     c'est he is, she is
un   **cadeau** gift, present
     ce sont they are, these are, those are
un   **chat** cat
un   **cheval** horse
des **cheveux (m.)** hair
un   **chien** dog
un(e) **cousin(e)** cousin

une **date** date
     décembre December
un   **demi-frère** half-brother
une **demi-sœur** half-sister
     diligent(e) hardworking

     égoïste selfish
     en on
un(e) **enfant** child
     être to be
     Nous sommes le (+ *date*). It's the
     (+ date).

une **famille** family
une **femme** wife; woman
     février February
une **fille** daughter
un   **fils** son
un   **frère** brother

     généreux, généreuse generous
une **grand-mère** grandmother
un   **grand-père** grandfather
     gris(e) gray
la   **Guadeloupe** Guadeloupe

     intelligent(e) intelligent

     janvier January
     juillet July

     juin June

un   **kilomètre** kilometer

     leur their

     mai May
un   **mari** husband
     mars March
la   **Martinique** Martinique
     méchant(e) mean
un   **membre** member
une **mère** mother
un   **million** million
un   **mois** month
     mon, ma; mes my

     n'est-ce pas? isn't that so?
     noir(e) black
     notre; nos our
     nous us
     novembre November

     octobre October
un   **oiseau** bird
un   **oncle** uncle

     parce que because
un   **parent** parent; relative
     paresseux, paresseuse lazy
un   **père** father
une **photo** photo, picture
un   **poisson** fish
     un poisson rouge goldfish
     premier, première first

     que how
     Que je suis bête! How dumb I am!

     ressembler à to look like, to resemble
     rouge red
     roux, rousse red (hair)

     septembre September
une **sœur** sister
     son, sa; ses his, her, one's, its
     sympa (sympathique) nice

une **tante** aunt
     timide timid, shy
     ton, ta; tes your
     tous les deux both

les **vacances (f.)** vacation
     vert(e) green
     votre; vos your

des **yeux (m.)** eyes

Unité 6

Tu viens d'où?

In this unit you will be able to:

➤ identify nationalities

➤ ask and tell where someone is from

➤ identify professions

➤ ask for information

➤ give information

➤ explain something

➤ invite

➤ express emotions

NATIONAL STANDARDS
C2.1

Workbook Activity 1

 Grammar & Vocabulary Exercises 1-2

 Audiocassette/CD Countries and Nationalities

Transparencies 25-26

Teacher's Notes

1. The countries and nationalities portrayed here represent a sampling of those your students may identify with. In **Unité 11** a list of francophone countries and nationalities is given, with an emphasis on francophone Africa. If you have students with African heritage, you may want to introduce the appropriate terms from **Unité 11** at this point. If you have students whose native countries and nationalities appear in neither this lesson nor in **Unité 11**, you may want to present the corresponding French terms at this time. 2. **L'Amérique (f.)** is often used instead of **les États-Unis**. 3. Some other related terms in French include **danois(e)** (*Danish*), **hollandais(e)** (*Dutch*), **libanais(e)** (*Lebanese*), **grec/grecque** (*Greek*), **israélien(ne)** (*Israeli*), **brésilien(ne)** (*Brazilian*), **coréen(ne)** (*Korean*), **égyptien(ne)** (*Egyptian*), **portugais(e)** (*Portuguese*), **suisse** (*Swiss*), **belge** (*Belgian*), **luxembourgeois(e)** (*Luxembourger*), **russe** (*Russian*), **cambodgien(ne)** (*Cambodian*), **laotien(ne)** (*Laotian*) and **amérindien(ne)** (*Native American*). African-American is **afroaméricain(e)**. 4. How to say you are from a certain city, town, state or country is explained in this lesson's **Structure**. 5. A communicative function that is recycled in this lesson is "giving information" and "pointing out family members."

Leçon A

In this lesson you will be able to:

➤ **ask for information**

➤ **ask and tell where someone is from**

➤ **identify nationalities**

Elle vient des États-Unis.   *Il vient du Mexique.*
                                 Elle vient d'Allemagne.

It's the beginning of the school year in Tours. At a meeting of international exchange students, Petra, Sandy and José are showing each other pictures of their families.

Sandy: C'est qui sur la photo?

José: C'est ma famille... mon père et ma belle-mère.

Petra: Vous venez d'où?

José: Nous venons du Mexique. Mon père et moi, nous sommes mexicains, et ma belle-mère est japonaise. Et toi, Petra, tu viens d'où? Est-ce que tu es allemande?

Petra: Oui, je viens d'Allemagne. Voilà ma famille.

Sandy: Tu ressembles à ta mère. Moi, je ressemble à mon père. Je viens des États-Unis. Je suis de Dallas.

Situated in the Loire Valley, Tours is the capital of the Touraine region of France. The area around Tours has many beautiful castles, such as

Enquête culturelle

Azay-le-Rideau, like the other Renaissance castles, was built in the 16th century.

Workbook Activities 2-3

Audiocassette/CD Dialogue

TPR

Masculine or Feminine?

To practice listening skills with masculine and feminine adjectives of nationality, say various adjectives introduced in this lesson. Have students raise their left hand if they hear a masculine adjective; have them raise their right hand if they hear a feminine adjective.

NATIONAL STANDARDS
C1.2, C2.2, C4.2

Connections

Foreign Students

If there are foreign exchange students at your school or in your city, you may want to invite them to speak to your class about their country and customs. In preparation for this discussion, have each of your students write five questions to ask the international students. (If any of these students are from francophone countries, your students might write their questions in French.)

Comparisons

Cultural Journal

If your students are keeping a cultural journal and did the connections activity dealing with foreign students, you might have them write answers to these questions following their discussion with these international students: What did you learn about each country that you didn't know before? What surprised you the most? What would you like or dislike about living in each country?

NATIONAL STANDARDS
C2.1, C2.2, C4.2

Chenonceaux and Chambord. The city's cultural and intellectual life centers around its university, which attracts students from all over the world. Many American teachers and students study in Tours.

The castle of Chenonceaux is built on a bridge over the river Cher.

Chambord is the largest of the Loire castles with 440 rooms.

European teenagers have many opportunities to travel to other countries. Because of the relatively small size of the European continent, it doesn't take long by car or train to arrive in another country. Europeans often vacation in neighboring countries. Rather than simply visiting famous monuments, people in Europe often like to explore quaint villages, camp in quiet parks or get to know other people. Therefore, Europeans find

an immediate use for speaking a second language, and international study programs are very popular.

Complétez les phrases avec la lettre du mot convenable d'après le dialogue.
(Complete the sentences with the letter of the appropriate word according
to the dialogue.)

1. José vient du....
2. José et son père sont....
3. La... de José est japonaise.
4. Petra est....
5. Petra vient d'....
6. Petra ressemble à sa....
7. Sandy ressemble à son....
8. Sandy vient des....

   a. États-Unis
   b. allemande
   c. mère
   d. Mexique
   e. belle-mère
   f. père
   g. mexicains
   h. Allemagne

Azteca   **Mexicain**
7, rue Sauval Paris 1er, tél : 01 42 36 11 16.
Ce charmant restaurant propose une agréable cuisine mexicaine. Musiciens et chanteurs le soir. *A nice
restaurant serving a good Mexican cuisine.*
■ Menus déj. / *Luncheon menus* : 8,84 & 13,57 €.

Manuel vient d'Espagne. Il est
espagnol.

---

2 Match the letter of the sentence that describes each person's nationality
with the sentence that tells the country he or she comes from.

1. Rolf vient d'Allemagne.
2. Gina vient d'Italie.
3. Tim vient des États-Unis.
4. Francisco vient d'Espagne.
5. Diana vient d'Angleterre.
6. Liu vient de Chine.
7. Sei vient du Japon.
8. Yolanda vient du Mexique.

   a. Il est espagnol.
   b. Elle est mexicaine.
   c. Elle est anglaise.
   d. Elle est japonaise.
   e. Elle est italienne.
   f. Il est allemand.
   g. Il est chinois.
   h. Il est américain.

LA BOCCA

RESTAURANT ITALIEN - BAR
59, rue Montmartre 75002 Paris
Tel: 01 42 36 71 88
Fermé le dimanche

Andreas est le frère de Rolf. Il est aussi
allemand.

CHEZ NGO
*Haute gastronomie chinoise et thaïlandaise.
Spécialités de poissons frais et crustacés vivants,
préparées par 2 chefs, l'un chinois l'autre thaïlandais.*

NATIONAL STANDARDS
C1.1, C1.2

175

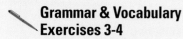
Workbook
Activities 4-5

Grammar & Vocabulary
Exercises 3-4

Audiocassette/CD
Activities 3-4

Computer Software
Activity 1

Answers

3 Answers will vary.

4 1. Je viens avec Charles.
2. David et Renée viennent ensemble.
3. Sandrine vient avec Latifa.
4. Charles et moi, nous venons ensemble.
5. Tu viens avec Delphine.
6. Bruno vient avec Louis.
7. Françoise et Cécile viennent ensemble.
8. Delphine et toi, vous venez ensemble.

3 | *C'est à toi!*
1. Tu viens d'où?
2. Tes parents, ils viennent d'où?
3. Tu ressembles à un membre de ta famille?
4. Tu étudies le français, l'espagnol ou l'allemand?
5. Ton professeur d'anglais, il/elle est américain(e)?

Structure

Present tense of the irregular verb *venir*

The verb **venir** (*to come*) is irregular.

venir			
je	**viens**	Je **viens** d'Allemagne.	*I come from Germany.*
tu	**viens**	Tu **viens** d'où?	*Where are you from?*
il/elle/on	**vient**	Juan **vient** du Mexique.	*Juan comes from Mexico.*
nous	**venons**	Nous **venons** ensemble.	*We're coming together.*
vous	**venez**	Vous ne **venez** pas demain?	*Aren't you coming tomorrow?*
ils/elles	**viennent**	Ils **viennent** chez moi.	*They're coming to my house.*

Tout vient à point
à qui sait attendre demain
vendredi 13.

Pratique

4 | Some of your friends are meeting at a café after school. Tell who's coming with whom.

Thérèse vient avec Dominique.

1. je/avec Charles
2. David et Renée/ensemble
3. Sandrine/avec Latifa
4. Charles et moi, nous/ensemble
5. tu/avec Delphine
6. Bruno/avec Louis
7. Françoise et Cécile/ensemble
8. Delphine et toi, vous/ensemble

Modèle:
Théo et Stéphanie/ensemble
Théo et Stéphanie viennent ensemble.

Qui vient? (Paris)

5 With a partner, take turns asking and telling who's coming to the school dance. Follow the models.

1. Margarette/non
2. tu/oui
3. Daniel et toi, vous/oui
4. Abdou/non
5. Anne-Marie et Benjamin/non
6. Nathalie et moi, nous/oui
7. Béatrice et Karine/oui
8. le prof de français/non

Non, pas moi. Je ne viens pas à la danse.

Modèles:

Clément/oui
Student A: Clément vient?
Student B: Oui, il vient.

Chloé et Alain/non
Student B: Chloé et Alain viennent?
Student A: Non, ils ne viennent pas.

De + definite articles

The preposition **de** (*of, from*) does not change before the definite articles **la** and **l'**.

C'est l'ordinateur **de la** fille.   *It's the girl's computer.*
Où est le cahier **de l'**élève?   *Where is the student's notebook?*

Before the definite articles **le** and **les**, however, **de** changes form. **De** combines with **le** and **les** as follows:

de + le = du	*from (the), of (the)*
de + les = des	*from (the), of (the)*

Je viens **des** États-Unis.   *I'm from the United States.*
José vient **du** Mexique.   *José is from Mexico.*

To say that someone is from a country with a masculine name, use a form of **venir de** with the definite article: **Je viens du Canada. Elle vient des États-Unis**. To say that someone is from a country with a feminine name, do not use the definite article after **de** or **d'**: **Il vient de Chine. Elles viennent d'Angleterre.** (To say that someone is from a certain city or town, use a form of **être de**: **Je suis de Chicago.**)

Nous venons du Japon.

QUELQUES IMAGES DE LA RENTRÉE

L'ÉPÉE DU NINJA

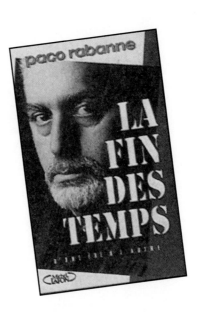

paco rabanne

LA FIN DES TEMPS

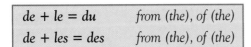

Workbook Activity 6

Grammar & Vocabulary Exercises 5-6

Audiocassette/CD Activity 5

Computer Software Activity 2

Answers

5 1. Margarette vient?
Non, elle ne vient pas.
2. Tu viens?
Oui, je viens.
3. Daniel et toi, vous venez?
Oui, nous venons.
4. Abdou vient?
Non, il ne vient pas.
5. Anne-Marie et Benjamin viennent?
Non, ils ne viennent pas.
6. Nathalie et moi, nous venons?
Oui, vous venez.
7. Béatrice et Karine viennent?
Oui, elles viennent.
8. Le prof de français vient?
Non, il ne vient pas.

Teacher's Note

Point out to students that the **s** in **des** is pronounced [z] before a vowel sound: **Où sont les boissons des enfants?**

[z]

Connections

Countries

To continue the activity described earlier in this lesson where students each chose a country and designed its flag on note cards, give students a copy of a world map and have them locate their country. Then tell students to interview each other, asking where their partner is from (**Tu viens d'où?**). Partners also show each other their country on the map.

NATIONAL STANDARDS
C1.1, C1.2, C4.1

Audiocassette/CD Activity 7

Answers

6 1. C'est le chien du père.
2. C'est l'oiseau des filles.
3. C'est le cheval de la tante.
4. C'est le chat de l'oncle.
5. C'est le poisson rouge des cousins.
6. C'est le chien de la grand-mère.
7. C'est l'oiseau du grand-père.

7 1. Gilberte vient du Canada.
2. Josh vient des États-Unis.
3. Diego vient du Mexique.
4. Jane vient d'Angleterre.
5. Christophe vient de France.
6. Ingrid vient d'Allemagne.
7. Stefano vient d'Italie.
8. Carmen vient d'Espagne.

Cooperative Group Practice

Sentence Construction
To vary Activity 6, you might put students in small groups of four or five. First, have the group members bring pictures from the back issues of magazines (or have them make drawings) showing nouns that they can express in French, for example, pets, foods, beverages or classroom objects. Next have them make a set of note cards each containing a family member, for example, **la mère**, **les oncles**, **le beau-père**. Then each student chooses one picture and one note card and makes a sentence saying that the object belongs to the family member, for example, **C'est l'ordinateur du grand-père**. When all pictures and cards have been used, groups can exchange them and begin the activity again.

NATIONAL STANDARDS
C1.1, C1.2

178

Modèle:

Minou
C'est le chat de la mère.

Dagobert, c'est l'oiseau de la sœur.

Modèle:

Ingrid vient d'Allemagne.

Pratique

6 Tell whom each pet belongs to in this French family.

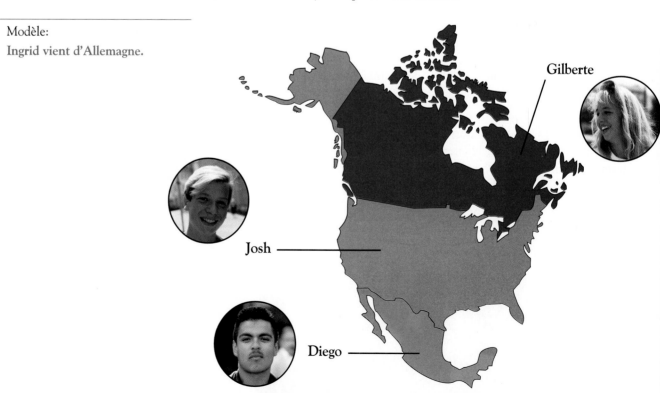

1. Rex
2. Happy
3. Ouragan
4. Pompon

5. Roger
6. Sultan
7. Sylvestre

7 Tell what country each person comes from.

Gilberte

Josh

Diego

Jane

Ingrid

Christophe

Stefano

Carmen

Workbook Activity 7

Grammar & Vocabulary Exercises 7-9

Teacher's Note

More information on intonation in question formation is presented in the **Prononciation** section of this lesson.

Cooperative Group Practice

Forming Questions

You may want to have students practice forming questions in small groups of four or five using the same pictures of nouns that they worked with earlier in this lesson. Have each student choose a picture and ask other members of the group if the object belongs to them, for example, **Est-ce que c'est ton chien**? The student answering the question responds either **Oui, c'est mon chien** or **Non, ce n'est pas mon chien**. For additional practice in forming questions, students may ask the same questions using **n'est-ce pas**, for example, **C'est ton chien, n'est-ce pas**?

Forming questions

Questions can be divided into two groups:

1. questions that can be answered by "yes" or "no"
    Is it raining?
2. questions that ask for information
    What time is it?

In spoken French there are three basic ways to ask a question that can be answered by "yes" or "no":

1. Make your tone of voice rise at the end of a sentence.
    (It rises at the end of all "yes" or "no" questions.)

    C'est ta famille sur la photo? *Is this your family in the photo?*

2. Put the expression **est-ce que** right before the subject of the sentence. **Est-ce que** has no meaning by itself; it serves only to change a statement into a question. Before a word beginning with a vowel sound, **est-ce que** becomes **est-ce qu'**.

    Est-ce que Normand   *Is Normand Canadian?*
    est canadien?
    Est-ce qu'il est de Montréal? *Is he from Montreal?*

NATIONAL STANDARDS
C1.1, C1.2, C4.1

Answers

8 1. Est-ce que tu joues au basket?
2. Est-ce que tu nages?
3. Est-ce que tu danses?
4. Est-ce que tu vas au cinéma?
5. Est-ce que tu manges au fast-food?
6. Est-ce que tu regardes la télé?
7. Est-ce que tu étudies?
8. Est-ce que tu téléphones?

9 1. Avec qui est-ce que tu joues au basket?
2. Comment est-ce que tu nages?
3. Comment est-ce que tu danses?
4. Avec qui est-ce que tu vas au cinéma?
5. Pourquoi est-ce que tu manges au fast-food?
6. À quelle heure est-ce que tu regardes la télé?
7. Où est-ce que tu étudies?
8. À qui est-ce que tu téléphones?

Teacher's Note

You may want to give students examples of question formation with other interrogative expressions that they have seen, such as **qu'est-ce que** and **quel(le)**. For example, *Qu'est-ce que* **tu aimes faire?** À *quelle* **heure est-ce que tu viens?**

NATIONAL STANDARDS
C1.1, C1.2, C4.1, C5.1

180

Vous venez des États-Unis, n'est-ce pas?

Modèle:

skier
Est-ce que tu skies?

Modèle:

skier (pourquoi)
Pourquoi est-ce que tu skies?

3. Add the expression **n'est-ce pas** to the end of a sentence. **N'est-ce pas** basically means "isn't that so" and may be interpreted in various ways, depending on context.

C'est ta sœur, **n'est-ce pas?**   *She's your sister, isn't she?*
Vous venez du Mexique, **n'est-ce pas?**   *You're from Mexico, aren't you?*

In spoken French you form a question that asks for information by using a specific question word followed by **est-ce que**, a subject and a verb. Some question words you have already seen are **comment**, **qui**, **pourquoi**, **combien** and **où**.

Où est-ce que tu vas?   *Where are you going?*
Avec **qui est-ce que** tu joues au tennis?   *With whom are you playing tennis?*

Pratique

8 You are going to conduct a survey about what teenagers do in their free time. Prepare some questions for your survey.

1. jouer au basket
2. nager
3. danser
4. aller au cinéma
5. manger au fast-food
6. regarder la télé
7. étudier
8. téléphoner

Est-ce que tu joues au tennis?

Oui, je joue avec ma sœur.

9 Now prepare some follow-up survey questions to ask the participants if they answer "yes" to any of your original questions.

1. jouer au basket (avec qui)
2. nager (comment)
3. danser (comment)
4. aller au cinéma (avec qui)
5. manger au fast-food (pourquoi)
6. regarder la télé (à quelle heure)
7. étudier (où)
8. téléphoner (à qui)

Communication

10 A group of French-speaking international exchange students is going to visit your French class. You volunteered to make name tags for the visitors and to introduce them to your classmates. To practice your introductions, look at each name tag you made and then give the appropriate information.

Bonjour! Je m'appelle
Jacques Delorme
français
Paris

Bonjour! Je m'appelle
Margaret Tate
anglaise
Northampton

Bonjour! Je m'appelle
Paola Malpezzi
italienne
Milan

Bonjour! Je m'appelle
Jun An
chinoise
Beijing

Bonjour! Je m'appelle
Karl Kohl
allemand
Bonn

Bonjour! Je m'appelle
María Herrera
mexicaine
Veracruz

Bonjour! Je m'appelle
Diego Botero
espagnol
Madrid

Bonjour! Je m'appelle
Akio Kusumoto
japonais
Tokyo

Bonjour! Je m'appelle
Loan Cao
vietnamienne
Hô Chi Minh-Ville

Modèle:

Bonjour! Je m'appelle
Renée Tremblay
canadienne
Montréal

Voilà Renée Tremblay. Elle vient du Canada. Elle est de Montréal.

Paired Practice

Survey

Have each student list the names of ten classmates on the back of his or her world map that was used in the connections activity on page 177. Then have each student interview these ten classmates asking where they are from and record the responses next to the list of names on the back of the map. After students finish their interviews, have them return to their seats and chart each classmate by number on the map. For example, if the second student interviewed is from China, a "2" is written next to China on the map.) Finally, put students in pairs and have them tell each other where their ten classmates are from.

NATIONAL STANDARDS
C1.1, C1.2, C5.1

Modèle:

Jacques et sa mère

Student A: Tiens, Jacques ressemble à sa mère!
Student B: Oui, il a ses cheveux blonds.
Student A: Il vient d'où?
Student B: Il vient de France.

11 Some of the international exchange students that are visiting your class have brought family pictures along with them. With a partner, look at these pictures and then take turns discussing some of the family resemblances you notice. Also see if you can remember where each student is from. Follow the model.

Paola et sa grand-mère

Karl et son père

Loan et son père

Margaret et sa sœur

María et son frère

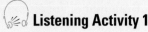
Audiocassette/CD
Prononciation

Listening Activity 1

Quiz
Leçon A

2 You and your friend Melissa Montoya are applying for a homestay program in Paris. At the end of the application form you are asked to write a short composition in French about yourself. Melissa has already finished her composition, but you haven't started yours. Take a look at Melissa's composition for ideas. Then write your own paragraph.

> *Je m'appelle Melissa Montoya. Je suis américaine. J'ai 15 ans. Mes parents sont Eduardo et Kay Montoya. J'ai un frère, Andy, et deux sœurs, Katie et Ana. Nous avons un chat qui s'appelle Harley. Mon professeur de français s'appelle Madame Darber. J'ai six cours : français, anglais, histoire, biologie, maths, musique. J'aime faire du footing et du vélo. J'aime aussi lire, aller au cinéma, regarder la télé et écouter de la musique. Je voudrais aller à Paris parce que j'aime la France et le français.*

Intonation

Prononciation

In spoken French the voice rises slightly after each group of related words. The voice then falls back to the beginning pitch to start the next phrase. Finally, at the end of the statement, the voice falls to the lowest point. This rising and falling of the voice is called intonation. The lines above the sentence show how the voice rises and falls. Say each of these sentences.

Clarisse ressemble à sa mère.

Elle a ses yeux bleus et ses cheveux bruns.

Mon père et moi, nous sommes américains, et ma belle-mère est japonaise.

In French there are basically two intonation patterns for questions. Questions requiring a "yes" or "no" answer have a rising intonation pattern. Say each of these questions:

On y va?

Est-ce que tu as faim?

Information-seeking questions have a falling intonation pattern. Say each of these questions:

Où est le cahier?

Qui aime étudier?

NATIONAL STANDARDS
C1.1, C1.2, C4.1

Teacher's Notes

1. Two words for "profession" are **une profession** and **un métier**. The first one usually refers to intellectual work, and the second one usually refers to manual labor or a trade. 2. The two occupations that students already know (**un prof, une prof, un professeur; un serveur, une serveuse**) are not presented visually. 3. **Médecin** is the formal word used to refer to a physician; however, the word **docteur (m.)** is heard more frequently. When talking to a doctor directly, refer to the person as **Docteur.** A common slang expression for a doctor is **un toubib.** 4. The words **un policier** and **une policière** are general names for any member of the police force. In France the police force is divided into several branches. Police officers in a city, often seen directing traffic, are called **agents de police.** A slang term for a police officer in French is **un flic. Les gendarmes,** technically soldiers since they are part of the army, usually patrol rural areas and deal with emergencies. 5. Some of the feminine forms of these nouns of profession may also refer to the wife of the man who has that occupation. For example, **une boulangère** may refer either to a female baker or to a baker's wife.

Leçon B

In this lesson you will be able to:

➤ **identify professions**

➤ **ask for information**

➤ **give information**

➤ **explain something**

une dentiste

une fermière

un agent de police

un cuisinier

une femme d'affaire

un avocat

un homme au foyer

un médecin

une journaliste

une infirmière

une comptable

une coiffeuse

une informaticienne

un ingénieur

un agent de police	un agent de police
un avocat	une avocate
un coiffeur	une coiffeuse
un comptable	une comptable
un cuisinier	une cuisinière
un dentiste	une dentiste
un fermier	une fermière
un homme au foyer	une femme au foyer
un homme d'affaires	une femme d'affaires
un infirmier	une infirmière
un informaticien	une informaticienne
un ingénieur	un ingénieur
un journaliste	une journaliste
un médecin	un médecin
un prof	une prof
un professeur	un professeur
un serveur	une serveuse

Teacher's Notes

1. Some other related terms include **un pharmacien, une pharmacienne** (*pharmacist*); **un menuisier** (*carpenter*); **un musicien, une musicienne** (*musician*); **un(e) secrétaire** (*secretary*); **un(e) artiste** (*artist*); **un(e) peintre** (*painter*); **un pilote** (*pilot*); **un pêcheur** (*fisherman*); **un instituteur, une institutrice** (*elementary school teacher*); **un commerçant, une commerçante** (*shopkeeper*); **un boulanger, une boulangère** (*baker*); **un boucher, une bouchère** (*butcher*); **un chanteur, une chanteuse** (*singer*); **un chef** (*chef*); **un danseur, une danseuse** (*dancer*); **un ouvrier, une ouvrière** (*factory worker*); **un architecte** (*architect*); **un pompier** (*firefighter*); **un chauffeur** (*driver*); **un vendeur, une vendeuse** (*sales-clerk*); **un caissier, une caissière** (*cashier*); **un mécanicien, une mécanicienne** (*mechanic*); **un(e) fonctionnaire** (*civil servant*) and **un acteur, une actrice** (*actor, actress*). 2. A communicative function that is recycled in this lesson is "pointing out family members."

Game

Quelle est ma profession?

To practice nouns of profession and question formation, you might have students play this game. Have them pick a profession for which they have learned the French equivalent. Then each one in turn goes in front of the class to answer questions from classmates who try to discover his or her profession. A questioner may ask, for example, **Est-ce que tu travailles au bureau?** The student in front of the class can answer with either **oui** or **non**, with a complete sentence or with a complete sentence that gives further information.

NATIONAL STANDARDS
C1.1, C1.2, C4.1

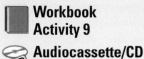

**Workbook
Activity 9**

**Audiocassette/CD
*Dialogue***

Teacher's Notes

1. In asking the question **Quelle est la profession de tes parents?**, you assume that each parent has only one profession. If you ask the question **Quelles sont les professions de tes parents?**, you imply that each parent may have more than one profession. 2. Point out to your students that when the verb **parler** is modified by an adverb, the definite article is retained before the name of a language. 3. Some French businesses close during the summer (especially in August) to allow all employees to take their vacations. 4. Health care in France is regulated primarily by the government through the social security system. 5. Some workers' benefits may be curtailed by the French government due to their cost and the aging of the French population.

Connections

Minimum Wage

You may want to put students in small groups and have them do research and report on the minimum wage in francophone countries and/or countries that border France.

Petra, Sandy and José continue to exchange information about their families.

Petra: Mon père, il est homme d'affaires. Il voyage beaucoup. Ma mère travaille beaucoup aussi. Elle est femme au foyer. Et tes parents, José?

José: Mon père est informaticien et ma belle-mère est dentiste. Sandy, quelle est la profession de tes parents?

Sandy: Je n'ai pas de mère. Mon père est prof de français.

Petra: Tiens, c'est pourquoi tu parles si bien le français!

 Enquête culturelle

Students over the age of 14 may work during their school vacations. Since school is required until the age of 16, people younger than 16 do not work full-time. The official work week in France is 35 hours, but naturally the actual number of hours spent working depends on the specific job and worker. In offices and stores, the work day typically begins around 8:00 A.M. or 9:00 A.M. and finishes between 5:00 P.M. and 7:00 P.M. All people who are salaried for 12 months are given six weeks of vacation. Many people take up to four weeks of vacation in the summer; the

How many hours is this hairdresser open on Monday?

other weeks must be taken at a different time of the year. In addition, employers must pay salaried employees for 11 holidays each year. Another benefit that French workers receive is the opportunity to take continuing education courses. By law, French firms must offer these courses to their employees, who may, for example, perfect their professional knowledge or learn a foreign language.

**RECHERCHE
Ingénieur en électronique**
- Savoir-faire sur système d'exploitation:
  MS DOS,langage C et assembleur.
- Conception d'équipements à base de cir-
  cuits analogiques, digitals et microprocesseurs
- Expérience exigée : cinq ans.
**MAGNER ÉLECTRONIQUE
11, rue des Îles
60340 Saint-Leu-d'Esserent**

ADIA RESTAURATION

RESTAURATION recrute
**CUISINIERS
ETAGERES**
Références exigées
Tél. pour rendez-vous
PARIS : 01.48.87.81.37
AULNAY : 01.48.79.07.42

1 *Répondez par "vrai" ou "faux" d'après le dialogue.*
(Answer "true" or "false" according to the dialogue.)

1. Le père de Petra est informaticien.
2. La mère de Petra voyage beaucoup.
3. La belle-mère de José n'est pas femme au foyer.
4. Le père de José est dentiste.
5. Le père de Sandy est professeur de français.
6. Sandy ne parle pas très bien le français.

2 Match the picture and the description to answer the question **Quelle est sa profession?**

1.
2.
3.
4.
5.
6.
7.
8.
9.

a. Monsieur Rajy est ingénieur.
b. Mademoiselle Sorlot est dentiste.
c. Monsieur Géraud est médecin.
d. Monsieur Odier est fermier.
e. Madame Toussaint est femme d'affaires.
f. Monsieur Dupont est avocat.
g. Madame Pinot est comptable.
h. Mademoiselle Blot est journaliste.
i. Madame Vasconi est professeur.

Connections

Career Planning
Have students write in French the names of five professions that interest them. Be prepared to provide them with the names of professions they haven't learned to express in French. Then, under each profession, have them list in French what courses offered in high school are useful to someone wanting to enter that profession.

NATIONAL STANDARDS
C1.1, C1.2, C2.1, C2.2,
C4.2

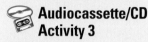

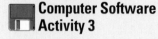

3 | *C'est à toi!*

1. Quelle est la profession de tes parents?
2. Est-ce que tu préfères être journaliste ou comptable?
3. Est-ce que tu préfères être agent de police ou médecin?
4. Est-ce que tu voyages beaucoup?
5. Dans la salle de classe, qui parle bien le français?

Est-ce qu'ils sont agents de police ou médecins? (Paris)

Structure

Indefinite articles in negative sentences

The indefinite articles **un**, **une** and **des** become **de** or **d'** (*a, an, any*) in a negative sentence.

Tu as **un** frère?	Non, je n'ai pas **de** frère.
Est-ce que Marcel a **une** tante?	Non, il n'a pas **de** tante.
M. Rondeau a **des** enfants?	Non, il n'a pas **d'**enfants.

However, **un**, **une** and **des** do not change after a form of the verb **être** in a negative sentence.

Ce sont des photos de mes parents; ce ne sont pas **des** photos de mes profs.

These are pictures of my parents; they're not pictures of my teachers.

Je n'ai pas de devoirs.

Pratique

4 Because of a mix-up in the school cafeteria, many students are missing a part of their lunch. Tell what each person doesn't have.

Modèle:

Mélanie

Mélanie n'a pas de sandwich.

1. Jérôme

4. Suzanne

2. Anne-Marie

5. Assane

3. je

6. tu

5 With a partner, take turns asking and telling whether or not you have the following relatives and pets. Follow the model.

1. une sœur
2. un oiseau
3. un chat
4. des oncles
5. un cheval
6. des poissons rouges
7. une cousine
8. un chien

Modèle:

un frère

Student A: **Est-ce que tu as un frère?**
Student B: **Oui, j'ai un frère. Et toi, est-ce que tu as un frère?**
Student A: **Non, je n'ai pas de frère.**

Est-ce que tu as une sœur?

Non, je n'ai pas de sœur, mais voilà une photo de mon frère.

NATIONAL STANDARDS
C1.1, C1.2

189

**Workbook
Activities 11-12**

**Grammar & Vocabulary
Exercises 14-17**

**Audiocassette/CD
Activity 6**

**Computer Software
Activities 4-5**

Answers

6 1. Quel coiffeur?
2. Quelle journaliste?
3. Quels agents de police?
4. Quelle prof?
5. Quel médecin?
6. Quels hommes d'affaires?
7. Quelles avocates?
8. Quelles informaticiennes?

Teacher's Notes

1. Point out liaison after **quels** or **quelles** before a word beginning with a vowel sound. 2. If you or your students made flash cards or have pictures of the foods and beverages that were introduced in **Unité 3**, use them to practice the forms of **quel** orally. Put the pictures into the following categories: sandwiches, beverages, desserts and fruits. Then ask students (or put students in pairs and have them ask each other) which they prefer as you show them two pictures from each category. For example, as you show pictures of mineral water and orange juice, say **Tu préfères quelle boisson**? Students respond by saying **Je préfère l'eau minérale/le jus d'orange**. 3. After **c'est**, the modifying adjective may either precede or follow the noun. 4. Point out liaison after **est** before a word beginning with a vowel sound. 5. **C'** is also used with people's names: **C'est Monique**. 6. The word that names the nationality or profession after **il/elle est** is not modified.

NATIONAL STANDARDS
C1.1, C1.2, C4.1

190

	Masculine	Feminine
Singular	quel	quelle
Plural	quels	quelles

Modèle:
Véronique parle avec un professeur.
Quel professeur?

Voilà M. Lussac. Il est avocat.

The interrogative adjective *quel*

The adjective **quel** means "which" or "what" and is used to ask questions. **Quel** comes before the noun it describes.

Tu préfères **quel** coiffeur?	*Which hairdresser do you prefer?*
Quelle femme d'affaires voyage beaucoup?	*Which businesswoman travels a lot?*

The forms of **quel** may also come directly before the verb **être**. In this case **quel** agrees with the noun after **être**.

Quelle est la profession de tes parents?	*What are your parents' occupations?*

Pratique

6 Bruno is trying to tell you who's talking to whom, but he isn't being very clear. Ask him to be more specific.

1. Adja parle avec un coiffeur.
2. Ariane et Alain parlent avec une journaliste.
3. Paul parle avec des agents de police.
4. Monique parle avec une prof.
5. Mme Manet et son fils parlent avec un médecin.
6. Le prof de français parle avec des hommes d'affaires.
7. M. Lafitte parle avec des avocates.
8. Jean parle avec des informaticiennes.

C'est vs. *il/elle est*

Both **c'est** and **il/elle est** mean "he is" or "she is" as well as "it is."

Use **c'est** when the noun that follows is modified by an article, an adjective or both. In a negative sentence, **c'est** becomes **ce n'est pas**.

C'est ma dentiste; **c'est** une Italienne.	*She's my dentist; she's Italian.*
C'est un bon infirmier; **ce n'est pas** un médecin.	*He's a good nurse; he's not a doctor.*

Use **il/elle est** when the following word is an adjective or a noun that functions as an adjective (for example, the name of a nationality or an occupation).

Elle est italienne.	*She's Italian.*
Elle est dentiste.	*She's a dentist.*
Il est bavard.	*He's talkative.*

The corresponding plural forms are **ce sont** and **ils/elles sont**.

Ce sont des avocats.	*They are lawyers.*
Ils sont américains.	*They are American.*

Note that a noun of nationality is capitalized but an adjective of nationality is not.

C'est un **Japonais.** **Il est** japonais.	*He's Japanese.*

Pratique

7 With a partner, talk about the occupations of various people. Student A asks questions and Student B answers them. Follow the model.

1. Mme Robert (prof de français/prof d'anglais)
2. Mlle Chartrier (coiffeuse/infirmière)
3. Jean-Michel (cuisinier/serveur)
4. M. et Mme Tremblay (médecins/dentistes)
5. M. Godot (ingénieur/comptable)
6. Mme Peyrot et Mme Renault (femmes au foyer/femmes d'affaires)
7. Mlle Olivari (informaticienne/journaliste)

Jean-Michel est coiffeur.

Modèle:

M. Nataf (avocat/agent de police)
Student A: Voilà Monsieur Nataf. Il est avocat?
Student B: Non, il est agent de police.

8 Complete Béatrice's descriptions of the following people. Follow the model.

1. C'est Max. ... un bon élève. ... très beau! Max est de Montréal. ... canadien. ... un garçon timide. ... bavard.

2. C'est Madame Tran. ... une infirmière. ... médecin. ... une femme très intelligente. ... vietnamienne. ... la femme de mon prof de maths.

3. Ce sont mes parents. ... des fermiers. ... très diligents. Ma mère vient d'Espagne. ... espagnole. Mais mon père, ... un Français. ... des parents super!

4. Ce sont Clémence et Magali. ... mes cousines. ... étudiantes, mais elles travaillent aussi. Clémence travaille dans un café. ... serveuse. Magali travaille aussi dans un café, mais ... serveuse. ... une cuisinière.

Modèle:

C'est Madame Gagner. **C'est** la mère de David, un garçon dans mon cours d'anglais. **Elle est** française. **Ce n'est pas** une femme au foyer. **C'est** une femme d'affaires. **Elle est** très sympa.

CENTRE HOSPITALIER PRIVÉ
DES YVELINES
20, AV. MAURICE-BERTAUX
78500 SARTROUVILLE
15' gare St-Lazare, RER
recherche
INFIRMER (E) D.E.
+ 2 ans expérience.
Salaire brut 1829 €.
INFIRMER (E) D.E.
BLOC OPÉRATOIRE
Salaire brut 1829 €
+ astreintes.
Tél. pour R.-V. 01.39.14.21.27.

Communication

9 You are starting to think seriously about possible careers. Look at this list of ten occupations and on a separate sheet of paper rank them from one to ten in order of your preference.

dentiste	infirmier, infirmière
avocat, avocate	informaticien, informaticienne
fermier, fermière	comptable
professeur	journaliste
cuisinier, cuisinière	coiffeur, coiffeuse

10 For each of your top five career choices in Activity 9, determine what three classes in high school you might need to take in order to enter this profession.

11 Your assignment for current events day in social studies class is to find a newspaper article about jobs. To give your assignment a global perspective, you found an article in a French newspaper that reports the results of a survey taken in France. Two hundred students were surveyed about their parents' occupations. Read the article that follows and then, in order to share the results with students in your social studies class, make two bar graphs on a separate sheet of paper that show how many people are in each profession. In the first one, graph the occupations of the men; in the second one, graph the occupations of the women.

> **Bourges, le 23 septembre**
>
> Deux cents élèves ont participé à un sondage hier pour indiquer les professions et les métiers de leurs parents. Cent élèves de lycée technique, 50 élèves de collège et 50 élèves d'école primaire ont rempli ce sondage. Voilà les résultats.
>
> | **Les Hommes** | **Les Femmes** |
> |---|---|
> | Il y a beaucoup de médecins et d'informaticiens parmi les hommes. Il y a 34 informaticiens et 28 médecins. Vingt de ces hommes sont dentistes, 10 sont avocats, six sont professeurs et cinq sont ingénieurs. Dans ce groupe il y a neuf journalistes, trois infirmiers, sept agents de police et 14 comptables. Quinze hommes travaillent comme cuisiniers et huit sont fermiers. Cinq travaillent à la maison comme hommes au foyer et 13 ne travaillent pas. | Les femmes ont aussi beaucoup de professions différentes. Les professions les plus populaires pour les femmes sont médecin, professeur et ingénieur. Vingt-deux de ces femmes sont médecins, 21 sont professeurs et 20 sont ingénieurs. Dans ce groupe il y a 12 infirmières, 12 dentistes et sept journalistes. Il y a aussi 13 coiffeuses, 15 serveuses, sept comptables, deux fermières et neuf cuisinières. Dix-sept sont femmes au foyer et 16 ne travaillent pas. |

2 Here are some employment ads from a newspaper in Nice. Study them and then answer the questions that follow by giving the letter of the appropriate ad.

a.
Clinique Nice cherche infirmier, service chirurgie, temps plein, poste à pourvoir à partir du 26 août. Tél. 04.93.13.65.20 de 9 à 16 heures.

b.
Cherche serveuse. Se présenter RESTAURANT DE PARIS, 28 rue d'Angleterre, Nice, ce jour à partir de 18h.

c.
Hôtel 4 étoiles recherche secrétaire réception, expérience, anglais courant, libre de suite pour saison, tél. 04.93.50.02.02. Vence.

d.
Cherche apprenti(e) coiffeur(euse). 1ère année et 3ème année. Tél. 04.93.31.12.65.

e.
CNRS pour laboratoire de recherche Sophia-Antipolis recrute sur concours, un assistant ingénieur en Biologie, ayant bonnes connaissances en biologie moléculaire, culture de cellules, biologie et physiologie cellulaires (DUT ou équivalence). 04.93.95.77.05.

f.
INTERNATIONAL HOUSE, 90 écoles de langues dans 20 pays, recrute en septembre pour son centre de Nice, secrétaire commerciale bilingue confirmée. Ecrire 22 boulevard Dubouchage, Nice.

g.
Restaurant poissons Cagnes-Sur-Mer, cherche cuisinier ou commis de cuisine qualifié, de langue maternelle française, pour saison, libre de suite, bien rémunéré. Tél. pour rendez-vous, au 04.93.07.36.59 le matin avant 12h00.

h.
Clinique Nice cherche un infirmier psychiatrique ou DE, jour, temps complet. Tél. 04.93.13.65.00.

i.
Restaurant cherche jeune cuisinier, connaissances pâtisserie, sérieuses références contrôlables. Tél. 04.93.67.14.06.

1. Which ads are for cooking positions?
2. Which ads are for secretarial positions?
3. Which ad is for an apprentice hair stylist?
4. Which ad is for an organization looking for a biological engineer?
5. Which ad is for a waitressing job?
6. Which ad is for a surgical nurse?
7. Which other ad is for a nurse?
8. Which ads are for jobs that require a knowledge of English?

Listening Activity 2

Answers

12 1. g, i
2. c, f
3. d
4. e
5. b
6. a
7. h
8. c, f

NATIONAL STANDARDS
C1.2, C2.1, C2.2, C3.2, C5.1

Connections

France and Neighboring Countries

You may want to make copies of a map of western Europe for your students and have them fill in the names of the countries surrounding France, mountain ranges in France and bodies of water in and around France that are mentioned in the cultural reading. Have them use crayons, colored markers or colored pencils to fill in the countries in one color, mountains in another color and bodies of water in yet a different color.

TPR

Geography of France

Fill in a map of western Europe showing France's neighboring countries, mountain ranges and bodies of water. Then make an overhead transparency from it. (Instead, you may make a transparency from one of the maps students have done in the connections activity on France and neighboring countries.) Show the transparency to the class and call on students to come to the overhead projector and indicate certain geographical features on the map. For example, say **Montrez-moi la Seine**. One student points to the Seine on the map and says **Voilà la Seine**.

NATIONAL STANDARDS
C1.2, C2.1, C2.2, C3.1, C4.2

194

 ### *Mise au point sur... la France et ses voisins*

Rugged coastlines, sunlit beaches, snowcapped mountains and fields of lavender: this is the landscape of France. In the shape of a hexagon, France is bordered on three sides by water and on three sides by land. This diverse country, slightly smaller than the state of Texas, contains a variety of picturesque scenery.

To the north of France lies the English Channel, called **la Manche** by the French because it narrows from the Atlantic Ocean to the North Sea much like a shirt sleeve. Here the beaches blur under a frequent foggy haze and the coastline is rocky. Nevertheless, the cities of Saint-Malo, Étretat and Deauville attract thousands of tourists each year. A 31-mile-long tunnel under the English Channel now joins Folkestone, England, with Calais, France. The French wanted an easy way to cross the Channel for hundreds of years, but it was only recently that the English agreed to be joined "by land" to the continent. The sleek Eurostar bullet train makes the trip between London and Paris in just under four hours.

During the Hundred Years War (1337-1453), the English were going to destroy the city of Calais, but six men volunteered to be killed to save it. The Queen later intervened on their behalf and they were never killed. Rodin's life-size statue, *les Bourgeois de Calais*, honors their memory. (Calais)

A typical Eurostar train has 18 cars and almost 800 seats.

England, France and many of their neighbors have joined to form the European Union, an organization which promotes the economic growth of its members. Most of the barriers to the movement of money, goods, people and services among EU members have been removed, forming the largest single market in the world. Citizens of the 15 EU countries may travel to other member nations without passports, may work in other EU countries and are not required to pay import or export taxes on products purchased in other member countries.

Belgium, Luxembourg, Germany, Switzerland and Italy border France on the east. French is spoken in France, Belgium, Luxembourg and Switzerland. Three mountain ranges, **les Vosges** (between France and Germany), **le Jura** (between France and Switzerland) and **les Alpes** (between France and Italy) form natural boundaries between France and its neighbors. Skiing and mountain climbing are popular hobbies in these regions.

Corsica is an island in the Mediterranean.

The highest mountains in western Europe, the Alps extend from France into Switzerland, Italy and Austria.

To the south of France lie the Mediterranean Sea, the tiny principality of Monaco and the island of Corsica. The beaches of the French Riviera, stretching from near the city of Toulon to the Italian border, appeal to vacationers from all over the world. Colors seem brighter in the south of France and even the food, spiced with olive oil, garlic and tomatoes, has a unique flavor. Monaco is an independent country where citizens speak French. Napoléon Bonaparte was born in Corsica, a department of France.

Monaco, ruled by Prince Rainier, covers less than one square mile.

The mountains called **les Pyrénées** form a natural boundary between France and Spain on the west. The resort city of Biarritz and the port city of Bordeaux, famous for its vineyards, are on the Atlantic Ocean.

...any French people prefer to ski and hike in *les Pyrénées* because it's ...s expensive than in *les Alpes*. (Col du Pourtalet)

Teacher's Note

The 15 members of the EU are Germany, Belgium, France, Italy, Luxembourg, the Netherlands, Denmark, Great Britain, Ireland, Greece, Spain, Portugal, Austria, Finland and Sweden.

Connections

GATT
You may want to put students in small groups and have them do research and report on GATT (General Agreement on Tariffs and Trade).

Cooperative Group Practice

Commercials
Put your students in small groups of four or five. Have each group prepare a two-minute commercial in English about one of the countries surrounding France. In the commercial students should try to convince their audience to visit this country, while describing the language(s) spoken there, geographical characteristics, food, weather, customs, etc. After each group has presented its commercial to the entire class, have the class vote for the country, other than France, that they would most like to visit.

NATIONAL STANDARDS
C2.1, C2.2, C3.1, C4.2

Answers

Teacher's Note

The cities of Marseille and Lyon may also be written with a final "s" in English.

There are several important rivers in France. **La Seine** divides the capital city of Paris in half before it meanders north to the city of Le Havre on the English Channel. Along the tranquil banks of **la Loire**, the longest river in France, kings had beautiful châteaux built during the Renaissance. **Le Rhône** empties into the Mediterranean Sea near the city of Marseille, the largest French port. Two other important rivers in France are **la Garonne**, near Bordeaux, and **le Rhin**, which forms a border between France and Germany.

The Gulf Stream from the Atlantic Ocean keeps the climate of France quite mild throughout the year. However, **le mistral**, a powerful wind, blows dry air through the mountains of **le Massif Central** in central France during the spring and summer.

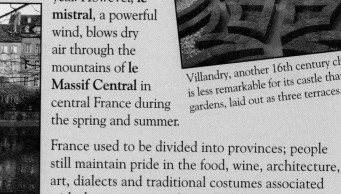

Villandry, another 16th century châtea[u] is less remarkable for its castle than for gardens, laid out as three terraces.

Strasbourg, in the province of Alsace, reflects both French and German heritage.

France used to be divided into provinces; people still maintain pride in the food, wine, architecture, art, dialects and traditional costumes associated with these provinces. Several of the more well-known French provinces are Brittany and Normandy to the north, Provence to the south, Aquitaine to the west, and Alsace and Lorraine to the east. Alsace and Lorraine have belonged to either Germany or France at various times throughout history; many of the people in these provinces speak both German and French, as well as local dialects.

Today France is divided into smaller **départements** for governmental purposes. You can tell what department people are from by the last two numbers of their license plates and also by the first two numbers of their zip codes.

A combination of the traditional and the contemporary, beautiful countryside and bustling cities, France, the largest country in western Europe, is rightly called **la Belle France**.

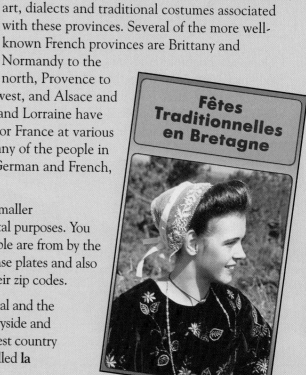

Fêtes Traditionnelles en Bretagne

3   Answer the following questions.

1. France is in the shape of what geometrical figure?
2. Why do the French call the English Channel **la Manche**?
3. What is the purpose of the European Union?
4. What are three European countries, other than France, where citizens speak French?
5. What three mountain ranges are located in the eastern part of France?
6. What is the name of the small principality located in the southern part of France?
7. How is the food in the southern part of France unique?
8. What river divides the city of Paris in half?
9. What two cities are important French ports?
10. What is responsible for France's moderate climate?
11. Why are the French proud to be associated with the former provinces?
12. How is France divided for governmental purposes today?
13. What is France often called?

Knowing French would make it easier to visit Lucerne, Switzerland.

The "N" on this bridge, one of 33 that cross the Seine in Paris, stands for Napoléon.

14   Here is France's weather report for October 30. Answer the questions that follow.

1. All temperatures in this weather report are given in Celsius degrees (°C). What five French cities had temperatures of 10°C?
2. With the exception of Bastia on the island of Corsica, which city had the warmest temperature?
3. What was the temperature in Biarritz?
4. For soccer players was the weather better in Rennes or Bordeaux?
5. It was 9°C in Dijon. What else can you say about the weather there?
6. What city is located on the Rhône River between Lyon and Marseille? What was the temperature in this city?
7. What city is located near the border between France and Belgium? What was the weather like there?
8. In what two mountain ranges did it snow?
9. The accompanying chart shows cities from 12 of the countries that belong to the European Union and their temperatures from October 29. At what time were these temperatures recorded?
10. In what city was the temperature 22°C?
11. Was it warmer in Greece or Spain?

Answers

14 1. It was 10°C in Brest, Nantes, Paris, Reims and Saint-Étienne.
2. Nice had the warmest temperature.
3. The temperature in Biarritz was 13°C.
4. The weather was better in Rennes.
5. The sky was cloudy.
6. Valence is located on the Rhône River between Lyon and Marseille. It was 13°C in Valence.
7. Lille is located near the border between France and Belgium. It was partly cloudy there.
8. It snowed in **les Alpes** and **les Pyrénées**.
9. These temperatures were recorded at 1:00 P.M.
10. It was 22°C in Rome.
11. It was warmer in Greece.

Teacher's Note

Specific information on the Celsius and Fahrenheit scales is presented in **Leçon C**.

NATIONAL STANDARDS
C2.1, C2.2, C3.1, C3.2, C4.2

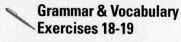

**Grammar & Vocabulary
Exercises 18-19**

**Audiocassette/CD
Seasons**

Leçon C

In this lesson you will be able to:

➤ **give information**

➤ **invite**

➤ **express emotions**

le printemps

l'été (m.)

l'automne (m.)

l'hiver (m.)

NATIONAL STANDARDS
C1.2, C4.1

Quel temps fait-il?

Il fait beau.

Il fait chaud.

Il fait froid.

Il fait frais.

Il fait mauvais.

Il fait du soleil.

Il neige.

Il fait du vent.

Il pleut.

Workbook Activity 14

 Audiocassette/CD *Quel temps fait-il?*

Cooperative Group Practice

Four Corners

To practice the names of the seasons and various weather expressions associated with each one, have students pick their favorite season. Then designate each corner of the room as a different season. Students go to the corner that represents their favorite season. (It doesn't matter if the groups vary in size as long as there are at least two students in each group.) Next students form pairs and each one tells his or her partner why he or she prefers this specific season. Then two pairs get together and each student tells the new pair why his or her partner prefers that season. Finally, a spokesperson from each of the four groups tells the entire class why students from that group prefer that season.

Weather

Put students in small groups and have them bring to class pictures of various weather conditions that they can describe in French. Have them make flash cards using these pictures. Then put the flash cards face down in a pile. Each student in turn takes a flash card, tells what season it is and then makes one statement about the weather in the picture. For example, **C'est l'hiver. Il fait très froid.** Afterward, groups can exchange flash cards and do the activity again. (You will want to save these pictures for use later on.)

NATIONAL STANDARDS
C1.1, C1.2, C1.3, C4.1

Audiocassette/CD
Dialogue

Transparency 31

Video

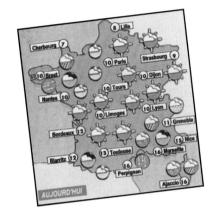

Petra, Sandy and José are talking about how they spend their free time.

Sandy: Il fait beau à Tours en automne. Après les cours je fais souvent du vélo.
José: Moi aussi. Et quand il fait mauvais, je joue aux jeux vidéo.
Petra: J'aime aussi faire du vélo. Mais je n'ai pas de vélo ici.
José: Ma famille a un autre vélo.
Sandy: Alors, on fait un tour ensemble aujourd'hui?
Petra: D'accord. Quelle chance! J'ai déjà deux amis à Tours.

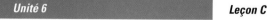
Enquête culturelle

Temperatures (**les températures**) in all French-speaking countries and most other countries in the world are calculated on the basis of the Celsius scale. Like all scales in the metric system, invented by the French, the Celsius scale is based on a division of measurements into hundredths or thousandths. Water freezes at 0° Celsius and boils at 100° Celsius. (It freezes at 32° Fahrenheit and boils at 212° Fahrenheit.)

Many people ride bicycles in France both for pleasure and as a means of transportation. Mopeds (**les mobylettes**) are another popular way to get around. **Les mobs**, as they are often called, get through traffic easily and relatively quickly. Teenagers find **les mobs** to be economical, easy to park and simple to operate. People over the age of 14 may operate **une mobylette** without a driver's license as long as they drive under 45 kilometers per hour and wear a helmet.

For a French teenager a moped offers freedom and independence.

1 Answer the following questions.

1. At what temperature (Celsius) does water boil?
2. What are two advantages of driving a **mobylette**?
3. How old must a person be to drive a **mobylette**?
4. Do you need a driver's license to drive a **mobylette**?
5. If you are over the age of 14 but don't have a driver's license, what is the speed limit you must observe when driving a **mobylette**?

2 *Répondez en français.*

1. Sandy, José et Petra, ils sont où?
2. Quel temps fait-il à Tours en automne?
3. Est-ce que Sandy fait souvent du vélo?
4. Qui joue aux jeux vidéo quand il fait mauvais?
5. Qui n'a pas de vélo à Tours?
6. Quand est-ce qu'on fait un tour ensemble?
7. Qui sont les deux amis de Petra à Tours?

3 *Quel temps fait-il? Répondez en français.*

 1.
 3.
 5.

 2.
 4.
 6.

4 *Complétez le dialogue suivant.*

Fred: Tu... d'où?
Maria: Je viens.... Je suis.... Et toi?
Fred: Je viens.... Je suis....
Maria: Quel temps fait-il chez toi en...?
Fred: Il fait.... Moi, j'aime.... Qu'est-ce que tu aimes faire en...?
Maria: Moi, j'aime... en....

Audiocassette/CD Activity 2

Answers

1 Possible answers:
1. Water boils at 100°C.
2. **Mobylettes** are economical and easy to park.
3. To drive a **mobylette** you must be at least 14 years old.
4. No, you do not need a driver's license to drive a **mobylette**.
5. The speed limit is 45 kilometers per hour.

2 1. Ils sont à Tours.
2. Il fait beau à Tours en automne.
3. Oui, elle fait souvent du vélo.
4. José joue aux jeux vidéo quand il fait mauvais.
5. Petra n'a pas de vélo à Tours.
6. On fait un tour ensemble aujourd'hui.
7. Sandy et José sont les deux amis de Petra à Tours.

3 Possible answers:
1. Il neige.
2. Il fait du vent.
3. Il fait du soleil.
4. Il pleut.
5. Il fait froid.
6. Il fait chaud.

4 Possible answers:
Tu viens d'où?
Je viens d'Italie. Je suis italienne. Et toi?
Je viens des États-Unis. Je suis américain.
Quel temps fait-il chez toi en hiver?
Il fait froid. Moi, j'aime skier. Qu'est-ce que tu aimes faire en automne?
Moi, j'aime lire en automne.

NATIONAL STANDARDS
C1.1, C1.2, C2.1, C2.2, C3.1, C4.2

Workbook Activity 15

Grammar & Vocabulary Exercises 20-22

Audiocassette/CD Activity 5

Computer Software Activity 6

Answers

5 Answers will vary.

Teacher's Notes

1. Point out to students that **faire** is one of the few verbs in French whose **vous** form does not end in **-ez**. Can your students name the other verb they have already learned whose **vous** form does not end in **-ez**? (It is **être**.) 2. You might have students repeat after you the forms of **faire**. Note especially the sound [ε] of **ai** in the **je**, **tu**, **il/elle** and **vous** forms and the sound [ə] of **ai** in the **nous** form. You may want to give affirmative forms to be changed to negative forms and do subject substitution exercises. You may also have students give plural forms for singular ones and vice versa. 3. You may want to point out that a form of **faire** is not always necessary when answering questions such as **Qu'est-ce que tu fais?** (For example, **Je regarde la télé.**) 4. Other expressions with **faire** that students have already learned but that do not appear in this presentation include **faire du roller**, **faire du shopping**, **faire les devoirs**, **il fait beau**, **il fait du soleil**, **il fait du vent**, **il fait frais**, **il fait froid** and **il fait mauvais**.

NATIONAL STANDARDS
C1.1, C1.2, C4.1

5 | *C'est à toi!*

1. Est-ce que tu préfères l'automne ou le printemps? Pourquoi?
2. Qu'est-ce que tu aimes faire en été?
3. Qu'est-ce que tu aimes faire en hiver?
4. Tu as un vélo?
5. Est-ce que tu aimes jouer aux jeux vidéo?
6. Est-ce que tu travailles après les cours?

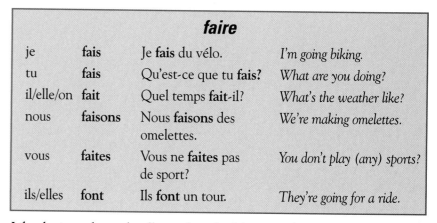

François aime faire du vélo en été. (Martinique)

Il fait très chaud en Guadeloupe. (Cascade Écrevisses)

Structure

Present tense of the irregular verb *faire*

The basic meaning of the irregular verb **faire** is "to do" or "to make," but it has other meanings as well.

faire			
je	**fais**	Je **fais** du vélo.	*I'm going biking.*
tu	**fais**	Qu'est-ce que tu **fais**?	*What are you doing?*
il/elle/on	**fait**	Quel temps **fait**-il?	*What's the weather like?*
nous	**faisons**	Nous **faisons** des omelettes.	*We're making omelettes.*
vous	**faites**	Vous ne **faites** pas de sport?	*You don't play (any) sports?*
ils/elles	**font**	Ils **font** un tour.	*They're going for a ride.*

Like the irregular verbs **aller** and **avoir**, **faire** is used in many expressions where a different verb is used in English. You have already seen expressions with **faire** when talking about participating in various activities, prices and what the weather's like.

Tu **fais** du footing?	*Are you going running?*
Ça **fait** combien?	*How much is it/that?*
Il **fait** chaud.	*It's (The weather's) hot/warm.*

Pratique

6 It's noon. Tell what the following people are making for lunch.

1. Jean-Michel

2. je

3. Ahmed et Aïcha

4. nous

5. tu

6. vous

7. Benjamin et Olivier

Modèle:
Christine

Christine fait un hamburger.

---

7 It's Saturday afternoon. Tell what various people are doing by combining each subject in column A with the appropriate form of one of the expressions in column B.

A	B
Grégoire	faire du vélo
tu	faire les devoirs
nous	faire du shopping
Karine et Denise	faire du roller
vous	faire un tour
je	faire du sport
ils	faire du footing

Modèle:
Grégoire fait du roller.

---

8 With a partner, take turns asking and telling what you normally do in certain types of weather. Follow the model.

1. Il fait chaud.
2. Il fait froid.
3. Il pleut.
4. Il fait beau.
5. Il fait mauvais.

Modèle:

Il neige.
Student A: Qu'est-ce que tu fais quand il neige?
Student B: Je skie. Et toi?
Student A: Je joue aux jeux vidéo.

Audiocassette/CD Activities 6, 8

Answers

6 Possible answers:
1. Jean-Michel fait un steak.
2. Je fais une crêpe.
3. Ahmed et Aïcha font des hot-dogs.
4. Nous faisons une salade.
5. Tu fais une omelette.
6. Vous faites des sandwichs.
7. Benjamin et Olivier font une quiche.

7 Answers will vary.

8 Answers will vary.

Cooperative Group Practice

Sentence Construction

Put your students in small groups and have each group make a set of note cards. On each card students write the name of a different activity that uses **faire**, for example, **faire un tour**. (Students should also use the names of activities they have learned in **Unité 2**.) Then have each group make a second set of note cards on which they write a different noun or pronoun subject. (They may have already made this set of cards in **Leçon A**.) Each student in the group selects at random one card from each set and makes a complete sentence. For example, **nous/faire du vélo — Nous faisons du vélo**.

NATIONAL STANDARDS
C1.1, C1.2

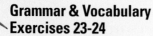

Teacher's Notes

1. Examples of verbs that may be followed by the inverted subject pronoun **je** include **Ai-je...?**, **Vais-je...?**, **Sais-je...?** and **Suis-je...?** 2. Tell students that when an **-er** verb already ends in the sound [t], a **t** is still added. For example, **Écoute-*t*-il bien?** 3. Point out that the final **t** of the plural **ils/elles** verb form is pronounced in inversion, for example, **Sont-ils ici?**
[t]

Cooperative Group Practice

Forming Questions
Put students in groups of four. Have each student write three sentences, each one on a separate note card. Each sentence should be about one of the other three students in the group. For example, **Raoul aime jouer aux jeux vidéo**. All cards are placed face down. Then each student chooses one at random and makes it into an inverted question (**Raoul aime-t-il jouer aux jeux vidéo?**) that another student in the group answers. (If a student draws a card about himself or herself, he or she should make it into a question using **est-ce que**, for example, **Est-ce que je ressemble à mon frère?**, that another student in the group answers). Afterward, groups can exchange note cards and do this activity again.

NATIONAL STANDARDS
C1.1, C1.2, C4.1

204

Forming questions with inversion

A more formal way to ask a question in French, especially in written French, is to invert, or reverse, the order of the verb and its subject pronoun. With simple inversion the order is:

> **verb + subject pronoun**

Quelle heure est-il? *What time is it?*
      [t]
Avez-vous faim? *Are you hungry?*
Mangeons-nous au fast-food? *Shall we eat at the fast-food restaurant?*

Note that a hyphen connects the verb and its subject pronoun.

Inverting the pronoun **je** and its verb is not common. Form **je** questions either by making your tone of voice rise at the end or by using **est-ce que**.

When the **il**, **elle** or **on** form of the verb ends with a vowel, a **t** is added between the verb and its subject pronoun. This **t** is pronounced.

Ressemble-*t*-il à son père? *Does he look like his father?*
     [t]
A-*t*-il les cheveux blonds? *Does he have blond hair?*
  [t]

If the subject of the sentence is a noun, inversion is formed by adding the appropriate subject pronoun after the verb. This pronoun agrees with the subject noun in gender and in number.

Les filles font-**elles** du sport? *Do the girls play sports?*
Valérie joue-*t*-**elle** au basket? *Is Valérie playing basketball?*

A-t-elle les yeux noirs?

LE CINEMA SERAIT-IL ENFIN RECONNU COMME LE SEPTIEME ART ?
Frank Borzage

Pratique

9 Find out if your friends are doing what you think they're doing by forming questions using inversion.

Modèle:
Anne/étudier la biologie
Anne étudie-t-elle la biologie?

1. Valérie/finir les devoirs
2. Christophe/parler avec le prof
3. Fatima/travailler
4. Marc et Fabrice/jouer au foot
5. Cécile et Patricia/faire un tour
6. Laurent/écouter de la musique
7. Stéphanie et Nadia/venir au café
8. Chloé et Daniel/manger des frites

Sophie mange-t-elle une pomme?

10 You're talking to your French pen pal on the phone. Unfortunately, you have a bad connection. Rephrase each question you ask using inversion.

1. —Est-ce que tu danses bien?
   —Pardon?
2. —Tes amis et toi, vous allez souvent en boîte?
   —Pardon?
3. —Tu fais du sport?
   —Pardon?
4. —Tu étudies beaucoup?
   —Pardon?
5. —Tes professeurs sont sympa?
   —Pardon?
6. —Est-ce que tu ressembles à ton frère?
   —Pardon?
7. —Est-ce que ton frère est méchant?
   —Pardon?
8. —Ton frère et toi, vous avez un chien?
   —Pardon?
9. —Est-ce que ta famille voyage beaucoup?
   —Pardon?
10. —Tu viens ici?
    —Pardon?

Modèle:
—Tu aimes le rock?
—Pardon?
—Aimes-tu le rock?

11 Get to know your partner better by asking and answering questions. Student A asks questions using inversion. Student B asks questions using **est-ce que**. Follow the model.

1. avec qui/aller au cinéma
2. quand/étudier
3. quels professeurs/aimer bien
4. à qui/ressembler
5. où/aller en vacances

Modèle:
quels sports/faire
Student A: Quels sports fais-tu?
Student B: Je fais du footing et du roller. Quels sports est-ce que tu fais?
Student A: Je joue au tennis.

Communication

12 With two partners, play the roles of an American student and two French-speaking exchange students. It's the last class of the day. The American student asks what the two exchange students are doing after class. After they respond, the American student suggests an activity for all of them to do together. The exchange students either agree or disagree, depending on the weather. If someone disagrees, that person suggests another activity. Finally, all three students decide what they are going to do after class.

Modèle:
Student A: Salut, Cédric! Qu'est-ce que tu fais après les cours aujourd'hui?
Student B: Moi, j'ai besoin de faire les devoirs.
Student A: Et toi, Farid?
Student C: Je regarde la télé.
Student A: Moi, je joue au foot. On joue ensemble?
Student B: Ah zut! Il pleut.
Student C: Pas possible! Alors, on va au fast-food?
Student A: Super! J'ai faim.
Student B: Moi aussi. Allons-y ensemble!

13 You want to know your classmates' favorite seasons. Write the names of the four seasons. Then poll as many of your classmates as you can in five minutes to find out their favorite season. For example, **Est-ce que tu préfères l'été, l'hiver, le printemps ou l'automne? Je préfère l'été**. As each classmate answers your question, make a check by the appropriate response. After you have finished asking questions, count how many people like each season and be ready to share your findings with the rest of the class.

Audiocassette/CD Activities 10-11

Answers

9 1. Valérie finit-elle les devoirs?
2. Christophe parle-t-il avec le prof?
3. Fatima travaille-t-elle?
4. Marc et Fabrice jouent-ils au foot?
5. Cécile et Patricia font-elles un tour?
6. Laurent écoute-t-il de la musique?
7. Stéphanie et Nadia viennent-elles au café?
8. Chloé et Daniel mangent-ils des frites?

10 1. —Danses-tu bien?
2. —Tes amis et toi, allez-vous souvent en boîte?
3. —Fais-tu du sport?
4. —Étudies-tu beaucoup?
5. —Tes professeurs sont-ils sympa?
6. —Ressembles-tu à ton frère?
7. —Ton frère est-il méchant?
8. —Ton frère et toi, avez-vous un chien?
9. —Ta famille voyage-t-elle beaucoup?
10. —Viens-tu ici?

11 1. Avec qui vas-tu au cinéma? Avec qui est-ce que tu vas au cinéma?
2. Quand étudies-tu? Quand est-ce que tu étudies?
3. Quels professeurs aimes-tu bien? Quels professeurs est-ce que tu aimes bien?
4. À qui ressembles-tu? À qui est-ce que tu ressembles?
5. Où vas-tu en vacances? Où est-ce que tu vas en vacances?
Students' responses to these questions will vary.

NATIONAL STANDARDS
C1.1, C1.2

Workbook
Activity 17

Audiocassette/CD
Sur la bonne piste

Listening Activity 3A

Quiz
Leçon C

Computer Software
Activity 8

Teacher's Notes

1. You may want students to work in pairs as they answer the questions. Note that the first four questions have specific answers. However, there is still some room for subjectivity. The last three questions are interpretation questions, and students should be encouraged to come up with a variety of answers. To holistically grade this activity, refer to the suggestions on page 162. 2. Optional activity. You might have students play a guessing game similar to **Qui suis-je?** based on the reading. Have each pair of students cut a sheet of paper into nine squares and write the name of one of Paul Piedbois' guests on each square. The squares of paper are folded and put in an envelope or a bag. Students take turns picking a name from the envelope or bag and having their partners guess who it is by asking yes or no questions. For example, if Student A has the square of paper with "Martin Nanteuil" written on it, his or her conversation with Student B might be:

Student B: C'est un Français?
Student A: Oui.
Student B: Il est musicien?
Student A: Non.
Student B: C'est Martin
Nanteuil?
Student A: Oui.

NATIONAL STANDARDS
C1.1, C1.2, C3.1

206

---

14 Your new pen pal from Guadeloupe is curious to find out if the seasons change where you live and what the weather is like. In a note to your pen pal, tell what the weather is like during the four seasons in your area. Give a typical temperature for each season using the Celsius scale. (**Il fait... degré(s) Celsius.**) Also mention what your favorite indoor and outdoor activities are during the various seasons.

 Sur la bonne piste

Reading is made up of at least three speeds: skimming, scanning and digesting. Skimming—reading very quickly—is a high-speed technique used to figure out context. (For most readings, skimming should be the first technique you use.) Scanning—hunting for a precise idea or word—is a medium-speed technique used to search for specific information. (Scanning helps you answer questions about a reading.) Digesting—reading very thoroughly to accomplish a task—is a low-speed technique. Digesting requires a lot of time and should not be the first or the only reading technique you use. If you approach a reading with the intent of digesting all the details, you waste both time and thinking energy. Instead, first skim the reading and make use of a very helpful skill: predicting. Reading becomes easier and much more interesting when you try to guess what comes next!

The following reading is a dialogue that takes place at a party. As you skim the dialogue, stop after each person's portion of the conversation. Then look at who will speak next and predict what that person will say. Finally, continue reading to find out if your prediction was correct.

La Soirée de Papa

Chez les Piedbois. Paul Piedbois, le père d'Olivier, ouvre la porte.

M. Piedbois: Bonsoir, Charles!

M. Théron: Salut, Paul!

M. Piedbois: Entre! Tu préfères un coca, une limonade ou un café?

M. Théron: Une limonade, s'il te plaît. Tiens, qui est ce beau garçon, Paul?

M. Piedbois: C'est mon fils.

Olivier: Bonsoir, Monsieur. Je m'appelle Olivier. Et vous?

M. Théron: Je m'appelle Charles Théron.

M. Piedbois: Monsieur Théron est musicien professionel.

Olivier: Musicien? C'est super génial! Papa, tu peux me présenter aux autres invités?

M. Piedbois: D'accord. Ah, Martin! Je te présente mon fils, Olivier. Il s'intéresse beaucoup aux professions de mes amis.

M. Nanteuil: Martin Nanteuil. Enchanté de faire ta connaissance, Olivier. Je suis dentiste.

Olivier: Enchanté!

M. Piedbois: Et voilà Fernando Ortiz. Il est ingénieur.

Olivier: Il est français?

M. Piedbois: Non, mexicain. Tu vois la femme brune?

Olivier: Oui.

M. Piedbois: C'est Danielle Graedel. On l'appelle "Dana." Elle vient de Suisse.

Olivier: Quelle est sa profession?

M. Piedbois: C'est une interprète. Elle parle français, italien, allemand, japonais et russe. Et là-bas, l'homme aux yeux noirs, c'est Marco Casati. Il est de Florence. Il assiste à une conférence de pharmaciens demain. Voilà Cathy Collins, une Anglaise. Mademoiselle Collins désire être prof de français à Londres, mais pour le moment elle est serveuse.

Olivier: Et la femme blonde?

M. Piedbois: C'est Astrid Schiller, une copine de Cathy. C'est une cuisinière.

Olivier: Elle est anglaise aussi?

M. Piedbois: Non, elle est allemande. Et voilà Hisatake Tanaka. Il vient du Japon. C'est un pilote pour Air France. À côté il y a Mercedes Pizano, une Espagnole. Elle est comptable.

Olivier: C'est une soirée internationale, papa! Tu as des copains intéressants!

---

15 Scan the reading to find answers to the following questions.

1. Where is Fernando Ortiz from? Where is Cathy Collins from?
2. Who has a nickname?
3. What is Danielle Graedel's profession? Which guests could she talk to in their native language?
4. Who is Italian? Who is Swiss? Who is Japanese?
5. Cathy Collins and Astrid Schiller are friends. How do you suppose they know each other?
6. Why does Olivier like his father's party?
7. What do you think Paul Piedbois does for a living?

Nathalie et Raoul

Answers

15 Possible answers:

1. Fernando Ortiz is from Mexico. Cathy Collins is from England.
2. Danielle Graedel has a nickname.
3. Danielle Graedel is an interpreter. She could talk to Paul Piedbois, Olivier Piedbois, Charles Théron, Martin Nanteuil, Marco Casati, Astrid Schiller and Hisatake Tanaka in their native language.
4. Marco Casati is Italian. Danielle Graedel is Swiss. Hisatake Tanaka is Japanese.
5. Cathy Collins is a server and Astrid Schiller is a cook. They might work at the same restaurant or café.
6. He finds the guests interesting.
7. Paul Piedbois knows people from all over the world. He could be a pilot for an international airline.

Teacher's Note

Here is the English version of this cartoon: (At the soccer stadium. Nathalie isn't very interested in the game.) Raoul, what time is it? Uhm . . . 3:15. Go, Dominique! Watch out, Fabrice! I love soccer! Don't you, Nathalie? Yes, it's fantastic. When is the game going to end? It's not very nice out. Raoul, what time is it? Uhm . . . 3:30. Look, Nathalie! The French are playing really well! Yes, yes. Darn! It's beginning to rain. Raoul, what time is it? Uhm . . . 3:40. What a game! Yes, it's extraordinary. Oh dear! It's raining a lot, and it's windy. Why doesn't the game end?! The weather is really bad! Raoul, what time . . . . Oh! The French two, the Americans zero! The French win! The French win . . . and the girl loses.

NATIONAL STANDARDS
C1.2, C3.1, C5.2

Answers

1. vrai
2. vrai
3. vrai
4. vrai
5. faux
6. vrai
7. faux
8. faux
9. faux
10. faux

C'est à moi!

Now that you have completed this unit, take a look at what you should be able to do in French. Can you do all of these tasks?

➤ I can tell someone's nationality.
➤ I can ask and tell what country and what city someone is from.
➤ I can identify someone's profession.
➤ I can ask for and give information about various topics, including the weather.
➤ I can explain why.
➤ I can invite someone to do something.
➤ I can express emotions.

Here is a brief checkup to see how much you understand about French culture. Decide if each statement is **vrai** or **faux**.

Juanita María est mexicaine.

Which Loire castle spans a river?

1. Chenonceaux and Chambord are two of the many beautiful castles located in the Loire Valley.
2. Teenagers in Europe frequently vacation in neighboring countries and therefore find it practical to speak a second language.
3. All people who receive a salary for 12 months are entitled to six weeks of vacation each year.
4. France is bordered on three sides by water: the English Channel, the Atlantic Ocean and the Mediterranean Sea.

The Seine River empties into the English Channel at Le Havre.

5. The European Union is a new underwater tunnel that connects France and England.
6. French is spoken in four European countries: France, Belgium, Luxembourg and Switzerland.
7. The three mountain ranges in France are **les Vosges, le Jura** and **le Rhône**.
8. Today France is divided into provinces for governmental purposes.
9. Temperatures are measured in degrees Fahrenheit in most European countries.
10. You must be at least 16 years old to operate a **mobylette** in France.

Communication orale

Businesspeople from foreign countries often visit the United States to learn more about our institutions and way of life. In addition to business establishments, they occasionally visit schools. To be prepared for an upcoming visit to your school from businesspeople representing various countries, have a conversation with your partner about these guests. Here is a list of guests and the countries they are from.

M. Jouffret - France

Mlle Castillo - Mexico

Mlle DiPiazza - Italy

M. Kraft - Germany

Mme Paquette - Canada

M. Cortés - Spain

Mme Chatton - France

M. Alonso - Mexico

Mlle Ounsworth - England

Mme Liu - China

M. Pagnucci - Italy

Mlle Peltier - Canada

Take turns naming at least eight different visitors. Tell their names, what countries and cities they are from, their professions, the languages they speak and the family members, if any, who are coming along with them. Follow the model.

Modèle:

Student A: M. Jouffret vient de France. Il est de Marseille. Il parle français et anglais. Il vient ici avec sa femme et son fils.

Student B: Quelle est sa profession?

Student A: M. Jouffret est informaticien.

NATIONAL STANDARDS
C1.1, C2.1, C2.2, C3.1

Communication écrite

Unfortunately, your French teacher was absent on the day the school administrator met with the staff to go over all the details about the prospective visit from international businesspeople to your school. Write a note to your teacher telling him or her who all these visitors are, what cities and countries they are from, what languages they speak, what their professions are and what family members, if any, are coming with them. Also tell your teacher which businessperson you would like to speak with.

Communication active

To identify someone's nationality, use:

Il est français.
C'est un Français.   *He is French.*

Elle est japonaise.
C'est une Japonaise.   *She is Japanese.*

To ask where someone is from, use:
Tu viens/Vous venez d'où?   *Where are you from?*

To tell where someone is from, use:
Il/Elle est de New York.   *He/She is from New York.*
Il/Elle vient du Canada.   *He/She is from Canada.*

Lien vient de Chine, et Mark vient du Canada.

Il/Elle vient de Chine.   *He/She is from China.*
Il/Elle vient d'Angleterre.   *He/She is from England.*
Il/Elle vient des États-Unis.   *He/She is from the United States.*

To identify someone's profession, use:

Il est avocat.
C'est un avocat.   *He's a lawyer.*

Elle est journaliste.
C'est une journaliste.   *She's a journalist.*

To ask for information, use:

C'est qui?	*Who is it?*
Quelle est la profession de Monsieur Desmarais?	*What is Mr. Desmarais' occupation?*
Il fait beau, **n'est-ce pas?**	*It's nice, isn't it?*
Est-ce que tu es allemande?	*Are you German?*
Quand viens-tu?	*When are you coming?*

M. Desmarais est informaticien.

To give information, use:

Il voyage beaucoup.	*He travels a lot.*
Elle travaille beaucoup.	*She works a lot.*
Je n'ai pas de mère.	*I don't have a mother.*
Il fait beau en automne.	*It's nice in autumn.*
Il fait mauvais en hiver.	*The weather's bad in the winter.*

To explain something, use:

C'est pourquoi tu parles si bien le français!	*That's why you speak French so well!*

To invite someone to do something, use:

On fait un tour **ensemble?**	*Do you want to take a trip together?*

To express emotions, use:

Quelle chance!	*What luck!*

Communication électronique

1. **Nuageux** and **couvert** mean "cloudy."
2. The noun **pluies** means "showers."
3. "Thunderstorms" are **orages**.
4. The abbreviation for "west" in French is "O" (not "W," as in English).

Answers will vary.

À moi de jouer!

Possible conversations:

— Salut! Je m'appelle Pia. Et toi? Tu t'appelles comment?

— Je m'appelle Fernando. Je viens du Mexique. Je suis mexicain. Et toi? Tu viens d'où?

— Je viens d'Italie. Je suis italienne. Quelle est la profession de tes parents?

— Ma mère est femme au foyer et mon beau-père est dentiste. Et tes parents?

— Mon père est journaliste et ma mère est avocate.

. . . .

— Salut! Je m'appelle Hans. Et toi? Tu t'appelles comment?

— Je m'appelle Jun. Je viens de Chine. Je suis chinoise. Et toi? Tu viens d'où?

— Je viens d'Allemagne. Je suis allemand. Quelle est la profession de tes parents?

— Mon père est homme d'affaires et ma mère est cuisinière. Et tes parents?

— Ma mère est médecin et je n'ai pas de père.

Teacher's Note

After students have finished writing their two dialogues, you may want to ask each pair to perform one of the dialogues they created in front of the entire class.

NATIONAL STANDARDS
C1.1, C1.2, C1.3, C2.1

212

Communication électronique

On page 199 of your textbook you learned basic weather expressions in French. In order to understand a French weather report, you should also know some additional weather vocabulary. To see certain weather symbols and their descriptions, go to this Internet site:

http://www.meteo.fr/guide/guide_pictos.html

After viewing this site, answer the following questions.

1. What are two French words that mean "cloudy"?
2. What noun means "showers"? (It's related to the French verb **pleut**.)
3. What is the French word for "thunderstorms"?
4. Look at the wind direction chart. Which direction in French is not abbreviated the same as it is in English?

Now check out today's weather in France by going to this Internet site:

http://www.meteo.fr

After clicking on "Le temps," look at the weather map and then answer the following questions.

1. What will the high temperature be today in Paris?
2. What is this temperature in Fahrenheit? (Multiply by 9, divide by 5 and add 32.)
3. In what parts of France will it be sunny?
4. Where will there be precipitation?

À moi de jouer!

Let's see how much French you have learned about countries, nationalities and professions! Work with a partner to complete each dialogue below with appropriate expressions from this unit. In each scene, two foreign exchange students meet and exchange information about where they're from and their parents' occupations. Since all of them are from different countries, the only language they have in common is French. (You may want to refer to the *Communication active* on pages 210-11 and the vocabulary list on page 213.)

Vocabulaire

à in
un agent de police police officer
l' Allemagne (f.) Germany
allemand(e) German
américain(e) American
un(e) ami(e) friend
anglais(e) English
l' Angleterre (f.) England
après after
au in (the)
aujourd'hui today
l' automne (m.) autumn, fall
autre other
   un(e) autre another
un(e) avocat(e) lawyer

c'est that's
le Canada Canada
canadien, canadienne Canadian
la chance luck
chaud(e) warm, hot
la Chine China
chinois(e) Chinese
un coiffeur, une coiffeuse hairdresser
un(e) comptable accountant
un cuisinier, une cuisinière cook

de (d') a, an, any
un(e) dentiste dentist
des from (the), of (the)
du from (the), of (the)

en in
l' Espagne (f.) Spain
espagnol(e) Spanish
est-ce que? (phrase introducing a question)
les États-Unis (m.) United States
l' été (m.) summer

faire un tour to go for a ride
Quel temps fait-il? What's the weather like? How's the weather?
Il fait beau. It's (The weather's) beautiful/nice.
Il fait chaud. It's (The weather's) hot/warm.
Il fait du soleil. It's sunny.
Il fait du vent. It's windy.
Il fait frais. It's (The weather's) cool.
Il fait froid. It's (The weather's) cold.
Il fait mauvais. It's (The weather's) bad.
une femme au foyer housewife

une femme d'affaires businesswoman
un fermier, une fermière farmer
frais, fraîche cool, fresh
français(e) French
la France France
froid(e) cold

l' hiver (m.) winter
un homme man
   un homme au foyer househusband
   un homme d'affaires businessman

ici here
un infirmier, une infirmière nurse
un informaticien, une informaticienne computer specialist
un ingénieur engineer
l' Italie (f.) Italy
italien, italienne Italian

le Japon Japan
japonais(e) Japanese
un(e) journaliste journalist

mauvais(e) bad
un médecin doctor
mexicain(e) Mexican
le Mexique Mexico

neiger: Il neige. It's snowing.

parler to speak, to talk
pleuvoir: Il pleut. It's raining.
le printemps spring
une profession occupation

quand when

si so
le soleil sun
souvent often
sur in

le temps weather
   Quel temps fait-il? What's the weather like? How's the weather?
un tour trip
travailler to work

venir to come
le vent wind
le Vietnam Vietnam
vietnamien, vietnamienne Vietnamese
voyager to travel

Unité 7

On fait les magasins.

In this unit you will be able to:

➤ express likes and dislikes

➤ agree and disagree

➤ express need

➤ express intentions

➤ invite

➤ inquire about and compare prices

➤ ask for information

➤ give information

➤ ask someone to repeat

➤ choose and purchase items

NATIONAL STANDARDS
C2.1, C2.2

Workbook Activity 1

Grammar & Vocabulary Exercises 1-4

Audiocassette/CD
Les vêtements,
Les magasins

Transparencies 32-33

Teacher's Notes

1. Students learned the expression **faire du shopping** in **Unité 2**. In French-speaking Canada, people use the verb **magasiner**. 2. The expression "to go window-shopping" in French is **faire du lèche-vitrines**. 3. The words for "jeans" and "pants" in French are singular. 4. **Chapeau** and **manteau** form their plurals by adding an **x**. 5. **Un pull** is the shortened form of **un pull-over**. In French-speaking Canada, **un chandail** is often used for **un pull**. 6. The plural form of **un tee-shirt** is **des tee-shirts**. 7. **Un sweat** may also be called **un sweat-shirt**. 8. Other related terms are **un chemisier** (*blouse*), **une cravate** (*tie*), **un survêtement, un jogging** (*warm-up suit*), **une ceinture** (*belt*), **un imper, un imperméable** (*raincoat*), **des gants (m.)** (*gloves*), **un foulard** (*lightweight scarf*), **une écharpe** (*thick scarf*), **un mouchoir** (*handkerchief*), **une casquette** (*cap*), **un collant** (*tights*), **des lunettes (f.)** (*glasses*), **des lunettes de soleil (f.)** (*sunglasses*), **des verres de contact (m.)**, **des lentilles (f.)** (*contact lenses*), **un bijou** (*piece of jewelry*), **un collier** (*necklace*), **un bracelet** (*bracelet*), **une montre** (*watch*), **une bague** (*ring*) and **des boucles d'oreille (f.)** (*earrings*). 9. Communicative functions that are recycled in this lesson are "asking for information" and "accepting and refusing an invitation."

NATIONAL STANDARDS
C1.2, C4.1

216

Leçon A

In this lesson you will be able to:

➤ **express intentions**

➤ **express need**

➤ **invite**

➤ **express likes and dislikes**

les vêtements (m.)

les magasins (m.)

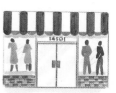

une boutique

un grand magasin

un centre commercial

Workbook Activity 2

Audiocassette/CD *Dialogue*

Teacher's Note

Trouver (*to find*) has both a literal and a figurative meaning in French. The sentence **Je ne trouve pas le livre** means "I can't find the book." The question **Comment est-ce que tu trouves cette chemise?** asks for an opinion: "How do you like this shirt?"

TPR

Les vêtements

If you have flash cards of all the clothing items, you might give students commands, such as **Montrez-moi le costume**, while holding up the man's suit card and another card. Students respond by pointing to the card that shows the man's suit. Displaying all the cards for students to see, you might continue the activity by giving commands to individual students, such as **Mets le costume avec la chemise**. Students could then demonstrate comprehension by manipulating the flash cards as directed.

Lamine and Ariane are talking about what they're going to wear to a party.

Lamine: **Je vais aller au centre commercial pour chercher un jean et un tee-shirt pour samedi soir. Et toi, qu'est-ce que tu vas porter à la boum?**

Ariane: **Moi, j'ai un pull mais j'ai besoin d'une jupe.**

Lamine: **Allons ensemble au grand magasin! On va peut-être trouver quelque chose là-bas.**

Ariane: **D'accord. J'aime bien faire les magasins!**

Enquête culturelle

There are huge shopping malls in France but fewer than in the United States. However, small specialized stores still do a brisk business. Just as in the United States, you can go to **le pressing** or **la teinturerie** (*dry cleaner's*) to have your clothes dry-cleaned, **le tailleur** (*tailor*) to have your clothes altered and **la cordonnerie** (*shoe repair shop*) to have your shoes repaired.

What might you expect to find in a shop called "Chaussetterie"?

Shopping Excursion

Put your students in small groups of four or five. Each group member brings pictures of clothing items. Then group members decide together on prices in euros and mark each item. Finally, the shopping excursion begins as one student in each group stays behind to be the salesclerk in the boutique while the other group members go shopping from boutique to boutique (group to group). Each shopper has a conversation with the salesclerk in that particular boutique, asking for an item, inquiring about its price and either buying or not buying it.

Like other teenagers around the world, French teens follow fashion trends closely. They like to dress up for special occasions. In general, the French place more importance on having quality clothing that is the latest style than on having many different outfits.

Certain areas of larger French cities attract teenagers and young adults. For example, **le Quartier latin**, near the University of Paris, is an area where students often find clothes, international restaurants and entertainment which appeal to their contemporary tastes.

Along pedestrian streets in *le Quartier latin*, you can shop, go to movies and eat in international restaurants. (Paris)

Open-air markets, featuring fresh fruits and vegetables as well as seafood and meat, are located in most French-speaking cities. In large cities, neighborhood markets may be open every day except Monday. In smaller towns, markets may be open only one day a week. At **le marché aux puces** (*flea market*) you can purchase a variety of

At *le marché aux puces* vendors expect customers to bargain. (Tours)

items ranging from antique lamps to secondhand clothing. At such outdoor markets buyers often try bargaining with vendors to get a reduced price. These lively markets attract many tourists and shoppers who have figured out a way to stretch their income.

1 | *Répondez en français.*

1. Qui va faire les magasins?
2. Qu'est-ce que Lamine va porter à la boum?
3. La boum, c'est quand?
4. Qu'est-ce qu'Ariane a déjà pour la boum?
5. De quoi Ariane a-t-elle besoin?
6. Ariane et Lamine, est-ce qu'elles vont au grand magasin ou à la boutique?

---

2 | Identify each numbered item you see in the illustration.

Modèle:

Ce sont des bas.

---

3 | Choose the letter of the item of clothing that each person must be wearing.

1. Sabrina skie. Elle porte....
   a. une jupe   b. un anorak   c. une robe

2. Mamadou nage. Il porte....
   a. une veste   b. des baskets   c. un maillot de bain

3. Michèle joue au volley. Elle porte....
   a. un blouson   b. des bas   c. un short

4. Nadia porte des tennis. Elle porte aussi....
   a. des chaussettes   b. des bottes   c. des bas

5. Il fait froid. Catherine porte une robe et aussi....
   a. un ensemble   b. un sweat   c. un manteau

6. Sylvie porte une jupe et aussi....
   a. un pull   b. un pantalon   c. un costume

7. Diana voyage beaucoup. Elle porte un ensemble: des chaussures, un tailleur et....
   a. des tennis   b. un chapeau   c. un tee-shirt

8. Édouard va au café avec ses parents. Il porte un pantalon et....
   a. une chemise   b. un jean   c. un tailleur

Audiocassette/CD Activity 1

Answers

1 1. Lamine et Ariane vont faire les magasins.
2. Lamine va porter un jean et un tee-shirt à la boum.
3. La boum, c'est samedi soir.
4. Ariane a déjà un pull.
5. Ariane a besoin d'une jupe.
6. Ariane et Lamine vont au grand magasin.

2 1. Ce sont des chaussures.
2. Ce sont des baskets.
3. C'est une robe.
4. C'est un tee-shirt.
5. C'est un jean.
6. C'est un blouson.
7. C'est une jupe.
8. C'est un pantalon.

3 1. b
2. c
3. c
4. a
5. c
6. a
7. b
8. a

NATIONAL STANDARDS
C1.1, C1.2

Workbook Activity 3

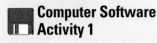
Grammar & Vocabulary Exercises 5-8

Audiocassette/CD Activity 4

Computer Software Activity 1

Answers

4 Answers will vary.

Teacher's Notes

1. You may want to review the forms of **aller** with your students before beginning this section.
2. The simple future tense will be introduced in the third level of *C'est à toi!* 3. Review with your students the names of activities that they can express in French (especially those from **Unité 2** on pages 20, 32 and 42-43). Then ask students what they are going to do **après les cours/vendredi soir/samedi/dimanche**. They answer using **aller** plus an infinitive.

Cooperative Group Practice

Forming Questions

Put your students in small groups and have each group make a set of note cards. On each card students write a different infinitive the class has already learned. Then, as each student in the group chooses one of the cards at random, he or she makes a question using a form of **aller** plus the indicated infinitive. The group's secretary records the question on the note card. After all cards have been used, groups exchange note cards and students in each group take turns answering the set of questions they have received.

NATIONAL STANDARDS
C1.1, C1.2, C4.1

220

---

4 | *C'est à toi!*

1. Est-ce que tu aimes faire les magasins?
2. Où est-ce que tu préfères faire les magasins, au centre commercial, au grand magasin ou à une boutique?
3. Qu'est-ce que tu portes aujourd'hui?
4. Qu'est-ce que ton ami(e) porte aujourd'hui?
5. Qu'est-ce que tu portes quand tu vas à une boum?
6. Qu'est-ce que tu portes en été?

Qu'est-ce que Christian porte aujourd'hui?

Structure

Aller + infinitive

One way to express what you are going to do in the near future is to use the present tense form of **aller** that agrees with the subject plus an infinitive.

Je vais faire les magasins.	*I'm going to go shopping.*
Qu'est-ce que tu vas chercher?	*What are you going to look for?*

To make a negative sentence, put **ne (n')** before the form of **aller** and **pas** after it.

André ne va pas porter son costume noir.	*André's not going to wear his black suit.*

La famille va faire du vélo. (Beaune)

vous allez faire le voyage de votre vie.

Pratique

5 Tell what the following people are going to do this weekend.

1. nous

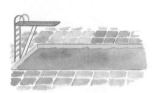

2. je

3. Nadine et Jeanne

4. Normand et Gilbert

5. tu

6. Vincent

7. vous

Modèle:

Véro
Véro va écouter de la musique.

6 Forecasters have predicted that the storm of the decade will hit your area tomorrow. Knowing that everyone will be stranded at home, tell whether or not the following people are going to do what they had planned.

1. Antonine et Marie/téléphoner à leurs amis
2. nous/étudier
3. vous/skier
4. Mme Delacroix/dormir
5. je/faire des crêpes
6. Étienne/sortir avec Sara
7. Emmanuel et Fabrice/manger au café
8. tu/aller à la boum de Monique

Modèles:

M. Martin/écouter de la musique
Monsieur Martin va écouter de la musique.

les filles/faire les magasins
Les filles ne vont pas faire les magasins.

Audiocassette/CD Activities 5-6

Answers

5 Possible answers:
1. Nous allons jouer au basket.
2. Je vais nager.
3. Nadine et Jeanne vont faire les magasins.
4. Normand et Gilbert vont faire du vélo.
5. Tu vas lire.
6. Vincent va faire les devoirs.
7. Vous allez regarder la télé.

6 1. Antonine et Marie vont téléphoner à leurs amis.
2. Nous allons étudier.
3. Vous n'allez pas skier.
4. Madame Delacroix va dormir.
5. Je vais faire des crêpes.
6. Étienne ne va pas sortir avec Sara.
7. Emmanuel et Fabrice ne vont pas manger au café.
8. Tu ne vas pas aller à la boum de Monique.

Cooperative Group Practice

Create a Story

Put your students in small groups of four or five. Give each group three pictures (for example, a girl, a bike and a boutique) and have them complete a story together based on these pictures. The first student begins by saying a sentence in either the present tense or in the near future. The second student repeats the first student's sentence before adding his or her own sentence, etc. After all members of the group have contributed a sentence to the story, it might be interesting to record the stories and play them back for the entire class.

NATIONAL STANDARDS
C1.1, C1.2, C1.3

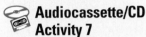

Modèle:

nager

Student A: Est-ce que tu
vas nager?
Student B: Oui, je vais nager.
Et toi, est-ce que tu
vas nager?
Student A: Non, je ne vais
pas nager.

7 With a partner, take turns asking and telling whether or not you're going to
do certain things during your next vacation.

1. skier
2. aller au centre commercial
3. voyager
4. jouer au foot

5. faire les devoirs
6. regarder la télé
7. travailler

Thérèse et Marianne vont faire du shopping.

À + definite articles

The preposition **à** (*to, at, in*) does not change before the definite articles
la and **l'**.

Allons ensemble **à la** boutique!	*Let's go to the boutique together!*
Pas possible. Je finis mes devoirs **à l'**école.	*Not possible. I'm finishing my homework at school.*

Before the definite articles **le** and **les**, however, **à** changes form.
À combines with **le** and **les** as follows:

à + le = au	*to (the), at (the), in (the)*
à + les = aux	*to (the), at (the), in (the)*

Qui va **au** centre commercial?	*Who is going to the mall?*
Jean et moi, nous allons **aux** grands magasins.	*Jean and I are going to the department stores.*

Au and **aux** are used before countries with masculine names.

Tu vas **aux** États-Unis ou **au** Canada?	*Are you going to the United States or to Canada?*

Pratique

8 Tell where some of your friends are going, choosing from the locations in the following list.

la boum de Marc	la boutique	le cinéma	l'école
le Mexique	le fast-food	les États-Unis	

Modèle:

Ariane va parler espagnol.
Elle va au Mexique.

1. Béatrice et Éric vont danser samedi soir.
2. Catherine et Florence ont faim.
3. Salim va parler anglais.
4. Yasmine a besoin de chercher un jean et un tee-shirt.
5. Magali et Patrick désirent regarder un film de Spielberg.
6. Thomas a besoin de parler avec le prof d'informatique.

9 You are in charge of giving away items left over from the school's rummage sale. Tell which items you're going to give to the following people.

Modèle:

le frère de Stéphanie
Je vais donner le blouson au frère de Stéphanie.

1. les profs de français
2. la prof de musique
3. le fils de la prof de biologie
4. l'informaticien de l'école
5. le prof de géographie
6. la sœur de David

Communication

10 Your French pen pal has sent you a message by e-mail to find out what American students wear when they do certain things. Make a list of four items of clothing that you normally wear, according to each situation.

> jouer au basket
> aller à l'école
> aller à une boum
> aller au café avec les parents

Quand Jean-Claude fait du vélo, il porte un tee-shirt, un short, des chaussettes et des tennis. (Montréal)

11 Imagine that you work at a travel agency. Clients ask you what they should pack when planning a trip to certain French-speaking vacation spots during the winter and spring travel seasons. According to the weather report you receive from each city's tourist bureau, select at least three clothing items for male travelers and three clothing items for female travelers to take to each destination.

1. À Québec, au Canada, il fait très froid et il neige beaucoup en hiver. Il fait -15° C.
2. À Fort-de-France, à la Martinique, il fait du soleil et il fait très chaud en hiver. Il fait 28° C.
3. À la Nouvelle-Orléans, aux États-Unis, il fait beau et il fait chaud au printemps. Il fait 24° C.
4. À Paris, en France, il fait frais et il pleut au printemps. Il fait 12° C.

Il fait chaud à la Nouvelle-Orléans au printemps.

12 With a partner, have a phone conversation about going shopping. Student A needs to go to the mall to buy some clothes and calls Student B to see if he or she would like to go along. Student B also needs to buy something and agrees to go with Student A. Decide on a time and tell each other good-bye.

 Prononciation

The sound [ɔ]

The sound [ɔ], or "open o," is just one of the sounds corresponding to the letter **o** in French. It is called "open o" because your mouth must be more open than closed to form it. Say each of these words:

robe   anorak   short   costume   botte   porter

The sound [õ]

The sound [õ] is an open nasal sound. It is represented by the letters **on** and **om**. In either case, the **n** or **m** is not pronounced and the sound [õ] comes out through your nose. Say each of these words:

pantal**on**   all**ons**   blous**on**   Jap**on**   combien   comptable

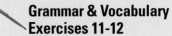

Workbook Activity 6

Grammar & Vocabulary Exercises 11-12

Audiocassette/CD *Les couleurs,* Adjectives

Transparencies 34-35

les couleurs (f.)

bleu(e) marron vert(e)
gris(e) rouge noir(e)
beige blanc, blanche
violet, violette orange
rose jaune

Il est petit.   Il est grand.

Elle est courte.   Elle est longue.

Il est vieux.   Il est nouveau.

Il est bon marché.

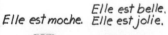
Soldes   Il est cher.

$29.99 $140.00

Elle est moche.   Elle est belle. Elle est jolie.

petit	petite
grand	grande
joli	jolie
beau	belle
moche	moche
nouveau	nouvelle
vieux	vieille
court	courte
long	longue
cher	chère
bon marché	bon marché

Leçon B

In this lesson you will be able to:

➤ **express likes and dislikes**

➤ **inquire about and compare prices**

➤ **agree and disagree**

Teacher's Notes

1. The colors **orange** and **marron** are invariable. For example, **Elle porte des chaussettes orange et marron.** 2. Another word for "brown" is **brun(e)**. It is generally used to describe hair color. 3. The names of some colors that are more specific are **rouge vif** (*bright red*), **vert clair/foncé** (*light/dark green*) and **bleu marine** (*navy blue*). 4. Students have already learned the irregular forms of the adjective **beau**. The irregular forms of the adjectives **nouveau** and **vieux** will be explained in the **Structure** section of this **leçon**. 5. The adjective **bon marché** is invariable. For example, **Les chaussures sont bon marché.** 6. Communicative functions that are recycled in this lesson are "expressing intentions" and "expressing need."

Game

Qu'est-ce qu'on porte?

To practice words for clothing and colors, put your class in a circle and ask two students to come to the center. Have these two students sit with their backs to each other. Then each student describes what the other is wearing and the color of each item. If either student has difficulty remembering, students in the circle may prompt him or her by asking leading questions. Repeat the activity with other pairs.

NATIONAL STANDARDS
C1.1, C1.2, C4.1

225

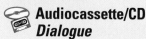
Teacher's Notes

1. Another way to say that something is cheap or inexpensive is to make the expression **être cher** negative. 2. You may want to point out that **le dollar** is the basic unit of money in Canada. The value of the Canadian **dollar** is less than that of the American dollar. 3. The exclamation **Beurk!** may also be spelled **Berk!**

Madame Desrosiers is shopping with her son Jean at a boutique in Montreal.

Madame Desrosiers:	J'adore la chemise bleue! Et elle est bon marché. Elle coûte 18 dollars.
Jean:	Beurk! Je ne vais pas acheter ça! Elle est moche. Mais j'ai besoin d'une nouvelle chemise.
Madame Desrosiers:	Il y a beaucoup de belles chemises ici - noires, blanches, vertes....
Jean:	C'est vrai. Tiens, j'aime la grande chemise noire.
Madame Desrosiers:	C'est combien? C'est en solde?
Jean:	Non, elle est assez chère... 40 dollars.

 Enquête culturelle

There are many opportunities for shopping in Montreal, the second largest French-speaking city in the world. Beneath Montreal's busy streets in the midtown area, and literally carved from the rock that supports them, lies the world's largest subterranean city. Shopping, strolling, eating, doing business and finding entertainment are easy at any time of the day or night, with no worries about the cold Canadian winters. Department stores, hotels, restaurants, movie theaters and many businesses are located in and around large

Underground Montreal is essentially one large shopping mall.

squares, such as the **Place Ville-Marie** and the **Place Bonaventure**. The four-line **métro** (*subway*) system and a series of walkways, stairways and elevators connect this underground complex. Decorations, such as stained glass windows, murals and ceramic artworks, beautify the modern **métro**

stations, each designed by a different architect. Aboveground, concrete and glass skyscrapers top the subterranean complex. The idea of an underground structure separating road traffic from pedestrian traffic is not new. Five centuries ago, the Italian artist Leonardo da Vinci envisioned a two-level city.

Montreal has immense skyscrapers aboveground; underground lies another complete city.

When items are **en solde** (*on sale*) in French shops, they are sometimes displayed on the sidewalk in front of the store marked with the sign **Soldes** to attract customers.

What word tells you that this shop is having a sale?

NATIONAL STANDARDS
C2.1, C2.2, C4.2

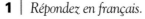

1 | *Répondez en français.*

1. Qui fait les magasins?
2. Qui aime la chemise bleue?
3. La chemise bleue, est-elle chère ou bon marché?
4. Est-ce que Jean aime la chemise bleue?
5. Pourquoi est-ce que Jean ne va pas acheter la chemise bleue?
6. La chemise noire, est-elle grande ou petite?
7. Combien coûte la chemise noire?

2 | Write the name of the person that fits each description.

Renée   *Fabienne*   *Ahmed*   *Thierry*

1. Son pull est bleu.
2. Il porte des baskets noires.
3. Elle est petite.
4. Son tee-shirt est blanc.
5. Il porte un vieux jean.
6. Sa jupe est longue.
7. Il est grand.
8. Sa jupe est courte.

3 | *C'est à toi!*

1. Avec qui fais-tu souvent les magasins?
2. Où vas-tu pour acheter des vêtements?
3. Est-ce que tu aimes acheter des vêtements en solde?
4. Qui porte un tee-shirt aujourd'hui?
5. Qui porte un jean aujourd'hui? Est-il nouveau ou vieux?
6. Qu'est-ce que tu portes aujourd'hui?

Claire fait souvent les magasins avec son amie Catherine.

LES IMBALLABLES.
DES GALERIES

N° **56**

Authentic Line

Le blouson long
100 % coton.

90,71 €

N° 57, pull côte anglaise, 65 % soie, 35 % coton, 29,73 €. N° 58, chemise 100 % coton, 29,73 €.
N° 59, pantalon gabardine lavée, 100 % coton, 37,35 €.

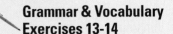
**Workbook
Activity 8**

**Grammar & Vocabulary
Exercises 13-14**

**Computer Software
Activities 3-4**

Structure

Irregular adjectives

You already know that most feminine adjectives are formed by adding an **e** to masculine adjectives.

gris	grise
bleu	bleue

You also know that if a masculine adjective ends in **-e**, the feminine adjective is identical.

rouge	rouge
moche	moche

Some irregular adjectives never change form, even in the plural.

orange	orange
marron	marron
super	super
sympa	sympa
bon marché	bon marché

Some feminine adjectives are formed by doubling the final consonant of a masculine adjective and adding an **e.**

bon	bon**ne**
quel	quel**le**
violet	violet**te**
italien	italien**ne**

To form a feminine adjective from a masculine adjective that ends in **-er,** change the ending to **-ère.**

cher	ch**ère**
premier	prem**ière**

Some other masculine adjectives also have irregular feminine forms.

blanc	**blanche**
frais	**fraîche**
long	**longue**

The adjectives **nouveau** and **vieux,** like the adjective **beau,** have irregular feminine forms as well as irregular forms before a masculine noun beginning with a vowel sound.

Masculine Singular before a Consonant Sound	Masculine Singular before a Vowel Sound	Feminine Singular
un **beau** magasin	un **bel** homme	une **belle** affiche
un **nouveau** pantalon	un **nouvel** ami	une **nouvelle** robe
un **vieux** costume	un **vieil** anorak	une **vieille** photo

The irregular masculine plural forms of these adjectives are **beaux, nouveaux** and **vieux.**

les **beaux** vêtements   les **nouveaux** élèves   les **vieux** pulls

[z]

Le Vieux Bistro

14, rue du Cloître Notre-Dame Paris 4ème
Tél : 01 43 54 18 95, M° Cité.

NATIONAL STANDARDS
C1.2, C1.3, C4.1

Audiocassette/CD Activity 5

Answers

4 Sophie va porter un pull noir, une chemise blanche, un pantalon blanc, un chapeau noir, des chaussettes blanches et des tennis blancs.

Jérémy va porter une veste violette, un tee-shirt violet, un jean bleu, des chaussettes violettes et des baskets blanches.

5 1. Madame Duval a une vieille robe. Elle a besoin d'une nouvelle robe.
2. Monsieur Bureau a un vieil ordinateur. Il a besoin d'un nouvel ordinateur.
3. Anne a un vieux sac à dos. Elle a besoin d'un nouveau sac à dos.
4. Sabrina a un vieil anorak. Elle a besoin d'un nouvel anorak.
5. Monsieur Piedbœuf a une vieille veste. Il a besoin d'une nouvelle veste.
6. Dikembe a un vieux vélo. Il a besoin d'un nouveau vélo.

Paired Practice

Fashion Show

Have your students plan a fashion show to help them practice clothing vocabulary and colors. Put students in pairs. Have each student write a description of what he or she is wearing and give it to his or her partner. Then as each student models what he or she is wearing for the entire class, his or her partner reads the description. (Prepare a list of phrases or comments in French that might be said during an actual fashion show for students to adapt and use in their descriptions.)

Pratique

4 Sophie and Jérémy are going out tonight. Tell what they are going to wear.

les vêtements de Sophie

les vêtements de Jérémy

Modèle:
Sophie va porter un pull noir....

5 Tell what old things the following people have. Then say that they need new ones.

Modèle:

Bruno
Bruno a un vieux sweat. Il a besoin d'un nouveau sweat.

1. Mme Duval

4. Sabrina

2. M. Bureau

5. M. Piedbœuf

3. Anne

6. Dikembe

6 With a partner, take turns asking and telling what you think about the items of clothing you see in the store window. When answering each question, use the appropriate form of one of the following adjectives.

| beau | moche | cher | bon marché | long | court |

1.

2.

3.

4.

Position of adjectives

In French, adjectives usually follow the nouns they describe.

> Donnez-moi une boisson **chaude**.
> Je voudrais un café **noir**.
> Mario est un serveur **italien**.

Some frequently used adjectives precede the nouns they describe. These adjectives often express *beauty*, *age*, *goodness* and *size*. (You can remember these categories easily by associating them with the word "bags.") Some of these adjectives are **beau**, **joli**, **nouveau**, **vieux**, **bon**, **mauvais**, **grand** and **petit**.

Ma **petite** sœur va faire les magasins.	*My little sister is going to go shopping.*
Elle cherche un **nouveau** jean.	*She's looking for new jeans.*
Elle trouve un **beau** pull rose.	*She finds a beautiful pink sweater.*
Quelles **bonnes** soldes!	*What good sales!*

Modèle:

Student A: Comment est-ce que tu trouves la chemise beige?
Student B: Elle est très chère. Comment est-ce que tu trouves la chemise jaune?
Student A: Elle est bon marché.

LA PETITE VALISE POUR UN GRAND TOUR DU MONDE

▪ **Workbook Activity 9**

✎ **Grammar & Vocabulary Exercises 15-17**

▯ **Computer Software Activity 5**

Answers

6 Possible answers:
1. Comment est-ce que tu trouves la veste grise? Elle est très belle. Comment est-ce que tu trouves la veste bleue? Elle est très moche.
2. Comment est-ce que tu trouves la jupe verte? Elle est très longue. Comment est-ce que tu trouves la jupe violette? Elle est très courte.
3. Comment est-ce que tu trouves le pantalon orange? Il est très moche. Comment est-ce que tu trouves le pantalon marron? Il est très beau.
4. Comment est-ce que tu trouves le pull rose? Il est très cher. Comment est-ce que tu trouves le pull rouge? Il est bon marché.

Teacher's Notes

1. You may want to tell students that **bon** is pronounced like **bonne** when it precedes a masculine noun beginning with a vowel sound: **un bon ami**. The **d** in **grand** is pronounced [t] before a masculine noun beginning with a vowel sound: **un grand élève**. 2. **Autre** is another adjective that precedes its noun. 3. Collect the pictures of clothing items that students brought for the shopping excursion activity in **Leçon A**. So that students can practice formation and position of adjectives, show them these pictures one at a time. Students identify the item and its color.

NATIONAL STANDARDS
C1.1, C1.2, C4.1

Answers

7 1. Oui, c'est un garçon timide!
2. Oui, c'est une prof bavarde!
3. Oui, c'est une fille méchante!
4. Oui, c'est un homme diligent!
5. Oui, c'est un élève paresseux!
6. Oui, c'est un professeur super!
7. Oui, c'est une femme généreuse!
8. Oui, c'est un ami sympa!

8 1. Pauline a un joli chat.
2. Alice a une nouvelle affiche.
3. André a un grand sac à dos.
4. Manu a un petit chien.
5. Alexandre a une bonne cassette.
6. Jamila a un bel oiseau.

Game

Auction

To give students additional practice with the formation and position of adjectives and in persuading someone to buy something, you might hold a class auction. Put about 25 objects (or pictures of objects) in a bag. These objects may range in value from expensive to worthless. Give all students 75 euros in play money. Then have each student randomly select an object from the bag. One at a time students try to sell their object to their classmates for the highest price. The seller describes the object, using as many adjectives as possible to make it sound appealing. The object goes to the highest bidder.

Pratique

7 Agree with what the French exchange student says about some of the people in your school. Use the indicated noun in each of your sentences.

Modèle:

Lisa est intelligente. (une élève)
Oui, c'est une élève intelligente!

1. Matt est timide. (un garçon)
2. Mrs. Johnson est bavarde. (une prof)
3. Amy est méchante. (une fille)
4. Mr. Ross est diligent. (un homme)
5. Paul est paresseux. (un élève)
6. Mr. Gray est super. (un professeur)
7. Ms. Lell est généreuse. (une femme)
8. Ryan est sympa. (un ami)

Mr. Gray est aussi un prof intelligent.

8 Tell what each child has for show-and-tell, using the appropriate form of the indicated adjective.

Modèle:

Joséphine/une photo (vieux)
Joséphine a une vieille photo.

1. Pauline/un chat (joli)
2. Alice/une affiche (nouveau)
3. André/un sac à dos (grand)
4. Manu/un chien (petit)
5. Alexandre/une cassette (bon)
6. Jamila/un oiseau (beau)

– Chouette, une petite valise! Chouette, une petite valise! Chouette, une petite valise!

Aïcha a trois beaux petits chats.

9 Describe the items you find in the school's lost-and-found department as you look for your missing sweater. Use two adjectives from the list that follows in each of your descriptions. Make sure the adjectives agree with the nouns they describe.

vieux	jaune	joli	blanc	grand	bleu	nouveau	vert
bon	noir	beau	mauvais	rouge	moche	petit	marron

Modèle:

Il y a un grand sweat vert.

1.

3.

5.

2.

4.

6.

Present tense of the verbs *acheter* and *préférer*

The endings of the verbs **acheter** (*to buy*) and **préférer** (*to prefer*) are regular, but there is an **accent grave** over the final **e** (**è**) in the stem of the **je, tu, il/elle/on** and **ils/elles** forms.

Tu préfères le bleu ou le vert?   *Do you prefer the blue (one) or the green (one)?*

Je n'achète pas ça!   *I'm not buying that!*

Mme Bourgue achète une nouvelle chemise blanche. (Angers)

Les femmes préfèrent les hommes qui lisent l'Auto-Journal...

"Je pense à moi, j'achète lorrain".

Workbook Activity 10

Grammar & Vocabulary Exercises 18-19

Computer Software Activity 6

Answers

9 Answers will vary.

Teacher's Notes

1. You may want to point out to students that the **e** in the stem of **acheter** is not pronounced in the infinitive or in the **nous** and **vous** forms. This **e** is pronounced [ɛ], however, in the other four forms. The accent grave is added when the ending is silent. 2. The final **é** in the stem of **préférer** is pronounced [e] in the infinitive and in the **nous** and **vous** forms because the ending is pronounced. But this **é** changes to **è** and is pronounced [ɛ] in the other four forms because the ending is silent. 3. When the names of colors are used as nouns, they are masculine.

TPR

Missing Accents

On an overhead transparency write complete sentences that each contain a different form of **acheter** and **préférer** but leave off any accents. As you uncover one sentence at a time, point to the final **e** in the verb's stem. If there should be an accent on that **e**, students raise their hands slanting them in the direction the accent should go. If no accent is needed, students do not raise their hands.

NATIONAL STANDARDS
C1.1, C1.2, C4.1

Cooperative Group Practice

Qu'est-ce qu'on préfère?

So that students can practice using the verbs **acheter** and **préférer**, put them in small groups. Use the same pictures of clothing items that students brought for the shopping excursion activity in **Leçon A**, mix them up and place them face down. Each student in the group selects two pictures at random and tells which item he or she isn't buying and which one he or she prefers. For example, (pants/sweater) **Je n'achète pas le pantalon vert parce que je préfère le pull jaune.** Finally, another student in that group repeats what the first student has said. (**Nadine n'achète pas le pantalon vert parce qu'elle préfère le pull jaune.**)

NATIONAL STANDARDS
C1.1, C1.2

234

Pratique

10 Say that although the following people prefer the items on the left, they're buying the items on the right.

Modèle:

Valérie
Valérie préfère la robe bleue, mais elle achète la robe rouge.

1. Mamadou

2. tu

3. je

4. nous

5. Yasmine

6. Charles et Bruno

7. vous

8. Myriam et Delphine

Communication

Modèle:
Chantal: Quelle couleur préfères-tu?
Marc: Moi, je préfère le vert.
. . . .
Chantal: Trois élèves préfèrent le vert, quatre élèves préfèrent le noir....

11 To find out what your classmates' favorite colors are, take a sheet of paper and list as many colors as you can think of in French. Then poll as many of your classmates as you can. In your survey:

1. Ask each classmate what color he or she prefers.
2. As each person answers your question, make a check on your paper by the appropriate color.
3. After you have finished asking questions, count how many people like each color and be ready to share your findings with the rest of the class.

2 It's near the end of your trip to France. You decide to do some comparative clothes shopping before you spend the 100 euros you saved to buy clothes with. Your two favorite stores are a big department store and a small boutique. Compare the items that you see at each store. Then, on a separate sheet of paper, make a list of what you are going to buy at each one. In the column **Au grand magasin**, write each item along with its color and price. Do the same in the column **À la boutique**. Finally, total each column and make sure the combined amount doesn't exceed 100 euros.

Grand magasin

Boutique

13 With a partner, discuss what you decided to purchase in Activity 12. From the lists you made, read each item you are going to buy to your partner and get his or her opinion.

Modèle:

Student A: Je vais acheter le tee-shirt bleu au grand magasin.

Student B: J'adore le tee-shirt bleu, et il est bon marché.

Mise au point sur... les vêtements

Whether they are digging through racks of secondhand clothes at the **marché aux puces**

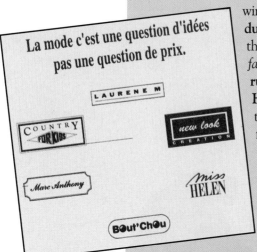
La mode c'est une question d'idées pas une question de prix.

LAURENE M

COUNTRY FOR KIDS

new look CREATION

Marc Anthony

miss HELEN

Bout'Chou

on the outskirts of Paris or window-shopping (**faire du lèche-vitrines**) at the **haute couture** (*high fashion*) shops along the **rue du Faubourg Saint-Honoré** in the heart of the city, French teenagers follow fashion trends (**la mode**) and strive to achieve their individual "look" (**le look**).

French teens find that window-shopping is a great way to catch up on the latest styles.

French teens, like their American counterparts, spend quite a bit of their free time and money on clothes.

The *rues piétonnes* usually have a wide selection of shops and restaurants without the interference of traffic and parked cars. (Montréal)

GALERIES Lafayette

In larger cities, they go to the **centre commercial** to shop. In smaller towns, they often browse along the **rues piétonnes** (*streets reserved only for pedestrians*), looking in department stores or boutiques for a unique outfit at an affordable price.

Different stores cater to people with a wide variety of tastes. You can find anything from a discarded designer dress to old army boots at the open-air markets. Small boutiques offer personalized service and specialized lines of clothing. Here customers may shop in a more relaxed setting as salespeople hand them clothing from racks and shelves to try on or purchase.

Les grands magasins, such as the Galeries Lafayette, Printemps, and the Samaritaine, have branches all over France and sell a large variety of goods. The oldest department store in the world, Au Bon Marché in Paris, opened in 1852

❀PRINTEMPS

OU TROUVER CE QUE VOUS CHERCHEZ ?

64, Boulevard Haussmann - 75009 PARIS
Ouvert de 9h35 à 19h - du Lundi au Samedi
Nocturne le Jeudi jusqu'à 22h
Métro : Havre-Caumartin - RER : Auber

and is famous for its extensive **épicerie** (*food market*) that sells everything from **escargots** (*snails*) to champagne. When you shop in a **grand magasin**, a salesclerk helps you select the item you want to buy, then brings it to a cashier. Usually stores also wrap the purchase free of charge when you say that it's for a gift. This comes in handy if you have been invited to a French home for a meal and want to bring something to your hosts, as is the custom. **Les grandes surfaces** (*large supermarket and discount stores*), also called **hypermarchés**, offer customers moderate prices along with a wide selection of merchandise.

56 HYPERMARCHÉS A VOTRE SERVICE — *Géant Casino*

In small towns, shops normally close for two hours at noon, but in large cities, department stores stay open all day. Stores are open until 9:00 P.M. or 10:00 P.M. at a **centre commercial**, but most small shops close between 6:00 P.M. and 7:00 P.M.

BAGATELLE

BOUTIQUE DE MODE FRANCAISE

Prêt à porter
pour hommes et femmes

Angle des rues Maréchal Foch et
Jacques Cartier
tél : 011(508) 41-20-83
Fax 011 (508) 41-33-10
97500 Saint-Pierre et Miquelon

(Fermé le lundi matin)

The entire world looks to French fashion houses, such as Cardin, Dior, Lacroix, Chanel, Saint Laurent and Nina Ricci, for the latest styles. Fashion shows twice a year in Paris attract buyers from all around the globe to see the **défilés** (*showings*). Most designers also create **prêt-à-porter** (*ready-to-wear*) clothing which is more affordable for the average customer. If you can't get a ticket to a fashion show, you can always go to Angelina. In the spring and fall, you can get a seat near the window of this tea salon on the **rue de Rivoli** and watch models and designers rushing off to exhibit the latest collections.

ANGELINA
R. Rumpelmayer

FONDÉE EN 1903

Restaurant, Salon de thé, Traiteur,
226, Rue de Rivoli — PARIS 1er — Tél. 01 42 60 82 00
Palais des Congrès — PARIS 17e — Tél. 01 40 68 22 50
Galeries LAFAYETTE — PARIS 8e — Tél. 01 42 82 30 32
Place de Mexico — PARIS 16e — Tél. 01 47 04 89 42

Quiz
Leçon B

Answers

14 Possible answers:

1. Teenagers often go to the **marché aux puces** in Paris to find secondhand clothing.
2. The boutiques of the leading fashion designers are located along the **rue du Faubourg Saint-Honoré**.
3. The French term for streets reserved only for pedestrians is **rues piétonnes**.
4. Some people prefer to shop in a small boutique because of the personalized service and specialized lines of clothing.
5. In a small boutique it's the salesperson who takes clothing from racks and shelves.
6. Two French department stores are the Galeries Lafayette and Printemps.
7. The concept of a department store originated in France.
8. It is customary to bring a gift.
9. Two famous French designers are Cardin and Dior.
10. **B.C.B.G.** are the initials used to describe a rather expensive, conservative style of clothing.

Teacher's Note

B.C.B.G. is the acronym for **bon chic bon genre.**

NATIONAL STANDARDS
C2.1, C2.2, C4.2

238

But French teenagers are interested in more than high fashion. For school, casual clothing is the usual attire; many students wear jeans to class. On weekends and for parties, students have a chance to show off their own personal style. Some prefer an upscale, conservative look called **B.C.B.G.** Others favor a more radical style. For French teenagers, tastes in **fringues** (slang for *clothes*) vary just as they do in the rest of the world.

French teens try to create their own distinctive look.

14 Answer the following questions.

1. Where do teenagers often go in Paris to find secondhand clothing?
2. Along what street in Paris are the boutiques of the leading fashion designers located?
3. What is the French term for streets reserved only for pedestrians?
4. Why do some people prefer to shop in a small boutique?
5. In a small boutique is it the customer or the salesperson who takes clothing from racks and shelves?
6. What are the names of two French department stores?
7. In what country did the concept of a department store originate?
8. If you are invited to eat at a French person's home, what is it customary to bring?
9. What are the names of two famous French designers?
10. What are the initials used to describe a rather expensive, conservative style of clothing?

What's the name of one of the more well-known French department stores? (Paris)

5 **Au Vieux Campeur** is a sporting goods chain with stores located throughout Paris. Each individual store specializes in certain areas. Match the people with the address of the store they should visit, based on what they want or need.

Les boutiques Au Vieux Campeur à Paris

50 rue des Écoles
(Face au collège de France et à la Sorbonne, angle rue St-Jacques)
- Toutes les **chaussures** de montagne et randonnée pédestre.
- Toutes les **chaussures** de marche.
- Chaussettes, guêtres, jambières et lacets. Chevillères, genouillères, semelles, cirages.

75 rue St Jacques
Tout le **Vélo Tout Terrain** y compris chaussures et vêtements.
Atelier de montage, réparation et entretien.

2 rue de Latran
(Angles rue Jean-de-Beauvais et rue du Sommerard).
Librairie, cartothèque, orientation :
- Livres, guides, topos, cartes se rapportant à nos activités.
- Cartes marines.
- Instruments d'orientation et de mesure (boussoles, altimètres, podomètres ...).
- Instruments optiques (jumelles, etc).
- GPS : Global Position System.
- Porte-cartes, cartes postales.

80+80 Bis bd St Germain
- **Les tentes.**
- Mâts, piquets et tissus de tentes.
Tout ce qui concerne le portage :
Sacs à dos, porte-bébés, sacs de voyage, sacs marins ...
Toutes les **sacoches** individuelles :
- Bandoulières, ceintures, porte-argent.
- Tous les sacs photo.
Tout ce qui concerne le **couchage** :
- Sacs, draps, matelas, moustiquaires, lits.
- Hamacs.

3 rue de Latran
Les vêtements, les vêtements, les vêtements.
- Les vêtements de **randonnée.**
- Les vêtements de **montagne.**
- Les vêtements de **grimpe.**
- Les vêtements **légers,** de **détente,** de **loisirs.**
- Les vêtements pour **pays chauds.**
- Les vêtements de **protection** (pluie et froid).
- Chapellerie.
- Gants, moufles.
- Les vêtements "outdoor".
- **Atelier de retouches.**

19 rue du Sommerard
Tout pour le **jogging, running**
(matériel, vêtements et chaussures)
en particulier montres, chronos, pulsomètres.

21 rue du Sommerard
Tout pour le **tennis et le squash**
(matériel, vêtements et chaussures).
Atelier de cordage et de réparation.

6 rue de Latran
(Vitrine aussi 11 rue du Sommerard)
- Tout pour le **ski** (piste, fond et rando).
- Tout pour le **surf** (snowboard).
- Matériel, vêtements et chaussures.

1. M. and Mme Thibault are going camping and need to buy a tent and two backpacks.
2. Issa needs to have her mountain bike repaired.
3. Mlle Bernier needs to have her tennis racket restrung.
4. Fabrice wants to buy some new ski poles.
5. M. Martin wants to buy some running shoes and a windbreaker.
6. The Dubois family is planning a trip to Normandy and wants to find some guidebooks and maps of the region.
7. Jean-Philippe is spending the month of January in Montreal and needs to buy some new winter clothing, including a coat and some gloves.
8. Martine is going hiking and needs to buy some thick socks.

a. 6, rue de Latran
b. 3, rue de Latran
c. 50, rue des Écoles
d. 19, rue du Sommerard
e. 80 + 80 bis, boulevard Saint-Germain
f. 2, rue de Latran
g. 21, rue du Sommerard
h. 75, rue Saint-Jacques

NATIONAL STANDARDS
C1.2, C2.1, C2.2, C3.2

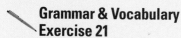

Workbook Activity 12

Grammar & Vocabulary Exercise 21

Audiocassette/CD Dialogue

Teacher's Notes

1. To express what size you wear, you can also say **Je porte du 42**. 2. Another word for "size" (**la pointure**) will be explained in the **Enquête culturelle**. 3. Communicative functions that are recycled in this lesson are "inquiring and comparing prices" and "agreeing and disagreeing."

Connections

En dollars, s'il vous plaît!

At the front of your room mount the same pictures of clothing items (and their prices) that students brought for the shopping excursion activity in **Leçon A**. Have each student choose five or six items to purchase in France, listing the item, its color and how much it costs in euros. Then have students convert each item's price and the total price to dollars. To be as realistic as possible, students should find the current rate of exchange for the euro in a newspaper in your school library or from a bank. Since students may have to do a similar activity when they come through customs as they return from France, find a customs declaration form and make copies for your students. Have them fill out the form, making sure the total in dollars is over $400 so that they can figure out the ten percent tax that they need to pay to the customs agent.

Leçon C

In this lesson you will be able to:

➤ **choose and purchase items**

➤ **ask someone to repeat**

➤ **ask for information**

➤ **give information**

A salesclerk in a small boutique offers to help Théo.

Le vendeur:	Oui, Monsieur?
Théo:	Je cherche un pantalon gris. Je fais du 42.
Le vendeur:	Voici les pantalons. Excusez-moi, quelle taille?
Théo:	42, s'il vous plaît.
Le vendeur:	Ah... voilà un 42 en gris.
Théo:	C'est combien, Monsieur?
Le vendeur:	33 euros 39.
Théo:	D'accord. Est-ce que vous vendez aussi des chaussures?
Le vendeur:	Non, nous ne vendons pas de chaussures ici.

Théo va dans une petite boutique pour chercher un pantalon.

If you haven't heard what someone has said, you may ask the person to repeat by saying **Pardon?** or **Excusez-moi?** You may also say **Comment?**, or in less formal situations, **Quoi?** or **Hein?**

Enquête culturelle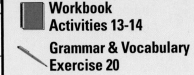

To ask a salesclerk the size of an item of clothing, you say **C'est quelle taille?** To ask the size of a pair of shoes, you say **C'est quelle pointure?** The accompanying chart compares sizes in the United States with those in France and Great Britain.

Size comparison
Table de comparaison de tailles

Women's dresses, knitwear and blouses.
Robes, chemisiers et tricots femmes.

F	36	38	40	42	44	46	48
GB	10	12	14	16	18	20	22
USA	8	10	12	14	16	18	20

Women's stockings. Bas et collants femmes.

F	1	2	3	4	5
USA	8½	9	9½	10	10½

Women's shoes. Chaussures femmes.

F	35½	36	36½	37	37½	38	39
GB	3	3½	4	4½	5	5½	6
USA	4	4½	5	5½	6	6½	7½

Men's shoes. Chaussures hommes.

F	39	40	41	42	43	44	45
GB	5½	6½	7	8	8½	9½	10½
USA	6	7	7½	8½	9	10	11

Men's suits. Costumes hommes.

F	36	38	40	42	44	46	48
GB	35	36	37	38	39	40	42
USA	35	36	37	38	39	40	42

Men's shirts. Chemises hommes.

F	36	37	38	39	40	41	42
USA	14	14½	15	15½	16	16½	17

Men's sweaters. Tricots hommes.

F	36	38	40	42	44	46
GB	46	48	51	54	55	59
USA	46	48	51	54	56	59

Many English words related to clothing originally came from French. For example, we use the word **chic** for "stylish," **boutique** for a "shop" and **béret** for the small round cap that was first worn in **les Pyrénées**. The French also gave us the word for "jeans." French tailors created denim pants, called **gênes**, which were named after the city of Genoa, Italy. They were first worn there by sailors during the Middle Ages. Later the word was modified to "jeans." The fabric that is used to make jeans was originally called **serge de Nîmes** after the town in France where it was loomed. This was eventually shortened to "denim."

Bérets, traditionally worn by older men, are becoming more and more fashionable among younger women. (Saint-Jean-de-Luz)

Workbook Activities 13-14

Grammar & Vocabulary Exercise 20

Video

Teacher's Note

Have your students make a gift size chart that they might carry when traveling to France. First, students list all the friends and family members for whom they might want to buy gifts. Then have students find out and record the shoe size, T-shirt size and blouse/shirt size for each person on their list.

Paired Practice

À la boutique

You may want to put your students in pairs and have them create a dialogue between a customer and a salesclerk in a clothing store. Make sure each pair talks about the size, color and price of at least one item. Students should bring appropriate props to use as they present their dialogues for the entire class.

NATIONAL STANDARDS
C1.1, C1.2, C2.1, C2.2, C3.2

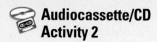
Answers

1 1. If you didn't hear what your teacher said the first time, you would say **Excusez-moi?**, **Pardon?** or **Comment?**

2. If you didn't hear what your friend said the first time, you would say **Quoi?** or **Hein?**

3. To refer to an article of clothing, use the word **taille**.

4. If a woman wears a size 38 shoe in France, she wears a size 6½ shoe in the United States.

5. If a man wears a size 15 shirt in the United States, he wears a size 38 shirt in France.

6. If a woman wears a size 38 dress in France, she wears a size 10 dress in the United States.

7. If a man wears a size 9 shoe in the United States, he wears a size 43 shoe in France.

8. Some French words related to clothing that are commonly used in English are **chic**, **boutique** and **béret**.

9. **De** and **Nîmes** were combined to give us the word "denim."

2 1. e
2. c
3. a
4. f
5. b
6. d

1 Answer the following questions.

1. What would you say if you didn't hear what your teacher said the first time?

2. What would you say if you didn't hear what your friend said the first time?

3. What is the French word for "size" if you are referring to an article of clothing?

4. If a woman wears a size 38 shoe in France, what size does she wear in the United States?

5. If a man wears a size 15 shirt in the United States, what size does he wear in France?

6. If a woman wears a size 38 dress in France, what size does she wear in the United States?

7. If a man wears a size 9 shoe in the United States, what size does he wear in France?

8. What are several French words related to clothing that are commonly used in English?

9. What two French words were combined to give us the word "denim"?

2 *Choisissez la bonne réponse.*

1. Qui cherche un pantalon?   a. gris
2. Qui parle à Théo?   b. 33,39 euros
3. De quelle couleur est le pantalon?   c. le vendeur
4. Théo, quelle taille fait-il?   d. des chaussures
5. Combien coûte le pantalon?   e. Théo
6. Qu'est-ce que Théo cherche aussi?   f. du 42

Mon blouson est de la taille 40.

3 | What would you say in French in the following situations?

1. You suggest to a friend that you go shopping together at the mall.
2. You tell a salesclerk that you're looking for some black jeans.
3. You didn't hear what a salesclerk said and ask him or her to repeat.
4. You ask a salesclerk the size of a shirt.
5. You ask a salesclerk how much a sweater costs.
6. You tell a salesclerk that you are going to buy the yellow ski jacket.
7. You ask a salesclerk if he or she also sells socks.

Excusez-moi? Ça coûte combien?

Le blouson coûte 182,94 euros.

4 | *C'est à toi!*

1. Est-ce que tu travailles dans une boutique, un magasin ou un grand magasin?
2. Est-ce que tu aimes acheter des vêtements?
3. Qu'est-ce que tu cherches quand tu vas dans une petite boutique?
4. Le pantalon coûte 33 euros 39. Est-ce qu'il est cher ou bon marché?
5. Qu'est-ce que tu préfères porter à l'école, un ensemble ou un jean et un sweat?
6. Est-ce que tu préfères porter un vieux jean ou un nouveau jean?

Je préfère porter un vieux jean.

Structure

Present tense of regular verbs ending in *-re*

The infinitives of many French verbs end in **-re**. Most of these verbs, such as **vendre** (*to sell*), are regular. To form the present tense of a regular **-re** verb, first find the stem of the verb by removing the **-re** ending of the infinitive.

Workbook
Activity 15

Grammar & Vocabulary
Exercises 22-25

Audiocassette/CD
Activity 4

Computer Software
Activity 7

Answers

3 Possible answers:
1. Allons ensemble au centre commercial!
2. Je cherche un jean noir.
3. Excusez-moi?
4. La chemise, c'est quelle taille?
5. Combien coûte le pull?
6. Je vais acheter l'anorak jaune.
7. Est-ce que vous vendez aussi des chaussettes?

4 Answers will vary.

NATIONAL STANDARDS
C1.1, C1.2, C4.1

Answers

5 1. Alors, ils vendent des jeux vidéo.
2. Alors, elle vend des livres.
3. Alors, il vend des baskets.
4. Alors, elles vendent des cartes.
5. Alors, ils vendent des vélos.
6. Alors, elle vend des ordinateurs.

Teacher's Notes

1. Point out to students that only the endings **-ons** and **-ez** are pronounced. There are only four different oral forms of **vendre**. The **d** is silent in the singular forms and pronounced [d] in the plural forms. The **d** is pronounced [t] in the inverted forms of **il/elle/on**: **Où vend-on des chemises?** 2. You might have students repeat after you the sentences in the chart. You might also do some exercises from affirmative to negative or from singular to plural.

Cooperative Group Practice

Qu'est-ce qu'on vend?

So that students can practice using the verb **vendre**, put them in small groups. Use the same pictures of clothing items that students brought for the shopping excursion activity in **Leçon A**, mix them up and place them face down. Each student in the group selects two pictures at random and tells what he or she is selling. For example, (socks/jeans) **Je vends des chaussettes et des jeans.** Finally, another student in that group repeats what the first student has said. (**Patrick vend des chaussettes et des jeans.**)

NATIONAL STANDARDS
C1.1, C1.2, C4.1

244

Joanne vend des fringues. (Brive-la-Gaillarde)

Modèle:

Sophie travaille à Bananas.
Alors, elle vend des maillots de bain.

Now add the endings (**-s, -s, —, -ons, -ez, -ent**) to the stem of the verb depending on the corresponding subject pronouns. Note that no ending is added to the stem in the **il/elle/on** form.

vendre			
je	**vends**	Je **vends** des vêtements.	*I sell clothes.*
tu	**vends**	Qu'est-ce que tu **vends**?	*What are you selling?*
il/elle/on	**vend**	On **vend** des baskets ici?	*Do they sell hightops here?*
nous	**vendons**	Oui, nous **vendons** des chaussures.	*Yes, we sell shoes.*
vous	**vendez**	Vous ne **vendez** pas de pulls?	*Don't you sell sweaters?*
ils/elles	**vendent**	Ils **vendent** des jeans.	*They sell jeans.*

Pratique

5 Tell what the following people sell, based on where they work.

1. Christine et Jean-Michel travaillent à Joué Club.
2. Mme Picard travaille à Vendredi.
3. Thierry travaille à Marathon.
4. Béatrice et sa sœur travaillent à Géo.
5. Abdoul et Khadim travaillent à Cycles Laurent.
6. Mlle Lambert travaille à Ordimega.

6 The French Club at your school is sponsoring a **marché aux puces** to raise money for a trip to France. Tell what the club members are selling.

Audiocassette/CD
Activity 6

Modèle:

Jean-Paul
Jean-Paul vend des cahiers.

Answers

6 1. Margarette vend des stylos.
2. Nous vendons des trousses.
3. Je vends des affiches.
4. Pierre et Amine vendent des cassettes.
5. Tu vends des tee-shirts.
6. Guillaume vend des sandwichs.
7. Vous vendez des calendriers.
8. Delphine et Françoise vendent des poissons rouges.

1. Margarette

5. tu

2. nous

6. Guillaume

3. je

7. vous

4. Pierre et Amine

8. Delphine et Françoise

Communication

7 With a partner, play the roles of an American student who is shopping at a ski resort in the French Alps and the salesclerk at the resort's boutique. The customer's brother wants a nice French ski jacket and has given the customer enough money to buy it. During the course of the conversation, the customer and the salesclerk should talk about what size ski jacket the customer's brother wears, what color he prefers and the prices of various jackets. Finally, the customer decides on a jacket and purchases it.

NATIONAL STANDARDS
C1.1, C1.2

245

Workbook Activity 16

Transparency 36

Listening Activity 3A

Quiz
Leçon C

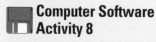
Computer Software Activity 8

Teacher's Note

At the end of Activity 8 you may want to take your own survey to find out about students' shopping habits and tastes in clothes.

Modèle:

Jacques: Tu aimes les shorts très grands?

Christiane: Oui, j'aime les shorts très grands. (Writes her name beside number 1.)

Je porte très souvent un tee-shirt noir.

8 *Trouvez une personne qui....* Interview your classmates to find out about their shopping habits and tastes in clothes. On a separate sheet of paper, number from 1 to 14. Circulate around the classroom asking your classmates one at a time the questions that follow. When someone answers a question affirmatively, have that person write his or her name next to the number of the appropriate question. Continue asking questions, trying to find a different person who answers each question affirmatively.

Est-ce que tu...

1. aimes les shorts très grands?
2. portes souvent un tee-shirt noir?
3. préfères porter un sweat?
4. vas faire du shopping aujourd'hui?
5. aimes le jaune?
6. as un pull rouge?
7. as un pantalon beige?
8. aimes les manteaux longs?
9. as un chapeau?
10. as un anorak bleu?
11. vas souvent au centre commercial?
12. aimes faire les magasins?
13. as des baskets?
14. aimes acheter les vêtements en solde?

Est-ce qu'Estelle et Lydie ont un anorak bleu?

 Sur la bonne piste

One of the major keys to understanding a reading is being able to evaluate it. Asking yourself whether you agree or disagree with the information in the reading will give you a reason to look at it in more depth. For instance, if a store advertisement claims that a shirt is stylish and guarantees popularity, you, the reader, need to evaluate this statement. Do you like the style of the shirt? Some readers may not. Can a shirt really make you popular? Most readers would doubt this. Evaluating information as you read it is called critical reading. Critical reading helps you separate fact from opinion. When you no longer simply accept what you read and begin to form your own opinions about it, you are using more advanced reading and thinking skills (especially if what you are reading is written in another language!).

The reading that follows is part of an article from a back-to-school issue of a French magazine. Read critically the three clothing descriptions.

Dans la mode c'est déjà la rentrée!

Bon chic, bon genre au masculin, c'est LA BLANCHE PORTE. Aucun problème avec le proviseur, ton succès est assuré !

Veste en maille côtelée sur une chemise en coton rayé et jean (27,14 €, 24,24 € et 22,71 €). Chaussures La Blanche Porte.

À prévoir dans la penderie, la tenue BASIC... souhaitable pour un examen ou un premier entretien professionnel !

Veste en lainage à col tailleur et poches plaquées (76,07 €, Tissaïa) sur un petit pull chaussette à encolure polo en laine mélangée. Pantalon de forme cigarette en coton strech (82,32 € chacun, Bensimon). Écharpe et chaussettes Soki. Bottines Un Matin d'Été.

Chassez le naturel... En disciple de l'écologie, PRISUNIC le rattrape au galop ! Fausse fourrure, laine rustique et motifs ethniques pour le confort...

Parka molletonné avec capuche bordée de fausse fourrure sur un pull irlandais en laine rustique et une minijupe portefeuille en lainage (64,79 €, 49,55 € et 34,91 €). Collant Pingouin. Bottes Un Matin d'Été.

Answers

9 Possible answers:
1. The French word for "short boot" is **bottine**.
2. The most expensive outfit is the one from Basic. The least expensive outfit is the one from La Blanche Porte.
3. The fur on the parka from Prisunic is fake. According to the article, this outfit is ecologically correct.
4. This claim is based on the assumption that students who wear upscale, conservative clothing never get in trouble.
5. Answers will vary.
6. Answers will vary.

Teacher's Notes

1. Have students work in pairs as they answer the questions. The first three questions have specific answers. However, there is still some room for subjectivity. The last three questions are interpretation questions, and students should be encouraged to come up with a variety of answers. To holistically grade Activity 9, refer to the suggestions on page 162.
2. Readers often compare similar texts, especially advertisements. When readers compare the similarities and differences of various texts, they clarify details specific to each one, which defines its context and content. To practice reading efficiency, you may want to have students compare the two women's outfits in the magazine article, noting similarities and differences.

9 Answer the following questions.
1. You know that the French word for "boot" is **botte**. What is the French word for "short boot"?
2. Which of the three outfits is the most expensive? Which is the least expensive?
3. Is the fur on the parka from Prisunic real or fake? Is this outfit ecologically correct?
4. According to the article, wearing the outfit from La Blanche Porte guarantees that you won't have any problems with your school principal. What assumption is this claim based on?
5. Which outfits, if any, are appropriate to wear...
   a. to school?
   b. to a job interview?
   c. to a party?
   d. at home while watching television?
6. Does one of these outfits reflect your own personal style? Why or why not?

Nathalie et Raoul

C'est à moi!

Now that you have completed this unit, take a look at what you should be able to do in French. Can you do all of these tasks?

➤ I can tell what I like and what I dislike.

➤ I can agree with someone.

➤ I can say what I need.

➤ I can say what someone is going to do.

➤ I can invite someone to do something.

➤ I can inquire about and compare prices.

➤ I can ask for and give information about various topics, including colors and sizes of clothing.

➤ I can ask someone to repeat.

➤ I can choose and purchase clothing.

Brigitte et Véro vont manger chinois.

Here is a brief checkup to see how much you understand about French culture. Decide if each statement is **vrai** or **faux**.

1. Small specialized stores still flourish in France even though there are giant shopping malls.
2. Generally the French prefer having stylish clothing of good quality rather than simply having a lot of different outfits.
3. At **le marché aux puces** customers are expected to bargain with vendors.
4. Montreal is the largest French-speaking city in the world.
5. Living and shopping in Montreal can be done entirely underground if you choose to remain in the subterranean part of the city.
6. If you see the sign **Soldes** on items displayed on the sidewalk in front of a French store, it means that someone else has already purchased them.

Does the sign in the window mean this store has been sold? (Paris)

🎧 **Listening Activity 3B**

Answers

1. vrai
2. vrai
3. vrai
4. faux
5. vrai
6. faux
7. vrai
8. faux
9. faux
10. vrai

Teacher's Notes

1. If you have access to a French catalogue that contains clothing items, reproduce certain pages and pass them out to your students. Also distribute a copy of the catalogue's order form. Then have students select specific clothing items from the catalogue and complete the order form by filling in the necessary information. 2. Have students write their own magazine articles on school clothing. Have them create three outfits by cutting out pictures of clothing from magazines or catalogues. Students should describe the outfits in French, telling what each article of clothing is, who makes it, what color it is and how much it costs. 3. Here is the English version of the cartoon on page 248: (At Raoul's house) To begin with, I take a bath. Next, I brush my teeth and my hair. How handsome I am! What am I going to wear? A shirt, but what color? Maybe blue. Nathalie loves blue. An old pair of jeans . . . brown shoes . . . and a little cologne. Yes, it's true, I'm very stylish! I'm irresistible! Where are you going, Raoul? To a dance club, Mom. With whom? Uhm . . . with some friends, Mom. Nathalie's going, too? Yes, Mom. Here's 20 euros. Have a good time, my angel. Thanks, Mom. You really understand your children!

NATIONAL STANDARDS
C1.1, C2.1, C2.2, C4.2

7. At Parisian department stores, such as the Galeries Lafayette and Printemps, you can find men's and women's fashions.
8. Department stores in large French cities close for two hours at noon.
9. Shoe sizes are the same in both France and the United States.
10. The French gave us the word for "jeans."

Communication orale

Imagine that you and your partner live in Montreal and are planning to go to the **Place Ville-Marie** on a big shopping spree tomorrow. Have a conversation in which each of you talks about several items of clothing you have that are old. Also give some other information about these items, for example, their color. Then say that you need new ones. Suggest that you go shopping together tomorrow. Next name several stores that you are going to shop at and tell what they sell. Finally, set a time to meet tomorrow.

Communication écrite

No one is at home when you and your partner decide to go to the **Place Ville-Marie** on your shopping spree tomorrow. Write a note in French to the rest of your family in which you tell them what you are going to do and why. Begin by saying at what time and where you and your friend are going shopping. Then mention what clothes you have that are old and say that you need new ones. Next tell the cost of each item you are going to buy. Finally, name several stores where you are going to shop and say what they sell.

Communication active

To say what you like, use:

J'aime bien faire les magasins.	*I really like to go shopping.*
J'adore la chemise bleue.	*I love the blue shirt.*

Mme Sevran adore la chemise blanche. (Angers)

To say what you dislike, use:
Beurk!   *Yuk!*

To agree with someone, use:
C'est vrai.   *This is/It's/That's true.*

To say you need something, use:
J'ai besoin d'un pull.   *I need a sweater.*
J'ai besoin d'une chemise.   *I need a shirt.*

To express intentions, use:
Je vais aller au centre   *I'm going to go to the mall.*
commercial.

To invite someone to do something, use:
Allons ensemble au   *Let's go to the department store*
grand magasin!   *together!*

To inquire about prices, use:
C'est combien?   *How much is it?*
C'est en solde?   *Is it on sale?*

Aux Galeries Lafayette les
chapeaux sont en solde.

To compare prices, use:
Il/Elle est assez cher/chère.   *It's rather expensive.*
Il/Elle est bon marché.   *It's cheap.*

To ask for information, use:
Quelle taille?   *What size?*
Est-ce que **vous vendez** aussi   *Do you also sell shoes?*
des chaussures?

To give information, use:
Je fais du 42.   *I wear size 42.*

To ask someone to repeat, use:
Excusez-moi?   *Excuse me?*

To choose and purchase an item, use:
Je cherche un pantalon gris.   *I'm looking for gray pants.*

Communication électronique

Communication électronique

1. This store features a "Webcamer" in the store, an online personal shopper that provides customers with an interactive shopping experience.
2. The three questions are "Quoi," "Quand" and "Qui."
3. Printemps is open six days a week.
4. It is open on Thursday until 10:00 P.M.
5. Answers will vary.

À moi de jouer!

Possible conversation:

— J'ai besoin d'une nouvelle chemise. Comment est-ce que tu trouves la chemise blanche?

— Elle est très belle. Tu fais quelle taille?

— Du 38. Pardon, Monsieur, la chemise blanche, c'est combien?

— C'est en solde, Mademoiselle. Elle est bon marché... 27,44 euros.

— D'accord.

— Tiens, j'adore la chemise bleue! Et toi?

— C'est pas mal.

— Monsieur, j'ai besoin d'une 40.

— Voilà, Mademoiselle. C'est en solde. Ça fait 18,29 euros.

— Bon d'accord. Merci, Monsieur.

Teacher's Note

After students have finished writing their dialogues, you may want to ask them to role-play their dialogues in front of the class.

NATIONAL STANDARDS
C1.1, C1.3, C2.2, C3.2,
C4.2, C5.1, C5.2

252

Communication électronique

Do you think that the French like to go shopping for the same things that you do? Do you think French stores and boutiques are similar to ours and have the same kinds of products? Are their prices higher or lower? To find out answers to these questions, go to the Internet site for Printemps, a popular Parisian department store:

http://www.printemps.fr/

After exploring this site, answer the following questions.

1. What unique feature does this store offer daily from 10 A.M. until 7 P.M.?
2. Now click on this feature and then on "Le shopping interactif" icon. What three questions are asked in French?
3. Return to the home page and click on "Le site du Grand Magasin" and then "Accès, plans." How many days of the week is this store open?
4. How many nights is it open?
5. Return to the home page and click on the "Boutiques" link. Then click on "La Boutique en Ligne" and choose either "Mode Femme" or "Mode Homme." Describe one item you would like to buy, including the item's color and price.

À moi de jouer!

To show that you are able to go shopping for clothes in a French-speaking country, work in groups of three to complete the dialogue on the right with appropriate expressions from this unit. Two students are talking to each other and to the salesclerk, saying what they need, telling what they like, giving sizes, asking about prices and finally purchasing something. (You may want to refer to the *Communication active* on pages 250-51 and the vocabulary list on page 253.)

Vocabulaire

	acheter to buy		**là-bas** over there	
	adorer to love		**long, longue** long	
un	**anorak** ski jacket			
	assez rather, quite	un	**magasin** store	
	aux to (the), at (the), in (the)		un grand magasin department store	
		un	**maillot de bain** swimsuit	
des	**bas (m.)** (panty) hose	un	**manteau** coat	
des	**baskets (f.)** hightops		**marron** brown	
	beige beige		**moche** ugly	
	Beurk! Yuk!			
	blanc, blanche white		**nouveau, nouvel, nouvelle** new	
un	**blouson** jacket (outdoor)			
	bon marché cheap		**orange** orange	
une	**botte** boot			
une	**boum** party	un	**pantalon** (pair of) pants	
une	**boutique** shop, boutique		**petit(e)** short, little, small	
			peut-être maybe	
un	**centre commercial** shopping center, mall		**porter** to wear	
			pour (in order) to	
un	**chapeau** hat	un	**pull** sweater	
une	**chaussette** sock			
une	**chaussure** shoe		**quelque chose** something	
une	**chemise** shirt			
	cher, chère expensive	une	**robe** dress	
	chercher to look for		**rose** pink	
une	**chose** thing			
	quelque chose something	un	**short** (pair of) shorts	
un	**costume** man's suit	un	**soir** evening	
une	**couleur** color	des	**soldes (f.)** sale(s)	
	court(e) short	un	**sweat** sweatshirt	
un	**dollar** dollar	une	**taille** size	
		un	**tailleur** woman's suit	
	en solde on sale	un	**tee-shirt** T-shirt	
un	**ensemble** outfit	des	**tennis (m.)** tennis shoes	
	excusez-moi excuse me		**trouver** to find	
	faire du (+ *number*) to wear size (+ number)	un	**vendeur, une vendeuse** salesperson	
			vendre to sell	
	faire les magasins to go shopping	une	**veste** (sport) jacket	
		des	**vêtements (m.)** clothes	
	grand(e) tall, big, large		**vieux, vieil, vieille** old	
			violet, violette purple	
	il y a there is, there are		**voici** here is/are	
			vrai(e) true	
	jaune yellow			
un	**jean** (pair of) jeans			
	joli(e) pretty			
une	**jupe** skirt			

Unité 8

On fait les courses.

In this unit you will be able to:

➤ ask for information

➤ give information

➤ express likes and dislikes

➤ agree and disagree

➤ identify objects

➤ ask for permission

➤ ask for a price

➤ state prices

➤ inquire about and compare prices

➤ make a complaint

➤ insist

➤ negotiate

➤ choose and purchase items

NATIONAL STANDARDS
C2.2

Workbook
Activity 1

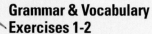
Grammar & Vocabulary
Exercises 1-2

Audiocassette/CD
Seafood, *Les légumes*

Transparencies 37-38

NATIONAL STANDARDS
C1.2, C4.1

256

Leçon A

In this lesson you will be able to:

➤ **ask for information**

➤ **give information**

➤ **agree and disagree**

➤ **identify objects**

➤ **ask for permission**

les légumes (m.)

les haricots verts (m.)

les carottes (f.)

les petits pois (m.)

les tomates (f.)

les pommes de terre (f.)

les oignons (m.)

les champignons (m.)

OK, je vais acheter ces tomates et cet oignon pour la soupe.

Madame Laurier and her daughter Madeleine are at the supermarket in Marseille.

Mme Laurier: **Qu'est-ce que tu veux manger ce soir?**

Madeleine: **Euh... tu peux faire une bouillabaisse?**

Mme Laurier: **OK, je vais acheter ces tomates et cet oignon pour la soupe. Maintenant on va chercher les crabes et les poissons.**

Madeleine: **Nous pouvons acheter des oranges aussi?**

Mme Laurier: **Oui, ton père veut toujours un fruit après le repas.**

Enquête culturelle

Marseille is France's largest seaport and oldest city. Tourists often visit **le Vieux Port**, a small port near the center of the city filled with recreational and fishing boats, and **la Canebière**, the main commercial street lined with many shops. Ships from all over the world dock at the modern, international port nearby. One of the well-known churches of the city, **Notre-Dame-de-la-Garde**, has a golden statue of the Virgin Mary on its steeple. This statue still guides sailors safely to the port, since it can be seen far out into the Mediterranean Sea. The French national anthem, the "Marseillaise," received its name from the city of Marseille.

Early in the morning people head to *le Vieux Port* to buy fresh fish. (Marseille)

Workbook Activities 2-4

Audiocassette/CD Dialogue

Teacher's Notes

1. You may want to point out to students that the word **euh** replaces "uhm" to fill pauses in conversations. 2. Another word for "soup" is **le potage**. 3. Students have already learned the word **une orange** in **Unité 3**. 4. Marseille is France's third largest city and was founded by the Greeks in the seventh century B.C. 5. **Le Vieux Port** was the main port of Marseille until the nineteenth century. 6. Two kilometers out into the sea is the island of If with its famous castle, the setting for the Alexandre Dumas novel *The Count of Monte-Cristo*.

Paired Practice

Qu'est-ce que c'est?

Have your students cut out pictures of the vegetables introduced in this lesson. Put students in pairs and have them take turns asking and answering the question **Qu'est-ce que c'est?** as they show one another each item they have cut out. (Save these pictures for future use.)

TPR

Masculine or Feminine?

To identify the gender of the vegetables introduced in this lesson, say these nouns with their plural definite articles. Have students raise their left hand if they hear a masculine noun; have them raise their right hand if they hear a feminine noun. To vary this TPR activity, you might have students raise a green card if the noun is masculine or a red card if the noun is feminine.

NATIONAL STANDARDS
C1.1, C1.2, C2.1, C2.2, C4.2

Bouillabaisse is a highly seasoned, healthy fish stew.

Regional specialties from all over the country may be found in French food stores as well as in restaurants. **Bouillabaisse**, a fish soup, is a specialty of Marseille. **Pâté de foie gras**, a pork and goose liver pâté, comes from the

59,46 € **Foie gras de canard**
51% morceaux
Le kg

Thoumieux
SPECIALITE DE CASSOULET
et CONFIT DE CANARD
Tous les jours jusqu'à minuit Tél. 01.47.05.49.75
79, rue Saint-Dominique (7ᵉ)

city of Strasbourg. **Cassoulet**, from the southwestern part of France, is a stew made from duck, goose or sausage and white beans. **Quiche lorraine**, a quiche containing bacon, onions and cheese, was created in the province of Lorraine. **Bœuf bourguignon**, a meat stew cooked in red wine, originated in the Burgundy region.

There are different types of *quiche* depending on the region and ingredients used. (Angers)

Pains spéciaux au blé complet

Ingrédients: Farine complète de blé (67%), farine de blé, matière grasse végétale, sucre, levure et sel.

Valeur nutritive par 100 g:
Protéines	12 g
Matières grasses	7 g
Hydrates de carbone	75 g
dont fibres	7 g
1640 kJ (390 kcal)	

A conserver dans un endroit sec.

A consommer de préférence avant fin: voir la face principale du paquet.

e **225 g**

Healthy ingredients are often emphasized on food packages in France, just as they are in the United States. Labels in grocery stores highlight expressions such as **pas d'additifs** (*no additives*), **1% de matière grasse** (*1% fat content*) and **fort en vitamines** (*high in vitamins*).

1 | *Répondez en français.*

1. Qu'est-ce que Mme Laurier va faire ce soir?
2. La bouillabaisse, c'est un dessert?
3. Quels légumes est-ce qu'il y a dans une bouillabaisse?
4. Qu'est-ce qu'il y a aussi dans une bouillabaisse?
5. Quel fruit est-ce que Mme Laurier et Madeleine vont acheter?
6. Qu'est-ce que les Français mangent souvent après le repas?

2 | *Choisissez la bonne réponse.*

1. Les... sont des légumes longs.
2. Les... sont des fruits.
3. Les... sont des légumes orange.
4. L'... est un légume blanc.
5. Les... sont des légumes blancs.
6. Les... sont des légumes rouges.
7. Les frites sont des....
8. On trouve les... dans la Méditerranée.

   a. tomates
   b. oignon
   c. haricots verts
   d. crabes
   e. carottes
   f. oranges
   g. champignons
   h. pommes de terre

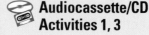

Il y a des poissons dans une bouillabaisse. (Lyon)

7,93 €
COLINOT

LE KG
0,90 €

TOMATES
Origine : France
Catégorie1. Calibre 57 et +.

D'où viennent les crabes? (Bayonne)

3 | Say how much you like each of the following foods, using **J'aime beaucoup**, **J'aime un peu** or **Je n'aime pas.**

1. les petits pois
2. les crevettes
3. les légumes
4. les champignons
5. les poissons
6. les oignons
7. les fruits

Qui n'aime pas les fruits frais? (Pornichet)

Workbook
Activity 5

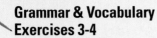

**Grammar & Vocabulary
Exercises 3-4**

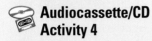

**Audiocassette/CD
Activity 4**

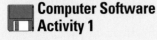

**Computer Software
Activity 1**

Answers

4 Answers will vary.

Teacher's Notes

1. The difference between the sound [ø] in **veux** and **veut** and the sound [œ] in **veulent** will be explained in the **Prononciation** section of this **unité**. 2. You may want to point out to students that **vouloir** may be followed by a noun or by an infinitive. 3. Point out that the **t** in **veut** and **veulent** is pronounced only in the inverted form.

Si tu veux, tu peux être mon parrain.

260

---

4 | *C'est à toi!*

1. Est-ce que tu manges beaucoup de légumes?
2. Quels légumes aimes-tu?
3. Est-ce que tu préfères le poisson ou le steak?
4. Quand est-ce que tu aimes manger de la soupe, en été ou en hiver?
5. Dans ta famille, qui aime les oranges?
6. Qu'est-ce que tu vas manger ce soir?

Est-ce que tes parents aiment les oranges? (Lyon)

Structure

Present tense of the irregular verb *vouloir*

The verb **vouloir** (*to want*) is irregular.

vouloir			
je	veux	Je **veux** un sandwich.	*I want a sandwich.*
tu	veux	Qu'est-ce que tu **veux**?	*What do you want?*
il/elle/on	veut	Ton père **veut** un fruit.	*Your father wants (a piece of) fruit.*
nous	voulons	Nous ne **voulons** pas ces tomates.	*We don't want these tomatoes.*
vous	voulez	Où **voulez**-vous manger?	*Where do you want to eat?*
ils/elles	veulent	Ils **veulent** faire une quiche.	*They want to make a quiche.*

You already know one form of the verb **vouloir** that you use when you ask for something: **Je voudrais....** (*I would like . . . .*) The French often use this form, which is more polite than **je veux**.

Qu'est-ce que vous voulez?

Pratique

5 You and your friends are trying to decide where to have lunch. Tell who wants to eat at a café and who wants to eat at a fast-food restaurant.

1. Christine

2. nous

3. Jamila et Latifa

4. tu

5. David

6. je

7. Laurent et Philippe

8. vous

Modèles:

Clément
Clément veut manger au fast-food.

Luc et Marie-Alix
Luc et Marie-Alix veulent manger au café.

6 Tell what the following people want, depending on whether they are hungry or thirsty.

1. Édouard a soif. (une eau minérale/une crêpe)
2. J'ai soif. (une orange/un café)
3. Mme Pinetti et son fils ont faim. (des jus d'orange/des légumes)
4. Tu as faim. (des crevettes/un jus de pomme)
5. Nous avons soif. (des pommes de terre/des limonades)
6. Vous avez faim. (des fruits/des boissons)

Modèles:

Patricia a soif. (un dessert/un coca)
Elle veut un coca.

M. et Mme Lavigne ont faim.
(des frites/un jus de raisin)
Ils veulent des frites.

Workbook
Activity 6

Grammar & Vocabulary
Exercises 5-6

Computer Software
Activity 2

Answers

7 1. Monsieur Prat peut acheter l'ordinateur.
2. Vous pouvez acheter le vélo.
3. Thibault et son frère peuvent acheter le CD.
4. Je peux acheter le jean.
5. Madame Wolff peut acheter le chapeau.
6. Les sœurs de Nicolas peuvent acheter l'oiseau.
7. Nous pouvons acheter le cheval.
8. Tu peux acheter le stylo.

Oui, je peux aller au cinéma.

Modèle:

Abdou (quinze euros)
Abdou peut acheter le sac à dos.

Present tense of the irregular verb *pouvoir*

The verb **pouvoir** (*to be able to*) is irregular. In the following examples note the different meanings of **pouvoir** in English.

	pouvoir		
je	**peux**	Je **peux** sortir?	*May I go out?*
tu	**peux**	Tu **peux** aller au cinéma?	*Can you go to the movies?*
il/elle/on	**peut**	Il ne **peut** pas inviter ses amis.	*He can't invite his friends.*
nous	**pouvons**	Nous **pouvons** acheter des oranges?	*Can we buy some oranges?*
vous	**pouvez**	**Pouvez**-vous venir demain?	*Are you able to come tomorrow?*
ils/elles	**peuvent**	Ils **peuvent** travailler ensemble.	*They can work together.*

Pratique

7 Tell which is the most expensive item the following people can buy, based on how much money they have.

1. M. Prat (sept cent soixante-dix euros)
2. vous (cent sept euros)
3. Thibault et son frère (vingt et un euros)
4. je (soixante-dix euros)
5. Mme Wolff (trente euros)
6. les sœurs de Nicolas (trente-huit euros)
7. nous (six cent dix euros)
8. tu (cinq euros)

8 The grocery store is closing in five minutes. You and your friends still have to buy some of the things you need to prepare a dinner of fish soup, bread, fruit, cheese and mineral water. Decide who in column A can look for each item in column B.

A	B
Gilbert	les carottes
Étienne et Diane	les tomates
je	les oignons
Thierry et toi, vous	les crabes
tu	les poissons
Florence	les oranges
Louis et moi, nous	le fromage
Stéphanie et Nadia	l'eau minérale

Modèle:

Gilbert peut chercher les oranges.

Demonstrative adjectives

Demonstrative adjectives are used to point out specific people or things. **Ce**, **cet** and **cette** mean "this" or "that"; **ces** means "these" or "those." These adjectives agree with the nouns that follow them.

	Singular		Plural
Masculine before a Consonant Sound	Masculine before a Vowel Sound	Feminine	
ce chien	cet anorak	cette robe	ces crabes

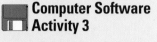

ce sac matelot en cadeau !

20.40 ● Arte 22.25 105 mn

Cet obscur objet du désir

cette semaine   N° 2510 0,30 €

Pratique

9 Help your great-grandmother with her grocery shopping by telling her the prices of the food she chooses. Complete each of your sentences with the appropriate demonstrative adjective (**ce**, **cet**, **cette** or **ces**).

1. ... jambon coûte 6,10 €.
2. ... tomate coûte 0,30 €.
3. ... crabe coûte 5,34 €.
4. ... haricots verts coûtent 1,07 €.
5. ... oignon coûte 0,46 €.
6. ... poisson coûte 3,51 €.
7. ... pommes de terre coûtent 1,68 €.
8. ... orange coûte 0,46 €.
9. ... champignons coûtent 1,22 €.

Find out whether or not you and your partner like the same clothes. Take

Ces champignons coûtent un euro vingt-deux.

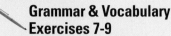

Workbook Activity 7

Grammar & Vocabulary Exercises 7-9

Audiocassette/CD Activities 8-9

Computer Software Activity 3

Answers

8 Answers will vary.

9 1. Ce
2. Cette
3. Ce
4. Ces
5. Cet
6. Ce
7. Ces
8. Cette
9. Ces

Teacher's Note

Point out to students that there is liaison after **cet**: **cet oignon**. There is also liaison after **ces** when the next word begins with a vowel sound: **ces affiches**.

Cooperative Group Practice

Forming Questions

Put your students in small groups and have each group make a set of note cards. On each card students write a different infinitive the class has already learned. (Students may have already made and used these cards for previous additional activities.) As each student in the group chooses one of the cards at random, he or she makes a question using a form of **pouvoir** plus the indicated infinitive. The group's secretary records the question on the note card. After all cards have been used, groups exchange note cards and students in each group take turns answering the set of questions they have received.

NATIONAL STANDARDS
C1.1, C1.2, C4.1

Answers

10 1. Tu aimes cette veste?
   Tu aimes ce pull?
2. Tu aimes ce maillot de bain?
   Tu aimes ces bottes?
3. Tu aimes ces baskets?
   Tu aimes cette jupe?
4. Tu aimes ce jean?
   Tu aimes ce chapeau?
5. Tu aimes ces chaussures?
   Tu aimes cette robe?
6. Tu aimes cette chemise?
   Tu aimes cet anorak?
Students' responses to these questions will vary.

NATIONAL STANDARDS
C1.1, C1.2, C2.2

---

10 Find out whether or not you and your partner like the same clothes. Take turns asking and answering questions about the pictured items.

Modèle:

Student A: Tu aimes ce short?
Student B: Oui, j'aime ce short. Tu aimes ces chaussettes?
Student A: Non, je n'aime pas ces chaussettes.

1.   4.

2.   5.

3.   6.

Communication

11 You are spending the summer with the Garrigues family in the south of France. Mme Garrigues is going to make a fish soup for dinner and asked you to pick up ingredients at the supermarket. Since she was in a hurry this morning, she left you only the recipe (on the left). You've already made a list of what ingredients you have (on the right). Comparing the recipe with what's on hand, write your grocery list.

Modèle:

Nous avons besoin de 15 crevettes....

La Soupe	Nous avons...
20 crevettes	5 crevettes
2 crabes	1 poisson blanc
3 poissons blancs	1 oignon
2 oignons	2 tomates
2 tomates	2 pommes de terre
2 carottes	
3 pommes de terre	

2 Interview two of your classmates to find out if they like certain foods. Make a grid like the partial one that follows. Write down the names of ten foods. Ask your classmates if they like each of these foods. As they answer each question, write their names in the appropriate column.

Est-ce que vous aimez...		
	oui	non
les crevettes?	*Francis*	*Yasmine*
le fromage?	*Yasmine, Francis*	

3 To help you and your partner decide what you are going to do tonight, take turns asking and answering questions. Student A asks if Student B would like to do certain things. Student B either accepts, saying **Oui, je veux bien,** or refuses, saying **Non, je ne peux pas,** depending on the response indicated.

1. aller au centre commercial (J'ai besoin d'un nouveau jean.)
2. venir chez moi (Je travaille à 18 heures.)
3. aller au fast-food (J'ai faim.)
4. étudier avec moi (J'ai une interro demain.)
5. aller en boîte (C'est trop cher.)
6. faire une bouillabaisse (Je vais au café avec la famille.)
7. nager (Je n'ai pas de maillot de bain.)

Modèles:

Danièle: Est-ce que vous aimez les crevettes?
Francis: Moi, j'aime les crevettes.
Yasmine: Et moi, je n'aime pas les crevettes.

Danièle: Est-ce que vous aimez le fromage?
Yasmine: Moi, j'aime le fromage.
Francis: Et moi aussi, j'aime le fromage.

Modèles:

aller au cinéma (On passe un bon film au Gaumont.)
Student A: Tu veux aller au cinéma?
Student B: Oui, je veux bien. On passe un bon film au Gaumont.

faire du vélo (Je n'ai pas de vélo.)
Student A: Tu veux faire du vélo?
Student B: Non, je ne peux pas. Je n'ai pas de vélo.

Prononciation

The sound [ø]

The vowel combination **eu** is pronounced [ø] when it's in the last syllable of a word ending in **-eu, -eut** or **-eux**. Say each of these words:

v**eu**t	chev**eu**x
bl**eu**	d**eu**x
p**eu**x	génér**eu**x

The sound [œ]

In most other cases **eu** is pronounced [œ] before a final pronounced consonant other than [z]. The vowel combination **œu** is always pronounced [œ]. Say each of these words:

p**eu**vent	taill**eu**r
coul**eu**r	vend**eu**r
v**eu**lent	s**œu**r

Answers

13 1. Tu veux aller au centre commercial?
Oui, je veux bien. J'ai besoin d'un nouveau jean.
2. Tu veux venir chez moi?
Non, je ne peux pas. Je travaille à 18 heures.
3. Tu veux aller au fast-food?
Oui, je veux bien. J'ai faim.
4. Tu veux étudier avec moi?
Oui, je veux bien. J'ai une interro demain.
5. Tu veux aller en boîte?
Non, je ne peux pas. C'est trop cher.
6. Tu veux faire une bouillabaisse?
Non, je ne peux pas. Je vais au café avec la famille.
7. Tu veux nager?
Non, je ne peux pas. Je n'ai pas de maillot de bain.

Teacher's Note

You might have students use the results of their interviews in Activity 12 to report their findings. For example, **Francis aime les crevettes. Yasmine n'aime pas les crevettes. Yasmine et Francis aiment le fromage....**

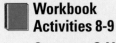

Teacher's Notes

1. Point out that the **f** in **œuf** is pronounced only in the singular. 2. **Yaourt** is pronounced [jauR(t)]. 3. Students have already learned the words **le fromage** and **le jambon** in **Unité 3**. 4. You may want to point out to students that **gâteau** and **morceau** form their plurals by adding an **x**. 5. Differences between **une boucherie** and **une charcuterie** will be explained in the main cultural reading in this **unité**. **Le porc** and **le jambon** sold at a **boucherie** are uncooked. Cooked pork products, including ham, are found at the **charcuterie**. 6. A store that features fish is **une poissonnerie**. 7. Other food-related terms include **la crème** (*cream*), **le petit pain** (*roll*), **l'agneau (m.)** (*lamb*), **le riz** (*rice*), **la farine** (*flour*), **les pâtes (f.)** (*pasta, noodles*) and **l'épicerie (f.)** (*grocery store*). 8. Communicative functions that are recycled in this lesson are "asking for information" and "expressing intentions."

TPR

Masculine or Feminine?

To identify the gender of the foods introduced in this lesson, say these nouns without their articles. Have students raise their left hand if they hear a masculine noun; have them raise their right hand if they hear a feminine noun.

Leçon B

In this lesson you will be able to:

➤ **agree and disagree**

➤ **express likes and dislikes**

➤ **insist**

➤ **give information**

Combien de confiture as-tu?

J'ai trop de confiture.

J'ai beaucoup de confiture.

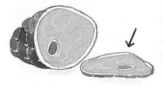

J'ai assez de confiture.

J'ai un peu de confiture.

une tranche de
jambon

un morceau de
fromage

une boîte de
petits pois

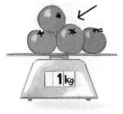

un kilo de
tomates

un pot de
moutarde

une bouteille d'eau
minérale

Paired Practice

Qu'est-ce que c'est?

You might have your students cut out pictures of the foods introduced in this lesson. Put students in pairs and have them take turns asking and answering the question **Qu'est-ce que c'est?** as they show one another each item they have cut out. To vary this activity, students can take turns showing an item and asking a "oui" or "non" question about it. For example (showing a picture of a cake), **Est-ce que c'est un gâteau?**

Cooperative Group Practice

Les magasins

Put your students in small groups and have each group choose one of the types of stores presented in this lesson. Group members should discuss what the store's exterior and display windows would look like. Then they will design and draw on construction paper or poster board a culturally-authentic storefront for their establishment, giving it a French name. In their drawing they will also include names, pictures and prices of various sale items.

NATIONAL STANDARDS
C1.1, C1.2, C2.2, C4.1

Teacher's Notes

1. **Maman** is the French word for "Mom"; **papa** is the French word for "Dad." 2. **Ouais** (*Yeah*) is a slang expression for "yes." 3. Point out to students that when **le** precedes a part of the day, for example, **le matin**, it means "in the (morning)." 4. Point out to students that the verb **attendre** follows the same pattern as the verb **vendre** that was introduced in **Unité 7**.

Madame Rousseau and her son Benjamin are talking about going grocery shopping.

Benjamin: Où est-ce qu'on va faire les courses, maman?
Mme Rousseau: D'abord, on va aller à la boulangerie acheter du pain et des croissants.
Benjamin: Ouais! J'aime bien les croissants le matin.
Mme Rousseau: Puis, on va acheter des yaourts et un peu de fromage, peut-être du camembert, à la crémerie.
Benjamin: Moi, j'aime aussi le pâté. On ne va pas acheter de pâté?
Mme Rousseau: Si, si, mais attends! Nous pouvons aussi aller à la charcuterie.

BOULANGERIE PATISSERIE
Rodrigue DETCHEVERRY
5 rue Gabriel Oyarzabai
Téléphone : 41-65-53 - MIQUELON

 Enquête culturelle

The expression **Repas sans pain, repas de rien** ("A meal without bread is nothing") shows the importance of bread in the French diet. Although French bread comes in many shapes and sizes, the most common

The French buy their *baguettes* fresh every day. (Angers)

La boulangerie - pâtisserie

LA PIÈCE
0,30 €
BAGUETTE DE CAMPAGNE
FABRICATION CARREFOUR
250 g
Soit le kg : 1,22 €

type, the **baguette**, is a long, thin loaf of bread with a crisp crust. This hard crust keeps the bread fresh without being wrapped; people can be seen carrying **baguettes** tucked under their arms or nibbling on the ends of them as they walk home from the **boulangerie**. The bread has such a good taste that the French usually don't butter it, except for breakfast. Other sweeter types of bakery products are just as delicious. A **pain**

You can make your own version of a *pain au chocolat* by baking chocolate chips inside a crescent roll.

au chocolat tastes like a **croissant** and has a piece of chocolate in the center.

Children often eat them for snacks. **Un éclair** is a cream-filled pastry, **un chausson aux pommes** resembles an apple turnover and **une brioche** is a soft, round roll.

Would you choose a chocolate or mocha *éclair*? (Angers)

Camembert is a soft cheese with a thin, edible skin.

Fruit and cheese, other staples in the French diet, are often served as dessert at the end of a meal. Most regions of France produce their own special cheese, with some 360 different kinds in all to choose from. Camembert, Pont-l'Évêque and Neufchâtel are three of the many famous types of cheese from the northern province of Normandy. Brie, the most famous of all French cheeses, comes from the Parisian area. Roquefort, one of the better-known blue cheeses from the **Massif Central**, is made from sheep's milk.

Instead of cheese, the French often eat yogurt for dessert. French yogurt is generally thinner than the custard-type yogurt found in the United States. In general, French teenagers drink less milk than American teens but consume more cheese and yogurt. They generally eat their yogurt plain, but sometimes sweeten it with a little sugar, honey, jam or jelly.

Comparisons

Cultural Journal

If your students are keeping a cultural journal, you might have them write an answer to this question: If you were having a French-speaking family over to your home for dinner and wanted to serve them a typical American meal, what would you prepare for them and why?

NATIONAL STANDARDS
C2.1, C2.2, C3.1, C4.2

Audiocassette/CD Activity 2

Answers

1 Possible answer:
Madame Rousseau et Benjamin vont faire les courses. D'abord, ils vont acheter du pain et des croissants à la boulangerie. Puis, ils vont acheter des yaourts et un peu de fromage à la crémerie. Benjamin aime les croissants et le pâté.

2 1. Tu préfères le pain ou les croissants?
Moi, je préfère....
2. Tu préfères le fromage ou le yaourt?
Moi, je préfère....
3. Tu préfères le poulet ou le saucisson?
Moi, je préfère....
4. Tu préfères les oranges ou les pommes?
Moi, je préfère....
5. Tu préfères la tarte aux fraises ou le gâteau?
Moi, je préfère....
6. Tu préfères l'eau minérale ou le coca?
Moi, je préfère....
7. Tu préfères le jambon ou le pâté?
Moi, je préfère....
8. Tu préfères la moutarde ou le ketchup?
Moi, je préfère....

3 1. c
2. e
3. b
4. a
5. d

NATIONAL STANDARDS
C1.1, C1.2

1 Write a four-sentence paragraph in French that summarizes the conversation between Madame Rousseau and Benjamin. Begin by telling what they are going to do. Then mention what they are going to buy at the bakery and at the dairy store. Also name two foods that Benjamin likes.

2 You're planning a picnic with some of your friends. Before you go grocery shopping, take turns with your partner asking and telling which foods and beverages each of you prefers.

Modèle:

Thomas: Tu préfères le lait ou le jus d'orange?
Amina: Moi, je préfère le jus d'orange.

1.

2.

3.

4.

5.

6.

7.

8.

Combien de tranches de jambon vas-tu acheter? (Angers)

3 Match the expression of quantity on the left with the appropriate food or beverage on the right.

1. un pot de...
2. une tranche de...
3. une boîte de...
4. une bouteille d'...
5. un morceau de...

a. eau minérale
b. tomates
c. confiture
d. camembert
e. jambon

4 | *C'est à toi!*

1. Dans ta famille, qui fait les courses?
2. Est-ce que tu aimes le fromage français?
3. Est-ce que tu préfères le bœuf, le poulet ou le poisson?
4. Est-ce que tu préfères le ketchup ou la moutarde avec les hamburgers?
5. Est-ce que tu manges beaucoup de pain?
6. Est-ce que tu manges assez de fruits et de légumes?

Structure

The partitive article

There are some nouns that can't be counted, such as bread, ice cream and water. We often use the words "some" or "any" before these nouns. In French, "some" or "any" is expressed by combining **de** with a singular definite article (**le, la** or **l'**). This forms the partitive article which indicates a part, a quantity or an amount of something.

Masculine before a Consonant Sound	Feminine before a Consonant Sound	Masculine or Feminine before a Vowel Sound
du café	**de la** soupe	**de l'**eau minérale

On va acheter **du** pain.	*We're going to buy (some) bread.*
Vous avez **de la** glace?	*Do you have (any) ice cream?*
Je voudrais **de l'**eau minérale.	*I would like (some) mineral water.*

As you can see in the preceding examples, the partitive article (**du, de la** or **de l'**) is required in French but is often omitted in English.

When talking about things that can be counted, such as potatoes and carrots, "some" or "any" is expressed by **des**, the plural of the indefinite article **un(e)**. Here, too, "some" or "any" is often omitted in English.

Je veux **des** pommes de terre.	*I want (some) potatoes.*

Partitive articles are often used after certain verbs and expressions to indicate quantity: **vouloir, acheter, manger, donner, désirer, avoir, voici, voilà** and **il y a.** Partitive articles are not used after the verbs **aimer, adorer** and **préférer,** which refer to things in general.

Il y a **de la** soupe?	*Is there (any) soup?*
Benjamin adore **la** bouillabaisse.	*Benjamin loves fish soup.*

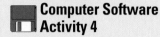

Mme Planchon fait les courses dans sa famille.

Vous voulez de la soupe?

Voici des pommes de terre. (Sarlat)

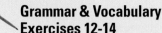

Workbook Activity 11

Grammar & Vocabulary Exercises 12-14

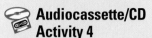
Audiocassette/CD Activity 4

Computer Software Activity 4

Answers

4 Answers will vary.

Teacher's Notes

1. Point out that there is liaison between **des** and a plural noun beginning with a vowel sound.
2. Point out to students that partitive articles are not used after **vouloir, acheter, manger, donner, désirer, avoir, voici, voilà** and **il y a** when referring to whole items. For example, **Christine mange la tarte** and **Je voudrais une salade.**

Cooperative Group Practice

On fait les courses.

Put students in the same small groups that they were in for the cooperative group activity earlier in this lesson where they designed a French storefront. Now have them add a list of names, prices and pictures of other foods that are sold at their store. Then have one student in each group remain at the storefront to be the sales-clerk as the others go around the classroom shopping at the various stores. Each customer should purchase at least one item at each store, saying to the clerk, for example, **Je voudrais acheter du pain à 0,57 €.** The clerk gives the customer the appropriate item and responds **Bon, voilà votre pain.** At the end of the activity, each student shows and tells the other group members what he or she has purchased, for example, **Voilà du pain.**

NATIONAL STANDARDS
C1.1, C1.2, C4.1

Modèle:
Lundi il y a du jambon, des carottes et de la glace à la vanille.

Modèle:
Tu veux du poulet?

Modèle:
à la boucherie
Je vais acheter du bœuf.

Pratique

5 Your teacher always posts the school lunch menu in French. You're the first one to see this week's menu. Report what's being served in the cafeteria each day. Monday has been done for you.

lundi	mardi	mercredi	jeudi	vendredi
jambon	porc	hamburgers	poulet	poisson
carottes	haricots verts	frites	petits pois	pommes de terre
glace à la vanille	fromage	glace au chocolat	pain	tarte aux fraises
	raisins		yaourts	

6 You're at a family picnic. Help your young cousin get something to eat and drink by asking him if he wants some of each item on the picnic table.

7 You're going to do your weekly grocery shopping at many stores. As you look at each one, say that you're going to buy some of what is indicated.

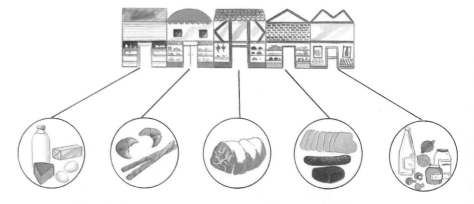

1. à la boulangerie
2. à la crémerie
3. au supermarché
4. à la charcuterie

Workbook Activity 12

Grammar & Vocabulary Exercises 15-16

Audiocassette/CD Activity 9

Computer Software Activity 5

8 Complete each short dialogue, using the appropriate articles from the following list.

du	de la	des	le	la	les

1. Karine: Nous pouvons manger... hamburgers ce soir, maman?
   Mme Renard: Oui. Alors, j'ai besoin d'acheter... ketchup et... moutarde au supermarché.

2. Mlle Javert: Avez-vous... tartes aux fraises aujourd'hui?
   M. Arnaud: Non, Mademoiselle, mais voici... tartes aux pommes.

3. Luc: J'adore... quiche.
   Brigitte: Moi, je préfère... omelettes.

4. M. Senghor: Voilà... petits pois.
   Khadim: Je n'aime pas... légumes verts. Il y a... carottes?

5. Amine: Tu veux... soupe?
   Florence: Oui, j'aime bien... bouillabaisse.

6. Serveur: Vous désirez... beurre?
   Mme Carnot: Oui, Monsieur. Donnez-moi aussi... confiture, s'il vous plaît.

7. Mme Vollet: Tu veux... jambon?
   Fred: Non, merci. Je n'aime pas beaucoup... porc.

Voulez-vous manger des carottes? (Sarlat)

The partitive article in negative sentences

You've already learned that in negative sentences, **des** becomes **de** or **d'**.

Je ne veux pas **de** pommes de terre. — *I don't want (any) potatoes.*

The partitive articles **du**, **de la** and **de l'** also change to **de** or **d'** in negative sentences.

On ne va pas acheter **de** fromage. — *We're not going to buy (any) cheese.*

Il n'y a pas **d'**eau minérale. — *There isn't any mineral water.*

Pratique

9 Olivier is a vegetarian. Tell whether or not he eats the foods that are indicated.

1. porc
2. steak
3. pâté
4. pain
5. légumes
6. fruits
7. jambon
8. camembert
9. glace
10. bœuf

Modèles:

frites
Il mange des frites.

saucisson
Il ne mange pas de saucisson.

Teacher's Notes

1. Students already know that the indefinite articles **un** and **une** become **de** or **d'** in negative sentences. Remind students that definite articles, however, remain the same. For example, **Je n'aime pas *les* haricots verts.** 2. You may want to tell students that after the verb **être** in a negative sentence, the partitive does not change. For example, **Ce n'est pas *du* bœuf.** (*This isn't beef.*)

NATIONAL STANDARDS C1.1, C1.2, C4.1

Answers

10 1. Il y a de la moutarde?
Oui, il y a de la moutarde.
Il y a du ketchup?
Non, il n'y a pas de ketchup.
2. Il y a du lait?
Non, il n'y a pas de lait. Il y a du jus d'orange?
Oui, il y a du jus d'orange.
3. Il y a du fromage?
Oui, il y a du fromage. Il y a des œufs?
Non, il n'y a pas d'œufs.
4. Il y a de l'eau?
Non, il n'y a pas d'eau. Il y a du coca?
Non, il n'y a pas de coca.
5. Il y a des pommes de terre?
Non, il n'y a pas de pommes de terre. Il y a des tomates?
Oui, il y a des tomates.
6. Il y a des crevettes?
Oui, il y a des crevettes. Il y a du poisson?
Non, il n'y a pas de poisson.
7. Il y a du pâté?
Non, il n'y a pas de pâté. Il y a du bœuf?
Oui, il y a du bœuf.

Teacher's Notes

1. You may point out to students that **de** becomes **d'** before a word beginning with a vowel sound. 2. To politely refuse when someone offers you something, you may also say simply **Merci** with the appropriate intonation. To accept, say **Oui, merci; Oui, s'il te/vous plaît** or **Oui, je veux bien**. 3. You may want to tell students that the noun after **de** may be singular or plural. 4. Tell students that **très** and **trop** are never used before **beaucoup**. 5. You may want to point out to students that after one of these expressions of quantity, the definite article that normally precedes the noun is dropped.

NATIONAL STANDARDS
C1.1, C1.2, C4.1

274

Modèle:

salade/beurre
Student A: Il y a de la salade?
Student B: Oui, il y a de la salade. Il y a du beurre?
Student A: Non, il n'y a pas de beurre.

Combien d'œufs voulez-vous?

10 With a partner, take turns asking and answering questions about what's in the refrigerator.

1. moutarde/ketchup
2. lait/jus d'orange
3. fromage/œufs
4. eau/coca
5. pommes de terre/tomates
6. crevettes/poisson
7. pâté/bœuf

Expressions of quantity

To ask "how many" or "how much," use the expression **combien de** before a noun.

Combien de croissants est-ce que tu veux?	*How many croissants do you want?*
Il y a **combien d'**œufs dans cette omelette?	*How many eggs are there in this omelette?*

To tell "how many" or "how much," use one of these general expressions of quantity before a noun:

assez de	*enough*
beaucoup de	*a lot of, many*
(un) peu de	*(a) little, few*
trop de	*too much, too many*

Je voudrais **un peu de** fromage.	*I would like a little cheese.*
Non, merci, j'ai **assez** d'eau.	*No thanks, I have enough water.*

Certain nouns express a specific quantity. They are followed by **de** and a noun.

un morceau de	*a piece of*
une tranche de	*a slice of*
un pot de	*a jar of*
une boîte de	*a can of*
une bouteille de	*a bottle of*
un kilo de	*a kilogram of*

Donnez-moi **une tranche de** jambon.	*Give me a slice of ham.*
Je veux acheter **un kilo** d'oranges.	*I want to buy one kilo of oranges.*

Pratique

1 With a partner, take turns asking and telling how much food is left on the buffet table.

Modèle:

salades/quiches
Student A: Il y a combien de salades?
Student B: Il y a quatre salades. Il y a combien de quiches?
Student A: Il y a une quiche.

1. omelettes/sandwichs
2. croissants/crevettes
3. poissons/oranges
4. gâteaux/tartes

2 Imagine that you work at a market and are taking inventory. Tell your boss how many of each vegetable or fruit you have using **trop de**, **assez de** or **peu de**.

Modèle:

Nous avons peu de haricots verts.

1.

2.

3.

4.

5.

6.

7.

8.

9.

10.

275

Cooperative Group Practice

Sentence Construction

So that students can practice using nouns of quantity, put them in small groups. First, have them make simple line drawings of each noun of quantity and put the drawings in one stack. Then, put the food pictures students used in the previous cooperative group activity in another stack. Each student takes one item from each stack and makes an appropriate sentence with these two elements using **vouloir** or **avoir**, for example, **un kilo de/pâté — Je veux un kilo de pâté**. Finally, another student in that group repeats what the first student has said. (**Catherine veut un kilo de pâté.**)

Modèle:

café
Donnez-moi un kilo de café, s'il vous plaît.

13 Because your neighborhood grocer has rearranged his store, you can't find any of the items you want. Ask him to give you each item you're looking for, using one of the quantities from the following list.

un pot de	une tranche de	une boîte de
un kilo de	une bouteille de	

1. pommes de terre
2. jus de pomme
3. mayonnaise
4. jambon

5. confiture
6. petits pois
7. coca
8. pâté

Vous voulez deux kilos de pommes de terre, Madame?

Communication

On va acheter des fruits au marché. (Pornichet)

14 You and the other 20 students that you're traveling through France with have picnic lunches at noon. You are all responsible for planning the daily menus as well as shopping for the food and beverages. You and your partner signed up to plan and shop for tomorrow's picnic lunch, which will consist of a variety of sandwiches, fruits, cheeses, desserts and beverages. With your partner, make the grocery list. Be sure to include the amount of each item you need, for example, **10 tranches de jambon, 7 baguettes, 4 bouteilles de coca**, etc.

15 With your partner, categorize the food and beverages you chose in the previous activity according to where you are going to buy them. On a separate sheet of paper, write the headings **crémerie, pâtisserie, boulangerie, charcuterie, marché** and **supermarché**. Then put each food or beverage item under the place where you're going to buy it.

16 Before you go shopping for your groceries, you and your partner want to practice a typical conversation between a customer and a shopkeeper or merchant at one of the places you will visit. In the course of your conversation:

1. Greet each other.
2. The customer says that he or she wants a specific quantity of each item he or she wants to buy there.
3. The shopkeeper says that he or she either has or doesn't have each item. If the shopkeeper doesn't have a certain item, the customer should ask for something similar.
4. The customer asks for the total amount.
5. The shopkeeper tells the amount.
6. Say good-bye to each other.

Ce fromage, c'est combien?

Workbook Activity 14

Listening Activity 2

Game

Memory Chain

To practice vocabulary for food items and the partitive, you and your students can play this memory game. You begin by saying one food item that you would like, for example, **Je voudrais du pain.** The first student repeats what you have said and adds another item: **Je voudrais du pain et du coca.** The second student repeats what you and the first student have said and adds one item he or she would like, etc. (Students with more limited abilities may want to write down each object as it is said.) Every time a student is unable to repeat what has been said before, he or she is eliminated. If this game is played with teams, the team with the most players at the end of the allotted time is the winner.

Mise au point sur... les courses

It's easy to find tasty things to eat in France, the country known throughout the world for its good food. However, it may be more difficult deciding where to shop. From open-air markets to specialty food shops, from corner grocery stores to large supermarkets, choices are everywhere.

Open-air markets generally offer the freshest food, with farmers bringing their products directly to the customer. Along with the fresh produce, reasonable prices also attract customers, who sometimes bargain to get an even better buy. Merchants set up stands of regional specialties as well as seasonal fruits, vegetables, meat, seafood and cheese. Few of the products are refrigerated, not even the meat. Often located on a public square, markets open early in the morning. Shoppers arrive with their shopping basket (**un sac à provisions**) in hand, as shopping bags are usually not provided.

Markets in other French-speaking countries reflect the local character. In Senegal, Morocco and Algeria, the smell of exotic spices, the shouts of the merchants tempting customers to their stalls and the bright colors of the merchandise itself all offer a lively shopping experience. Markets on the Caribbean islands of Guadeloupe and Martinique sell tuna, lobster, clams and other products from the sea, as well as bananas, papayas, mangoes, avocados, guavas and yams.

Specialty shops, also popular in French-speaking countries, are often family-owned and operated. Customers appreciate the individualized service they receive at these shops. To buy bakery products, such as bread and rolls, let your nose guide you to **la boulangerie.**

The pungent aroma of spices fills the air in this market in Pointe-à-Pitre. (Guadeloupe)

NATIONAL STANDARDS
C1.1, C1.2, C2.1, C2.2, C4.2

Answers

17 Possible answers:

1. A French-speaking shopper can bargain for a lower price at an open-air market.
2. No, few of the products at an open-air market are refrigerated.
3. Markets are often located on a public square.
4. Shopping bags are usually not furnished.
5. A typical African market has exotic spices, merchants shouting to tempt customers to their stalls and colorful merchandise.
6. Three kinds of food that can be found in Caribbean markets are tuna, papayas and yams.
7. A **boucherie** sells a variety of meat, whereas a **charcuterie** has prepared pork products, delicatessen food, prepared salads and cold meat dishes.
8. Two supermarket chains in France are Monoprix and Carrefour.
9. You go to the **caisse**.
10. The bottled water and cheese sections of a French supermarket are larger than those in American supermarkets. The cold cereal and snack food sections are smaller.

Comparisons

Cultural Journal

If your students are keeping a cultural journal, you might have them write about the following situation: Imagine that you work in a specific shop or store. Write your journal entry from the point of view of this employee. Tell why you chose that particular store, what you sell or what you do there, and what the best and worst parts of your job are.

NATIONAL STANDARDS
C1.2, C2.1, C2.2, C4.2

For special pastries, as well as cakes, pies and cookies, head for **la pâtisserie**. For most meat products, stop in **la boucherie** where the butcher will be happy to advise you on the appropriate cut of meat for a certain recipe and will cut and wrap it for you. **La boucherie chevaline**, a specialized butcher shop, offers only horse meat. For prepared pork products or deli food, including salads and cold meat dishes, go to **la charcuterie**.

BOULANGERIE
REMY BECK
7 rue Amiral Muselier

Meilleure Tripe du Monde
17
CHARCUTERIE FINE
Centre Commercial
GRACE DE DIEU
14300 CAEN
L. AMAGLIO
Tél: 02 31 52 18 13

French pastries are like individual works of art.

Convenient corner grocery stores (**les épiceries**) stock many different products. Sidewalk stands in front of these stores sell fruits and vegetables to passersby.

This *épicerie* even offers home delivery. (Paris)

COURS DES HALLES · ÉPICERIE
LIVRAISONS A DOMICILE

Supermarkets, like Monoprix, Uniprix and Prisunic, sell a variety of merchandise under one roof. Shoppers usually pay a small deposit to rent a shopping cart (**un chariot**) which they fill at different departments before paying at the checkout (**la caisse**). In many ways, French supermarkets resemble those in the United States. In fact, one French supermarket chain, Carrefour, has a store in Pennsylvania. Carrefour stores are so large that some supervisors wear roller skates to move quickly back and forth to help cashiers in the many checkout lines. Yet, in other ways, French supermarkets differ from their counterparts in the United States. For example, the long rows of bottled water, the large cheese section and the limited variety of cold cereal and snack food reflect traditional French shopping habits. Frozen foods (**les produits surgelés**) have become increasingly popular as busy lifestyles limit the time spent on meal preparation.

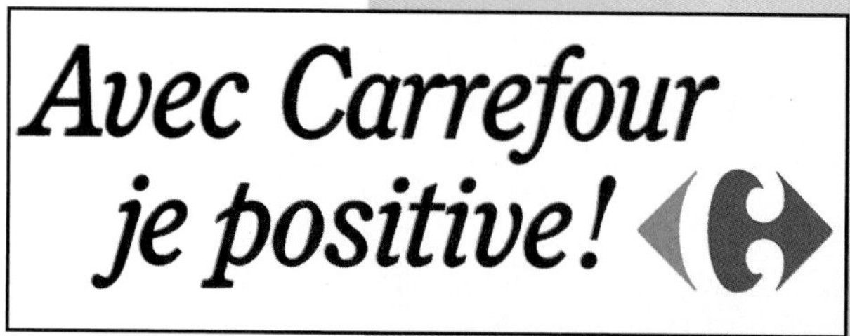
Avec Carrefour
je positive!

CONSIGNE GRATUITE

To rent a shopping cart, you insert a coin. When you return the cart, you get your money back.

Whether customers pick a place to shop based on fresh products, a large selection, individualized help or convenience, they will find a place to buy good food close to home.

17 Answer the following questions.

1. Where can a French-speaking shopper bargain for a lower price, at an open-air market, a specialty shop, a corner grocery store or a supermarket?
2. Are products at an open-air market refrigerated?
3. Where are markets often located?
4. Why do shoppers often bring their own **sac à provisions** with them?
5. How would you describe a typical African market?
6. What are three kinds of food that can be found in Caribbean markets?
7. What is the difference between a **boucherie** and a **charcuterie**?
8. What are the names of two supermarket chains in France?
9. Where do you go to pay for your purchases at a supermarket?
10. What section of a French supermarket is larger than its American counterpart? What section is smaller?

Depending on the quality of their produce, vendors may be willing to bargain at an open-air market.

18 Here are two grocery store receipts, one from Monoprix and the other from Prisunic. Answer the questions that follow.

At Monoprix:

1. What brand of mineral water did the customer buy?
2. How much did the bread cost?
3. How many grams did the Babybel cheese weigh?
4. What was the date of the customer's purchase?
5. In what city is this Monoprix?

At Prisunic:

1. How many packages of Lavazza coffee did the customer purchase?
2. How much was the customer's bill?
3. How many euros did the customer give the cashier?
4. How many euros did the customer receive in change?
5. At what time did the customer check out?

NATIONAL STANDARDS
C1.2, C2.1, C2.2, C3.2

Workbook
Activity 15

 Grammar & Vocabulary
Exercises 20-21

Audiocassette/CD
Les fruits

Teacher's Notes

1. Students learned **les raisins**, **les pommes** and **les oranges** in **Unité 2**. **Les fruits** and **les fraises** were presented in **Leçons A** and **B**, respectively, of this **unité**. 2. When a definite article precedes a noun of quantity, for example, **le kilo**, it means "per" or "a/an." 3. The French word for "grapes" (**les raisins**) is a false cognate. 4. The names of some other fruits in French are **le citron** (*lemon*), **la framboise** (*raspberry*), **l'ananas (m.)** (*pineapple*), **l'abricot (m.)** (*apricot*), **le pamplemousse** (*grapefruit*), **la prune** (*plum*), **le pruneau** (*prune*), **les raisins secs (m.)** (*raisins*), **la papaye** (*papaya*), **la mangue** (*mango*), **l'avocat (m.)** (*avocado*) and **la goyave** (*guava*). 5. Communicative functions that are recycled in this lesson are "agreeing and disagreeing" and "expressing intentions."

Paired Practice

Qu'est-ce que c'est?

Have your students cut out pictures of the fruits introduced in this lesson. Put students in pairs and have them take turns asking and answering the question **Qu'est-ce que c'est**? as they show one another each item they have cut out.

TPR

Masculine or Feminine?

To identify the gender of the fruits introduced in this lesson, say these nouns with their plural definite articles. Have students raise their left hand if they hear a masculine noun; have them raise their right hand if they hear a feminine noun.

National Standards
C1.1, C1.2, C4.1

280

Leçon C

In this lesson you will be able to:

➤ ask for a price

➤ state prices

➤ make a complaint

➤ inquire about and compare prices

➤ negotiate

➤ choose and purchase items

---

les fruits (m.)

les cerises (f.)   *les pêches (f.)*

les fraises (f.)   *les pommes (f.)*

1,52 € le kilo   1,52 € le kilo

les melons (m.)   *les pastèques (f.)*

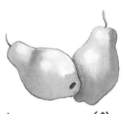

les poires (f.)   *les raisins (m.)*

2,29 € le kilo

les oranges (f.)   *les bananes (f.)*

Les bananes sont plus chères que les pastèques.
Les melons sont aussi chers que les pastèques.
Les melons sont moins chers que les bananes.

■ **Workbook Activity 16**

📻 **Audiocassette/CD** *Dialogue*

📺 **Video**

Vous désirez?

Combien coûtent les melons, s'il vous plaît?

le marché

Monsieur Gagnon is shopping for fruit at an open-air market in Guadeloupe.

Le marchand:	**Bonjour, Monsieur. Vous désirez?**
M. Gagnon:	**Combien coûtent les melons, s'il vous plaît?**
Le marchand:	**Les melons... euh... 1,52 euros le kilo.**
M. Gagnon:	**Mais ils sont déjà mûrs. Je trouve que c'est trop cher. Est-ce que je peux acheter deux kilos pour 2,50 euros?**
Le marchand:	**D'accord, Monsieur.**
M. Gagnon:	**Et les bananes, combien coûtent-elles?**
Le marchand:	**Les bananes sont plus chères que les melons. Elles coûtent 2,29 euros le kilo.**
M. Gagnon:	**Bon, alors je vais aussi acheter deux kilos de bananes.**

The Caribbean island of Guadeloupe, made up of two main islands and some smaller ones, is one of France's overseas departments in the West Indies (**les Antilles**). Its tropical climate encourages the growth of many fruits and vegetables. Some of the island's other exports are cocoa, coffee and sugar cane.

FRANCE-ANTILLES

LE QUOTIDIEN D'INFORMATION DES ANTILLES

Since most people in Guadeloupe have fruit trees and gardens near their homes, they need to shop for only some of their fruits and vegetables. When they go shopping at an open-air market, they usually bargain with the merchants. Fruit prices in the Caribbean vary according to the season and the type of fruit. In the metric system, **un kilogramme (un kilo)** equals 2.2 U.S. pounds. **Une livre** (*metric pound*) is the equivalent of half a kilogram or 500 grams.

Enquête culturelle

Bananas are one of Guadeloupe's principal fruits.

Teacher's Note

Used as an adjective describing a noun, the forms of **cher** agree with the noun. When **cher** is used as an adverb describing the verb **coûter**, it is invariable. Note that **cher** is also invariable when used after the expression **c'est**.

Cooperative Group Practice

Food Chain

Put students in one large circle that includes you as well. Then take the pictures of food items that students have already made. As you pass the first picture to the student next to you, identify it, for example, **les cerises**. The student who receives the picture must repeat what you said, turn to the student next to him or her and reidentify the picture (**les cerises**). (The picture will eventually make its way back to you.) After you have given the first picture to the student next to you, immediately pass a second picture to this student and identify it. Your neighbor repeats what you said and passes the picture to the next student while identifying it. Continue to add new pictures. The activity ends when all pictures are returned to you. (You may want to vary this activity by having everyone whisper the name of each item. Then the last person says the item's name aloud.)

NATIONAL STANDARDS
C1.2, C2.1, C2.2, C3.1, C4.2

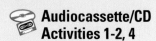

Audiocassette/CD Activities 1-2, 4

Answers

1 1. faux
2. vrai
3. vrai
4. faux
5. faux
6. vrai

2 Possible answers:
1. du bœuf, un poulet
2. du pâté, du saucisson
3. des pommes, des cerises
4. un gâteau, une tarte aux fraises
5. du lait, des œufs
6. un pot de moutarde, une bouteille d'eau minérale

3 Possible answers:
1. Combien coûtent les pêches?
2. Les melons coûtent combien le kilo?
3. Est-ce que les bananes sont plus chères que les melons?
4. Si, si, les bananes sont trop mûres.
5. Ces fraises sont trop chères.
6. Est-ce que je peux acheter deux kilos de poires pour 3 euros?

4 Answers will vary.

282

Est-ce que ces pêches sont mûres?

---

1 | *Répondez par "vrai" ou "faux" d'après le dialogue.*

1. Les melons coûtent 2,29 euros le kilo.
2. Monsieur Gagnon trouve que les melons sont trop chers.
3. Monsieur Gagnon peut acheter deux kilos de melons pour 2,50 euros.
4. Les bananes sont moins chères que les melons.
5. Monsieur Gagnon va acheter trois kilos de bananes.
6. Les bananes vont coûter 4,58 euros.

---

2 | Write the names in French of two products you could buy at each of the following places. **La boulangerie** has been done for you.

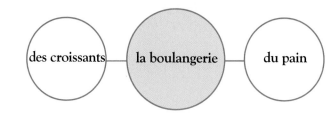

des croissants — la boulangerie — du pain

1. la boucherie
2. la charcuterie
3. le marché
4. la pâtisserie
5. la crémerie
6. le supermarché

---

3 | What would you say in French in the following situations?

1. You want to know the price of the peaches.
2. You want to know how much the melons cost per kilogram.
3. You want to know if the bananas are more expensive than the melons.
4. The merchant has just told you that the bananas are not too ripe. You insist that they are too ripe.
5. You tell the merchant that these strawberries are too expensive.
6. You want to know if you can buy two kilograms of pears for 3 euros.

---

4 | *C'est à toi!*

1. Quels fruits aimes-tu?
2. Est-ce que tu préfères les bananes ou les pêches?
3. Est-ce que tu manges beaucoup de fruits?
4. Quel(s) fruit(s) vas-tu manger aujourd'hui?
5. Est-ce que ta famille achète des fruits au supermarché ou au marché?
6. Après le repas, est-ce que tu manges un fruit ou un dessert?

Structure

Comparative of adjectives

To compare people and things in French, use the following constructions:

plus (*more*)	+	adjective	+	**que** (*than*)
moins (*less*)	+	adjective	+	**que** (*than*)
aussi (*as*)	+	adjective	+	**que** (*as*)

In the following examples, note how the adjective agrees with the first noun in the comparison.

La banane est **plus mûre que** la pêche. — *The banana is riper than the peach.*

Les raisins sont **moins chers que** les cerises. — *Grapes are less expensive than cherries.*

Le marchand est **aussi grand qu'**Abdou. — *The merchant is as tall as Abdou.*

M. Grenier est plus grand que sa femme. (Angers)

Pratique

5 Compare the prices of school supplies at Monoprix with those at the Papeterie Roche. Tell whether they are more expensive, less expensive or as expensive.

	Monoprix	Papeterie Roche
crayons	0,45 €	0,53 €
stylos	2,27 €	2,27 €
trousses	2,74 €	3,35 €
cahiers	1,05 €	0,75 €
calendriers	5,95 €	8,38 €
dictionnaires	13,42 €	13,42 €
cartes	3,96 €	3,20 €

Modèle:

Les crayons à Monoprix sont **moins chers que** les crayons à la Papeterie Roche.

1. Les stylos à Monoprix sont… les stylos à la Papeterie Roche.
2. Les trousses à Monoprix sont… les trousses à la Papeterie Roche.
3. Les cahiers à Monoprix sont… les cahiers à la Papeterie Roche.
4. Les calendriers à Monoprix sont… les calendriers à la Papeterie Roche.
5. Les dictionnaires à Monoprix sont… les dictionnaires à la Papeterie Roche.
6. Les cartes à Monoprix sont… les cartes à la Papeterie Roche.

Même si on paye moins cher on a le droit d'être satisfait à 100 %.

SATISFACTION
MONOPRIX
GARANTIE

Answers

5 1. aussi chers que
2. moins chères que
3. plus chers que
4. moins chers que
5. aussi chers que
6. plus chères que

Teacher's Notes

1. Tell students that **que** becomes **qu'** when the word that follows begins with a vowel sound. 2. Point out to students that there is liaison after **plus** and **moins** when the word that follows begins with a vowel sound. 3. Have your students name five teachers in your school who are of various heights. Then have students compare these teachers' heights, for example, **Monsieur Lake est plus grand que Madame Hartmann**. 4. You may want to tell students that **une papeterie** is a store that specializes in school and office supplies.

Cooperative Group Practice

Plus ou moins cher?

You might do a follow-up to the cooperative group shopping activity in **Leçon B** where students visited various stores buying one item at each one. When they return to their groups with their purchases and identify them for the other students, they can add more information that compares the prices of the items that they bought. For example, **Le pain est moins cher que les crevettes**.

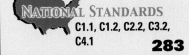

NATIONAL STANDARDS
C1.1, C1.2, C2.2, C3.2, C4.1

Answers

6 Michèle est aussi grande que Robert.
Laurent est plus grand que Robert.
Sandrine est plus grande que Robert.
Marc est aussi grand que Robert.
Étienne est moins grand que Robert.
Renée est moins grande que Robert.

7 1. Les pommes sont aussi petites que les oranges.
2. Les poires sont plus belles que les raisins.
3. La tarte est moins jolie que le gâteau.
4. Les petits pois sont plus frais que les haricots verts.
5. Les pêches sont aussi mûres que les bananes.
6. Les oignons sont plus petits que les champignons.
7. Le poulet est moins cher que le bœuf.

NATIONAL STANDARDS
C1.1, C1.2

284

Modèle:

Martine est moins grande que Robert.

6 Tell whether each of Robert's friends is taller, as tall as or shorter than he is. Use a form of the adjective **grand** in each of your comparisons.

Martine   Michèle   Laurent   Robert   Sandrine   Marc   Étienne   Renée

7 As you walk through the grocery store, comment on how the first items you see compare with the second ones. Use the appropriate form of the indicated adjective in each of your comparisons.

Modèle:

2,90 € le kilo   2,90 € le kilo

cher
Les cerises sont aussi chères que les fraises.

1. petit

2. beau

3. joli

4. frais

5. mûr

6. petit

1,52 € le kilo   4,42 € le kilo

7. cher

Communication

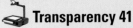

8 | You're planning a party for ten of your friends. Before you go grocery shopping, look at the supermarket ads that follow. Realizing that your friends don't all like to eat the same things and that you have only 25 euros to spend, write your shopping list. Be sure to specify the quantity of each item you plan to buy and its price. Then add up the total.

BEURRE PRESIDENT,
doux ou 1/2 sel,
le lot de 2 x 250 gr,
soit le kg : 4,48 €

2,24 €

Le lot

MOUTARDE DE DIJON
Amora
le verre T.V. de 195 g
soit le kg : 3,09 €

0,60 €

PAIN DE MIE SPECIAL SANDWICH
les 300 g soit le kg : 2,52 €

0,75 €

PIZZA CAPRICCIOSA
Marie
la pièce de 380 g soit le kg : 7,58 €

2,88 €

PECHES JAUNES
Cal. A - France
le kg

1,21 €

JAMBON ✻ SUPERIEUR BARBECUE A.C.
le kg

6,08 €

YAOURTS FRUITS
Montorval
les 8×125 g - 1 kg

1,52 €

**Workbook
Activity 18**

Listening Activity 3A

**Quiz
Leçon C**

**Computer Software
Activity 8**

Teacher's Note

You may want students to work in pairs as they answer the questions in Activity 10. Note that the first seven questions have specific answers. However, there is still some room for subjectivity. The last question is personalized. To answer questions 1 through 4, students should scan the reading for specific words. To answer questions 5 through 7, students may need to make use of some of the reading strategies they have learned in previous units: looking at the context of the reading, forming mental pictures and recognizing cognates. Encourage students to avoid translating the recipe into English and not to look up words they don't know. To holistically grade this activity, refer to the suggestions on page 162.

9 With a partner, play the roles of a person in charge of bringing a fruit salad to a family reunion and a merchant at an open-air market. The customer needs to buy enough of five kinds of fruits to make a salad for 25 people. In the course of your conversation:

1. The customer says that he or she would like some of five kinds of fruits and asks the prices.
2. The merchant tells the prices.
3. The customer comments that at least one of the fruits is too expensive.
4. The merchant gives at least one reason why that fruit is a good buy.
5. The customer complains about at least one of the fruits, saying that it is too ripe.
6. The merchant offers the customer a better price for that fruit.
7. The customer tells what he or she is going to buy and the quantity of each item.
8. The merchant totals the bill and the customer pays.

On peut trouver des fruits très frais au marché.

 Sur la bonne piste

When you read in French, your instinct probably tells you to translate all the words into English. Because you have been reading in English since you were very young, and because English has helped you understand many things, translation may appear to be a very appealing option. However, there is one big problem with translating a French reading into English: you have to know what every French word means! Translating while you read is like riding a bicycle with training wheels while competing in the **Tour de France**—you won't tip over or crash, but you'll never win the race. Right now it may seem risky to let your mind's bicycle speed down new terrain by thinking in French. You may get the urge to put on those training wheels and translate what you read. But eventually you'll discover that thinking in French, not translating into English, is the fastest, most comfortable and most effective way to read in French.

Try to think in French as you read the following salad recipe three times. Resist the temptation to translate it word for word into English. The information in the recipe will become clearer each time you read it.

NATIONAL STANDARDS
C1.1, C1.2, C3.1

Salade paysanne grecque

★

Pour 4 personnes. Préparation : 10 mn

- 4 grosses tomates fermes
- 16 olives noires de Kalamata
- 150 g de feta (fromage grec)
- 2 gros oignons frais
- 1/2 concombre
- 1 citron
- 4 cuil. à soupe d'huile d'olive
- 2 branches de basilic
- sel
- poivre

1. Lavez les tomates, épongez-les, coupez-les en quatre et recoupez chaque quartier en deux.

2. Pelez le concombre et coupez-le en rondelles. Pelez les oignons, coupez-les en rondelles et défaites celles-ci en anneaux.

3. Coupez la feta en petits cubes.

4. Pressez le citron. Salez et poivrez le jus obtenu. Ajoutez l'huile et mélangez avec une fourchette pour bien émulsionner la sauce.

5. Mélangez les tomates, le concombre, les oignons, les olives et le fromage dans un plat creux. Arrosez de sauce. Hachez le basilic avec des ciseaux, parsemez-en la salade et servez.

10 | Answer the following questions.

1. How long does it take to make this salad?
2. Should you buy green or black olives?
3. Do you need French cheese?
4. Which ingredients could you buy at a fruit and vegetable market? Which could you buy at a dairy store?
5. After you wash and dry the tomatoes, how should you cut them?
6. Should you grate the cheese?
7. What part of the lemon do you use?
8. Does this salad appeal to you? Why or why not?

Nathalie et Raoul

Answers

1. vrai
2. vrai
3. vrai
4. faux
5. faux
6. faux
7. faux
8. faux
9. vrai
10. faux

Teacher's Notes

Here is the English version of the cartoon on page 287: Mom, I'm going to go to the mall with Raoul. Say, do you want to go grocery shopping for me? You can buy a new pair of jeans. Here's the credit card. OK! That's cool! (Thirty minutes later . . . .) First, let's go to Benetton! Look, Raoul, there's a sale at Naf Naf! This pair of jeans is super! And this shirt . . . I love the color! When are we going to go grocery shopping for your mother? These boots are cheap! I'm going to buy them! And when are you going to buy the potatoes and green beans for your mother? Do you like my new clothes, Raoul? Hey, why are you looking at me like that? Where are the vegetables for your mother? Oh no!

C'est à moi!

Now that you have completed this unit, take a look at what you should be able to do in French. Can you do all of these tasks?

➤ I can ask for and give information about what someone can and wants to do.

➤ I can tell what I like.

➤ I can agree with someone.

➤ I can point out specific things.

➤ I can ask for permission.

➤ I can ask for, state and compare prices.

➤ I can make a complaint.

➤ I can insist on something.

➤ I can negotiate prices.

➤ I can choose and purchase various things.

Here is a brief checkup to see how much you understand about French culture. Decide if each statement is **vrai** or **faux**.

1. Marseille is France's oldest city and largest seaport.
2. Some well-known French foods are named after the provinces they come from: **quiche lorraine** comes from Lorraine and **bœuf bourguignon** is from Burgundy.
3. Regional specialties, such as **bouillabaisse** and **pâté de foie gras**, can be purchased in French grocery stores and ordered in restaurants.
4. French grocery stores rarely stock reduced-calorie or low-fat products since the French are well known for their heavy sauces and rich pastries.
5. The long, thin loaf of bread with the crisp crust that we often call "French bread" is called a **croissant** in French.
6. Camembert, Brie and Roquefort are three of the more than 300 different kinds of yogurt produced in France.

7. French teenagers drink as much milk as American teens do.
8. French people now do all of their grocery shopping in large supermarkets instead of going to small shops and markets.

Since French people generally drink more mineral water than Americans, they often buy enough for one or two weeks.

9. French supermarkets sell more bottled water and usually have a smaller variety of cold cereal than American supermarkets.
10. Because of its climate, Guadeloupe must buy most of its fresh fruits and vegetables from France.

Communication orale

With a partner, play the roles of a student who is planning to have a party to celebrate his or her friend's birthday and a grocer at the corner store. The student is going to order by phone several trays of party food and some beverages. During the course of your phone conversation, turn away from each other and talk as though you are on the phone.

1. The student dials the number of the grocery store, saying the numbers out loud in pairs.
2. The grocer answers the phone by saying hello and giving the name of the store.
3. The student identifies himself or herself and explains that he or she needs to buy some meat and cheese, fruits and vegetables, desserts and beverages for a party.
4. The grocer asks what day the party is.
5. The student gives the date of the party and then asks for the prices of specific items.
6. The grocer gives the prices.
7. The student orders the amount of the kinds of meat and cheese, fruits and vegetables, desserts and beverages that he or she wants.
8. The grocer gives the price of each item and then gives the total.
9. The student thanks the grocer and both say good-bye.

Communication écrite

Imagine that you are going to give a party to celebrate a special event. The first step in getting ready for your party is to design and write an invitation to send to your guests. On the invitation say that you're having a party and what special event you're celebrating. Be sure to mention what day and where the party is and at what time. Also include the foods and beverages you'll be serving. Remember to add RSVP and your name and phone number at the end of the invitation.

NATIONAL STANDARDS
C1.1, C1.2, C2.1

Communication active

To ask for information, use:

Qu'est-ce que tu veux manger ce soir? — *What do you want to eat tonight?*

Tu peux faire une bouillabaisse? — *Can you make fish soup?*

To give information, use:

Il veut toujours un fruit après le repas. — *He always wants (a piece of) fruit after a meal.*

Nous pouvons aussi aller à la charcuterie. — *We can also go to the delicatessen.*

To say what you like, use:

Moi, j'aime aussi le pâté. — *Me, I like pâté, too.*

To agree with someone, use:

OK. — *OK.*

Ouais. — *Yeah.*

To identify objects, use:

Je vais acheter **ces** tomates et **cet** oignon pour la soupe. — *I'm going to buy these tomatoes and this onion for the soup.*

To ask for permission, use:

Nous pouvons acheter des oranges aussi? — *Can we buy oranges, too?*

To ask for a price, use:

Combien coûte la pastèque? — *How much does the watermelon cost?*

Combien coûtent les melons? — *How much do the melons cost?*

Les carottes? Elles coûtent 1,84 euros le kilo. (Paris)

To state prices, use:

Ils/Elles coûtent 2,29 **euros** le kilo. — *They cost 2,29 euros per kilo.*

To compare prices, use:

Le fromage est **plus cher que** le beurre.
Cheese is more expensive than butter.

Les raisins sont **aussi chers que** les pastèques.
Grapes are as expensive as watermelons.

Les pommes sont **moins chères que** les cerises.
Apples are less expensive than cherries.

To make a complaint, use:

Les melons sont **déjà mûrs**.
The melons are already ripe.

Je trouve que c'est trop cher.
I think it's too expensive.

Les cerises sont déjà mûres.

To insist on something, use:

Si!
Yes!

To negotiate a price, use:

Est-ce que je peux acheter deux kilos de melons **pour 2,29 euros?**
May I buy two kilos of melons for 2,29 euros?

To choose and purchase items, use:

Je vais acheter trois kilos de bananes.
I am going to buy three kilos of bananas.

NATIONAL STANDARDS
C1.2, C4.1

Communication électronique

Communication électronique

1. The English equivalents are fruits and vegetables; delicatessen, butcher shop, catering; dairy; fish; pastry, cookies; desserts, sherbet, ice cream; and sweets, chocolates.
2. Answers may include margarine, deli ham, milk and bottled water.
3. They can be prepared in 15 to 20 minutes.
4. Answers may include salad and chicken.
5. Exotic foods may also come from India, Mexico, the Antilles (West Indies) and Réunion.
6. Answers will vary.

À moi de jouer!

Possible conversation:

— Bonjour, Mademoiselle. Vous désirez?

— Je voudrais des fruits. Est-ce que les poires sont bonnes aujourd'hui?

— Mais oui, Mademoiselle.

— Combien coûtent-elles, s'il vous plaît?

— Euh... 5,49 euros le kilo.

— Voyons... je trouve que ces poires sont trop mûres et un peu trop chères. Et les pommes, combien coûtent-elles?

— Elles sont moins chères que les poires. Elles coûtent 2,74 euros le kilo.

— Alors je vais acheter deux kilos de pommes et un kilo de haricots verts, s'il vous plaît.

— D'accord, Mademoiselle.

292

You've just learned about various French foods and grocery shopping in France. Now let's visit the French supermarket Monoprix! Go to this Internet site:

http://www.monoprix.com/il_y_a_quoi/marques/frame/index.htm

After exploring the site, answer the following questions.

1. First click on "Monoprix Gourmet." What are the English equivalents for the seven main sections of gourmet foods?
2. Return to the home page and click on "Monoprix bien vivre chaque jour." Look at the pictures. Which of these products does your local grocery store carry?
3. Return to the home page and click on "Monoprix Vite Prêt." How can these products revolutionize cooking?
4. What are several of the pictured items?
5. Return to the home page and click on "Monoprix Exotique." Foods in this department come from Asia and what other parts of the world?
6. Would you shop for groceries at this store? Why or why not?

À moi de jouer!

Show how much you have learned about shopping for produce in France by writing a dialogue with one of your classmates based on the scene on the right about shopping at an open-air market. One person plays the role of the shopper and the other plays the role of the vendor. In your dialogue, ask and give information about the produce, ask and give prices, compare prices and finally purchase some fruits and vegetables. (You may want to refer to the *Communication active* on pages 290-91 and the vocabulary list on page 293.)

Vocabulaire

	assez de enough
	attendre to wait (for)
	aussi as
une	**baguette** long, thin loaf of bread
une	**banane** banana
	beaucoup de a lot of, many
le	**beurre** butter
le	**bœuf** beef
une	**boîte** can
une	**boucherie** butcher shop
une	**bouillabaisse** fish soup
une	**boulangerie** bakery
une	**bouteille** bottle
le	**camembert** Camembert cheese
une	**carotte** carrot
	ce, cet, cette; ces this, that; these, those
une	**cerise** cherry
un	**champignon** mushroom
une	**charcuterie** delicatessen
	combien de how much, how many
la	**confiture** jam
les	**courses: faire les courses** to go grocery shopping
un	**crabe** crab
une	**crémerie** dairy store
une	**crevette** shrimp
un	**croissant** croissant
	d'abord first
	des any
	du some, any
	euh uhm
	faire les courses to go grocery shopping
une	**fraise** strawberry
un	**fruit** fruit
un	**gâteau** cake
des	**haricots verts (m.)** green beans
le	**ketchup** ketchup
un	**kilogramme (kilo)** kilogram
le	**lait** milk
un	**légume** vegetable
	maintenant now
	maman (f.) Mom
un(e)	**marchand(e)** merchant

un	**marché** market
le	**matin** in the morning
un	**matin** morning
la	**mayonnaise** mayonnaise
un	**melon** melon
	moins less
un	**morceau** piece
la	**moutarde** mustard
	mûr(e) ripe
un	**œuf** egg
un	**oignon** onion
	OK OK
	ouais yeah
le	**pain** bread
une	**pastèque** watermelon
le	**pâté** pâté
une	**pâtisserie** pastry store
une	**pêche** peach
des	**petits pois (m.)** peas
(un)	**peu de** (a) little, few
	plus more
une	**poire** pear
les	**pois (m.): des petits pois (m.)** peas
une	**pomme de terre** potato
le	**porc** pork
un	**pot** jar
un	**poulet** chicken
	pouvoir to be able to
	puis then
	que than, as, that
un	**repas** meal
le	**saucisson** salami
ce	**soir** tonight
la	**soupe** soup
un	**supermarché** supermarket
une	**tarte (aux fraises)** (strawberry) pie
la	**terre: une pomme de terre** potato
une	**tomate** tomato
	toujours always
une	**tranche** slice
	trop too
	trop de too much, too many
	vouloir to want
le	**yaourt** yogurt

Unité 9

À la maison

In this unit you will be able to:

➤ invite

➤ accept and refuse
   an invitation

➤ greet someone

➤ greet guests

➤ introduce someone else

➤ offer and accept a gift

➤ identify objects

➤ describe daily routines

➤ tell location

➤ express intentions

➤ agree and disagree

➤ offer food and beverages

➤ excuse yourself

NATIONAL STANDARDS
C2.1

Grammar & Vocabulary
Exercises 1-5

Audiocassette/CD
L'appartement, Les pièces

Teacher's Notes

1. Another word for an apartment building is **une résidence**. 2. **Le séjour** is the shortened form of **la salle de séjour**. 3. Communicative functions that are recycled in this lesson are "giving information" and "expressing likes and dislikes."

TPR

Home Furnishings

On a piece of paper make simple line drawings of all the furnishings that have been introduced in this lesson. On another piece of paper make a floor plan of a house or apartment. Make yourself an overhead transparency of each sheet. Also make copies for every student. Both you and your students cut out each piece of furniture on the first sheet. Then describe in French where each piece of furniture goes. As students listen to your directions, they place each piece of furniture in the appropriate spot on their floor plan. (You should do this also, placing your pieces of furniture on the overhead transparency that you will show the class at the end of the activity so students can check their work.)

NATIONAL STANDARDS
C1.2, C4.1

Leçon A

In this lesson you will be able to:

➤ **invite**

➤ **identify objects**

un appartement

un immeuble

un balcon

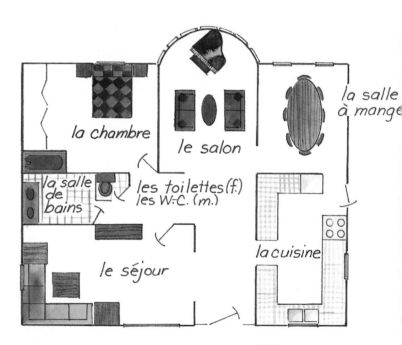

la chambre

le salon

la salle à manger

la salle de bains

les toilettes (f.)
les W.-C. (m.)

la cuisine

le séjour

les pièces (f.)

une photo
une lampe
une table
un tapis
un fauteuil
un canapé

une douche
un bureau
une chaise
une baignoire
une / armoire
une stéréo
un lit

un placard
une cuisinière
un évier
un micro-onde
un frigo
un four

Workbook Activities 1-3

Audiocassette/CD Furniture and Appliances

Transparencies 42-45

Teacher's Notes

1. **Un frigo** is the abbreviated form of **un réfrigérateur**. 2. **Un micro-onde** is the abbreviated form of **un four à micro-ondes**. 3. The following words have been introduced in earlier **unités: une fenêtre, une porte, une photo, une télé, un magnétoscope, un bureau, une chaise** and **une stéréo**. 4. Other related terms are **la moquette** (*wall-to-wall carpeting*), **le plancher** (*wood floor*), **le carrelage** (*tiled floor*), **une étagère** (*shelves*), **une bibliothèque** (*bookcase*), **une glace, un miroir** (*mirror*), **un piano** (*piano*), **des rideaux (m.)** (*curtains*), **une commode** (*chest of drawers*), **une radio** (*radio*), **une télécommande** (*remote control*), **un ascenseur** (*elevator*) and **des volets (m.)** (*shutters*).

Cooperative Group Practice

Qu'est-ce qu'il y a dans la maison?

Put students in small groups. Then combine groups so that two of them are working together. Each small group begins by finding a picture of a room that contains some of the items presented in this lesson. Next, small groups show their pictures to each other for 10-15 seconds. At the end of this time the pictures are turned face down. Each group works together to write a list of as many items from the picture as they can remember. After the lists are completed, students can check to see how closely their lists correspond to the pictured items.

NATIONAL STANDARDS
C1.2, C1.3, C4.1

297

Nadine Mairet is giving her parents a tour of her new apartment.

Nadine: Vous voulez faire le tour de mon appartement maintenant? Voici le salon. J'ai toujours votre vieux canapé, mais j'ai de nouveaux fauteuils.

Mme Mairet: Tu as aussi de belles photos de ton voyage en Espagne.

Nadine: Et voici la cuisine. J'ai même un micro-onde.

M. Mairet: Avec la chambre, la salle de bains et les W.-C., cet appartement est assez grand. Tu aimes bien habiter ici?

Nadine: Oui, pour moi, ça va bien.

GAGNEZ 15%

en achetant
1 canapé
+ 2 fauteuils
à partir de

~~1170 €~~

995 €

🔍 *Enquête culturelle*

It usually costs more to live in **le centre-ville** (*downtown*) of a French city than in **la banlieue** (*suburbs*). Many people reside in apartment buildings which surround **une cour** (*central courtyard*). They frequently purchase, rather than rent, their apartments. Single people often prefer living in a studio apartment, consisting of

PROCHE CENTRE VILLE
maison de 8 pièces, salon, sal[?]
à manger, séjour de famille,
cuisine, 5 chambres, 2 bains,
jardin agréable
PRIX : 240 869 €

Living in *le centre-ville* usually costs more than living in *la banlieue*. (Paris)

Memory Chain

Put your students in small groups of five or six and have them play this game to test their memories. The first student begins by naming an object in his or her bedroom. For example, **Dans ma chambre il y a un lit**. The second student repeats what the first student has said and adds one item in his or her bedroom. For example, **Dans ma chambre il y a un lit et un bureau**. The third student repeats what the first and second students have said and adds one more item, etc. For example, **Dans ma chambre il y a un lit, un bureau et une télé**. (Students with more limited abilities may want to write down each object as it is said.)

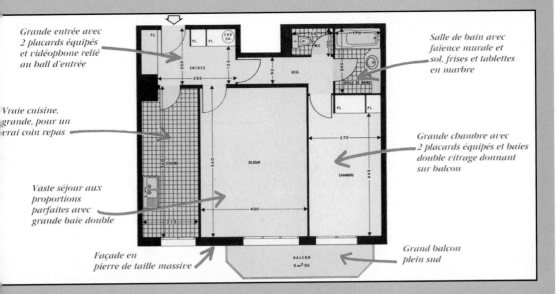

Grande entrée avec 2 placards équipés et vidéophone relié au hall d'entrée

Salle de bain avec faïence murale et sol, frises et tablettes en marbre

Vraie cuisine, grande, pour un vrai coin repas

Grande chambre avec 2 placards équipés et baies double vitrage donnant sur balcon

Vaste séjour aux proportions parfaites avec grande baie double

Façade en pierre de taille massive

Grand balcon plein sud

only a kitchenette, a main room and a bathroom. Even for a small studio apartment in the heart of a large city, the cost is high since rent is based on the apartment's location, not on its facilities. Apartment buildings are protected from both noise and intruders by an outer wall. To enter the buildings, residents often use a numbered security system rather than a key. They punch in a code number in a box which is installed near the front door.

Although some bedrooms have closets, many French people keep their clothes in a tall, free-standing piece of furniture called **une armoire**.

What do French teens have in their bedrooms? According to a recent survey, 100% have a desk and a lamp. Over 80% own a stereo, stuffed animals, books and posters. About 40% have a TV and video games. One in five French teens has a computer.

Annick, like almost half of all French teens, has a TV in her bedroom.

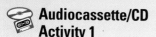

Audiocassette/CD Activity 1

Answers

1 1. Les parents de Nadine, M. et Mme Mairet, font le tour de l'appartement.
2. Le tour commence dans le salon.
3. Dans le salon il y a le vieux canapé de ses parents et de nouveaux fauteuils.
4. Non, elle a aussi des photos de son voyage en Espagne.
5. Dans la cuisine de Nadine il y a un micro-onde.
6. Il y a trois pièces dans l'appartement.
7. Non, l'appartement est assez grand.
8. Oui, elle aime bien son appartement.

Cooperative Group Practice

Survey

Have your students each make a grid. Across the top, have them write the names of five of their classmates; from top to bottom, have them write the names of ten objects that they might have in their bedrooms. Each student interviews the five classmates listed on his or her grid, asking each one if he or she has each of the indicated objects. (For example, **Robert, tu as une lampe?**) The interviewee responds accordingly. (For example, **Oui, j'ai une lampe./Non, je n'ai pas de lampe.**) Each student records his or her interviewees' answers on the grid and summarizes the results which he or she may be asked to share with the entire class.

The French *salle de bains* doesn't have a toilet.

Most French houses and apartments have two separate bathrooms. **La salle de bains** contains a bathtub, a sink, a bidet and a vanity. **Un bidet** is a small, toilet-shaped tub where you sit to take a sponge bath. Hand-operated showers are often attached to the bathtub faucet. Instead of a washcloth, people use **un gant de toilette** (*bath mitt*). The second bathroom, **les W.-C.**, is smaller and has only a toilet and a sink. **W.-C.** (often pronounced "vay-say") is the abbreviated form of "water closet," the British word for a bathroom. To ask to use a public bathroom, say **Où sont les toilettes, s'il vous plaît?**

Le bidet (between the sink and the tub) is used for personal hygiene.

When counting the rooms of a house or an apartment, the French do not include the bathroom.

In public places a variety of words may appear on restroom doors. The word **Hommes** or **Messieurs** or a picture of a man designates the men's restroom; the word **Femmes** or **Dames** or a picture of a woman shows which restroom is for women. You may also see the word **Toilettes** or **W.-C.**, which refers to facilities that may be used by either sex.

In public places the signs *Toilettes* and *W.-C.* indicate the restrooms.

MORIZET
agréable 3 pièces, 80 m2 environ, 2ème étage dans immeuble ravalé, entrée spacieuse, grand séjour ouvert sur balcon, 2 belles chambres, cuisine équipée, parking sous-sol
PRIX : 243 918 €

1 | *Répondez en français.*
1. Qui fait le tour de l'appartement de Nadine?
2. Où est-ce que le tour commence?
3. Qu'est-ce qu'il y a dans le salon?
4. Est-ce que Nadine a aussi des photos de son voyage en Allemagne?
5. Qu'est-ce qu'il y a dans la cuisine de Nadine?
6. Combien de pièces est-ce qu'il y a dans l'appartement?
7. Est-ce que l'appartement est petit?
8. Est-ce que Nadine aime son appartement?

2 *Trouvez dans la liste suivante le mot qui complète correctement chaque phrase.*

cuisine	séjour
chambre	photos
immeuble	fauteuils
magnétoscope	four
frigo	lampe

1. Nadine habite dans un appartement. Son appartement est dans un....
2. Il y a quatre... dans la pièce.
3. On trouve un micro-onde dans la....
4. Est-ce qu'il y a une vidéocassette dans le...?

A PARTIR DE
289,65 €
PAL/SECAM/MESECAM
PLUS DE 30 MAGNÉTOSCOPES

5. On regarde la télé au....
6. J'ai un grand lit dans ma....
7. Nous avons beaucoup de... de notre voyage en Italie.
8. J'aime lire, mais j'ai besoin d'une....
9. Maman fait un gâteau. Le gâteau est maintenant dans le....
10. Pierre veut du lait. Le lait est dans le....

K
34,91 €

K   Eclairage raffiné et classique pour cette lampe bougeoir à abat-jour plissé.
Pied en résine synthétique. Abat-jour coton. Haut. 50 cm. Ø 28 cm .
saumon 650.7719
bordeaux 650.7727
vert 651.1864
Prix   34,91 €

3 *C'est à toi!*

1. Est-ce que tu habites dans un appartement?
2. Qu'est-ce qu'il y a dans ton salon?
3. Dans quelle pièce est-ce que tu regardes la télé?
4. Où est-ce que ta famille mange?
5. Est-ce que ta famille a un micro-onde?
6. De quelle couleur est ta chambre?
7. Est-ce que tu as des affiches dans ta chambre?
8. Est-ce que tu as un bureau dans ta chambre?

La famille Dufresne mange dans leur cuisine.

Audiocassette/CD Activity 3

Answers

2 1. immeuble
   2. fauteuils
   3. cuisine
   4. magnétoscope
   5. séjour
   6. chambre
   7. photos
   8. lampe
   9. four
   10. frigo

3 Answers will vary.

Paired Practice

Chez moi

You might ask your students to pick one room in their real or imaginary house or apartment and make a drawing of it, labeling in French as many items as they can. To expand this activity, you might put students in pairs after they have made their drawings. Students should not show their drawings to each other. Student A begins by describing his or her room and furnishings to Student B. Student B has a blank sheet of paper and draws the room and furnishings as Student A describes them. For example, **La lampe est sur la table**. Then students reverse roles. At the end of the activity, students compare their drawings with their partners'.

NATIONAL STANDARDS
C1.1, C1.2, C3.2

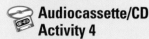
Workbook
Activity 5

Grammar & Vocabulary
Exercises 6-7

Audiocassette/CD
Activity 4

Computer Software
Activity 1

Answers

4 1. Les Ramos ont de
   nouvelles tables.
   2. Les Ramos ont de
   nouveaux tapis.
   3. Les Ramos ont de
   nouveaux fauteuils.
   4. Les Ramos ont de
   nouvelles chaises.
   5. Les Ramos ont de
   nouveaux canapés.
   6. Les Ramos ont de
   nouvelles armoires.

Teacher's Notes

1. In colloquial French it is not
uncommon to hear **des** before a
plural adjective that precedes a
noun. 2. You may point out to
students that **de** becomes **d'**
before an adjective beginning
with a vowel sound.

Cooperative Group Practice

Scrambled Sentences

Write a series of scrambled sentences on an overhead transparency.
Each sentence should be composed
of a subject, verb, plural adjective
and plural noun. It should not include **des** or **de (d')**. (For example,
belles/avoir/photos/tu.) Put students in small groups and have
them unscramble each sentence
as you uncover it on the transparency. Students can either say the
reordered sentence including **des**,
de or **d'** or write it out.

NATIONAL STANDARDS
C1.1, C1.2, C4.1

302

Structure

De + plural adjectives

Des becomes **de** before most plural adjectives that precede a noun.

Tu as toujours **de** vieilles chaises?	*Do you still have (some) old chairs?*
Oui, mais j'ai **de** nouvelles lampes.	*Yes, but I have (some) new lamps.*

When an adjective that precedes a noun is an inseparable part of that noun, **des** does not become **de** or **d'**.

Je voudrais **des** petits pois.	*I would like (some) peas.*

Remember to use **des** before a noun whose plural adjective comes afterward.

On va acheter **des** légumes frais.	*We're going to buy (some) fresh vegetables.*

Pratique

4 Last week the Ramos family went shopping for new furniture. As each delivery truck arrives at their house, tell what new things they have.

Modèle:

Les Ramos ont de nouvelles lampes.

1.

4.

2.

5.

3.

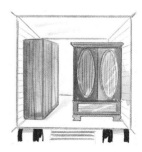
6.

Voilà de nouveaux vêtements. (Angers)

Nadine likes old things, and her favorite color is green. Tell what old or green items there are in her apartment.

1. Dans la salle de bains il y a....
2. Dans la cuisine il y a....
3. Dans la chambre il y a....

Modèle:

Dans le salon il y a de vieux fauteuils, de vieux tapis et des tables vertes.

Communication

6 Charles is going to move into his first apartment and is trying to find some inexpensive furniture. He made a list of everything he needs (on the left). His mother made a list of the things the family has but no longer needs (on the right). With a partner, play the roles of Charles and his mother. Charles tells his mother each item he needs and asks for it. Then his mother tells him whether or not he can have it.

J'ai besoin d'....

un fauteuil
une chaise
un lit
une stéréo
une table
un tapis
un micro-onde
un canapé
une lampe
un magnétoscope

On a....

un fauteuil noir
un bureau
une petite table
une télé
un frigo
une lampe
une vieille armoire

Modèles:

Charles: J'ai besoin d'un fauteuil. Est-ce qu'on a un fauteuil?
Maman: Oui, tu peux avoir le fauteuil noir.

Charles: J'ai besoin d'une chaise. Est-ce qu'on a une chaise?
Maman: Non, on n'a pas de chaise.

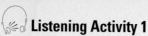
7 After you and your partner have completed Activity 6, make a list of the items that Charles needs to buy, based on what his family can't furnish.

8 Imagine that you and a friend are going to move into your own apartment. You've saved up 990 euros to spend on furniture. The store where you are going to shop is advertising certain specials. Using the store's ads, make a list of each item you are going to purchase along with its price. Then total your purchases, remembering not to exceed your limit.

la table ronde avec allonge

E À PARTIR DE
227,15 €
LA TABLE + 4 CHAISES

le fauteuil
205,81 €

le tapis à partir de
89,94 €

le meuble TV Hi-Fi
à partir de
144,83 €

**STOP
AFFAIRE**
le lit à partir de
151,69 €

STOP
AFFAIRE
l'armoire à partir de
303,37 €

STOP
AFFAIRE
à partir de
151,69 €

VALEUR SÛRE

simple caisson en pin naturel ou laqué

le canapé à partir de
288,13 €

Prononciation

The sound [ə]

The vowel **e** without an accent mark is pronounced [ə] when it comes at the end of a one-syllable word, such as **de, je** or **le**.

It is also pronounced [ə] when it appears at the end of the first syllable in a word of more than one syllable. Say each of these words:

fenêtre	cerise
premier	devant
crevette	besoin

Silent "e"

The vowel **e** without an accent mark is usually silent, that is, unpronounced, when it comes at the end of a word containing more than two letters, such as **pièce, salle** or **immeuble**.

It is also silent when it appears after the first syllable of certain words and before the last one. Say each of these words:

maintenant	médecin
acheter	vêtements
omelette	boucherie

Teacher's Note

The word **appartement** is an exception to this rule since the first **e** is pronounced [ə].

NATIONAL STANDARDS
C1.2, C2.2, C3.2, C4.1

**Workbook
Activity 6**

**Grammar & Vocabulary
Exercises 8-10**

Audiocassette/CD
La maison

Leçon B

In this lesson you will be able to:

➤ **invite**

➤ **accept and refuse an invitation**

➤ **greet someone**

➤ **greet guests**

➤ **introduce someone else**

➤ **offer and accept a gift**

➤ **excuse yourself**

➤ **offer food and beverages**

NATIONAL STANDARDS
C1.2, C4.1

Monsieur and Madame Poitras have invited their new neighbors, Monsieur and Madame Giraud, to their home for dinner.

Mme Poitras:	**Bonsoir, Monsieur. Bonsoir, Madame. Bienvenue! Je vous présente mon mari, Raymond. Raymond, Anne-Marie et Étienne Giraud.**
M. Giraud:	**Enchanté. Bonsoir, Monsieur. Voici des fleurs, Madame.**
Mme Poitras:	**Oh, que vous êtes gentils! Raymond, prends le vase rouge, s'il te plaît. Il est sur la table.**
M. Poitras:	**Bien sûr. Entrez donc, allons au salon.**
Mme Poitras:	**Euh..., pardon, j'ai encore quelques petites choses à faire dans la cuisine. Prenez des chips. Vous voulez un jus de fruit?**
Mme Giraud:	**Oui, je veux bien.**

Every region of France has its unique style of house that is constructed with building materials from that region. In the northern part of the country, many houses have stone or brick exteriors. In Normandy, dark wooden trim commonly decorates white stucco dwellings with sloped roofs. In Brittany, even contemporary houses sometimes have thatched roofs that resemble those of

Enquête culturelle

A typical characteristic of houses in Normandy is white stucco decorated with dark wooden trim in an "X" shape.

Workbook Activities 7-9

 Audiocassette/CD Dialogue

Teacher's Notes

1. To greet guests, you might also say **Entrez, je vous en prie, Asseyez-vous** or **Ça me fait plaisir de vous voir**. 2. You may want to review with your students the informal introductions that were presented in **Unité 1**. 3. Another common expression for excusing oneself is the more formal **Je vous prie de m'excuser**. A typical response is **Il n'y a pas de mal** or the more formal **Je vous en prie**. Some people believe that **Je m'excuse** is inappropriate because you cannot excuse yourself; it is up to the other person to excuse you. Nevertheless, this expression is commonly used in everyday speech. When you are excusing yourself for something you have done, you may say **Je suis désolé(e)**, which corresponds closely to "I'm sorry." Possible responses are **Ce n'est rien, Ce n'est pas grave, Ne vous en faites pas** or **Ne t'en fais pas**. A polite way to correct someone who has made an error is to say **Je regrette**. (For example, in talking to a server at a restaurant, you might say **Je regrette, mais ce n'est pas l'addition pour notre table**.) Saying **Je regrette** also implies that the listener might not be happy to hear the information that follows. 4. To ask your guests what refreshments they would like to have, you may also use the expressions **Qu'est-ce que vous voulez boire?** or **Qu'est-ce que je vous offre?** As you place food on the table, you may say to your guests **Servez-vous**.

NATIONAL STANDARDS
C1.2, C2.1, C4.2

homes from the past. In the south of France, awnings as well as flat roofs made of reddish orange tiles protect houses from the hot sun. Two especially distinctive French styles of houses are the **chalet alpin**, a cottage in the Alps, and the **mas provençal,** a picturesque farmhouse in the Provence region of southern France.

Alpine chalets have a distinctive shape and a long, flower-covered balcony.

The first or ground floor of a building in French-speaking countries is called **le rez-de-chaussée**. The floor directly above is **le premier étage**, and the next floor is **le deuxième étage**. Beneath **le rez-de-chaussée**, families store wine and other beverages and food items in **la cave** (*cellar*).

More French people own vacation homes than any other national group. Often this home is located in the region of the country where the family comes from originally. Many of these homes have been passed down from generation to generation. Other people buy vacation apartments on one of the French coasts. Many city dwellers tolerate holiday and weekend traffic jams to spend time at their vacation home.

It's appropriate to take a bouquet of cut flowers when you're invited to a French home for dinner.

You've already learned that when you are invited to someone's home for a meal in a French-speaking country, you should bring a small gift for your hosts. Most guests bring flowers or have them sent the following day. However, don't choose chrysanthemums! They are appropriate only at funerals.

In French-speaking countries, **les apéros** is a general term used to refer to many kinds of small crackers (**les biscuits salés**), chips (**les chips**) and other snacks which are served to guests before a meal. Small quantities of these snacks are put in little bowls or on tiny plates for guests to munch on.

1 Reread the conversation between the Poitras and Giraud families. Then answer the following questions, telling who does what.

1. Qui est à la porte des Poitras?
2. Qui présente son mari?
3. Qui a des fleurs pour M. et Mme Poitras?
4. Qui est gentil?
5. Qui va chercher le vase rouge?
6. Qui invite M. et Mme Giraud à aller au salon?
7. Qui a quelques petites choses à faire dans la cuisine?
8. Qui veut un jus de fruit?

2 Tell exactly where certain people or things are in or around the house, depending on what's happening.

1. M. Bouchard présente M. Duval à sa femme.
2. Le petit oiseau est dans l'arbre.
3. Hervé écoute un CD.
4. La famille mange ensemble.
5. Nathalie trouve les vieux vêtements de sa grand-mère.
6. Les enfants regardent la télé.
7. Le chat est sous la voiture.

Modèle:

Denise a faim.
Denise est dans la cuisine.

Les chats sont sur le fauteuil. Donc, ils sont dans le salon.

3 *C'est à toi!*

1. Est-ce que tu habites dans une maison ou dans un appartement?
2. Quelles pièces est-ce qu'il y a dans ta maison ou ton appartement?
3. Combien de chambres est-ce qu'il y a dans ta maison ou ton appartement?
4. Est-ce que ta maison ou ton appartement a un balcon?
5. Est-ce que ta maison ou ton appartement a un garage?
6. Est-ce que tu as une voiture?
7. À qui est-ce que tu donnes des fleurs?
8. Est-ce que tu manges souvent des chips?

La famille Aknouch a une nouvelle voiture. (La Rochelle)

Answers

1 1. M. et Mme Giraud sont à la porte des Poitras.
2. Mme Poitras présente son mari.
3. M. Giraud a des fleurs pour M. et Mme Poitras.
4. M. et Mme Giraud sont gentils.
5. M. Poitras va chercher le vase rouge.
6. M. Poitras invite M. et Mme Giraud à aller au salon.
7. Mme Poitras a quelques petites choses à faire dans la cuisine.
8. Mme Giraud veut un jus de fruit.

2 Possible answers:
1. M. Bouchard est dans l'entrée.
2. Le petit oiseau est dans le jardin.
3. Hervé est dans sa chambre.
4. La famille est dans la salle à manger.
5. Nathalie est dans le grenier.
6. Les enfants sont dans le séjour.
7. Le chat est dans le garage.

3 Answers will vary.

 **NATIONAL STANDARDS**
C1.1, C1.2

Workbook
Activity 10

Grammar & Vocabulary
Exercises 11–14

Audiocassette/CD
Activity 4

Computer Software
Activity 2

Answers

4 1. Clémence prend du poisson.
2. Je prends du poisson.
3. Abdou prend du bœuf.
4. Florence et moi, nous prenons du poisson.
5. Cécile et Sébastien prennent du bœuf.
6. Tu prends du bœuf.
7. Alexandre et Karine prennent du poisson.
8. Benjamin et toi, vous prenez du bœuf.

Teacher's Notes

1. You may want to point out the nasal sound [ã] in the singular forms, the non-nasal sound [ə] in **prenons** and **prenez**, and the non-nasal sound [ɛ] in **prennent**.
2. You may also want to point out that the singular forms of **prendre** are like those of regular **-re** verbs. There is no **d** in the irregular plural forms. 3. Tell students that partitive articles are often used after the forms of **prendre**. 4. The verb **emmener**, not **prendre**, is used to express the idea of taking someone somewhere. For example, **Tu emmènes les enfants à l'école?** You may also want to tell students that **passer** or **avoir**, not **prendre**, is used to express the idea of taking a test. For example, **Je passe/J'ai une interro**. To express the idea of passing a test, use the expression **réussir à**.

NATIONAL STANDARDS
C1.1, C1.2, C4.1

310

Claire prend une chemise de son armoire. (Strasbourg)

Modèles:

Florence
Florence prend du poisson.

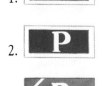

Benjamin
Benjamin prend du bœuf.

Structure

Present tense of the irregular verb *prendre*

The verb **prendre** (*to take*) is irregular. Note that it can also mean "to have" when referring to something to eat or drink.

prendre			
je	**prends**	Je **prends** la voiture.	*I'm taking the car.*
tu	**prends**	Tu **prends** des photos?	*Are you taking (some) pictures?*
il/elle/on	**prend**	Il **prend** le vase rouge.	*He takes the red vase.*
nous	**prenons**	Nous **prenons** des chips.	*We're having (some) snacks.*
vous	**prenez**	Qu'est-ce que vous **prenez**?	*What are you having?*
ils/elles	**prennent**	Ils **prennent** du café.	*They're having (some) coffee.*

The **d** is pronounced [t] in the inverted forms of **il/elle/on**:
Prend-on une glace?
　　[t]

Pratique

4 At Ariane and Raoul's wedding dinner, the guests have a choice of fish or beef. Tell what the people at your table are having to eat.

1.  Clémence　　　5. Cécile et Sébastien

2. je　　　6. tu

3.  Abdou　　　7. Alexandre et Karine

4. Florence et moi　　　8. Benjamin et toi

Audiocassette/CD Activities 5-6

5 You and your relatives are meeting in La Rochelle for a family reunion. Tell whether or not certain people are driving there, based on what you see.

1. ma belle-sœur

2. ma grand-mère et mon grand-père

3. je

4. mon oncle Raoul

5. ma sœur et sa fille

6. mon père, ma belle-mère et moi

Modèles:

ma tante Élise
Ma tante Élise prend la voiture.

mon cousin Laurent et sa femme
Mon cousin Laurent et sa femme ne prennent pas la voiture.

La Rochelle, en Charente-Maritime, est un port sur l'Atlantique.

Answers

5 1. Ma belle-sœur prend la voiture.
2. Ma grand-mère et mon grand-père ne prennent pas la voiture.
3. Je prends la voiture.
4. Mon oncle Raoul ne prend pas la voiture.
5. Ma sœur et sa fille ne prennent pas la voiture.
6. Mon père, ma belle-mère et moi, nous prenons la voiture.

6 Vous prenez le porc ou le bœuf?
Vous prenez les petits pois ou les carottes?
Vous prenez le fromage ou le yaourt?
Vous prenez le gâteau ou la glace?
Student B's responses to these questions will vary.

6 With a partner, play the roles of a server in a restaurant and a customer who has ordered a meal at a fixed price. Student A, the server, asks Student B, the customer, what he or she wants to have for each course.

Menu à 15 euros

pâté ou salade de tomates
porc ou bœuf
petits pois ou carottes
fromage ou yaourt
gâteau ou glace

Modèle:
Student A: Vous prenez le pâté ou la salade de tomates?
Student B: Je prends la salade de tomates.

Les enfants prennent le bœuf. (Urcuit)

Cooperative Group Practice

Packing List

Put your students in small groups. Have each student choose a country that he or she would like to visit and the season in which he or she would like to travel. Then each student names the country and the season and says what clothing he or she is taking. For example, **Je vais en Italie cet été. Je prends des tee-shirts, des shorts, des jupes et des chaussures.** Finally, another student in that group repeats what the first student has said. (**Monique va en Italie cet été. Elle prend des tee-shirts, des shorts, des jupes et des chaussures.**)

NATIONAL STANDARDS
C1.1, C1.2, C1.3

Workbook
Activities 11-13

Grammar & Vocabulary
Exercises 15-17

Audiocassette/CD
Activity 7

Computer Software
Activity 3

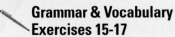
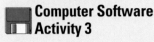

Answers

7 1. Donnez vos blousons à ma belle-mère!
2. Allez au salon!
3. Parlez avec tout le monde!
4. Mangez des chips!
5. Prenez des boissons!
6. Écoutez mes nouveaux CDs!
7. Dansez!

Teacher's Notes

1. You may want to review with your students the differences between **tu** and **vous**. 2. Point out to students that **ne** becomes **n'** before a verb beginning with a vowel sound. 3. You may want to tell students that the verb **avoir** has irregular imperative forms: **Aie! Ayez! Ayons!** The verb **être** also has irregular imperative forms: **Sois! Soyez! Soyons!** (**Soyez les bienvenus!** is another way to say "Welcome!")

TPR

Les ordres

If you have pictures or flash cards of the items in a home or apartment that were introduced in **Leçon A**, display them for all students to see. Then give commands to individual students that use these visuals. For example, **Anne, prends la table!** and **Donne la table à Jérôme!** Students demonstrate comprehension by manipulating the visuals as directed.

NATIONAL STANDARDS
C1.1, C1.2, C4.1

312

Achetez de nouvelles chaussettes!

Modèle:

entrer
Entrez!

The imperative

Imperative verb forms are used to give commands and make suggestions. Each French verb has three imperative forms whose subjects are understood to be **tu, vous** and **nous.** These subjects, however, are not used with commands. Compare the following present tense forms of the verb **étudier** with their corresponding commands.

Present Tense	Imperative	
tu étudies	**Étudie!**	*Study!*
vous étudiez	**Étudiez!**	*Study!*
nous étudions	**Étudions!**	*Let's study!*

As you can see, the **nous** and **vous** imperative forms of verbs ending in **-er** are exactly the same as their corresponding present tense forms. However, the **tu** imperative form does not end in **-s.**

The imperative forms of verbs ending in **-ir** and **-re** are exactly the same as their corresponding present tense forms: **Finis! Finissez! Finissons!** and **Vends! Vendez! Vendons!**

The **nous** form of the imperative is used to make a suggestion and means "Let's + *verb*."

Form the negative imperative by putting **ne** before the verb and **pas** after the verb.

Ne va **pas** chez les Giraud!   *Don't go to the Girauds!*

Pratique

7 As guests arrive at your party, make sure they have a good time by telling them to do the following things.

1. donner vos blousons à ma belle-mère
2. aller au salon
3. parler avec tout le monde
4. manger des chips
5. prendre des boissons
6. écouter mes nouveaux CDs
7. danser

Prends du gâteau!

8 Based on what Marcel tells you, advise him to do or not to do certain things.

1. J'ai soif. (prendre de l'eau)
2. Je n'aime pas les fast-foods. (manger au Quick)
3. Je veux acheter un nouveau jean. (faire les magasins)
4. Il y a des soldes. (acheter ce pull)
5. J'ai beaucoup de vidéocassettes. (vendre le magnétoscope)
6. Je ne veux pas danser. (aller en boîte)
7. Je n'aime pas le rock. (écouter le reggae)
8. Il pleut. (entrer donc)

Modèles:

Il y a une interro demain. (étudier)
Alors, étudie!

Je n'ai pas faim. (finir le dessert)
Alors, ne finis pas le dessert!

Vous voulez danser? Alors, allez en boîte!

9 For each place you and your friends go to this weekend, suggest one thing to do there.

1. la maison de Jean-Christophe
2. le centre commercial
3. le fast-food
4. le grand magasin
5. la pâtisserie
6. le cinéma
7. la boum de Sylvie
8. le café

Modèle:

la boîte
Dansons!

Dansons!

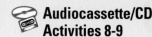 **Audiocassette/CD**
Activities 8-9

Answers

8 1. Alors, prends de l'eau!
  2. Alors, ne mange pas au Quick!
  3. Alors, fais les magasins!
  4. Alors, achète ce pull!
  5. Alors, ne vends pas le magnétoscope!
  6. Alors, ne va pas en boîte!
  7. Alors, écoute le reggae!
  8. Alors, entre donc!

9 Answers will vary.

Cooperative Group Practice

Forming Commands

So that students can practice giving commands, put them in small groups. First, have each student in the group make five note cards, each of which contains an infinitive and **tu, nous** or **vous**. Have all group members combine their cards. Then each student takes one card at random and makes an appropriate command using these two elements plus any other additional words, for example, **étudier/nous — Étudions le français ce soir**! To vary this activity, you can tell students to add **ne... pas** to the bottom of two of their note cards in order to make negative commands. When students have completed this activity, they can exchange note cards with another group and begin forming commands again.

NATIONAL STANDARDS
C1.1, C1.2

Answers

12 Possible answers:

1. ch.
2. sdb
3. cuis.
4. RdC
5. dche
6. imm.
7. 1ᵉʳ ét.
8. gge
9. pces
10. s/sol
11. séj.

Communication

10 Imagine the house or apartment of your dreams! On a separate sheet of paper, draw the floor plan of your ideal residence, labeling all the rooms in French. It may have one or two floors. Then choose any room in this house or apartment and make a larger drawing of it on another piece of paper, adding whatever you would buy to decorate and furnish the room. You may either draw the decorations and furniture or find pictures of them in back issues of magazines to cut out and attach to your drawing.

11 After you have completed the drawing of your ideal house or apartment, write a paragraph in French describing it. Also write about the specific room you chose to draw in detail, mentioning what decorations and furniture are in it. You may also want to tell the colors of various items.

12 In reading the classified ads for houses and apartments in French newspapers, you notice that many of the names of rooms and related expressions are abbreviated. Write one abbreviation used for each of the expressions that follow.

> 11ᵉ REPUBLIQUE: très bel imm., grd, 2 pces 42m², cuis. 108.238 €

> Réf 410 - BLANC-MESNIL - Appt F4, à rénov., entrée, cuis., séj., 3 chbres, sdb, wc, cft, cave, gar. + park. priv. 85.371 €

> 30m Paris Nord, pavillon 4 pièces, cuisine, RdC douche wc, 1ᵉʳ ét. bains wc, 508m² terrain, s/sol cave 94.518 €

> GAGNY pr. ctre. Pav. Ind. 300m² de terr., s/sol tot. av. cuis. d'été + chem., dche, wc, cave. RdC: dble séj. + chem. sur terrasse, cuis. amén., 1 ch., bureau, SdB + wc. Etage: 3 ch., cab. de toil., wc, plac. gge 2 voit. A saisir 131.106 €

1. chambre
2. salle de bains
3. cuisine
4. rez-de-chaussée
5. douche
6. immeuble
7. premier étage
8. garage
9. pièces
10. sous-sol
11. séjour

Workbook Activity 14

**Transparency 46**

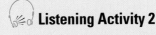**Listening Activity 2**

Now that you know how French classified ads in the real estate section look, write your own ad in French for the house or appartment of your dreams that you designed and described in Activities 10 and 11. Remember to use appropriate abbreviations as seen in Activity 12.

Meals play an important part in a French person's day. He or she can relax and talk with family and friends, enjoy well-prepared food served on a beautifully set table and observe dining customs that have been handed down from generation to generation.

Mise au point sur... les repas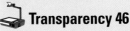

Paired Practice

Apartment Search

After students have written their own classified ads, post each one along with the student's name on the bulletin board. Students can examine the ads and choose the two that sound the most appealing. For each house or apartment a student is interested in, he or she will find the owner and interview him or her by asking a series of questions, including where the house or apartment is located, how many rooms it has, its price, when it is available, when it can be seen, etc.

Breakfast **(le petit déjeuner)** is often a light meal. At home, adults usually have coffee, coffee with milk **(le café au lait)** or tea **(le thé)**. Children drink fruit juices or hot chocolate **(le chocolat chaud)**. Although some French people choose to eat a bowl of cereal in the morning, most of them prefer to cut crusty **baguettes** into thick slices and cover them with butter and jam. Other choices include dry toast **(les biscottes)** and toasted bread **(le pain grillé)**. Occasionally, perhaps on Sunday mornings, one member of the family goes to the bakery for fresh **croissants**. Since warm beverages are usually served in large, deep bowls, many people like to dip their bread in their coffee or hot chocolate when they are at home. People who have breakfast at a hotel eat either in their room or in a small dining area. The usual hotel breakfast consists of part of a **baguette**, a **croissant**, butter, jam and a beverage.

Laurier d'Or
de la Qualité et de la Tradition Boulangère

COPALINE

COPALINE
LA BAGUETTE DU CHEF

KRISPROLLS®
pogen Pains Grillés Suédois

Bread usually comes with butter only at breakfast.

Lunch **(le déjeuner)** is still the largest meal of the day when families are able to get together. In the past, families gathered at home for the noon meal. Today, however, many women work outside of the home, students eat at school or at cafés, and businesses in urban areas remain open over the noon hour. Therefore, families usually reserve long lunches for weekends and special occasions.

NATIONAL STANDARDS
C1.1, C1.3, C2.1, C2.2, C3.1, C4.2, C5.1

Cooperative Group Practice

Venez chez nous!

Put your students in pairs and have them imagine that they are Monsieur and Madame Poitras (from the dialogue at the beginning of this lesson). The Poitras are inviting Monsieur and Madame Giraud to their home for dinner. Each pair of students will design, write and decorate the Poitras' invitation, telling the occasion, the date, the time, what will be served, the address and the telephone number. You may want to post each pair's invitation for all students to see.

Qu'est-ce que tu prends?

Put your students in small groups and have them open their textbooks to any restaurant menu. Have students take turns ordering what they would like from the menu, using the verb **prendre**. For example, **Je prends un sandwich au jambon, une limonade et une glace au chocolat, s'il vous plaît.** Then have another student in the group repeat what the first student has said. For example, **Laurent prend un sandwich au jambon, une limonade et une glace au chocolat.**

Since the French usually don't eat dinner until 7:30 or 8:00 P.M., students often enjoy a small snack (**le goûter**) after school. Rather than just grabbing food from the cupboard or refrigerator, teenagers often stop for something sweet at a **pâtisserie** or sit down at home or at a café for a bite to eat and a beverage.

Families often spend time during the evening meal, **le dîner**, discussing what they did during the day. A typical main meal, either lunch or dinner, may last several hours and consists of various courses. First of all comes an

hors-d'œuvre, such as soup, **crudités** or **pâté**, or an **entrée**, such as a small slice of quiche. Then the main dish (**le plat principal**), usually meat and vegetables, is served. A salad of lettuce mixed with vinegar and oil dressing (**vinaigrette**) usually follows the main course, although sometimes the salad may be served before or with the main course. Different kinds of cheeses are offered next; each person takes just a small portion of his or her favorites. A dessert, such as fruit, ice cream or pastries, tops off the meal.

Snails, *les escargots*, are a popular entrée.

A bottle of water or mineral water accompanies most meals. Children sometimes drink fruit juices or soft drinks; adults often drink wine. Coffee is served at the end of the meal.

Fresh bread accompanies every meal. Instead of being sliced, bread is usually broken into individual pieces and served in a basket. Bread plates are generally used only in elegant restaurants; at home, each person puts his or her bread right on the table.

Cheese and fruit are served at the end of a meal.

A beautiful table setting enhances the presentation of the food. Fresh flowers often serve as a centerpiece. Most families use cloth napkins. Each family member has his or her own napkin which may be kept in a napkin ring or a cloth holder.

French families have adopted certain eating habits and traditions that have been passed on from one generation to the next. They set the table differently in France than in the United States. Teaspoons or dessert forks go horizontally above the plate, and forks and spoons are turned face down. French silverware is slightly larger and heavier than American silverware. For formal meals the French use different dishes for each course. They usually cut and eat each piece of meat separately, keeping the fork, tines down, in the left hand. They even scoop up vegetables, such as peas, on the fork. Instead of leaving one hand in their lap, they keep both hands above or resting on the table during the meal.

The French use a tablecloth and napkins even for ordinary meals at home. (Paris)

At the end of the meal, they place the fork and knife horizontally across the plate.

French cooking is famous throughout the world, and the opportunity to relax and talk at the table, the presentation of the food and the chance to maintain family traditions are as important to the French as a well-prepared meal.

---

4 Answer the following questions.

1. What is a typical French breakfast for an adult?
2. When French people eat breakfast at home, how do they serve warm beverages?
3. What is a typical French breakfast served at a hotel?
4. When is lunch still the largest meal of the day?
5. At what time do most French people eat their evening meal?
6. At a French dinner, what might be served as an **hors-d'œuvre**?
7. What is the French expression for the main course of a meal?
8. What are two desserts that might be served in France?
9. What kind of napkins do the French use?
10. How is a French table setting different from a table setting in the United States?
11. Do the French switch the fork from one hand to the other while eating?
12. How can you tell that someone has finished eating in France?

A typical French breakfast is a *baguette*, butter, jam and coffee.

NATIONAL STANDARDS
C2.1, C4.2

Answers

15 1. Dinner is the larger of the two meals.
    2. This flight arrives in Paris in the morning.

In the first meal:

    1. The first course is a green salad.
    2. The two choices for the main course are filet mignon and shrimp.
    3. Vegetables are served with either main course.
    4. The dessert is ice cream.

In the second meal:

    1. Fruit juices are offered.
    2. Butter and jam accompany the pastries.

15 Look at the menus from an international flight between the United States and France. Answer the questions that follow.

DÎNER

Salade verte de saison
avec sauce "Caesar"

•

Plats Principaux

Filet mignon
sauce chutney à la mangue

Crevettes à la creole
avec jalapeno et riz à la coriandre

Servis avec des légumes sélectionnés

•

Glace

PETIT-DÉJEUNER

Avant votre arrivée nous avons le plaisir
de vous offrir des jus de fruits rafraîchis,
la pâtisserie du jour, confiture et beurre.

---

1. Which is the larger of the two meals that are served on this flight?
2. Based on the order in which the two meals are served, at approximately what time of day does this flight arrive in Paris?

In the first meal:
    1. What is the first course?
    2. What are the two choices for the main course?
    3. What is served with either main course?
    4. What is the dessert?

In the second meal:
    1. What beverages are offered?
    2. What accompanies the pastries?

NATIONAL STANDARDS
C1.2, C2.1, C3.2, C4.2

le couvert

le poivre   le sel   un bol   une nappe   un verre   une tasse   une cuiller   une serviette   le sucre   un couteau   une fourchette   une assiette

La fourchette est à gauche de l'assiette.
Le couteau est à droite de l'assiette.
La cuiller est au-dessus de l'assiette.

le petit déjeuner   le déjeuner

le goûter   le dîner

Leçon C

In this lesson you will be able to:

➤ **express intentions**

➤ **describe daily routines**

➤ **tell location**

➤ **agree and disagree**

 Workbook Activity 15

 Grammar & Vocabulary Exercises 18-21

 Audiocassette/CD *Le couvert, Les repas*

Transparencies 47-48

Teacher's Notes

1. Tell your students that the expression "to set the table" is either **mettre la table** or **mettre le couvert**. 2. Point out to students that **couteau** forms its plural by adding an **x**. 3. Another spelling for **cuiller** is **cuillère**. 4. Another related term is **la soucoupe** (*saucer*). 5. In Quebec, breakfast is called **le déjeuner**, lunch is called **le dîner** and dinner is called **le souper**. Dinner is also called **le souper** in Switzerland. 6. A communicative function that is recycled in this lesson is "asking for information."

Cooperative Group Practice

On met la table.

Put students in four groups. The first three groups are competing teams, and the fourth group serves as judges. In three corners of the classroom have the three teams each create the most attractive table setting that they can imagine. Everything should be in its proper place, and students can include any props they may design to decorate their table setting. Students in each team then explain in French their table setting to the judges, identifying each item and telling its position. After hearing the three presentations, the judges decide which table setting wins.

NATIONAL STANDARDS
C1.2, C1.3, C2.1, C4.2

Workbook Activity 16

Audiocassette/CD
Dialogue

Video

Teacher's Note

Couscous was described in **Unité 3**.

TPR

Mettez la table!

You may want to bring plastic tableware to class. Then give your students commands related to setting the table. Students show that they understand your commands by placing the appropriate tableware in the correct location. For example, **Mettez la serviette à droite du couteau!**

Cooperative Group Practice

Le Maghreb

Put your students in groups of three or four and have them go to the instructional materials center to do research in English on **le Maghreb**. Divide the region into the following topics (adding others, if you like): food, family life, holidays, geography and climate, religion, education, housing, and economy. After students complete their research, have each group prepare and give a short oral presentation to the entire class.

NATIONAL STANDARDS
C1.2, C2.1, C2.2, C3.1, C4.2

Arabéa Mamoudi and her younger brother, Djamel, live in Rabat, Morocco. They are helping their parents get ready to entertain luncheon guests to celebrate the end of Ramadan. Djamel is going to set the dining room table while Arabéa finishes preparing the meal.

Djamel: **Qu'est-ce que j'ai besoin de mettre sur la table pour le déjeuner?**

Arabéa: **On va manger du couscous. Mets les verres, les serviettes et les cuillers, s'il te plaît.**

Djamel: **Je mets aussi les assiettes pour le fruit?**

Arabéa: **Bien sûr.**

Enquête culturelle

Le Maroc (*Morocco*), **l'Algérie** (*Algeria*) and **la Tunisie** (*Tunisia*) make up a region in North Africa called **le Maghreb**. Each year thousands of tourists flock to this sunlit area. They explore the markets and the Muslim sections (**les médinas**) of the cities in **le Maghreb**, admire the artwork, stone-cuttings and ancient fortresses of the region and relax at its beaches on the Mediterranean Sea.

Casablanca is the largest North African city west of Egypt.

Morocco's two largest cities are Casablanca and the capital, Rabat. They both lie on the Atlantic Ocean. The country gained its independence from France in 1956. Arabic is the official language of Morocco, yet many people also speak French and Spanish.

Ramadan is the ninth month of the Islamic year. During this sacred month, Muslims don't eat or drink from sunrise to sunset. On the day after the end of Ramadan, **l'Aïd el-Fitr**, people celebrate by eating from morning until night. The noon meal often consists of **couscous**, which is served in a large bowl placed in the

Eating *couscous* marks the end of Ramadan. (La Rochelle)

Baklava is a sweet made of thin pastry, honey and nuts. (Morocco)

middle of the table. Everyone eats out of the same bowl with spoons. For dessert, people have fruit, often watermelon. In the afternoon, young people visit their friends and relatives. Even if they stay for only a few minutes, they have time to enjoy mint tea, the national beverage of Morocco, and cookies, cakes or baklava, a honey and nut pastry.

---

1 *Choisissez la bonne réponse d'après le dialogue et l'Enquête culturelle.*

1. Qui parle?
   a. une femme et son mari
   b. une sœur et son frère
   c. deux amis

2. Où habite la famille Mamoudi?
   a. en France
   b. à Casablanca
   c. à Rabat

3. Quelle heure est-il?
   a. 11h30
   b. 15h00
   c. 20h00

4. Où est-ce que Djamel travaille?
   a. dans le séjour
   b. dans la salle à manger
   c. dans la salle de bains

5. Où est-ce qu'Arabéa travaille?
   a. dans le salon
   b. dans la cuisine
   c. dans le grenier

6. Comment est-ce qu'on mange du couscous?
   a. avec les cuillers
   b. avec les verres
   c. avec les serviettes

7. Le dessert, c'est quoi?
   a. du fromage
   b. de la glace
   c. de la pastèque

La famille Mamoudi va manger dans la salle à manger.

Comparisons

Concept Mapping

To help students categorize the information they have learned from the reports given on **le Maghreb**, create a series of graphic organizers dealing with this region. The central concept is labeled **le Maghreb**, and the eight concept maps are labeled according to the topics covered in the students' presentations. Have each student complete the concept maps with relevant information he or she has learned from the oral presentations. As a follow-up activity, you might have each student use his or her concept maps to write a paper in English about **le Maghreb**.

Cultural Journal

Find a native informant to talk about a specific region of **le Maghreb**. Before the speaker comes to class, put your students in small groups. Each group should take notes and form questions on a certain aspect of the culture, for example, food, family life, holidays, geography and climate, religion, education, housing, and economy. After the speaker's presentation, students may write their observations in their cultural journals. They may also want to consider how a person's background affects how a culture is described. For example, how would the information students learned be different if the speaker had been a teacher, a doctor, an artisan, a farmer or a student?

NATIONAL STANDARDS
C1.2, C2.1, C2.2, C4.2

Answers

2 Possible answers:

1. une assiette; une fourchette, un couteau
2. un bol; une cuiller
3. une tasse
4. une assiette; une fourchette
5. une assiette; une fourchette, un couteau
6. un verre
7. un bol; une cuiller

3 Answers will vary.

Teacher's Notes

1. You may want to point out that the plural forms of **mettre** are like those of regular **-re** verbs. The singular stem is irregular. 2. You may want to point out that the **t** is silent in the singular forms and pronounced in the plural forms as well as in the inverted forms **met-il**, **met-elle** and **met-on**. 3. You may want to mention that **sur** is not used after **mettre** when it concerns putting on clothes. 4. Use the same plastic tableware that was suggested in the previous TPR activity **Mettez la table!**, or have students cut out pictures of tableware. Then ask students to set the table in the French manner. As they place each piece of tableware, they should tell in French where it goes. For example, **On met la fourchette à gauche de l'assiette.**

NATIONAL STANDARDS
C1.1, C1.2, C4.1

Modèle:

le steak
une assiette; une fourchette, un couteau

Où est-ce qu'il met la cassette?

METTEZ DU SUPER DANS VOTRE LAVE-VAISSELLE.

---

2 | Tell what serving dish or container the following items are served in or on and what utensils are used, if any, to eat or drink them.

1. le jambon
2. le couscous
3. le café
4. les haricots verts
5. la pizza
6. le lait
7. la glace

Pour manger une salade de haricots verts, on a besoin d'une assiette et d'une fourchette.

3 | *C'est à toi!*

1. Qu'est-ce que tu prends au petit déjeuner?
2. Est-ce que tu préfères un grand déjeuner ou un grand dîner?
3. Où est-ce que tu prends le goûter?
4. À quelle heure est-ce que tu prends le dîner?
5. Est-ce que tu mets souvent la table?
6. Est-ce que tu veux manger du couscous?

Où est-ce qu'on prend le goûter? (Paris)

Structure

Present tense of the irregular verb *mettre*

The verb **mettre** (*to put, to put on, to set*) is irregular.

	mettre		
je	**mets**	Je **mets** la table.	*I'm setting the table.*
tu	**mets**	Où **mets**-tu les cuillers?	*Where are you putting the spoons?*
il/elle/on	**met**	Il **met** le sel avec le poivre.	*He puts the salt with the pepper.*
nous	**mettons**	Nous **mettons** des baskets.	*We're putting on hightops.*
vous	**mettez**	**Mettez**-vous un jean?	*Are you putting on jeans?*
ils/elles	**mettent**	Ils **mettent** les fleurs dans le vase.	*They put the flowers in the vase.*

Pratique

4 It's Claude Garnier's birthday. Tell who's putting what on the table to get ready for his party.

1. M. Garnier

2. je

3. nous

4. les sœurs de Claude

5. vous

6. Mme Garnier et Daniel

7. tu

Modèle:

la grand-mère de Claude
La grand-mère de Claude met la nappe.

---

5 Everyone bought something at the grocery store. Tell whether they're putting what they bought in the refrigerator or in the cupboard.

1. Zakia et Karima/les yaourts
2. nous/les boîtes de petits pois
3. je/les œufs
4. M. Baribeau/le steak
5. tu/le poulet
6. Diane/le poivre
7. M. et Mme Charpentier/ le fromage
8. vous/les chips

Claire met le jus d'orange dans le frigo. (Strasbourg)

Modèles:

Mme Surprenant/le lait
Madame Surprenant met le lait dans le frigo.

Daniel et Alain/le sel
Daniel et Alain mettent le sel dans le placard.

Answers

6 1. Où est-ce que je mets le bureau?
Où est-ce que je mets l'armoire?
2. Où est-ce que je mets la table?
Où est-ce que je mets le fauteuil?
3. Où est-ce que je mets le canapé?
Où est-ce que je mets le micro-onde?
4. Où est-ce que je mets la lampe?
Où est-ce que je mets le tapis?
5. Où est-ce que je mets les chaises?
Où est-ce que je mets la télé?
Students' responses to these questions will vary.

Teacher's Note

As your students complete Activity 8, you may want them to compare their drawings with the illustration on page 319.

324

Modèle:

le lit/la stéréo
Student A: Où est-ce que je mets le lit?
Student B: Mets le lit dans la chambre. Où est-ce que je mets la stéréo?
Student A: Mets la stéréo dans le salon.

Où est-ce qu'on met la table et les chaises?

Modèle:

Student A: On a besoin de combien de fourchettes?
Student B: On a besoin de 16 fourchettes.

Modèle:

Student A: Où est-ce que je mets les deux fourchettes?
Student B: Mets les deux fourchettes à gauche de l'assiette.

---

6 Imagine that you and your partner are helping a friend move into an apartment. Take turns asking and telling whether you should put certain appliances and pieces of furniture in the living room, the kitchen or the bedroom.

1. le bureau/l'armoire
2. la table/le fauteuil
3. le canapé/le micro-onde
4. la lampe/le tapis
5. les chaises/la télé

Communication

7 Imagine that you and your partner are in charge of setting the table for a formal dinner party for eight people. Talk about exactly what you need to set the table with, decide how many of each item you need and write down this information.

8 Before you and your partner set the table for your formal dinner, see if you can remember what a typical French place setting looks like by drawing it. On a separate sheet of paper, draw a plate. Then take turns asking and telling each other where each item goes in relation to another. As you determine the correct placement of each item, add it to your drawing.

9 Review the information you learned about French eating habits in the **Mise au point sur... les repas** section on pages 315-17. Then form small groups of four or five students. With your group members, make one list of French eating habits and another list of American ones. Use only vocabulary words and expressions that you have already learned in French. For example, you might write **À la maison les Français prennent le café ou le chocolat dans un bol** and **Les Américains prennent le café ou le chocolat dans une tasse.** When your group has written as many sentences as possible, put them in graphic form. Draw two intersecting circles. Then write the sentences that describe only the French in one circle, the sentences that describe only Americans in the other circle, and the sentences that describe both the French and Americans where the circles intersect.

Les Français   Les Américains

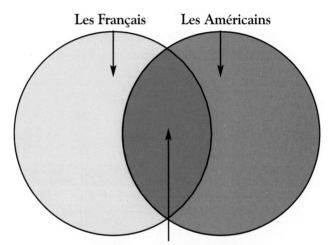

Les Français et les Américains

 ***Sur la bonne piste***

When you read, how do you figure out the meaning of words you don't know? One way is to take advantage of the clues their context provides. In the following plot summary, certain words are underlined. Some of them may be new to you. See if you can use the context of the summary to find a synonym—a word that has the same meaning—to logically replace each one.

> What a <u>Utopian</u> place for an adventure—the French Riviera—with its eternal sunshine, sandy beaches, and that wonderful <u>azure</u> of the Mediterranean! But our friends' summer <u>escapades</u> happen to lead them to the exact <u>locale</u> of a plutonium-smuggling <u>rendezvous</u>! And who happens to be at the meeting? Their host, Monsieur Cau. Is this man a spy, a foreign agent involved in smuggling atomic products? What happens to him <u>hinges</u> entirely on the <u>proficiency</u> of our young friends.

You probably found synonyms for at least some of the underlined words without too much difficulty. Although the summary is in English, you can use this technique when you read in French, too. In the reading that follows, taken from a brochure on vacation housing, the underlined words are ones you probably haven't seen before. The rest are either words you already know or obvious cognates. As you read the passage, practice the technique of inference—that is, using the context of the words you *do* know to help you understand the ones you *don't* know.

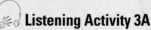

Workbook Activity 18

 Listening Activity 3A

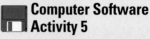 **Quiz** *Leçon C*

Computer Software Activity 5

Game

Password

For each pair of students prepare a set of note cards. Fold each note card in half. On the outside write a category, for example, **le couvert**. On the inside write six words that belong to that category, for example, **la fourchette, l'assiette, le couteau, la cuiller, le verre** and **la tasse**. Student A begins by telling Student B the category. Then Student A gives Student B some synonyms or short descriptions in French of the words on the inside of the card to help Student B guess each of the six words. (Other categories might be clothing items, foods, family members, classroom objects, sports, months, countries, rooms in a house, etc.)

NATIONAL STANDARDS
C1.1, C1.2, C2.1, C3.1, C5.1

325

Le logement

Cent appartements <u>répartis</u> dans 13 chalets sur 2 ou 3 étages sont regroupés <u>autour</u> du <u>pavillon</u> central. Vous <u>serez</u> <u>logé</u> dans un trois-pièces pour 5 ou 6 personnes.

<u>Chaque</u> <u>logement</u> <u>comprend</u>: une salle de séjour-chambre des parents <u>meublée</u> de 2 lits ou d'un canapé-lit, d'une table et de chaises; une chambre d'enfants avec 2 lits <u>superposés</u>; un <u>coin</u>-cuisine équipé d'un bloc-évier-réfrigérateur-<u>plaque</u> 2 <u>feux</u> incorporés et placard de <u>rangement</u> du matériel de cuisine; une salle d'eau avec w.-c. séparé.

10 Draw a floor plan of the apartment described in the reading, using the context of the words you know to infer the meaning of the others. Be sure to include in your floor plan the furniture and appliances that are mentioned.

Nathalie et Raoul

C'est à moi!

Now that you have completed this unit, take a look at what you should be able to do in French. Can you do all of these tasks?

➤ I can invite someone to do something.

➤ I can accept an invitation.

➤ I can greet someone by saying good evening.

➤ I can welcome guests.

➤ I can introduce people to each other.

➤ I can offer and accept a gift.

➤ I can identify objects, including types of housing, rooms, pieces of furniture and appliances.

➤ I can describe daily routines.

➤ I can tell where things are located, such as items in a place setting.

➤ I can say what someone is going to do.

➤ I can agree with someone.

➤ I can offer someone something to eat and drink.

➤ I can excuse myself.

Bonsoir, Adèle. Bienvenue!

Here is a brief checkup to see how much you understand about French culture. Decide if each statement is **vrai** or **faux**.

1. Many people in France live in apartment buildings and often buy their apartments.
2. Most French homes and apartments have two different types of bathrooms.
3. To ask to use the bathroom in French, you say **Où est la salle de bains, s'il vous plaît?**
4. The style of houses in France differs from region to region depending on construction materials.
5. The second floor of a French building is called **le premier étage**.
6. If you are invited to a French home for a meal, it's appropriate to bring or send chrysanthemums to your hosts.
7. A typical French breakfast consists of eggs, bacon, pancakes and fruit juice.
8. The French often serve the salad and cheese courses after their main course.
9. **Le Maghreb** is a region in North Africa that includes **le Maroc, l'Algérie** and **la Tunisie**.
10. Muslims celebrate the month of Ramadan by eating **couscous**, fruit and desserts for their noon meal.

Listening Activity 3B

Answers
1. vrai
2. vrai
3. faux
4. vrai
5. vrai
6. faux
7. faux
8. vrai
9. vrai
10. faux

Teacher's Notes

1. Your students may enjoy creating their own captions for each of the "Nathalie et Raoul" cartoons. Or you may want to find appropriate cartoons from newspapers and/or magazines. Remove the captions or use white correction fluid to delete the dialogues. Put students in small groups to compose new captions or dialogues in French. Post each group's cartoon for all to see. 2. Here is the English version of the cartoon on page 326: What a splendid day! Yeah, it's super nice out. Look at the flowers! No wind! No mosquitoes! And no brothers! What are we going to eat? There are sandwiches and fruit. Do you want the ham sandwich or the pâté sandwich? The ham, please. The ham? You want the ham sandwich? Yes. Darn! So, you don't like pâté? Uhm . . . yes. Yuk! Then have the pâté. No, it's for you. How nice you are! But take the pâté. I insist! Here you are. Do you want the apple or the peach? The peach, please. The peach? You want the peach? Oh no! This girl is unbelievable!

NATIONAL STANDARDS
C1.1, C2.1, C2.2, C4.2

327

Jeopardy

After your students have given their presentations on **le Maghreb** (page 320), they might play this game. Construct a game board out of cardboard, cloth or similar material. It should be large enough to accommodate five rows of pockets vertically and five rows of pockets horizontally. Making and lining up the pockets is the next step in setting up the game. The five pockets in each vertical row should each contain a question, all in the same category. (This makes for a total of 25 questions representing five different categories.) Above the top row of each set of horizontal pockets, attach (with paper clips or pins) a card labeling each category. Next, write questions from areas that you want to quiz, for example, food, education, holidays, geography and religion. For every category, try to write questions along a scale of increasing difficulty and place them accordingly in the pockets. Customarily, the question at the top of any row is the easiest of the five of its kind. Divide the class into two teams. Have a student from one team choose a category and whichever question from it that he or she wants to try. Then do the same for the other team. Whenever a question is missed, give the next player in line on the opposing team a chance at it. A correct answer increases the team's point total.

Communication orale

With a partner, play the roles of a French-speaking exchange student and an American host student. It's the day the exchange student arrives in the American student's home town. Begin your conversation at the airport where the American student greets the exchange student and welcomes him or her to the United States. Then continue your conversation on the way home. The exchange student, curious to find out what his or her new home is like, asks questions about his or her room and what's in it. The American student answers, giving as much specific information as possible.

Communication écrite

Imagine that Abdel-Cader Mamoude, a French-speaking Moroccan exchange student, is coming to live with your family for the year. Before arriving in the United States, he writes you a letter asking what his room in your home or apartment is like. Write a response to Abdel-Cader in French. Describe his room, saying where each piece of furniture and electronic appliance is in relation to something else. You may also want to enclose a floor plan of his room to help him visualize his new surroundings.

Communication active

Bienvenue!

To invite someone to do something, use:

Vous voulez faire le tour de mon appartement?	*Do you want to take a tour of my apartment?*
Entrez donc!	*Then come in!*
Allons au salon.	*Let's go to the living room.*

To accept an invitation, use:

Oui, je veux bien.	*Yes, I'm willing.*

To greet someone, use:

Bonsoir!	*Good evening!*

To greet guests, use:

Bienvenue!	*Welcome!*

To introduce someone else, use:

Je vous présente.... Raymond, Anne-Marie.	*Let me introduce you to . . . . Raymond, this is Anne-Marie.*

To offer a gift, use:

Voici des fleurs, Madame.	*Here are some flowers, Ma'am.*

To accept a gift, use:

Oh, que vous êtes gentil!	*Oh, how nice you are!*

Voici le canapé.

To identify objects, use:

> **Voici** la cuisine. *Here's the kitchen.*

To describe daily routines, use:

> **Je mets** les verres, les serviettes et les assiettes.

I'm putting the glasses, napkins and plates on (the table).

To tell location, use:

> La fourchette est **à gauche** de l'assiette.

The fork is (to the) left of the plate.

> Le couteau est **à droite** de l'assiette.

The knife is (to the) right of the plate.

To express intentions, use:

> **On va** manger du couscous. *We're going to eat couscous.*

Je vais prendre une autre baguette.

To agree, use:

> **Bien sûr.** *Of course.*

To offer food, use:

> **Prenez** des chips. *Have some snacks.*

To offer a beverage, use:

> **Vous voulez** un jus de fruit? *Do you want fruit juice?*

To excuse yourself, use:

> **Pardon**, j'ai encore quelques choses à faire.

Excuse me, I still have some things to do.

NATIONAL STANDARDS
C1.2, C4.1

Communication électronique

1. He draws his artistic inspiration from the Italian Renaissance (and also Flemish painting of the fifteenth century).
2. Two of his common themes include landscapes and flowers.
3. Answers will vary.
4. Answers will vary.
5. You may contact M. Besenval by regular mail, telephone, fax or e-mail.
6. The address is 32, rue de Sévigné in Paris.

À moi de jouer!

Possible paragraphs:

Dans le salon il y a un tapis, un canapé, un fauteuil et des photos. Une chaise est devant le bureau. Une lampe est sur une table. Il y a un vase et des fleurs sur une autre table.

Dans la salle à manger il y a une table et des chaises. Une nappe est sur la table. Une serviette et une fourchette sont à gauche de l'assiette et un couteau est à droite de l'assiette. Une cuiller est au-dessus de l'assiette. Il y a aussi une tasse, un verre, un bol, le poivre et le sel.

Communication électronique

Imagine that you win the lottery and decide to move to France! In decorating your house or apartment, you'll probably need some new furniture. Jean-Pierre Besenval is one of the last remaining French artists who maintains the tradition of fine hand-painted furniture. Explore his original, one-of-a-kind offerings by going to this Internet site:

http://www.meublespeints.com/francais/index.html

After viewing this site, answer the following questions.

1. M. Besenval draws his artistic inspiration from which country and which historical period?
2. Now click on "Meubles" and then click on each piece to see a close-up of it. What appear to be the two most common themes of the artist?
3. Which one of these pieces would you like to buy? How much does it cost?
4. From which century does this piece of furniture date?
5. Click on "Nous Contacter." If you would like to order, what are four ways in which to contact M. Besenval?
6. Finally click on "Boutique" to see the actual shop. What is its address?

À moi de jouer!

It's your turn to show what you've learned in this unit about French homes by writing a paragraph that describes what you see in each room below. First describe everything you see in the living room. Then do the same for the dining room with the table setting, remembering to identify as many objects as possible by saying where they are in relation to other things. (You may want to refer to the *Communication active* on pages 328-29 and the vocabulary list on page 331.)

Vocabulaire

à droite to (on) the right
à gauche to (on) the left
un appartement apartment
un arbre tree
une armoire wardrobe
une assiette plate
au-dessus de above

une baignoire bathtub
un bain: une salle de bains bathroom
un balcon balcony
bien: bien sûr of course
Bienvenue! Welcome!
un bol bowl
bonsoir good evening

un canapé couch, sofa
une chambre bedroom
des chips (m.) snacks
le couscous couscous
un couteau knife
un couvert table setting
une cuiller spoon
une cuisine kitchen
une cuisinière stove

de (d') some
le déjeuner lunch
   le petit déjeuner breakfast
dessus: au-dessus de above
le dîner dinner, supper
donc so, then
une douche shower
la droite: à droite to (on) the right

enchanté(e) delighted
encore still
une entrée entrance
entrer to enter, to come in
un escalier stairs, staircase
un étage floor, story
un évier sink

faire le tour to take a tour
un fauteuil armchair
une fleur flower
un four oven
une fourchette fork
un frigo refrigerator

un garage garage
la gauche: à gauche to (on) the left
gentil, gentille nice
le goûter afternoon snack
un grenier attic

habiter to live

un immeuble apartment building

un jardin garden, lawn
le jus de fruit fruit juice

une lampe lamp
un lit bed

une maison house
manger: une salle à manger dining room
même even
mettre to put (on), to set
un micro-onde microwave

une nappe tablecloth

le petit déjeuner breakfast
une pièce room
un placard cupboard
le poivre pepper
prendre to take, to have (food or drink)

que: Que vous êtes gentils! How nice you are!
quelques some

le rez-de-chaussée ground floor

s'il te plaît please
une salle à manger dining room
une salle de bains bathroom
un salon living room
un séjour family room
le sel salt
une serviette napkin
un sous-sol basement
le sucre sugar
sûr: bien sûr of course

une table table
un tapis rug
une tasse cup
les toilettes (f.) toilet
toujours still
le tour tour

un vase vase
un verre glass
une voiture car
vouloir bien to be willing
vous to you
un voyage trip

les W.-C. (m.) toilet

Unité 10

La santé

In this unit you will be able to:

➤ **express astonishment and disbelief**

➤ **express emotions**

➤ **point out something**

➤ **make a complaint**

➤ **explain a problem**

➤ **congratulate and commiserate**

➤ **express concern**

➤ **express need and necessity**

➤ **give advice**

➤ **express reassurance**

➤ **make a prediction**

➤ **make an appointment**

➤ **state exact and approximate time**

➤ **give information**

NATIONAL STANDARDS
C2.1

Workbook Activities 1-2

 Grammar & Vocabulary Exercises 1-2

Audiocassette/CD
Le corps

Transparencies 49-50

Teacher's Notes

1. **Genou** forms its plural by adding an **x**. 2. Another word for "toe" is **l'orteil (m.)**. 3. Students learned several idiomatic expressions with **avoir** in Unité 4 (**avoir faim** and **avoir soif**) that you may want to review with them before introducing the new idiomatic expressions with **avoir** in this lesson (**avoir froid** and **avoir chaud**). 4. Other related terms are **le pouce** (*thumb, big toe*), **le gros orteil** (*big toe*), **le coude** (*elbow*), **la cheville** (*ankle*), **le poignet** (*wrist*), **la taille** (*waist*), **la cuisse** (*thigh*) and **la poitrine** (*chest*). 5. Communicative functions that are recycled in this lesson are "agreeing and disagreeing" and "inviting."

Cooperative Group Practice

Les Monstres

Put students in small groups of four or five. Have each group write on a piece of paper four or five body parts that a human would not have, for example, **trois têtes** or **huit doigts**. Collect these pieces of paper. Randomly distribute a piece of paper to each group and have the group members draw a monster using the information on their paper. Finally, each group shows their monster to the entire class while describing it in French. For example, **Elle a trois têtes, mais elle n'a pas de jambes.**

NATIONAL STANDARDS
C1.2, C4.1

334

Leçon A

In this lesson you will be able to:

➤ **express astonishment and disbelief**

➤ **express emotions**

➤ **express reassurance**

➤ **point out something**

➤ **express need and necessity**

➤ **give advice**

 Workbook Activity 3

Grammar & Vocabulary Exercises 3-4

 Audiocassette/CD *Dialogue*

Sébastien's older brother, Francis, is teaching him how to ski near the city of Chamonix in the Alps.

Sébastien:	**Oh là là!**
Francis:	**Tu as froid?**
Sébastien:	**Non, ce n'est pas ça.**
Francis:	**Alors, tu as peur?**
Sébastien:	**Oui, un peu.**
Francis:	**Mais non, c'est facile. Regarde! Il faut prendre les bâtons dans les mains et garder les jambes solides.**
Sébastien:	**Il faut baisser la tête?**
Francis:	**Oui, mais pas trop. Allons-y!**
Sébastien:	**Au secours!**

Teacher's Notes

1. Chamonix is the site of the national skiing school, which is a boarding school for promising young skiers. 2. Traditionally, the French use **il est** before an adjective in a general expression, but in everyday speech **c'est** before an adjective is commonly heard. 3. Definite articles, not possessive adjectives, usually precede parts of the body in French. 4. Pronounce the double **s** in **baisser** as [s] so as not to confuse **baisser** with **baiser**. 5. French speakers usually shout **Au secours!** or **Aidez-moi!** when they need help. However, **Au feu!** (*Fire!*) draws the largest response from bystanders.

Game

Jacques dit....

Play the French version of "Simon says" with your students. Begin by saying **Jacques dit...** and giving your students a command in the **vous** form. Students should perform the action ordered. If you do not say **Jacques dit...** before giving a command, however, students should ignore your command. Keep giving orders till you spot someone who either performs incorrectly or makes a motion when you have not said **Jacques dit....** He or she then comes to the front of the room and gives orders until someone else slips up. Command forms that you might practice with students before beginning the game include **Levez-vous, Restez, Tournez, Ouvrez, Marchez, Allez, Regardez, Indiquez, Gardez, Couvrez, Enlevez, Jetez, Prenez, Touchez, Sautez, Levez, Baissez, Fermez** and **Asseyez-vous.**

Enquête culturelle

The French capital of mountain climbing and a popular international winter sports resort, Chamonix is situated in **les Alpes** in the eastern part of the country. From Chamonix, the highest cable car (**le téléphérique**) in the world carries people several thousand meters up the slopes of the **Aiguille du Midi**, one of the highest peaks in **les Alpes**, to ski, hike and enjoy the spectacular view.

Skiers take *un téléphérique* to the top of a mountain. (Cauterets)

CHAMONIX MONT-BLANC

74400 - Off. de T. : 04 50 53 00 24
C'est une ville à la montagne, avec le toit des Alpes pour soleil, l'alpinisme pour symbole et 350 km de sentiers pour décor. Le carrefour des passions.
Visiter : Le musée alpin. L'observatoire de l'Aiguille du Midi. Le Montenvers.
Voir : 24-26/06 Festival des sciences ; 16-18/07 Rencontres de la petite édition ; 15/08 Fête des guides.
Idées : VTT, stage trial+cross-country +descente+raid, 4j, 83,85 €. Tennis, stage P. Barthès, 5j à mi-temps, 213,43 €. Golf, 4j, 4h/j, 236,30 €. Raft+hydro, 3j, 300,32 €, transports+déjeuners compris.

CHAMONIX MONT-BLANC   Alt. 1 035 m

NATIONAL STANDARDS C1.2, C3.1, C3.2, C4.2

Comparisons

Les classes de neige

Put your students in small groups of three or four and have them brainstorm a one-week schedule during **les classes de neige**. They should come up with an hour-by-hour list of activities, special events and classes. The schedules may be posted for all students to see. The class may want to vote on which schedule is the most appealing.

Cultural Journal

If your students are keeping a cultural journal, you might have them read the following proverbs and then write in their journals what value or values they think these proverbs suggest: 1. Birds of a feather flock together. 2. Time is money. 3. Don't cry over spilt milk. 4. Don't put all your eggs in the same basket. 5. A bird in the hand is worth two in the bush. 6. No sooner said than done. (For example, the proverb "You've made your bed — now lie in it" suggests that you control your own destiny and are responsible for the consequences of your actions.)

TPR

Où met-on les couleurs?

Have students cut up construction paper of various colors into small pieces. Then give commands to tell students where on their body to place the scraps of paper. For example, **Mettez le rouge sur la tête!** When all the colors have been used, students can verify that they have put the pieces of paper on the indicated spots by looking at their classmates.

336

Résidence composée de petits immeubles-chalets merveilleusement située, au départ des pistes de ski et des remontées mécaniques. Tous les commerces et centres d'animation à proximité. (Existe en studios, 2 pièces-mezzanine).

VAL-CENIS
L'immense domaine skiable de Savoie

36 435 €
2 pièces coin-montagne balcon

Le Mont Blanc, the highest mountain in **les Alpes**, rises over 15,000 feet and stands on the border of France, Switzerland and Italy. This mountain received its name (in English, "White Mountain") because its peak remains snow covered the entire year.

When French schools are closed for a week during winter vacation in February, many students go skiing in **les Alpes** and **les Pyrénées**. During the regular school year some schools offer organized

Le ski alpin is a popular sport in a country with five major mountain ranges.

Many mountain peaks in France are named *aiguilles* because they resemble needles. (Chamonix)

excursions, such as **les classes de neige**, where students have academic classes in the morning and ski in the afternoon. Most teenagers in France would rather downhill ski (**le ski de piste** or **le ski alpin**) than cross-country ski (**le ski de fond**). Skiing is also a popular winter sport in Switzerland, the site of many world-class ski slopes.

TOUTES LES INFORMATIONS SUR LES STATIONS DE MONTAGNE SKI FRANCE
3615 CORUS

Mains froides, cœur chaud

The French proverb **Mains froides, cœur chaud** means "Cold hands, warm heart." This proverb suggests that the way the body feels does not always reflect a person's emotions. Therefore, you may be cold on the outside but still have a warm and friendly personality.

Répondez par "vrai" ou "faux" d'après le dialogue.

1. Francis et Sébastien sont à Paris.
2. Chamonix est en Italie.
3. Sébastien a froid.
4. Sébastien a peur.
5. Francis trouve que skier, c'est facile.
6. Il faut prendre les bâtons dans les mains.
7. Il faut beaucoup baisser la tête.

Il faut prendre les bâtons dans les mains.

Match the letter of the object with the part of the body it is associated with.

a.

c.

f.

b.

d.

g.

1. la tête
2. la main
3. le genou
4. le pied
5. le doigt
6. les jambes
7. le dos
8. le cou

e.

h.

3 *C'est à toi!*

1. Tu trouves qu'il est facile de skier?
2. Est-ce que tu skies bien ou mal?
3. Qu'est-ce que tu portes quand tu skies?
4. Quand est-ce que tu as peur?
5. Est-ce que tu as chaud ou froid maintenant?
6. Est-ce que tu étudies trop?
7. Est-ce que tu manges de la pizza avec les doigts ou avec une fourchette?

Monsieur Belanger porte un anorak quand il skie.

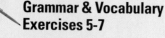

Answers

4 Answers will vary.

5 1. Est-ce qu'il faut de la mayonnaise pour faire une pizza?
   Non. Pour faire une pizza, il ne faut pas de mayonnaise.
2. Est-ce qu'il faut des pommes de terre pour faire des frites?
   Oui. Pour faire des frites, il faut des pommes de terre.
3. Est-ce qu'il faut des raisins pour faire du jus d'orange?
   Non. Pour faire du jus d'orange, il ne faut pas de raisins.
4. Est-ce qu'il faut de la moutarde pour faire un gâteau?
   Non. Pour faire un gâteau, il ne faut pas de moutarde.
5. Est-ce qu'il faut du pain pour faire un sandwich?
   Oui. Pour faire un sandwich, il faut du pain.
6. Est-ce qu'il faut du poisson pour faire une bouillabaisse?
   Oui. Pour faire une bouillabaisse, il faut du poisson.
7. Est-ce qu'il faut des pêches pour faire une tarte aux fraises?
   Non. Pour faire une tarte aux fraises, il ne faut pas de pêches.
8. Est-ce qu'il faut de l'eau pour faire du café?
   Oui. Pour faire du café, il faut de l'eau.

NATIONAL STANDARDS
C1.1, C1.2, C4.1

338

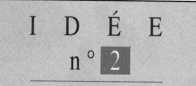

IDÉE n° 2

Il faut toujours profiter des bonnes opportunités.

Modèle:

J'ai soif.
Il faut prendre une boisson.

Modèles:

des œufs/une omelette

Student A: Est-ce qu'il faut des œufs pour faire une omelette?
Student B: Oui. Pour faire une omelette, il faut des œufs.

de la confiture/une salade

Student B: Est-ce qu'il faut de la confiture pour faire une salade?
Student A: Non. Pour faire une salade, il ne faut pas de confiture.

Structure

Present tense of the irregular verb *falloir*

The verb **falloir** (*to be necessary, to have to*) has only one present tense form. **Il faut** means "it is necessary," "one has to/must" or "we/you have to/must." **Il faut** usually is followed by an infinitive.

Il faut garder les jambes solides.   *You have to keep your legs steady.*
Il ne faut pas baisser la tête.   *You must not lower your head.*

Pratique

4 For each of Ariane's statements, tell her one thing she should do.

1. J'ai faim.
2. Je voudrais faire une quiche.
3. Il n'y a pas de légumes dans le frigo.
4. Je veux regarder le nouveau film de Gérard Depardieu.
5. J'ai besoin de nouvelles chaussures.
6. Il fait très froid.
7. J'ai une interro demain.

Il faut acheter des légumes. (Paris)

5 With a partner, take turns asking and telling whether or not you need certain items in order to make certain things.

1. de la mayonnaise/une pizza
2. des pommes de terre/des frites
3. des raisins/du jus d'orange
4. de la moutarde/un gâteau
5. du pain/un sandwich
6. du poisson/une bouillabaisse
7. des pêches/une tarte aux fraises
8. de l'eau/du café

Pour faire un sandwich, il faut du pain.

Audiocassette/CD
Prononciation

Listening Activity 1

Quiz
Leçon A

Communication

6 | You and one of your classmates have volunteered to visit elementary schools during National Foreign Language Week to present a short program in French. With your partner, create a song, rap or poem in French about parts of the body. In your song, rap or poem, name as many parts of the body as you can, using only words and expressions that you have already learned. Finally, perform your song or rap or read your poem, pointing to each part of the body as it is mentioned.

7 | With a partner, play the roles of an American student who is spending spring break skiing in the Laurentian Hills in Quebec and a French-Canadian student who is also skiing there. Their conversation begins when the two students meet on the slopes, introduce themselves and say where they're from. Then the American confesses that he or she can't ski very well. The French Canadian asks if the American is afraid. The American admits that he or she is, but just a little. The French Canadian offers reassurance and gives the American several helpful suggestions and encouragement.

Teacher's Notes

1. In the expression **il faut**, **il** is an impersonal subject pronoun meaning "it/one/we/you," not "he." 2. Before you begin Activity 5, review with your students the use of partitive articles in negative sentences. 3. The French **s** is usually silent at the end of a word. 4. Review with your students some examples of liaison in which a final **s** is pronounced [z] before a vowel sound. For example, **les amis** and **elles habitent**.   [z]
[z]

Prononciation

The sounds [s] and [z]

The French **s** is pronounced either [s] or [z] depending on what comes before or after it.

Pronounce **s** as [s] when it begins a word. Say each of these words:

solide	serviette
santé	sous-sol
Sylvie	seize

Pronounce **s** as [s] when it is followed by a consonant. Say each of these words:

escalier	disquette
pastèque	espagnol
baskets	costume

Pronounce **s** as [s] when it is doubled. Say each of these words:

baisser	assez
rez-de-chaussée	bouillabaisse
croissant	tasse

Pronounce **s** as [z] when it comes between vowels. Say each of these words:

cuisine	blouson
maison	chose
vase	magasin

Cooperative Group Practice

Qu'est-ce qu'il faut faire?

Put students in small groups of four or five. Give each group a sheet of paper and have students make two columns on it. In the first column have students write ten situations in French, for example, **J'ai froid**. In the second column have students write ten solutions (a solution for each situation) using **il faut**, for example, **Il faut mettre un manteau**. (Tell students to make sure the solutions are not directly across from the corresponding situations.) After each group has written ten situations and ten solutions, have them exchange papers with another group and match the new situations and solutions. Finally, students in each group can read their situations and solutions to the entire class.

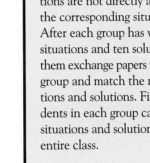

NATIONAL STANDARDS
C1.1, C1.2, C1.3, C4.1, C5.1

Workbook
Activity 5

Grammar & Vocabulary
Exercises 8-10

Audiocassette/CD
Negative Expressions,
La figure

Teacher's Notes

1. You may want to review with students the negative expression **ne... pas** before introducing new negative expressions. 2. The word **quelque chose** was introduced in **Unité 7**. The word **des yeux (m.)** was introduced in **Unité 5**. 3. You may want to point out that **la figure** is a false cognate. 4. Other related terms are **la langue** (*tongue*), **le sourire** (*smile*), **les lèvres (f.)** (*lips*), **le visage** (*face*), **les taches de rousseur (f.)** (*freckles*), **le menton** (*chin*), **le cil** (*eyelash*), **le sourcil** (*eyebrow*) and **le front** (*forehead*). 5. Communicative functions that are recycled in this lesson are "greeting someone," "agreeing and disagreeing" and "asking for information."

Game

Parts of the Head or Body

To practice expressions for parts of the head and to review expressions for parts of the body, you may want to play this game with your students. Divide the class into two teams. Have one person from each team go to the board. When you call out the name of a part of the head or body, both students try to draw it as quickly as possible. The first student to draw it correctly gets a point for his or her team. The team with the most points at the end of the allotted time is the winner.

NATIONAL STANDARDS
C1.2, C4.1

Leçon B

In this lesson you will be able to:

➤ **make an appointment**

➤ **state exact and approximate time**

➤ **explain a problem**

➤ **congratulate and commiserate**

➤ **give information**

Il y a quelqu'un à la porte.

Il trouve quelque chose.

Il n'y a personne à la porte.

Il ne trouve rien.

Il neige souvent à Boston.

Il y a toujours de la place.

Il ne neige jamais à Fort-de-France.

Il n'y a plus de place.

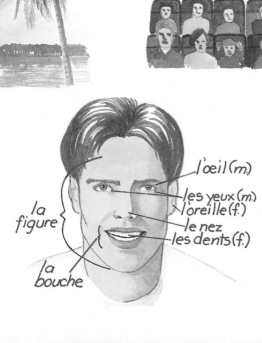

l'œil (m.)
les yeux (m.)
l'oreille (f.)
le nez
les dents (f.)
la figure
la bouche

It's Thursday morning. Madame Graedel wants to make an appointment with her dentist in Lausanne, Switzerland.

La réceptionniste:	Allô? Cabinet du docteur Odermatt.
Mme Graedel:	Bonjour, Madame. Je voudrais prendre rendez-vous avec Monsieur Odermatt, s'il vous plaît.
La réceptionniste:	Oui, Madame. Quand est-ce que vous voulez venir?
Mme Graedel:	Aussitôt que possible. J'ai mal aux dents.
La réceptionniste:	Je regrette, mais nous n'avons rien ce matin.
Mme Graedel:	Alors, cet après-midi?
La réceptionniste:	Monsieur Odermatt n'est jamais ici le jeudi après-midi. Est-ce que vous pouvez venir demain matin à 9h30?
Mme Graedel:	Bien sûr.

The city of Lausanne sits on the hills overlooking the north shore of Lake Geneva in Switzerland. Of glacial origin, beautiful Lake Geneva attracts many tourists. Also called **le lac Léman**, Lake Geneva is approximately 70 kilometers long. On the western side of the lake, close to France, lies the city of Geneva (Genève). Many organizations, such as the Red Cross, the World Health Organization and the European headquarters of the United Nations, have their main offices here.

The waterspout in Lake Geneva shoots 130 meters into the air. (Genève)

Enquête culturelle

Even though Switzerland is not a member of the United Nations, its *Palais des Nations* is the seat of the UN in Europe.

key
TOURS S.A.
GENÈVE

7, rue des Alpes
(Square du Mont-Blanc)
Tel 731 41 40 Fax 732 27 07

342

Audiocassette/CD Activity 3

Answers

1 Possible answer:

Le dentiste s'appelle Monsieur Odermatt. Madame Graedel a besoin de prendre rendez-vous avec Monsieur Odermatt parce qu'elle a mal aux dents. Elle ne peut pas prendre rendez-vous avec le dentiste ce matin parce qu'il n'a plus de place. Elle ne peut pas prendre rendez-vous avec le dentiste cet après-midi parce qu'il n'est jamais au cabinet le jeudi après-midi. Elle peut prendre rendez-vous avec le dentiste demain matin à 9h30.

2 1. oreilles
2. tête
3. bouche
4. yeux
5. pieds, jambes
6. doigts
7. dents

3 Answers will vary.

Teacher's Note

About 65 percent of the Swiss speak German, 10 percent speak Italian and less than 5 percent speak Romansh, an offshoot of Latin.

Game

Jacques dit....

You may want to play this TPR game again with your students. Include the expressions for parts of the head that are introduced in this lesson. (The game was explained in **Leçon A** of this unit.)

Switzerland has four official languages. About 20 percent of the Swiss speak French; most of these people live in western Switzerland near the French border. German is the language of the majority of people in northern Switzerland. Almost all of those in the south of the country speak Italian, while a small portion of the population in the eastern part of the country uses Romansch.

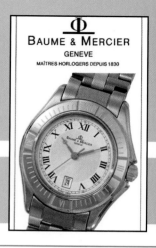

In addition to its spectacular scenery, Switzerland is famous for its watch industry, its delicious chocolates and its stable banking system.

1 Write a five-sentence paragraph in French that summarizes the conversation between the dentist's receptionist and Madame Graedel. Begin by telling the dentist's name. Then say why Madame Graedel needs to make an appointment with him. Next explain why she is unable to see him this morning. Then tell why she is unable to see him this afternoon. Finally, give the time when she is able to schedule an appointment.

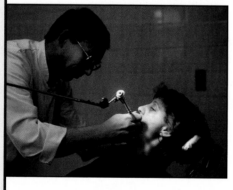

Mme Robin a mal aux dents.

2 *Complétez les phrases avec le mot convenable.*

tête	oreilles	jambes	dents	yeux	bouche	doigts	pieds

1. On écoute avec les....
2. On porte un chapeau sur la....
3. On parle avec la....
4. On regarde la télé avec les....
5. On fait du footing avec les... et les....
6. On joue aux jeux vidéo avec les....
7. On téléphone au dentiste quand on a mal aux....

3 *C'est à toi!*

1. Quand est-ce que tu prends rendez-vous avec le/la dentiste?
2. Est-ce que tu as souvent mal aux dents?
3. Est-ce que tu as peur de prendre rendez-vous avec le/la dentiste?
4. Ton/ta dentiste, il/elle s'appelle comment?
5. De quelle couleur sont tes yeux?
6. Quand il n'y a plus de place dans un café, est-ce que tu attends ou est-ce que tu vas à un autre café?

J'ai les yeux bleus.

Structure

Verbs + infinitives

Many French verbs may be followed directly by an infinitive. Here is a list of the verbs you have already learned that may be followed by an infinitive.

adorer	J'**adore faire** du shopping.
aimer	**Aimez**-vous **prendre** rendez-vous avec le dentiste?
aller	Maman **va téléphoner** à la réceptionniste.
désirer	Nous **désirons finir** aussitôt que possible.
falloir	Il ne **faut** pas **baisser** la tête.
pouvoir	Est-ce que vous **pouvez venir** demain matin?
préférer	Mes amis **préfèrent faire** du roller.
venir	Mes cousins **viennent regarder** mes photos.
vouloir	Qu'est-ce que tu **veux faire** maintenant?

Qu'est-ce que M. et Mme Barde préfèrent prendre pour le petit déjeuner?

Pratique

4 Get to know your partner better. Take turns asking and answering questions.

1. aller/étudier le français aujourd'hui
2. pouvoir/sortir avec tes amis ce soir
3. aller/faire du shopping samedi
4. vouloir/être médecin
5. aimer/voyager
6. désirer/aller en vacances à Chamonix
7. adorer/skier
8. préférer/jouer au foot ou faire du footing

Modèles:

adorer/faire du roller

Student A: Est-ce que tu adores faire du roller?

Student B: Oui, j'adore faire du roller.

aimer/aller au cinéma

Student B: Est-ce que tu aimes aller au cinéma?

Student A: Non, je n'aime pas aller au cinéma.

Leïla et son cousin vont faire du shopping. (La Rochelle)

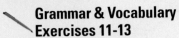
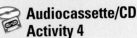

Answers

4 1. Est-ce que tu vas étudier le français aujourd'hui?
2. Est-ce que tu peux sortir avec tes amis ce soir?
3. Est-ce que tu vas faire du shopping samedi?
4. Est-ce que tu veux être médecin?
5. Est-ce que tu aimes voyager?
6. Est-ce que tu désires aller en vacances à Chamonix?
7. Est-ce que tu adores skier?
8. Est-ce que tu préfères jouer au foot ou faire du footing?
Students' responses to these questions will vary.

Teacher's Notes

1. You may want to point out that the subject pronoun in inversion and the second half of a negative expression may come between the conjugated verb and the infinitive that follows. 2. **Devoir**, to be introduced in **Leçon C**, may also be followed by an infinitive. 3. Verbs followed by **à** or **de** before an infinitive will be presented later.

NATIONAL STANDARDS
C1.1, C1.2, C4.1

Answers

5 Answers will vary.

Modèle:

jouer au tennis
Je n'aime pas jouer au tennis.
Je préfère jouer au basket.

5 You've been asked to take part in a survey about the typical activities of teenagers. Express your feelings about the activities on the survey, using the appropriate form of the verbs in the following list. Use each of the verbs at least once.

adorer	aimer	falloir	préférer

1. aller aux boums
2. écouter le rock
3. danser
4. aller au cinéma
5. manger de la pizza
6. faire les magasins
7. travailler
8. regarder la télé
9. faire les devoirs
10. étudier pour les interros

Claire adore faire les magasins. (Strasbourg)

Negative expressions

You've already learned one French expression used to make a verb negative: **ne (n')... pas**. There are other negative expressions that follow the same pattern as **ne (n')... pas**. Compare the following expressions.

Affirmative	Negative
souvent (*often*) **toujours** (*always*)	**ne (n')... jamais** (*never*)
toujours (*still*)	**ne (n')... plus** (*no longer, not anymore*)
quelqu'un (*someone, somebody*)	**ne (n')... personne** (*no one, nobody, not anyone*)
quelque chose (*something*)	**ne (n')... rien** (*nothing, not anything*)

Il n'y a personne dans la voiture.

Tu vas souvent au cinéma avec tes parents?   *Do you often go to the movies with your parents?*

Non, je ne vais jamais au cinéma avec mes parents.   *No, I never go to the movies with my parents.*

Vous avez toujours de la place?   *Do you still have room?*

Non, nous n'avons plus de place.   *No, we don't have room anymore.*

Il y a quelqu'un devant toi?   *Is there someone in front of you?*

Non, il n'y a personne devant moi.   *No, there's no one in front of me.*

Tu prends quelque chose?   *Are you having something (to eat)?*

Non, je ne prends rien.   *No, I'm not having anything (to eat).*

Ce restaurant a toujours de la place. (Tours)

"On n'est jamais séparés plus d'une semaine"

Ne m'invitez plus à la **campagne!**

Note that in each of these negative expressions, **ne (n')** comes before the verb and **jamais, plus, personne** or **rien** follows the verb.

Remember that indefinite articles (**un, une, des**) and partitive articles (**du, de la, de l'**) become **de** or **d'** in a negative sentence.

Ton père fait toujours du sport?   *Does your father still play sports?*

Non, il ne fait plus de sport.   *No, he no longer plays sports.*

Personne may also be used after a preposition.

Je ne parle à personne.   *I'm not talking to anyone.*

Pratique

6 For two weeks Élodie kept track of how often she did certain things. Then she plotted her findings on a bar graph. Make a general statement about the frequency of each of Élodie's activities, using **toujours, souvent, ne (n')... pas souvent** or **ne (n')... jamais.**

Modèle:
Élodie ne prend pas souvent le petit déjeuner.

- prendre le petit déjeuner
- porter des baskets
- aller à l'école
- regarder la télé après les cours
- faire du shopping au centre commercial
- téléphoner aux amis après le dîner
- finir les devoirs
- faire du sport

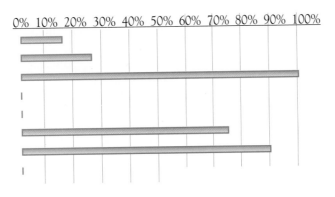

0% 10% 20% 30% 40% 50% 60% 70% 80% 90% 100%

**Audiocassette/CD
Activity 8**

Answers

7 Vous avez toujours des CDs?
Non, je regrette, nous n'avons plus de CDs.

Vous avez toujours des bâtons?
Oui, nous avons toujours des bâtons.

Vous avez toujours des fauteuils?
Non, je regrette, nous n'avons plus de fauteuils.

Vous avez toujours des lampes?
Non, je regrette, nous n'avons plus de lampes.

Vous avez toujours des vélos?
Oui, nous avons toujours des vélos.

Vous avez toujours des tapis?
Non, je regrette, nous n'avons plus de tapis.

Vous avez toujours des magnétoscopes?
Non, je regrette, nous n'avons plus de magnétoscopes.

Vous avez toujours des verres?
Oui, nous avons toujours des verres.

Vous avez toujours des armoires?
Non, je regrette, nous n'avons plus d'armoires.

8 1. Non, je ne cherche rien dans le grenier.
2. Non, je ne veux rien.
3. Non, je n'achète rien au supermarché.
4. Non, je n'invite personne à la boum.
5. Non, je ne fais rien ce soir.
6. Non, je ne présente personne à mes parents.
7. Non, je ne ressemble à personne dans ma famille.
8. Non, je n'étudie avec personne.

NATIONAL STANDARDS
C1.1, C1.2

346

---

7 Pied-à-terre is going out of business. Student A plays the role of a customer and Student B plays the role of a salesperson who works at this store. Student A asks whether or not the store still has some of each item listed in the newspaper ad that follows. Student B answers, knowing that the only things left are sports equipment and dinnerware.

Modèles:

Student A: Vous avez toujours des stéréos?
Student B: Non, je regrette, nous n'avons plus de stéréos.

Student A: Vous avez toujours des assiettes?
Student B: Oui, nous avons toujours des assiettes.

Pied-à-terre
SOLDES! LIQUIDATION TOTALE!

stéréo	**assiettes**
CDs	**bâtons**
fauteuils	**lampes**
vélos	**tapis**
magnétoscopes	
verres	**armoires**

31, RUE R. DELAGNES
TÉL: 04.93.24.86.02

Modèles:

Tu manges quelque chose?
Non, je ne mange rien.

Tu attends quelqu'un?
Non, je n'attends personne.

8 You're in a bad mood. Answer each question negatively using **ne (n')... rien** or **ne (n')... personne**.

1. Tu cherches quelque chose dans le grenier?
2. Tu veux quelque chose?
3. Tu achètes quelque chose au supermarché?
4. Tu invites quelqu'un à la boum?
5. Tu fais quelque chose ce soir?
6. Tu présentes quelqu'un à tes parents?
7. Tu ressembles à quelqu'un dans ta famille?
8. Tu étudies avec quelqu'un?

Non, je ne fais rien ce soir.

Communication

Using your imagination, draw a monster with various parts of the body that are unusual, for example, three small heads, one long leg, five eyes, etc. Next write a description in French of your monster, for example, **Il a trois petites têtes, une jambe très longue, cinq yeux...** etc. Then form groups of three. Each group member reads his or her description while the other two draw this monster based on what they hear. Afterward, students compare the original monsters with the drawings the other two group members have made and note similarities and differences.

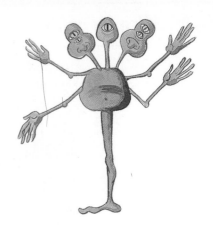

0 Write a paragraph about your activities. Name five things that you never do, five things that you used to do but don't do any more and five things that you always do. You might begin to organize your thoughts by writing lists that have the following headings: **ne (n')... jamais, ne (n')... plus** and **toujours.** Use the information from your three lists to write your paragraph.

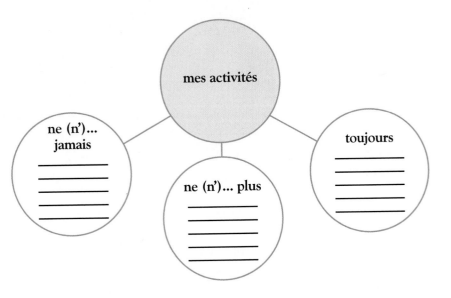

11 With a partner, have a phone conversation about a patient making an appointment to see a dentist. Student A plays the role of someone with a toothache and Student B plays the role of the dentist's receptionist. The patient calls the dentist's office, begins the conversation by saying hello, states his or her problem and then asks for an appointment. The receptionist and the patient discuss various times and days. They finally decide on a time that is convenient for both the dentist and the patient.

 **Listening Activity 2**

Teacher's Notes

1. You may want students to use colored markers in their drawings, specifying a color for each part of the body when they do Activity 9.
2. You may want students to draw on large white sheets of paper so that the drawings can be displayed for all to see.

Cooperative Group Practice

Inside-Outside Circle

Have each student write a question at the top of a note card. This question should use one of the affirmative expressions. The answer to this question, written at the bottom of the card, should include one of the negative expressions. For example, **Tu aimes quelqu'un?/ Non, je n'aime personne.** Collect the note cards. Have students form two circles with the same number of students in each one, one circle inside the other. Students face their partner. Distribute the note cards, one to each student. The outside student asks the question to the inside student. After the inside student answers correctly, he or she asks the question to the outside student. After the outside student answers correctly, all students exchange cards with their partner and the outside students move one person to the right. Asking and answering questions continue until students return to their original partners.

NATIONAL STANDARDS
C1.1, C1.2, C1.3

347

Workbook Activity 11

Teacher's Note

The French are worried about the deterioration of their social security system. Its cost is rising rapidly because people tend to abuse and take advantage of it.

Connections

National Health Care

You may want your students to do research on the national health care programs of both France and Canada. (Students may want to compare these programs to the current U.S. health care program.) Students should report their findings to the entire class. Another possible topic for student research is **le SIDA** (*AIDS*) and the success of the Pasteur Institute in Paris.

Comparisons

Cultural Journal

You may want to organize class debates on one or more of these health-related topics: 1. the advantages and disadvantages of socialized medicine, 2. the advantages of natural and/or preventative medicine vs. the use of drugs and/or operations to cure illnesses, 3. the salaries of doctors and others in the medical profession. If your students are keeping a cultural journal, you might have them write a personal response to questions posed in the debates.

NATIONAL STANDARDS
C2.1, C3.1, C4.2

Mise au point sur... la santé

Kayaking is an exciting way to exercise. (Limousin)

Like Americans, French people are increasingly conscious of physical fitness. By receiving adequate health care, watching their eating habits and exercising on a regular basis, **garder la ligne** (*keeping in shape*) has become a way of life for the French.

The French system of national health care provides medical treatment for everyone who needs it. All taxpayers contribute to the social security system (**la Sécurité sociale**, or **"la sécu"**), which covers most of the costs of visits to doctors and dentists, as well as prescription medicines. To avoid serious illnesses, many people try to keep healthy by eating nutritious foods and exercising.

The cost of most doctors' visits is covered by the social security system.

In recent years French cooking has changed to reflect a growing interest in healthy foods. In many French kitchens, products that are low in fat and high in fiber have replaced traditional heavy sauces and rich dairy products. Although a typical French meal normally consists of several courses, the portions tend to be quite small. Also, most French people snack very little between meals. When they do have **une petite faim** (*a little hunger*), they usually reach for a piece of fruit rather than for an artificially sweetened or salty snack.

Exercise is another way for the French to maintain physical well-being. Rather than relying on cars for transportation, many people choose to walk to their destinations. Health clubs provide aerobics and dance classes, as well as weight training equipment. Some people work out in their own homes with the help of exercise videos and TV programs. Many people exercise by taking advantage of inexpensive community facilities, such as public tennis courts and swimming pools. Soccer, cycling and martial arts clubs are popular with teenagers. Common family vacation activities offer other forms of exercise, such as mountain climbing (**l'alpinisme**), skiing, and windsurfing (**la planche à voile**). French people of all ages play **boules** (called **pétanque** in southern France), a form of lawn bowling.

Playing *boules* is another great way to get outdoor exercise.

ALPINISME ET ESCALADE

Many French adults visit health spas to receive treatments for various ailments, such as liver, heart and digestive problems. During their stay, they rest, diet, drink mineral water and take thermal baths. The Romans were the first to recognize the benefits of the warm waters of the French city of Digne-les-Bains in the department of Alpes-de-Haute-Provence. The spas of this city, open from March to November, are famous for treating rheumatism and respiratory illnesses. Often people supplement a cleansing, relaxing visit to a health spa with more vigorous exercise during the rest of the year.

EURO THERMES

LE RENDEZ-VOUS SANTÉ

Onze stations thermales

AIX-EN-PROVENCE - BAGNERES-DE-BIGORRE - LA BOURBOULE
CAPVERN-LES-BAINS - CAUTERETS - CHATEL-GUYON - CILAOS - DIGNE-LES-BAINS
LES EAUX-BONNES - ROCHEFORT-SUR-MER - CALDAS-DA-FELGUEIRA

Une agence à Paris

Onze indications thérapeutiques

Rhumatologie - Phlébologie - O.R.L. voies respiratoires - Appareil digestif
Maladies métaboliques - Affections psychosomatiques
Appareil réno-urinaire - Gynécologie - Dermatologie - Stomatologie
Troubles du développement chez l'enfant

87, av. du Maine - 75014 PARIS
01 43 27 12 50 Pour en savoir plus :

Yet, with all their efforts to stay fit, the French face significant health-related issues. The increasing number of fast-food restaurants and their popularity with teenagers worry people who are concerned with nutrition. Smoking is also a serious problem for this age group. The French government has a monopoly on the sale of cigarettes. Nevertheless, strict laws have been passed limiting tobacco advertising and forbidding smoking in certain places. Strong anti-smoking campaigns have been launched to reduce the number of people who smoke.

At school or work and during their leisure hours, many French people spend both time and energy on maintaining good health. Regular medical and dental visits, participation in sports and a healthy diet all contribute to the goal of physical well-being.

Nutritionists agree that many fast-food items have a high fat content and "empty" calories.

---

12   Answer the following questions.

1. How do French people keep in shape?
2. Who is covered under the French national health care system?
3. What health-related expenses are covered by the French social security system?
4. How big are the portions of food in a typical French meal?
5. Do the French often snack between meals?
6. Rather than relying on cars, how do many French people get to their destinations?
7. What are three sports in which the French participate to maintain physical well-being?
8. What is **boules**?
9. What are four things people do at a health spa?
10. What are two concerns about the health of French teenagers in general?

Answers

13 1. You should eat a lot of fruits and vegetables for the vitamins.
2. You should schedule a visit with your doctor once a year.
3. As a result of excess weight, your heart tires easily.
4. You should avoid tobacco and alcohol.
5. You should walk one-half hour each day.
6. You should get eight hours of sleep each night.
7. No, you shouldn't season your food with lots of salt.
8. Answers will vary.

13 Here are ten ways to keep your heart healthy. After reading the suggestions and looking at the pictures, answer the questions that follow.

Pour votre cœur... dix conseils-santé.

1 Mangez des fruits et des légumes pour les vitamines.

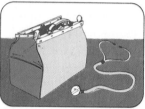
2 Voyez votre médecin une fois par an.

3 Contrôlez votre poids: l'excès fatigue le cœur.

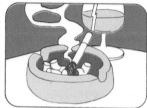
4 Réduisez tabac et alcool.

5 Ménagez-vous chaque jour quelques pauses-détente.

6 Faites le plein d'air pur pendant le week-end.

7 Pratiquez tous les jours une demi-heure de marche.

8 Dormez au moins huit heures par nuit.

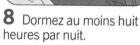
9 Ne consommez pas trop de sel.

10 Évitez l'excès de cholestérol.

1. Why should you eat a lot of fruits and vegetables?
2. How many times a year should you schedule a visit to your doctor?
3. What part of your body tires easily as a result of excess weight?
4. What two products should you avoid?
5. How long should you walk each day?
6. How many hours of sleep should you get each night?
7. Should you season your food with lots of salt?
8. How many of these suggestions do you follow?

Il a mal à la tête.

Il a mal au cœur.

Il a mal aux dents.

Il a mal au dos.

Il a mal à la gorge.

Il a mal aux oreilles.

Leçon C

In this lesson you will be able to:

➤ **express concern**

➤ **make a complaint**

➤ **explain a problem**

➤ **express need and necessity**

➤ **make a prediction**

➤ **give advice**

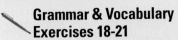

Workbook
Activities 12-14

Grammar & Vocabulary
Exercises 18-21

Audiocassette/CD
Où as-tu mal?

Transparencies 51-52

Teacher's Notes

1. Other related terms are
l'estomac (m.) (*stomach*), **avoir**
une angine (*to have a bad sore*
throat, to have tonsillitis), **être en**
forme (*to feel well*), **une maladie**
(*illness*), **des boutons (m.)** (*pimples*),
une ordonnance (*prescription*),
un médicament (*medicine*), **une**
aspirine (*aspirin*), **un kleenex**
(*Kleenex*), **un mouchoir** (*hand-*
kerchief), **tousser** (*to cough*),
éternuer (*to sneeze*) and **un/une**
malade (*patient, sick person*).
2. Communicative functions
that are recycled in this lesson
are "asking for information" and
"expressing intentions."

NATIONAL STANDARDS
C1.2, C4.1

351

Paired Practice

Qu'est-ce que tu as?

Working in pairs, students can take turns miming a specific ailment as their partners guess what it is. For example, one student looks sad and covers his or her ears. The other student says **Tu as mal aux oreilles.**

Game

Jacques dit....

You may want to play this TPR game again with your students. Include the expressions for parts of the body that are introduced in this lesson. (The game was explained in **Leçon A** of this unit.)

Cooperative Group Practice

Making Excuses

Tell your students to imagine that they are feeling a bit mischievous and are planning excuses to give the school nurse so that they can be sent home. Put your students in small groups of three of four and have them come up with as many plausible excuses as possible. After groups have completed their lists, they may share them orally with the entire class.

Elle est malade.

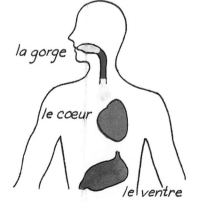

Workbook Activity 15

Audiocassette/CD
Dialogue, Enquête culturelle

Video

Martine Bekhechi doesn't feel well, and her mother asks her what's wrong.

Martine:	**Atchoum!**
Mme Bekhechi:	**À tes souhaits! Qu'est-ce que tu as?**
Martine:	**Je ne suis pas en bonne forme. J'ai mal au cœur.**
Mme Bekhechi:	**Tu as de la fièvre? Je dois prendre ta température.**
Martine:	**J'ai des frissons aussi.**
Mme Bekhechi:	**C'est peut-être la grippe. Tu dois rester au lit. Moi, je vais téléphoner au médecin.**

Teacher's Notes

1. French speakers say **Atchoum!** (*Achoo!*) when they sneeze. This word is for passive recognition only. 2. Another common response when someone sneezes is **À tes amours!** (*Bless you!*) In Switzerland, people respond by saying **Santé!** 3. You may want to point out that **rester** is a false cognate. 4. You may want to tell your students that many French doctors still make house calls on a regular basis and charge only a slightly higher fee than for office calls. 5. You may want to put your students in small groups and have each group design and draw a colorful poster to illustrate one of the picturesque health expressions in the **Enquête culturelle**.

Most stomachaches in France are blamed on the liver. When someone says that he or she has **une crise de foie** (literally, a liver attack), everyone understands that the person probably is experiencing indigestion rather than serious liver trouble.

Enquête culturelle

The French use many colorful expressions to describe their health. Here are a few samples.

Il a les jambes en compote.	*His legs feel like jelly.*
Elle n'est pas dans son assiette.	*She's not feeling well.*
Elle a une fièvre de cheval.	*She has a very high temperature.*
Il a des fourmis dans les jambes.	*He has pins and needles in his legs.*
Elle est clouée au lit.	*She has to stay in bed.*
Il a un chat dans la gorge.	*He has a frog in his throat.*
Son estomac fait des nœuds.	*Her stomach is tied in knots.*

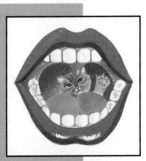

In French-speaking countries, a pharmacy (**une pharmacie**) has a bright green cross on the front of the building. When the cross is lit, the pharmacy is open.

To find a pharmacy, look for the bright green cross.

Answers

1 Possible answers:

1. Martine est malade.
2. Martine n'est pas en bonne forme.
3. Elle a mal au cœur.
4. Sa mère va prendre la température de Martine.
5. Oui, elle a des frissons.
6. Elle va rester au lit.
7. Mme Bekhechi va téléphoner au médecin.

2 Possible answers:

1. Elle a de la fièvre.
2. Il est fatigué.
3. Il a mal au ventre.
4. Elle a mal à la tête.
5. Il a mal à la gorge.
6. Elle a mal aux dents.

Connections

Herb Teas

Ask your students to call or visit a local health food store to find out what herb teas are available. They should also ask about the uses of various herb teas. Assign several students to bring some mint leaves or camomile and sugar, a teapot and paper cups to class to make **une infusion**. To make herb tea, pour boiling water over the herbs, let it steep for several minutes and add sugar to taste.

Comparisons

Cultural Journal

Invite the health teacher, the school nurse or a member of the health profession to your class to give a brief presentation and lead a discussion on alternative medical treatments. Have your students write a personal response to the class discussion in their cultural journal.

NATIONAL STANDARDS
C1.1, C1.2, C2.1, C2.2, C3.1, C4.2

354

Because many French people believe that certain plants can help relieve some aches and pains, most specialty stores and markets have herbal sections. Herbal teas are often given to people who don't feel well. Any tea made with natural herbs is called **une infusion**.

ELEPHANT
THÉ
VERT A LA MENTHE
AVEC DES FEUILLES DE MENTHE
THÉ AROMATISÉ A LA MENTHE
L'alliance gourmande de la saveur du thé vert et de la fraîcheur tonique de la menthe.
Conseils de préparation :
Utilisez un sachet par tasse.
Versez de l'eau frémissante sur le sachet. Laissez infuser de 3 à 5 minutes selon votre goût.

The French sometimes use alternative medical treatments to complement traditional medicine. In one such treatment, **l'homéopathie** (*homeopathy*), a person takes small doses of a remedy which provokes the same symptoms as the sickness that the patient wants to fight. By taking these pills, the person eventually builds up a resistance to the illness. Although many people believe in this type of cure, others think that this form of medicine is largely psychosomatic. Stomach ailments, colds and headaches might all be treated by **l'homéopathie**. Sections of some pharmacies and entire specialty stores are devoted to this form of treatment.

Many pharmacies offer homeopathic treatments. (Angers)

1 | *Répondez en français.*

1. Qui est malade?
2. Martine, qu'est-ce qu'elle a?
3. Où a-t-elle mal?
4. Qui va prendre la température de Martine?
5. Est-ce que Martine a des frissons?
6. Où est-ce que Martine va rester?
7. Mme Bekhechi va téléphoner à qui?

Clémence a des frissons et elle a mal à la tête. Donc, elle téléphone au médecin.

2 | According to the descriptions of the following people, tell what is probably wrong with them.

Modèle:
Le nez de Joël est très rouge.
Il a un rhume.

1. Chloé a une température de 39°.
2. Laurent Fignon finit le Tour de France.
3. Khaled mange trop de chocolat.
4. Sonia étudie beaucoup pour l'interro de maths.
5. Robert ne peut pas parler.
6. Mme Graedel prend rendez-vous avec le dentiste.

3 C'est à toi!

1. Comment vas-tu aujourd'hui?
2. Tu es fatigué(e) aujourd'hui?
3. Tu as souvent mal à la tête?
4. Est-ce que tu as beaucoup de rhumes en hiver?
5. Quand tu as de la fièvre, qui prend ta température?
6. Ton médecin, il/elle s'appelle comment?
7. Quand tu es malade, est-ce que tu aimes regarder la télé?

Même quand il est malade, Christian aime regarder la télé.

Structure

Present tense of the irregular verb *devoir*

The verb **devoir** (*to have to*) is irregular. It is often followed by an infinitive to express obligation.

devoir			
je	**dois**	Je **dois** téléphoner au médecin.	*I have to call the doctor.*
tu	**dois**	Tu **dois** rester au lit.	*You must stay in bed.*
il/elle/on	**doit**	Il **doit** prendre sa température.	*He must take his temperature.*
nous	**devons**	Nous **devons** étudier.	*We have to study.*
vous	**devez**	Vous **devez** prendre quelque chose.	*You should eat something.*
ils/elles	**doivent**	Qu'est-ce qu'ils **doivent** faire?	*What do they have to do?*

Laurent doit faire son lit.

UN PARFUM DOIT ÊTRE UNE ŒUVRE D'ART

Pratique

4 You work in Docteur Odermatt's dental office. It's time to send out reminders to people who haven't seen the dentist in the past six months. Based on how long it's been since their last checkup, tell whether or not the following patients have to make an appointment.

Modèle:

Sophie et David Tulipe doivent prendre rendez-vous avec le dentiste.

Sophie et David Tulipe	deux ans
M. et Mme Chevalier	un mois
Benjamin Robillard	trois semaines
Mlle Parsy	dix mois
Nadia et Myriam Vernon	cinq jours
M. Vega	quatre ans
Normand et Robert Bouchard	une semaine
Mme Picot	sept mois
Philippe Nino	un an

Workbook
Activities 16-17

Grammar & Vocabulary
Exercises 22-25

Audiocassette/CD
Activity 3

Computer Software
Activity 5

Answers

3 Answers will vary.

4 M. et Mme Chevalier ne doivent pas prendre rendez-vous avec le dentiste.

Benjamin Robillard ne doit pas prendre rendez-vous avec le dentiste.

Mlle Parsy doit prendre rendez-vous avec le dentiste.

Nadia et Myriam Vernon ne doivent pas prendre rendez-vous avec le dentiste.

M. Vega doit prendre rendez-vous avec le dentiste.

Normand et Robert Bouchard ne doivent pas prendre rendez-vous avec le dentiste.

Mme Picot doit prendre rendez-vous avec le dentiste.

Philippe Nino doit prendre rendez-vous avec le dentiste.

Teacher's Notes

1. Point out that the **t** in **doit** and **doivent** is pronounced only in the inverted form. 2. You might tell students that if **devoir** is followed by a noun, it means "to owe." For example, **Fabrice doit vingt euros à sa mère**. (*Fabrice owes his mother 20 euros.*) 3. Working in pairs, students can take turns asking and answering questions about what they have to do on certain days of the week. For example, **Qu'est-ce que tu dois faire le samedi?/Je dois travailler le samedi.**

NATIONAL STANDARDS
C1.1, C1.2, C4.1

Cooperative Group Practice

Qu'est-ce qu'on doit faire?

Put your students in two large groups. Have each student write on a piece of paper what he or she has to do on one specific day this week. For example, **Je dois aller chez le médecin jeudi.** Collect each group's papers and distribute them randomly to members of that group. Using the information on the pieces of paper, group members take turns asking who has to do what. For example, **Qui doit aller chez le médecin jeudi?** The student who wrote that information answers **Moi, je dois aller chez le médecin jeudi.**

Teacher's Note

You may want your students to decorate the posters they make in Activity 7 by either making a drawing or finding pictures to illustrate each of their sentences.

5 Tell which two items the indicated people should buy at the **marché aux puces** in order to spend all the money they have with them.

Modèle:

la prof (18 €)
La prof doit acheter le pot et la robe.

1. nous (17 €)
2. tu (16 €)
3. les parents de Martine (22 €)
4. je (10 €)
5. vous (12 €)

Communication

Modèle:

Marie-Hélène: Tu as mal à la tête?
Abdou: Oui, j'ai mal à la tête.
. . . .
Marie-Hélène: Deux élèves ont mal à la tête....

6 You want to know how your classmates are feeling today. On a separate sheet of paper, copy the seven indicated expressions that deal with health concerns. Then poll five of your classmates to determine whether or not they have any of these problems. As a classmate answers each of your seven questions, make a check if the answer is affirmative. After you have finished asking questions, count how many people are experiencing each of these problems and be ready to share your findings with the rest of the class.

mal à la tête	✔✔
mal au ventre	
mal à la gorge	
mal aux dents	
un rhume	
fatigué(e)	
malade	

To observe Health Education Week, you and your classmates are having a contest to see who can create the best poster in French to promote good health. Choose any five of the health concerns listed in Activity 6. Then write two sentences for each one that tell what you should do or what you should not do to avoid that problem.

Modèle:

mal aux dents
Je dois prendre rendez-vous avec le dentiste.
Je ne dois pas manger beaucoup de chocolat.

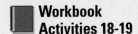 **Workbook Activities 18-19**

 Listening Activity 3A

 Quiz *Leçon C*

Computer Software Activity 6

When you were young, before you learned how to read, you probably spent a lot of time looking through storybooks. Even though you couldn't read the words, you were able to figure out what the stories were about. How? By looking at the pictures, of course! In fact, over time you could probably tell the stories yourself, just by referring to the illustrations or photos that accompanied them. Taking advantage of information contained in visual references can help you do two things: 1) predict what you will be reading about, and 2) figure out the meaning of unknown words. Examining pictures before you begin a French reading will put your mind on the right track; referring to them while you read will help keep it there.

Before you read the magazine article that follows, use the illustrations to predict the main idea. Then, as you read the article, use them to figure out the meaning of words you don't know in order to understand the details.

Sur la bonne piste

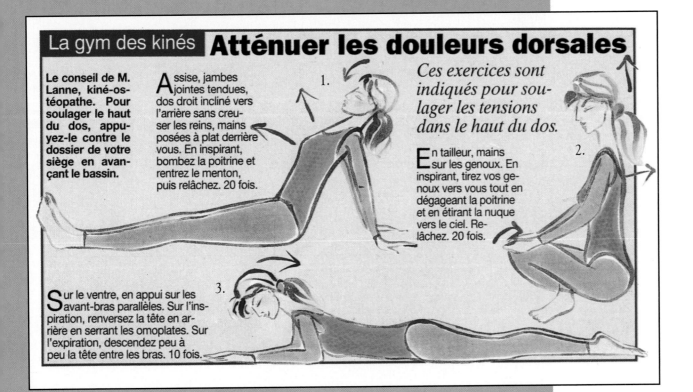

La gym des kinés Atténuer les douleurs dorsales

Le conseil de M. Lanne, kiné-ostéopathe. Pour soulager le haut du dos, appuyez-le contre le dossier de votre siège en avançant le bassin.

Assise, jambes jointes tendues, dos droit incliné vers l'arrière sans creuser les reins, mains posées à plat derrière vous. En inspirant, bombez la poitrine et rentrez le menton, puis relâchez. 20 fois.

Ces exercices sont indiqués pour soulager les tensions dans le haut du dos.

En tailleur, mains sur les genoux. En inspirant, tirez vos genoux vers vous tout en dégageant la poitrine et en étirant la nuque vers le ciel. Relâchez. 20 fois.

Sur le ventre, en appui sur les avant-bras parallèles. Sur l'inspiration, renversez la tête en arrière en serrant les omoplates. Sur l'expiration, descendez peu à peu la tête entre les bras. 10 fois.

 **NATIONAL STANDARDS** C1.2, C1.3, C2.1, C3.1, C3.2, C4.2, C5.1

Answers

8 1. a. Exercise 2 requires you to squat.
   b. Exercise 1 requires you to sit down.
   c. Exercise 3 requires you to lie on your stomach.

2. a. Exercise 3 requires you to tip your head backward.
   b. Exercise 1 requires you to tip your head forward.
   c. Exercise 2 requires you to raise your head by stretching your neck.

3. You should repeat exercises 1 and 2 twenty times and exercise 3 ten times.

4. You should do it slowly.

5. The exercises are for the (upper) back.

6. The exercises relieve back tension.

7. The French word for "forearm" is **avant-bras**.

8. Answers will vary.

Teacher's Notes

1. You may want students to work in pairs as they answer the questions. Note that the first seven questions have specific answers. However, there is still some room for subjectivity. The last question is an interpretation question, and students should be encouraged to come up with a variety of answers. To holistically grade this activity, refer to the suggestions on page 162. 2. Optional activity. You may want to have students do the exercises described in the magazine article. Put students in pairs and have them figure out together how to perform the exercises by reading the article and referring to the illustrations.

8 Use the illustrations to help you answer the following questions.

1. Which exercise requires you to . . .
   a. squat?
   b. sit down?
   c. lie on your stomach?

2. Which exercise requires you to . . .
   a. tip your head backward?
   b. tip your head forward?
   c. raise your head by stretching your neck?

3. How many times should you repeat each exercise?

4. When you drop your head between your arms during exercise 3, should you do it quickly or slowly?

5. What part of the body are the exercises for?

6. What do the exercises relieve?

7. You know that the French word for "arm" is **bras**. What is the French word for "forearm"?

8. People in what occupations could benefit most from doing these exercises?

Nathalie et Raoul

C'est à moi!

Now that you have completed this unit, take a look at what you should be able to do in French. Can you do all of these tasks?

➤ I can express astonishment.

➤ I can express emotions.

➤ I can point out something.

➤ I can make a complaint.

➤ I can explain a health-related problem.

➤ I can express sympathy.

➤ I can express concern.

➤ I can say what needs to be done.

➤ I can give advice.

➤ I can reassure someone.

➤ I can make a prediction.

➤ I can make an appointment.

➤ I can state approximate time.

➤ I can give information about various topics, using negative expressions.

J'ai mal aux dents.

Here is a brief checkup to see how much you understand about French culture. Decide if each statement is **vrai** or **faux**.

1. Chamonix is a winter sports resort located in **les Pyrénées** in southwestern France.
2. **Le Mont Blanc** got its name because it remains snow covered all year long.
3. Cross-country skiing is more popular with French teens than downhill skiing is.
4. Geneva, Switzerland, serves as the headquarters for many international organizations.
5. Everyone in Switzerland speaks French.
6. The French have a national health care system that provides medical treatment for everyone.
7. Many French people visit health spas to treat liver, heart and digestive ailments by resting, dieting and taking thermal baths.
8. Fortunately, French teens in general do not have a serious smoking problem.
9. When people have indigestion or a stomachache in France, they usually blame it on their liver.
10. **L'homéopathie** is an alternative medical treatment in which patients build up a resistance to the illness they are suffering from.

Alpine peaks are covered with snow all year long. (Switzerland)

Lausanne, a large French-speaking Swiss city, is known for its castle and cathedral.

Listening Activity 3B

Answers

1. faux
2. vrai
3. faux
4. vrai
5. faux
6. vrai
7. vrai
8. faux
9. vrai
10. vrai

Teacher's Note

Here is the English version of the cartoon on page 358: You look sick, Raoul. What's the matter with you? I have an upset stomach. Me, too, Ma'am. I also have the chills. And me, I have a headache. Oh dear! You three have to go to the infirmary. Yes, Ma'am. OK, Ma'am. Yes, Ma'am. (At the infirmary) You're not in good shape. Stay in bed. I'm going to call your parents. Thank you, Miss. OK, Miss. Thank you, Miss. Oh no! It's an epidemic! Things are going very badly! I have an upset stomach! Where's the bathroom?! Help! I'm not feeling well! Achoo! I have a very high temperature! (School is closed.)

NATIONAL STANDARDS
C1.1, C2.1, C2.2, C3.1, C4.2

Communication orale

With a partner, play the roles of an American student and a French tour guide. The student has just arrived in France on the last stop of a ten-country, three-week European tour. The tour group encountered various weather conditions, ate many different types of food and spent long hours riding on the tour bus. The student, consequently, is not feeling at all well and begins the conversation by saying so. The tour guide asks the student what the matter is, and the student tells what symptoms he or she has. The tour guide tells the student what the problem must be, what he or she should or should not do to get better and whether or not it's necessary to make an appointment to see a doctor.

Communication écrite

Imagine that you are a French tour guide who has just spoken with a sick American student. Each night the tour company you work for requires you to write a memo telling what problems you encountered during the day. Write a report to your tour company telling which student is sick, how he or she is feeling, what the matter is, what symptoms he or she is experiencing, what problem he or she has, what he or she should or should not do to get better and whether or not the student needs to make an appointment to see a doctor.

Communication active

Stéphane a mal à la gorge.

To express astonishment, use:

Oh là là!   *Wow! Oh no! Oh dear!*

To express emotions, use:

J'ai peur.   *I'm afraid.*

To point out something, use:

Regarde!   *Look!*

To make a complaint, use:

Je ne suis pas en bonne forme. *I'm not in good shape.*

To explain a problem, use:

J'ai mal aux dents.   *I have a toothache.*
J'ai mal au cœur.   *I feel nauseous.*

To commiserate, use:

Je regrette.   *I'm sorry.*

To express concern, use:

Qu'est-ce que tu as?   *What's the matter with you?*

To express need and necessity, use:

Il faut garder les jambes solides.   *You need (it is necessary) to keep your legs steady.*

Je dois prendre ta température.   *I need to take your temperature.*

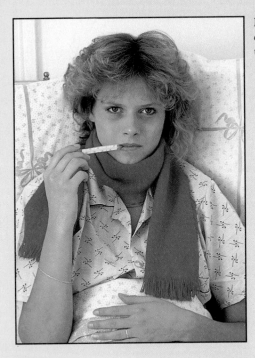

Margarette est malade;
elle doit prendre sa
température.

To give advice, use:

Tu dois rester au lit.   *You have to stay in bed.*
Il faut baisser la tête.   *You must lower your head.*
Mais pas trop.   *But not too much.*

To express reassurance, use:
Mais non, c'est facile.   *(But) no, it's easy.*

To make a prediction, use:
C'est peut-être la grippe.   *Maybe it's the flu.*

To make an appointment, use:
**Je voudrais prendre
rendez-vous avec....**   *I'd like to make an appointment
with . . .*

To state approximate time, use:
Aussitôt que possible.   *As soon as possible.*

To give information, use:
Nous **n'**avons **plus** de place
ce matin.   *We don't have any more room
this morning.*

Monsieur Odermatt **n'**est **jamais**
ici le jeudi après-midi.   *Mr. Odermatt is never here on
Thursday afternoon.*

Il **n'**y a **personne** ici.   *There's no one here.*

Je **ne** fais **rien.**   *I'm not doing anything.*

Communication électronique

For several centuries all of Europe has loved to bathe in the warm, therapeutic waters of southwestern France. Eurothermes operates eight thermal spas that are each built around a natural water source. To learn more about these spas, go to this Internet site:

http://www.eurothermes.com/indexE.htm

After exploring this site, answer the following questions.

1. Which Eurothermes spa is not within the borders of France? Where is it?
2. Click on "Histoire." For how many years have these warm waters been used for medicinal purposes?
3. Which government program offers reimbursement for visits to thermal spas?
4. Now click on the site of one of these spas, Ax-les-Thermes. This spa is well known because of the temperature of its water. How warm is it?
5. Click on "Hébergement." How many two-star hotels are there in Ax-les-Thermes?
6. Finally click on "Retour" and then on "Évasion Bien-être" to find information on ten other health spas in France. What are four health problems that can be treated here?
7. The thermal spa at Ax-les-Thermes can also treat these other health problems. Click on this city. At what price does the "Bien-être et Santé" package start?

À moi de jouer!

Now it's your turn to put together everything that you have learned about health by completing the two dialogues below with appropriate expressions from this unit. In the first scene, Éric calls to make an appointment to see his doctor. In the second scene he complains to his doctor and points out his problems, and his doctor gives him advice. (You may want to refer to the *Communication active* on pages 360-61 and the vocabulary list on page 363.)

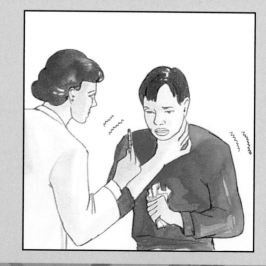

Vocabulaire

À tes souhaits! Bless you!
l' **après-midi (m.)** afternoon
Au secours! Help!
aussitôt que as soon as
avoir bonne/mauvaise mine to look well/sick
avoir chaud to be warm, hot
avoir froid to be cold
avoir mal (à...) to hurt, to have a/an . . . ache, to have a sore . . .
    avoir mal au cœur to feel nauseous
avoir peur (de) to be afraid (of)

baisser to lower
un **bâton** ski pole
une **bouche** mouth
un **bras** arm

un **cabinet** (doctor or dentist's) office
chaud: avoir chaud to be warm, hot
un **cœur** heart
    avoir mal au cœur to feel nauseous
un **corps** body
un **cou** neck

une **dent** tooth
devoir to have to
un **docteur** doctor
un **doigt** finger
    un doigt de pied toe
un **dos** back

une **épaule** shoulder

facile easy
falloir to be necessary, to have to
fatigué(e) tired
faut: il faut it is necessary, one has to/must, we/you have to/must
la **fièvre** fever
une **figure** face
une **forme: être en bonne/mauvaise forme** to be in good/bad shape
des **frissons (m.)** chills
froid: avoir froid to be cold

garder to keep
un **genou** knee
une **gorge** throat
la **grippe** flu

jamais: ne (n')... jamais never
une **jambe** leg

une **main** hand
mal: avoir mal (à...) to hurt, to have a/an . . . ache, to have a sore . . .
malade sick
la **mine: avoir bonne/mauvaise mine** to look well/sick

ne (n')... jamais never
ne (n')... personne no one, nobody, not anyone
ne (n')... plus no longer, not anymore
ne (n')... rien nothing, not anything
un **nez** nose

un **œil** eye
Oh là là! Wow! Oh no! Oh dear!
une **oreille** ear

une **personne: ne (n')... personne** no one, nobody, not anyone
la **peur: avoir peur (de)** to be afraid (of)
un **pied** foot
    un doigt de pied toe
la **place** room, space
plus: ne (n')... plus no longer, not anymore
prendre rendez-vous to make an appointment

Qu'est-ce que tu as? What's the matter with you?
quelqu'un someone, somebody

un(e) **réceptionniste** receptionist
regarder to look (at)
regretter to be sorry
un **rendez-vous** appointment
    prendre rendez-vous to make an appointment
rester to stay, to remain
un **rhume** cold
rien: ne (n')... rien nothing, not anything

la **santé** health
le **secours: Au secours!** Help!
solide steady
un **souhait: À tes souhaits!** Bless you!

une **température** temperature
une **tête** head
trop too much

un **ventre** stomach

Teacher's Notes

Songs

A. "Alouette." You may want to teach your students the French-Canadian folk song "Alouette" to practice body parts. Verse 1: Alouette, gentille alouette, alouette, je te plumerai. Je te plumerai la tête, je te plumerai la tête. Et la tête, et la tête, alouette, alouette, oh... Verse 2: Alouette, gentille alouette, alouette, je te plumerai. Je te plumerai le bec, je te plumerai le bec. Et le bec, et le bec, et la tête, et la tête, alouette, alouette, oh... Verse 3: Je te plumerai le cou... Verse 4: Je te plumerai les ailes... Verse 5: Je te plumerai le dos... Verse 6: Je te plumerai les pattes... Verse 7: Je te plumerai la queue.

B. "Head and shoulders, knees and toes." This is another traditional children's song that may be used to practice body parts. Tête, épaules, genoux et pieds, genoux et pieds (bis), J'ai deux yeux, un nez, une bouche et deux oreilles, Tête, épaules, genoux et pieds, genoux et pieds.

NATIONAL STANDARDS C1.2, C3.1, C5.2

Unité 11

En vacances

In this unit you will be able to:

➤ write postcards

➤ describe past events

➤ sequence events

➤ ask for information

➤ inquire about details

➤ tell location

➤ give directions

➤ give addresses

➤ identify objects

➤ express likes and dislikes

➤ state a preference

➤ express emotions

NATIONAL STANDARDS
C2.1

Workbook Activity 1

 Grammar & Vocabulary Exercises 1-3

 Audiocassette/CD *L'Europe, La gare*

Transparencies 53-55

Teacher's Notes

1. There are two other French-speaking regions in Europe, Andorra and Monaco. **L'Andorre (f.)** is located between France and Spain in **les Pyrénées** and has only about 40,000 inhabitants. **Monaco (m.)** is a principality on the French Riviera near the Italian border. 2. Realia to have on hand when introducing this lesson includes a map of Europe and a French train schedule. 3. Communicative functions that are recycled in this lesson are "asking for information," "stating exact time" and "asking and telling the date."

Connections

National Tourist Offices

You may ask your students to write to the national tourist offices of Belgium, Luxembourg and Switzerland to obtain more information about these francophone countries. Here are their addresses: Belgian Tourist Office, 780 Third Avenue, New York, NY 10017; Luxembourg National Tourist Office, 17 Beekman Place, New York, NY 10022; Switzerland Tourism Office, 608 Fifth Avenue, New York, NY 10020.

NATIONAL STANDARDS
C1.2, C3.1, C3.2, C4.2, C5.1

Leçon A

In this lesson you will be able to:

➤ **describe past events**

➤ **tell location**

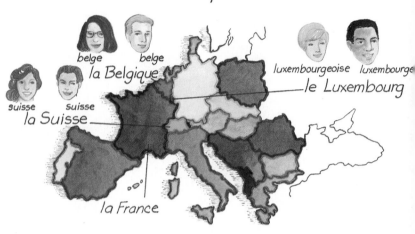

l'Europe (f.)

belge *belge*
la Belgique

luxembourgeoise *luxembourge*
le Luxembourg

suisse *suisse*
la Suisse

la France

un horaire

un train

la gare

Diane and Nicolas are talking about what they did during vacation.

Diane: **Tiens, Nicolas! Quand est-ce que tu es rentré de vacances?**

Nicolas: **Ma famille et moi, nous sommes rentrés hier soir. Le train est arrivé à la gare à 22h05.**

Diane: **Vous êtes allés en Belgique, n'est-ce pas?**

Nicolas: **Oui, nous sommes partis pour Bruxelles le 29 octobre. C'est une belle ville. Et toi, tu es restée ici?**

Diane: **Oui, je suis sortie avec des amis la veille de la Toussaint. C'est tout.**

Teacher's Notes

1. In *C'est à toi!* we present the **passé composé** with **être** in this **unité** and the **passé composé** with **avoir** in the following **unité**. In keeping with a natural, function-based approach to learning, students will learn how to express where they have been before learning how to say what they have done. 2. The verb **rentrer** often implies that the subject is returning home. To stress this idea even more, a speaker may say **Je rentre chez moi**. 3. Review with your students the 24-hour clock that was presented in **Leçon C** of **Unité 4**. 4. Your students may be curious about the present tense forms of the irregular verbs **partir** and **sortir**. They are **pars, pars, part, partons, partez, partent** and **sors, sors, sort, sortons, sortez, sortent**. 5. Bruxelles is pronounced [bʀysɛl]. 6. **La veille de la Toussaint** is All Saints' Eve, October 31. It does not resemble the American Halloween celebration. Be sure your students don't confuse **veille** with **ville** (also in this dialogue) or with **vieille**.

Two French holidays begin the month of November: **la Toussaint** (*All Saints' Day*) on November 1 and **le jour des Morts** (*the Day of the Dead*) on November 2. On these two days the French remember their war dead as well as deceased relatives and loved ones. Flowers, especially chrysanthemums, are placed on the graves of family and friends. Students celebrate the holidays by taking a week of vacation.

Enquête culturelle

Many French people travel by train. Some people who live in the suburbs of Paris take the train to work instead of drive a car. The **SNCF (Société nationale des chemins de fer français)**, a state-owned company, operates the French rail system, known for its trains that are on schedule, convenient and affordable. France has the most extensive network of tracks in Europe, and many people choose to travel by train when on vacation. France's modern **TGV (Train à grande vitesse)** runs 24 hours a day, covers all parts of France and extends into other European countries. It reaches speeds of up to 322 m.p.h., but usually goes about 186 m.p.h.

The TGV has a superior suspension system for a smooth ride.

SNCF C'EST POSSIBLE !

NATIONAL STANDARDS
C1.2, C2.1, C3.1, C4.2

Connections

Belgium, Luxembourg and Switzerland

To give your students some idea about the size of Belgium, Luxembourg and Switzerland, find and bring to class a European road map. (Your local AAA may be able to help you.) Point out to your students four or five cities in Belgium and calculate how far it is from one city to another. Do the same for Luxembourg and Switzerland. After you have done this, have your students make a list of ten of these cities along with the francophone country in which each one is located.

Traditional *gaufres* are square, but these popular desserts may come in various shapes.

HISTOIRES BELGE
différentes chaque jour

Belgium lies northeast of France on the North Sea. Belgians are divided primarily into two groups, according to which language they speak. The French-speaking Walloons live in the southern part of the country; the Dutch-speaking Flemings live in northern Belgium. Another country known for its good food, Belgium is the capital of French fries and **gaufres,** thick waffles covered with syrup, fresh fruit or cream. Belgian chocolates have a worldwide reputation.

Brussels, the capital of Belgium, is the country's economic, cultural and political center. Organizations such as the European Union (EU) and the North Atlantic Treaty Organization (NATO) have headquarters in or near the city. Ornate buildings that date from the 1500s, sidewalk cafés, and bird and flower markets decorate the city's main square (**la Grand-Place**). In 1815 Napoléon Bonaparte suffered his final defeat near Brussels in the city of Waterloo.

The historic buildings in Brussels' *Grand-Place* are in the Flemish Baroque style and decorated with gold.

La famille Gautier est rentrée de vacances.

1 *Trouvez dans la liste suivante l'expression qui complète correctement chaque phrase.*

hier soir	français	22h05	Toussaint
le 29 octobre	Nicolas	Belgique	Diane

1. ... est rentré de vacances.
2. Nicolas et sa famille sont rentrés....
3. Le train est arrivé à....
4. Nicolas est allé en....
5. Nicolas est parti....
6. En Belgique on parle....
7. ... est sortie avec des amis.
8. La... est le premier novembre.

Identify each numbered country you see in the illustration.

Modèle:
C'est la France.

Audiocassette/CD Activity 3

Answers

2 1. C'est la Belgique.
  2. C'est l'Allemagne.
  3. C'est l'Espagne.
  4. C'est le Luxembourg.
  5. C'est l'Italie.
  6. C'est la Suisse.
  7. C'est l'Angleterre.

3 Answers will vary.

Comparisons

Cultural Journal

If your students are keeping a cultural journal, you might have them try to find examples of art, music and/or literature from the francophone countries introduced in this lesson. Then have students write their personal observations about these art forms in their journals.

---

3 *C'est à toi!*

1. Est-ce que tu préfères l'école ou les vacances?
2. Est-ce que tu prends souvent le train?
3. À quelle heure est-ce que tu vas rentrer après les cours aujourd'hui?
4. Est-ce que tu vas sortir avec tes amis ce vendredi soir?
5. Est-ce que tu restes à la maison la veille de la Toussaint?
6. Qu'est-ce que tu fais la veille de la Toussaint?

NATIONAL STANDARDS
C1.1, C1.2, C3.1, C4.2

Workbook
Activities 3-6

Grammar & Vocabulary
Exercises 4-9

Computer Software
Activities 1-2

Teacher's Notes

1. Review the forms of **être** with your students before beginning this section. 2. Mention that the past participles of **-er** verbs sound exactly like the infinitives. 3. Traditionally, a past participle does not agree with the subject pronoun **on**. But in current French you may encounter agreement between the past participle and the subject's implied gender and number. 4. Tell students that not all verbs conjugated with **être** express motion. For example, the verb **rester** means "to stay" or "to remain." 5. In this **leçon** we list only those eight **être** verbs that have been previously introduced. You may choose to also include the other eight verbs in the phrase DR. & MRS. VANDERTRAMP (or, if you prefer, MRS. D. R. VANDERTRAMP) that are conjugated with **être** (**devenir**, **revenir**, **mourir**, **naître**, **descendre**, **tomber**, **retourner** and **monter**). Each letter in this phrase represents the first letter of a verb conjugated with **être**. The verb **revenir** will be introduced in **Leçon B**. You may want to include **passer** in this list even though its meaning "to pass" or "to go (by)" isn't presented until second-level French. (When it means "to show (a movie)" or "to spend (time)," **passer** is conjugated with **avoir**.) To help students to learn which verbs are conjugated with **être**, use the drawing of a house. Verbs that use **être** express movement into, from or within the house as well as a change of condition.

Structure

Passé composé with *être*

The **passé composé** is a verb tense used to tell what happened in the past. This tense is composed of two words: a helping verb and a past participle. To form the **passé composé** of certain verbs, use the appropriate present tense form of the helping verb **être** and the past participle of the main verb.

Vous **êtes allé** en Belgique.   *You went to Belgium.*

(helping verb)   (past participle of **aller**)

To form the past participle of **-er** verbs, drop the **-er** of the infinitive and add an **é**: **aller → allé**. The past participle of the verb agrees in gender (masculine or feminine) and in number (singular or plural) with the subject. For a masculine singular subject, add nothing to the past participle; for a masculine plural subject, add an **s**. For a feminine singular subject, add an **e**; for a feminine plural subject, add an **es**. Here is the **passé composé** of **aller**. Note in the chart that both the form of **être** and the ending of the past participle agree with the subject.

Denise est allée au marché. (Pointe-à-Pitre)

			aller	
je	suis	allé	Je **suis allé** en France.	*I went to France.*
je	suis	allée	Je **suis allée** chez moi.	*I went home.*
tu	es	allé	Marc, tu **es allé** à Paris?	*Marc, did you go to Paris?*
tu	es	allée	Nora, tu **es allée** au cinéma?	*Nora, did you go to the movies?*
il	est	allé	Ahmed n'**est** jamais **allé** en Europe.	*Ahmed has never gone to Europe.*
elle	est	allée	Elle **est allée** à la gare.	*She went to the train station.*
on	est	allé	Où **est**-on **allé**?	*Where did they go?*
nous	sommes	allés	Nous **sommes allés** en boîte.	*We went to the dance club.*
nous	sommes	allées	Nous ne **sommes** pas **allées** en Suisse.	*We didn't go to Switzerland.*
vous	êtes	allé	Monsieur Diouf, où **êtes**-vous **allé**?	*Mr. Diouf, where did you go?*
vous	êtes	allée	Vous **êtes allée** au centre commercial, Mme Gras?	*Did you go to the mall, Mrs. Gras?*
vous	êtes	allés	Vous n'**êtes** pas **allés** à la boulangerie?	*You didn't go to the bakery?*
vous	êtes	allées	Comment **êtes**-vous **allées** au Canada?	*How did you go to Canada?*
ils	sont	allés	Ils **sont allés** à l'école.	*They went to school.*
elles	sont	allées	Quand les filles **sont**-elles **allées** au café?	*When did the girls go to the café?*

To form the past participle of most **-ir** verbs, drop the **-ir** and add an **i**: **partir** → **parti**. (For some verbs that end in **-ir,** add a **u**.)

Most of the verbs that use **être** in the **passé composé** *express motion or movement* of the subject from one place to another. Here are the verbs you have already learned that use the helping verb **être,** along with their past participles. (You will learn more of these verbs later.)

Infinitive	Past Participle
all**er**	all**é**
arriv**er**	arriv**é**
entr**er**	entr**é**
rentr**er**	rentr**é**
rest**er**	rest**é**
part**ir**	part**i**
sort**ir**	sort**i**
but: ven**ir**	ven**u**

To make a negative sentence in the **passé composé**, put **ne (n')** before the form of **être** and **pas** after it.

Ma sœur **n'**est **pas** rentrée de vacances hier.	*My sister didn't come back from vacation yesterday.*
Le train **n'**est **pas** arrivé à la gare à 22h00.	*The train didn't arrive in the station at 10:00 P.M.*

To ask a question in the **passé composé** using inversion, put the subject pronoun after the form of **être**.

Thierry **est**-il déjà **parti**?	*Did Thierry leave already?*
Et toi, pourquoi n'**es**-tu pas **restée** à la boum?	*And why didn't you stay at the party?*

The **passé composé** has more than one meaning in English.

Ils **sont sortis**.	{ *They have gone out.* / *They went out.*
Sont-ils **sortis**?	*Did they go out?*

Mme Dagorne est sortie de la boucherie.

Teacher's Notes

1. There is often liaison after forms of **être** before a past participle beginning with a vowel sound. For example, **elle est allée**, **ils sont allés**.   [t]   [t]

2. To practice agreement in the **passé composé** with verbs that use **être**, make a transparency of various subject pronouns and **passé composé** forms with no agreement indicated. (For example, **elles sont venu__**.) Have students say what agreement, if any, is needed. (For example, **venu avec -es**.)

Cooperative Group Practice

Est-ce que tu es allé(e) à...?

To practice asking and answering questions in the **passé composé**, have each student make a list of five cities in the United States or in your state (or suggest five of the cities in Belgium, Luxembourg and Switzerland that you listed earlier in the preceding connections activity), putting them in a horizontal line at the top of a piece of paper. Next each student makes a list of five classmates, writing the names in a vertical line at the left of the piece of paper to form a grid. Then each student interviews the five listed classmates, asking them if they have gone to each of the cities. For example, **Est-ce que tu es allé(e) à Albany**? Students put check marks in the grid to show what cities their partners have visited. After the interviews have been completed, ask your students to write a summary of their surveys, telling who has or has not been to each city.

NATIONAL STANDARDS
C1.1, C1.2, C4.1

Audiocassette/CD Activity 4

Cooperative Group Practice

Forming Questions

So that students can practice forming questions in the **passé composé**, put them in groups of eight. Each group prepares two sets of eight note cards. Each of the cards in the first set contains a group member's name; each of the cards in the second set has a verb that is conjugated with **être** in the **passé composé**. Each student in the group selects two cards at random and asks a question in the **passé composé** to the student whose name is on the card. For example, **Richard/sortir — Richard, est-ce que tu es sorti hier soir?** The student whose name is on the card answers.

372

Pratique

4 Yesterday was the first day of vacation. Tell whether the following people left for Belgium or for Switzerland.

Modèles:

Karine

Karine est partie pour la Belgique.

M. Dumont

M. Dumont est parti pour la Suisse.

 1. Bruno

 4. M. Vert

 2. Mme Clerc

 5. le prof de français

 3. Amina

 6. la prof d'allemand

5 You took a poll to find out whether or not your classmates went out on Friday night. Give the results of your poll by completing the sentences that follow.

Modèles:

Sylvie et Salim **sont sortis**.
Sabrina et Nicole **ne sont pas sorties**.

Est-ce que tu es sortie vendredi soir, Karine?

Oui, je suis sortie vendredi soir. Pourquoi?

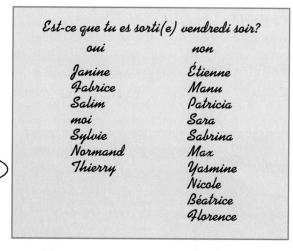

Est-ce que tu es sorti(e) vendredi soir?

oui	non
Janine	Étienne
Fabrice	Manu
Salim	Patricia
moi	Sara
Sylvie	Sabrina
Normand	Max
Thierry	Yasmine
	Nicole
	Béatrice
	Florence

1. Florence et Béatrice....
2. Thierry et moi, nous....
3. Étienne et Max....
4. Fabrice et Normand....
5. Manu et Patricia....
6. Janine et moi, nous....
7. Sara et Yasmine....

6 When did people arrive at school this morning? To find out, complete the following short dialogues with the appropriate forms of the verb **arriver**.

1. Sonia: Tu... à sept heures et demie?
   Daniel: Non, je... à sept heures vingt.
2. Jean-François: Vous... à quelle heure, Madame?
   Mme Graedel: M. Laurier et moi, nous... à huit heures moins le quart.
3. M. Smith: Vous... à huit heures?
   Élise et Anne: Oui, nous... à huit heures.
4. Thibault: Vous... à sept heures et demie, Monsieur?
   M. Deslauriers: Non, je... à huit heures moins vingt.
5. Malick: Tu... à quelle heure?
   Margarette: Je... à sept heures vingt.
6. Ariane: Vous... à sept heures et quart, Monsieur?
   M. Pinot: Oui, je... à sept heures et quart.

Modèle:

Ahmed: Tu **es arrivée** à quelle heure?
Caroline: Je **suis arrivée** à sept heures et demie.

---

7 Based on their purchases, tell where the following people went shopping.

1. mon ami et moi, nous

5. Mlle Paganelli

2. Frédéric et toi, vous

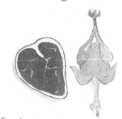

6. je

Modèle:

Chloé
Chloé est allée à la crémerie.

3. Isabelle et sa sœur

7. Mohamed et son demi-frère

4. le beau-père de Denise

Audiocassette/CD Activity 7

Answers

6 1. es arrivé, suis arrivé
2. êtes arrivée, sommes arrivés
3. êtes arrivées, sommes arrivées
4. êtes arrivé, suis arrivé
5. es arrivée, suis arrivée
6. êtes arrivé, suis arrivé

7 1. Mon ami et moi, nous sommes allés à la pâtisserie.
2. Frédéric et toi, vous êtes allés au supermarché.
3. Isabelle et sa sœur sont allées à la boulangerie.
4. Le beau-père de Denise est allé au marché.
5. Mlle Paganelli est allée au grand magasin.
6. Je suis allé(e) à la boucherie.
7. Mohamed et son demi-frère sont allés à la charcuterie.

Cooperative Group Practice

Où es-tu allé(e)?

Put your students in small groups of four or five. Give each group a set of pictures showing various places to shop. Each student in the group chooses one of the pictures at random and says that he or she went to the place to buy a certain object. For example, **Je suis allé(e) au marché pour acheter des tomates.** Finally, as a review, the student to the left of each speaker asks why he or she went to the place and the student to the right answers.

NATIONAL STANDARDS
C1.1, C1.2

Audiocassette/CD Activity 8

Answers

8 1. Es-tu rentré(e) à la maison après les cours vendredi après-midi?
Et toi, es-tu rentré(e) à la maison après les cours vendredi après-midi?

2. Es-tu sorti(e) avec des amis vendredi soir?
Et toi, es-tu sorti(e) avec des amis vendredi soir?

3. Es-tu allé(e) à une boum?
Et toi, es-tu allé(e) à une boum?

4. Es-tu entré(e) dans une boutique?
Et toi, es-tu entré(e) dans une boutique?

5. Es-tu resté(e) à la maison samedi soir?
Et toi, es-tu resté(e) à la maison samedi soir?

6. Es-tu venu(e) à l'école?
Et toi, es-tu venu(e) à l'école?

7. Es-tu parti(e) en vacances?
Et toi, es-tu parti(e) en vacances?

Students' responses to these questions will vary.

9 Adja Mutumbo est partie à 2h30 de Dakar. Elle est arrivée à Atlanta à 16h39.

Damien Vau est parti à 8h00 de Paris. Il est arrivé à Denver à 14h00.

Sabine Kaas est partie à 8h25 de Bruxelles. Elle est arrivée à Boston à 17h00.

Patrick Boucher est parti à 11h45 de Genève. Il est arrivé à Cincinnati à 17h45.

Nicole Bertrand est partie à 11h45 de Nice. Elle est arrivée à San Francisco à 14h45.

Henri Tremblay est parti à 13h45 de Montréal. Il est arrivé à Salt Lake City à 15h05.

374

Modèle:

aller au cinéma

Student A: Es-tu allé(e) au cinéma?

Student B: Oui, je suis allé(e) au cinéma. Et toi, es-tu allé(e) au cinéma?

Student A: Non, je ne suis pas allé(e) au cinéma.

Modèle:

Martine Vannier est partie à 13h55 de Paris. Elle est arrivée à Chicago à 20h00.

---

8 Find out what your partner did last weekend. Take turns asking and answering questions.

1. rentrer à la maison après les cours vendredi après-midi
2. sortir avec des amis vendredi soir
3. aller à une boum
4. entrer dans une boutique
5. rester à la maison samedi soir
6. venir à l'école
7. partir en vacances

Aurélie et Leïla sont sorties samedi soir. (La Rochelle)

Communication

9 Your French teacher, Mlle Hopen, is a program coordinator for an organization that sponsors French-speaking students who visit the United States. You have offered to help her with part of her report on an international group that just arrived. Mlle Hopen has asked you to write a memo detailing each student's departure and arrival times to send to the program director in Paris. Based on the information she has given you, prepare this memo to send to France.

Élève	Départ	Ville	Arrivée	Ville
Martine Vannier	13h55	Paris	20h00	Chicago
Adja Mutumbo	02h30	Dakar	16h39	Atlanta
Damien Vau	08h00	Paris	14h00	Denver
Sabine Kaas	08h25	Bruxelles	17h00	Boston
Patrick Boucher	11h45	Genève	17h45	Cincinnati
Nicole Bertrand	11h45	Nice	14h45	San Francisco
Henri Tremblay	13h45	Montréal	15h05	Salt Lake City

Audiocassette/CD
Prononciation

 Listening Activity 1

Quiz
Leçon A

10 You want to know what your classmates did last weekend. On a separate sheet of paper, create a chart like the one that follows and copy the six indicated expressions. Then poll five of your classmates to determine whether or not they did any of these activities. Write the names of the five classmates at the top of your chart. As a classmate answers each of your six questions, make a check in the appropriate column if he or she answers affirmatively. After you have finished asking questions, count how many people answered each question affirmatively and be ready to share your findings with the rest of the class.

	Théo	Jérémy	Sandrine	Sonia	Max
aller chez un ami	✔		✔		✔
rester à la maison vendredi soir					
aller au centre commercial					
sortir samedi soir					
aller au fast-food					
sortir dimanche avec les parents					

Modèle:

Myriam: Est-ce que tu es allé chez un ami?

Théo: Oui, je suis allé chez un ami.

. . . .

Myriam: Trois élèves sont allés chez un ami....

chez
Clément
——

11 Now use the results of your survey in Activity 10 to write a report on what your classmates did last weekend. For each question you asked, specify who answered affirmatively and who answered negatively.

Modèle:

Théo, Sandrine et Max sont allés chez un ami. Jérémy et Sonia ne sont pas allés chez un ami....

The sound [ɛ̃]

The nasal sound [ɛ̃] is represented by **in** when it appears before a consonant or at the end of a word. The **n** is not pronounced; the sound [ɛ̃] comes out through your nose. Say each of these words:

jar**din** **in**firmier
printemps mat**in**
informaticienne maga**sin**

The sound [ɛ̃] is also found in words containing the letters **ain** when they occur before a consonant or at the end of a word. Say each of these words:

tr**ain** salle de b**ain**s
Touss**aint** p**ain**
m**ain**tenant mexic**ain**

The sound [jɛ̃]

Words that end in **-ien** contain the sound [jɛ̃]. The only difference between the sounds [ɛ̃] and [jɛ̃] is the **i** in the **-ien** ending. Say each of these words:

informatic**ien** b**ien**
ch**ien** ital**ien**
canad**ien** comb**ien**

Prononciation

Game

Le jeu aux dés

You might have your students play this dice game to practice the **passé composé** of verbs that use **être**. First put students in pairs. Then give all pairs two dice, each a different color, say green and red. Next, show the class a transparency you have made with two columns, one green and the other red. The green column reads: 1 = **je**, 2 = **tu**, 3 = **il/elle**, 4 = **nous**, 5 = **vous** and 6 = **ils/elles**. The red column reads: 1 = **aller**, 2 = **partir**, 3 = **venir**, 4 = **arriver**, 5 = **sortir** and 6 = **rester**. With each roll of the dice, two colors and two sets of dots appear. Four dots on a green die and six dots on a red die mean, for example, that the roller must say the corresponding subject and verb shown on the transparency, i.e., **nous sommes resté(e)s**. If done correctly, he or she earns the total point value of the dice (i.e., 4 + 6 = 10). Players take turns at the dice and keep a running count of their own score. They can build up their scores quickly by rolling doubles. In the case of two twos, the roller should respond **tu es parti(e)**, thus earning four points. The lucky roller has the opportunity to double his or her score by giving the corresponding plural or singular form of the subject and verb, i.e., **vous êtes parti(e)(s)(es)**. When time runs out, the winning pair is the one with the highest total score.

NATIONAL STANDARDS
C1.1, C1.2, C1.3, C4.1

Grammar & Vocabulary Exercises 10-11

Audiocassette/CD
L'aéroport, Ordinal Numbers

Teacher's Notes

1. Students learned **premier**, **première** in **Unité 5**. 2. A communicative function that is recycled in this lesson is "identifying nationalities."

Leçon B

In this lesson you will be able to:

➤ write postcards

➤ express emotions

➤ tell location

➤ describe past events

➤ sequence events

➤ express likes and dislikes

➤ state a preference

un avion

un passepo[rt]

l'aéroport (m.)

premier / première   deuxième   troisième   quatrième   cinquième

sixième   septième   huitième   neuvième   dixième

Workbook Activity 7

 Audiocassette/CD *L'Afrique*

 Transparencies 56-57

Teacher's Note

The former **Zaïre** became **la République Démocratique du Congo** in 1997. Inhabitants of the new country are officially called **Congolais(e)**, but they still may refer to themselves as **Zaïrois(e)**.

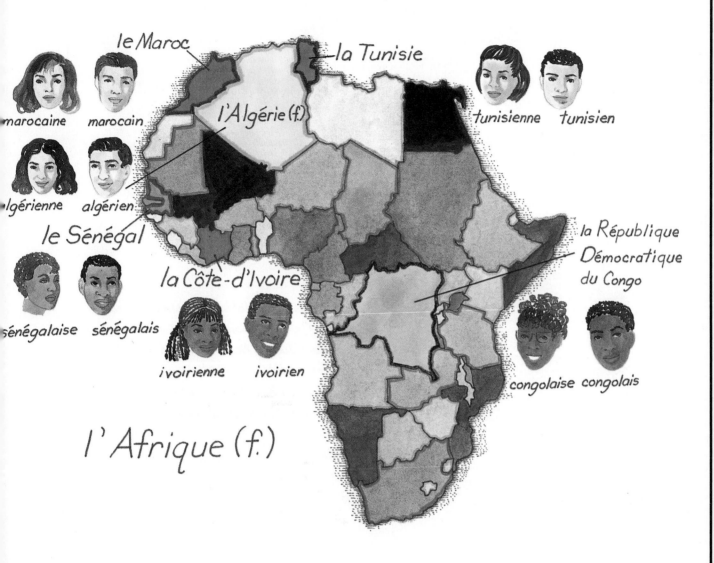

le Maroc

la Tunisie

l'Algérie (f.)

marocaine   marocain

tunisienne   tunisien

lgérienne   algérien

le Sénégal

la République Démocratique du Congo

la Côte-d'Ivoire

sénégalaise   sénégalais

ivoirienne   ivoirien

congolaise   congolais

l'Afrique (f.)

NATIONAL STANDARDS
C1.2, C3.1, C4.1

**Workbook
Activity 8**

**Audiocassette/CD
Postcard**

Teacher's Notes

1. The word **le séjour** meaning "family room" was introduced in **Unité 9**. In this letter it means "stay." 2. You might tell students that **revenir** is a member of the **venir** verb family. 3. **Gros bisous** is a more colloquial form of **Grosses bises**. Both expressions are used to end a personal letter in French. **Amitiés** (*Best wishes*) is a more formal expression used to end such a letter.

Alexandre is sending his friend Marie-Claire a postcard from his trip to West Africa with his parents.

Chère Marie-Claire,

Ce petit séjour est formidable ! L'avion est parti de Roissy-Charles de Gaulle, et nous sommes arrivés à l'aéroport à Abidjan en Côte-d'Ivoire. Nous sommes restés chez ma grand-mère qui est ivoirienne. Quatre jours après nous sommes partis pour Dakar. Le premier jour au Sénégal on est allé à Cayar, un petit village. Le deuxième jour nous sommes revenus à Dakar. Hier on est allé à Saint-Louis pour faire le tour de la ville. L'Afrique me plaît beaucoup ! Je n'ai pas envie de rentrer !

Grosses bises,
Alexandre

 Enquête culturelle

Planes from all over the world use the international airports of Roissy-Charles de Gaulle and Orly. Both on the outskirts of Paris, Roissy is to the north and Orly is to the south of the city. Air France and Air Inter are the two French nationally owned airlines.

AIR FRANCE ///

Escalators enclosed in glass tubes crisscross the center of the main terminal at Roissy-Charles de Gaulle.

NATIONAL STANDARDS
C1.2, C2.2, C4.2

The Ivory Coast received its name from French sailors who traded for ivory in this West African country in the fifteenth century. It became independent from France in 1960 and has rapidly developed into one of

C.A.T.H. VOYAGES
COMPAGNIE AFRICAINE DE TOURISME D'HOTELLERIE ET DE VOYAGES
TEL. 32.70.73 TELEX 23760
01 BP 2636 ABIDJAN 01 - COTE D'IVOIRE

hotel ibis
COTE D'IVOIRE

the most prosperous and progressive countries in the region. Abidjan, called the "Pearl of Africa," is the Ivory Coast's largest city and the main seaport on the Atlantic Ocean. Tourists enjoy water sports on Abidjan's beautiful beaches.

Mme Diouf speaks the Senegalese national language, Wolof.

Although Senegal also became independent from France, it keeps close cultural and economic ties with the country that governed it for 300 years. About the size of South Dakota, Senegal has a landscape that varies from dry land in the north near the Sahara Desert, to grassy plains in the center, to rain forests in the southwest. Its seven million people belong to a variety of ethnic groups. French is taught in schools and used in government, business and the media. However,

★★★★ **LAGON 2 - DAKAR**
56 chambres sur la mer
climatisation centrale
Son Bar *"Le Clipper"* - Son restaurant *"Le Niokolo"*
Ambiance de gaieté
SHICA Société Hotellière et Immobilière de la Chaine des Alizés
Route de la Corniche est
Tél. : 21 58 31 - 21 34 14 - 22 17 80 - 21 60 31
Télex 214 LAGON SG BP 3115 DAKAR SENEGAL

most Senegalese also speak Wolof, the national language. From the modern capital of Dakar to the seventeenth century French settlement at Saint-Louis to the tiny fishing village of Cayar, from peanut farms to wildlife preserves, Senegal is a country full of contrasts.

NATIONAL STANDARDS
C2.1, C3.2, C4.2

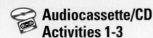
Audiocassette/CD Activities 1-3

Answers

1 1. Ils sont allés en Afrique.
2. L'avion est parti de Roissy-Charles de Gaulle.
3. Ils sont arrivés à l'aéroport à Abidjan en Côte-d'Ivoire.
4. La grand-mère d'Alexandre habite en Côte-d'Ivoire.
5. Après quatre jours en Côte-d'Ivoire ils sont allés à Dakar.
6. Le premier jour au Sénégal sa famille est allée à Cayar.
7. Oui, il aime beaucoup l'Afrique.
8. Non, il ne veut pas rentrer.

2 1. Elle est belge.
2. Il est ivoirien.
3. Elle est tunisienne.
4. Il est suisse.
5. Il est luxembourgeois.
6. Elle est marocaine.
7. Elle est congolaise.
8. Il est algérien.
9. Elle est sénégalaise.

3 Answers will vary.

1 *Répondez en français.*

1. Est-ce qu'Alexandre et ses parents sont allés en Afrique ou est-ce qu'ils sont allés en Europe?
2. De quel aéroport est-ce que l'avion est parti?
3. Où est-ce qu'Alexandre et sa famille sont arrivés?
4. Qui habite en Côte-d'Ivoire?
5. Où est-ce qu'Alexandre et ses parents sont allés après quatre jours en Côte-d'Ivoire?
6. Où est-ce que la famille d'Alexandre est allée le premier jour au Sénégal?
7. Est-ce qu'Alexandre aime l'Afrique?
8. Est-ce qu'Alexandre veut rentrer?

2 Based on which country they come from, describe the nationality of the following people.

1. Brigitte vient de Belgique.
2. Abdou vient de Côte-d'Ivoire.
3. Yasmine vient de Tunisie.
4. Bernard vient de Suisse.
5. Paul vient du Luxembourg.

Modèle:

Hanako vient du Japon.
Elle est japonaise.

Amina est sénégalaise.

Brigitte est belge.

6. Malika vient du Maroc.
7. Sonia vient de République Démocratique du Congo.
8. Salim vient d'Algérie.
9. Amina vient du Sénégal.

3 *C'est à toi!*

1. Est-ce que tu as des amis sénégalais ou ivoiriens?
2. Est-ce que tu es allé(e) en Afrique?
3. Aimes-tu voyager en avion?
4. Est-ce que tu préfères voyager avec ta famille ou avec tes amis?
5. Vas-tu souvent chez ta grand-mère?
6. Ta grand-mère et ton grand-père, d'où viennent-ils?
7. Qu'est-ce que tu as envie de faire après les cours aujourd'hui?

NATIONAL STANDARDS
C1.1, C1.2

380

Structure

Ordinal numbers

You have already learned cardinal (or counting) numbers in French (**un, deux, trois**, etc.). Numbers like "first," "second" and "third" are called ordinal numbers because they show the order in which things are placed. All ordinal numbers in French, except **premier** and **première**, end in **-ième**. To form most ordinal numbers, add **-ième** to the cardinal number. If a cardinal number ends in **-e**, drop this **e** before adding **-ième.** Here are cardinal numbers and their corresponding ordinal numbers from "first" through "tenth." Note that "first," "fifth" and "ninth" are formed irregularly.

un, une	→	premier (m.), première (f.)
deux	→	deuxième
trois	→	troisième
quatre	→	quatrième
cinq	→	cinquième
six	→	sixième
sept	→	septième
huit	→	huitième
neuf	→	neuvième
dix	→	dixième

C'est mon **premier** voyage en Afrique.

This is my first trip to Africa.

Le **deuxième** jour nous sommes revenus à Dakar.

On the second day we came back to Dakar.

Pratique

4 | Tell the order of each day of the week using the appropriate ordinal number. (Remember that Monday is the first day of the week on the French calendar.)

1. vendredi
2. dimanche
3. mercredi
4. samedi
5. jeudi
6. lundi

Modèle:

mardi
Mardi est le deuxième jour de la semaine.

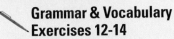
Workbook
Activities 9-10

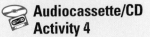
Grammar & Vocabulary
Exercises 12-14

Audiocassette/CD
Activity 4

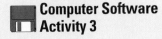
Computer Software
Activity 3

Answers

4 1. Vendredi est le cinquième jour de la semaine.
2. Dimanche est le septième jour de la semaine.
3. Mercredi est le troisième jour de la semaine.
4. Samedi est le sixième jour de la semaine.
5. Jeudi est le quatrième jour de la semaine.
6. Lundi est le premier jour de la semaine.

Teacher's Notes

1. Students have already learned that **le premier** is used in expressing "the first" of any month. 2. You may want to point out that ordinal numbers come before the nouns they describe. 3. You may want to tell students that the letter **x** in **deuxième, sixième** and **dixième** is pronounced [z]. 4. Another word for **deuxième** is **second(e)**. 5. You may want to explain French abbreviations of ordinal numbers. Point out the difference between the abbreviations **1ᵉʳ** and **1ᵉʳᵉ** (*first*). All the others end in **-ᵉ** or **-ᵉᵐᵉ**, for example, **2ᵉ** or **2ᵉᵐᵉ**. 6. You may want to expand Activity 4 by naming a month of the year and seeing who can give its order. For example, **mars** — **Mars est le troisième mois.**

NATIONAL STANDARDS
C1.1, C1.2, C3.2, C4.1

382

Answers

5 1. L'avion suisse est le troisième.
2. L'avion luxembourgeois est le cinquième.
3. L'avion japonais est le huitième.
4. L'avion mexicain est le deuxième.
5. L'avion espagnol est le sixième.
6. L'avion belge est le neuvième.
7. L'avion anglais est le premier.
8. L'avion allemand est le quatrième.

Paired Practice

Où es-tu allé(e)?

Have partners practice using prepositions before countries. Tell each pair to list as many countries as they can in French. Then have partners take turns asking and telling each other if they have been to each of these countries. For example, **Maroc — Est-ce que tu es allé(e) au Maroc? Non, je ne suis pas allé(e) au Maroc.**

Cooperative Group Practice

Où est-on rentré?

Put your students in small groups to practice using prepositions before countries. Each group prepares two sets of note cards. The first set of cards has all the masculine adjectives of nationality that the group can think of; the second set has all the corresponding feminine adjectives of nationality. After both sets of note cards have been combined, each student selects one card at random and gives the imaginary person's nationality and to which country he or she returned, based on the adjective written on the card. For example, **tunisien — Il est tunisien. Il est rentré en Tunisie.**

NATIONAL STANDARDS
C1.1, C1.2

5 Planes from various countries are in France for an air show. As they wait to take off, give each plane's place in line.

Modèle:
l'avion américain

L'avion américain est le septième.

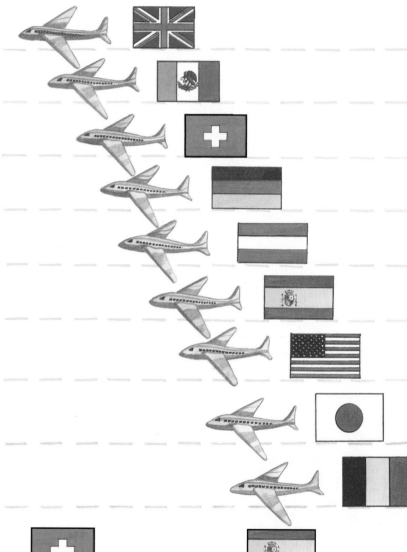

1. l'avion suisse

2. l'avion luxembourgeois

3. l'avion japonais

4. l'avion mexicain

5. l'avion espagnol

6. l'avion belge

7. l'avion anglais

8. l'avion allemand

Prepositions before cities, countries and continents

You have already learned that **au** is used to express "to" or "in" before countries with masculine names. Use **aux** if the country has a masculine plural name.

Tu vas **au** Sénégal?   *Are you going to Senegal?*

Non, je vais **aux** États-Unis.   *No, I'm going to the United States.*

Use **en** before countries or continents with feminine names.

Nous allons **en** Côte-d'Ivoire **en** Afrique.   *We're going to the Ivory Coast in Africa.*

Use **à** before the names of cities.

On est allé **à** Abidjan.   *We went to Abidjan.*

M. et Mme Foch vont aux États-Unis.

Pratique

6 Tell which of the following cities each person lives in, based on the country he or she is from.

Tokyo	Paris	Genève	Berlin
Boston	Toronto	Madrid	Rome

1. Mme Anderson vient des États-Unis.
2. Alejandro vient d'Espagne.
3. Monika vient d'Allemagne.
4. Mauro vient d'Italie.
5. Mlle Callaghan vient du Canada.
6. M. Hamada vient du Japon.
7. Bernard vient de Suisse.

Modèle:

M. Arnaud vient de France.

Il habite à Paris.

7 All the foreign exchange students are getting ready to go home at the end of the school year. Tell what country each student is returning to.

1. Tatsuo, l'élève japonais
2. Phong, l'élève vietnamienne
3. Karim, l'élève tunisien
4. Zakia, l'élève congolaise
5. Isabelle, l'élève belge
6. Ousmane, l'élève sénégalais
7. Assia, l'élève marocaine
8. Nora, l'élève algérienne
9. Ricardo, l'élève espagnol
10. Charles, l'élève anglais

Modèle:

Fabrice, l'élève luxembourgeois

Il rentre au Luxembourg.

Will rentre au Canada dans une semaine.

Workbook
Activity 11

Grammar & Vocabulary
Exercises 15-17

Audiocassette/CD
Activity 7

Computer Software
Activity 4

Answers

6 1. Elle habite à Boston.
    2. Il habite à Madrid.
    3. Elle habite à Berlin.
    4. Il habite à Rome.
    5. Elle habite à Toronto.
    6. Il habite à Tokyo.
    7. Il habite à Genève.

7 1. Il rentre au Japon.
    2. Elle rentre au Vietnam.
    3. Il rentre en Tunisie.
    4. Elle rentre en République Démocratique du Congo.
    5. Elle rentre en Belgique.
    6. Il rentre au Sénégal.
    7. Elle rentre au Maroc.
    8. Elle rentre en Algérie.
    9. Il rentre en Espagne.
    10. Il rentre en Angleterre.

Teacher's Notes

1. Tell students that all countries whose names end in **-e** are feminine, except **le Mexique** and **le Cambodge**. Conversely, most countries whose names do not end in **-e** are masculine. Most European countries are feminine, whereas most American countries are masculine. 2. **En** is used before countries with masculine singular names beginning with a vowel sound: **en Iran, en Israël, en Afghanistan**, etc. 3. If a city has a definite article as part of its name, use **à la, au** or **aux**: **Je vais *à la* Nouvelle-Orléans, *au* Havre et *aux* Saintes-Maries-de-la-Mer.**

NATIONAL STANDARDS
C1.1, C1.2, C4.1

Audiocassette/CD Activity 8

Answers

8 1. Bruxelles est au Mexique?
Non, Bruxelles est en Belgique.
2. Dallas est aux États-Unis?
Oui, Dallas est aux États-Unis.
3. Tours est en Allemagne?
Non, Tours est en France.
4. Dakar est en Italie?
Non, Dakar est au Sénégal.
5. Montréal est au Canada?
Oui, Montréal est au Canada.
6. Lausanne est au Japon?
Non, Lausanne est en Suisse.
7. Rabat est en Chine?
Non, Rabat est au Maroc.

Cooperative Group Practice

Francophone Countries

Divide your class into small groups. Have each group select a different francophone country and do some research on the country's exports, population, climate, art, music, literature, unit of money, political system, famous sites and historical facts. Each group should then present information about their country to the entire class.

Connections

Labeling Francophone Countries

Put your students in four different groups. Give each group an outline map of a specific area: Europe, Africa, Southeast Asia, North America and the Caribbean. List the francophone countries (in English or in French) that are found in each area at the bottom of that map. Have students in each group label these francophone countries on their map. (They may also make a miniature flag of each of their countries, mount it on a toothpick and attach it to the country.) Finally, post all maps on the bulletin board.

NATIONAL STANDARDS
C1.1, C1.2, C3.1, C3.2, C4.2

384

Modèles:

Abidjan/la Côte-d'Ivoire
Student A: **Abidjan est en Côte-d'Ivoire?**
Student B: **Oui, Abidjan est en Côte-d'Ivoire.**

Paris/la République Démocratique du Congo
Student B: **Paris est en République Démocratique du Congo?**
Student A: **Non, Paris est en France.**

Modèle:

Le premier jour nous sommes arrivés à Dakar, au Sénégal.

---

8 With a partner, take turns asking and answering questions about where certain cities are located.

1. Bruxelles/le Mexique
2. Dallas/les États-Unis
3. Tours/l'Allemagne
4. Dakar/l'Italie
5. Montréal/le Canada
6. Lausanne/le Japon
7. Rabat/la Chine

Communication

9 You and your family spent ten days traveling through Africa visiting various French-speaking countries. During your trip you kept a journal. Now that you're back home, you need to write a summary to put at the top of each day's entry to help you remember details. For each day, write where you were (city or village, and country). Use the map to help you remember your itinerary as you write your summaries. (Make sure that the order of the countries you visited and the time spent in each one are realistic.) The first day has been done for you.

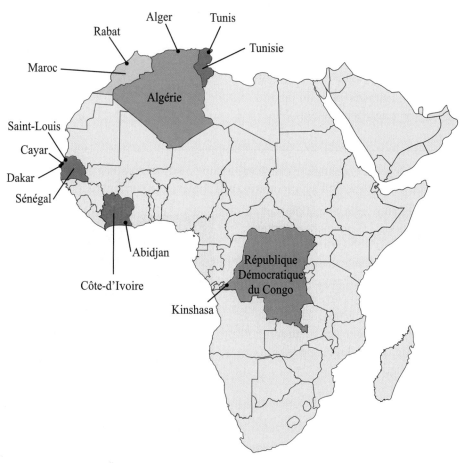

You didn't have time during your trip to French-speaking Africa to buy any postcards. Once you returned home, you decided to make your own. Do some research on one of the countries you visited: Senegal, the Ivory Coast, the Democratic Republic of the Congo, Morocco, Tunisia or Algeria. Look for current information on this country in your school's resource center or instructional materials center. Then design an original postcard. On one side, draw something that you found interesting about this country (for example, the scenery). On the other side, write a friend's name and address and a message in French about your visit to this country. In your note, be sure to describe your drawing, tell where you went and say how much you liked what you saw and did.

Mise au point sur... le monde francophone

The rich vocabulary, colorful expressions and precise structures of the French language extend beyond the borders of France itself. During hundreds of years of colonial expansion, the French people spread their language and culture throughout the world. Today, nearly 200 million people use French in their daily lives; millions more understand this international language. Even humor, certain manners of thinking and gestures are shared by the variety of people around the globe who communicate in French.

Some French citizens, such as those in Corsica, live beyond France's borders. This Mediterranean island, near the west coast of Italy, is one of metropolitan France's 96 administrative divisions (**départements**). Outside of Europe, some French citizens live in France's overseas departments (**Départements d'Outre-Mer**): Martinique and Guadeloupe in the Caribbean, Réunion in the Indian Ocean and French Guiana in South America. Residents of these departments enjoy all the rights that mainland French citizens have.

People in France's overseas territories (**Territoires d'Outre-Mer**) also maintain close cultural and economic ties with France. Although they have no voice in French politics, the French government protects them in times of international crisis. Among these territories are French Polynesia, a group of islands in the South Pacific, and New Caledonia, an island near Australia.

In Europe, several countries bordering France have designated French as one of their official languages. People in parts of Belgium, Luxembourg and Switzerland speak French at home and when they travel or do business in neighboring countries. In the tiny principality of Monaco, near the Italian border but surrounded on three sides by France, the only official language is French.

In North America, many Canadians speak both French and English. Throughout the country, communication in government, business, schools and entertainment is usually

The principality of Monaco includes Monaco, Monte-Carlo and the port.

Teacher's Notes

1. Actually, Corsica accounts for two of France's **départements**, 2A and 2B. 2. The island of Saint Barthélemy in the Caribbean is in the department of Guadeloupe; the island of Saint Martin, also in the Caribbean, is divided between France and the Netherlands. 3. Tahiti is an island in French Polynesia. 4. Wallis and Futuna Islands in the South Pacific and the French Southern and Antarctic Territories are other French overseas territories. 5. The islands of Saint Pierre and Miquelon near the eastern coast of Canada and the island of Mayotte off the eastern coast of Africa are called territorial collectivities, a designation somewhere in between overseas departments and overseas territories.

Paired Practice

Flags of Francophone Countries
Put your students in pairs. Give each student a colored copy of the flag of a francophone country. As the student describes the flag (design and colors) to his or her partner, the partner draws it. (Students with more advanced language ability may want to describe their flags in French.) When both drawings are completed, partners may compare them to the originals.

NATIONAL STANDARDS
C1.1, C1.2, C1.3, C2.1, C2.2, C3.1, C4.2

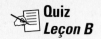

Quiz
Leçon B

Answers

11 Possible answers:

1. The French language and culture originally spread through colonial expansion.
2. Corsica is located in the Mediterranean.
3. French Guiana is in South America.
4. Two of the French overseas territories are French Polynesia and New Caledonia.
5. Many people speak French in Belgium, Luxembourg and Switzerland.
6. French is the only official language in the Province of Quebec.
7. New England and Louisiana were settled by the French and French Canadians.
8. Some cities in the United States that have French names are Pierre, Des Moines, Saint Louis and Boise.
9. Various ethnic groups in some African countries still use French as the common language of communication.
10. Three former French colonies in Southeast Asia are Vietnam, Cambodia and Laos.

In Louisiana many street signs point to the area's French heritage.

INDOCHINE TOURS
HIT VOYAGES
Spécialiste du VIETNAM, du LAOS et du CAMBODGE.
Circuits à la carte
Voyages d'affaires
Billets - Visa - Hôtel
EXPERIENCE ET RAPIDITE
Tél : 01 43 54 17 17   Fax : 01 43 25 22 16

French is everywhere in Quebec, even on billboards.

JE RÉUSSIS TOUS MES EXAMENS!

L'examen dentaire, c'est important.

bilingual. In the Province of Quebec, French is the native language of almost 80 percent of the population and has been named the only official language.

French and French-Canadian settlers in New England brought the French language and culture to the United States. Both Creoles, descendants of the original French settlers, and Cajuns, whose French-Canadian ancestors were called "Acadians," now live in Louisiana. In fact, Louisiana was named after the French king Louis XIV. Names of cities such as Pierre (South Dakota), Des Moines (Iowa), Saint Louis (Missouri) and Boise (Idaho) reflect the French presence in America.

France once had the largest colonial empire in Africa. People in more than 20 African countries speak French, even though all these countries have gained their independence. Because these people represent various ethnic groups, French is often used as the common language of communication. Many people in **le Maghreb** and on the large island of Madagascar off the eastern coast of Africa communicate in French on a daily basis. In West Africa, the French influence still remains strong in the Ivory Coast, the Democratic Republic of the Congo and Senegal.

France's former colonial empire extended far beyond the African continent. Today many people living in Haiti in the Caribbean and in Vietnam, Cambodia and Laos in Southeast Asia also speak French.

People all over the world use French in their daily lives. As the world continues to become smaller and smaller through faster means of communication and greater travel opportunities, the French language remains a key to understanding for vast numbers of people.

French is the official language of Haiti, but many people speak Creole. (Port-au-Prince)

11 Answer the following questions.

1. How did the French language and culture originally spread throughout the world?
2. What French department is located in the Mediterranean?
3. Which overseas department of France is in South America?
4. What are two of the French overseas territories?
5. What are the names of three European countries (other than France) where many people speak French?
6. In what Canadian province is French the only official language?
7. What are the two major areas of the United States settled by the French and French Canadians?
8. What cities do you know in the United States that have French names?
9. Why do various ethnic groups in some African countries still use French?
10. What are three former French colonies in Southeast Asia?

12 Look at the Air France schedule of flights from Paris to five different French-speaking cities throughout the world. To answer the questions that follow, you will need to know that on the schedule the days of the week are numbered from one (Monday) to seven (Sunday), **départ** means "departure," an **A** or a **G** after the departure time indicates Roissy-Charles de Gaulle, an **S** after the departure time indicates Orly, and **arrivée** means "arrival."

1. You can fly from Paris to four of these cities every day of the week. Which city does not have daily service?
2. At what time does a flight from Paris to Casablanca leave every day of the week? From which airport does this flight leave?
3. On what two days is there only one flight from Paris to Montreal?
4. If you want to fly to Montreal on Monday, from which airport would you leave?
5. At what time does the plane for Papeete leave Paris on Friday?
6. How many flights from Paris to Dakar leave on Saturday?
7. Does the 10:15 A.M. flight from Paris to Abidjan get in earlier or later than the flight leaving Paris at 10:45 A.M.?
8. If you want to fly to Dakar on Sunday and arrive there in the early afternoon, at what time would your flight leave?
9. If you want to fly to Abidjan on a 747 but don't want to fly at night, what day would you leave?
10. The 12:30 P.M. flight from Paris to Montreal arrives at 2:05 P.M. Why is there only about an hour and a half difference between departure and arrival times for this transatlantic flight?

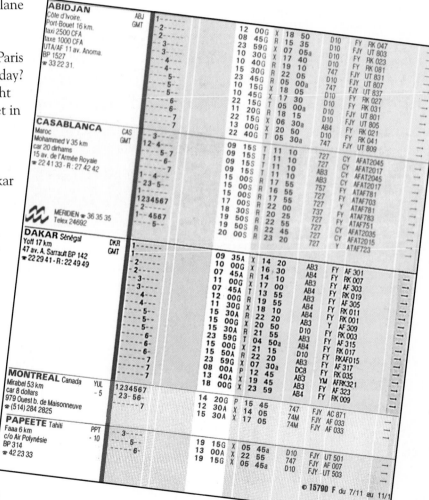

Answers

12 1. Papeete does not have daily service.
2. The daily flight from Paris to Casablanca leaves at 6:30 P.M. This flight leaves from Orly.
3. There is only one flight from Paris to Montreal on Monday and Thursday.
4. You would leave from Roissy-Charles de Gaulle.
5. The plane leaves for Papeete on Friday at 1:00 P.M.
6. There are three flights from Paris to Dakar on Saturday.
7. The 10:15 A.M. flight from Paris to Abidjan gets in later than the flight leaving Paris at 10:45 A.M.
8. Your flight would leave at 8:00 A.M.
9. You would leave on Wednesday.
10. There is only about an hour and a half difference between departure and arrival times for this flight because there is a six-hour time difference between Paris and Montreal.

Comparisons

Cultural Journal

If your students are keeping a cultural journal, you might have them think about the questions that follow and then write answers to them: Knowing that the French language and culture were often spread through colonial expansion, why do you think some French citizens might have chosen to live in another part of the world? What kinds of mixed feelings might these immigrants have had toward their new country? What kinds of mixed feelings might the indigenous people of these countries have toward the people of France?

NATIONAL STANDARDS
C2.2, C3.2, C4.2

Workbook
Activities 13-15

Grammar & Vocabulary
Exercises 18-22

Audiocassette/CD
In the City (A), Directions

Transparencies 60-61

Teacher's Notes

1. In conversational French **les traveller's** is often used instead of **les chèques de voyage.** 2. You may want to tell your students that some banks will not exchange traveler's checks, but **un bureau de change** will always accept them. 3. To help students distinguish between a **restaurant** and a **café**, you might tell them that a **restaurant** usually has tablecloths and customers are expected to order a complete meal there. 4. You might want to expand upon the directions presented by introducing **le sud-ouest** (*southwest*), **le sud-est** (*southeast*), **le nord-ouest** (*northwest*) and **le nord-est** (*northeast*). 5. A communicative function that is recycled in this lesson is "expressing thanks."

NATIONAL STANDARDS
C1.2, C4.1, C4.2

Leçon C

In this lesson you will be able to:

➤ **inquire about details**

➤ **identify objects**

➤ **tell location**

➤ **give addresses**

➤ **ask for information**

➤ **give directions**

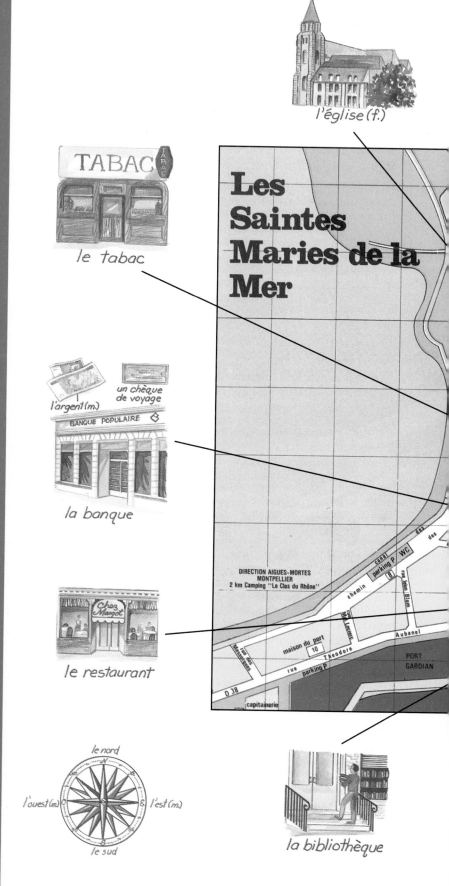

l'église (f.)

le tabac

l'argent (m.)   *un chèque de voyage*

la banque

le restaurant

la bibliothèque

Les Saintes Maries de la Mer

le nord
l'ouest (m.)   l'est (m.)
le sud

un musée

la librairie

le stade

la piscine

la mairie

la place

un timbre

la poste

la plage   la mer

Teacher's Notes

1. You may want to point out that **librairie** is a false cognate. 2. Students already learned **la place** meaning "room" or "space" in **Unité 10**.

TPR

The Living City

Make signs that have the names of buildings or places in the city. Punch two holes in the top of each sign and insert a string so that the sign can be worn. Distribute the signs to your students. As you ask where each building or place is (**Où est le musée?**), the student wearing the appropriate sign stands up. (Students will want to keep their signs for a subsequent activity.)

Cooperative Group Practice

The Living City

Put your students in groups of six or eight. Have them wear the building or place signs that you used in the preceding TPR activity. Prepare a set of location cards for each group. The cards tell where each building or place is located in the city in relation to something else. For example, **Le stade est près du musée et à droite de la mairie**. As group members take turns reading the location cards, those students mentioned must put themselves in the appropriate location.

NATIONAL STANDARDS
C1.2, C4.1, C4.2

**Workbook
Activity 16**

**Grammar & Vocabulary
Exercise 23**

 Audiocassette/CD
Dialogue

Video

 NATIONAL STANDARDS
C1.2, C2.1, C2.2, C3.1,
C4.2

390

13460 Les Saintes-Maries-de-la-Mer
CAMARGUE
FRANCE

The Borde family from Luxembourg is camping near Les Saintes-Maries-de-la-Mer, the capital of the Camargue region of southern France. M. Borde questions M. Rivoire, the director of the campground, about the camping facilities and the nearby town.

M. Borde:　**Qu'est-ce que vous avez à faire ici au camping pour les enfants?**

M. Rivoire:　**Vous voyez, tout droit, il y a une piscine.**

M. Borde:　**Oui, je vois la piscine. Et est-ce que je peux toucher des chèques de voyage dans le village?**

M. Rivoire:　**Oui, la banque n'est pas loin. Elle est près d'ici... à 1,5 kilomètres à l'est du camping sur l'avenue Frédéric Mistral.**

M. Borde:　**Et pour acheter des timbres?**

M. Rivoire:　**La poste est près de la mairie. Vous prenez l'avenue de la République, puis vous tournez à droite sur l'avenue Léon Gambetta.**

M. Borde:　**Merci, Monsieur.**

 Enquête culturelle

One of Europe's oldest and smallest countries, Luxembourg lies northeast of France. Known as **le cœur vert de l'Europe** because of its landscape of thick forests and rolling hills, its capital city is also called Luxembourg.

Located in the delta formed by **le Rhône** as it enters the Mediterranean Sea, the Camargue region is famous for its environmental reserve and bird sanctuary, white horses, groups of semi-wild black bulls guarded by men on horseback, rose flamingos, marshes and vast rice paddies.

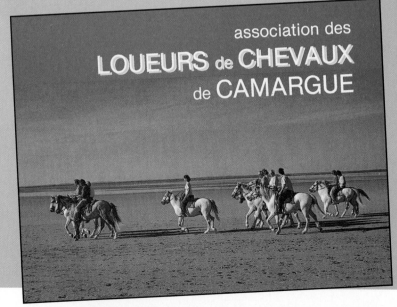

association des
LOUEURS de CHEVAUX de CAMARGUE

Les Saintes-Maries-de-la-Mer is named after Marie-Jacobé and Marie-Salomé, who came across the Mediterranean Sea by boat in the early Christian era. Residents say that the local church contains the relics of the two Maries and of Sara, their servant,

LOU SIMBÈU
Petites et grandes promenades à cheval
Ferrades - Fêtes provençales

Les Saintes-Maries
Etang
Rte d'Aigues-Mortes
Le Petit Rhône
près du Tombeau du Marquis de Baroncelli
1.5 km des Stes-Maries-de-la-Mer
Tél.: 04.90.97.86.99
LOU SIMBÈU Arènes Mer

Gypsies make their way to Les Saintes-Maries-de-la-Mer twice each year.

who became the patron saint of the Gypsies. Annual Gypsy pilgrimages to the town take place in May and October.

HOTEL MEDITERRANEE ★★ NN
4, boulevard Frédéric Mistral - Près du Port
13460 LES SAINTES-MARIES-DE-LA-MER
Tél.: 04.90.97.82.09 Ouvert de février à novembre et vacances fin d'année
TAXI «MEDITERRANEE»
LOCATION DE VELOS

Streets in France are often named after famous people. For example, the **avenue Frédéric Mistral** in Les Saintes-Maries-de-la-Mer honors a famous French poet who won the Nobel Prize in literature in 1904. Mistral wrote in Provençal, a French dialect spoken in southern France.

You can change money and traveler's checks in France at **la banque** or **le bureau de change** (*money exchange*). Or, using a credit card, you can get money from an ATM (**un distributeur**) at a more favorable exchange rate.

An automated teller machine in French is called *un distributeur* or *un guichet automatique*. (Paris)

POUR TÉLÉPHONER CHOISISSEZ VOTRE HEURE
TELECARTE 50 UNITÉS

At a post office you can buy stamps, send letters and packages, use public telephones, buy **télécartes** (*phone cards to use in public phone booths*) and use the Minitel. Some French people even pay their gas and telephone bills at the post office.

Teacher's Notes

1. Marie-Jacobé was the sister of the Virgin Mary. The two women were expelled from Judea. Upon their arrival in Europe, they attempted to convert the inhabitants to Christianity.
2. Streets in France may also be named after important historical events or a particular locality.

TPR

Using a *Télécarte*

You may want to do a Gouin series with your students on using a **télécarte** at a French public phone. Make a copy of a **télécarte** for each student. (You might tell students that one side of these cards usually has a design that depicts historical or cultural events.) Then use a large sheet of paper to make an imaginary French pay phone with push-button numbers and a **télécarte** slot in the bottom right-hand corner. Also make a detachable phone receiver. Next, model the procedure for making a phone call with a **télécarte** by saying these sentences as you demonstrate the appropriate actions: 1. Décrochez. 2. Introduisez la carte. 3. Numérotez. 4. Attendez. 5. Parlez. 6. Raccrochez. 7. Prenez votre carte. After you have modeled the appropriate actions, have the students perform them with you. Then give the commands and have students perform the actions. Finally, you may want to introduce students to the written forms of these commands. Have students practice reading the commands, and then have students work in pairs with one partner reading the commands and the other partner performing the actions.

NATIONAL STANDARDS
C1.2, C2.1, C2.2, C3.1, C3.2, C4.2

Game

Treasure Hunt

To practice following directions in French, your students might want to participate in a **cherche au trésor**. Divide your class into four teams. (If possible, you might want to move your students outside the classroom.) Begin by giving each team a written clue, for example, **Allez à la table et regardez sous le dictionnaire.** (The second clue will be found under the dictionary.) Each team should uncover four to six clues in order to get to their final destination — **le trésor.** If two or more teams have the same final destination but different clues, they can race to see who is the first to finish.

Stamps and phone cards are also sold at **le tabac (le bureau de tabac)**. A distinctive reddish-orange sign with the word **TABAC** on it makes these shops easy to recognize at a distance.

A French *tabac* usually sells newspapers, magazines, postcards, candy, lottery tickets, stamps and *télécartes*.

1 | *Qu'est-ce que c'est?* Identify the places you see in the illustrations.

Modèle:

C'est une bibliothèque.

1.

2.

3.

4.

5.

6.

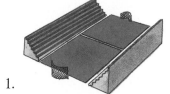
7.

8.

9.

Audiocassette/CD
Activity 4

2 Imagine that you are a teenager in the Borde family that is camping near Les Saintes-Maries-de-la-Mer. Write a postcard to your friend Yvette back home. In your postcard,

1. give the date.
2. greet Yvette.
3. tell her that your family is at the campground near Les Saintes-Maries-de-la-Mer.
4. tell her that there is a swimming pool at the campground.
5. tell her that you like camping a lot.
6. tell her that your father needs to go to the bank to cash traveler's checks.
7. tell her that he is also going to the post office to buy some stamps.
8. say that you'll see her soon.
9. give a closing and sign your name.

Est-ce que le camping vous plaît beaucoup? (Collonges-la-Rouge)

3 Write a sentence in French telling what you do at each of the following places.

1. l'aéroport
2. la poste
3. la banque
4. le centre commercial
5. la librairie
6. le stade
7. le restaurant
8. l'école

Modèle:

la gare
Je prends le train à la gare.

4 *C'est à toi!*

1. Sur quelle avenue est ta maison ou ton appartement?
2. Ton école est à combien de kilomètres de ta maison ou de ton appartement?
3. Est-ce que ton école est au nord, au sud, à l'est ou à l'ouest de ta maison ou de ton appartement?
4. Qui est à gauche de toi en cours de français?
5. Est-ce que tu préfères acheter des livres à la librairie ou lire à la bibliothèque?
6. Est-ce que tu vas souvent à la banque?
7. Est-ce que tu aimes le camping?
8. Est-ce que tu préfères nager à la piscine ou à la mer?

Étienne est à gauche de Joanne.

Answers

2 Possible answer:

le 5 août

Chère Yvette,
   Ma famille est au camping près des Saintes-Maries-de-la-Mer. Il y a une piscine au camping. Le camping me plaît beaucoup. Mon père a besoin d'aller à la banque pour toucher des chèques de voyage. Il va aussi à la poste pour acheter des timbres. À bientôt.
      Grosses bises,
      Marc

3 Possible answers:

1. Je prends l'avion à l'aéroport.
2. J'achète des timbres à la poste.
3. Je touche des chèques de voyage à la banque.
4. Je fais du shopping au centre commercial.
5. J'achète des livres à la librairie.
6. Je joue au foot au stade.
7. Je mange au restaurant.
8. J'étudie à l'école.

4 Answers will vary.

NATIONAL STANDARDS
C1.1, C1.2

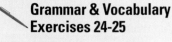

Workbook Activity 17

Grammar & Vocabulary Exercises 24-25

Audiocassette/CD Activity 6

Computer Software Activity 5

Answers

5 1. voit des livres
2. voyez des baguettes
3. voient une serveuse
4. vois la réceptionniste
5. voit la mer
6. voient beaucoup de timbres
7. vois des avions

6 1. Tu vois la piscine.
2. Les garçons voient le stade.
3. Karima et moi, nous voyons la plage.
4. Djamel et toi, vous voyez la poste.
5. Clarence voit l'église.
6. Je vois la bibliothèque.
7. Sara et son cousin voient le musée.
8. Véro voit la banque.

Teacher's Notes

1. You may want to point out that there are only three different oral forms of **voir**. Emphasize the sounds [waj] in **voyons** and **voyez**. 2. You might point out that **y** replaces **i** when the verb form is composed of two syllables.

Gaz de France.

Voir Autrement, Voir plus Loin.

23, rue Philibert-Delorme 75840 Paris Cedex 17

Modèle:

Magali est au centre commercial.
Elle voit des boutiques.

Modèle:

Béatrice et son frère/mer
Béatrice et son frère voient la mer.

Structure

Present tense of the irregular verb *voir*

The verb **voir** (*to see*) is irregular.

voir			
je	vois	Je **vois** la piscine.	*I see the swimming pool.*
tu	vois	Tu ne **vois** pas la banque?	*Don't you see the bank?*
il/elle/on	voit	Elle ne **voit** jamais ses cousins.	*She never sees her cousins.*
nous	voyons	Nous **voyons** tout le monde.	*We see everybody.*
vous	voyez	Qu'est-ce que vous **voyez**?	*What do you see?*
ils/elles	voient	Ils **voient** le train.	*They see the train.*

Pratique

5 As you report where certain people are, tell what they see, choosing from the following list of people and things.

des livres	beaucoup de timbres	la mer	des avions
la réceptionniste	des boutiques	une serveuse	des baguettes

1. Abdel-Cader est à la librairie. Il....
2. Vous êtes à la boulangerie. Vous....
3. M. et Mme Potvin sont au restaurant. Ils....
4. Je suis au cabinet du docteur Vaillancourt. Je....
5. Cécile est à la plage. Elle....
6. Les demi-sœurs de Catherine sont à la poste. Elles....
7. Tu es à l'aéroport. Tu....

6 You and your friends are meeting at a café in Les Saintes-Maries-de-la-Mer. Because you're all coming from different places in town, you take different routes. Tell what you see on your way to the café.

1. tu/piscine
2. les garçons/stade
3. Karima et moi/plage
4. Djamel et toi/poste
5. Clarence/église
6. je/bibliothèque
7. Sara et son cousin/musée
8. Véro/banque

Communication

7   You and some of your classmates are working together on a project for French class. You're planning to all get together after school today at your house to complete it. Since these classmates have never been to your house before, write a note that you can copy and pass out to them, giving detailed directions from school to your house.

8   You and your French host family have been visiting the Camargue region and staying in Les Saintes-Maries-de-la-Mer. Since you are going to leave the area today, you have decided to take some final pictures. You're staying at a hotel near the tennis courts on the **Avenue du Docteur Cambon**. You plan to meet your family at **Les Arènes** near the center of town. Using the map, explain to them how to get from the hotel to where you will be.

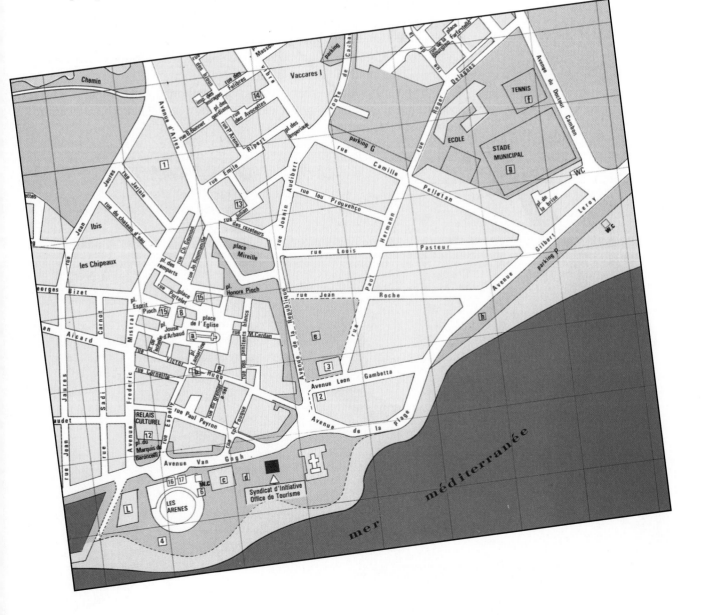

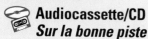

Workbook
Activity 18

🎧 **Audiocassette/CD**
Sur la bonne piste

Teacher's Notes

1. You may choose to read the poem aloud to students while playing appropriate background music. 2. Even after using the listed reading strategies, students may still have difficulty understanding the following words: **les clapotis** (*lapping*), **mourir** (*to die*), **wouawoua** (*the sound made by waves*), **sablonneuse** (*sandy*), **la nuit** (*night*), **l'Aube** (*dawn*), **naît** (*is born*) and **le sommeil** (*sleep*). 3. If you think that students still need more guidance before reading *Dors mon enfant*, you may want to provide them with specific examples taken from the poem showing how each of the eight reading strategies can help them understand it. 4. You may want students to work in pairs as they answer the questions on page 397. Note that some of the questions have specific answers. However, there is still some room for subjectivity. Other questions are interpretation questions, and students should be encouraged to come up with a variety of answers. To holistically grade this activity, refer to the suggestions on page 162. 5. Optional activity. You may want to have students make two lists of the indicators or hints that lead to the conclusion that *Dors mon enfant* is an African lullaby. In their first list, have students specify indicators that the poem is African. In their second list, have them specify indicators that the poem is a lullaby. Remind students to refer to both the poem and the illustration.

NATIONAL STANDARDS
C1.2, C3.1, C3.2, C4.2

Sur la bonne piste

In previous units you learned about and practiced a variety of strategies to help you read in French. Now try to make use of all of them as you read "Dors mon enfant," an African poem.

Cameroonian author Elalongué Epanya Yondo wrote "Dors mon enfant" during Cameroon's struggle for independence from France and England in the late 1950s and early 1960s. (Cameroon is a country in western equatorial Africa. The official languages of Cameroon are French and English.)

Use the following reading strategies to help you understand what the poem means:

1. Take advantage of the clues provided by the *illustration* to predict what the poem is about and to figure out the meaning of words you haven't seen before.
2. *Skim* the poem to figure out its context.
3. Identify *cognates* to try to make sense of the poem as a whole.
4. *Think in French* as you read the poem. Resist the temptation to translate it word for word into English.
5. Avoid "seeing" the poem through the eyes of an American. Instead, try to form mental pictures that take into account possible *cultural differences*.
6. Practice the technique of *inference*: use the context of the words you know to help you understand the ones you don't know.
7. Read the poem critically—that is, *evaluate* the information it contains.
8. *Scan* the poem to hunt for precise ideas or words that will help you answer the questions that follow it.

DORS MON ENFANT

Dors mon enfant dors
Quand tu dors
Tu es beau
Comme un oranger fleuri.

Dors mon enfant dors
Dors comme
La mer haute
Caressée par les clapotis
De la brise
Qui vient mourir en woua-woua
Au pied de la plage sablonneuse.

Dors mon enfant dors
Dors mon beau bébé noir
Comme la promesse
D'une nuit de lune
Au regard de l'Aube
Qui naît sur ton sommeil.

Dors mon enfant dors
Tu es si beau
Quand tu dors
Mon beau bébé noir dors.

Elalongué Epanya Yondo, Kamerun! Kamerun!
©Présence Africaine

Scan the poem to find answers to the following questions.

1. What does the illustration suggest that the poem is about? If the poem is a song, what kind of song do you think it is?
2. Try to "see" the illustration as it would be drawn if the poem were set in the United States. What cultural differences are there between your mental picture and the illustration? Are there any similarities?
3. Can you figure out what the word **dors** means in the title of the poem? Look for clues in the illustration and use the context of the other words you already know in the title to help you. (Hint: **dors** is a form of an infinitive you've seen before.)
4. What words in the poem are cognates?
5. The poem states that the child is beautiful. Is this a fact or an opinion? If it is an opinion, whose opinion is it?
6. A simile compares two different things that share some quality. A simile often uses the word "like." In the poem the mother first compares the beauty of her son to a flowering orange tree, using the word **comme**. What two other comparisons does the mother make?
7. Cameroon is very close to the equator. What can you see in the illustration and find in the poem itself about the climate and location of the country?
8. The poem represents the hope of the mother for her son's future. Recalling the political conditions during which the author wrote the poem, do you see a relationship between the child and Cameroon? What is it?

Nathalie et Raoul

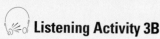

Listening Activity 3B

Answers

1. vrai
2. faux
3. vrai
4. faux
5. vrai
6. vrai
7. faux
8. vrai
9. vrai
10. vrai

Teacher's Notes

1. Optional activity. Some students can quickly form mental pictures of what they read about. Others need more time to form these pictures, and still other students have problems forming mental pictures at all. To help students improve their imaging skills, you may want to have them select a calming image from the poem on page 396 and then draw or paint it. Be sure to have students identify which lines of the poem they are trying to portray artistically. 2. Optional activity. You may want to have students create their own similes in French. To prepare students for this activity, write the phrase **L'enfant est beau comme....** on the board. Then have students come up with as many completions to this sentence as they can, comparing the beauty of a child to anything else that is appropriate and that they can express in French. Finally, have students create their own similes, comparing two unlike things using only vocabulary words they have seen before.

C'est à moi!

Now that you have completed this unit, take a look at what you should be able to do in French. Can you do all of these tasks?

➤ I can write a postcard.

➤ I can talk about what happened in the past.

➤ I can talk about things sequentially.

➤ I can ask for detailed information.

➤ I can tell location.

➤ I can give directions.

➤ I can give addresses.

➤ I can identify objects.

➤ I can tell what I like.

➤ I can state my preference.

➤ I can express emotions.

Here is a brief checkup to see how much you understand about French culture. Decide if each statement is **vrai** or **faux**.

1. The **SNCF**, the government-owned company that operates French trains, is well known for its prompt, affordable service.
2. Belgians are divided into four groups according to the languages they speak.
3. During the fifteenth century French sailors named the Ivory Coast for the ivory they traded there.
4. Senegal has close economic and cultural ties with France because it is one of the few African colonies still governed by France.
5. Almost 200 million people speak French around the world.
6. France is divided into nearly 100 administrative divisions called **départements**.
7. Although French is spoken in many African countries, France is the only French-speaking country in Europe.
8. In North America, the French influence is especially strong in the Province of Quebec in Canada and in Louisiana.
9. Les Saintes-Maries-de-la-Mer is a town near the mouth of the Rhône River that hosts Gypsy pilgrimages.
10. You can buy **télécartes** at the post office and at **le tabac**.

Communication orale

Imagine that you and your partner have returned from trips to a French-speaking country. One partner went to a French-speaking country in Europe, and the other partner went to a French-speaking country in Africa. Begin your conversation by greeting each other. Then ask and tell where (in what country and city) you arrived. Next ask and tell where you went in the country you visited. Finally, ask and tell when you returned home. Finish your conversation by asking and telling each other how much you like what you saw and did. (If you've already been on a trip to a French-speaking country, you will probably want to talk about this country in your conversation. Be sure to include some of your experiences there.)

Communication écrite

Your teacher overheard some of your conversation about your trips to a French-speaking country and wants to find out more information about both trips. Write out in French a description of both trips, based on the information you gave your partner and heard from your partner in your previous conversation. Also add any additional information about the places you both visited that you learned during your study of French-speaking countries. Finally, mention two other French-speaking countries you would like to see and tell why you would like to see them.

Communication active

To write postcards, use:

Cher (Chère)...,	*Dear . . . ,*
Grosses bises,	*Big kisses,*

To describe past events, use:

Je **suis sorti(e)** avec mes amis.	*I went out with my friends.*
Nous **sommes allés** au cinéma.	*We went to the movies.*
On **est revenu** à minuit.	*We came back at midnight.*
Vous **êtes rentrés** en Suisse.	*You returned to Switzerland.*
L'avion **est parti** de Roissy-Charles de Gaulle.	*The plane left Roissy-Charles de Gaulle.*
Il **est arrivé** à Genève à 20h00.	*It arrived in Geneva at 8:00 P.M.*
Chantal **est entrée** dans l'aéroport.	*Chantal entered the airport.*
Ses frères **sont venus** aussi.	*Her brothers came also.*
Pourquoi **es-tu resté** chez toi?	*Why did you stay home?*

To sequence events, use:

Le premier jour....	*The first day . . . .*
Après quatre **jours....**	*After four days . . . .*
Hier....	*Yesterday . . . .*
Aujourd'hui....	*Today . . . .*
Demain....	*Tomorrow . . . .*

Le Concorde est parti de Roissy.

Teacher's Note

Here is the English version of the cartoon on page 397: I have good news and bad news, Nathalie. Oh really? What's the good news? I'm leaving on vacation with my family. And the bad news? Dad says we're leaving . . . tomorrow. We'll come back in two weeks. Oh no! I'll write you every day! And me, I can't wait for you to return! (The first day of Raoul's vacation.) (The fifth day of Raoul's vacation.) (The tenth day of Raoul's vacation.) Hi, Nathalie! Are things all right? No, not at all. Aren't you happy to see me? Yes! But I have bad news. I'm leaving on vacation with my family . . . tomorrow. We really don't have any luck.

Cooperative Group Practice

Crossword Puzzle

Put your students in small groups and give each group some graph paper and a certain amount of time to develop a crossword puzzle that uses at least ten new words from this **unité**. Have groups exchange puzzles. See which group can complete their new puzzle first.

NATIONAL STANDARDS
C1.1, C1.2, C1.3, C2.1, C4.1

To ask for information, use:

Et pour acheter des timbres?   *And (where do I go) to buy stamps?*

To inquire about details, use:

Qu'est-ce que vous avez   *What's there to do here?*
à faire ici?

To tell location, use:

Mon père est parti **pour**   *My father left for Brussels in Belgium.*
Bruxelles **en** Belgique.
Les Caron sont arrivés **à**   *The Carons arrived in Boston in the*
Boston **aux** États-Unis.   *United States.*
Après une semaine, ils sont   *After one week, they went to the*
allés à la plage **au** Mexique.   *beach in Mexico.*
Il y a une banque **près d'ici.**   *There's a bank near here.*
La banque n'est pas **loin.**   *The bank isn't far.*
Il/Elle est à 5 kilomètres.   *It's 5 kilometers.*

Le cinéma? Allez tout droit.
Il est à deux kilomètres.

Il/Elle est au nord.	*It's (to the) north.*
Il/Elle est à l'est.	*It's (to the) east.*
Il/Elle est au sud.	*It's (to the) south.*
Il/Elle est à l'ouest.	*It's (to the) west.*
Il/Elle est à gauche.	*It's on the left.*
Il/Elle est à droite.	*It's on the right.*
Il/Elle est tout droit.	*It's straight ahead.*

To give directions, use:

Allez tout droit.   *Go straight ahead.*
Vous prenez l'avenue Foch.   *You take Foch Avenue.*
Vous tournez à droite/gauche   *You turn right/left on Maine Avenue.*
sur l'avenue du Maine.

La banque est sur l'avenue du Maine. (Pointe-à-Pitre)

To give an address, use:

Il/Elle est sur l'avenue   *It's on Victor Hugo Avenue.*
Victor Hugo.

To identify objects, use:

Il y a une piscine.   *There is a swimming pool.*

Il y a une piscine.

To say what you like, use:

L'Afrique **me plaît** beaucoup!   *I like Africa a lot!*

To state a preference, use:

J'ai envie de rentrer!   *I want to come home!*

To express emotions, use:

Ce séjour **est formidable!**   *This stay is terrific!*

Communication électronique

1. Answers will vary.
2. Flags are used to rank these Web sites. One flag means "see," two flags means "interesting" and three flags means "absolutely necessary."
3. Senegal's approximate population is about ten million.
4. Ninety-seven percent of the Senegalese are younger than 65.
5. The Wolofs account for 36% of the Senegalese population.
6. Eighty percent of the Senegalese speak Wolof.
7. Peanuts and peppers are responsible for giving Senegalese food its flavor.

À moi de jouer!

Fatima est congolaise. Elle habite en République Démocratique du Congo. Elle est de....

Abdou est sénégalais. Il habite au Sénégal. Il est de....

Malika est ivoirienne. Elle habite en Côte-d'Ivoire. Elle est de....

Leïla est marocaine. Elle habite au Maroc. Elle est de....

Bruno est Suisse. Il habite en Suisse. Il est de....

Thierry est belge. Il habite en Belgique. Il est de....

Communication électronique

In this unit you learned about Senegal, a French-speaking country on the western coast of Africa. To explore a comprehensive Web site about this country, go to:

http://altern.org/stalin/senegal.htm

After viewing this site, answer the following questions.

1. How many active links are offered to other sites about Senegal?
2. When you click on one of these links, you see a certain number of Senegalese flags. What do these flags indicate?
3. Click on "Peuples" and then on "La population." What is the approximate population of Senegal?
4. Senegal's population is younger than the population of the United States. What percent of the Senegalese is younger than 65?
5. Which is the largest ethnic group in Senegal?
6. Return to "Peuples" and click on "Parler le Wolof." What percent of the Senegalese speak Wolof? Now click on some of the French expressions you recognize and hear how they are said in Wolof.
7. Return to the home page and click on "Gastronomie." Then click on "Le Sénégal dans votre assiette." What two pictured items are responsible for giving Senegalese food its flavor?

À moi de jouer!

Let's see how much you have learned about nationalities, countries and cities in the francophone world! For each highlighted country, first identify the person's nationality, then tell what country he or she lives in and finally say that he or she is from any city in that country. Follow the model. (You may want to refer to the *Communication active* on pages 399-401, the vocabulary list on page 403 and the map of Africa on page 384.)

Modèle:

Caroline est française.
Elle habite en France.
Elle est de Fontainebleau.

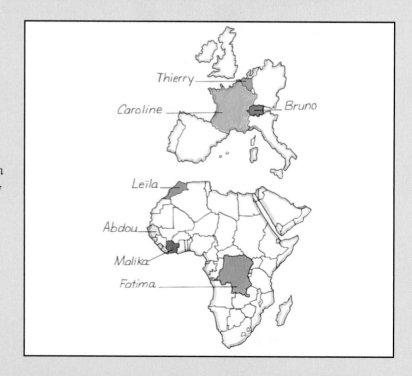

Vocabulaire

un	**aéroport** airport			**neuvième** ninth
l'	**Afrique (f.)** Africa		le	**nord** north
l'	**Algérie (f.)** Algeria			
	algérien, algérienne Algerian		l'	**ouest (m.)** west
l'	**argent (m.)** money			
une	**avenue** avenue			**partir** to leave
un	**avion** airplane		un	**passeport** passport
	avoir envie de to want, to feel like		une	**piscine** swimming pool
			une	**place** (public) square
une	**banque** bank		une	**plage** beach
	belge Belgian			**plaît: ... me plaît.** I like . . . .
la	**Belgique** Belgium		une	**poste** post office
une	**bibliothèque** library			**près (de)** near
une	**bise** kiss			
				quatrième fourth
un	**camping** campground			
un	**chèque (de voyage)** (traveler's) check			**rentrer** to come home, to return, to come back
	cher, chère dear		la	**République Démocratique du Congo** Democratic Republic of the Congo
	chez at the house/home of			
	cinquième fifth			
	congolais, congolaise Congolese		un	**restaurant** restaurant
la	**Côte-d'Ivoire** Ivory Coast			**revenir** to come back, to return
	deuxième second		un	**séjour** stay
	dixième tenth		le	**Sénégal** Senegal
				sénégalais(e) Senegalese
une	**église** church			**septième** seventh
l'	**envie (f.): avoir envie de** to want, to feel like			**sixième** sixth
			un	**stade** stadium
l'	**est (m.)** east		le	**sud** south
l'	**Europe (f.)** Europe			**suisse** Swiss
			la	**Suisse** Switzerland
	formidable great, terrific			
			un	**tabac** tobacco shop
une	**gare** train station		un	**timbre** stamp
	gros, grosse big, large			**toucher** to cash
				tourner to turn
	hier yesterday		la	**Toussaint** All Saints' Day
un	**horaire** schedule, timetable			**tout** all, everything
	huitième eighth			**tout droit** straight ahead
			un	**train** train
	ivoirien, ivoirienne Ivorian			**troisième** third
			la	**Tunisie** Tunisia
une	**librairie** bookstore			**tunisien, tunisienne** Tunisian
	loin far			
le	**Luxembourg** Luxembourg		la	**veille** night before
	luxembourgeois(e) Luxembourger		un	**village** village
			une	**ville** city
une	**mairie** town hall			**voir** to see
le	**Maroc** Morocco			
	marocain(e) Moroccan			
	me: ... me plaît. I like			
une	**mer** sea			
un	**musée** museum			

NATIONAL STANDARDS
C2.2

Unité 12

À Paris

In this unit you will be able to:

➤ write journal entries

➤ describe past events

➤ sequence events

➤ express need and necessity

➤ ask for information

➤ give opinions

➤ compare things

NATIONAL STANDARDS
C2.2

Teacher's Notes

1. You may want to point out to students that **tombeau**, **bateau** and **tableau** form their plurals by adding an **x**. 2. **Un tableau** (*painting*) is the word usually used when talking about a specific painting. **La peinture** (*painting*) refers to painting in general. For example, **J'adore la peinture impressionniste, surtout les tableaux de Monet.** Students learned the word **tableau** meaning "(chalk)board" in **Unité 4**. 3. **Un billet** is any kind of ticket (e.g., theater, plane, train, concert). **Un ticket** is generally a smaller ticket obtained from a machine or torn off from a roll for the movies, bus or parking. In everyday speech, the French use both words. In formal speech, one says **un ticket de métro** but **un billet de chemin de fer**. 4. You may want to remind students that a train station is **une gare**, but **une station** refers to a subway station (**station de métro**). 5. Communicative functions that are recycled in this lesson are "telling time on the hour," "expressing likes and dislikes," "expressing emotions" and "expressing need and necessity."

Leçon A

In this lesson you will be able to:

➤ **write journal entries**

➤ **describe past events**

➤ **sequence events**

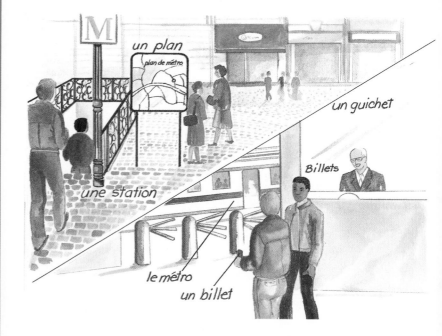

Karine Couty, a student from Papeete, Tahiti, is spending the month of July in France. In her journal she describes some of her experiences in Paris.

le 5 juillet

Ce matin j'ai quitté l'hôtel à neuf heures. D'abord, j'ai marché sur l'avenue des Champs-Élysées de l'arc de triomphe au Drugstore. Là, j'ai mangé, puis, j'ai continué mon chemin jusqu'au Louvre où j'ai regardé de beaux tableaux. J'aime la Joconde de Léonard de Vinci. Puis, j'ai décidé de prendre le métro pour voir le tombeau de Jim Morrison au cimetière du Père-Lachaise, mais j'ai perdu mon plan de métro. Alors je suis allée au guichet du métro, et j'ai demandé un nouveau plan.

Paris est vraiment la "Ville lumière"! J'ai fini la journée en bateau sur la Seine d'où j'ai regardé beaucoup de beaux monuments : la tour Eiffel, Notre-Dame, les jardins des Tuileries, et même la

BATEAUX-MOUCHES®

PARIS

PONT DE L'ALMA–RIVE DROITE

☎ 01.42.25.96.10

Karine a regardé l'arc de triomphe sur la place Charles de Gaulle. (Paris)

 Workbook Activity 1

Grammar & Vocabulary Exercise 2

 Audiocassette/CD Journal

Teacher's Notes

1. Information on many of the sites that Karine describes is found in this lesson's **Enquête culturelle** and in this unit's **Mise au point sur... Paris**. 2. Realia to have on hand when presenting this lesson includes a map of Paris, a **métro** map, some **métro** tickets and a **Père-Lachaise** map. 3. Capitalization of the names of monuments and sites is taken from *le Petit Robert, Dictionnaire universel des noms propres*. 4. You may want to point out to students that the verb **quitter** (*to leave*) is usually followed by the name of a person or place. 5. You may want to point out to students that two verbs of motion in this journal entry, **quitter** and **marcher**, are both conjugated with **avoir** in the **passé composé**. 6. **L'avenue des Champs-Élysées** is often referred to as simply **les Champs-Élysées**. 7. Léonard de Vinci is the French spelling of the Italian name Leonardo da Vinci (1452-1519). 8. You may want to point out to students that the verbs **quitter**, **marcher** and **demander** are false cognates. 9. Paris is called the "City of Light" because so many of its monuments are illuminated at night.

 NATIONAL STANDARDS
C1.2, C2.2, C3.2, C4.2

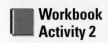

Workbook Activity 2

Connections

French Art

Viewing the paintings of Gauguin is an excellent way for students to review the names of colors in French. Transform your classroom into a museum by hanging up as many Gauguin prints as you can find. Prepare a museum guide sheet for each student. Horizontally, across the top of the sheet, list the colors in French. Complete the grid by listing the names of the various paintings vertically along the left side. As students walk from one painting to the next, have them check off the colors that are in each one. Also leave space for students to write a personal comment beside the name of each painting. For example, **J'aime beaucoup** or **Le cheval est très beau**.

petite statue de la Liberté. Quel paradis! D'après mon professeur de français, il faut venir à Paris au moins trois fois : une fois quand on est jeune, une fois quand on est amoureux et une fois quand on a de l'argent et qu'on peut vraiment vivre bien! Imagine, c'est seulement ma première fois ici....

Aux jardins des Tuileries on voit souvent des enfants qui jouent avec de petits bateaux. (Paris)

Enquête culturelle

Papeete, the largest city on the South Pacific island of Tahiti, is the capital of French Polynesia. Many Tahitians work in tourism, the island's major industry. Blessed with luxuriant vegetation and spectacular waterfalls, Tahiti has been portrayed as a tropical paradise by many painters and writers, including the French artist Paul Gauguin and the American author James Michener.

Papeete, one of the most populated urban centers in the South Pacific, exports vanilla and coconut. (Tahiti)

As its name implies, **le Drugstore** in Paris sells some over-the-counter products, such as aspirin. However, this contemporary café primarily serves light meals and American-style ice cream specialties.

The French name for the *Mona Lisa*, a painting by the Italian artist Leonardo da Vinci, is *la Joconde*. Probably the best-known painting in the **Louvre**, it became famous because of the woman's mysterious smile.

The French king François I not only brought the painting back from Italy, but the artist as well. Da Vinci spent the last years of his life in France.

Most people who see the *Mona Lisa* are surprised at how small it is. (Paris)

The Paris subway system, called the **métro** (the shortened form of **métropolitain**), is known for its efficiency, speed, cleanliness and reasonable fares. The first **métro** line opened in 1900; today, over 300 stations dot the city. Most of them are named after streets, squares, monuments, famous people, historical places and the former gates (**portes**) to the city. Modern express lines, called **R.E.R.**, have recently been added to the **métro** system. They

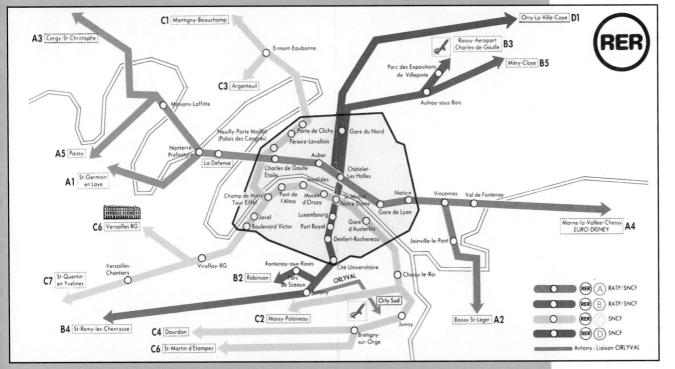

Teacher's Notes

1. Da Vinci was a Renaissance artist. 2. The Paris **métro** is the world's third oldest subway system and was built for a World's Fair. Subway tickets are also valid on Paris buses. Travelers should not discard their **métro** tickets because a controller may stop and ask to see them at any time.

Cooperative Group Practice

The Unveiling

Before beginning to talk about French art, you may want to try to sharpen your students' powers of observation. Divide your class into three or four small groups. Prepare a tray to show each group. On the tray make an attractive display of 25-30 items for which students know the French names. (This is a good chance to review vocabulary from previous **unités**.) As you uncover the tray for each group, say that this is the unveiling of a work of art and that students should observe closely. Let each group spend only about one minute examining the tray. Then students in each group work together to compile a list of as many objects as they can remember that were on the tray. The group with the longest and most accurate list wins.

NATIONAL STANDARDS
C1.1, C2.2, C3.1, C3.2

Grammar & Vocabulary Exercise 1

Teacher's Notes

1. Visitors can obtain maps of **Père-Lachaise** to direct them to the graves they want to see. But you don't need a map to find Jim Morrison's tomb. Graffiti and arrows on other tombstones will point you in the right direction.
2. The French sculptor Bartholdi's small Statue of Liberty is on the **pont de Grenelle** on the Seine. There is an even smaller scale model of the Statue of Liberty in **le jardin du Luxembourg**.

Connections

Music

You may want to play some music by Jim Morrison and the Doors for your students (especially for those who have never heard of the Doors). On a different note, songs about Paris (for example, those by the American composer Cole Porter who lived there during the 1920s) may interest students. French composers, such as Frédéric Chopin, make interesting studies in and of themselves. Their works provide wonderful background music for students to listen to as they write their journal entries.

NATIONAL STANDARDS
C2.1, C2.2, C3.1, C4.2, C5.2

This train's final destination is *Château de Vincennes*. (Paris)

serve the suburbs and make fewer stops in the center of Paris than do the other lines. To ride the subway, you first buy a ticket or **un carnet** (a group of ten tickets). Although each **métro** line has a number, you refer to the line by the stations at each end of it. Follow the signs for the end point in the direction in which you are going. To transfer from one line to another, follow the **correspondance** signs. The **métro** runs from 5:00 A.M. to 1:00 A.M.

You're never more than 500 yards from a *métro* station in Paris.

Le cimetière du Père-Lachaise is the largest cemetery in Paris. Here lie the remains of such famous people as the composer

Jim Morrison's tomb, the most popular site in *Père-Lachaise,* is still frequently decorated by people who appreciate his music. (Paris)

Frédéric Chopin and the playwright Molière. Many American tourists visit the tomb of Jim Morrison, a singer with the rock group the Doors. He died in Paris in 1971.

A replica of Bartholdi's Statue of Liberty is on the *pont de Grenelle* in Paris.

The French gave the United States the Statue of Liberty in 1886. A small copy of the statue stands in Paris as a continuing reminder of the friendship between the two countries.

1 | *Répondez par "vrai" ou "faux" d'après le journal de Karine.*

1. Karine est en vacances à Tahiti.
2. Karine a quitté l'hôtel à dix heures.
3. L'arc de triomphe est sur l'avenue des Champs-Élysées.
4. Karine aime *la Joconde* de Léonard de Vinci.
5. Le tombeau de Jim Morrison est au Louvre.
6. Karine a perdu son plan de métro.
7. Karine a fini la journée en bateau sur le Rhône.
8. C'est la troisième fois que Karine est à Paris.

Le bateau est devant le musée d'Orsay. (Paris)

2 | Choose where certain people are going, according to what they want to do.

1. François veut voir le tombeau de Molière.
2. Julien veut faire un tour en bateau.
3. Mathieu et ses parents veulent mettre leurs vêtements dans l'armoire.
4. Grégoire veut faire les magasins.
5. Marguerite veut regarder des tableaux.
6. M. Dupleix veut acheter un billet.
7. Les enfants veulent jouer.

    a. la Seine
    b. le musée
    c. le guichet
    d. l'avenue des Champs-Élysées
    e. le cimetière
    f. le jardin
    g. l'hôtel

3 | *C'est à toi!*

Voulez-vous voir le Louvre? (Paris)

1. Combien de fois est-ce que tu es allé(e) au cinéma ce mois?
2. Est-ce que tu préfères aller au musée ou au cinéma?
3. Quels tableaux aimes-tu?
4. Est-ce que tu préfères aller en vacances à Tahiti ou à Paris? Pourquoi?
5. Quel monument à Paris veux-tu voir?
6. L'avenue où tu habites s'appelle comment?
7. À quelle heure est-ce que tu quittes la maison pour aller à l'école?

411

Teacher's Notes

1. You may want to review the forms of **avoir** with your students before beginning this section. 2. You may want students to see or write out all the **passé composé** forms of **finir** and **vendre**. 3. You might have students repeat after you the sentences in the chart. You might also do some exercises from affirmative to negative, declarative to interrogative, singular to plural or present tense to **passé composé**.

Comparisons

Le passé composé

After your students have seen a variety of sentences in the **passé composé**, ask them if they can make any generalizations about what kind of verbs use **avoir** to form the **passé composé**. (Hint: What part of speech appears in these sentences that does not appear in sentences that use **être** in the **passé composé**?)

Avoir ou être?

Prepare a transparency that has two columns, one for verbs that use **avoir** in the **passé composé** and the other for verbs that use **être**. As a quick review, ask your students how many regular **-er**, **-ir** and **-re** verbs they can think of. As each verb is named, write it in the appropriate column.

412

Structure

Passé composé with *avoir*

You have learned that the **passé composé** expresses what happened in the past. This tense is made up of a helping verb and the past participle of the main verb. You use the appropriate present tense form of the helping verb **être** with certain verbs. But the majority of verbs form their **passé composé** with the helping verb **avoir**.

> J'**ai** regardé des monuments.   *I looked at some monuments.*

(helping verb)   (past participle of **regarder**)

Remember that to form the past participle of **-er** verbs, drop the **-er** of the infinitive and add an é: regarder → regardé.

The past participle of verbs that use **avoir** in the **passé composé** does not agree with the subject. Therefore, the past participle stays the same while the form of **avoir** changes according to the subject. Here is the **passé composé** of **regarder**.

regarder				
j'	ai	regardé	J'**ai regardé** mon plan.	*I looked at my map.*
tu	as	regardé	**As**-tu **regardé** la télé?	*Did you watch TV?*
il/elle/on	a	regardé	Malika **a regardé** l'affiche.	*Malika looked at the poster.*
nous	avons	regardé	Nous **avons regardé** la tour Eiffel.	*We looked at the Eiffel Tower.*
vous	avez	regardé	Qu'est-ce que vous **avez regardé?**	*What did you watch?*
ils/elles	ont	regardé	Ils **ont regardé** les tableaux.	*They looked at the paintings.*

Remember that to form the past participle of most **-ir** verbs, drop the **-ir** and add an **i**: finir → fini.

Most infinitives that end in **-re** form their past participles by dropping the **-re** and adding a **u**: vendre → vendu, perdre → perdu, attendre → attendu.

To make a negative sentence in the **passé composé**, put **n'** before the form of **avoir** and **pas** after it.

> Les élèves **n'**ont **pas** fini le tour.   *The students didn't finish the tour.*

To ask a question in the **passé composé** using inversion, put the subject pronoun after the form of **avoir**.

> Quand le prof **a**-t-il **perdu** son plan de Paris?   *When did the teacher lose his Paris map?*

Pratique

4 Tell what the following tourists lost while they were on vacation.

1. Amina/des CDs
2. les parents d'Amina/de l'argent
3. je/mon sac à dos
4. M. Smith/son passeport
5. Fabrice et toi, vous/des chèques de voyage
6. tu/une chaussette
7. M. et Mme Orgeval/leur plan de la ville
8. ma famille et moi, nous/nos billets d'avion

Je n'ai pas perdu mon sac à dos.

Modèle:

Jean-François/un tee-shirt
Jean-François a perdu un tee-shirt.

5 Some tourists chose to walk while they were in Paris. Others bought **métro** tickets and took the subway. Tell whether or not the following people walked.

1. Amina
2. les parents d'Amina
3. je
4. M. Smith

5. Fabrice et toi, vous
6. tu
7. M. et Mme Orgeval
8. ma famille et moi, nous

Modèle:

Jean-François
Jean-François n'a pas marché.

6 Tell what certain people did last Friday, based on where they went. Choose from the activities in the following list.

finir les devoirs	nager
attendre le train	danser
acheter des timbres	manger un hamburger
toucher des chèques de voyage	regarder des tableaux

1. Khadim est allé au fast-food.
2. Les Dupont sont allés au Louvre.
3. Florence et sa sœur sont allées à la plage.
4. Mlle Wang est allée à la banque.
5. Luc et Patrick sont allés à la bibliothèque.
6. Mme Lannion et sa fille sont allées à la gare.
7. Marc est allé au tabac.

Modèle:

Sophie est allée en boîte.
Elle a dansé.

Florence et sa sœur ont nagé à la plage. (Canet-Plage)

Audiocassette/CD Activity 4

Answers

4 1. Amina a perdu des CDs.
2. Les parents d'Amina ont perdu de l'argent.
3. J'ai perdu mon sac à dos.
4. M. Smith a perdu son passeport.
5. Fabrice et toi, vous avez perdu des chèques de voyage.
6. Tu as perdu une chaussette.
7. M. et Mme Orgeval ont perdu leur plan de la ville.
8. Ma famille et moi, nous avons perdu nos billets d'avion.

5 1. Amina a marché.
2. Les parents d'Amina ont marché.
3. Je n'ai pas marché.
4. M. Smith n'a pas marché.
5. Fabrice et toi, vous avez marché.
6. Tu as marché.
7. M. et Mme Orgeval n'ont pas marché.
8. Ma famille et moi, nous n'avons pas marché.

6 1. Il a mangé un hamburger.
2. Ils ont regardé des tableaux.
3. Elles ont nagé.
4. Elle a touché des chèques de voyage.
5. Ils ont fini les devoirs.
6. Elles ont attendu le train.
7. Il a acheté des timbres.

Audiocassette/CD Activities 7-8

Answers

7 1. Le premier jour Raoul a skié. Le deuxième jour il a dormi. Le troisième jour il a téléphoné.
2. Le premier jour Christine et Saleh ont étudié. Le deuxième jour elles ont mangé au café. Le troisième jour elles ont écouté de la musique.
3. Le premier jour mes amis et moi, nous avons joué aux jeux vidéo. Le deuxième jour nous avons nagé. Le troisième jour nous avons travaillé au fast-food.

8 1. Es-tu venu(e) à l'école hier?
2. As-tu fini tes devoirs hier?
3. As-tu joué au foot hier?
4. Es-tu allé(e) au fast-food hier?
5. Es-tu resté(e) à la maison hier?
6. As-tu regardé la télé hier?
7. As-tu travaillé hier?
8. Es-tu sorti(e) avec des amis hier?
Students' responses to these questions will vary.

Comparisons

Making Agreement

Write a variety of sentences in the **passé composé** on an overhead transparency, some that use **avoir** and some that use **être**. Do not make agreement between past participles and subjects. For each sentence ask students if any agreement is needed. For example, **Nous avons joué__ au foot. Ma sœur est sorti__ hier.**

NATIONAL STANDARDS
C1.1, C1.2, C4.1

414

Modèle:

Le premier jour Raoul a skié. Le deuxième jour il....

---

7 The teachers at your school attended a workshop on Monday. Describe what you and some of your friends did each day of your three-day weekend. The first description has been started for you.

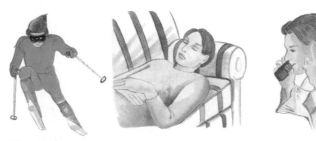

1. Raoul

2. Christine et Saleh

3. mes amis et moi, nous

Modèles:

étudier le français
Student A: **As-tu étudié le français hier?**
Student B: **Oui, j'ai étudié le français hier./Non, je n'ai pas étudié le français hier.**

aller au cinéma
Student B: **Es-tu allé(e) au cinéma hier?**
Student A: **Oui, je suis allé(e) au cinéma hier./Non, je ne suis pas allé(e) au cinéma hier.**

---

8 With a partner, take turns asking and telling whether or not you did certain things yesterday. (Remember that some verbs use **être** as their helping verb in the **passé composé**.)

1. venir à l'école
2. finir tes devoirs
3. jouer au foot
4. aller au fast-food
5. rester à la maison
6. regarder la télé
7. travailler
8. sortir avec des amis

Teacher's Note

At the end of Activity 10 you may want to take your own survey to find out how many students or which ones did each of the listed things.

Communication

9 Imagine that you've just returned home after a one-week stay in Paris with some of your classmates. During your trip you were so busy going places and seeing things that you didn't have time to write in your journal. Instead, you just wrote brief notes. Now that you have more time, put your notes from the first two days into sentences so that you will have a more complete account of what you did.

> *1ᵉʳ jour - 12.7*
>
> *banque - chèques de voyage*
> *Louvre - la Joconde*
> *librairie - plan de Paris*
> *jardins des Tuileries - fleurs,*
> *   enfants*
> *restaurant - Le Petit Zinzin,*
> *   poulet, frites, coca*

> *2ᵉ jour - 13.7*
>
> *avenue des Champs-Élysées*
> *magasin - Prisunic, tee-shirt*
> *   arc de triomphe*
> *Drugstore - glace au chocolat*
> *tabac - timbres*
> *cinéma - film américain*

10 *Trouvez une personne qui....* (Find someone who . . . .) Interview your classmates to find out who did various things this past weekend. On a separate sheet of paper, number from 1 to 15. Circulate around the classroom asking your classmates, one at a time, questions based on the phrases that follow. When someone says that he or she did a specific thing, have that person write his or her name next to the number of the appropriate phrase. Continue asking questions, trying to find a different person who did each thing.

Modèle:

Jean-Paul: Tu as joué au basket?
Clémence: Oui, j'ai joué au basket.
(Writes her name beside number 1.)

1. jouer au basket
2. manger de la pizza
3. rester au lit samedi matin
4. acheter des vêtements
5. travailler
6. sortir avec des amis
7. aller au cinéma
8. regarder la télé
9. étudier le français
10. aller au centre commercial
11. dormir jusqu'à dix heures dimanche
12. perdre quelque chose
13. aller au fast-food
14. finir les devoirs
15. nager

Oui, j'ai joué au basket samedi après-midi.

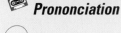

Audiocassette/CD
Prononciation

Listening Activity 1

Quiz
Leçon A

11 Write a paragraph in which you describe what you did this past weekend. For each day, tell where you went, what you did at each place and whether or not you worked. Add any interesting details. Some verbs you may be able to include are **regarder, parler, jouer, manger, étudier, travailler, dormir, voyager, acheter, finir, aller, rentrer, rester** and **sortir.** While writing your paragraph in the **passé composé**, be sure to use the appropriate helping verb to describe each action.

Benoît a joué au foot samedi.

Prononciation

The sound [k]

The sound [k] is written as **c** (before **a, o** or **u**), **k** or **qu.** The sound [k] in French is different from the English sound "k." In producing the French sound, no air escapes from the mouth. To see if you pronounce the French [k] correctly, hold a sheet of paper about two inches in front of your mouth. Then say the following sentences without making the paper move.

De **qu**elle **c**ouleur est le **c**ostume?

Caroline et **C**olette prennent du **c**o**c**a et du **k**etchup.

Les **c**arottes **c**oûtent un euro **qu**arante.

Combien de **C**anadiens ont des **c**oiffeurs améri**c**ains?

À **qu**elle heure **c**ommence le **c**ours?

The paper should move only when you pronounce the English equivalent of each of these words:

café	Canada
cuisine	cassette
camping	cousin

NATIONAL STANDARDS
C1.3, C4.1

✎ **Grammar & Vocabulary Exercise 10**

📼 **Audiocassette/CD**
Le 14 juillet

Teacher's Notes

1. The plural of **un bal** is **des bals**; the plural of **un feu** is **des feux**.
2. A communicative function that is recycled in this lesson is "writing journal entries" and "telling time on the hour."

Leçon B

In this lesson you will be able to:

➤ **describe past events**

➤ **sequence events**

➤ **express need and necessity**

NATIONAL STANDARDS
C1.2, C2.1, C4.1

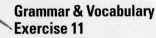

Workbook Activity 6

Grammar & Vocabulary Exercise 11

Audiocassette/CD Journal

Teacher's Notes

1. Point out to your students that **monter** (*to go up*) is conjugated with **être** in the **passé composé**. 2. You will want to point out to your students that the verb **visiter** is used only when you visit a place. To visit a person, use **rendre visite à** or **aller voir**. 3. L'**arche de la Défense** forms a straight line with l'**arc de triomphe** and l'**arc de triomphe du Carrousel**.

Karine continues to write in her journal, describing a busy week in Paris.

le 17 juillet

J'ai passé une bonne semaine. Lundi j'ai vu le Centre Pompidou où je suis montée jusqu'au cinquième étage pour bien voir Paris. Puis, j'ai pris un coca sur la place et j'ai regardé des musiciens. Mardi matin je suis allée à la Défense où j'ai visité l'arche et les magasins modernes. Mardi soir il y a eu un bal dans la rue. J'ai dansé jusqu'à trois heures du matin ! Puis, j'ai été obligée de prendre un taxi pour rentrer à l'hôtel, parce qu'on a fermé le métro. Mercredi j'ai regardé le grand défilé du 14 juillet, la fête nationale de la France. On a fait beaucoup de bruit! Puis, le soir j'ai vu un beau feu d'artifice. Jeudi j'ai visité le musée d'Orsay pour voir les tableaux impressionnistes. Vendredi j'ai vu le tombeau de Napoléon aux Invalides et la statue du __Penseur__ au musée Rodin. Une semaine bien chargée, n'est-ce pas?

GRAND FEU D'ARTIFICE DE LA FÊTE NATIONALE

Karine a vu un très beau feu d'artifice mercredi soir. (Paris)

Enquête culturelle 🔍

Several modern neighborhoods, such as **la Défense**, have been built on the outskirts of Paris. With its enormous **arche de la Défense**, skyscrapers, apartments, businesses and shops, **la Défense** has changed the skyline of contemporary Paris.

■ **Workbook Activity 7**

Connections

The French Revolution

You may want to contact your Social Studies Department to ask the history teacher if he or she would be interested in joining classes with you to hold an integrated lesson on the French Revolution. After the presentation, you might have your students write their reactions to it in their cultural journal.

L'arche de la Défense was built directly in line with l'arc de triomphe, la place de la Concorde and l'arc de triomphe du Carrousel. (Paris)

On July 14 the French celebrate their national holiday. They honor the day in 1789 when the people of Paris captured the **Bastille**, the royal prison. Although only seven non-political prisoners were there at that time, the capture of the old fortress symbolized the beginning of the French Revolution and a spirit of freedom for everyone. The monarchy eventually fell, and the people established a more democratic form of government. Although the **Bastille** itself was demolished shortly after being stormed, a 170-foot column today stands on the **place de la Bastille.**

On *la place de la Bastille* stands the bronze *colonne de Juillet*, topped with a gilded spirit of liberty that commemorates those who died there in July, 1830. (Paris)

NATIONAL STANDARDS
C2.1, C2.2, C3.1, C4.2

Audiocassette/CD Activity 1

Answers

1 1. b
  2. d
  3. g
  4. h
  5. i
  6. f
  7. c
  8. a
  9. e

Teacher's Notes

1. The route of the Bastille Day parade usually proceeds from the **arc de triomphe de l'Étoile** down the **Champs-Élysées** to the **place de la Concorde**. The parade normally lasts between one and two hours. 2. **La garde républicaine** is traditionally a crowd favorite. This group of 30 men with their trumpets is part of the president's escort. As part of its regular duty, the group escorts foreign dignitaries who come to Paris and guards the Élysée palace.

Connections

"La Marseillaise"

Have your students listen to a recording of the "Marseillaise," the French national anthem. (You may want to hand out copies of the words.)

NATIONAL STANDARDS
C1.2, C2.1, C3.1, C3.2, C5.2

Students from the *École Polytechnique* dazzle the crowds during the Bastille Day parade. (Paris)

On Bastille Day, Parisians line the parade route hours in advance to have the best possible view of the annual military parade. A flyover with jets trailing blue, white and red smoke starts the parade. Then the French president comes down the parade route, usually **l'avenue des Champs-Élysées**. Both male and female members of the police, the Foreign Legion, **la garde républicaine** and other military units are presented for the inspection of the president and the French people, along with various military hardware. Smaller towns often hold military parades as well. In the evening fireworks explode across the sky. Street dances take place the nights of July 13 and 14. The firefighters of Paris, for example, sponsor dances which last well into the morning hours. People of all ages dance to a variety of music in celebration of their freedom.

Auguste Rodin a fait la statue du *Penseur*. (Paris)

1   *Répondez aux questions avec la lettre de l'expression convenable d'après le journal de Karine.*

1. À quel étage du Centre Pompidou est-ce que Karine est montée?
2. Qui est-ce que Karine a regardé sur la place?
3. Où est-ce qu'il y a une arche moderne?
4. Où est-ce qu'il y a eu un bal?
5. Jusqu'à quelle heure est-ce que Karine a dansé?
6. Comment est-ce que Karine est rentrée?
7. Où sont les tableaux impressionnistes?
8. Où est le tombeau de Napoléon?
9. Où est la statue du *Penseur*?

   a. aux Invalides
   b. au cinquième
   c. au musée d'Orsay
   d. des musiciens
   e. au musée Rodin
   f. en taxi
   g. à la Défense
   h. dans la rue
   i. jusqu'à trois heures du matin

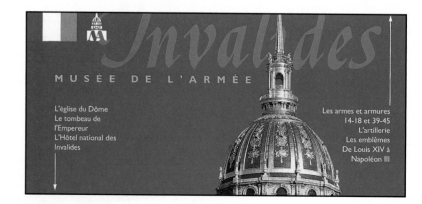

Invalides

MUSÉE DE L'ARMÉE

L'église du Dôme
Le tombeau de l'Empereur
L'Hôtel national des Invalides

Les armes et armures
14-18 et 39-45
L'artillerie
Les emblèmes
De Louis XIV à Napoléon III

Identify each of the things or people that Karine saw during her stay in Paris.

Modèle:

C'est un taxi.

1.

2.

3.

4.

5.

6.

7.

8.

 Audiocassette/CD Activity 2

Answers

2 1. C'est un bateau.
  2. C'est un feu d'artifice.
  3. C'est une statue.
  4. C'est un billet.
  5. C'est un bal.
  6. C'est un défilé.
  7. C'est un tableau.
  8. Ce sont des musiciens.

NATIONAL STANDARDS
C1.1

Answers

3 Answers will vary.

4 1. M. Lefebvre a fait les courses hier.
2. Les étudiants ont fait les devoirs hier.
3. J'ai fait du sport hier.
4. Ta belle-sœur et toi, vous avez fait du shopping hier.
5. Mes cousins et moi, nous avons fait du vélo hier.
6. Tu as fait un tour en bateau hier.
7. Mme Boucher et son mari ont fait du footing hier.

422

3 *C'est à toi!*

1. Qu'est-ce que tu fais le 4 juillet?
2. Est-ce que tu préfères regarder un défilé ou un feu d'artifice?
3. Est-ce que tu aimes danser?
4. Quel musicien est-ce que tu préfères?
5. Est-ce que tu aimes les tableaux impressionnistes?
6. Dans ta famille, qui fait beaucoup de bruit?
7. Est-ce que tu as passé une bonne semaine? Pourquoi ou pourquoi pas?

Structure

Irregular past participles

Some verbs that form their **passé composé** with **avoir** have irregular past participles.

Ces élèves ont eu une interro aujourd'hui.

Verb	Past Participle	Passé Composé	
avoir	eu	Il y **a eu** un grand défilé.	*There was a big parade.*
être	été	J'**ai été** obligé de prendre le métro.	*I had to (was obliged to) take the subway.*
faire	fait	On n'**a** pas **fait** beaucoup de bruit.	*They didn't make a lot of noise.*
prendre	pris	Karine **a pris** un café.	*Karine had coffee.*
voir	vu	**As**-tu **vu** le feu d'artifice?	*Did you see the fireworks?*

Pratique

4 Tell what the following people did yesterday.

1. M. Lefebvre/les courses
2. les étudiants/les devoirs
3. je/du sport
4. ta belle-sœur et toi, vous/du shopping
5. mes cousins et moi, nous/du vélo
6. tu/un tour en bateau
7. Mme Boucher et son mari/du footing

Modèle:

Karine/du roller
Karine a fait du roller hier.

On a fait un tour en bateau sur la Seine.

5 The Troussard family spent a week in Paris. To find out what they did, complete each sentence with the **passé composé** of the appropriate verb from the following list.

avoir	être	faire	prendre	voir

1. M. Troussard... obligé de passer une semaine à Paris. Donc, sa femme et ses fils sont venus à Paris aussi.
2. Ils... le métro pour aller à leur hôtel.
3. La famille Troussard... beaucoup de monuments à Paris.
4. Djamel Troussard... des photos de la tour Eiffel.
5. Le 14 juillet les Troussard sont allés aux Champs-Élysées où il y... un grand défilé.
6. Au défilé, les garçons... beaucoup de bruit!
7. Puis, le soir il y... un feu d'artifice.
8. Le 15 juillet les Troussard... un tour en bateau sur la Seine.

6 Marie-Claude made a list of everything she wanted to do yesterday. This morning she checked off those things she was able to get done. Tell whether or not Marie-Claude did the things she wanted to do.

> *dormir jusqu'à dix heures du matin*
> ✔ *prendre rendez-vous avec le médecin*
> *faire les magasins*
> *voir le nouveau film au Gaumont*
> ✔ *finir les devoirs*
> *téléphoner à Cécile*
> ✔ *attendre Daniel à l'aéroport*

Communication

7 Your French-speaking pen pal is curious to know what Americans do to celebrate their national holiday on July 4. Write your pen pal a short letter in which you describe what you, your friends and your family did last Fourth of July. Also tell about some of the special events that took place in your town or city during this holiday, even if you didn't take part in them.

8 With a partner, talk about what you did this past weekend. In preparation, each partner needs to bring to class three props, either real objects or drawings of them, that serve as reminders of some things he or she did. Student A begins by telling Student B about the activity that each of his or her props represents. After each of Student A's sentences, Student B asks Student A a specific follow-up question about that activity, and Student A responds. Then switch roles.

Gérard a pris beaucoup de photos.

Modèle:

Elle n'a pas dormi jusqu'à dix heures du matin.

Modèle:

Student A: (shows Student B a movie ad from the newspaper) Je suis allée au cinéma vendredi soir.
Student B: Tu as vu quel film?
Student A: J'ai vu *The Perfect Storm*.

Listening Activity 2

Answers

5 1. a été
2. ont pris
3. a vu
4. a pris
5. a eu
6. ont fait
7. a eu
8. ont fait

6 Elle a pris rendez-vous avec le médecin.
Elle n'a pas fait les magasins.
Elle n'a pas vu le nouveau film au Gaumont.
Elle a fini les devoirs.
Elle n'a pas téléphoné à Cécile.
Elle a attendu Daniel à l'aéroport.

Cooperative Group Practice

Memory Chain

Put your students in small groups of five or six and have them play this memory game about an imaginary trip to Paris. The first student begins by saying a sentence in the **passé composé**. (The verb can have a regular or an irregular past participle.) For example, **Je suis allé(e) à Paris**. The second student repeats what the first student has said and adds another sentence. For example, **Je suis allé(e) à Paris et j'ai vu Notre-Dame**. The third student repeats what the first and second students have said and adds one more sentence, etc. For example, **Je suis allé(e) à Paris et j'ai vu Notre-Dame et j'ai pris le métro**. (Students with more limited abilities may want to write down each sentence as it is said.)

NATIONAL STANDARDS
C1.1, C1.2, C1.3, C4.2

Workbook Activities 10-11

Transparencies 62-63

Teacher's Notes

1. The American author Ernest Hemingway (1899-1961) moved to Paris in 1921. He lived there off and on for the next eight years. While in Paris, Hemingway wrote *In Our Time* and *The Sun Also Rises*, and he began *A Farewell to Arms*. Much later, his book *A Moveable Feast* described his life in Paris. He wrote about the cultural and literary scene of the decade immediately after World War I, cafés where he wrote, and other expatriates, such as Gertrude Stein and F. Scott Fitzgerald. In his writing Hemingway focused attention on physical sensations: the tastes, smells and sights of the City of Light. Because he perfected his writing style while he lived there, and because he said that it was "the city I love best in all the world," Hemingway carried the memories of his years in Paris with him for the rest of his life.

2. Quotations from other Americans about Paris include Josephine Baker's "J'ai deux amours: mon pays et Paris" and Ralph Waldo Emerson's "Il y a entre Londres et Paris cette différence que Paris est fait pour l'étranger et Londres pour l'Anglais. L'Angleterre a bâti Londres pour son propre usage; la France a bâti Paris pour le monde entier."

3. **Notre-Dame**, the setting for Victor Hugo's novel *The Hunchback of Notre Dame*, was completed in 1245. The cathedral is 427 feet long and 158 feet wide and can hold 9,000 people. Its towers are 226 feet high. In front of **Notre-Dame** is the point from which all distances in France are measured.

NATIONAL STANDARDS
C2.2, C3.1, C4.2

Mise au point sur... Paris

"If you are lucky enough to have lived in Paris as a young man, then wherever you go for the rest of your life, it stays with you, for Paris is a moveable feast," wrote the American author Ernest Hemingway. Long considered to be the cultural capital of the world, Paris still attracts people interested in the arts. Visitors come from all over the globe to see the famous sights of this cosmopolitan city.

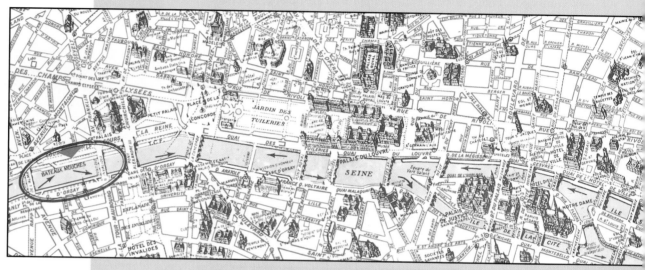

The origins of Paris go back many centuries. The city received its name from the **Parisii**, a Gallic tribe that settled on the **île de la Cité** over 2,000 years ago. The larger of the two islands in the Seine, the **île de la Cité** is called the "cradle" of Paris because the city's history began here. Tourists admire the quaint seventeenth century buildings on the smaller, more residential **île Saint-Louis**. Sightseers needing a break stop at Le Berthillon, a popular establishment known for its delicious ice cream.

Several monuments draw visitors to the **île de la Cité**. The cathedral of **Notre-Dame**, begun in the twelfth century, is a triumph of Gothic architecture with its ribbed vaulting and flying buttresses. These structures support the weight of the cathedral from the outside, allowing for thinner, higher walls filled with richly colored stained glass windows. Gargoyles, waterspouts sculpted in the form of long-necked creatures, and intricately carved statues decorate the church's façade.

The **Sainte-Chapelle**, a tiny church on the **île de la Cité**, was built in the thirteenth century to house relics from the religious Crusades. Another jewel of Gothic architecture, it contains enough stained glass windows to

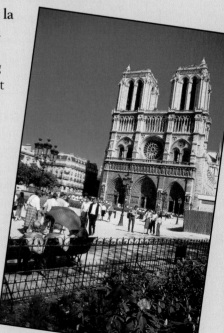

The western façade of the cathedral of *Notre-Dame* features three large doors, two tall towers and a central rose window. (Paris)

caisse nationale des **monuments historiques** et des sites ◇

SAINTE CHAPELLE
entrée

PLEIN TARIF

VALABLE LE 15/01/2002

VENDU LE 15/01/2002 A 11h57

CAISSE No 13　　　0081　　951300004564

ticket à conserver en cas de contrôle

cover three basketball courts. Since most people couldn't read during the Middle Ages, biblical stories were illustrated through the scenes on these windows, as well as on those of other Gothic churches.

Just a block away lies the **Conciergerie**, which was a state prison during the French Revolution. You can still visit cell number VI where Queen Marie-Antoinette, wife of King Louis XVI, spent her last days before being guillotined in 1793.

seine rive gauche
3, rue Louise Weiss - 75013 Paris
face 161, rue du Chevaleret -01.44.23.80.02
RESTAURANT SALON DE THÉ - Référencé Gault et Millau
ASSIETTES COMPOSÉES RAFFINÉES
PÂTISSERIES MAISON
TERRASSE, OUVERT TOUT L'ÉTÉ

Bargain hunters often like to browse at the stands of the *bouquinistes*. (Paris)

The Seine River divides Paris in half before it continues northwest to the English Channel. The Right Bank (**rive droite**) is north of the Seine; the Left Bank (**rive gauche**) is south of the Seine. More than 30 bridges, such as the **Pont-Neuf** (the oldest) and the **pont Alexandre-III** (the newest and most elaborate), join the two sides of the river. **Les bouquinistes** (*booksellers*) line the banks of the Seine with their stands full of secondhand books, posters, old prints and postcards.

On the Right Bank of the Seine is the **place Charles-de-Gaulle** where Napoléon had the **arc de triomphe** built to commemorate his military victories. Under the arch lies the Tomb of the Unknown Soldier. This square used to be called the **place de l'Étoile** because 12 avenues radiate from its center. The most famous of these streets, the **avenue des Champs-Élysées**, stretches to the **place de la Concorde**, where over one thousand French people were guillotined during the French Revolution. The largest square in western Europe, the **place de la Concorde** has an Egyptian obelisk and beautiful fountains at its center.

The Tomb of the Unknown Soldier is marked by an eternal flame and a daily bouquet of flowers. (Paris)

The obelisk at the center of *la place de la Concorde* stands 75 feet tall, weighs over 220 tons and is covered with Egyptian hieroglyphics. (Paris)

Teacher's Note

The **Louvre** originally was a fortress erected in 1200. It consisted of a tower and a keep, surrounded by a heavy wall. Transformed into a royal residence in the 1360s by Charles V, this second **Louvre** also has disappeared. The oldest part of the building standing today was begun in 1546. The **Louvre** became a public museum after the French Revolution.

Game

Concentration

Put your students in pairs to play this memory game. Have each pair make a grid with 16 squares. Students write the name of a Parisian monument on each one of the first eight squares and a description of each monument on one of the other eight squares. For example, **Notre-Dame**; Gothic cathedral. Students cut out the 16 squares and place them one by one face down on the playing surface. Partner A chooses two squares at random, hoping to have a match between monument and description. If there is a match, Partner A gets one point, keeps the squares and takes an additional turn. If there is no match, Partner A replaces the squares and then it's Partner B's turn. Pairs continue playing until all matches have been made.

NATIONAL STANDARDS
C2.1, C2.2, C3.1, C3.2, C4.2

426

The **jardins des Tuileries**, the former gardens of French royalty, extend farther east along the river. Next to the gardens is the enormous **musée du Louvre** with its modern steel and glass pyramid designed by the American architect I. M. Pei.

The exterior of the *Louvre* combines classical and modern architecture. (Paris)

Formerly a royal palace, the **Louvre** houses one of the most extensive art collections in the world. Among its treasures are paintings, such as the *Mona Lisa*, sculptures, such as *Winged Victory*, period furniture, antiquities and the crown jewels of France. If you were to spend three minutes in front of each painting in the museum, it would take you over two and one-half months to view all of them.

On the northern edge of the city, the basilica of **Sacré-Cœur** overlooks Paris from the hill of **Montmartre**, an artistic quarter of the city.

The white-domed basilica of *Sacré-Cœur* overlooks the *place du Tertre*, the artists' quarter. (Paris)

The Right Bank has contemporary buildings as well as historical landmarks. The **Centre national d'art et de culture Georges Pompidou**, familiarly called **Beaubourg**, was designed in a bold, functional style of architecture. The pipes, ducts, pillars and stairways of the glass structure are exposed; each is painted a different color according to its function (water, heating, air-conditioning, etc.). A "caterpillar" escalator brings visitors to the top of the building for a fabulous view of the city. The **Centre Pompidou** contains a computer music center, the city's biggest public library and a modern art museum. The square in front of the building remains a perpetual showcase, with street performers entertaining the public at all hours of the day and night.

Centre Georges Pompidou

PATHÉ, PREMIER EMPIRE DU CINÉMA

jusqu'au 6 mars
une exposition
et
300 films en Salle Garance
copies rares,
films des premiers temps,
films muets
avec accompagnement musical en direct

Street performers, such as jugglers, flame throwers, musicians and artists, attract crowds in front of the *Centre Pompidou*. (Paris)

Both the **musée d'Orsay** and the **musée Rodin** are on the Left Bank (**rive gauche**) of the Seine. Built in a former train station, the **musée d'Orsay** features artwork from the years 1848 to 1914. Paintings from such well-known artists as Claude Monet, Vincent Van Gogh, Pierre Auguste Renoir, Édouard Manet, Edgar Degas and Henri de Toulouse-Lautrec hang in this airy museum. The **musée Rodin** and its gardens contain some of the most famous pieces sculpted by Auguste Rodin, such as *The Thinker*, *The Burghers of Calais* and *The Gates of Hell*.

The tomb of Napoléon is located in the **hôtel des Invalides**, a former military hospital and now a military museum. Napoléon's remains are contained within six coffins, one inside the other.

Built by Gustave Eiffel for the World's Fair of 1889, the **tour Eiffel** is the symbol of Paris. Tourists take an elevator to the observation deck on the third level of the tower for a spectacular view of the city, or they may stop at the scenic restaurants on the first and second levels. For many years the tallest structure in the world, the Eiffel Tower was originally scorned by many artists and writers who were offended by its geometric structure. Nevertheless, **la Grande Dame de Paris** has been used for a variety of purposes over the years, serving as a military observation station during World War I, a meteorological post, and a radio and television transmitting station. With new lights illuminating the tower from within, the Eiffel Tower sparkles in the night sky, reminding people that Paris is **la Ville lumière.**

Le musée d'Orsay opened in 1986 and quickly became one of Paris' most popular attractions.

The *tour Eiffel*, the tallest monument in Paris at 985 feet, is the symbol of the city.

An ancient yet beautiful and dynamic city, the Paris of today, including its suburbs, has over 10 million people and is the intellectual, economic, cultural and political center of France. As the German writer Goethe said, **Paris est la capitale du monde.**

Teacher's Notes

1. The body of Napoléon was brought to the domed church in the center of the **hôtel des Invalides** in 1840. He had wanted to be buried near the Seine. His coffins are of tin-sheeted iron, mahogany, ebony, oak and lead, all encased within dark red porphyry. His body was put into many coffins to preserve it better and to duplicate the manner in which the pharaohs of Egypt were buried. 2. Remarkably, the **tour Eiffel**, one of the tallest structures in the world, weighs a mere 7,000 tons.

Connections

French Art

You may want to check local libraries and art museums for slides and videos of various French artists and their work to show to your students. The art teacher in your school may agree to give a presentation on French art to your class. If your students are keeping a cultural journal, you might have each one pick out the piece of art that he or she likes the best and explain why.

Cooperative Group Practice

Métro to the Monuments

Divide your class into four groups. Give each group two maps: one of Paris and one of the **métro**. Then have students in each group go through the **Mise au point sur... Paris** and make a list of 12 of the major monuments and sites in Paris. Using the two maps, have each group find and write the name of the closest **métro** stop to each monument or site. Afterward, have groups compare **métro** stops for the monuments or sites they have listed in common.

NATIONAL STANDARDS
C2.1, C2.2, C3.1, C3.2, C4.2

Transparency 64

Quiz
Leçon B

Answers

9 Possible answers:
1. The **Parisii** settled on the **île de la Cité**.
2. The **île de la Cité** is called the "cradle" of Paris because the city's history began here.
3. The **île Saint-Louis** is the smaller of the two islands in the Seine.
4. Two characteristics of Gothic architecture are ribbed vaulting and flying buttresses.
5. Most people couldn't read during the Middle Ages.
6. Queen Marie-Antoinette was imprisoned in the **Conciergerie**.
7. The oldest bridge in Paris is the **Pont-Neuf**.
8. Napoléon had the **arc de triomphe** built to commemorate his military victories.
9. Many people were guillotined in the **place de la Concorde**.
10. Two famous works of art in the **Louvre** are the *Mona Lisa* and *Winged Victory*.
11. Crowds gather outside the **Centre Pompidou** to watch the street performers.
12. Claude Monet and Vincent Van Gogh are two artists who have paintings displayed at the **musée d'Orsay**.
13. Napoléon's tomb is in the **hôtel des Invalides**.
14. The **tour Eiffel** is considered to be the symbol of Paris.
15. Hemingway probably meant that if you've ever lived in Paris, the memories of your stay there will be with you for the rest of your life.

NATIONAL STANDARDS
C2.1, C2.2, C3.1, C3.2, C4.2

428

Napoléon wanted to be buried near the Seine, and his tomb is in the *hôtel des Invalides* on the Left Bank. (Paris)

9 Answer the following questions.
1. What Gallic tribe settled on the **île de la Cité**?
2. Why is the **île de la Cité** called the "cradle" of Paris?
3. What is the name of the smaller of the two islands in the Seine?
4. What are two characteristics of Gothic architecture?
5. Why were biblical stories told in the stained glass windows of churches?
6. Where was Queen Marie-Antoinette imprisoned?
7. What is the oldest bridge in Paris?
8. Why did Napoléon have the **arc de triomphe** built?
9. Where were many people guillotined during the French Revolution?
10. What are two famous works of art in the **Louvre**?
11. Why do crowds gather outside the contemporary **Centre Pompidou**?
12. What are the names of two artists whose paintings are displayed at the **musée d'Orsay**?
13. Where is Napoléon's tomb?
14. Which monument is considered to be the symbol of Paris?
15. What did Ernest Hemingway mean when he said ". . . Paris is a moveable feast"?

Stained glass windows in the *Sainte-Chapelle* illustrat[e] stories from the Bible in 1,134 scenes. (Paris)

10 Look at the **métro** map of Paris on the next page and answer the following questions.
1. What station is at the opposite end of the line from Porte d'Orléans (on the Left Bank)?
2. How many **métro** lines serve Pasteur (on the Left Bank)?
3. Are there more or less than 15 stations on the line whose end points are Pont de Levallois-Bécon and Gallieni (line 3)?
4. The Voltaire station is on the Right Bank. What are the names of the stations at the end points of the line that passes through this station? What is the number of this line?
5. If you wanted to go from Concorde to Hôtel de Ville (both on the Right Bank), in what direction would you go? (Give the name of the station at the line's end point.)
6. If you were going from Rambuteau to Père-Lachaise (both on the Right Bank), in what direction would you go first? At what station would you transfer? In what direction would you finally go?
7. If you were going from Victor Hugo (on line 2 on the Right Bank) to Jacques Bonsergent (on line 5 on the Right Bank), in what direction would you go first? At what station would you transfer? In what direction would you finally go?

M (RER) Paris

Answers

10 Possible answers:

1. The station at the opposite end of the line is Porte de Clignancourt.
2. Two lines serve Pasteur.
3. There are more than 15 stations on line 3.
4. The stations at the end points of the line are Pont de Sèvres and Mairie de Montreuil. This is line 9.
5. You would go in the direction Château de Vincennes.
6. You would first go in the direction Mairie des Lilas. You would transfer at République. You would finally go in the direction Gallieni.
7. You would first go in the direction Nation. You would transfer at Stalingrad. You would finally go in the direction Place d'Italie.

NATIONAL STANDARDS
C2.1, C2.2, C3.1, C3.2

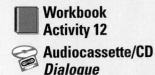

**Workbook
Activity 12**

Audiocassette/CD
Dialogue

Teacher's Notes

1. Communicative functions that are recycled in this lesson are "describing past events" and "giving information." 2. You may want to review with your students both the literal and figurative meanings of **trouver** in French. Danielle is using the figurative meaning as she asks Karine for her opinion. 3. You may want to point out to your students the new meaning of **jardin** (*park*) introduced in this dialogue. 4. You may want to have each student choose a different Parisian monument or site, do research on it and then give a brief oral presentation in English to the entire class. Students should use pictures or slides to illustrate their comments. (You may want to videotape students' presentations.)

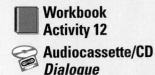

National Standards
C1.2

430

Leçon C

In this lesson you will be able to:

➤ **ask for information**

➤ **give opinions**

➤ **compare things**

➤ **sequence events**

Karine returns to Tahiti and tells her friend Danielle about her trip to Paris.

Danielle: **Comment est-ce que tu as trouvé Paris?**
Karine: **Je pense que c'est la plus belle ville du monde.**
Danielle: **Qu'est-ce que tu as fait?**
Karine: **J'ai vu beaucoup de monuments. La semaine dernière j'ai aussi visité le jardin du Luxembourg. Ce n'est pas le plus grand jardin de Paris, mais il est très joli.**
Danielle: **Quels quartiers sont les plus modernes?**
Karine: **Le Forum des Halles et la Villette.**

Le Forum des Halles, au centre de Paris, est un quartier très moderne.

Enquête culturelle

Students from the nearby **Quartier latin** often relax in the **jardin du Luxembourg**. Children push toy boats across the park's large pond with long sticks. In addition to the many public parks in Paris, there are two larger wooded areas, the **bois de Boulogne** on the west side of the city and the **bois de Vincennes** on the east side. Both offer lakes, restaurants, zoos and sporting opportunities for people who want to spend some time away from the busy inner city.

The *jardin du Luxembourg*, a convenient, tranquil garden, provides a perfect place for university students to study or relax. (Paris)

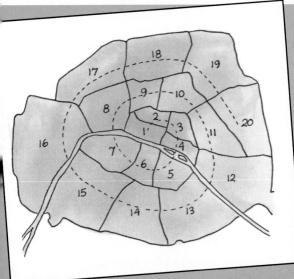

The city of Paris is divided into 20 **arrondissements** (*districts*) for governmental purposes and many **quartiers** (*quarters*) for cultural or artistic reasons. For example, many artists live and work in the **quartier** of **Montmartre**.

Le Forum des Halles is a contemporary, underground shopping mall with restaurants, cafés, snack bars, boutiques and movie theaters on four levels. It also has a branch of Fnac, a large specialty store for those who love music, books, photography and TV. At Fnac you can choose from a wide variety of CDs and also order concert tickets.

La Villette, in the northeastern part of Paris, houses the **Cité des Sciences**, an ultramodern "hands-on" science museum. Here teenagers also enjoy **la Géode**, a movie theater where films are projected 180 degrees above and around the audience.

Workbook
Activities 13-14

Grammar & Vocabulary
Exercises 18-20

Video

Teacher's Notes

1. There are also popular puppet shows for children in the **jardin du Luxembourg**. 2. The **arrondissements** start with number one near the **Louvre**, then spiral clockwise around the city. 3. Review another modern **quartier** of Paris, **la Défense**, introduced in **Leçon B**.

Comparisons

Cultural Journal

If your students are keeping a cultural journal, have them write their reaction to the following situation. Imagine that your trip to Paris is almost over. Write a list of ten things you need to do before you return home. Consider both practical needs, such as confirming return flight reservations, and personal needs, such as getting the addresses of new people you have met or returning to your favorite spot just one more time.

TPR

Rive gauche, rive droite ou île de la Cité?

After you have reviewed with your students where all the famous monuments and sites of Paris are located, you might have them do the following activity. As you name a specific place, have students raise their left hand if it is located on the Left Bank; have them raise their right hand if it is located on the Right Bank; have them raise both hands if it is located on the **île de la Cité**.

NATIONAL STANDARDS
C1.2, C2.1, C2.2, C3.1, C4.2

Workbook Activity 15

Grammar & Vocabulary Exercises 21-25

Audiocassette/CD Activity 3

Computer Software Activity 4

Answers

1 1. e
 2. c
 3. h
 4. d
 5. b, a
 6. g, f

2 Possible answer:

Karine pense que Paris est la plus belle ville du monde. Karine a vu beaucoup de monuments et le jardin du Luxembourg. Le jardin du Luxembourg n'est pas le plus grand jardin de Paris, mais il est très joli. Deux quartiers modernes sont le Forum des Halles et la Villette.

3 Answers will vary.

Teacher's Note

Before beginning the section on the superlative of adjectives, have your students review the comparative of adjectives (**Unité 8**). In addition, review which adjectives precede nouns (for example, **beau, joli, nouveau, vieux, bon, mauvais, grand** and **petit**) and which ones follow them (**Unité 7**).

Comparisons

The Superlative

Ask students to compare the way the superlative is expressed both in English and in French. Does the English superlative depend on the position of the adjective?

NATIONAL STANDARDS
C1.1, C1.2, C1.3, C4.1

432

Veux-tu voir le Sacré-Cœur? (Paris)

Tous les mois dans le magazine

PHOTO

les plus belles images du monde

---

1 | *Complétez les phrases avec la lettre du mot convenable d'après le dialogue.*

  1. Qu'est-ce que Karine... de Paris?
  2. Quelle est la plus belle ville du...?
  3. Qu'est-ce que Karine... fait à Paris?
  4. Karine a... beaucoup de monuments.
  5. La semaine... elle a visité le... du Luxembourg.
  6. La Villette et le... sont des... très modernes.

  a. jardin
  b. dernière
  c. monde
  d. vu
  e. pense
  f. quartiers
  g. Forum des Halles
  h. a

2 | Write a four-sentence paragraph in French that summarizes what Karine tells Danielle about her trip to Paris. Begin by telling what Karine thinks of Paris. Then mention two things that she saw. Next describe the Luxembourg Gardens. Finally, give the name of two modern quarters of Paris.

3 | *C'est à toi!*

  1. Quel monument de Paris est-ce que tu veux voir?
  2. Quel monument de ta ville ou de ton village est-ce que tu as visité?
  3. Comment est-ce que tu trouves ta ville ou ton village?
  4. Quel quartier de ta ville ou de ton village est le plus beau?
  5. Qu'est-ce que tu as fait hier soir?
  6. Est-ce que tu as déjà vu ton professeur d'anglais aujourd'hui?

Structure

Superlative of adjectives

To tell that a person or thing has the most of a certain quality compared to all others, use the superlative construction:

le/la/les + **plus** + adjective

Je pense que *la Joconde* est **le plus beau** tableau.

I think that the Mona Lisa *is the most beautiful painting.*

If an adjective usually precedes a noun, its superlative form also precedes it. If an adjective usually follows a noun, so does its superlative form. Both the definite article and the adjective agree in gender and in number with the noun they describe.

Le Louvre est **le plus grand** musée.

The **Louvre** *is the largest museum.*

Le Forum des Halles et la Villette sont les quartiers **les plus modernes**.

Le Forum des Halles and *la Villette are the most modern neighborhoods.*

Sometimes the superlative is followed by a form of **de** (*in*).

Paris est la plus belle ville **du** monde.

Paris is the most beautiful city in the world.

Pratique

4 | Describe some of the students and teachers in your school using the superlative construction.

1. M. Poirier (prof généreux)
2. Jérémy et Denise (élèves timides)
3. Anne-Marie et Monique (jolies filles)
4. le professeur de maths et le professeur de dessin (professeurs intelligents)
5. Daniel et Amine (beaux garçons)
6. Mlle Vigier (grande prof)

Modèle:

Caroline (petite fille)
Caroline est la plus petite fille de l'école.

David (garçon bavard)
David est le garçon le plus bavard de l'école.

5 | Comment on some of the sites in Paris. Use a superlative form of one of the adjectives from column A and a noun from column B in stating each of your opinions.

A	B
beau	le cimetière
moderne	l'arche
grand	l'église
joli	le musée
petit	l'avenue
	le monument
	la place
	le quartier
	le jardin

1. la Villette
2. Notre-Dame
3. le cimetière du Père-Lachaise
4. la Cité des Sciences
5. le jardin du Luxembourg
6. la Sainte-Chapelle
7. la tour Eiffel
8. l'arche de la Défense
9. l'avenue des Champs-Élysées
10. la place de la Concorde

Modèle:

le Louvre
Le Louvre est le plus grand musée de Paris.

L'arche de la Défense est l'arche la plus moderne de Paris.

6 | Find out what your partner's opinions are on certain topics. Take turns asking and answering questions using the superlative construction.

1. couleur (moche)
2. repas (grand)
3. élèves (diligent)
4. cours (facile)
5. mois (beau)
6. CD (formidable)
7. légume (mauvais)
8. baskets (cher)

La plus belle ville, c'est Paris.

Modèles:

ville (beau)
Student A: Quelle ville est la plus belle?
Student B: La plus belle ville, c'est Paris.

professeur (sympa)
Student B: Quel professeur est le plus sympa?
Student A: Le professeur le plus sympa, c'est M. Johnson.

Audiocassette/CD Activities 4, 6

Answers

4 1. M. Poirier est le prof le plus généreux de l'école.
2. Jérémy et Denise sont les élèves les plus timides de l'école.
3. Anne-Marie et Monique sont les plus jolies filles de l'école.
4. Le professeur de maths et le professeur de dessin sont les professeurs les plus intelligents de l'école.
5. Daniel et Amine sont les plus beaux garçons de l'école.
6. Mlle Vigier est la plus grande prof de l'école.

5 Possible answers:
1. La Villette est le quartier le plus moderne de Paris.
2. Notre-Dame est la plus belle église de Paris.
3. Le cimetière du Père-Lachaise est le plus grand cimetière de Paris.
4. La Cité des Sciences est le musée le plus moderne de Paris.
5. Le jardin du Luxembourg est le plus joli jardin de Paris.
6. La Sainte-Chapelle est la plus petite église de Paris.
7. La tour Eiffel est le plus grand monument de Paris.
8. L'arche de la Défense est l'arche la plus moderne de Paris.
9. L'avenue des Champs-Élysées est la plus belle avenue de Paris.
10. La place de la Concorde est la plus grande place de Paris.

6 Answers are on page 434.

NATIONAL STANDARDS
C1.1, C1.2

Answers

6 1. Quelle couleur est la plus moche?
2. Quel repas est le plus grand?/Quels repas sont les plus grands?
3. Quels élèves sont les plus diligents?/Quelles élèves sont les plus diligentes?
4. Quel cours est le plus facile?/Quels cours sont les plus faciles?
5. Quel mois est le plus beau?/Quels mois sont les plus beaux?
6. Quel CD est le plus formidable?
7. Quel légume est le plus mauvais?
8. Quelles baskets sont les plus chères?
Students' responses to these questions will vary.

Teacher's Notes

1. Have students bring photos or drawings they have made of the attractions they chose to write about in Activity 7, attaching these photos or drawings to their descriptions. Then conduct a poster contest for which each student creates a travel poster using his or her photos or drawings and their descriptions. 2. You, too, may want to participate in the contest described in Activity 8 and bring one of your baby pictures. 3. Appoint one student to record the name of the winner in each category.

434

Bienvenue à Amiens

AMIENS

Communication

7 | Your local tourist bureau has asked your class to help write a French travel brochure about your city, town or area that will be distributed to French-speaking tourists who pass through. Write five sentences in French using the superlative construction. In each sentence describe one of the most important tourist attractions in your area. You might tell which sites are the newest, oldest, most beautiful, largest, smallest, etc.

8 | With your classmates, hold an "ultimate" baby contest. Bring to class a picture of you taken when you were either a baby or a toddler. In small groups, come up with five questions using the superlative that students in other groups will be able to answer by looking at your group's baby pictures. (For example, you might ask **Qui a les cheveux les plus blonds?**) Then, select a group member to read these five questions to the entire class. After each group has presented its questions, you and your classmates should choose the ten best questions to use in the contest. In preparation, post your photo on the class bulletin board for your teacher to number and for everyone to see. When the contest begins, one student reads the ten questions, and everyone else votes for the winning baby in each category.

Workbook Activity 16

Audiocassette/CD
Sur la bonne piste

Sur la bonne piste

You have already learned several reading strategies that can help you figure out the meaning of French words you don't know, including recognizing cognates and determining the context of the reading. However, there will be times when these strategies won't help you. When all else fails and you need to know the meaning of a word in order to understand the reading as a whole, there is another skill that can help you: using a French-English dictionary.

You may not think you need any special skill to use a dictionary. This is not true! Imagine the different meanings a French speaker will find when looking up the word "kid" in an English dictionary. As a noun, "kid" can mean either "child" or "young goat." As a verb, "kid" means "to joke." Similarly, you know that the French word **glace** means "ice cream." But if you look up **glace** in a French dictionary, you will discover that it can also mean "ice," "glass" or "mirror." The meaning of a word depends entirely on how it is used in a sentence.

The paragraph that follows is the beginning of a historical overview of the **Louvre**. To learn how to use a dictionary effectively, concentrate on the three highlighted examples in this paragraph. After you read it, refer to the dictionary hints that show you how to look up these three words.

XIIIᵉ siècle:

Le château royal du Louvre, fondé par Philippe-Auguste, est situé à Paris sur la rive droite de la Seine et **protège** la ville à l'ouest. La **grosse** tour centrale de cette forteresse **carrée** sert de prison, d'arsenal et de chambre au trésor.

Here are some hints on how to use a French-English dictionary:

1. *Before you look up a word, try to figure out what part of speech it is (noun, verb, adjective, etc.).* As a clue, use the word's position in the sentence. For example, look at the word **carrée**. In the French dictionary there are different meanings for the word as an adjective and as a noun. Looking at its position in the sentence, you'll notice that **carrée** follows **forteresse**, a cognate for the English noun "fortress." You know that most adjectives follow the nouns they describe. Thus, you can figure out that **carrée**, in this sentence, functions as an adjective meaning "square."

2. *Remember that verbs are listed in the dictionary in their infinitive form.* Once you have determined that a word is a verb, try to figure out what its infinitive is before you look it up, keeping in mind that all infinitives end in **-er**, **-ir** or **-re**. For example, when trying to figure out the infinitive of the verb form **protège**, you should remember that certain forms of **-er** verbs end in **-e**. Thus, you might logically guess that the infinitive of this word is **protéger**, which means "to protect."

3. *Realize that adjectives (and nouns) that have both masculine and feminine forms are listed in the dictionary in their masculine singular form.* For example, once you have determined that **grosse** is a feminine adjective, try to figure out what it's masculine form is before you look it up in the dictionary. You know that some feminine adjectives are formed by doubling the final consonant of a masculine adjective and adding an **e**. So, you might logically guess that the masculine form of **grosse** is **gros**.

NATIONAL STANDARDS
C1.2, C2.2, C3.1

Teacher's Notes

1. You may want students to work in pairs as they answer the questions on page 437. Note that the first seven questions have specific answers. However, there is still some room for subjectivity. The last question allows students to use the dictionary skills they have learned to look up key words from the reading they don't understand. To holistically grade this activity, refer to the suggestions on page 162. 2. You might want to encourage students to use a French-English dictionary only as a last resort after having tried the many other reading strategies they learned in previous **unités**. You might also want to point out specific abbreviations for parts of speech that are given after the word and before its definition(s), for example, *nf, nm, adj, vi, vt, adv*, etc.

4. *When you look up a word in the dictionary, be sure to check all its possible meanings.* Don't just assume that the first meaning given is the one you need. For example, the adjective **grosse** can mean "big," "large," "thick," "heavy" or "fat." Use the context of the sentence it appears in to figure out which meaning applies. **Grosse** modifies **la tour**, which you know means "tower." This information can help you determine that the correct meaning for **grosse** in this sentence is "big" or "large."

Now read the rest of the historical description of the **Louvre**. Use all the reading strategies you have learned up to this point to figure out the meaning of words you don't know.

XIVᵉ siècle:

Charles V embellit le château et le transforme en demeure habitable.

XVIᵉ siècle:

François Iᵉʳ démolit la forteresse et commence le palais. Amateur d'art italien, il y installe ses tableaux préférés, *la Joconde* incluse. Pierre Lescot élève la partie sud-ouest de la Cour Carrée.

Fin du XVIᵉ, début du XVIIᵉ siècle:

Pour joindre le Louvre au Palais des Tuileries, la Petite Galerie et la Grande Galerie sont construites le long de la Seine.

XVIIᵉ siècle:

Louis XIII et Louis XIV donnent à la Cour Carrée ses proportions actuelles. Claude Perrault est un des auteurs de la Colonade qui, à l'est, fait face à l'église Saint-Germain-l'Auxerrois.

XVIIIᵉ siècle:

Napoléon Iᵉʳ achève la Cour Carrée et son décor. Il commence l'aile Richelieu qui longe la rue de Rivoli. Demeure des rois de France, siège des Académies, le Louvre devient musée pendant la Révolution en 1793.

XIXᵉ siècle:

Napoléon III et ses architectes terminent les travaux à l'ouest. Les Tuileries brûlent en 1871 et l'unité de cet immense ensemble de palais est rompue.

XXᵉ siècle:

Ieoh Ming Pei, architecte américain d'origine chinoise, construit une pyramide moderne de verre dans la cour du musée en 1989. Elle fonctionne comme entrée principale et librairie. En 1993 l'aile Richelieu est remise à neuf. Le Carrousel, centre commercial de luxe souterrain, est bâti.

Aujourd'hui:

Le musée devient un des plus riches du monde. Les collections justement célèbres ne font que croître.

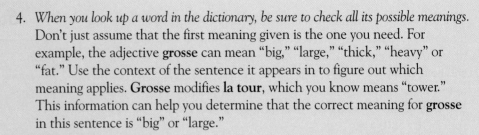
NATIONAL STANDARDS
C1.2, C2.2, C3.1

9   Now make a list of the words you still don't know that you feel are essential to understanding the reading as a whole. By answering the following questions, the meaning of some of these words may become clear.

1. Realizing that the word **embellit** is a verb form, what do you think its infinitive is?
2. The word **amateur** can mean either "amateur" or "lover (of something)." Which meaning applies here?
3. The word **élève** can function as a noun or as a verb. Which part of speech applies here?
4. The word **actuelles** is an adjective. What is its masculine singular form?
5. The word **ensemble** can function as an adverb or as a noun. Which part of speech applies here?
6. The word **neuf** can mean either "nine" or "new." Which meaning applies here?
7. The word **devient** looks similar to a verb form you have already learned. What is it? What do you think its infinitive is?
8. Choose three of the words you still don't understand from the list you made and answer the following questions about each word.
   a. What part of speech is the word?
   b. If it is a verb form, what is its infinitive?
   c. If it is an adjective, what is its masculine singular form?
   d. When you look it up in a French-English dictionary, how many different meanings does it have?
   e. Which meaning applies here?

Nathalie et Raoul

Answers

1. faux
2. vrai
3. faux
4. vrai
5. vrai
6. faux
7. vrai
8. faux
9. faux
10. vrai

Teacher's Notes

Here is the English version of the cartoon on page 437: Nathalie, we're going to spend our vacation in Paris. It's up to you to decide what to do during our stay. Hmmm . . . . I can imagine the perfect week . . . . Shopping on the **Champs-Élysées** . . . with Raoul. Visiting the **musée d' Orsay** . . . with Raoul. And going for a romantic ride on the Seine at night . . . with Raoul. Well then, what do I want to do during my vacation? Spend time with Raoul! Nathalie, are you listening to me? Are you still there? Have you decided? Yes, Dad. Uhm . . . I prefer to stay here . . . with Raoul! I don't understand teenagers . . . especially those in love!

C'est à moi!

Now that you have completed this unit, take a look at what you should be able to do in French. Can you do all of these tasks?

➤ I can write a journal entry.

➤ I can talk about what happened in the past.

➤ I can talk about things sequentially.

➤ I can say what needs to be done.

➤ I can ask for information.

➤ I can give my opinion by saying what I think.

➤ I can make comparisons by saying who or what has the most of a certain quality.

Vous êtes obligé(e) de visiter le musée d'Orsay! (Paris)

Here is a brief checkup to see how much you understand about French culture. Decide if each statement is **vrai** or **faux**.

1. *La Joconde*, the French name for Leonardo da Vinci's masterpiece, can be found in the **musée d'Orsay** in Paris.
2. The **R.E.R.**, an expansion of the Paris **métro** system, serves the suburbs with fewer stops in the center of the city.
3. France and the United States both have their national holiday on July 4.
4. The French celebrate Bastille Day with a military parade, fireworks and street dances.
5. **Notre-Dame,** the **Sainte-Chapelle** and the **Conciergerie** are all located on the **île de la Cité** in the Seine River.

What cathedral is located on the *île de la Cité?* (Paris)

6. Napoléon's **arc de triomphe** is the site where he had over one thousand people guillotined during the French Revolution.
7. The **Centre Pompidou** has a modern, functional style of architecture with its pipes, ducts, pillars and stairways on the outside of the building.
8. To view the paintings by such great French artists as Monet, Renoir and Toulouse-Lautrec, visit the **Louvre**.
9. The **tour Eiffel** is best known because both the Tomb of the Unknown Soldier and the tomb of Jim Morrison lie underneath it.
10. Modern **quartiers** of Paris include **la Défense, la Villette** and **le Forum des Halles.**

Communication orale

Imagine that you and your partner have returned from separate one-week trips to Paris. One partner went there as part of a group of tourists specifically interested in seeing the sites. The other partner went there to visit a former French exchange student and stayed with the student's family. Consequently, both partners have different memories of Paris. The second partner didn't see as many sites as the first partner, but took part in more family-related activities and did things that French teenagers do. Begin your conversation by greeting each other. Then ask and tell each other how you liked Paris. Next ask and tell when you arrived in Paris. Finally, ask and tell where you went and what you saw and did. Finish your conversation by asking and telling each other when you returned home.

Communication écrite

Your teacher is curious to find out what you and your partner did in Paris and how you liked the city. Write a composition in French that describes the similarities and differences between your trip and your partner's trip, based on the information you exchanged in your previous conversation. To help you organize your composition, you may first want to make intersecting circles. In the first circle list only the things that you did and saw; in the second circle list only the things that your partner did and saw; in the section where the circles intersect list the things that both of you did and saw.

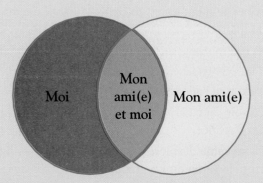

Moi — Mon ami(e) et moi — Mon ami(e)

Cooperative Group Practice

The Writing Process

To help your students understand the process of writing a composition, put them in small groups of three or four. Give each group a composition you have written about someone's imaginary trip to Paris. The composition should have four paragraphs, each with four or more supporting ideas. Some descriptions should be written in the **passé composé**. Under each paragraph leave a space for students to write the topic sentence. Along with each paragraph include a web with a center circle and four supporting circles.

For each paragraph students should write the topic sentence in the center circle and then identify four supporting ideas from the rest of the paragraph and write them in the other spaces of the web.

Comparisons

Writing Supporting Sentences

To give your students practice writing sentences that support a topic sentence, give them these four topic sentences that someone has written about an imaginary trip to Paris: 1. **Je pense que Paris est la plus belle ville du monde.** 2. **Hier j'ai vu quatre beaux monuments à Paris.** 3. **Je suis allé(e) à la tour Eiffel.** 4. **J'ai acheté beaucoup de CDs.** Then have students expand each of these topic sentences by writing four supporting sentences that give more information about the topic.

NATIONAL STANDARDS
C1.1, C1.2, C1.3, C2.1, C2.2, C3.1, C4.2

Communication active

To write journal entries, use:

le 5 juillet	*July 5*

To describe past events, use:

J'ai regardé de beaux tableaux.	*I looked at some beautiful paintings.*
J'ai fini la journée en bateau sur la Seine.	*I finished the day on a boat on the Seine.*
J'ai perdu mon plan de métro.	*I lost my subway map.*

Karine a vu le pont Alexandre-III. (Paris)

J'ai vu le Centre Pompidou.	*I saw the **Centre Pompidou**.*
J'ai pris un café sur la place.	*I had coffee on the square.*
Il y a eu un bal dans la rue.	*There was a street dance.*
J'ai été obligé(e) de rentrer.	*I had to (was obliged to) come back.*
On a fait beaucoup de bruit.	*People made a lot of noise.*
Je suis monté(e) au cinquième étage.	*I went up to the fifth floor.*

To sequence events, use:

D'abord, j'ai marché sur l'avenue des Champs-Élysées.	*First I walked on the **Champs-Élysées**.*
Puis, j'ai continué mon chemin jusqu'au Louvre.	*Then I continued on my way (up) to the **Louvre**.*
Alors, je suis allée au guichet du métro.	*Then I went to the subway ticket window.*
Mardi matin je suis allé(e) à la Défense.	*Tuesday morning I went to **la Défense**.*
Mercredi j'ai regardé le défilé.	*Wednesday I watched the parade.*
Le soir j'ai vu un beau feu d'artifice.	*In the evening I saw some beautiful fireworks.*
La semaine dernière j'ai aussi visité le jardin du Luxembourg.	*Last week I also visited the Luxembourg Gardens.*

To express need and necessity, use:

J'ai été obligé(e) de prendre un taxi à l'hôtel.

I had to (was obliged to) take a taxi to the hotel.

To ask for information, use:

Comment est-ce que tu as trouvé Paris?

How did you like Paris?

To give opinions, use:

Je pense que c'est la plus belle ville du monde.

I think that it's the most beautiful city in the world.

Paris est la plus belle ville du monde, n'est-ce pas?

To compare things, use:

Le Louvre est **le plus grand** musée de Paris.

*The **Louvre** is the largest museum in Paris.*

Nathalie et Raoul

Cooperative Group Practice

Forming Questions Using the Superlative

Put your students in groups of four or five. Have each group make two stacks of note cards: each card in the first stack has an adjective that precedes its noun; each card in the second stack has an adjective that follows its noun. (Tell students not to use the adjective **bon**.) Have each student randomly choose a card (from alternating stacks). Using the adjective he or she chooses, the student will ask a question in the superlative form. For example, **beau — Quelle est la plus belle ville du monde?** One person in the group serves as recorder and lists all the questions. After all cards have been used to make questions, groups exchange lists of questions. Then students take turns reading questions formed by other groups and answering them.

Teacher's Note

Here is the English version of this cartoon: We spent a wonderful year together. That's true. Let's see . . . . What was the first word you said to me? "Good-bye," of course! You thought I was stupid. No, I thought you were charming! I found out that you hate soccer. And if I remember correctly, you don't like pâté! But you love to go shopping. And you, you like to go to the movies, even if you never have enough money! I have good memories of our time together, Nathalie. They'll stay with me forever. And me, too, Raoul. You're my first love. That can never change. Good-bye. Good-bye.

NATIONAL STANDARDS
C1.2, C4.1, C5.2

Communication électronique

Answers will vary.

Communication électronique

Throughout **Unité 12** you have learned about the important sites in Paris. Now it's your chance to choose which ones you want to visit. To see a helpful map of the most popular attractions in Paris, go to this Internet site:

http://www.paris.org/Maps/MM/MMF.html

Now assume that you are going to spend several days sightseeing in Paris. From the 44 sites located on this map and described in the accompanying links, pick three that you want to explore: one monument, one church and one museum. Then answer the following questions for each place you are going to visit

1. Why would you like to visit this site?
2. In which **arrondissement** is it located?
3. What is its address?
4. What is the name of the nearest **métro** stop?
5. How much is the entrance fee?
6. When was it built?
7. What can you find inside this structure? For what is it famous?

À moi de jouer!

À moi de jouer!

Possible journal entry:

C'est aujourd'hui ma première journée à Paris. Ce matin j'ai décidé de prendre le métro pour aller au Louvre. J'ai acheté des billets au guichet et j'ai attendu le train. Le métro est très moderne.

Tout le monde a visité le Louvre aujourd'hui. J'ai vu *la Joconde* de Léonard de Vinci. C'est assez petit mais très beau.

À midi nous sommes allés au café près de la Seine. J'ai pris un sandwich au jambon, des frites et un cocoa. Super!

Cet après-midi nous avons vu les monuments de Paris d'un bateau-mouche sur la Seine. Nous avons vu la tour Eiffel, la place de la Concorde, Notre-Dame et la petite statue de la Liberté. Quelle ville formidable! Je pense que Paris est la plus belle ville du monde!

Imagine that you're visiting Paris for the first time. Write an entry in your journal about where you went, what you saw and what you did today. Also give your opinion on what you've just seen or done. Use what you see in each of the four illustrations on the right to help you remember the day's highlights. (You may want to refer to the *Communication active* on pages 440-41 and the vocabulary list on page 443.)

NATIONAL STANDARDS
C1.1, C1.3, C2.2, C3.2, C5.1

Vocabulaire

	amoureux, amoureuse in love	
un	**arc** arch	
une	**arche** arch	
	au moins at least	
un	**bal** dance	
un	**bateau** boat	
un	**billet** ticket	
un	**bruit** noise	
un	**centre** center	
	chargé(e) full	
un	**chemin** path, way	
un	**cimetière** cemetery	
	continuer to continue	
	d'après according to	
	de (d') in, by	
	décider (de) to decide	
un	**défilé** parade	
	demander to ask for	
	dernier, dernière last	
	du in (the)	
	fermer to close	
une	**fête** holiday, festival	
un	**feu d'artifice** fireworks	
une	**fois** time	
un	**guichet** ticket window	
un	**hôtel** hotel	
	imaginer to imagine	
	impressionniste Impressionist	
un	**jardin** park	
	jeune young	
une	**journée** day	
	jusqu'à up to, until	
la	**liberté** liberty	
une	**lumière** light	
	marcher to walk	
un	**métro** subway	
	moderne modern	
	moins: au moins at least	
le	**monde** world	
	monter to go up	
un	**monument** monument	
un	**musicien, une musicienne** musician	
	national(e) national	

	obligé(e): être obligé(e) de to be obliged to, to have to	
le	**paradis** paradise	
	passer to spend (time)	
	penser (à) to think (of)	
	perdre to lose	
un	**plan** map	
	plus: le/la/les plus (+ *adjective*) the most (+ adjective)	
un	**quartier** quarter, neighborhood	
	quitter to leave (a person or place)	
une	**rue** street	
	seulement only	
une	**station** station	
une	**statue** statue	
un	**tableau** painting	
un	**taxi** taxi	
un	**tombeau** tomb	
une	**tour** tower	
un	**triomphe** triumph	
	visiter to visit (a place)	
	vivre to live	
	vraiment really	

Grammar Summary

Subject Pronouns

Singular	Plural
je	nous
tu	vous
il/elle/on	ils/elles

Indefinite Articles

Singular		Plural
Masculine	Feminine	
un	une	des

Definite Articles

Singular			Plural
Before a Consonant Sound		Before a Vowel Sound	
Masculine	Feminine		
le	la	l'	les

À + Definite Articles

Singular			Plural
Before a Consonant Sound		Before a Vowel Sound	
Masculine	Feminine		
au	à la	à l'	aux

De + Definite Articles

Singular			Plural
Before a Consonant Sound		Before a Vowel Sound	
Masculine	Feminine		
du	de la	de l'	des

Partitive Articles

Before a Consonant Sound		Before a Vowel Sound
Masculine	Feminine	
du pain	**de la** glace	**de l'**eau

In negative sentences the partitive article becomes *de (d')*.

Expressions of Quantity

combien	how much, how many
assez	enough
beaucoup	a lot, many
(un) peu	(a) little, few
trop	too much, too many

These expressions are followed by *de (d')* before a noun.

Question Words

combien	how much, how many
comment	what, how
où	where
pourquoi	why
qu'est-ce que	what
quand	when
quel, quelle	what, which
qui	who, whom

Question Formation

1. By a rising tone of voice
   Vous travaillez beaucoup?
2. By beginning with *est-ce que*
   Est-ce que vous travaillez beaucoup?
3. By adding *n'est-ce pas?*
   Vous travaillez beaucoup, n'est-ce pas?
4. By inversion
   Travaillez-vous beaucoup?

Possessive Adjectives

Singular			Plural
Masculine	Feminine before a Consonant Sound	Feminine before a Vowel Sound	
mon	ma	mon	mes
ton	ta	ton	tes
son	sa	son	ses
notre	notre	notre	nos
votre	votre	votre	vos
leur	leur	leur	leurs

Demonstrative Adjectives

	Masculine before a Consonant Sound	Masculine before a Vowel Sound	Feminine
Singular	ce	cet	cette
Plural	ces	ces	ces

Quel

	Masculine	Feminine
Singular	quel	quelle
Plural	quels	quelles

Agreement of Adjectives

	Masculine	Feminine
add **e**	Il est bavard.	Elle est bavarde.
no change	Il est suisse.	Elle est suisse.
change **-er** to **-ère**	Il est cher.	Elle est chère.
change **-eux** to **-euse**	Il est paresseux.	Elle est paresseuse.
double consonant + **e**	Il est gros.	Elle est grosse.

Irregular Feminine Adjectives

Masculine before a Consonant Sound	Masculine before a Vowel Sound	Feminine
blanc		blanche
frais		fraîche
long		longue
beau	bel	belle
nouveau	nouvel	nouvelle
vieux	vieil	vieille

Position of Adjectives

Most adjectives usually follow their nouns. But adjectives expressing beauty, age, goodness and size precede their nouns. Some of these preceding adjectives are:

autre	joli
beau	mauvais
bon	nouveau
grand	petit
gros	vieux
jeune	

Comparative of Adjectives

plus	+	adjective	+	**que**
moins	+	adjective	+	**que**
aussi	+	adjective	+	**que**

Superlative of Adjectives

le/la/les	+	**plus**	+	adjective

Regular Verbs—Present Tense

-er parler			
je	parle	nous	parlons
tu	parles	vous	parlez
il/elle/on	parle	ils/elles	parlent

-ir finir			
je	finis	nous	finissons
tu	finis	vous	finissez
il/elle/on	finit	ils/elles	finissent

-re perdre			
je	perds	nous	perdons
tu	perds	vous	perdez
il/elle/on	perd	ils/elles	perdent

Irregular Verbs

acheter			
j'	achète	nous	achetons
tu	achètes	vous	achetez
il/elle/on	achète	ils/elles	achètent

aller			
je	vais	nous	allons
tu	vas	vous	allez
il/elle/on	va	ils/elles	vont

avoir			
j'	ai	nous	avons
tu	as	vous	avez
il/elle/on	a	ils/elles	ont

devoir			
je	dois	nous	devons
tu	dois	vous	devez
il/elle/on	doit	ils/elles	doivent

être			
je	suis	nous	sommes
tu	es	vous	êtes
il/elle/on	est	ils/elles	sont

faire			
je	fais	nous	faisons
tu	fais	vous	faites
il/elle/on	fait	ils/elles	font

falloir	
il	faut

mettre			
je	mets	nous	mettons
tu	mets	vous	mettez
il/elle/on	met	ils/elles	mettent

pleuvoir	
il	pleut

pouvoir			
je	peux	nous	pouvons
tu	peux	vous	pouvez
il/elle/on	peut	ils/elles	peuvent

préférer			
je	préfère	nous	préférons
tu	préfères	vous	préférez
il/elle/on	préfère	ils/elles	préfèrent

prendre			
je	prends	nous	prenons
tu	prends	vous	prenez
il/elle/on	prend	ils/elles	prennent

venir			
je	viens	nous	venons
tu	viens	vous	venez
il/elle/on	vient	ils/elles	viennent

voir			
je	vois	nous	voyons
tu	vois	vous	voyez
il/elle/on	voit	ils/elles	voient

vouloir			
je	veux	nous	voulons
tu	veux	vous	voulez
il/elle/on	veut	ils/elles	veulent

Regular Imperatives

-er parler	-ir finir	-re perdre
parle	finis	perds
parlez	finissez	perdez
parlons	finissons	perdons

Verbs + Infinitive

adorer	devoir	regarder
aimer	falloir	venir
aller	pouvoir	vouloir
désirer	préférer	

Negation in Present Tense

ne... jamais	Je **ne** vois **jamais** Hélène.
ne... pas	Vous **ne** mangez **pas**.
ne... personne	Il **n'y** a **personne** ici.
ne... plus	Tu **ne** fais **plus** de footing?
ne... rien	Nous **ne** faisons **rien**.

Numbers

0 = zéro	18 = dix-huit	71 = soixante et onze
1 = un	19 = dix-neuf	72 = soixante-douze
2 = deux	20 = vingt	80 = quatre-vingts
3 = trois	21 = vingt et un	81 = quatre-vingt-un
4 = quatre	22 = vingt-deux	82 = quatre-vingt-deux
5 = cinq	30 = trente	90 = quatre-vingt-dix
6 = six	31 = trente et un	91 = quatre-vingt-onze
7 = sept	32 = trente-deux	92 = quatre-vingt-douze
8 = huit	40 = quarante	100 = cent
9 = neuf	41 = quarante et un	101 = cent un
10 = dix	42 = quarante-deux	102 = cent deux
11 = onze	50 = cinquante	200 = deux cents
12 = douze	51 = cinquante et un	201 = deux cent un
13 = treize	52 = cinquante-deux	1.000 = mille
14 = quatorze	60 = soixante	1.001 = mille un
15 = quinze	61 = soixante et un	2.000 = deux mille
16 = seize	62 = soixante-deux	1.000.000 = un million
17 = dix-sept	70 = soixante-dix	2.000.000 = deux millions

Ordinal Numbers

1er	= premier		6e	= sixième
2e	= deuxième		7e	= septième
3e	= troisième		8e	= huitième
4e	= quatrième		9e	= neuvième
5e	= cinquième		10e	= dixième

Passé Composé—Regular Past Participles

jouer			
j'ai	joué	nous avons	joué
tu as	joué	vous avez	joué
il/elle/on a	joué	ils/elles ont	joué

finir			
j'ai	fini	nous avons	fini
tu as	fini	vous avez	fini
il/elle/on a	fini	ils/elles ont	fini

attendre			
j'ai	attendu	nous avons	attendu
tu as	attendu	vous avez	attendu
il/elle/on a	attendu	ils/elles ont	attendu

Passé Composé—Irregular Past Participles

Infinitive	Past Participle
avoir	eu
être	été
faire	fait
prendre	pris
voir	vu

Passé Composé with *Être*

aller		
je	suis	allé
je	suis	allée
tu	es	allé
tu	es	allée
il	est	allé
elle	est	allée
on	est	allé
nous	sommes	allés
nous	sommes	allées
vous	êtes	allé
vous	êtes	allés
vous	êtes	allée
vous	êtes	allées
ils	sont	allés
elles	sont	allées

Some of the verbs that use *être* as the helping verb in the *passé composé* are:

Infinitive	Past Participle
aller	allé
arriver	arrivé
entrer	entré
partir	parti
rentrer	rentré
rester	resté
sortir	sorti
venir	venu

Vocabulary
French/English

All words and expressions introduced as active vocabulary in *C'est à toi!* appear in this end vocabulary. The number following the meaning of each word or expression indicates the unit in which it appears for the first time. If there is more than one meaning for a word or expression and it has appeared in different units, the corresponding unit numbers are listed.

A

à to 2; at 4; in 6; *À bientôt.* See you soon. 1; *À demain.* See you tomorrow. 2; *à droite* to (on) the right 9; *à gauche* to (on) the left 9; *À tes souhaits!* Bless you! 10

acheter to buy 7

adorer to love 7

un **aéroport** airport 11

une **affiche** poster 4

l' **Afrique (f.)** Africa 11

l' **âge (m.)** age 5; *Tu as quel âge?* How old are you? 5

un **agent de police** police officer 6

ah oh 1

aimer to like, to love 2

l' **Algérie (f.)** Algeria 11

algérien, algérienne Algerian 11

l' **Allemagne (f.)** Germany 6

l' **allemand (m.)** German (language) 4

allemand(e) German 6

aller to go 2; *allons-y* let's go (there) 3

allô hello (on telephone) 1

alors (well) then 2

américain(e) American 6

un(e) **ami(e)** friend 6

amoureux, amoureuse in love 12

un **an** year 5; *J'ai... ans.* I'm ... years old. 5

l' **anglais (m.)** English (language) 4

anglais(e) English 6

l' **Angleterre (f.)** England 6

un **anniversaire** birthday 5

un **anorak** ski jacket 7

août August 5

un **appartement** apartment 9

après after 6

l' **après-midi (m.)** afternoon 10

un **arbre** tree 9

un **arc** arch 12

une **arche** arch 12

l' **argent (m.)** money 11

une **armoire** wardrobe 9

arriver to arrive 1

assez rather, quite 7; *assez de* enough 8

une **assiette** plate 9

attendre to wait (for) 8

au to (the), at (the) 2; in (the) 6; *au moins* at least 12; *au revoir* good-bye 1; *Au secours!* Help! 10; *au-dessus de* above 9

aujourd'hui today 6

aussi also, too 2; as 8

aussitôt que as soon as 10

l' **automne (m.)** autumn, fall 6

autre other 6; *un(e) autre* another 6

aux to (the), at (the), in (the) 7

avec with 4

une **avenue** avenue 11

un **avion** airplane 11

un(e) **avocat(e)** lawyer 6

avoir to have 4; *avoir besoin de* to need 4; *avoir bonne/mauvaise mine* to look well/sick 10; *avoir chaud* to be warm, hot 10; *avoir envie de* to want, to feel like 11; *avoir faim* to be hungry 4; *avoir froid* to be cold 10; *avoir mal (à...)* to hurt, to have a/an ... ache, to have a sore ... 10; *avoir mal au cœur* to feel nauseous 10; *avoir peur (de)* to be afraid (of) 10; *avoir quel âge* to be how old 5; *avoir soif* to be thirsty 4; *avoir... ans* to be ... (years old) 5

avril April 5

B

une **baguette** long, thin loaf of bread 8

une **baignoire** bathtub 9

un **bain: une salle de bains** bathroom 9

baisser to lower 10

un **bal** dance 12

un **balcon** balcony 9

une **banane** banana 8

une **banque** bank 11

des **bas (m.)** (panty) hose 7

le **basket (basketball)** basketball 2

des **baskets (f.)** hightops 7

un **bateau** boat 12

un **bâton** ski pole 10

bavard(e) talkative 5

beau, bel, belle beautiful, handsome 5

beaucoup a lot, (very) much 2; *beaucoup de* a lot of, many 8

un **beau-frère** stepbrother, brother-in-law 5

un **beau-père** stepfather, father-in-law 5

beige beige 7

belge Belgian 11

la **Belgique** Belgium 11

une **belle-mère** stepmother, mother-in-law 5

une **belle-sœur** stepsister, sister-in-law 5

ben: bon ben well then 2

le **besoin: avoir besoin de** to need 4

bête stupid, dumb 5

Beurk! Yuk! 7

le **beurre** butter 8

une **bibliothèque** library 11

bien well 1; really 2; *bien sûr* of course 9

Bienvenue! Welcome! 9

un **billet** ticket 12

la **biologie** biology 4

une **bise** kiss 11

blanc, blanche white 7

bleu(e) blue 5

blond(e) blond 5

un **blouson** jacket (outdoor) 7

le **bœuf** beef 8

une **boisson** drink, beverage 3

une **boîte** dance club 2; can 8

un **bol** bowl 9

bon, bonne good 2; *bon ben* well then 2; *bon marché* cheap 7

bonjour hello 1

bonsoir good evening 9

une **botte** boot 7

une **bouche** mouth 10

une **boucherie** butcher shop 8

une **bouillabaisse** fish soup 8

une **boulangerie** bakery 8

une **boum** party 7

une **bouteille** bottle 8

une **boutique** shop, boutique 7

un **bras** arm 10

un **bruit** noise 12

brun(e) dark (hair), brown 5

un **bureau** desk 4

C

c'est this is, it's 1; he is, she is 5; that's 6

ça that, it 3; *Ça fait....* That's/It's . . . . 3; *Ça fait combien?* How much is it/that? 3; *Ça va?* How are things going? 1; *Ça va bien.* Things are going well. 1

un **cabinet** (doctor or dentist's) office 10

un **cadeau** gift, present 5

un **café** café; coffee 3

un **cahier** notebook 4

un **calendrier** calendar 4

le **camembert** Camembert cheese 8

le **camping** camping 2

un **camping** campground 11

le **Canada** Canada 6

canadien, canadienne Canadian 6

un **canapé** couch, sofa 9

une **cantine** cafeteria 4

une **carotte** carrot 8

une **carte** map 4

une **cassette** cassette 4

un **CD** CD 4

ce, cet, cette; ces this, that; these, those 8

ce sont they are, these are, those are 5

cent (one) hundred 3

un **centre** center 12; *un centre commercial* shopping center, mall 7

une **cerise** cherry 8

une **chaise** chair 4

une **chambre** bedroom 9

un **champignon** mushroom 8

la **chance** luck 6

un **chapeau** hat 7

une **charcuterie** delicatessen 8

chargé(e) full 12

un **chat** cat 5

chaud(e) warm, hot 6; *avoir chaud* to be warm, hot 10

une **chaussette** sock 7

une **chaussure** shoe 7

un **chemin** path, way 12

une **chemise** shirt 7

un **chèque de voyage** traveler's check 11

cher, chère expensive 7; dear 11

chercher to look for 7

un **cheval** horse 5

des **cheveux (m.)** hair 5

chez to the house/home of 2; at the house/home of 11; *chez moi* to my house 2

un **chien** dog 5

la **chimie** chemistry 4

la **Chine** China 6

chinois(e) Chinese 6

des **chips (m.)** snacks 9

le **chocolat** chocolate 3

une **chose** thing 7; *quelque chose* something 7

ciao bye 1

un **cimetière** cemetery 12

le **cinéma** movies 2

cinq five 1

cinquante fifty 3

cinquième fifth 11

un **coca** Coke 3

un **cœur** heart 10; *avoir mal au cœur* to feel nauseous 10

un **coiffeur, une coiffeuse** hairdresser 6

combien how much 3; *combien de* how much, how many 8

comme like, for 3; *comme ci, comme ça* so-so 3

commencer to begin 4

comment what 1; how 3; *Comment vas-tu?* How are you? 3

un(e) **comptable** accountant 6

la **confiture** jam 8

congolais(e) Congolese 11

continuer to continue 12

une **corbeille** wastebasket 4

un **corps** body 10

un **costume** man's suit 7

la **Côte-d'Ivoire** Ivory Coast 11

un **cou** neck 10

une **couleur** color 7

un **cours** course, class 4

les **courses: faire les courses** to go grocery shopping 8

court(e) short 7

le **couscous** couscous 9

un(e) **cousin(e)** cousin 5

un **couteau** knife 9

coûter to cost 3

un **couvert** table setting 9

un **crabe** crab 8

un **crayon** pencil 4

une **crémerie** dairy store 8

une **crêpe** crêpe 3

une **crevette** shrimp 8

un **croissant** croissant 8

une **cuiller** spoon 9

une **cuisine** kitchen 9

un **cuisinier, une cuisinière** cook 6

une **cuisinière** stove 9

D

d'abord first 8

d'accord OK 1

d'après according to 12

dans in 4

danser to dance 2

une **date** date 5

de (d') of, from 4; a, an, any 6; some 9; in, by 12

décembre December 5

décider (de) to decide 12

un **défilé** parade 12

déjà already 3

le **déjeuner** lunch 9; *le petit déjeuner* breakfast 9

demain tomorrow 2

demander to ask for 12

demi(e) half 4; *et demi(e)* thirty (minutes), half past 4

un **demi-frère** half-brother 5

une **demi-sœur** half-sister 5

une **dent** tooth 10

un(e) **dentiste** dentist 6

dernier, dernière last 12

derrière behind 4

des some 3; from (the), of (the) 6; any 8

désirer to want 3; *Vous désirez?* What would you like? 3

un **dessert** dessert 3

le **dessin** drawing 4

dessus: au-dessus de above 9

deux two 1

deuxième second 11

devant in front of 4

devoir to have to 10

les **devoirs (m.)** homework 2

un **dictionnaire** dictionary 4

diligent(e) hardworking 5

dimanche (m.) Sunday 4

le **dîner** dinner, supper 9

dis say 2

une **disquette** diskette 4

dix ten 1

dix-huit eighteen 1

dixième tenth 11

dix-neuf nineteen 1

dix-sept seventeen 1

un **docteur** doctor 10

un **doigt** finger 10; *un doigt de pied* toe 10

un **dollar** dollar 7

donc so, then 9

donner to give 3; *Donnez-moi....* Give me 3

dormir to sleep 2

un **dos** back 10

une **douche** shower 9

douze twelve 1

la **droite: à droite** to (on) the right 9

du from (the), of (the) 6; some, any 8; in (the) 12

E

l' **eau (f.)** water 3; *l'eau minérale (f.)* mineral water 3

une **école** school 4

écoute listen 1

écouter to listen (to) 2; *écouter de la musique* to listen to music 2

une **église** church 11

égoïste selfish 5

Eh! Hey! 1

un(e) **élève** student 4

elle she, it 2

elles they (f.) 2

un **emploi du temps** schedule 4

en to (the) 2; on 5; in 6; *en solde* on sale 7

enchanté(e) delighted 9

encore still 9

un(e) **enfant** child 5

ensemble together 4

un **ensemble** outfit 7

une **entrée** entrance 9

entrer to enter, to come in 9

l' **envie (f.): avoir envie de** to want, to feel like 11

une **épaule** shoulder 10

un **escalier** stairs, staircase 9

l' **Espagne (f.)** Spain 6

l' **espagnol (m.)** Spanish (language) 4

espagnol(e) Spanish 6

est is 3

l' **est (m.)** east 11

est-ce que? (phrase introducing a question) 6

et and 2

un **étage** floor, story 9

les **États-Unis (m.)** United States 6

l' **été (m.)** summer 6

être to be 5; *Nous sommes le (+ date).* It's the (+ date). 5

un(e) **étudiant(e)** student 4

étudier to study 2; *Étudions....* Let's study 4

euh uhm 8

un **euro** euro 3

l' **Europe (f.)** Europe 11
un **évier** sink 9
excusez-moi excuse me 7

F

facile easy 10
la **faim: J'ai faim.** I'm hungry. 3
faire to do, to make 2; *faire du* (**+ number**) to wear size (+ number) 7; *faire du footing* to go running 2; *faire du roller* to go in-line skating 2; *faire du shopping* to go shopping 2; *faire du sport* to play sports 2; *faire du vélo* to go biking 2; *faire le tour* to take a tour 9; *faire les courses* to go grocery shopping 8; *faire les devoirs* to do homework 2; *faire les magasins* to go shopping 7; *faire un tour* to go for a ride 6
fait: Ça fait.... That's/It's . . . . 3; *Quel temps fait-il?* What's the weather like? How's the weather? 6; *Il fait beau.* It's (The weather's) beautiful/nice. 6; *Il fait chaud.* It's (The weather's) hot/warm. 6; *Il fait du soleil.* It's sunny. 6; *Il fait du vent.* It's windy. 6; *Il fait frais.* It's (The weather's) cool. 6; *Il fait froid.* It's (The weather's) cold. 6; *Il fait mauvais.* It's (The weather's) bad. 6
falloir to be necessary, to have to 10
une **famille** family 5
un **fast-food** fast-food restaurant 3
fatigué(e) tired 10
faut: il faut it is necessary, one has to/must, we/you have to/must 10
un **fauteuil** armchair 9
une **femme** wife; woman 5; *une femme au foyer* housewife 6; *une femme d'affaires* businesswoman 6

une **fenêtre** window 4
fermer to close 12
un **fermier, une fermière** farmer 6
une **fête** holiday, festival 12
un **feu d'artifice** fireworks 12
une **feuille de papier** sheet of paper 4
février February 5
la **fièvre** fever 10
une **figure** face 10
une **fille** girl 4; daughter 5
un **film** movie 2
un **fils** son 5
finir to finish 4
une **fleur** flower 9
une **fois** time 12
le **foot (football)** soccer 2
le **footing** running 2
une **forme: être en bonne/ mauvaise forme** to be in good/bad shape 10
formidable great, terrific 11
un **four** oven 9
une **fourchette** fork 9
frais, fraîche cool, fresh 6
une **fraise** strawberry 8
le **français** French (language) 4
français(e) French 6
la **France** France 6
un **frère** brother 5
un **frigo** refrigerator 9
des **frissons (m.)** chills 10
des **frites (f.)** French fries 3
froid(e) cold 6; *avoir froid* to be cold 10
le **fromage** cheese 3
un **fruit** fruit 8

G

un **garage** garage 9
un **garçon** boy 4
garder to keep 10
une **gare** train station 11
un **gâteau** cake 8
la **gauche: à gauche** to (on) the left 9

généreux, généreuse generous 5
un **genou** knee 10
gentil, gentille nice 9
la **géographie** geography 4
une **glace** ice cream 3; *une glace à la vanille* vanilla ice cream 3; *une glace au chocolat* chocolate ice cream 3
une **gorge** throat 10
le **goûter** afternoon snack 9
grand(e) tall, big, large 7
une **grand-mère** grandmother 5
un **grand-père** grandfather 5
un **grenier** attic 9
la **grippe** flu 10
gris(e) gray 5
gros, grosse big, fat, large 11
la **Guadeloupe** Guadeloupe 5
un **guichet** ticket window 12

H

habiter to live 9
un **hamburger** hamburger 3
des **haricots verts (m.)** green beans 8
l' **heure (f.)** hour, time, o'clock 3; *Quelle heure est-il?* What time is it? 3
hier yesterday 11
l' **histoire (f.)** history 4
l' **hiver (m.)** winter 6
un **homme** man 6; *un homme au foyer* househusband 6; *un homme d'affaires* businessman 6
un **horaire** schedule, timetable 11
un **hot-dog** hot dog 3
un **hôtel** hotel 12
huit eight 1
huitième eighth 11

I

ici here 6
il he, it 2

il y a there is, there are 7

ils they (m.) 2

imaginer to imagine 12

un **immeuble** apartment building 9

impressionniste Impressionist 12

un **infirmier,** une **infirmière** nurse 6

un **informaticien,** une **informaticienne** computer specialist 6

l' **informatique (f.)** computer science 4

un **ingénieur** engineer 6

intelligent(e) intelligent 5

une **interro (interrogation)** quiz, test 2

inviter to invite 2

l' **Italie (f.)** Italy 6

italien, italienne Italian 6

ivoirien, ivoirienne from the Ivory Coast 11

J

j' I 1

jamais: ne (n')... jamais never 10

une **jambe** leg 10

le **jambon** ham 3

janvier January 5

le **Japon** Japan 6

japonais(e) Japanese 6

un **jardin** garden, lawn 9; park 12

jaune yellow 7

le **jazz** jazz 2

je I 1

un **jean** (pair of) jeans 7

jeudi (m.) Thursday 4

jeune young 12

des **jeux vidéo (m.)** video games 2

joli(e) pretty 7

jouer to play 2; *jouer au basket* to play basketball 2; *jouer au foot* to play soccer 2; *jouer au tennis* to play tennis 2; *jouer au volley* to play volleyball 2; *jouer aux jeux vidéo* to play video games 2

un **jour** day 4

un(e) **journaliste** journalist 6

une **journée** day 12

juillet July 5

juin June 5

une **jupe** skirt 7

le **jus d'orange** orange juice 3; *le jus de fruit* fruit juice 9; *le jus de pomme* apple juice 3; *le jus de raisin* grape juice 3

jusqu'à up to, until 12

juste just, only 4

K

le **ketchup** ketchup 8

un **kilogramme (kilo)** kilogram 8

un **kilomètre** kilometer 5

L

là there, here 4

là-bas over there 7

le **lait** milk 8

une **lampe** lamp 9

le **latin** Latin (language) 4

le, la, l' the 2; *le* (**+ day of the week**) on (+ day of the week) 4; *le* (**+ number**) on the (+ ordinal number) 1

un **légume** vegetable 8

les the 2

leur their 5

la **liberté** liberty 12

une **librairie** bookstore 11

une **limonade** lemon-lime soda 3

lire to read 2

un **lit** bed 9

un **livre** book 4

loin far 11

long, longue long 7

une **lumière** light 12

lundi (m.) Monday 4

le **Luxembourg** Luxembourg 11

luxembourgeois(e) from Luxembourg 11

M

m'appelle: je m'appelle my name is 1

Madame (Mme) Mrs., Ma'am 1

Mademoiselle (Mlle) Miss 1

un **magasin** store 7; *un grand magasin* department store 7

un **magnétoscope** VCR 4

mai May 5

un **maillot de bain** swimsuit 7

une **main** hand 10

maintenant now 8

une **mairie** town hall 11

mais but 2

une **maison** house 9

mal bad, badly 3; *avoir mal (à...)* to hurt, to have a/an ... ache, to have a sore ... 10

malade sick 10

maman (f.) Mom 8

manger to eat 2; *manger de la pizza* to eat pizza 2; *une salle à manger* dining room 9

un **manteau** coat 7

un(e) **marchand(e)** merchant 8

un **marché** market 8

marcher to walk 12

mardi (m.) Tuesday 4

un **mari** husband 5

le **Maroc** Morocco 11

marocain(e) Moroccan 11

marre: J'en ai marre! I'm sick of it! I've had it! 4

marron brown 7

mars March 5

la **Martinique** Martinique 5

les **maths (f.)** math 4

un **matin** morning 8; *le matin* in the morning 8

mauvais(e) bad 6

la **mayonnaise** mayonnaise 8

me (to) me 11

méchant(e) mean 5

un **médecin** doctor 6

un **melon** melon 8

un **membre** member 5

même even 9

une **mer** sea 11

merci thanks 1

mercredi (m.) Wednesday 4

une **mère** mother 5

Messieurs-Dames ladies and gentlemen 3

un **métro** subway 12

mettre to put (on), to set 9

mexicain(e) Mexican 6

le **Mexique** Mexico 6

un **micro-onde** microwave 9

midi noon 3

mille (one) thousand 4

un **million** million 5

la **mine: avoir bonne/mauvaise mine** to look well/sick 10

minuit midnight 3

une **minute** minute 4

moche ugly 7

moderne modern 12

moi me, I 2

moins minus 4; less 8; *au moins* at least 12; *moins le quart* quarter to 4

un **mois** month 5

mon, ma; mes my 5

le **monde** world 12

Monsieur Mr., Sir 1

monter to go up 12

montrer to show 4; *Montrez-moi....* Show me 4

un **monument** monument 12

un **morceau** piece 8

la **moutarde** mustard 8

mûr(e) ripe 8

un **musée** museum 11

un **musicien, une musicienne** musician 12

la **musique** music 2

N

n'est-ce pas? isn't that so? 5

nager to swim 2

une **nappe** tablecloth 9

national(e) national 12

ne (n')... jamais never 10

ne (n')... pas not 2

ne (n')... personne no one, nobody, not anyone 10

ne (n')... plus no longer, not anymore 10

ne (n')... rien nothing, not anything 10

neiger: Il neige. It's snowing. 6

neuf nine 1

neuvième ninth 11

un **nez** nose 10

noir(e) black 5

non no 1

le **nord** north 11

notre; nos our 5

nous we 2; us 5

nouveau, nouvel, nouvelle new 7

novembre November 5

O

obligé(e): être obligé(e) de to be obliged to, to have to 12

octobre October 5

un **œil** eye 10

un **œuf** egg 8

oh oh 4; *Oh là là!* Wow! Oh no! Oh dear! 10

un **oignon** onion 8

un **oiseau** bird 5

OK OK 8

une **omelette** omelette 3

on they, we, one 2; *On y va?* Shall we go (there)? 2

un **oncle** uncle 5

onze eleven 1

orange orange 7

une **orange** orange 3

un **ordinateur** computer 4

une **oreille** ear 10

ou or 3

où where 4

ouais yeah 8

l' **ouest (m.)** west 11

oui yes 1

P

le **pain** bread 8

un **pantalon** (pair of) pants 7

par per 4

le **paradis** paradise 12

parce que because 5

pardon excuse me 1

un **parent** parent; relative 5

paresseux, paresseuse lazy 5

parler to speak, to talk 6

partir to leave 11

pas not 1

un **passeport** passport 11

passer to show (a movie) 2; to spend (time) 12

une **pastèque** watermelon 8

le **pâté** pâté 8

une **pâtisserie** pastry store 8

une **pêche** peach 8

une **pendule** clock 4

penser (à) to think (of) 12

perdre to lose 12

un **père** father 5

une **personne: ne (n')... personne** no one, nobody, not anyone 10

petit(e) short, little, small 7; *le petit déjeuner* breakfast 9

des **petits pois (m.)** peas 8

(un) **peu** (a) little 2; *(un) peu de* (a) little, few 8

la **peur: avoir peur (de)** to be afraid (of) 10

peut-être maybe 7

la **philosophie** philosophy 4

une **photo** photo, picture 5

la **physique** physics 4

une **pièce** room 9

un **pied** foot 10; *un doigt de pied* toe 10

une **piscine** swimming pool 11

une **pizza** pizza 2

un **placard** cupboard 9

la **place** room, space 10; *une place* (public) square 11

une **plage** beach 11

plaît: ... me plaît. I like 11

un **plan** map 12

pleuvoir: Il pleut. It's raining. 6

plus more 8; *le/la/les plus* (+ adjective) the most (+ adjective) 12; *ne (n')... plus* no longer, not anymore 10

une **poire** pear 8

les **pois (m.): des petits pois (m.)** peas 8

un **poisson** fish 5; *un poisson rouge* goldfish 5

le **poivre** pepper 9

une **pomme** apple 3; *une pomme de terre* potato 8

le **porc** pork 8

une **porte** door 4

porter to wear 7

possible possible 2

une **poste** post office 11

un **pot** jar 8

un **poulet** chicken 8

pour for 2; (in order) to 7

pourquoi why 2

pouvoir to be able to 8

préférer to prefer 2

premier, première first 5

prendre to take, to have (food or drink) 9; *prendre rendez-vous* to make an appointment 10

près (de) near 11

présenter to introduce 1

prie: Je vous en prie. You're welcome. 3

le **printemps** spring 6

un(e) **prof** teacher 4

un **professeur** teacher 4

une **profession** occupation 6

puis then 8

un **pull** sweater 7

Q

qu'est-ce que what 2; *Qu'est-ce que c'est?* What is it/this? 4; *Qu'est-ce que tu as?* What's the matter with you? 10

quand when 6

quarante forty 3

un **quart** quarter 4; *et quart* fifteen (minutes after), quarter after 4; *moins le quart* quarter to 4

un **quartier** quarter, neighborhood 12

quatorze fourteen 1

quatre four 1

quatre-vingt-dix ninety 3

quatre-vingts eighty 3

quatrième fourth 11

que how 5; than, as, that 8; *Que je suis bête!* How dumb I am! 5; *Que vous êtes gentils!* How nice you are! 9

quel, quelle what, which 3

quelqu'un someone, somebody 10

quelque chose something 7

quelques some 9

qui who, whom 2

une **quiche** quiche 3

quinze fifteen 1

quitter to leave (a person or place) 12

quoi what 4

R

un **raisin** grape 3

un(e) **réceptionniste** receptionist 10

regarder to watch 2; to look (at) 10

le **reggae** reggae 2

regretter to be sorry 10

un **rendez-vous** appointment 10; *prendre rendez-vous* to make an appointment 10

rentrer to come home, to return, to come back 11

un **repas** meal 8

la **République Démocratique du Congo** Democratic Republic of the Congo 11

ressembler à to look like, to resemble 5

un **restaurant** restaurant 11

rester to stay, to remain 10

revenir to come back, to return 11

le **rez-de-chaussée** ground floor 9

un **rhume** cold 10

rien: ne (n')... rien nothing, not anything 10

une **robe** dress 7

le **rock** rock (music) 2

le **roller** in-line skating 2

rose pink 7

rouge red 5

roux, rousse red (hair) 5

une **rue** street 12

S

s'appelle: elle s'appelle her name is 1; *il s'appelle* his name is 1

s'il te plaît please 9; *s'il vous plaît* please 3

un **sac à dos** backpack 4

une **salade** salad 3

une **salle à manger** dining room 9

une **salle de bains** bathroom 9

une **salle de classe** classroom 4

un **salon** living room 9

salut hi; good-bye 1

samedi (m.) Saturday 4

un **sandwich** sandwich 3; *un sandwich au fromage* cheese sandwich 3; *un sandwich au jambon* ham sandwich 3

la **santé** health 10

le **saucisson** salami 8

les **sciences (f.)** science 4

le **secours: Au secours!** Help! 10

seize sixteen 1

un **séjour** family room 9; stay 11

le **sel** salt 9

une **semaine** week 4

le **Sénégal** Senegal 11

sénégalais(e) Senegalese 11

sept seven 1

septembre September 5

septième seventh 11

un **serveur, une serveuse** server 3

une **serviette** napkin 9

seulement only 12

le **shopping** shopping 2

un **short** (pair of) shorts 7

si yes (on the contrary) 4; so 6

six six 1

sixième sixth 11

skier to ski 2

une **sœur** sister 5

la **soif: J'ai soif.** I'm thirsty. 3

un **soir** evening 7; *ce soir* tonight 8

soixante sixty 3

soixante-dix seventy 3

des **soldes (f.)** sale(s) 7

le **soleil** sun 6

solide steady 10

son, sa; ses his, her, one's, its 5

sortir to go out 2

un **souhait: À tes souhaits!** Bless you! 10

la **soupe** soup 8

sous under 4

un **sous-sol** basement 9

souvent often 6

un **sport** sport 2

un **stade** stadium 11

une **station** station 12

une **statue** statue 12

un **steak** steak 3; *un steak-frites* steak with French fries 3

une **stéréo** stereo 4

un **stylo** pen 4

le **sucre** sugar 9

le **sud** south 11

suisse Swiss 11

la **Suisse** Switzerland 11

super super, terrific, great 2

un **supermarché** supermarket 8

sur on 4; in 6

sûr: bien sûr of course 9

un **sweat** sweatshirt 7

sympa (sympathique) nice 5

T

t'appelles: tu t'appelles your name is 1

un **tabac** tobacco shop 11

une **table** table 9

un **tableau** (chalk)board 4; painting 12

une **taille** size 7

un **taille-crayon** pencil sharpener 4

un **tailleur** woman's suit 7

Tant mieux. That's great. 4

une **tante** aunt 5

un **tapis** rug 9

une **tarte (aux fraises)** (strawberry) pie 8

une **tasse** cup 9

un **taxi** taxi 12

te to you 1

un **tee-shirt** T-shirt 7

la **télé (télévision)** TV, television 2

téléphoner to phone (someone), to make a call 2

une **température** temperature 10

le **temps** weather 6; *Quel temps fait-il?* What's the weather like? How's the weather? 6

des **tennis (m.)** tennis shoes 7

le **tennis** tennis 2

la **terre: une pomme de terre** potato 8

une **tête** head 10

Tiens! Hey! 1

un **timbre** stamp 11

timide timid, shy 5

toi you 3

les **toilettes (f.)** toilet 9

une **tomate** tomato 8

un **tombeau** tomb 12

ton, ta; tes your 5

toucher to cash 11

toujours always 8; still 9

un **tour** trip 6; *le tour* tour 9

une **tour** tower 12

tourner to turn 11

tous les deux both 5

la **Toussaint** All Saints' Day 11

tout all, everything 11; *tout droit* straight ahead 11; *tout le monde* everybody 2

un **train** train 11

une **tranche** slice 8

travailler to work 6

treize thirteen 1

trente thirty 3

très very 3

un **triomphe** triumph 12

trois three 1

troisième third 11

trop too 8; too much 10; *trop de* too much, too many 8

une **trousse** pencil case 4

trouver to find 7

tu you 2

la **Tunisie** Tunisia 11

tunisien, tunisienne Tunisian 11

U

un **one** 1; a, an 2

une **a**, an, one 3

V

les **vacances (f.)** vacation 5

un **vase** vase 9

la **veille** night before 11

un **vélo** bicycle, bike 2

un **vendeur, une vendeuse** salesperson 7

vendre to sell 7

vendredi (m.) Friday 4

venir to come 6

le **vent** wind 6

un **ventre** stomach 10

un **verre** glass 9

vert(e) green 5

une **veste** (sport) jacket 7

des **vêtements (m.)** clothes 7

une **vidéocassette** videocassette 4

le **Vietnam** Vietnam 6

vietnamien, vietnamienne Vietnamese 6

vieux, vieil, vieille old 7

un **village** village 11

une **ville** city 11

vingt twenty 1

violet, violette purple 7

visiter to visit (a place) 12

vivre to live 12

voici here is/are 7

voilà here is/are, there is/are 3

voir to see 11

une **voiture** car 9

le **volley (volleyball)** volleyball 2

votre; vos your 5

voudrais would like 3

vouloir to want 8; *vouloir bien* to be willing 9

vous you 2; to you 9

un **voyage** trip 9

voyager to travel 6

voyons let's see 3

vrai(e) true 7

vraiment really 12

W

les **W.-C. (m.)** toilet 9

Y

le **yaourt** yogurt 8

des **yeux (m.)** eyes 5

Z

zéro zero 1

Zut! Darn! 4

Vocabulary

English/French

All words and expressions introduced as active vocabulary in *C'est à toi!* appear in this end vocabulary. The number following the meaning of each word or expression indicates the unit in which it appears for the first time. Verbs are listed in their infinitive forms even though a specific form may appear in an earlier unit. If there is more than one meaning for a word or expression and it has appeared in different units, the corresponding unit numbers are listed.

A

a un 2; une 3; de (d') 6; *a lot* beaucoup 2; *a lot of* beaucoup de 2

to be **able to** pouvoir 8

above au-dessus de 9

according to d'après 12

accountant un(e) comptable 6

ache: to have a/an . . . ache avoir mal (à...) 10

to be **afraid (of)** avoir peur (de) 10

Africa l'Afrique (f.) 11

after après 6

afternoon l'après-midi (m.) 10

age l'âge (m.) 5

ahead: straight ahead tout droit 11

airplane un avion 11

airport un aéroport 11

Algeria l'Algérie (f.) 11

Algerian algérien, algérienne 11

all tout 11; *All Saints' Day* la Toussaint 11

already déjà 3

also aussi 2

always toujours 8

American américain(e) 6

an un 2; une 3; de (d') 6

and et 2

another un(e) autre 6

any de (d') 6; des, du 8

anymore: not anymore ne (n')... plus 10

anyone: not anyone ne (n')... personne 10

anything: not anything ne (n')... rien 10

apartment un appartement 9; *apartment building* un immeuble 9

apple une pomme 3; *apple juice* le jus de pomme 3

appointment un rendez-vous 10; *to make an appointment* prendre rendez-vous 10

April avril 5

arch un arc, une arche 12

arm un bras 10

armchair un fauteuil 9

to **arrive** arriver 1

as aussi, que 8; *as soon as* aussitôt que 10

to **ask for** demander 12

at à 4; *at (the)* au 2, aux 7; *at least* au moins 12

attic un grenier 9

August août 5

aunt une tante 5

autumn l'automne (m.) 6

avenue une avenue 11

B

back un dos 10; *to come back* rentrer, revenir 11

backpack un sac à dos 4

bad mal 3; mauvais(e) 6; *It's bad.* Il fait mauvais. 6

badly mal 3

bakery une boulangerie 8

balcony un balcon 9

banana une banane 8

bank une banque 11

basement un sous-sol 9

basketball le basket (basketball) 2; *to play basketball* jouer au basket 2

bathroom une salle de bains 9

bathtub une baignoire 9

to **be** être 5; *to be . . . (years old)* avoir... ans 5; *to be able to* pouvoir 8; *to be afraid (of)* avoir peur (de) 10; *to be cold* avoir froid 10; *to be how old* avoir quel âge 5; *to be hungry* avoir faim 4; *to be in good/ bad shape* être en bonne/mauvaise forme 10; *to be necessary* falloir 10; *to be obliged to* être obligé(e) de 12; *to be sorry* regretter 10; *to be thirsty* avoir soif 4; *to be warm/hot* avoir chaud 10; *to be willing* vouloir bien 9

beach une plage 11

beans: green beans des haricots verts (m.) 8

beautiful beau, bel, belle 5; *It's beautiful.* Il fait beau. 6

because parce que 5

bed un lit 9

bedroom une chambre 9

beef le bœuf 8

to **begin** commencer 4

behind derrière 4

beige beige 7

Belgian belge 11

Belgium la Belgique 11

beverage une boisson 3

bicycle un vélo 2

big grand(e) 7; gros, grosse 11

bike un vélo 2

biking: to go biking faire du vélo 2

biology la biologie 4

bird un oiseau 5

birthday un anniversaire 5

black noir(e) 5

Bless you! À tes souhaits! 10

blond blond(e) 5

blue bleu(e) 5

board un tableau 4

boat un bateau 12

body un corps 10

book un livre 4

bookstore une librairie 11

boot une botte 7

both tous les deux 5

bottle une bouteille 8

boutique une boutique 7

bowl un bol 9

boy un garçon 4

bread le pain 8; *long, thin loaf of bread* une baguette 8

breakfast le petit déjeuner 9

brother un frère 5

brother-in-law un beau-frère 5

brown brun(e) 5; marron 7

building: apartment building un immeuble 9

businessman un homme d'affaires 6

businesswoman une femme d'affaires 6

but mais 2

butcher shop une boucherie 8

butter le beurre 8

to buy acheter 7

by de (d') 12

bye ciao 1

C

café un café 3

cafeteria une cantine 4

cake un gâteau 8

calendar un calendrier 4

call: to make a call téléphoner 2

Camembert cheese le camembert 8

campground un camping 11

camping le camping 2

can une boîte 8

Canada le Canada 6

Canadian canadien, canadienne 6

car une voiture 9

carrot une carotte 8

to cash toucher 11

cassette une cassette 4

cat un chat 5

CD un CD 4

cemetery un cimetière 12

center un centre 12; *shopping center* un centre commercial 7

chair une chaise 4

chalkboard un tableau 4

cheap bon marché 7

check: traveler's check un chèque de voyage 11

cheese le fromage 3; *Camembert cheese* le camembert 8; *cheese sandwich* un sandwich au fromage 3

chemistry la chimie 4

cherry une cerise 8

chicken un poulet 8

child un(e) enfant 5

chills des frissons (m.) 10

China la Chine 6

Chinese chinois(e) 6

chocolate le chocolat 3; *chocolate ice cream* une glace au chocolat 3

church une église 11

city une ville 11

class un cours 4

classroom une salle de classe 4

clock une pendule 4

to close fermer 12

clothes des vêtements (m.) 7

club: dance club une boîte 2

coat un manteau 7

coffee un café 3

Coke un coca 3

cold froid(e) 6; *It's cold.* Il fait froid. 6; *to be cold* avoir froid 10

cold un rhume 10

color une couleur 7

to come venir 6; *to come back* rentrer, revenir 11; *to come home* rentrer 11; *to come in* entrer 9

computer un ordinateur 4; *computer science* l'informatique (f.) 4; *computer specialist* un informaticien, une informaticienne 6

Congolese congolais(e) 11

to continue continuer 12

cook un cuisinier, une cuisinière 6

cool frais, fraîche 6; *It's cool.* Il fait frais. 6

to cost coûter 3

couch un canapé 9

course un cours 4

couscous le couscous 9

cousin un(e) cousin(e) 5

crab un crabe 8

crêpe une crêpe 3

croissant un croissant 8

cup une tasse 9

cupboard un placard 9

D

dairy store une crémerie 8

dance un bal 12; *dance club* une boîte 2

to dance danser 2

dark (hair) brun(e) 5

Darn! Zut! 4

date une date 5

daughter une fille 5

day un jour 4; une journée 12

dear cher, chère 11

December décembre 5

to **decide** décider (de) 12

delicatessen une charcuterie 8

delighted enchanté(e) 9

Democratic Republic of the Congo la République Démocratique du Congo 11

dentist un(e) dentiste 6

department store un grand magasin 7

desk un bureau 4

dessert un dessert 3

dictionary un dictionnaire 4

dining room une salle à manger 9

dinner le dîner 9

diskette une disquette 4

to **do** faire 2; *to do homework* faire les devoirs 2

doctor un médecin 6; un docteur 10

dog un chien 5

dollar un dollar 7

door une porte 4

drawing le dessin 4

dress une robe 7

drink une boisson 3

dumb bête 5; *How dumb I am!* Que je suis bête! 5

E

ear une oreille 10

east l'est (m.) 11

easy facile 10

to **eat** manger 2; *to eat pizza* manger de la pizza 2

egg un œuf 8

eight huit 1

eighteen dix-huit 1

eighth huitième 11

eighty quatre-vingts 3

eleven onze 1

engineer un ingénieur 6

England l'Angleterre (f.) 6

English anglais(e) 6; *English (language)* l'anglais (m.) 4

enough assez de 8

to **enter** entrer 9

entrance une entrée 9

euro un euro 3

Europe l'Europe (f.) 11

even même 9

evening un soir 7

everybody tout le monde 2

everything tout 11

excuse me pardon 1; excusez-moi 7

expensive cher, chère 7

eye un œil 10; *eyes* des yeux (m.) 5

F

face une figure 10

fall l'automne (m.) 6

family une famille 5; *family room* un séjour 9

far loin 11

farmer un fermier, une fermière 6

fast-food restaurant un fast-food 3

fat gros, grosse 11

father un père 5

father-in-law un beau-père 5

February février 5

to **feel: to feel like** avoir envie de 11; *to feel nauseous* avoir mal au cœur 10

festival une fête 12

fever la fièvre 10

few (un) peu de 8

fifteen quinze 1; *fifteen (minutes after)* et quart 4

fifth cinquième 11

fifty cinquante 3

to **find** trouver 7

finger un doigt 10

to **finish** finir 4

fireworks un feu d'artifice 12

first premier, première 5; d'abord 8

fish un poisson 5; *fish soup* une bouillabaisse 8

five cinq 1

floor un étage 9; *ground floor* le rez-de-chaussée 9

flower une fleur 9

flu la grippe 10

foot un pied 10

for pour 2; comme 3

fork une fourchette 9

forty quarante 3

four quatre 1

fourteen quatorze 1

fourth quatrième 11

France la France 6

French français(e) 6; *French (language)* le français 4; *French fries* des frites (f.) 3

fresh frais, fraîche 6

Friday vendredi (m.) 4

friend un(e) ami(e) 6

fries: French fries des frites (f.) 3; *steak with French fries* un steak-frites 3

from de (d') 4; *from (the)* des 3, du 6

front: in front of devant 4

fruit un fruit 8; *fruit juice* le jus de fruit 9

full chargé(e) 12

G

games: to play video games jouer aux jeux vidéo 2; *video games* des jeux vidéo (m.) 2

garage un garage 9

garden un jardin 9

generous généreux, généreuse 5

geography la géographie 4

German allemand(e) 6; *German (language)* l'allemand (m.) 4

Germany l'Allemagne (f.) 6

gift un cadeau 5

girl une fille 4

to **give** donner 3; *Give me . . . .* Donnez-moi.... 3

glass un verre 9

to **go** aller 2; *let's go (there)* allons-y 3; *Shall we go (there)?* On y va? 2; *to go biking* faire du vélo 2; *to go for a ride* faire un tour 6; *to go grocery shopping* faire les courses 8; *to go in-line skating* faire du roller 2; *to go out* sortir 2; *to go running* faire du footing 2; *to go shopping* faire du shopping 2, faire les magasins 7; *to go up* monter 12

goldfish un poisson rouge 5

good bon, bonne 2; *good evening* bonsoir 9; *good-bye* au revoir, salut 1

grandfather un grand-père 5

grandmother une grand-mère 5

grape un raisin 3; *grape juice* le jus de raisin 3

gray gris(e) 5

great super 2; formidable 11; *That's great.* Tant mieux. 4

green vert(e) 5; *green beans* des haricots verts (m.) 8

ground floor le rez-de-chaussée 9

Guadeloupe la Guadeloupe 5

H

hair des cheveux (m.) 5

hairdresser un coiffeur, une coiffeuse 6

half demi(e) 4; *half past* et demi(e) 4

half-brother un demi-frère 5

half-sister une demi-sœur 5

ham le jambon 3; *ham sandwich* un sandwich au jambon 3

hamburger un hamburger 3

hand une main 10

handsome beau, bel, belle 5

hardworking diligent(e) 5

hat un chapeau 7

to **have** avoir 4; *I've had it!* J'en ai marre! 4; *one has to, we/you have to* il faut 10; *to have (food or drink)* prendre 9; *to have a/an . . . ache, to have a sore . . .* avoir mal 10; *to have to* devoir, falloir 10; être obligé(e) de 12

he il 2; *he is* c'est 5

head une tête 10

health la santé 10

heart un cœur 10

hello bonjour 1; *hello (on telephone)* allô 1

Help! Au secours! 10

her son, sa; ses 5; *her name is* elle s'appelle 1

here là 4; ici 6; *here are* voilà 3, voici 7; *here is* voilà 3, voici 7

Hey! Eh!, Tiens! 1

hi salut 1

hightops des baskets (f.) 7

his son, sa; ses 5; *his name is* il s'appelle 1

history l'histoire (f.) 4

holiday une fête 12

home: at the home of chez 11; *to come home* rentrer 11; *to the home of* chez 2

homework les devoirs (m.) 2; *to do homework* faire les devoirs 2

horse un cheval 5

hot chaud(e) 6; *It's hot.* Il fait chaud. 6; *to be hot* avoir chaud 10

hot dog un hot-dog 3

hotel un hôtel 12

hour l'heure (f.) 3

house une maison 9; *at the house of* chez 11; *to my house* chez moi 2; *to the house of* chez 2

househusband un homme au foyer 6

housewife une femme au foyer 6

how comment 3; que 5; *How are things going?* Ça va? 1; *How are you?* Comment vas-tu? 3; *How dumb I am!* Que je suis bête! 5; *how many* combien de 8; *how much* combien 3, combien de 8; *How much is it/that?* Ça fait combien? 3; *How nice you are!* Que vous êtes gentils! 9; *How old are you?* Tu as quel âge? 5; *How's the weather?* Quel temps fait-il? 6

hundred: (one) hundred cent 3

hungry: I'm hungry. J'ai faim. 3; *to be hungry* avoir faim 4

to **hurt** avoir mal (à...) 10

husband un mari 5

I

I j', je 1; moi 2

ice cream une glace 3; *chocolate ice cream* une glace au chocolat 3; *vanilla ice cream* une glace à la vanille 3

to **imagine** imaginer 12

Impressionist impressionniste 12

in dans 4; à, en, sur 6; de (d') 12; *in (the)* au 6, aux 7, du 12; *in front of* devant 4; *in order to* pour 7; *in the morning* le matin 8

in-line skating le roller 2; *to go in-line skating* faire du roller 2

intelligent intelligent(e) 5

to **introduce** présenter 1

to **invite** inviter 2

is est 3; *isn't that so?* n'est-ce pas? 5

it elle, il 2; ça 3; *it is necessary* il faut 10; *it's* c'est 1; *It's . . . .* Ça fait.... 3; *It's bad.* Il fait mauvais. 6; *It's beautiful.* Il fait beau. 6; *It's cold.* Il fait froid. 6; *It's cool.* Il fait frais. 6; *It's hot.* Il fait chaud. 6; *It's nice.* Il fait beau. 6; *It's raining.* Il pleut. 6; *It's snowing.* Il neige. 6; *It's sunny.* Il fait du soleil. 6; *It's the (+ date).* Nous sommes le (+ *date*). 5; *It's warm.* Il fait chaud. 6; *It's windy.* Il fait du vent. 6

Italian italien, italienne 6

Italy l'Italie (f.) 6

its son, sa; ses 5

Ivory Coast la Côte-d'Ivoire 11; *from the Ivory Coast* ivoirien, ivoirienne 11

J

jacket (outdoor) un blouson 7; *ski jacket* un anorak 7; *sport jacket* une veste 7

jam la confiture 8

January janvier 5

Japan le Japon 6

Japanese japonais(e) 6

jar un pot 8

jazz le jazz 2

jeans: (pair of) jeans un jean 7

journalist un(e) journaliste 6

juice: apple juice le jus de pomme 3; *fruit juice* le jus de fruit 9; *grape juice* le jus de raisin 3; *orange juice* le jus d'orange 3

July juillet 5

June juin 5

just juste 4

K

to **keep** garder 10

ketchup le ketchup 8

kilogram un kilogramme (kilo) 8

kilometer un kilomètre 5

kiss une bise 11

kitchen une cuisine 9

knee un genou 10

knife un couteau 9

L

ladies and gentlemen Messieurs-Dames 3

lamp une lampe 9

large grand(e) 7; gros, grosse 11

last dernier, dernière 12

Latin (language) le latin 4

lawn un jardin 9

lawyer un(e) avocat(e) 6

lazy paresseux, paresseuse 5

least: at least au moins 12

to **leave** partir 11; *to leave (a person or place)* quitter 12

left: to (on) the left à gauche 9

leg une jambe 10

lemon-lime soda une limonade 3

less moins 8

liberty la liberté 12

library une bibliothèque 11

light une lumière 12

like comme 3

to **like** aimer 2; *I like ....* me plaît. 11; *What would you like?* Vous désirez? 3; *would like* voudrais 3

to **listen (to)** écouter 2; *listen* écoute 1; *to listen to music* écouter de la musique 2

little petit(e) 7; *a little* (un) peu 2, (un) peu de 8

to **live** habiter 9; vivre 12

living room un salon 9

long long, longue 7

longer: no longer ne (n')... plus 10

to **look (at)** regarder 10; *to look for* chercher 7; *to look like* ressembler à 5; *to look well/sick* avoir bonne/ mauvaise mine 10

to **lose** perdre 12

lot: a lot beaucoup 2; *a lot of* beaucoup de 2

love: in love amoureux, amoureuse 12

to **love** aimer 2; adorer 7

to **lower** baisser 10

luck la chance 6

lunch le déjeuner 9

Luxembourg le Luxembourg 11; *from Luxembourg* luxembourgeois(e) 11

M

Ma'am Madame (Mme) 1

to **make** faire 2; *to make a call* téléphoner 2; *to make an appointment* prendre rendez-vous 10

mall un centre commercial 7

man un homme 6

many beaucoup 8; *how many* combien de 8; *too many* trop de 8

map une carte 4; un plan 12

March mars 5

market un marché 8

Martinique la Martinique 5

math les maths (f.) 4

matter: What's the matter with you? Qu'est-ce que tu as? 10

May mai 5

maybe peut-être 7

mayonnaise la mayonnaise 8

me moi 2; me 11; *to me* me 11

meal un repas 8

mean méchant(e) 5

melon un melon 8

member un membre 5

merchant un(e) marchand(e) 8

Mexican mexicain(e) 6

Mexico le Mexique 6

microwave un micro-onde 9

midnight minuit 3

milk le lait 8

million un million 5

mineral water l'eau minérale (f.) 3

minus moins 4

minute une minute 4

Miss Mademoiselle (Mlle) 1

modern moderne 12

Mom maman (f.) 8

Monday lundi (m.) 4

money l'argent (m.) 11

month un mois 5

monument un monument 12

more plus 8

morning un matin 8; *in the morning* le matin 8

Moroccan marocain(e) 11

Morocco le Maroc 11

most: the most (+ adjective) le/la/les plus (+ *adjective*) 12

mother une mère 5

mother-in-law une belle-mère 5

mouth une bouche 10

movie un film 2; *movies* le cinéma 2

Mr. Monsieur 1

Mrs. Madame (Mme) 1

much: how much combien 3; combien de 8; *How much is it/that?* Ça fait combien? 3; *too much* trop de 8, trop 10; *very much* beaucoup 2

museum un musée 11

mushroom un champignon 8

music la musique 2

musician un musicien, une musicienne 12

must: one/we/you must il faut 10

mustard la moutarde 8

my mon, ma; mes 5; *my name is* je m'appelle 1

N

name: her name is elle s'appelle 1; *his name is* il s'appelle 1; *my name is* je m'appelle 1; *your name is* tu t'appelles 1

napkin une serviette 9

national national(e) 12

nauseous: to feel nauseous avoir mal au cœur 10

near près (de) 11

to be **necessary** falloir 10; *it is necessary* il faut 10

neck un cou 10

to **need** avoir besoin de 4

neighborhood un quartier 12

never ne (n')... jamais 10

new nouveau, nouvel, nouvelle 7

nice sympa (sympathique) 5; gentil, gentille 9; *How nice you are!* Que vous êtes gentils! 9; *It's nice.* Il fait beau. 6

night before la veille 11

nine neuf 1

nineteen dix-neuf 1

ninety quatre-vingt-dix 3

ninth neuvième 11

no non 1; *no longer* ne (n')... plus 10; *no one* ne (n')... personne 10

nobody ne (n')... personne 10

noise un bruit 12

noon midi 3

north le nord 11

nose un nez 10

not pas 1; ne (n')... pas 2; *not anymore* ne (n')... plus 10; *not anyone* ne (n')... personne 10; *not anything* ne (n')... rien 10

notebook un cahier 4

nothing ne (n')... rien 10

November novembre 5

now maintenant 8

nurse un infirmier, une infirmière 6

O

o'clock l'heure (f.) 3

to be **obliged to** être obligé(e) de 12

occupation une profession 6

October octobre 5

of de (d') 4; *of (the)* des, du 6; *of course* bien sûr 9

office (doctor or dentist's) un cabinet 10

often souvent 6

oh ah 1; oh 4; *Oh no! Oh dear!* Oh là là! 10

OK d'accord 1; OK 8

old vieux, vieil, vieille 7; *How old are you?* Tu as quel âge? 5; *I'm . . . years old.* J'ai... ans. 5; *to be . . . (years old)* avoir... ans 5; *to be how old* avoir quel âge 5

omelette une omelette 3

on sur 4; en 5; *on (+ day of the week)* le (+ day of the week) 4; *on sale* en solde 7; *on the (+ ordinal number)* le (+ number) 1

one un 1; on 2; une 3; *no one* ne (n')... personne 10

one's son, sa; ses 5

onion un oignon 8

only juste 4; seulement 12

or ou 3

orange une orange 3; orange 7; *orange juice* le jus d'orange 3

other autre 6

our notre; nos 5

outfit un ensemble 7

oven un four 9

over there là-bas 7

P

painting un tableau 12

pants: (pair of) pants un pantalon 7

panty hose des bas (m.) 7

paper: sheet of paper une feuille de papier 4

parade un défilé 12

paradise le paradis 12

parent un parent 5

park un jardin 12

party une boum 7

passport un passeport 11

pastry store une pâtisserie 8

pâté le pâté 8

path un chemin 12

peach une pêche 8

pear une poire 8

peas des petits pois (m.) 8

pen un stylo 4

pencil un crayon 4; *pencil case* une trousse 4; *pencil sharpener* un taille-crayon 4

pepper le poivre 9

per par 4

philosophy la philosophie 4

to **phone (someone)** téléphoner 2

photo une photo 5

physics la physique 4

picture une photo 5

pie une tarte 8; *strawberry pie* une tarte aux fraises 8

piece un morceau 8

pink rose 7

pizza une pizza 2; *to eat pizza* manger de la pizza 2

plate une assiette 9

to **play** jouer 2; *to play basketball* jouer au basket 2; *to play soccer* jouer au foot 2; *to play sports* faire du sport 2; *to play tennis* jouer au tennis 2; *to play video games* jouer aux jeux vidéo 2; *to play volleyball* jouer au volley 2

please s'il vous plaît 3; s'il te plaît 9

pole: ski pole un bâton 10

police officer un agent de police 6

pool: swimming pool une piscine 11

pork le porc 8

possible possible 2

post office une poste 11

poster une affiche 4

potato une pomme de terre 8

to **prefer** préférer 2

present un cadeau 5

pretty joli(e) 7

purple violet, violette 7

to **put (on)** mettre 9

Q

quarter un quart 4; un quartier 12; *quarter after* et quart 4; *quarter to* moins le quart 4

quiche une quiche 3

quite assez 7

quiz une interro (interrogation) 2

R

to **rain: It's raining.** Il pleut. 6

rather assez 7

to **read** lire 2

really bien 2; vraiment 12

receptionist un(e) réceptionniste 10

red rouge 5; *red (hair)* roux, rousse 5

refrigerator un frigo 9

reggae le reggae 2

relative un parent 5

to **remain** rester 10

to **resemble** ressembler à 5

restaurant un restaurant 11; *fast-food restaurant* un fast-food 3

to **return** rentrer, revenir 11

ride: to go for a ride faire un tour 6

right: to (on) the right à droite 9

ripe mûr(e) 8

rock (music) le rock 2

room une pièce 9; la place 10; *dining room* une salle à manger 9; *family room* un séjour 9; *living room* un salon 9

rug un tapis 9

running le footing 2; *to go running* faire du footing 2

S

saint: All Saints' Day la Toussaint 11

salad une salade 3

salami le saucisson 8

sale(s) des soldes (f.) 7; *on sale* en solde 7

salesperson un vendeur, une vendeuse 7

salt le sel 9

sandwich un sandwich 3; *cheese sandwich* un sandwich au fromage 3; *ham sandwich* un sandwich au jambon 3

Saturday samedi (m.) 4

say dis 2

schedule un emploi du temps 4; un horaire 11

school une école 4

science les sciences (f.) 4

sea une mer 11

second deuxième 11

to **see** voir 11; *let's see* voyons 3; *See you soon.* À bientôt. 1; *See you tomorrow.* À demain. 2

selfish égoïste 5

to **sell** vendre 7

Senegal le Sénégal 11

Senegalese sénégalais(e) 11

September septembre 5

server un serveur, une serveuse 3

to **set** mettre 9

setting: table setting un couvert 9

seven sept 1

seventeen dix-sept 1

seventh septième 11

seventy soixante-dix 3

shape: to be in good/bad shape être en bonne/ mauvaise forme 10

sharpener: pencil sharpener un taille-crayon 4

she elle 2; *she is* c'est 5

shirt une chemise 7

shoe une chaussure 7; *tennis shoes* des tennis (m.) 7

shop une boutique 7

shopping le shopping 2; *shopping center* un centre commercial 7; *to go grocery shopping* faire les courses 8; *to go shopping* faire du shopping 2, faire les magasins 7

short court(e), petit(e) 7

shorts: (pair of) shorts un short 7

shoulder une épaule 10

to **show** montrer 4; *Show me . . . .* Montrez-moi.... 4; *to show (a movie)* passer 2

shower une douche 9

shrimp une crevette 8

shy timide 5

sick malade 10; *I'm sick of it!* J'en ai marre! 4

sink un évier 9

Sir Monsieur 1

sister une sœur 5

sister-in-law une belle-sœur 5

six six 1

sixteen seize 1

sixth sixième 11

sixty soixante 3

size une taille 7

skating: in-line skating le roller 2; *to go in-line skating* faire du roller 2

ski: ski jacket un anorak 7; *ski pole* un bâton 10

to **ski** skier 2

skirt une jupe 7

to **sleep** dormir 2

slice une tranche 8

small petit(e) 7

snacks des chips (m.) 9; *afternoon snack* le goûter 9

snow: It's snowing. Il neige. 6

so si 6; donc 9; *so-so* comme ci, comme ça 3

soccer le foot (football) 2; *to play soccer* jouer au foot 2

sock une chaussette 7

soda: lemon-lime soda une limonade 3

sofa un canapé 9

some des 3; du 8; de (d'), quelques 9

somebody quelqu'un 10

someone quelqu'un 10

something quelque chose 7

son un fils 5

soon: as soon as aussitôt que 10

sore: to have a sore . . . avoir mal (à...) 10

to be **sorry** regretter 10

soup la soupe 8; *fish soup* une bouillabaisse 8

south le sud 11

space la place 10

Spain l'Espagne (f.) 6

Spanish espagnol(e) 6; *Spanish (language)* l'espagnol (m.) 4

to **speak** parler 6

to **spend (time)** passer 12

spoon une cuiller 9

sport un sport 2; *sport jacket* une veste 7; *to play sports* faire du sport 2

spring le printemps 6

square: public square une place 11

stadium un stade 11

staircase, stairs un escalier 9

stamp un timbre 11

station une station 12; *train station* une gare 11

statue une statue 12

stay un séjour 11

to **stay** rester 10

steady solide 10

steak un steak 3; *steak with French fries* un steak-frites 3

stepbrother un beau-frère 5

stepfather un beau-père 5

stepmother une belle-mère 5

stepsister une belle-sœur 5

stereo une stéréo 4

still encore, toujours 9

stomach un ventre 10

store un magasin 7; *department store* un grand magasin 7

story un étage 9

stove une cuisinière 9

straight ahead tout droit 11

strawberry une fraise 8; *strawberry pie* une tarte aux fraises 8

street une rue 12

student un(e) élève, un(e) étudiant(e) 4

to **study** étudier 2; *Let's study . . . .* Étudions.... 4

stupid bête 5

subway un métro 12

sugar le sucre 9

suit: man's suit un costume 7; *woman's suit* un tailleur 7

summer l'été (m.) 6

sun le soleil 6

Sunday dimanche (m.) 4

sunny: It's sunny. Il fait du soleil. 6

super super 2

supermarket un supermarché 8

supper le dîner 9

sweater un pull 7

sweatshirt un sweat 7

to **swim** nager 2

swimming pool une piscine 11

swimsuit un maillot de bain 7

Swiss suisse 11

Switzerland la Suisse 11

T

table une table 9; *table setting* un couvert 9

tablecloth une nappe 9

to **take** prendre 9; *to take a tour* faire le tour 9

to **talk** parler 6

talkative bavard(e) 5

tall grand(e) 7

taxi un taxi 12

teacher un(e) prof, un professeur 4

television la télé (télévision) 2

temperature une température 10

ten dix 1

tennis le tennis 2; *tennis shoes* des tennis (m.) 7; *to play tennis* jouer au tennis 2

tenth dixième 11

terrific super 2; formidable 11

test une interro (interrogation) 2

than que 8

thanks merci 1

that ça 3; ce, cet, cette, que 8; *that's* c'est 6; *That's ....* Ça fait.... 3; *That's great.* Tant mieux. 4

the le, la, l', les 2

their leur 5

then puis 8; donc 9; *(well) then* alors 2

there là 4; *there are* voilà 3, il y a 7; *there is* voilà 3, il y a 7; *over there* là-bas 7

these ces 8; *these are* ce sont 5

they on 2; *they (f.)* elles 2; *they (m.)* ils 2; *they are* ce sont 5

thing une chose 7; *How are things going?* Ça va? 1; *Things are going well.* Ça va bien. 1

to **think (of)** penser (à) 12

third troisième 11

thirsty: I'm thirsty. J'ai soif. 3; *to be thirsty* avoir soif 4

thirteen treize 1

thirty trente 3; *thirty (minutes)* et demi(e) 4

this ce, cet, cette 8; *this is* c'est 1

those ces 8; *those are* ce sont 5

thousand: one thousand mille 4

three trois 1

throat une gorge 10

Thursday jeudi (m.) 4

ticket un billet 12; *ticket window* un guichet 12

time l'heure (f.) 3; une fois 12; *What time is it?* Quelle heure est-il? 3

timetable un horaire 11

timid timide 5

tired fatigué(e) 10

to à 2; *in order to* pour 7; *to (the)* au, en 2, aux 7

tobacco shop un tabac 11

today aujourd'hui 6

toe un doigt de pied 10

together ensemble 4

toilet les toilettes (f.), les W.-C. (m.) 9

tomato une tomate 8

tomb un tombeau 12

tomorrow demain 2

tonight ce soir 8

too aussi 2; trop 8; *too many* trop de 8; *too much* trop de 8, trop 10

tooth une dent 10

tour le tour 9; *to take a tour* faire le tour 9

tower une tour 12

town hall une mairie 11

train un train 11; *train station* une gare 11

to **travel** voyager 6

traveler's check un chèque de voyage 11

tree un arbre 9

trip un tour 6; un voyage 9

triumph un triomphe 12

true vrai(e) 7

T-shirt un tee-shirt 7

Tuesday mardi (m.) 4

Tunisia la Tunisie 11

Tunisian tunisien, tunisienne 11

to **turn** tourner 11

TV la télé (télévision) 2

twelve douze 1

twenty vingt 1

two deux 1

U

ugly moche 7

uhm euh 8

uncle un oncle 5

under sous 4

United States les États-Unis (m.) 6

until jusqu'à 12

up to jusqu'à 12

us nous 5

V

vacation les vacances (f.) 5

vanilla ice cream une glace à la vanille 3

vase un vase 9

VCR un magnétoscope 4

vegetable un légume 8

very très 3; *very much* beaucoup 2

video games des jeux vidéo (m.) 2; *to play video games* jouer aux jeux vidéo 2

videocassette une vidéocassette 4

Vietnam le Vietnam 6

Vietnamese vietnamien, vietnamienne 6

village un village 11

to **visit (a place)** visiter 12

volleyball le volley (volleyball) 2; *to play volleyball* jouer au volley 2

W

to **wait (for)** attendre 8

to **walk** marcher 12

to **want** désirer 3; vouloir 8; avoir envie de 11

wardrobe une armoire 9

warm chaud(e) 6; *It's warm.* Il fait chaud. 6; *to be warm* avoir chaud 10

wastebasket une corbeille 4

to **watch** regarder 2

water l'eau (f.) 3; *mineral water* l'eau minérale (f.) 3

watermelon une pastèque 8

way un chemin 12

we nous, on 2

to **wear** porter 7; *to wear size (+ number)* faire du (+ number) 7

weather le temps 6; *The weather's bad.* Il fait mauvais. 6; *The weather's beautiful/nice.* Il fait beau. 6; *The weather's cold.*

Il fait froid. 6; *The weather's cool.* Il fait frais. 6; *The weather's hot/warm.* Il fait chaud. 6; *What's the weather like? How's the weather?* Quel temps fait-il? 6

Wednesday mercredi (m.) 4

week une semaine 4

Welcome! Bienvenue! 9; *You're welcome.* Je vous en prie. 3

well bien 1; *well then* alors, bon ben 2

west l'ouest (m.) 11

what comment 1; qu'est-ce que 2; quel, quelle 3; quoi 4; *What is it/this?* Qu'est-ce que c'est? 4; *What time is it?* Quelle heure est-il? 3; *What would you like?* Vous désirez? 3; *What's the matter with you?* Qu'est-ce que tu as? 10; *What's the*

weather like? Quel temps fait-il? 6

when quand 6

where où 4

which quel, quelle 3

white blanc, blanche 7

who, whom qui 2

why pourquoi 2

wife une femme 5

to be **willing** vouloir bien 9

wind le vent 6

window une fenêtre 4; *ticket window* un guichet 12

windy: It's windy. Il fait du vent. 6

winter l'hiver (m.) 6

with avec 4

woman une femme 5

to **work** travailler 6

world le monde 12

would like voudrais 3

Wow! Oh là là! 10

Y

yeah ouais 8

year un an 5; *I'm . . . years old.* J'ai... ans. 5; *to be . . . (years old)* avoir... ans 5

yellow jaune 7

yes oui 1; *yes (on the contrary)* si 4

yesterday hier 11

yogurt le yaourt 8

you tu, vous 2; *toi* 3; *to you* te 1, vous 9; *You're welcome.* Je vous en prie. 3

young jeune 12

your ton, ta, tes, votre, vos 5; *your name is* tu t'appelles 1

Yuk! Beurk! 7

Z

zero zéro 1

Grammar Index

Acknowledgments

The following teachers responded to our surveys by offering valuable comments and suggestions in the revision of the *C'est à toi!* series:

Rebecca Alford, Burlington High School, Burlington, KS; **James Anteau**, Power Middle School, Farmington Hills, MI; **Linda Attaway**, North Mesquite High School, Mesquite, TX; **Rochelle R. Barry**, Trumansburg Middle School, Trumansburg, NY; **Marie Beauzil**, Vailsburg Middle School, Newark, NJ; **Mary Ann Becker**, Academy of the Sacred Heart, Bloomfield Hills, MI; **Barbara Bellino**, Somerset High School, Somerset, MA; **Marlene J. Berasi**, Monte Vista Middle School, Tracy, CA; **Ellen Berna**, Sagewood Middle School, Parker, CO; **Vicki Blankenship**, Mansfield Middle School, Mansfield, MO; **Julia T. Bressler**, North Middlesex Regional High School, Townsend, MA; **R. L. Bryant**, Thurgood Marshall Middle School, Atlanta, GA; **Mary Kay Buckius**, Parker Vista West Middle School, Parker, CO; **Sister Jeanne Buisson**, C.S.C., Academy of the Holy Cross, Kensington, MD; **Angeline A. Burke**, Joliet Central High School, Joliet, IL; **Cecile Canales**, Greenway Middle School, Pittsburgh, PA; **Scott Capron**, Alameda High School, Lakewood, CO; **Rosalie Caputo**, Centennial High School, Pueblo, CO; **Fran Carlson**, St. Francis Senior High School, St. Francis, MN; **Kevin J. Carney**, Kelvyn Park High School, Chicago, IL; **Corinne Chace**, Lauvalton Hall, Milford, CT; **Carolyn Cimino**, Lyme - Old Lyme High School, Old Lyme, CT; **Pat Clark**, Rembrook School, W. Hartford, CT; **Marilyn Coartney**, Casey-Westfield High School, Casey, IL; **Debbie Cody**, South High School, Pueblo, CO; **Amy Coe**, Horace Mann High School, N. Fond du Lac, WI; **Rick Cohoun**, Lovington High School, Lovington, IL; **Alexandra (Sandy) Colomb**, Hopkins North Junior High School, Minnetonka, MN; **Virginia Cosgrove**, Scranton Preparatory School, Scranton, PA; **Erika D. Couey**, Ridgeland High School, Rossville, GA; **Dianne Couts**, Minerva High School, Minerva, OH; **Teresa A. Crowe**, Catholic Central High School, Springfield, OH; **Gloria Cunningham**, Farmington High School, Farmington, MI; **Lisa Curtiss**, Clearwater Central Catholic High School, Clearwater, FL; **Pat De la Cerda**, Poinciana Day School, West Palm Beach, FL; **Carol S. Dempsey**, Ridge High School, Basking Ridge, NJ; **Margaret Dodge**, Honeoye Central High School, Honeoye, NY; **Dawn M. Drexler**, Huth Middle School, Matteson, IL; **Judy Dudukovic**, Mehlville Senior High School, St. Louis, MO; **Heather Edwards**, Nelson County High School, Lovingston, VA; **James E. Ellis**, Mather High School, Chicago, IL; **Elizabeth A. Elvidge**, Newton High School, Newton, NJ; **Joan Faisant**, Carey High School, Carey, OH; **Claudie Finney**, Palm Beach Day School, Palm Beach, FL; **Dawn Floyd**, Lincoln-Way High School, New Lenox, IL; **Larry Friedman**, Hoover Middle School, Buffalo, NY; **Irene Garger**, Knoxville Middle School, Pittsburgh, PA; **Marie T. George**, North Country Union High School, Newport, VT; **Margaret Geyer**, Whitehall-Yearling High School, Whitehall, OH; **Karen Gibson**, Bishop DuBourg High School, St. Louis, MO; **Joanna Gipson**, The Honor Roll School, Sugar Land, TX; **James V. Goddard**, Howard A. Doolin Middle School, Miami, FL; **Sheila Gomez-Mira**, Keystone School, San Antonio, TX; **Patricia Goslin**, Upper Township Middle School, Petersburg, NJ; **Laura Graf**, Wentzville High School, Wentzville, MO; **Barbara Graff**, Caro Learning Center, Caro, MI; **Anne Graham**, William Chrisman High School, Independence, MO; **Mary Green**, O. E. Dunckel Middle School, Farmington Hills, MI; **Donna Grissom**, Wentzville Holt High School, Wentzville, MO; **Linda Guerrieri**, Champion High School, Warren, OH; **Joyce Hall**, Tattnall Square Academy, Macon, GA; **Peri V. Hartzell**, Field Kindley High School, Coffeyville, KS; **Kathy Hayes**, Oconto High School, Oconto, WI; **Annette Hegler**, Southwest Junior High School, Forest Lake, MN; **Barbara Herman**, North Farmington High School, Farmington, MI; **Annette Herr**, Kenmore West High School, Kenmore, NY; **Linda Herron**, Marshall School, Duluth, MN; **Sherry Hoff**, Cadott Junior/Senior High School, Cadott, WI; **Mignonne A. Holz**, Metz Junior High School, Manassas, VA; **Julie Horowitz**, Culver City High School, Culver City, CA; **Susan C. Johnson**, LaSalle-Peru Township High School, LaSalle, IL; **Paula Johnson-Fox**, Muskego High School, Muskego, WI; **Vera C. Kap**, Our Lady of the Elms High School, Akron, OH; **Edna-May L. King**, Lamoille Union High School, Hyde Park, VT; **Tad Kirkendoll**, Mesquite High School, Mesquite, TX; **Elaine Koehler**, Northwest High School, House Springs, MO; **Karen Kramer**, Fairborn High School, Fairborn, OH; **Pamela LaLonde**, Rombout Middle School, Beacon, NY; **Christine Leroueil**, LaKota Junior High School, Federal Way, WA; **Donna Lombardo**, Benjamin Franklin Middle School, Buffalo, NY; **Kathleen A. Lutz**, Sterling Heights High School, Sterling Heights, MI; **JoAnn Mancuso**, Cassadaga Valley Central School, Sinclairville, NY; **Marie Martin**, Giles High School, Pearisburg, VA; **Roberta**

Matt, Federal Way High School, Federal Way, WA; **Kathleen Mattern**, Mishicot High School, Mishicot, WI; **May Mavrogenis**, Clinton Central High School, Clinton, NY; **Donyce McCluskey**, West Canada Valley Central School, Newport, NY; **Kathleen J. McCrillis**, Miami East High School, Casstown, OH; **Carol McLeod**, Delphian School, Sheridan, OR; **Henry Menninger**, The School at Church Farm, Padi, PA; **Terry Meredith**, Aquinas High School, Augusta, GA; **Stephanie N. Mikesell**, National Trail High School, New Paris, OH; **Fabienne Modesitt**, Powhatan School, Boyce, VA; **Tamara Montgomery**, Northside College Prep High School, Chicago, IL; **Tola Mosadami**, Louise S. McGehee School, New Orleans, LA; **Jim Mozina**, Port Clinton High School, Port Clinton, OH; **Jon Muellerleile**, St. Michael - Albertville Senior High, Albertville, MN; **Julia Mullikin**, Herscher High School, Herscher, IL; **Carol Dean Nassau**, Oneonta Middle School, Oneonta, NY; **Mary Nichols**, Austin High School, Austin, TX; **Robin Noble**, Providence Catholic, New Lenox, IL; **Diane Odoerfer**, South Lake High School, St. Clair Shores, MI; **Mirta Pagnucci**, Oak Park River Forest High School, Oak Park, IL; **Catherine Pasture**, South Kingstown High School, Wakefield, RI; **Rebecca G. Philippone**, Greene Central High School, Greene, NY; **Amy B. Polcha**, King George High School, King George, VA; **Alla Pyatkovskaya**, Benedictine High School, Cleveland, OH; **Sonia Quinlan**, Linden High School, Linden, MI; **Mary Rebmann**, Hoover Middle School, Buffalo, NY; **Susan Reese**, Heritage Christian School, Canton, OH; **Paul H. Ribbeck**, Benjamin Franklin Middle School, Buffalo, NY; **M. Carmen L. Richards**, Gateway High School, Kissimmee, FL; **Kim Riley**, Archbishop Spalding High School, Severn, MD; **Judith A. Rinck**, Ocean City High School, Ocean City, NJ; **Suzanne Robert**, Preble Shawnee High School, Camden, OH; **Kristi Rumschlag**, Buckeye Central High School, New Washington, OH; **Kevin J. Ruth**, Newark Academy, Livingston, NJ; **Frank Sabina**, Carbondale Area High School, Carbondale, PA; **Frances Salvato**, Julian Junior High School, Oak Park, IL; **Lise B. Sanborn**, Concord High School and Rundlett Middle School, Concord, NH; **Eileen Sauret**, Kenmore West Senior High School, Kenmore, NY; **Aurora Schlegel**, Ocean Township High School, Oakhurst, NJ; **Susan Schmied**, South Oldham High School, Crestwood, KY; **Florence Schranz**, Chaparral High School, Parker, CO; **Pamela Schroeder**, Westosha Central High School, Salem, WI; **Mary Alice Schroeger**, Lansing High School, Lansing, KS; **Ramona Shaw**, Steelville R-3 High School, Steelville, MO; **Judy Shick**, Arlington Local, Arlington, OH; **Cari Simon**, Johnson-Williams Middle School, Berryville, VA; **Leslie Sims**, Totem Junior High School, Federal Way, WA; **Jackie Slade**, Blessed Sacrament, Walpole, MA; **Bev Smith**, Fairborn High School, Fairborn, OH; **Diane Smith**, Upper Sandusky High School, Upper Sandusky, OH; **Pamela St. Clair-Correa**, Rockbridge County High School, Alexandria, VA; **Carolyn K. Staker**, East High School, Portsmouth, OH; **Laura G. Stark**, Saint Mary's School, Raleigh, NC; **Joanne A. Stemer**, Warren Mott High School, Warren, MI; **Laurie Stolarz**, Our Lady of Nazareth Academy, Wakefield, MA; **Donna Stutzman**, Central High School, Pueblo, CO; **Pamela Sundheim**, Mattoon Senior High School, Mattoon, IL; **Roz Sunquist**, Mother McAuley High School, Chicago, IL; **Susan G. Thibo**, Lemon-Monroe High School, Monroe, OH; **Bassirou Thioune**, Cleveland High School, Reseda, CA; **Kirk Tooley**, Northville Central School, Northville, NY; **Karina Tulley**, Lincoln Way High School, New Lenox, IL; **Patricia Hunt Vana**, North Country Union High School, Newport, VT; **Lea Wainwright**, Caravel Academy, Bear, DE; **Cheryl Weisberg**, Birch Wathen Lenox School, New York, NY; **Darlene Weller**, Jefferson High School, Shenandoah Junction, WV; **Rita Peer Williams**, Eastern High School, Reedsville, OH; **Carol Wilson**, Charles City High School, Charles City, VA; **John Wilson**, Southeast Whitfield High School, Dalton, GA; **Mary Woznicki**, River View Middle School, Kaukauna, WI; **Carol Wright**, Gateway High School, Kissimmee, FL; **Jenny (Geneva) K. Yelle**, Frontier Regional School, S. Deerfield, MA; **Kimberly Young**, New Riegel High School, New Riegel, OH; **Catherine Ziegler**, Carterville High School, Carterville, IL; **Linda A. Zynda**, Kenmore East High School, Tonawanda, NY

Photo Credits

Cover: Kelly Stribling Sutherland, *Woman with Jazz Musicians*, original acrylic.

Abbreviations: top (t), bottom (b), left (l), right (r), center (c)

Air France: 399

Antin, Angel: 386 (t)

Armstrong, Rick: 148 (b), 329 (t), 411 (t)

Barbey: xx (b)

Barde, Jean-Luc/French Government Tourist Office: 343 (t)

Barnes, David/The Stock Market: 338 (b)

Berndt, Eric R./Unicorn Stock Photos: 84 (t)

Bordis, E./Leo de Wys Inc.: 43 (tl)

Bourgeois, Steve: xxi (c)

Brown, Steve/Leo de Wys Inc.: xxii (t), 18-19, 34

Burgess, Michele: xxiv (t, c, b), 379, 386 (c), 410 (tr), 420 (b), 422 (b), 424, 426 (c), 428 (r), 440

Camille/French Government Tourist Office: 433 (t)

Chirol/French Government Tourist Office: 418

Comnet/Leo de Wys Inc.: 6 (bc), 361

Damm, Fridmar/Leo de Wys Inc.: 307

Dratch, Howard/Leo de Wys Inc.: v (b)

Flipper, Florent/Unicorn Stock Photos: 420 (t)

Fly, James L./Unicorn Stock Photos: 359 (c)

French Government Tourist Office: xxi (b), 378, 410 (b), 411 (b)

Fried, Robert: viii (b), ix, x (b), 2 (t), 4, 10 (b), 14 (t), 22 (t), 25 (b), 28, 35 (t), 43 (tr), 47, 53, 56-57, 60 (tl, tr, b), 61 (t), 62, 70, 74, 75, 76, 78, 84 (b), 85 (t), 86 (b), 87 (t), 90, 96 (t), 125, 130-31, 135, 140 (tl, bl), 146 (t), 154 (t), 155 (t), 161, 174 (l), 176 (t), 188 (t, b), 195 (b), 196 (t, b), 197 (b), 208 (c, b), 217 (t), 218 (t, b), 227 (t), 238 (b), 240, 241, 254-55, 257, 259 (t, c), 260 (t), 263, 274, 276 (t), 277 (t, b), 281, 303, 311 (b), 322 (c), 345, 353, 367 (t), 369, 370, 381, 391 (b), 401 (t), 410 (tl), 419 (b), 425 (t), 426 (b), 427 (t, b), 428 (l), 430, 431, 438 (t), 441

Garnett, R./Visual Contact: 408 (b)

Garry, Jean-Marc: 155 (b)

Geppert, Rollin/Frozen Images: xxv (b)

Gerda, Paul/Leo de Wys Inc.: 359 (t)

Gratien/French Government Tourist Office: 348 (t)

Greenberg, Jeff/Unicorn Stock Photos: 368 (c)

Higgins, Jean/Unicorn Stock Photos: xxii (b)

Hill, Justine: 23, 25 (tl), 278 (t), 282, 321 (tr), 322 (t)

Hille, W./Leo de Wys Inc.: 144 (cr)

Johnson, Everett/Frozen Images: 407

Kraft, Wolfgang: 262

Larson, June: v (t), vi, 2 (cl, b), 11, 21 (b), 24 (tc), 83, 85 (t), 96 (cl), 104, 138, 145, 154 (b), 165, 166, 180 (t), 233, 249 (b), 250, 258 (b), 259 (b), 268 (b), 269 (tr), 270, 271 (c, b), 273, 276 (b), 278 (bl), 283, 290, 299 (t), 302, 317 (t), 338, 349, 398

Last, Victor: 36, 194 (l), 195 (c), 220 (b), 224, 244, 269 (tl), 300 (tr, b), 320, 367 (b), 393 (t), 408 (t), 410 (c), 413 (b)

Lyons, Dave/Unicorn Stock Photos: 197 (t)